Chinese Religion in Western Languages

MONOGRAPHS OF THE ASSOCIATION FOR ASIAN STUDIES

Published by and available from: The University of Arizona Press
1615 E. Speedway Blvd., Tucson, Arizona 85719

XLI. *Chinese Religion in Western Languages: A Comprehensive and Classified Bibliography of Publications in English, French and German through 1980*, by Laurence G. Thompson. 1984.

XL. *Kerajaan: Malay Political Culture on the Eve of Colonial Rule*, by A. C. Milner. 1982.

XXXIX. *Academies in Ming China: An Historical Essay*, by John Meskill. 1982.

XXXVIII. *An Anthology of Modern Writing From Sri Lanka*, edited by Ranjini Obeyesekere and Chitra Fernando. 1981.

XXXVII. *An Introduction to Javanese Law: A Translation of and Commentary on the Agama*, by M. C. Hoadley and M. B. Hooker. 1980.

XXXVI. *Burmese Sit-tans 1764—1826: Records of Rural Life and Administration*, by Frank N. Trager and William J. Koenig with the assistance of Yi Yi. 1979.

XXXV. *Robe and Plough: Monasticism and Economic Interest in Early Medieval Sri Lanka*, by R. A. L. H. Gunawardana. 1979.

XXXIV. *Code and Custom in a Thai Provincial Court*, by David M. Engel. 1978.

XXXIII. *Philippine Policy Toward Sabah: A Claim to Independence*, by Lela Garner Noble. 1977.

XXXII. *Political Behavior of Adolescents in China: The Cultural Revolution in Kwangchow*, by David M. Raddock. 1977.

XXXI. *Big City Government in India: Councilor, Administrator, and Citizen in Delhi*, by Philip Oldenburg. 1976.

XXX. *The New Jerusalem: Aspects of Utopianism in the Thought of Kagawa Toyohiko*, by George B. Bikle, Jr. 1976.

XXIX. *Dogen Kigen—Mystical Realist*, by Hee-Jin Kim. 1975.

XXVIII. *Masks of Fiction in DREAM OF THE RED CHAMBER: Myth, Mimesis, and Persona*, by Lucien Miller. 1975.

XXVII. *Politics and Nationalist Awakening in South India, 1852-1891*, by R. Suntharalingam. 1974.

XXVI. *The Peasant Rebellions of the Late Ming Dynasty*, by James Bunyan Parsons. 1970.

XXV. *Political Centers and Cultural Regions in Early Bengal*, by Barrie M. Morrison, 1970.

XXIV. *The Restoration of Thailand Under Roma I: 1782—1809*, by Klaus Wenk. 1968. O.P.

XXIII. *K'ang Yu-wei: A Biography and a Symposium*, translated and edited by Jung-pang Lo. 1967.

XXII. *A Documentary Chronicle of Sino-Western Relations (1644—1820)*, two volumes by Lo-shu Fu. 1966.

XXI. *Before Aggression: Europeans Prepare the Japanese Army*, by Ernst L. Presseisen, 1965. O.P.

XX. *Shinran's Gospel of Pure Grace*, by Alfred Bloom. 1965.

XIX. *Chiaraijima Village: Land Tenure, Taxation, and Local Trade, 1818—1884*, by William Chambliss. 1965.

XVII. *The British in Malaya: The First Forty Years*, K. G. Tregonning. 1965. O.P.

XVII. *Ch'oe Pu's Diary: A Record of Drifting Across the Sea*, by John Meskill. 1965. O.P.

XVI. *Korean Literature: Topics and Themes*, by Peter H. Lee. 1965. O.P.

XV. *Reform, Rebellion, and the Heavenly Way*, Benjamin Weems. 1964.

XIV. *The Malayan Tin Industry to 1914*, by Wong Lin Ken. 1965.

The Association for Asian Studies Monograph No. XLI
Frank Reynolds, Anthony Yu, Ronald Inden, Editors

Chinese Religion in Western Languages: A Comprehensive and Classified Bibliography of Publications in English, French, and German through 1980

LAURENCE G. THOMPSON

Published for the Association for Asian Studies by
THE UNIVERSITY OF ARIZONA PRESS
Tucson, Arizona

About the Compiler

LAURENCE G. THOMPSON, professor of East Asian Languages and Cultures at the University of Southern California, was a founding member of the Society for the Study of Chinese Religions and its president in 1984. Besides having published many articles on Chinese religion, Thompson is the author of *Chinese Religion: An Introduction* (third edition 1979) and *The Chinese Way in Religion* (1973), as well as the first edition of the present bibliography, *Studies of Chinese Religion,* now out of print.

The publication of this volume has been financed from a revolving fund that initially was established by a generous grant from the Ford Foundation.

Second printing 1987

THE UNIVERSITY OF ARIZONA PRESS

Library of Congress Cataloging in Publication Data

Thompson, Laurence G.
    Chinese religion in Western Languages.

    (Monographs of the Association for Asian Studies ; 41)
    Updated ed. of: Studies of Chinese religion. c1976.
    Includes index.
    1. China—Religion—Bibliography. I. Thompson,
Laurence G. Studies of Chinese religion. II. Title.
III. Series: Monographs of the Association for Asian
Studies ; no. 41.
Z7757.C6T55 1985   016.2'000951   84-24010
[BL1802]

ISBN 0-8165-0926-3

To My Friend
Fred Streng
With Respect and Appreciation

CONTENTS

PART ONE
BIBLIOGRAPHY AND GENERAL STUDIES

PART TWO
CHINESE RELIGION EXCLUSIVE OF BUDDHISM

PART THREE
CHINESE BUDDHISM

FOREWORD

The first version of this catalog was published by Dickenson in 1976 under the title, **Studies of chinese religion.** It covered publications through 1970. Unfortunately, for reasons that need not be detailed here, it was never widely available. It had been the compiler's intention in any case to continue the work, both to include items that had been overlooked in the first attempt, and to extend coverage through 1980. This new edition has been given a title that less ambiguously indicates its nature as a bibliography, while publication under the auspices of the Association for Asian Studies will assure better circulation and therefore greater usefulness. It will not be superfluous, in view of the circumstances, to repeat here much of what was said in the Preface to the original version.

The task of compiling such a bibliography was motivated mainly of course by the obvious need for it. It was also the compiler's intention to give sharper definition to the field of Chinese religion, which had always lacked focus in the sense that writers tended to confuse the Confucian Canon, writings of the philosophers, and religion properly speaking. Most treatments of "Confucius" and "Confucianism," as well as "Lao Tzu" and "Taoism" have suffered from this confusion. It is our view that religion can and should be distinguished from philosophy in the case of China as in the case of the West. Thus we have wished to deal here only with Chinese **religion,** and in all possible cases have excluded philosophical studies from our purview. However, because of the historical facts, the sections on Confucianism, Taoism, and Lao Tzu have necessarily become all-inclusive and constitute an exception to our general principle. And of course our section on Religious Thought attempts to include publications that may be considered "philosophy of religion."

Restricting the definition of the field will be helpful, but we have also expanded it to include many topics that hitherto have often been neglected in bibliographies dealing with Chinese religion. We trust that these categories will sharpen perception of the subject's many facets. We wish to emphasize that the system of classification used to bring out all aspects of Chinese religion was arrived at after the facts, and was not adopted because of any preconceived notions as to how the subject-matter should be arranged. In the new edition, therefore, some of the titles of the various sections have been altered the better to describe their contents, while in Part Two four new categories have been required by new developments in the field.

For the convenience of the user there is a considerable amount of cross-listing. In those cases where to follow this procedure fully would have resulted in undue duplication we have noted under the section headings additional categories to be consulted.

As in our other studies, we have here taken Chinese religion to be essentially a manifestation of the Chinese culture. We have considered only Buddhism, of all the foreign religions historically known in China, to have permeated this culture to such an extent that it became an integral part of Chinese religion. The other foreign religions have not, therefore, been included. Furthermore, we have limited our coverage to the religion of the Han Chinese, and have excluded materials pertaining to ethnic minorities and peripheral cultures. Several other topics are also excluded from the scope of this catalog:

1. In the section on Sects, Secret societies, and New Religion, the voluminous literature on the T'ai-p'ing rebellion.

2. The question of Fu-sang. For references consult Cordier's **Bibliotheca sinica** 4, col 2653-2658.

3. Studies deriving from writings of Chinese Buddhist pilgrims that do not concern Chinese religion.

4. Writings on medicine that do not include religious aspects of traditional theory.

5. General travel and descriptive literature in which religion is mentioned more or less incidentally.

6. General and historical treatments of art, and album-volumes, which include Buddhist art as part of their broad coverage. We hope, however, that the extensive bibliography of Chinese Buddhist art included in our Part Three will be a useful tool.

It would no doubt have been desirable to include items in Western languages other than the three here represented; but in fact the great bulk of the material is in English, French, and German. In our original Preface we expressed the hope that the best of numerous theses and dissertations on Chinese religion would eventually be published, and that we might have the opportunity to list them in a later version of our catalog. It is a pleasure to note that in fact many such works have been published subsequent to our first edition, and are included in the present one.

The word "comprehensive" in our sub-title must of course be taken as somewhat less than literally true. This edition is certainly more nearly comprehensive than the first attempt, but comprehensiveness is by the nature of the case a chimerical goal. Our hopes will be abundantly satisfied if the material here brought together proves useful in providing an overview of the state of the field to the terminal date, in furnishing leads for new researches, and in defining the discipline of Chinese religion in its whole extent and its various parts.

Laurence G. Thompson

University of Southern California

ACKNOWLEDGMENTS

In preparing the first version of this bibliography I had the very helpful assistance of Ms Justine Pinto, whose name appeared on the title page. Inasmuch as Ms Pinto is not responsible for any of the new material in this version, I have not thought it fair to her to indicate in this way that she participated in the new project. Of course this does not in the slightest degree lessen my obligation to her for her help in what is still more than half of the content of the present work, and I am pleased to have this opportunity to acknowledge that debt. The Faculty Research Fund of the College of Letters, Arts, and Sciences of the University of Southern California provided two small, but crucially important, grants in support of the first edition, while publication of that edition was made possible by an additional grant from The Institute for Advanced Studies of World Religions in New York. Preparation of camera-ready copy for the present edition was very costly, and I am greatly indebted to Irwin C. Lieb, Vice President and Provost of the College of Letters, Arts and Sciences of my university, for personally securing a grant to underwrite that processing, and to the President's Circle of U.S.C. for making the funds available. Several individuals helped in various ways, including professors Alvin Cohen and Julian Pas, who took the trouble to send information about a number of relevant items for inclusion in the catalog, and my wife Grace, who gave time to that most tedious of tasks, preparing the Index. Special appreciation is due to the compiler's dear friend Mark Kochan, who arranged for and supervised all the technical aspects of preparing the book for submission to the University of Arizona Press.

ABBREVIATIONS

A. GENERAL

abbrev/abbreviated
abrmt/abridgement
add/additional, additions
ann/année(s)
annot/annotated, annotations
anthol/anthology
app/appendix(es)
arch/architecture, architectural
art/article(s)
assoc/association

bd/band
betw/between
bibliog/bibliography
bk/book
bl-&-wh/black and white
budd/Buddhist, Buddhism

chap/chapter(s)
char/characters
chin/China, Chinese, chinois
chron/chronology
col/column(s), color
collab/collaboration, collaborator
comm/commentary
comp/compiled, compiler(s)
corr/corrected, corrigenda

d/date(d)
dept/department
diagr/diagram(s)
dyn/dynasty, dynasties

ed/edited, edition, editor(s)
engl/English, England
enl/enlarged
esp/especially
extr/extract(ed)

fasc/fascicule(s)
fig/figure(s)
fr/from

gloss/glossary
govt/government

HK/Hong Kong

illus/illustration(s), illustrated
incl/includes, including, included
indiv/individual
inscr/inscription
intl/international
intro/introduction

jap/Japan (ese)

lit/literature
lith/lithographs

mél/mélanges
MIT/Massachusetts Institute of Technology

natl/national
no/number(s)
n.d./no date
n.p./no place
n.s./new series
NY/New York

offpr/offprint
orig/original(ly)

p/page(s)
pl/plate(s)
pref/preface
proc/proceedings
pseud/pseudonym
pt/part(s)
publ/publication, published, publisher

ref/references
reimp/reimpression
relig/religion/religious
repr/reprint(ed)
republ/republished
rev/review(ed), revised

s/seite
sec/section(s)
sel/selected
sep/separate(ly)
ser/series
sér/série
soc/society/social ·
summ/summary
suppl/supplement

t/tome
trad/traduit
trans/transactions
tsl/translated, translation, translator

übers/übersetzt
univ/university
unk/unknown

vol/volume(s)

B. PUBLICATIONS*

AA	Artibus asiae	ARW	Archiv für religionswissenschaft
AAA	Archives of asian art	ArchOr	Archiv orientální
A&T	Art & thought, issued in honour of dr. ananda k. coomaraswamy on the occasion of his 70th birthday. London (1947)	ArtsAs	Arts asiatiques
		AS	Asiatische studien
		ASAB	Annales de la société royale d'archaeologie, bruxelles
AArch	Art and archaeology	ASBIE	Academia sinica, bulletin of the institute of ethnology (Taipei)
AB	Art bulletin		
AC	Aspects de la chine. Paris, musée guimet (1959)	ASBIHP	Academia sinica, bulletin of the institute of history and philology (Taipei)
ACASA	Archives of the chinese art society of america	AsFS	Asian folklore studies
		Asiatica	Asiatica; festschrift friedrich weller zum 80. geburstag überreicht. Leipzig (1954)
ACF	Annuaire du collège de france		
ACP	Annales de chimie et de physique	Asien	Lydia Brüll & Ulrich Kemper (ed) Asien. Tradition und fortschritt. Festschrift für horst hammitzsch zu seinem 60. geburstag. Wiesbaden (1971)
ACQ	Asian culture quarterly		
AC:SEC	David T. Roy & Tsuen-hsuin Tsien (ed) Ancient china: studies in early civilization. Chin univ hk (1978)		
		ASONT	Marjorie Topley (ed) Aspects of social organization in the new territories, hong kong. HK (1965)
ACSS	Annual of the china society, singapore		
ActaA	Acta asiatica	ASR	Archives de sociologie des religions
AdSin	Adversaria sinica	ASSR	Archives de sciences sociales des religions
AEO	Annales de l'extrême-orient		
AGP	Archives of general psychiatry	AsSur	Asian survey
AIPHO	Annuaire de l'institut de philologie et d'histoire orientale	ATOW	Wilhelm Bitter (heraus) Abendländische therapie und östliche weisheit; ein tagungstericht. Stuttgart (1967)
AJCM	American journal of chinese medicine		
AL	Annali lateranensi	ATS	Asian thought & society: an international review
AM	Asia major		
AMG	Annales du musée guimet	AUFS	American universities field staff
AMH	Annals of medical history	AV	Archiv für völkerkunde
AMHAV	Asia major, hirth anniversary volume (introductory vol of this journal, pref by editor Bruno Schindler d Oct 1922)	AWGN	Akademie der wissenschaft in göttingen, philologisch-historischeklasse, nachrichten
		BAAFC	Bulletin de l'association amicale franco-chinoise
AMS	Charles Leslie (ed) Asian medical systems. Univ calif (1976)		
		BAF	Bulletin asie-française
AMZ	Allgemeine missions-zeitschrift	BAIC	Bulletin of the art institute of chicago
ANA	Art news annual	B&J	Harish Chandra Das et al (ed) Buddhism and jainism. Cuttack, orissa (1976)
Ancestors	William H. Newell (ed)Ancestors. The hague (1976)		
		BAV	Boas anniversary volume; anthropological papers written in honor of franz boas . . . NY. (1906)
AnnEPHE	Annuaire, école pratique des hautes études		
AO	Acta orientalia (Copenhagen)	BCL	D.R. Bhandarker et al (ed) B.c. law volume. Calcutta, pt 1 (1945) pt 2 (1946)
AofA	Arts of asia		
AP	Aryan path	BCMA	Bulletin of the cleveland museum of art
APC	Annales de philosophie chrétienne	BCUP	Bulletin of the catholic university of peking
APQCSA	Asian & pacific quarterly of cultural and social affairs	BDIA	Bulletin of the denver institute of arts
		BDetIA	Bulletin of the detroit institute of arts
AQ	Art quarterly	BEA	Bulletin of eastern art
AQR	Asiatic quarterly review	BEFEO	Bulletin de l'école française d'extrême-orient
AR	Asiatic review		
AR-HR	Harry Partin (comp) Asian religions-history of religions: 1974 proceedings; preprinted papers for the section on asian religions-history of religions, annual meeting of american academy of religion. Florida state univ (1974)	BFoggMA	Bulletin of the fogg museum of art
		BHM	Bulletin of the history of medicine
		BIHM	Bulletin of the institute of the history of medicine
		BJP	British journal of psychiatry
		BLM	Blackwood's magazine
ArsO	Ars orientalis. The arts of islam and the east.	BM	Burlington magazine
		BMFA	Bulletin of the museum of fine arts (Boston)

*Book or journal titles consisting of more than one word have been abbreviated if they occur more than twice in this bibliography, except when a book as a whole is listed.

BMFEA	Bulletin of the museum of far eastern antiquities (Stockholm)
BMFJ	Bulletin de la maison franco-japonaise
BMMA	Bulletin of the metropolitan museum of art (N.Y.)
BMQ	British museum quarterly
BMSAP	Bulletin et mémoires de la société d'anthropologie de paris
BOR	Babylonian and oriental record
BROMA	Bulletin of the royal ontario museum of archaeology
BSAB	Bulletin de la société royale belge d'anthropologie, bruxelles
BSEIS	Bulletin de la société d'études indochinoises de saigon
BSOAS	Bulletin of the school of oriental and african studies (Univ london)
BT&AC	Leslie S. Kawamura & Keith Scott (ed) Buddhist thought and asian civilization: essays in honour of herbert v. guenther on his sixtieth birthday. Emeryville, calif (1977)
BTLVK	Bijdragen tot de taal-, land-en volkskunde
BUA	Bulletin de l'université l'aurore (Shanghai)
BTS—I	Michael Saso & David W. Chappell (ed) Buddhist and taoist studies-I. Univ hawaii (1977)
BTTSoc	Buddhist text translation society, affiliate of sino-american buddhist association, san francisco
BVAMG	Bibliothèque de vulgarisation des annales du musée guimet
CalR	Calcutta review
C&C	James D. Whitehead, Yu-ming Shaw & Norman J. Girardot (ed) China and christianity. Historical and future encounters. Notre dame univ (1979)
CB	Current background (U.S. consulate general, hong kong)
CBS	William P. Lebra (ed) Culture-bound syndromes, ethnopsychiatry, and alternate therapies. Univ hawaii (1976)
CBWK	Chinesische blätter für wissenschaft und kunst
CbyM	Timothy Richard. Conversion by the million in china. Shanghai, vol 1 (1907)
CC	Chinese culture (Taipei)
CCHC	Michael Loewe. Crisis and conflict in han china. London (1974)
CCJ	Chung chi journal
CCS	Collectanea commisionis synodalis. Peking (1935)
CCY	China christian yearbook
CD	B.C. Henry, The cross and the dragon. NY (1885)
CDA	Chinesisch-deutsch almanach
CE	Eugene N. Anderson jr & Marja L. Anderson. Mountains and water: essays on the cultural ecology of south coastal china.Taipei (1973)
CEB	Paul Demiéville. Choix d'études bouddhiques (1929-1970) Leiden (1973)
CEd	Chinese education
CES	Paul Demiéville. Choix d'études sinologiques (1921-1970) Leiden (1973)
CF	Ching feng

CFL&SC	David C. Buxbaum (ed) Chinese family law and social change. Univ washington (1978)
CFQ	California folklore quarterly
CHAS	Arthur Kleinman et al (ed) Culture and healing in asian societies. Cambridge, mass (1978)
ChBudd	W. Pachow. Chinese buddhism: aspects of interaction and reinterpretation. Washington d.c. (1980)
ChFor	China forum
ChLit	Chinese Literature: essays, articles, reviews. Madison, wis
CHM	Cahiers d'histoire mondiale
ChRec	Chinese recorder
ChRep	Chinese repository
ChRev	China review
CIHR	Congrès internationale d'histoire des religions
CISE	Congrès internationale des sciences ethnographiques, session de 1878
CJ	China journal
CL	Chinese Literature. Peking
CLG	Chinese law and government
CLIC	G. William Skinner (ed) The city in late imperial china. Stanford univ (1977)
CM	Charles A. Moore (ed) The chinese mind. Univ hawaii (1967)
CMBA	China Missionary; later China missionary bulletin; later Mission bulletin; later Asia
CME&W	Comparative medicine east and west
CMG	Conférences faites au musée guimet
CMH	China mission hand-book
CMI	Church missionary intelligencer
CMJ	Chinese medical journal
CN	China notes
CNA	China news analysis
CP	Arthur F. Wright and Denis Twitchett (ed) Confucian personalities. Stanford univ(1962)
CPOL	Congrès provinciale des orientalistes, lyon, (1878)
CQ	China quarterly
CR	Contemporary review
CRAIBL	Comptes rendus de l'académie des inscriptions et belles-lettres
CRJ	Contemporary religions in japan
CRecon	China reconstructs
CRWMS	W. Moese, G. Reinknecht & E. Schmitz-Seisser. Chinese regionalism in west-malaysia and singapore. Hamburg, MDGNVO 77 (1979)
CSA	Chinese sociology and anthropology
CSM	Chinese students' monthly
CSP	Chinese studies in philosophy
CSPSR	Chinese social and political science review
CSSH	Comparative studies in society and history
CTI	John K. Fairbank (ed) Chinese thought and institutions. Univ chicago (1957)
CToday	T.T. Lew et al. China today through chinese eyes. NY, 1st ser (n.d.--1922) 2nd ser, london (1926)
CW	Catholic world
CWayRel	Laurence G. Thompson (ed) The chinese way in religion. Encino and belmont, calif.(1973)

CWR	China weekly review
CYT	E.T. Williams, China yesterday and today.
Deviance	NY (1923 et seq; 4th ed (1928) Amy A. Wilson, Sidney L. Greenblatt & Richard R. Wilson (ed) Deviance and social control in chinese society. NY (1977)
DR	J.M. Reid (ed) Doomed religions: a series of essays on great religions of the world. NY and cincinnati (1884)
DV	Justus Doolittle (ed) Vocabulary and handbook of the chinese language. Foochow (1872)2 vol.
EA	East of asia
EarlyCC	Chang Kwang-chih. Early chinese civilization. Harvard univ (1976)
EArt	Eastern art
EB	Eastern Buddhist
EBio	Encyclopedia of bioethics. Georgetown univ (1978)
EC	Early china
ECA	Noel Barnard (ed) Early chinese art and its possible influence in the pacific basin. "Authorized taiwan edition" (1974) Orig publ (1972) repudiated by ed.
ECC	Derk Bodde. Essays on chinese civilization. Ed & intro Charles Le Blanc & Dorothy Borei
EH	Eastern horizon
EJ	Eranos jahrbuch
ELC	Edwin Joshua Dukes. Everyday life in china. London (1885)
EM	Encyclopédie moderne
EMM	Evangelisches missions-magazin
EMO	M.-M. Davy (direction) Encyclopédie des mystiques orientales. ?Paris (1975)
EncyA	Encyclopedia americana
EncyB	Encyclopaedia britannica
EncyP:HR	Encylopédie de la pléiade. Histoire des religions. Paris (1976)
EncyWA	Encyclopaedia of world art. NY (1959-68)
EORL	Études d'orientalisme, publiées par le musée guimet à la mémoire de raymond linossier. Paris (1932)
EP	Essays in philosophy of the university of chicago. Univ chicago (1929)
ER	Études religieuses
ESC	Études sociologiques sur la chine. Collected papers of Marcel Granet. Préface Louis Gerner, intro R.-A. Stein. Paris (1953)
ESCBP	Eugene N. Anderson jr. Essays on south china's boat people. Taipei (1972)
ESCH	Donald D. Leslie, Colin Mackerras & Wang Gung-wu (ed) Essays on the sources for chinese history. Australian natl univ (1973) univ south carolina (1975)
ET	Expository times
Etudes	Études des pères de la compagnie de jésus
EUF	Encyclopaedia universalis france. Paris (1968)
EW	Eastern world
EWCR	East-west center review

ExHum	Agehananda Bharati (ed) The realm of the extra-human: agents and audience. The hague (1976)
EZT	Essays on the history of buddhism presented to professor zenryu tsukamoto. Kyoto university (1961)
E&W	East and west
FA	France-asie
FA:BPB	René de Berval (ed) Présence du bouddhisme (FA 16, 1959)
FC	E.G. Kemp. The face of china. NY (1909)
FCR	Free china review
FE	Far east
FEER	Far eastern economic review
FEQ	Far eastern quarterly
FF	Fortschungen und fortschritte
FKCS	Maurice Freedman (ed) Family and kinship in chinese society. Stanford univ(1970)
FLJ	Folk-lore journal
FMB	Field museum bulletin.
FO	Ferne osten
FRWVSP	Folk religion and the worldview in the southwestern pacific. Tokyo(1968)
FS	Folklore studies
FT	Holmes Welch & Anna Seidel (ed) Facets of taoism. Essays in chinese religion. Yale univ (1979)
GBA	Gazette des beaux-arts
GC	Genevieve Wimsatt. A griffin in china. NY & london (1927)
GE	La grande encyclopédie
GM	Geographical magazine
H&SC	Tu Wei-ming. Humanity and self-cultivation: essays in confucian thought. Berkeley, calif (1979)
HCP:HR	Henri-Charles Puech (ed) Histoire des religions. T 1, Les religions antique . . . Paris (1970)
HERE	James Hastings (ed) Encyclopaedia of religion and ethics. 13 vol (1908-26)
HJ	Hibbert journal
HJAS	Harvard journal of asiatic studies
HKS	Symposium on historical, archaeological and linguistic studies on southern china, south east asia and the hong kong region. Hong kong (1967)
HLC	Isaac Taylor Headland. Home life in china. NY (1914)
HM	Histoire de la médecine
HMRC	Henri Maspero. Les religions chinoises. Mélanges posthumes sur les religions et l'histoire de la chine, t 1.Paris (1950)
HPEW	S. Radhakrishnan (ed) History of philosophy, eastern and western. London (1952)
HR	History of religions
HRAF	Human relations area files
HTR	Harvard theological review
HZ	Hansei zasshi
IA	Indian antiquary
IAC	Indo-asian culture
IAE	Internationales archiv für ethnographie
IAF	Internationales asien forum
I&C	Sarvapelli Radhakrishnan. India and china. Lectures delivered in china may 1944. Bombay, 3rd ed (1954)

I&S	Issues and studies
IAQR	Imperial and asiatic quarterly review
IBFQ	International buddhist forum quarterly
ICG	Indo-chinese gleaner
ICO	International congress of orientalists
ICHR	International congress for the history of religions
ICR	International congress of religions
IHQ	Indian historical quarterly
IJSP	International journal of social psychiatry
India antiqua	India antiqua. A volume of oriental studies presented to jean philippe vogel. Leiden (1947)
IntC	Mrs Archibald Little. Intimate china. London (n.d.--ca.1900)
IPQ	IPQ: International philosophical quarterly
IQB	Iqbal, later Iqbal review
IRM	International review of missions
JA	Journal asiatique
JAAS	Journal of asian and african studies
JAC	Journal of asian culture
JAFL	Journal of american folk-lore
JAK	Jahrbuch der asiatischen kunst
JAOS	Journal of the american oriental society
JAS	Journal of asian studies
JBBRAS	Journal of the bombay branch, royal asiatic society
JCE	Journal of chemical engineering
JCS	Journal of the china society, taipei
JCLTA	Journal of the chinese language teachers association
JCP	Journal of chinese philosophy
JCUHK	Journal of the chinese university of hong kong
JD	Journal of dharma
JEAC	Journal of esthetics and art criticism
JHI	Journal of the history of ideas
JHKBRAS	Journal of the hong kong branch, royal asiatic society
JHMAS	Journal of the history of medicine and allied sciences
JHP	Journal of humanistic psychology
JIA	Journal of the indian archipelago
JIBS	Journal of indian and buddhist studies: Indogaku bukkyōgaku kenkyū
JIC	Journal of intercultural studies
JISOA	Journal of the indian society of oriental art
JJRS	Journal of japanese religious studies
JMBRAS	Journal of the malayan branch, royal asiatic society
JMGS	Journal of the manchester geographical society
JNCBRAS	Journal of the north china branch, royal asiatic society'
JOR	Journal of oriental research (Madras)
JOS	Journal of oriental studies (Univ hong kong)
JOSA	Journal of the oriental society of australia
JPOS	Journal of the peking oriental society
JPTS	Journal of the pali text society
JR	Journal of religion
JRAS	Journal of the royal asiatic society
JRASB	Journal of the royal asiatic society of bengal
JRE	Journal of religious ethics

JRH	Journal of religious history
JRLB	John rylands library, bulletin
JSBRAS	Journal of the straits branch, royal asiatic society
JSMVL	Jahrbuch der stadtliches museums für völkerkunde zu leipzig
JSR:HS	Japan science review: humanistic studies
JSR:LPH	Japan science review: literature, philosophy and history
JSS	Journal of social science, national taiwan university college of law
JSEAS	Journal of southeast asian studies
JSSR	Journal for the scientific study of religion
JTP	Journal of transpersonal psychology
JWCBorder-ResS	Journal of the west china border research society
KdeO	Kunst des orients
KGUAS	Kwansei gakuin university annual studies
KT:OS	Keleti Tanu/manyok. Oriental studies
L&S	John McGowan. Lights and shadows of chinese life. Shanghai (1909)
LD	Light of dharma
LL&R	Sarah Allan & Alvin P. Cohen (ed) Legend, lore, and religion in china: essays in honor of wolfram eberhard on his seventieth birthday. San francisco (1979)
LO	M. Kern (ed) Das licht des ostens. Stuttgart (1922)
LTY:SP	Liu Ts'un-yan. Selected papers from the hall of harmonious wind. Leiden (1976)
MAI	Mémoires de littérature tirés des registres de l'académie des inscriptions
MAIBL	Mémoires de l'académie des inscriptions et belles-lettres
MB	Maha bodhi
MBM	Minoru Kiyota (ed) Mahayana buddhist meditation: theory and practice. Univ hawaii (1978)
MC	Missions catholiques
MCAM	Mémoires couronnés et autre mémoires, académie royale de belgique
MCB	Mélanges chinois et bouddhiques
MCC	Arthur Kleinman et al (ed) Medicine in chinese cultures: comparative studies of health care in chinese and other societies. Washington d.c. US dept of HEW (1975)
MCLC	Mémoires concernant l'histoire, les sciences, les arts, les moeurs, les usages etc des chinois, par les missionaires de pékin
MCSJ	Mémoires du comité sinico-japonais
MDGNVO	Mitteilungen der deutschen gesellschaft für natur- und völkerkunde ostasiens, tokyo
MEO	Message d'extrême-orient
MIHEC	Mélanges, paris universitaire institut des hautes études chinoises
MIOF	Mitteilungen, deutsche (preussische) akademie der wissenschaften zu berlin (institut für orientforschung)
MJ	Museum journal
MLA	Magazin für die literatur des auslandes
MMDFL	Hugo Kuhn and Kurt Schier (ed) Märchen, mythos, dichtung: festschrift zum 90. geburstag friedrich von der leyens. . . München (1963)

MN	Monumenta nipponica	PCIEEO	Première congrès internationale des études d'extrême-orient, hanoi (1902)
MRW	Missionary review of the world		
MS	Monumenta serica	PEW	Philosophy east and west
MS/CA	Actes du XXIXe ICO, sec organisée par Michel Soymié: chine ancienne (pre-modern china) Paris (1977)	PFEH	Australian natl univ, papers in far eastern history
		PFV	Paranavitana felicitation volume on art and architecture presented to senarat paranavitana. Colombo (1966)
MSGFOK	Mitteilungen der schweitzerischen gesellschaft der freunde ostasiatische kultur		
		PIAHA	Proceedings of the 2nd biennial conference, international association of historians of asia. Taipei (1963)
MSL	Mémorial sylvain lévi. Paris (1937)		
MSOS	Mitteilungen des seminars für orientalische sprachen	PIAJ	Proceedings of the imperial academy of japan
MSPD	Mélanges de sinologie offerts à monsieur paul demiéville. Paris. T 1 (1966) t 2 (1974)	PJGG	Philosophisches jahrbuch der görres-gesellschaft
		PMB	Philadelphia museum bulletin
MSVC	Wolfram Eberhard. Moral and social values of the chinese: collected essays. Taipei (1971)	PMSS	Jean Chesneaux (ed) Popular movements and secret societies in china 1840-1950. Stanford univ (1972)
MW	Middle way	PR	Peking review
NABCC	Arthur Kleinman & T.-Y. Lin (ed) Normal and abnormal behavior in chinese culture. Dordrecht (1980)	PrAnthro	Practical anthropology
		PRPCC	Clarence B. Day. Popular religion in pre-communist china. San francisco (1975)
Nachr-DGNVO	Nachrichten der deutschen gesellschaft für natur- und völkerkunde ostasiens, hamburg	PRS	Lewis Lancaster (ed) Prajñāpāramitā and related systems. Studies in honor of edward conze. Berkeley, calif (1977)
NC	Nineteenth century		
NC&O	Arthur E. Moule. New china and old. London (n.d.--ca.1900)	PS	Popular science monthly
		Psychologia	Psychologia; international journal of psychology in the orient
NC:CR	Michael Chu (ed) The new china: a catholic response. NY (1977)	PT	People's tribune
NCELYY	Frederick Wakeman, jr(ed) 'Nothing concealed': essays in honor of liu yü-yün. Taipei (1970)	PTP	Phi theta papers
		PW	Pacific world
		QJCA	Quarterly journal of current acquisitions, u.s. library of congress
NCH	North china herald		
NCR	New china review	QNCCR	Quarterly notes on christianity and chinese religion (Hong kong)
NEAJT	Northeast asia journal of theology		
NGM	National geographic magazine	RA	Revue archéologique
NH	Natural history	RAA	Revue des arts asiatiques
NLIP	Natural law institute proceedings (Univ notre dame)	R&Rev	Guenter Lewy. Religion and revolution. Oxford univ (1974)
NO	New Orient	RC	Relations de chine (Kiangnan)
NPMB	National palace museum bulletin (Taipei)	RCCS	Albert R. O'Hara. Research on changes of chinese society. Taipei (1971)
NQ	Notes and queries on china and japan		
NR	Nouvelle revue	RCDA	Religion in communist dominated areas
NRJ	National reconstruction journal	RDH	Revue des droits de l'homme
NZM	Neue zeitschrift für missionswissenschaft	RDM	Revue de deux mondes
		RDR	Ryūkoku daigaku ronshū, the journal of ryūkoku univ
OA	Oriental art		
OC	Open court	RE	Revue d'ethnologie
OE	Oriens extremus	RechScRelig	Recherches de sciences religieuse
OL	Orientalische literaturzeitung	Religion	Religion. A journal of religion and religions
OM	Overland monthly		
OR	Ostasiatische rundschau	Renditions	Renditions. A chinese-english translation magazine
OSCEP	Val Dastur Cursetji Pavri (ed) Oriental studies in honor of cursetji evachji pavri. London (1933)		
		REO	Revue de l'extrême-orient
OstL	Ostasiatische lloyd (shanghai)	RGI	Revue géographique internationale
OZ	Ostasiatische zeitschift	RH	Religious humanism
		RHR	Revue de l'histoire des religions
PA	Pacific affairs	RIC	Revue indochinoise
PAAAS	Proceedings of the american academy of arts and sciences	RMHA-PU	Record of the museum of historic art, princeton univ
PC	People's china	RMM	Revue de métaphysique et de morale
PCEW	Charles A. Moore (ed) Philosophy and culture east and west. Univ hawaii (1962)	ROA	Revue de l'orient et de l'algérie

RofR	Review of religion
RR	Revue des religions
RRCS	Arthur P. Wolf (ed) Religion and ritual in chinese society. Stanford univ (1974)
RS	Religious studies
RS&P	Richard H. Cox (ed) Religious systems and psychotherapy. Springfield, ill (1973)
RSJ	Religious studies in japan. Tokyo (1959)
RSR	Religious studies review
RSO	Revista degli studia orientali
RSW	Religious systems of the world. London and NY (1889 et seq)
R-WAW	Rheinisch-Westfälische akademie der wissenschaften
SA	Robert K. Sakai (ed) Studies on asia 1963. Univ nebraska (1963)
SAR	Sino-american relations
SAWW	Sitzungsberichte der . . . akademie der wissenschaften in wien (phil.-hist. klasse)
SCFRE	Wolfram Eberhard. Studies in chinese folklore and related essays. Indiana univ (1970)
SCMM	Survey of china mainland magazines (U.S. consulate general, hong kong)
SCMP	Survey of the china mainland press
SCR	Studies in comparative religion
SCT	Arthur F. Wright (ed) Studies in chinese thought. Univ chicago (1953)
SEAJT	South east asia journal of theology
SF	Uno Seiichi et al (ed) Studies on oriental culture. A collection of articles in commemoration of the seventieth birthday of dr. yoshijiro suzuki. Tokyo (1942) All art in jap except for 2
SG	S.G. Brandon (ed) The saviour god: comparative studies in the concept of salvation. Manchester univ (1963)
SIEW	Charles A. Moore(ed) with assistance of Aldyth V. Morris. The status of the individual in east and west. Univ hawaii (1968)
SIJ	Sino-indian journal
SinSon	Sinica sonderausgabe (1934)
SIS	Sino-indian studies
SJ	Silliman journal
SJFAW	Sino-japonica; festschrift andré wedemeyer zum 80. geburstag. Leipzig (1956)
SJV	Silver jubilee volume, kyoto university jimbun kagaku kenkyū-sho (1954)
SLC	Justus Doolittle. Social life of the chinese. NY, 2 vol (1865)
SM	Studia missionalia
SOERF	Maurice Freedman (ed) Social organization. Essays presented to raymond firth. London (1967)
SPRCM	Selections from peoples republic of china magazines
SR/SR	Sciences religieux/studies in religion
SS	Studia serica
SSBKD	Søren, Egerod (ed) Studia serica bernhard karlgren dedicata. Copenhagen (1959)
SSCRB	Society for the study of chinese religions, bulletin

SSM	Social science and medicine
SSM/FHF	Wolfgang Bauer (ed) Studia sino-mongolica: festschrift für herbert franke. Wiesbaden (1979)
SSMT	William Theodore deBary (ed) Self and society in ming thought. Columbia univ (1970)
StAs	Laurence G. Thompson (ed) Studia asiatica. Essays in felicitation of the seventy-fifth anniversary of professor ch'en shou-yi. San Francisco (1975)
SW	W.S. McCullough (ed) The seed of wisdom: essays in honor of t.j. meek. Univ toronto (1964)
SWJA	Southwestern journal of anthropology
Synthesis	Synthesis; the undergraduate journal in the history and philosophy of science
SyY:T&W	Ssu yü yen: Thought & word
T&T	Frank E. Reynolds & Theodore M. Ludwig (ed) Transitions and transformations in the history of religions. Essays in honor of joseph m. kitagawa. Leiden (1980)
TASJ	Transactions of the asiatic society of japan
TBMRD	Tōyō bunko, memoirs of the research department
TC	James T.C. Liu and Wei-ming Tu (ed) Traditional china. Englewood cliffs, n.j. (1970)
Tch'an	Tch'an (zen) Textes chinois fondamentaux, témoignages japonais, expériences vécues contemporaines. Hermès 7. Paris (1970)
TheE&TheW	The east and the west. A quarterly review for the study of missions
THM	T'ien hsia monthly
TICHK	Marjorie Topley (ed) Some traditional chinese ideas and conceptions in hong kong social life today. Honk kong (1967)
TJ	Tsinghua journal of chinese studies
TJR	Tenri journal of religion
TM	À travers le monde
TOCS	Transactions of the oriental ceramic society
TP	T'oung pao
TPJS	Transactions and proceedings of the japan society
TPZB	Toshihiko Izutsu. Toward a philosophy of zen buddhism. (1977)
TR	Tamkang review
TransKBRAS	Korea branch, royal asiatic society, transactions
TUAS	Tōyō university asian studies
UPUMB	University of pennsylvania museum bulletin
USJPRS	U.S. joint publications service
UW	Nancy A. Falk & Rita M. Gross (ed) Unspoken words. Women's religious life in non-western cultures. San francisco etc (1980)
VBA	Visva-bharati annals
VBQ	Visva-bharati quarterly
VBS	Vajra bodhi sea
VFCC	William Parish & Martin King Whyte. Village and family in contemporary china. Univ chicago (1978)

Waifs & strays	Frederic H. Balfour. Waifs and strays from the far east, being a series of disconnected essays on matters relating to china. Shanghai (1877).
WBKKGA	Wiener beiträge zur kunst- und kulturgeschichte asiens
WCS	Margery Wolf & Roxanne Witke (ed) Women in chinese society. Stanford univ (1975)
Wen-lin	Tse-tsung Chow (ed) Wen-lin; studies in the chinese humanities. Univ wisconsin (1968)
WinC	Constance F. Gordon-Cumming. Wanderings in china. Edinburgh & london, 2 vol (1886)
WMM	Wesleyan methodist magazine
WPDMD	Ram Jee Singh (ed) World perspectives in philosophy, religion and culture: essays presented to professor dhirenda mohan datta. Patna (1968)
WPR	John Henry Barrows (ed) The world's parliament of religions. Chicago (1893) 2 vol.
WZKM	Wiener zeitschrift für die kunde des morgenlandes
Yana	Yana. Zeitschrift für buddhismus und religiöse kultur auf buddhistischen grundlage
YE	Young east
Z&H	Harold Heifetz (comp) Zen and hasidism. Wheaton, ill (1978)
ZBK	Zeitschrift bildende kunst
ZCE	R.C. Zaehner (ed) Concise encyclopaedia of living faiths. London (1959)
ZDMG	Zeitschrift der deutschen morgenländischen gesellschaft
ZE	Zeitschrift für ethnologie
ZMK	Zeitschrift für missionskunde
ZMR	Zeitschrift für missionswissenschaft und religionswissenschaft
ZRGG	Zeitschrift für religious- und geistes-geschichte.

DETAILS CONCERNING SERIAL SOURCES

The following list assembles publication data for most of the serials named in the bibliography. Reference is made to our abbreviations in the left-hand column. Because it was not possible in many cases to determine date of termination, the absence of such an indication should not be taken as implying that the serial continued publication through 1980. Where we have been unable to find sufficient information to be useful, the serial has been omitted from this list.

ASBIE   Academia sinica. The institute of ethnology. Taipei. **Bulletin,** 1, march 1956-.

ASBIHP   Academia sinica. The institute of history and philology. Peking and taipei. **Bulletin** 1, october 1928-.

     Académie des inscriptions et belles-lettres. Paris-. Publ the following five ser:

CRAIBL   **Comptes-rendus des séances.** 1, 1857-.

     Histoire et mémoires. 1-51, 1666/1710-1784/93. Publ 1736-1843. Individual numbers with **Mémoires de littérature tirés des registres.** See below.

MAIBL   **Mémoires.** 1, 1803-. Publ 1815-. May be listed as new ser.

     Mémoires concernant l'asie orientale, inde, asie centrale, extrême-orient. 1-3, 1913-1919.

MAI   **Mémoires de littérature tirés des registres.** 1-81, 1666/1710-1773/1776. Repr from vol 1-41 of the **Histoire.**

     Académie des sciences. Paris. **Comptes-rendus hebdomadaires des séances,** 1, 1835-.

     Académie impériale des sciences. St. Petersburg. **Bulletin.** See Akademiia nauk. SSSR, Leningrad.

     Académie royale de belgique. Classe des lettres et des sciences morales et politiques. **Bulletin.** See académie royale des sciences . . . brussels.

     Académie royale des sciences, des lettres et beaux-arts de belgique, brussels. **Bulletin,** 1, 1832-98. Classe des lettres et des sciences morales et politiques, **Bulletin,** 1899-. Also publ:

MCAM   **Mémoires couronnés et autre mémoires,** 1840-1904. Title varies as **Mémoires couronnés et mémoires des savants étrangers.**

Academy   **Academy and literature.** London. 1, 1869-. Title varies.

ActaA   **Acta asiatica.** Tokyo. 1, 1960-.

ActaOr   **Acta orientalia** academiae scientiarum hungaricae. See Magyar tudomanyos. Akademia.

AO   **Acta orientalia.** Copenhagen. 1, 1922-.

     Acts of various congresses, institutions, etc. are listed by name or title of congress or institution.

     Adyar library bulletin. Madras. 1, february 1937.

     Akademie der wissenschaften (Royal Prussian Academy of Science) Berlin. See also under Institut für orientforschung. **Abhandlungen.** 1804-1907 in one volume a year including publications of various klasses. 1908- as **Abhandlungen** under Philosophisch-historische and physikalisch-mathematische klasse.

AWGN   Akademie der wissenschaft in göttingen,, philologisch-historischeklasse. **Nachrichten.**

     Akademie der wissenschaften. Leipzig. The name of the institute varies as Königlich sächsische gesellschaft der wissenschaften; Sächsische akademie der wissenschaften. **Berichte über die verhandlungen,** 1846-48. Philologisch-historische klasse, **Berichte..** 1, 1849-.

SAWW   Akademie der wissenschaften. Vienna. Philosophisch-historische klasse, **Sitzungsberichte.** 1, 1848-.

                Akademiia nauk. SSSR, Leningrad. **Bulletin.** Ser 3, 1, 1860-. Previously divided by class. **Izvestiia.** Ser 7, 1928-. Earlier titled **Bulletin.**

                All the year round. London. April 30, 1859-95.

AMZ   **Allgemeine missions-zeitschrift.** Berlin. 1-50, 1874-1923. Superseded by **Neue allgemeine missions-zeitschrift.**

                Ambix. Society for the study of alchemy and early chemistry. London. 1, May 1937-.

PAAAS   American academy of arts and sciences. **Proceedings.** See **Daedalus.**

                American anthropologist. Washington, n.y., pa. 1, 1888-.

                American antiquarian and oriental journal. n.p. 1, 1878-.

AJCM   **American journal of chinese medicine.** Grant city, n.j. 1.1, jan 1973. With 5.2, 1977, title changed to
CME&W   **Comparative medicine east and west.**

                American journal of economics and sociology. Lancaster, pa. 1, 1941-.

JR   **American journal of theology.** Baltimore. 1-15, 1880-95. Chicago. 1-24, 1897-1920, united with **Biblical world** to form **Journal of religion.**

                American magazine of art. See **Magazine of art.**

JAOS   American oriental society. New haven, conn. **Journal.** 1, 1843-.

AUFS   American university field staff. Reports service: **East Asia series.** N Y. August, 1952-.

                Anatomical record. Wistar institute of anatomy and biology. Baltimore; philadelphia. Nov 1906-.

                Ankara, Turkey. Université. Dil ve tarih-cografya fakultesi. **Dergisi.** 1, 1942-. Title page in french, Université d'ankara, **Revue de la faculté de langues, d'histoire et de géographie.**

                Annales, annuals, annuairie, etc. of institutions, societes, etc, see under the name or location of the organization.

ACP   **Annales de chimie et de physique.** Paris. 1, 1789-.

                Annales d'hygiène et de médecine coloniales. See **Annales de médecine et de pharmacie coloniales.**

AEO   **Annales de l'extrême-orient et de l'afrique.** Paris. 1, 1878-91. 1-3 as **Annales de l'extrême-orient; bulletin de la société académique indochinoise.**

                Annales de médecine et de pharmacie coloniales. Paris. 1, 1898-. 1-17 titled **Annales d' hygiène et de médecine coloniales.**

APC   **Annales de philosophie chrétienne.** Paris. 1-166, 1830-1913.

APC   **Annales des voyages de la géographie, de l'histoire et de l'archéologie.** Paris. 1-188, 1819-70. 1819-65 as **Nouvelles annales des voyages.**

AL   **Annali lateranensi.** (Rome lateran. Museo lateranense. Pontificio museo missionario ethnologico) 1, 1937-.

AMH   **Annals of medical history.** N Y. 1, 1917-.

                Année sociologique. Paris. Ann 1-12, 1896/97-1909/12; n.s. 1-2 1923-25; 3e sér 1940/48-. 1934-42 superseded by **Annales sociologique.**

                Antaios. Athens. 1, 1945-.

                Anthropological institute. **Journal.** See Royal anthropological institute of great britain and ireland and/or the ethnological society of london.

Anthropological quarterly. Washington, d.c. 1, 1928-.

Anthropologie. Paris. 1, 1890-. Suspended 1941-46.

Anthropos; ephemeris internationales ethnologica et linguistic. Salzburg, vienna, fribourg. 1, 1906-.

Antiquity; a quarterly review of archaeology. Gloucester. 1, 1927-.

Apollo; journal of the arts. London. 1, 1925-.

Archaeologia, or miscellaneous tracts relating to antiquity. London. 1, 1770-.

Archaeology. Cambridge, mass. 1, 1948-.

Archiv für geschichte der philosophie. Berlin. 1, 1888-. Vol 37-39 (1925-30) as **Archiv für geschichte der philosophie und soziologie:** vol 8-39 (1895-1930) as n.s. vol 1-32.

ARW   **Archiv für religionswissenschaft.** Heidelberger akademie der wissenschaften. Leipzig, etc. 1-37, 1898-1942.

AV   **Archiv für völkerkunde.** Museum für völkerkunde. Vienna. 1, 1946-.

ArchOr   **Archiv orientální.** Prague. Oriental institute, czechoslavak academy of sciences. 1, 1929-.

Archives d'anthropologie criminelle, de médecine légale et de psychologie normale et pathologique. Paris. 1-29, 1886-1914. 1886-92 as **Archives de l'anthropologie criminelle et des sciences pénales.**

ASSR   **Archives de sciences sociales des religions.** Succeeded **ASR.** T. 18, 1973-.

ASR   **Archives de sociologie des religions.** Paris. C.N.R.S., Groupe de sociologie des religions et groupe religions et développement. 1, 1956-. Title changed with t. 18, 1973 to **ASSR.**

Archives suisses d'anthropologie générale. Genève. 1, 1914-.

AAA   **Archives of asian art.** See Chinese art society of america.

AGP   **Archives of general psychiatry.** Chicago. American medical association. With july 1960- continues **A.M.A. archives of general psychiatry.**

ACASA   **Archives** of the Chinese art society of america. See Chinese art society of america.

Aristotelian society for the systematic study of philosophy. **Proceedings.** London. 1, 1887-; n.s. 1, 1900-.

Ars islamica. Michigan university research seminar in islamic art; Detroit institute of arts. Ann arbor. 1-15/16, 1934-51. Superseded by **Ars orientalis.**

ArsO   **Ars orientalis. The arts of islam and the east.** Washington, d.c., freer gallery, smithsonian institution, & univ of michigan dept of fine art. 1, 1954-.

AArch   **Art and archaeology.** Archaeological institute of america. Baltimore/washington d.c. 1-35, 1914-34.

Art and letters; india and pakistan. London, 1, 1925-26; n.s. 1, 1927+ 1925-47 as **Indian art and letters.**

AB   **Art bulletin.** College art association of america. N Y. 1913-.

Art in america. N Y. 1, 1913-.

ANA   **Art news (annual)** N Y. 1, 1902-.

AQ   **Art quarterly.** See Detroit institute of arts of the city of detroit.

Art studies; medieval, renaissance and modern. Ed members of the departments of fine arts at harvard and princeton universities. 1-8, 1923-31. Note also that these were issued as extra numbers of the **American journal of archaeology** in 1923, 1925-28.

Artes; monuments et mémoires. Copenhagen. 1-8, 1932-40.

AA   **Artibus asiae; quarterly of asian art and archaeology for scholars and connoisseurs.** Ascona, switzerland. 1925- There is also a ser of **Supplementa** issued from 1937.

ArtsAs   **Arts asiatiques.** Annales du musée guimet et du musée cernuschi. Paris. 1, 1954-.

AofA   **Arts of asia.** HK (Kowloon) 1.1 jan/feb 1971-. Issued bimonthly.

Ap   **Aryan path.** Bombay. 1, 1930-.

            Asia. N Y. See **Asia and the americas.** From march 1917 to october 1942 title was simply **Asia.**

            Asia. Asia society, N Y. 1, spring 1964-.

CMBA   **Asia.** Shanghai and hong kong. 1, 1948-. Title varies as follows: jan 1948-june 1949, **China missionary;** sep 1949-july 1953, **China missionary bulletin;** sep 1953-dec 1959, **Mission bulletin.**

            Asia; asian quarterly of culture and synthesis. Saigon. 1-4, 1951-55.

Asia   **Asia and the americas.** N Y. 1-46, 1898-1946. Title varies as follows: 1898-jan 1917, **Journal of the american asiatic association;** mar 1917-oct 1942, **Asia.**

AM   **Asia major.** London, Leipzig. 1-10, 1924-34/35; 1944; London 1, 1949-.

AMHAV   **Asia major; Hirth anniversary volume.** Oct 1922. The introductory issue, not included in vol numbering.

APQCSA   **Asian and pacific quarterly of cultural and social affairs.** Seoul. Asian and pacific cultural and social centre for the asian and pacific region. 1.1, summer 1969-.

ACQ   **Asian culture quarterly.** Taipei. Asian cultural center, asian parliamentarians union. 1.1, autumn 1973-.

AsFS   **Asian folklore studies.** Nagoya. Nanzan univ. Succeeded **FS** in 1963.

AH   **Asian horizon.** London. 1-3, spring 1948-winter 1950/51.

AQR   **Asian review.** London etc. 1, 1886-. Title varies as follows: 1886-90, 1913, **Asiatic quarterly review;**
AR   1891-1912, **Imperial and asiatic quarterly review;** or **Oriental and colonial record;** 1914-52, **Asiatic review.**

AsSur   **Asian survey.** Berkeley. 1, 1961-. Supersedes **Far eastern survey.**

ATS   **Asian thought and society: an international review.** Oneonta. State univ of ny. Dept of political science. 1.1, apr 1976-.

            Asiatic journal. See **Asiatic journal and monthly review.**

            Asiatic journal and monthly register. See **Asiatic journal and monthly review.**

            Asiatic journal and monthly review. London. 1816-45. Title varies as follows: ser 1-2, **Asiatic journal and monthly register;** ser 3, **Asiatic journal and monthly miscellany.** United with **Colonial magazine** and **East india review** to form **Colonial and asiatic review.**

AQR   **Asiatic quarterly review.** See **Asian review.** London.

AR   **Asiatic review.** See **Asian review.** London.

JRASB   Asiatic society of bengal, calcutta. 1936- as Royal asiatic society of bengal. **Asiatic researches;** or **Transactions** of the society. Calcutta. 1-20, 1788-1839. Superseded by **Journal.** Title varies. **Journal.** 1-33, 1832-64. Continued in the following: **Journal and proceedings,** n.s. 1-30, 1905-34; ser 3, 1, 1935-. **Proceedings.** 1865-1904. Continued in preceding title.

JBBRAS   Asiatic society of bombay. 1804-27, Literary society of bombay; 1827-1955, Royal asiatic society of great britain and ireland, bombay branch. **Journal.** 1841-1922/23; n.s. 1925-. Proc incl. **Transactions.** 1-3, 1804/5-1819-21.

Asiatic society of great britain and ireland. See Royal asiatic society of great britain and ireland.

TASJ   Asiatic society of japan. **Transactions.** 1, 1872/73-. Various series.

AS   **Asiatische studien; études asiatiques. Zeitschrift der schweizerischen gesellschaft für asienkunde; review de la société d'études asiatiques.** Bern. 1, 1947-.

Asiatisches magazin. Weimar. 1-2, 1802.

BAF   **Asie française; bulletin mensuel.** Paris, Comité de l'asie française. 1, 1901-, 1901-10 as **Bulletin** de la comité.

Asien. Berlin. 1-16, 1901-19. Superseded by **Ostasiatische rundschau.**

BAAFC   Association amicale franco-chinoise. **Bulletin.** See **Revue franco-chinoise.**

Association françoise des amis de l'orient. **Bulletin.** Paris. No 1-6, 1921-23; n.s. no 1-11, mar 1925-déc 1927; no 77, oct 1929. N.s. in **Revue des arts asiatiques** q.v. Nothing publ in 1924, 1928.

Association of american geographers. n.p. **Annals.** 1, 1911-.

Athenaeum; journal of literature, science, the fine arts, music and the drama. London. 1828-1921.

Atlantic monthly. Boston. 1, nov 1857-.

Ausland. Stuttgart. 1-66, 1828-93. Merged into **Globus.**

Aussenpolitik. Stuttgart. 1, 1950-.

BOR   **Babylonian and oriental record.** London. 1-9, 1886-1901.

Baessler-archiv; beiträge zur völkerkunde. Leipzig, berlin. 1-25, 1910-43; n.s. 1, 1952-.

Basavangudi, bangalore. Indian institute of culture. **Transactions.** See Indian institute of world culture.

Belgrade. Institut imeni N.P. Kondakova. **Annaly.** 1-11, 1927-40. 1927-36 as **Sbornik statei po arkheologii i vizantinoiedieniiu seminarium kondakovianum.**

Berichte der K. -Sach. ges. d. wiss. phil-hist.cl. see Akademie der wissenschaften. Leipzig. **Berichte.**

Berichte des rheinischen missionsgesellschaft. See Rheinische missionsgesellschaft.

Berlin. Staatliche museen. Ethnologische abtheilung. **Mitteilungen.** 1, 1885-86.

Berlin. Staatliche museen. Museum für völkerkunde. **Veröffentlichungen.** 1-12, 1889-1919. Vol 11 not publ. 12 publ in 1907.

MSOS   Berlin. Universität. Ausland-hochschule. Through 1935, this organization was the university's seminar für orientalische sprachen. **Mitteilungen.** 1, 1898-.

Berliner gesellschaft für anthropologie, ethnologie and urgeschichte. **Verhandlungen.** 1869-1902. May be bound with **Zeitschrift für ethnologie.**

Berliner museum (museen). Amtliche berichte aus den preussischen kunstsammlungen. Berlin. 1-64, 1880-1943.

Biblical world. Chicago. 1, 1882-1920. United with the **American journal of theology** to form the **Journal of religion.**

Bibliotheca sacra; a theological quarterly. Oberlin. 1, 1844-.

Bibliothèque d'école hautes. See Paris. École pratique des hautes études.

BVAMG   **Bibliothèque de vulgarisation des annales du musée guimet.** See Paris. Musée guimet.

BTLVK   **Bijdragen tot de taal-, land- en volkskunde von nederlandsche-indie.** The hague. 1, 1853-.

Biologie médicale. Paris. 1, 1903-.

BIM   **Blackwood's magazine.** Edinburgh, london. 1, 1817-. 1817-1905 as **Blackwood's edinburgh magazine.**

Bombay. University. **Journal.** 1, july 1932-. Also numbered in various sub-ser.

BMFA   Boston. Museum of fine arts. **Bulletin.** 1, 1903-.

British academy for the promotion of historical, philosophical and philological studies. London. **Proceedings.** 1, 1903-.

BJP   **British journal of psychiatry.** London. Publ by authority of the royal medico-psychological association. Continues **Journal of mental science** and **Asylum journal of mental science** with vol 109, 1963-.

British journal of sociology. London. 1, 1950-.

BMQ   **British museum quarterly.** London. 1, 1926-.

AIPHO   Brussels. Université libre. Institut de philologie et d'histoire orientales et slaves. **Annuaire.** 1, 1932/33-.

Buddhism in england. See **Middle way.**

The buddhist annual. Colombo. 1, 1964-.

Buddhist text society. Calcutta. **Journal.** 1-7, 1893-1906. The name of the organization varies and is superseded by the Indian research society.

BTTSoc   Buddhist text translation society. Affiliate of sino-american buddhist association, san francisco.

Buecherei (bücherei) der kultur und geschichte. Bonn, leipzig. 1-30, 1919-23?

BAF   **Bulletin asie-française.** See **Asie française.**

Bulletin de géographie historique et descriptive. See under France. Comité des travaux historiques et scientifiques.

Bulletin de l'académie impériale des sciences de st. petersburg. See Akademiia nauk, SSSR; Leningrad.

BAAFC   **Bulletin** de l'association amicale franco-chinoise. See **Revue franco-chinoise.**

BMFJ   **Bulletin** de la maison franco-japonaise. See under Tokyo. Maison franco-japonaise.

Bulletin de la société saint-jean-baptiste. See **Information nationale.**

Bulletin des missions. Bruges. 1, 1899-. Title varies.

BAAFC   **Bulletin franco-chinoise.** See **Revue franco-chinoise.**

Bulletin médical franco-chinois. Peking. 1, 1920-.

BEA   **Bulletin of eastern art.** Tokyo. No 1-19/20, 1940-41.

Bulletin of sung and yuan studies. Ithaca, ny. Cornell univ. Dept of history. Through vol 13, 1977, titled **Sung studies newsletter.** 1, may 1970-.

BHM   **Bulletin of the history of medicine.** Johns hopkins university. Institute of the history of medicine. 1, 1933-. From 1933-38 as **Bulletin of the institute of the history of medicine.**

             Bulletin of the john herron institute. See under indianapolis. Art association of indianapolis. John herron art institute.

             Bulletins of other societies, libraries, museums, etc. are listed by name or place of the institution.

BM   **Burlington magazine.** London. 1, 1903-.

CHM   **Cahiers d'histoire mondiale; journal of world history.** Superseded by **Cultures.** Paris. 1, 1953-1972.

CalR   **Calcutta review.** Calcutta. 1, 1844-.

CFQ   **California folklore quarterly.** Berkeley. Univ california. 1, jan 1942-.

             Canadian magazine of politics, science, art and literature. Toronto. 1-91, 1893-1939. 1925-37 titled **Canadian.**

             Canadian review of sociology and anthropology. 1, 1964-.

BCUP   Catholic university of peking. **Bulletin.** See under Peking.

CW   **Catholic world; monthly magazine of general literature and science.** N Y. 1, apr 1865-.

             Central asiatic journal. The hague. 1, 1955-.

             Century, a popular quarterly. N Y. 1-120, 1870-1930. Title varies as follows: 1870-81 as **Scribner's monthly;** 1881-1925 as **Century illustrated magazine;** 1925-29 as **Century monthly magazine.** United with **Forum** to form **Forum and century.**

             Century illustrated magazine. See **Century, a popular quarterly.**

             Century magazine. See **Century, a popular quarterly.**

BAIC   Chicago. Art institute. **Bulletin.** 1, 1907- 1-45 as **Bulletin** and now **Quarterly.**

             China analysen. Frankfurt-am-main. 1, 1962-.

CCY   **China Christian yearbook.** Shanghai. 1910-35. 1910-25 as **China mission yearbook.**

ChFor   **China forum.** Taipei. 1.1, jan 1974-. Publ semiannually.

             China informatie. Delft. 1, 1967-.

             China institute bulletin. China institute in america. N Y. 1936-47, 1949-.

CJ   **China journal.** Shanghai. 1-35, 1923-41. 1-5 as **China journal of science and arts.**

             China magazine. Hankow, chungking, N Y.1-19, 1938-49. 1-15 as **China at war.**

             China magazine. N Y. 1, 1924-. 1-10 as **China.**

             China mail. Hong kong.

CMH   **China mission hand-book.** Shanghai. 1, 1896. Only one published.

             China mission year book. See **China christian yearbook.**

CMBA   **China missionary** or **China missionary bulletin.** See **Asia.** Shanghai; hongkong.

             China monthly; the truth about china. N Y. 1-11, 1931-50.

CWR   **China monthly review.** Shanghai. 1-24, 1917-53. Title varies as follows: 1917-21, **Millard's review;** 1921-23, **Weekly review of the far east;** 1923-50, **China weekly review.**

CNA   **China news analysis.** Hongkong. 1, 1953-.

CN   **China notes.** NY. The china committee, far eastern office, division of foreign missions, national council
             of churches of christ/usa. 1.1, sept 1962-.

             China pictorial. Peking. 1951-.

CQ   **China quarterly.** London. 1, 1960-.

             China quarterly. Shanghai. 1-6, 1935-41.

CRecon   **China reconstructs.** Peking. 1, 1952-.

ChRev   **China review.** Hongkong. 1-25, 1872-1901.

             China review. London. 1-5, 1931-38.

ACSS   China society. Singapore. **Annual.** 1948-(Chung-kuo hsüeh-hui)

JCS   China society. Taipei. **Journal.** 1, 1961- Alternate listing under Chung-kuo hsüeh-hui, taipei.

             China society occasional papers. London. N.s. 1, 1942-.

             China today. N Y. 1937-42.

             China today. Taipei. 1958-.

CWR   **China weekly review.** *See* **China monthly review.**

             La chine; revue bi-mensuelle illustrée. Peking. 1-73, 1921-25.

             Chine et sibérie. Brussels. 1-2 (no 1-40), 1900-01.

             **Chinese and japanese repository of facts and events in science, history, and art, relating to eastern
             asia.** London. 1-2 (no 1-29) 1863-65.

ACASA   Chinese art society of america. N.Y. **Archives.** 1, 1945/46-. With vol 20, 1966/67, changed to **Archives**
AAA   **of asian art.**

             Chinese buddhist. pure karma buddhist association. Shanghai. 1-2, 1930-31(?)

CC   **Chinese culture.** Taipei. 1, 1957-.

CEd   **Chinese education.** White plains, ny. 1, spring 1968-. A journal of translations.

CLG   **Chinese law and government.** White plains, ny. 1, spring 1968-. A journal of translations.

CL   **Chinese literature.** Peking. Foreign languages press. 1, autumn 1951-. Monthly, each year numbered
             vol 1 through 12.

ChLit   **Chinese literature: essays, article, reviews.** Madison. Univ wisconsin. 1, jan 1979-.

CMJ   **Chinese medical journal.** Shanghai. 1, 1887-.

ChRec   **Chinese recorder.** Shanghai. 1-72, 1868-1941. Supersedes **Missionary recorder.**

ChRep   **Chinese repository.** Canton. 1-20, 1832-51.

             Chinese review. London. 1-4, 1914.

CSPSR   **Chinese social and political science review.** Peking. 1-24, 1916-41.

CSA   **Chinese sociology and anthropology.** White plains, ny. 1, fall 1968-. A journal of translations.

CSM   **Chinese students' monthly.** Baltimore. 1-26, 1905-30.

CSP   **Chinese studies in philosophy.** White plains, ny. 1, fall 1969-. A journal of translations.

     Chinese year book. Shanghai. 1-7, 1935/36-1944/45.

CDA   **Chinesische-deutscher almanach.** Frankfurt-am-main. China-institut. 19–; probably 1926.

     Chinesische blätter für wissenschaft und kunst. 1, 1925/27. Superseded by **Sinica.**

CF   **Ching feng.** Hong kong. 1957-. 1-7 has title **Quarterly notes on christianity and chinese religion and**
QNCCR   **culture.**

     Ch'ing hua hsüeh-pao. See **Tsinghua journal of chinese studies.**

     Ch'ing-shih wen-t'i. New haven. 1, 1965-.

     Christian century. Chicago. 1, 1884-.

     Christliche welt. Marburg. 1, 1886-.

CCJ   **Chung chi journal.** Hongkong. July, 1961-1976.

     Chung-kuo hsüeh-hui. See China society, taipei, or China society, singapore.

     Chung mei yüeh-k'an. Taipei. 1, 1956-. **West and east** is the engl title of this journal.

CMI   **Church missionary intelligencer.** See **Church missionary review.**

     Church missionary review. London. 1-78, 1849-1927. From 1849-1906 as **Church missionary**
     intelligencer.

     Church missionary society. London. **Annual report of the committee of the church missionary**
     society for africa and the east. 1, 1801-. Title varies as **Proceedings** of the society for missions to africa
     and the east, or **Proceedings** of the church missionary society.

     Ciba symposia. New jersey. 1-11, 1939-51. Engl companion vol to **Ciba zeitschrift.**

     Ciba zeitschrift. Basel. 1-11, 1933-52. See also **Ciba symposia.**

     Cina. Rome. Istituto italiano per il medio estremo oriente. 1-8, 1956-64.

     Claremont quarterly. Claremont, california. 1-11, 1956/57-64.

BCMA   Cleveland. Museum of art. **Bulletin.** 1, 1914-.

     Club alpin français. Paris. **Annuaire.** 1-30, 1874-1903.

     Colonial and asiatic review. See **Asiatic journal and monthly review.**

     Comité japonais des sciences historiques. A section of the XIe Congrès international des sciences
     historiques. Stockholm, 1960.

     Comité sinico-japonais. See Société sinico-japonaise. Paris.

     Common cause. Chicago. 1-4, 1947-51.

     Common cause. London, n.y. 1, 1944-.

CME&W   **Comparative medicine east and west.** NY. Neale watson academic publications. Continues **AJCM**
     (1973-77) Publ for the Institute for advanced research in asian science and medicine.

CSSH   **Comparative studies in society and history, an international quarterly.** The hague. 1, 1958-.

     Comptes rendus. See under name of institution or organization.

Concilium; internationale zeitschrift für theologie. Zürich, mainz. 1, 1965-.

CMG   **Conférences faites au musée guimet.** See under Paris. Musée guimet.

Conferenze tenute all' istituto italiano per il medio ed estremo oriente. See under Istituto italiano per il medio ed estremo oriente.

CIHR   Congrès international d'histoire des religions. (Société ernest renan) Paris, 1923. **Actes,** Paris, 1925, 2 vol. See also International congress for the history of religions.

Congrès international des sciences anthropologiques et ethnologiques. See International congress of anthropological and ethnological sciences.

ICO   Congrès international d'orientalistes. See International congress of orientalists.

CPOL   Congrès provincial des orientalistes français. Lyon, paris. **Compte rendu.** 1-3, 1875-78.

Congrès scientifique international des catholiques. 1888-. 4e congrès. Fribourg, 1897. **Compte rendu.** Fribourg, 1898, 11 vol in 3 vol.

CRJ   **Contemporary religions in japan.** Tokyo. 1, 1960-.

CR   **Contemporary review.** London. 1, 1866-.

La controverse et la contemporain. Paris. 1, 1845-89.

Cornhill magazine. London. 1, 1860-.

CB   **Current background.** Hong kong. American consulate general. No 1, 1950-.

Current science; science in the making. Bangalore, india. 1, july 1932-.

The cycle; a political and literary review. Shanghai. 1st ser may 1870-june 1871. All publ in 1871.

Daedalus. American academy of arts and sciences. Cambridge, mass. 1, no 1, may 1846-. The Academy's **Proceedings.**

Dan viet nam. École française d'extrême-orient. Hanoi. No 1-3, 1948-49.

BDetIA   Detroit institute of arts of the city of detroit. **Art quarterly.** 1, winter 1938-. **Bulletin.** 1, 1904- ; n.s.
AQ   1919-.

DGNVO   Deutsche gesellschaft für natur- und völkerkunde ostasiens. See under Gesellschaft für natur-und völkerkunde ostasiens.

ZDMG   Deutsche morgenländische gesellschaft. Leipzig. **Zeitschrift.** 1, 1847-.

Deutsche rundschau für geographie. Vienna, leipzig. 1-37, 1878-1915. 1-32 titled **Deutsche rundschau für geographie und statistik.**

Diogène. Paris. No 1, 1952-. French edition of **Diogenes.**

Diogenes: an international review of philosophy and humanistic studies. N.Y. No 1, 1952-.

Discovery; a popular journal of knowledge. London, cambridge. 1, 1920-.

Les documents du progrès. Paris. 1, 1909-. See following item. **Dokumente des fortschritte; internationale revue.** Berlin. 1-11, 1907-18. Affiliated with **Documents du progrès.** Paris. Occasionally art are duplicated. **Records of progress** is the american ed.

Dublin review. London. 1, 1836-.

EC   **Early china.** Berkeley. Univ of california. Institute of east asian studies. Publ for Society for the study of early china. 1, fall 1975-. Publ annually.

E&W   **East and west.** Rome. 1, 1950-.

EA   **East of asia; an illustrated quarterly.** Shanghai. 1-5, 1902-06. This is engl ed of **Ferne osten,** q.v.

EWCR   **East-west center review.** Honolulu. 1-4, 1964-68.

EArt   **Eastern art.** College art association of america. Philadelphia. 1-3, 1928-31.

EB   **Eastern buddhist.** Kyoto. Otani univ. 1, 1921-1937; n.s. 1, 1965-.

EH   **Eastern horizon.** HK. 1, 1960-.

EW   **Eastern world.** London. 1, 1947-.

Eclectic magazine of foreign literature. N Y. boston. 1-148, 1844-1907.

École des hautes études. See Paris. École pratique des hautes études.

BEFEO   École française d'extrême-orient. Hanoi. **Bulletin.** 1, 1901-.

École pratique des hautes études. See under Paris.

Education. France. Haut- commissariat de france pour l'indochine. Saigon. 1, 1948.

Eine heilige kirche. Munich. 1-22 no 2, 1919-41. Vol 1-15 as **Hochkirche.** Superseded by **Ökumenische einheit.**

Encounter. London. 1, 1953-.

Endeavour; revue trimestrielle, publiée en cinq langues et destinée à tenir registre du progrès des sciences au service du genre humain. Imperial chemical industries. London. vol 1, 1942-.

EJ   **Eranos-jahrbuch.** Zürich. 1933-.

Etc.; a review of general semantics. Chicago. 1, 1943-.

Ethics. Chicago. 1, 1890-. Vol 1-48, 1890-1938 titled **International journal of ethics.**

Ethnographie. Paris. 1-22, 1860-1903. N.s no 1, oct 1913-. Vol 1-2 as **Comptes rendus** of Société d'ethnographie; vol 3-8 as **Actes** of the society. Vol 1-22 also numbered in ser.

Ethnological society of london. **Journal.** 1848-71. 1861-69 as **Transactions.** This society united with the anthropological society of london to form the Royal anthropological institute of great britain and ireland.

Ethnologisches notizblatt. Königliche museum für völkerkunde. Königliche museum, berlin. 1-3, 1894-1904.

Ethnos. staten etnogtafiska museum. Stockholm. 1, 1936-.

AS   **Études asiatiques.** See **Asiatische studien.**

Études sociales. Paris, 1, 1881-. 1881-1930 as **La reforme sociale.**

Études   **Études des pères de la compagnie de jésus.** Paris. 1, 1856-. Title varies as follows: 1856-61 as **Études de théologie, de philosophie et d'histoire;** 1862-94 as **Études religieuses, philosophiques et historiques.**

ER   **Études religieuses.** See **Études des pères.** . . .

Evangelischen missionen, illustriertes familienblatt. Güterslah. 1, 1898-.

EMM   **Evangelisches missions-magazin.** Basel. 1816-1939. In 1940 merged with **NAM, ZMR,** and **Orient** (Potsdam?) to form **Evangelische missionszeitschrift.** Stuttgart. 1, 1940-.

Évidences. Paris. No 1, 1949-. Preceded in mar 1949 by one unnumbered issue.

	l'Explorateur: Journal géographique et commercial. Paris. 1-4, 1875-76.
ET	**Expository times.** Edinburgh. 1, oct 1889-.
FE	**The far east.** Shanghai? 1, no 1-12, 1905-06.
FEER	**Far eastern economic review.** Hongkong. 1, 1946-.
FEQ	**Far eastern quarterly.** See **Journal of asian studies.**
	Far eastern review. Shanghai. 1-38, 1904-41.
FO	**Ferne osten.** Shanghai. 1-3, 1902-05. See also **East of asia.**
	Fogg museum of art. See Harvard University. William H. Fogg art museum.
	Folk-lore; quarterly review of myth, tradition, institution and custom. London. 1, 1890-.
FLJ	**Folklore journal.** London. 1-7, 1883-89.
FS AsFS	**Folklore studies.** Catholic university. Museum of oriental ethnology. Peking, nagoya. 1, 1942-. In 1963, title changed to **Asian folklore studies.**
FF	**Forschungen und fortschritte; korrespondenzblatt der deutschen wissenschaft und technik.** Berlin. 1-41?, 1925-67(?)
	Fortnightly. London. 1-182, 1865-1954. From 1865-1934 titled **Fortnightly review.**
	France. Comité des travaux historiques et scientifiques. Section de géographie. **Bulletin.** 1, 1886-. From 1886-1912 titled **Bulletin de géographie historique et descriptive.**
FA	**France-asie; revue de culture et de synthèse franco-asiatique.** Saigon. 1, 1946-.
	Frankfurter hefte. Stadtisches völkermuseum. Frankfurter universität. 1-39, 1915-31. N.s. 1946-. 1, 1946-.
	Fraser's magazine. London. 1, 1869-82.
FCR	**Free China review.** Taipei. 1, 1951-.
	Freer galley of art. Washington, d.c. **Occasional papers.** 1, 1947-.
GBA	**Gazette des beaux-arts.** Paris. 1, 1859-1939. American ed NY. Ser 6, vol 22, 1942-.
	Geist des ostens. Munich. 1-2, 1913-15.
	Geisteswissenschaften. Leipzig. No 1-39, 1913-14.
	Geisteswissenschaftliche forschungen. Stuttgart. 1, 1936-.
	Gentleman's magazine. London. 1-303, 1731-1907.
	Geographical journal. Royal geographical society of london. London. 1, 1893-. Supersedes the society's **Proceedings.**
GM	**Geographical magazine.** London. 1-5, 1874-78. Superseded by the Royal geographical society of london, **Proceedings.**
	Geographical magazine. London. 1, 1935-.
	Géographie. Paris. 1-72,no 3, 1900-39. Supersedes **Bulletin** of the Société de géographie (Paris) See also listing under the Société.
MDGNVO Nachr DGNVO	Gesellschaft für natur- und völkerkunde ostasiens. Tokyo to 1945. Deutsche gesellschaft für natur-... is an earlier name of the institution. **Mitteilungen.** 1-32E, 1873/76-1943. Continued after 1945. **Nachrichten.** Tokyo, wiesbaden. No 1, 1926-. No 1-70, 1926-45 as **Nachrichten aus der gesellschaft.**
	Globus. Hildburghausen, brunswick. 1-98, 1861-1910. Merged into **Petermanns geographische mitteilungen.**

Goldthwaite's geographical magazine. N Y. 1-7, 1891-95.

Gregorianum Rome. 1, 1920-.

Gutenberg jahrbuch. Mainz. 1, 1926-.

Han-hiue. Paris. Université. Centre d'études sinologiques de Pékin. 1-3.4, 1944-49. Vol 1 titled **Bulletin** de la centre.

HZ   **Hansei Zasshi.** See **Orient.** Tokyo.

Harper's magazine. N Y. 1, 1850-, 1-101 as **Harper's new monthly magazine;** 102-28 as **Harper's monthly magazine.**

Harper's weekly. N Y., 1-62, 1857-.

Harvard divinity bulletin. Harvard university. Divinity school. Cambridge, mass. 1, 1935/36-. Title varies as follow: **Harvard divinity school annual; Harvard divinity school bulletin; Harvard divinity school.**

HJAS   **Harvard journal of asiatic studies.** Cambridge, mass. 1, 1936-

HTR   **Harvard theological review.** Harvard University. Theological school. 1, 1908-.

        Harvard university. Center for east-asian studies. **Papers on China.** 1, 1947-.

BFoggMA Harvard university. William H. Fogg art museum. **Bulletin.** 1, 1931-.

        Hermès; recherches sur l'expérience spirituelle. Paris. 1, 1963-.

HJ   **Hibbert journal; quarterly review of religion, theology and philosophy.** London, boston. 1, 1902-.

HM   **Histoire de la médecine.** Paris. 1, 1951-.

HR   **History of religions.** Chicago. 1, 1961-.

        History today. London. 1, 1951-.

        Hitotsubashi academy annals. Tokyo. **Annals.** 1-10, 1950-59. In 1960, vol one of the **Hitotsubashi journal of arts and sciences** partially superseded the **Annals.** May also be listed under Tokyo. Hitotsubashi Daigaku.

        Hobbies; the magazine for collectors. N.p. Begins with vol 36, 1931-.

        Hochland; monatschrift für alle gebiete des wissens, der literatur und kunst. Munich; kempton. 1, 1903-.

        l'Homme. Revue française d' anthropologie. Paris. École des hautes études en sciences sociales avec le concours du centre nationale de la recherche scientifique. 1, 1961-.

        Honolulu academy of arts. **Special Studies.** 1, 1947-. Supersedes its **Annual bulletin.** 1-3, 1939-41(?)

HRAF   Human relations area files, inc. Country survey series. New haven. 1, 1956-.

        Illustrated london news. London. 1, 1842-.

        Illustration. Paris 1-102, 1843-1944.

PIAJ   Imperial academy of japan. **Proceedings.** See Japan academy. Tokyo. **Proceedings.**

IAQR   **Imperial and asiatic quarterly review.** See **Asian review.** London.

IA   **Indian antiquary.** Bombay. 1-62, 1872-1933. Superseded by **New indian antiquary.**

Indian art and letters. *See* **Art and letters: India and pakistan.**

Indian culture. Calcutta. 1, 1934-.

IHQ   **Indian Historical quarterly.** Calcutta. 1, 1925-.

Indian institute of culture. *See* Indian institute of world culture.

Indian institute of world culture. Basavangudi, bangalore. **Transactions.** No 1, 1948-.

Indian journal of social research. Baraut, india. 1960-.

Indian journal of (the) history of medicine. Madras. 1, 1956-.

JISOA   Indian society of oriental art. Calcutta. **Journal.** 1-19, 1933-52/53. Superseded by **Rupam.**

Indianapolis. Art association of indianapolis. John herron art institute. **Bulletin;** 1, 1911-.

IAC   **Indo-asian culture,** New delhi. 1, 1952-.

ICG   **Indo-chinese gleaner.** Malacca. 1-3 (no 1-20) 1817-22.

Information nationale. Montreal. 1953-. Vol 1-10 as **Bulletin** de la société saint-jean-baptiste de montreal.

AIPHO   Institut de philologie et d'histoire orientales. *See* under Brussels. Université.

MIOF   Institut für orientforschung. Deutsche akademie der wissenschaften. Berlin. **Mitteilungen.** 1953-.

Institute of pacific research. China academy. Taipei. **Journal** or **Bulletin.** 1, 1967-.

IAE   **International archives of ethnography.** Leiden. 1, 1888-. Title varies as **Internationales archiv für ethnographie; Archives internationales d'ethnographie,** etc.

PIAHA   International association of historians of asia. **Conference proceedings.** 1st biennial conference. Manila. 1960. 2nd biennial conference. Taipei. 1962.

ICfO   International conference of orientalists in japan. **Transactions.** 1956.

ICHR   International congress for the history of religions. Proceedings title varies with host country. 1900-. 2nd congress Basel (1904) **Verhandlungen.** Basel (1905) 382p. 3rd congress. Oxford (1908) **Transactions.** Oxford (1908) 2 vol. 7th congress. Amsterdam (1950) **Proceedings.** Amsterdam (1951) 196p. 11th congress. Claremont, calif (1965) **Proceedings.** Leiden (1968?) 3 vol. See also under Congrès international d'histoire des religions, paris, 1923, for data on a congress which is not one of this ser.

International congress of anthropological and ethnological sciences. 1st congress. London. 1934. **Proceedings.** 2nd congress. Copenhagen. 1938. **Proceedings.** 6th congress. Paris. 1960. 3 vol **Proceedings.**

ICO   International congress of orientalists. Transactions. Title varies with host country. 2nd congress. London (1874) **Transactions.** 1876. 4th congress. Florence (1878) **Atti.** 2 vol 1880-81. 6th congress. Leiden (1883) **Actes.** 4 vol 1884-85. 9th congress. London (1892) **Transactions.** 2 vol 1893. 10th congress. Genève (1894) **Actes.** 3 vol (Leide) 1895-97. 11th congress. Paris (1897) **Actes.** 5 vol 1898-99. 13th congress. Hamburg (1902) **Verhandlungen** (Leiden) 1904. 14th congress. Algiers (1905) **Actes.** 3 vol in 4 (Paris) 1906-8. 18th congress. Leiden (1931) **Actes.** 1932. 21st congress. Paris (1948) **Actes.** 1949. 26th congress. New delhi (1964) **Daily Bulletins.**

International journal of ethics. *See* **Ethics**

IJSP   **International journal of social psychiatry.** London. 1, 1955-.

IPQ   **IPQ: International philosophical quarterly.** N Y. 1, 1961-.

IRM   **International review of missions.** Edinburgh. 1, 1912-.

IAF   **Internationales asien forum.**München. 1, jan 1970-.

               Ipek; jahrbuch für prähistorische und ethnographische kunst. Berlin. 1-2, 1925-69.

IQB   **Iqbal review.** Karachi, pakistan. 1960-. Alternately in engl and urdu.

               Isis, international review devoted to the history of science and civilization. Brussels, bern. 1, 1913-.

I&S   **Issues and studies.** Taipei. Institute of international relations. 1, oct 1964-.

Is.MEO   Istituto italiano per il medio e l'estremo oriente. Conferenze tenute all'is (tituto italiano per il) M(edio e l') e(stremo)o(riente) 1952-.

               Izvestiya (izvestiia) akademiya nauk. See under Akademiia nauk, SSSR Leningrad. **Izvestia.**

JAK   **Jahrbuch der asiatischen kunst.** Leipzig. 1-2. 1924-25.

JSMVL   **Jahrbuch der städtliches museum für völkerkunde.** See under Leipzig.

               Jahrbuch für psychologie, psychotherapie und medizinische anthropologie. Munich, etc. 1, 1952/53-. Title varies. Vol 1-6 (1952-59) as **Jahrbuch für psychologie und psychotherapie.**

               Jahresberichte der geschichtswissenschaft. Berlin. 1-36, 1878-1913.

               Jahrbuch für prähistorische ethnographische kunst. See **Ipek.**

               Janus; revue internationale de l'histoire des sciences, de la médecine, de la pharmacie et de la technique. Leiden. 1, 1896-.

PIAJ   Japan academy. Tokyo. **Proceedings.** 1, 1912-. From 1912-47 listed as published by the imperial academy of japan.

               Japan quarterly. Tokyo. 1, 1954-.

JSR:HS   **Japan science review: humanistic studies.** Tokyo. 1, 1950-. Vol 1-9, 1950-58 as **Japan science**
JSR:LPH   **review: literature, philosophy and history**

JSR:LPH   **Japan science review: literature, philosophy and history.** See **Japan science review: humanistic studies.**

TPJS   Japan society, London. **Transactions and Proceedings.** 1, 1892-.

               Japanese studies in the history of science. (Nippon kagakusi gakkai) Tokyo. 1, 1962-.

               John herron institute. See under Indianapolis.Art association.

JRLB   John rylands library. Manchester, england. **Bulletin.** 1, 1903-.

JA   **Journal asiatique.** Paris. 1, 1822-. 1828-35 as **Nouveau journal asiatique.**
NouvJA
               Journal des savans. Paris. 1665-1792. Superseded by **Journal des savants.**

               Journal des savants. Académie des inscriptions et belles - lettres. Paris. No 1-12, 1797; sér 2, 1, 1816-.

               Journal d'hygiène. Paris. 1-40, 1875-1914.

JSSR   **Journal for the scientific study of religion.** Washington, d.c. 1, oct 1961-. Official journal of the society for the scientific study of religion.

JAFL   **Journal of american folklore.** Boston, lancaster. 1, 1888-.

JEAC   **Journal of aesthetics and art criticism.** N Y. 1, 1941-.

JAAS **Journal of asian and african studies.** Leiden. 1, 1966-.

JAC **Journal of asian culture.** Los angeles. Univ california. Dept of oriental languages. 1, 1977-. Publ annually by graduate students of the dept.

JAS **Journal of asian studies.** Ann arbor. 1, 1941-. Years 1941-56 titled **Far eastern quarterly.**

JCE **Journal of chemical engineering, China.** Chinese institute of chemical engineers. Tientsin. 1, 1934-.

JCP **Journal of chinese philosophy.** Dordrecht & boston. 1.1 dec 1973-.

JD **Journal of dharma.** Bangalore. Dharmaram college. Dharma research association, center for the study of world religions. 1, 1975-.

JHP **Journal of humanistic psychology.** Brandeis univ. 1, spring 1961-.

JIBS **Journal of indian and buddhist studies (Indogaku bukkyōgaku kenkyū)** Tokyo. 1, 1952-.

  Journal of indian art and industries. London. 1-17, 1884-1916.

JIC **Journal of intercultural studies.** Hirakawa city, Kansai univ of foreign studies. Intercultural research institute. 1, 1974-. Publ annually.

JOR **Journal of oriental research.** See under University of madras. **Annals of oriental research.**

  Journal of oriental research. Kuppuswami sastri research intitute. Madras. 1, 1927-.

JOS **Journal of oriental studies.** HK univ. Centre of asian studies. 1, 1954-.

JR **Journal of religion.** Chicago. 1, 1921-.

JRE **Journal of religious ethics.** Waterloo, ont. 1, fall 1973. Published for the american academy of religion.

JRH **Journal of religious history.** University of Australia. Sydney. 1, 1960-.

  Journal of religious psychology including its anthropological and sociological aspects. Worcester, mass. 1-7, 1904-15.

JSS **Journal of social science.** National taiwan university. College of law. 1, 1956-. May be catalogued by chin title: **She-hui k'o-hsüeh lun-ts'ung.**

JSSEAS **Journal of southeast asian studies.** Singapore & ny. 1, mar 1970-.

JCLTA **Journal of the chinese language teachers association.** Univ pennsylvania. 1, fall 1966-.

JTP **Journal of transpersonal psychology.** Palo alto, calif. American transpersonal association. 1, spring 1969-.

  Journal of unified science. Leipzig, the hague. 1, 1930-. Supersedes **Annalen der philosophie und philosophischen kritik** (1-8 no 9/10, 1919- apr 1930). Vol 1-7 no 5/6, 1930- april 1939, as **Erkenntniss.**

  Journal société finno-ougrienne. See under Suomalais-ugrilainen seura. Helsingfors.

JHI **Journal of the history of ideas.** NY, lancaster. 1, 1940-.

JHMAS **Journal of the history of medicine and allied sciences.** N Y. 1, 1946-.

JIA **Journal of the indian archipelago and eastern asia.** Singapore. 1, 1847-. superseded by **Journal of eastern asia.** Singapore. 1, 1875-.

  Journals of societies and institutions are listed under the name or locations of their respective organizations.

  Kairos; religionswissenschaftliche studien. Salzburg. 1, 1964-.

Kairos; zeitschrift für religionswissenschaft und theologie. Salzburg. 1, 1959-.

Die katholischen missionen. Freiberg i.b; st. louis, mo.; aachen, etc. 1, July 1873-. Numbering irregular.

KT:OS   **Keleti tanu/manyok. Oriental studies.** Budapest. 1, 1977-.

Königlichen museum für völkerkunde. See under Berlin. Staatliche museem.

Kokka, an illustrated monthly journal of the fine and applied arts of Japan and other eastern countries. No 1, 1889-. Subtitle varies.

Koloniale rundschau. Berlin, leipzig. 1-34, 1909-43. May have the title **Kolonialdeutsche, wissenschaftliche beihefte.**

TransKBRAS   Korea branch, royal asiatic society. **Transactions.** Seoul. New series begins with vol 32, 1951-.

KdeO   **Kunst des orients.** Wiesbaden. 1, 1950-.

KGUAS   Kwansei gakuin university. Nishinomiya, japan. **Annual studies.** 1, 1953-.

Lancet. London, 1823-.

Laval theologique et philosophique. Quebec. 1, 1945-.

JSMVL   Leipzig. Städtisches museum für völkerkunde. **Jahrbuch.** 1-9, 1906-22/25; 10,1926/51-. **Mitteilungen.** No 1-17, 1960-64; 1965-.

Leipzig. Üniversität. **Wissenschaftliche zeitschrift. Gesellschafts und sprachwissenschaftliche reihe.** 1951/52.

Life. N Y. 1936-72.

LD   **Light of dharma.** San francisco. 1-6, 1901-07.

Littell's living age. Boston. 1844-1941.

Litterae orientales. Leipzig, wiesbaden. 1-84, ?-1939; n.s. no 1-44, 1953-1958.

BSOAS   London. University. School of oriental and african studies. **Bulletin.** 1, 1917-.

London. University. Warburg Institute. **Journal of the warburg and courtauld institutes.** 1, 1937-.

London and china express. London. 1-73, 1858-1931. Title varies.

Lotus. See under Société sinico-japonais. Paris.

Lyons. Université. **Annales.** 1-9, 1891-98; n.s. 1, **Sciences, médecine,** no 1-50, 1899-1934; n.s. 2, **Droit, lettres,** no 1-48, 1899-1934; Both superseded by n.s.3, **Science,** 1936-.

MacMillan's magazine. London, etc. 1, 1859-1907.

Magasin littéraire. Paris. 1-15, 1884-98. 1884-93 as **Magasin littéraire et scientifique.**

MLA   **Magazin; monatsschrift für literatur, kunst und kultur.** Berlin. 1832-1915. Title varies as follows: 1832-80, **Magazin für die literatur des auslandes,** 1881-90, **Magazin für die literatur des in- und auslandes;** 1890-1904, **Magazin für literatur;** 1904-05, **Neue magazin;** 1906-07, **Magazin für literatur des in- und auslandes.**

Magazine of art. Washington, NY 1-46 no 5, nov 1909- may 1953. 1909-15 as **Art and progress;** 1916-36 as **American magazine of art.**

ActaOr   Magyar tudomanyos akademia. Budapest. **Acta orientalia.** 1, 1950-.

Maharaja sayajirao university of baroda. **Journal.** 1, 1952-.

MB   **Maha Bodhi; a monthly journal of international buddhist brotherhood.** Calcutta. 1, 1892-. Title
            varies as follow: 1892-1901, **Journal of the Maha Bodhi society;** 1901-23, **Maha-bodhi and the
            united buddhist world.**

            Main currents in modern thought. N Y. 1, 1940-.

BMFJ   Maison franco-japonaise. See under Tokyo.

            Man. Royal anthropological institute of great britain and ireland. London. 1,1901-.

JMGS   Manchester geographical society. Manchester, england. **Journal.** 1, 1885-.

            Marco polo. Shanghai. 1, 1939-.

            Mariner's mirror. London. 1, 1911-.

MCB   **Mélanges chinois et bouddhiques.** Louvain. 1, 1932-. Monographic ser, issued irregularly.

MIHEC   **Mélanges,** Paris universitaire, institut des hautes études chinoise. See under Paris. Université.

            Mélanges sinologiques. Centre d'études sinologiques. Peking. 1951-.

            Mémoires concernant l'asie orientale, inde, asie-centrale, extrême-orient. See Académie des
            inscriptions et belles-lettres.

MCLC   **Mémoires concernant l'histoire, les sciences, les arts, les moeurs, les usages etc. des chinois; par
            les missionnaires de pékin.** Ed C. Batteux, L.G. Oudert, Feudrix de Brequigny, J. de Guignes, and A. J.
            Silvestresle Sacy. Paris. 1-16, 1776-1804.

MCAM   **Mémoires couronnés et autre mémoires.** See under Académie royale des sciences, des lettres et
            beaux-arts de belgique.

MAIBL   **Mémoires de l'académie des inscriptions et belles-lettres.** See under Académie des inscriptions . . .

MAI   **Mémoires de littérature tirés des registres de l'académie des inscriptions.** See under Académie des
            inscriptions et belles-lettres.

            Mémoires de la société d'émulation de roubaix. See under société d'émulation. . . .

            Merkur; deutsche zeitung für europäisches denken. Stuttgart, baden-baden. 1, 1947-.

WMM   **Methodist magazine.** London. 1, 1778-. Title varies as follows: 1778-97, **Arminian magazine;**
            1798-1821, **Methodist magazine;** 1822-1912, **Wesleyan methodist magazine;** 1914-26, **Magazine
            of the wesleyan methodist church.**

            Methodist review. N Y. 1-114, 1818- 1931. Title varies as follows: 1818-28, **Methodist magazine;**
            1830-40, **Methodist magazine and quarterly review;** 1841-84, **Methodist quarterly review.**

BMMA   Metropolitan museum of art. **Bulletin** See under New York.

MW   **Middle way.** London. 1, 1926-. Vol 1-17 as **Buddhism in england.**

            Ministry; a quarterly theological review for east and south africa. Moriji, basutoland. 1, 1960-.

            Minneapolis institute of art. Minneapolis. **Bulletin.** 1, 1905.

            Missiology. Continuation of **PrAnthro** beginning with vol 19, 1973-.

            Mission bulletin. Shanghai, hongkong. See **Asia.**

            Missionary recorder. Foochow 1, no 1-2, 1867. Superseded by **Chinese recorder.**

            Missionary research library. New York. **Bulletin.** 1, 1928-. This publication coincides with dating of
            Occasional bulletin.

MRW   **Missionary review of the world.** London, etc. 1-62, 1878-1939. 1878-87 as **Missionary review.**

MC   **Missions catholiques.** Paris. 1, 1868-.

	Mitteilungen aus der ethnologischen abteilung der königl- museen zu berlin. See Berlin. Staatliche museen. Ethnologische abteilung.
MSGFOK	**Mitteilungen** der schweizerischen gesellschaft der freunde ostasiatische kultur. See schweizerische gesellschaft für asien-kunde.
	Mitteilungen des instituts für orientforschung. East berlin. Deutsche akademie der wissenschaften zu berlin, institut für orientforschung. 1, 1953-.
MSOS	**Mitteilungen** des seminars für orientalische sprachen. See under Berlin. Universität. Ausland-hochschule.
MIOF	**Mitteilungen** deutsche preussiche akademie der wissenschaften zu berlin. See Institut für orientforschung.
MDGNVO	**Mitteilungen** der deutsche gesellschaft für natur- und völkerkunde ostasiens, tokyo. See Gesellschaft für natur-und völkerkunde.
	Modern china; an international quarterly of history and social science. Beverly hills, calif & london. Sage publications. 1, 1975-.
	Moderne welt. Cologne. 1, 1959-.
	Monde moderne et la femme d'aujourdhui. Paris. 1-28, 1895-1908. 1895-1905 as **Monde moderne.** Merged into **Revue hebdomadaire.**
	Monist, a quarterly magazine devoted to the philosophy of science. Chicago. 1-46, 1890-1936.
	Moniteur universel: Journal officiel. Paris. 1789-1868.
MN	**Monumenta nipponica.** Tokyo. 1, 1938-.
MS	**Monumenta serica.** Peking, nagoya, los angeles, st. augustin (germany) 1, 1935/36-.
	Muséon. Société des lettres et des sciences. Paris, louvain. 1, 1882-.
	Museum; tijdschrift voor filologie geschiedenis. Groningen, leyden. 1-64, 1893-1959?
	Museum journal. See under Pennsylvania. University. University museum.
BMFEA	Museum of far eastern antiquities. **Bulletin.** See under Stockholm.
BMFA	Museum of fine arts (Boston) **Bulletin.** See under Boston.
Nachr DGNVO	**Nachrichten** der deutsche gesellschaft für natur- und völkerkunde ostasiens. See Gesellschaft für natur-und völkerkunde ostasiens.
NGM	**National geographic magazine.** Washington, d.c. 1, 1888-.
	National medical journal. London. 1, 1914-.
	National medical journal of china. Shanghai. 1915-.
NPMB	**National palace museum bulletin.** Taipei. 1, 1966-. May be catalogued under Kuo-li ku-kung po-wu-yüan.
NRJ	**National reconstruction journal.** N Y. 1-8, 1942-47.
	National review. Shanghai. 1-20, ?-1916.
NH	**Natural history.** NY American museum of natural history. 1, apr 1900-.
NLIP	**Natural law institute proceedings.** Notre dame university. Law school (college of law) 1-15, 1947-51. Superseded by **Natural law forum.**

Nature. London. 1, 1869-.

Nature. Paris. 1, 1873-.

Neue orient. Berlin. 1-17, 1917-43.

Neue orient; abhandlungen zur geographie, kultur und wirtschaft der länden des ostens. Halle-a-saale. 1-13, 1905-18.

Neue schweizer rundschau. Zürich. 1-41, 1907-33; n.s. 1-22, 1933-55. 1907 as **Wissen und leben.**

NZM   **Neue zeitschrift für missionwissenschaft.** Beckenreid, switz. 1, 1945-.

New age. Communist party of india. New delhi. 1, sep 1952-? n.s. 1, apr 1964-.

New asia; an organ of oriental culture and thought. Calcutta. 1-2, 1939-40?

New century review. London. 1-8, 1897-1900.

NCR   **New china review.** Shanghai. 1-4, 1919-22.

NewIA   **New indian antiquary; a monthly journal of oriental research in archaeology, art, epigraphy.** Bombay. 1, 1938-. Supersedes **Indian antiquary.** See also **New Indian antiquary. Extra series.**

NewIA   **New indian antiquary. Extra Series.** Bombay 1, 1939-.

New orient. N Y. 1-3, 1923-27. Vol. 1 as **Orient; an international magazine of art and culture.** Superseded by **Oriental magazine.**

NO   **New orient.** Prague. 1, 1960-68.

New world; a quarterly review of religion, ethics and theology. Boston. 1-9, 1892-1900.

BMMA   New York. Metropolitan museum of art. **Bulletin.** 1, 1905-.

New zealand institute. See Royal society of new zealand.

NC   **Nineteenth century.** See **Twentieth century.** London.

Nineteenth century and after. See **Twentieth century.** London.

North american review. N Y. boston. 1, 1815-.

NCH   **North China herald.** Shanghai. 1850-?

NQ   **Notes and queries on china and japan.** Hongkong. 1-4, 1867-70.

NouvJA   **Nouveau journal asiatique.** See **Journal asiatique.**

NouvClio   **Nouvelle clio.** Brussels. 1, 1949-.

NR   **Nouvelle revue.** Paris. 1, 1879-.

Nouvelle revue française. Paris. 1-31, 1909-43. N.s. 1, 1953-. Title varies as **La nouvelle revue.**

Nouvelles annales des voyages. See **Annales des voyages, de la géographie, de l'histoire et de l'archéologie.**

Nucleus. American chemical society. Boston. 1, 1924-.

Numen; international review for the history of religions. Leyden, 1, 1954-.

Numismatic and antiquarian society of philadelphia. **Proceedings.** Philadelphia 1, 1865/66-.

Occult review. See **Rider's review.** London.

Occult review. Boston. 1888-97.

Österreichische monatschrift für den orient. Vienna. 1-44, 1875-1918.

Okurayama oriental research institute. **Proceedings.** 1, 1954-. Engl title of Okurayama gakuin. Yokohama. Okurayama Gakuin Kiyo.

OC   **Open court, a quarterly magazine.** Chicago. 1-50, 1887-1936.

Oriens. Leiden. 1, 1948-.

OE   **Oriens extremus.** Wiesbaden. 1, 1954-.

Orient. Hongkong. 1-6, 1950-56.

HZ   **Orient.** Tokyo, 1-16, ?-1901. Vol 1-13 titled **Hanzei zasshi.**

Orient et occident. Geneva. 1-2, 1934-36.

OA   **Oriental art.** London. 1-3, 1948-51; n.s. 1- 1955-.

TOCS   Oriental ceramic society. London. **Transactions.** 1, 1921-.

JOSA   Oriental society of australia. Sydney. **Journal.** 1, 1960-.

Orientalia suecana. Uppsala. 1, 1952-.

Orientalische archiv. Leipzig. 1-3, 1910-13.

OL   **Orientalistische literaturzeitung.** Berlin, leipzig. 1, 1898-.

Orientations. HK. Pacific communications ltd. 1.1, jan 1970-.

Oriente poliana. Istituto italiano per il medio e l'estremo oriente. Rome.

OstL   **Ostasiatische lloyd.** Shanghai. 1-31, 1866-1917.

Ostasiatische rundschau. Berlin. 1-25, 1920-44.

OZ   **Ostasiatische zeitschrift.** Berlin. 1, 1912-42/43.

Our missions. London. 1-24, 1894-1917.

Outlook, a weekly review of politics, art, literature and finance. London. 1-61, 1898-1928.

OM   **Overland monthly & out west magazine.** San francisco 1, 1868-.

PA   **Pacific affairs.** Honolulu, NY. 1, 1926-.

PW   **Pacific world.** Berkeley. 1-4, 1925-28

Paideuma; mitteilungen zur kulturkunde. Bamberg. 1, 1938-.

Pakistan journal of science. See **Pakistan journal of scientific research.**

Pakistan journal of scientific research. Pakistan association for the advancement of science. Lahore. 1, 1949-.

Pakistan philosophical journal. Lahore. 1, 1957-.

JPTS   Pali text society. London. **Journal.** 1882-1924/27.

Pantheon; international zeitschrift für kunst. Munich. 1, 1928-.

ACF   Paris. Collège de france. **Annuaire.** 1, 1901-.

Paris. École pratique des hautes études. Bibliothèque. **Sciences religieuses.** 1, 1889-.

AMG   Paris. Musée guimet. **Annales.** 1-51, 1880-1935? **Bibliothèque de vulgarisation.** 1, 1889-.
BVAMG   **Conférences faites au musée guimet.** 1898/99-1914; 1902-16.
CMG

MIHEC   Paris. Université. Institut des hautes études chinoises. **Mélanges.** 1, 1957-.

Parnassus. N Y. 1-13. 1929-41.

BCUP   Peking. Catholic university. **Bulletin.** 1-9, 1926-34.

JPOS   Peking oriental society. **Journal.** 1-4, 1885-98.

UPUMB   Pennsylvania. State university. University museum. **Museum journal.** 1-24, 1910-35. **Museum bulletin,** 1-22, 1930-55.

Pennsylvania museum bulletin. See **Philadelphia museum bulletin.**

La pensée; revue du (bon) rationalisme moderne. Paris. 1939- ; n.s. no 1, oct/dec 1944-.

PC   **People's china.** Peking. 1, 1950-57.

PT   **People's tribune.** Peking. 1, 1931-1941(?)

Petermanns geographische mitteilungen. Gotha. 1, 1855-. Title varies.

Pharmazeutische industrie. Aulendorf. 1, 1933-.

PTP   **Phi theta papers.** Berkeley. 1, 1950-. 1950, 1954-55 titled **Phi theta annual.**

PMB   **Philadelphia museum bulletin.** Philadelphia. 1, 1903-, From 1920-38 titled **Pennsylvania museum bulletin.**

Philosophical magazine. London. 1, 1798-. Ser varies.

Philosophical quarterly. Calcutta. 1, 1925-.

Philosophical studies of japan. Comp by the Japanese national commission for UNESCO. Tokyo. 1, 1959-.

Philosophisches jahrbuch der görres-gesellschaft. Munich, etc. 1, 1888-. Suspended 1943-45 and 1952.

PEW   **Philosophy east and west.** Honolulu. 1, 1951-.

PS   **Popular science monthly.** N Y. 1, 1872-.

PrAnthro **Practical anthropology.** Tarrytown, ny. 1953-72. Continued with vol 19, 1973, by **Missiology.**

Praxis der psychotherapie. Munich. 1, 1956-. 1-3 (1956-58) as **Psychotherapie.**

Proceedings of various societies and institutions are listed under the name or location of the organization in question.

Psyche. Heidelberg, stuttgart. 1, 1947-.

Psychoanalysis and the psychoanalytic review. N Y. 1, 1913-. 1913-57, titled **Psychoanalytic review.**

Psychoanalytic review. See **Psychoanalysis and the psychoanalytic review.**

Psychologia; international journal of psychology in the orient. Kyoto univ. 1, june 1957-.

Psychotherapie. See **Praxis der psychotherapie.**

QJCA **Quarterly journal of current acquisitions.** See under United States. Library of Congress.

QNCCR **Quarterly notes on christianity and chinese religion.** See **Ching feng.**

Quarterly review. London. 1, 1809-.

Quest. London. 1-21, 1909-30.

Quiver. London. 1, 1861-. N Y. 1-39, 1884-1926 is american ed of london publ.

Race. London. 1, 1959-.

RechScRelig **Recherches de science religieuse.** Paris. 1, 1910-.

RMHA-PU **Record of the museum of historic art, princeton university.**

Records of progress. See **Dokumente des fortschritte.**

Reforme sociale. See Études sociales.

RC **Relations de chine (Kiang-nan)** Paris. 1, 1903-27 (?)

Religion. A journal of religion and religions. London etc. 1, spring 1971-.

Religion in life; a christian quarterly. N Y. 1, 1932-

Religion und geisteskult. Göttingen. 1-8, 1907-14.

Religions. London. No 1-77, 1931-53.

RH **Religious humanism.** Yellow springs, ohio. Fellowship of religious humanists. 1, winter 1967-.

Religious studies. London. 1, 1965-.

RSR **Religious studies review.** Waterloo, ont. Council on the study of religion. 1, sept 1975-.

Rencontre orient-occident. Geneva. 1, 1954-.

Renditions. A chinese-english translation magazine. Univ hk. Translation centre. 1, autumn 1973-.

RofR **Review of religion.** N Y. 1-22, 1936-58.

Review of religions. Punjab. 1, 1902-.

La revue. (Ancient revue des revues) Paris. 1, ? Vol 46, pt 3, 1903-. Title changes to **La revue mondiale.**

La revue; littérature, histoire, arts et sciences des deux mondes. Paris. 1948-. Supersedes **Revue des deux mondes.**

La revue; littéraire et artistique. Paris. 1, 1882-.

Revue anthropologique. Paris. 1-50, 1891-1942; 1955-.

Revue apologétique. Paris. 1-68, 1905-39.

Revue apologétique. Brussels. 1-13, 1900-12.

RA **Revue archéologique.** Paris. 1944-.

Revue blanche. Paris. 1-30, 1891-1903.

Revue bleu, politique et littéraire. Paris. 1863-1939. Title varies.

Revue britannique. Paris. 1-77, 1825-1901.

Revue catholique. Université catholique. Louvain. 1-61, 1843-98.

Revue critique. Paris. 1866-1935.

RE   **Revue d'ethnographie.** Paris. 1-8, 1882-91.

Revue d'ethnographie et des traditions populaires. Paris 1-10, 1920-29. Supersedes **Revue des traditions populaires.**

Revue d'europe et d'amérique. Paris. 1-20, 1898-1908. Title varies.

Revue de l'art ancien et moderne. Paris. 1-71, 1897-1937.

REO   **Revue de l'extrême-orient.** Paris. 1882-87.

Revue de la faculté de langues, d'histoire et de géographie. See under Ankara. Université.

RHR   **Revue de l'histoire des religions.** Musée guimet. Paris. 1, 1880-.

ROA   **Revue de l'orient et de l'algérie et des colonies.** Paris. 1843-65.

RMM   **Revue de métaphysique et de morale.** Paris. 1, 1893-.

Revue de paris. Paris. 1, 1894-.

Revue de théologie et de philosophie. Genève. 1868-1911; 1913-.

RAA   **Revue des arts asiatiques.** Paris. 1-13, 1924-42. Superseded by **Arts asiatiques.** See also Association française des amis de l'orient, **Bulletin.**

RDM   **Revue des deux mondes.** Paris. 1829-1948.

Revue des études ethnographiques et sociologiques. Paris. 1-2, 1908-09. Superseded by **Revue d'ethnographie et de sociologie.** 1-5, 1910-14.

Revue des questions historiques. Paris. 1866-.

RR   **Revue des religions.** Paris. 1-8, 1889-96.

Revue des revues. Paris. 1-50, 1876-1925.

Revue des traditions populaires. Paris. 1-34, 1886-1919. Superseded by **Revue d'ethnographie et des traditions populaires.**

Revue du clergé français. Paris. 1-103, 1895-1920.

Revue du monde catholique. Paris. 1-64, 1861-1925.

Revue du sud-est asiatique et de l'extrême-orient. Brussels. 1961-.

Revue encyclopédique. See **Revue universelle.** Paris.

Revue française de l'étranger et des colonies. Paris. 1885-1914.

Revue franco-chinoise. Association amicale franco-chinoise. Paris. 1, 1907-. 1907-15 as the association's **Bulletin.**

Revue de géographie commerciale. See Société de géographie commerciale de bordeaux.

RGI   **Revue géographique internationale.** Paris. 1-28, no 1-326, 1876-1903.

Revue hebdomadaire. Paris. 1892-1939.

RIC   **Revue indochinoise.** Hanoi. 1, 1893-.

Revue maritime et coloniale. Paris. no 1-202, 1861-1914; n.s. no 1-236, 1920-39.

Revue nationale chinoise. Shanghai. 1, 1929-. Suspended jan-june 1938.

Revue orientale et américaine. Paris. 1859-99. Title and ser vary.

Revue politique et parlementaire. Paris. 1, 1894-.

Revue scientifique. Paris. 1863-1954.

Revue universelle. Paris. 1891-1905. To 1900 as **Revue encyclopédique.**

Rheinische missionsgesellschaft. Barmen, germany. **Berichte.** 1, 1828/30-. Vol 1-8 (1829/30-36/37) as **Jahresbericht.**

R-WAW   Rheinisch-Westfälische akademie der wissenschaften.

Rider's review. London. 1, 1905-. Title varies as follows: 1-58.2 and 63-75.5 as **Occult review;** 58.3-62 as **London Forum.**

RSO   **Revista degli studi orientali.** Roma. 1, 1907-.

Rocznik orjentalistyczny. Krakow. 1, 1914/15-.

SM   Rome. Pontifica università gregoriana. **Studia missionalia.** 1, 1943-.

Royal anthropological institute of great britain and ireland. London. **Journal.** 1, 1871-. **Proceedings.** 1965-.

Royal geographical society. London. **Proceedings.** 1-22, 1855/57-77/78; n.s. 1-14, 1879-92. See also **Geographical magazine** and **Geographical journal** publ by the society.

JRASB   Royal asiatic society of bengal. See Asiatic society of bengal.

RAS   Royal asiatic society of great britain and ireland. **Journal.**London. 1-20, 1834-63; n.s. 1-21, 1864-89; 1889-. **Transactions.** London. 1-3, 1827-33. Superseded by **Journal.** Publications of branches of the RAS are as follows:

JBBRAS   Bombay branch. See under Asiatic society of bombay.

China branch. Shanghai. **Transactions.** 1-6, 1847-59. **Journal,** see North China branch.

JHKBRAS   Hong kong branch. Hongkong. **Journal.** 1, 1960/61-.

JMBRAS   Malayan branch. Singapore. **Journal.** 1, 1923-. Supersedes the Straits branch.

JNCBRAS   North China Branch. Shanghai. **Journal.** 1-2, 1858-60; n.s. 1, 1864-. Vol 1 as **Shanghai literary and scientific society journal.** 1886-95 as the China branch, **Journal.**

JSBRAS   Straits branch. Singapore. **Journal.** 1-86, 1878-1922. Superseded by the Malayan branch.

BROMA   Royal ontario museum of archaeology. See under Toronto. Royal ontario museum.

Royal society of new zealand. Wellington. **Transactions and proceedings.** 1, 1868-.

Rupam. Calcutta. 1920-30. Superseded by the Indian society of oriental art. **Journal.**

Rythmes du monde. Lyons. April, 1946-.

RDR   **Ryūkoku daigaku ronshū; the journal of ryūkoku univ.**

S.E.T.; structure et évolution des techniques. Association pour l'étude des techniques. Paris. 1, 1949-.

Saeculum; jahrbuch für universal geschichte. Freiburg, 1, 1950-.

Saturday review of literature. N Y. 1925-1973.

Schweitzerische gesellschaft der freunde ostasiatische kultur. *See* Schweitzerische gesellschaft für asienkunde.

MSGFOK   Schweitzerische gesellschaft für asienkunde. Founded 1939 as above and changed to asienkunde in 1947. **Mitteilungen.** St. gall. No 1-8, 1937-46. Superseded by **Asiatische studien.**

Science catholique. Paris. 1-20, 1886-1906.

Sciences religieuses. *See* under Paris. École pratique des hautes études.

SR/SR   **Sciences religieux/studies in religion.** Waterloo, ont. Wilfrid laurier univ. 1, 1971-.

'Scientia,' revista di scienza. Bologna. 1, 1907-.

Scientific monthly. Washington, etc. 1-85, 1915-1957. Merged into **Science.**

SCCM   **Selections from china mainland magazines.** Hongkong. No 1, 1955-.

SPRCM   **Selections from peoples republic of china magazines.** HK. American consulate general. Publ quarterly. jan/mar 1974-sept 1977.

Seminarium kondakovianum. *See* under Belgrade.

Seminars für orientalische sprachen. *See* under Berlin. Universität.

Shanghae almanac for 1854 (1855) and miscellany. Shanghai. 1851-62. Subtitle varies. *See also* **Shanghai miscellany.**

Shanghai literary and scientific society. **Journal.** 1, 1858. First vol of the **Journal** of the North china branch of the royal asiatic society.

Shanghai miscellany. 1-2, 1834-57. 1853-56 included in **Shanghae almanac.** 1857 publ sep.

Siam respository. Bangkok. 1-6, 1869-74.

Siam society. Bangkok. **Journal.** 1, 1904-.

BUA   Shanghai. Université de l'aurore. **Bulletin.** 1909-.

SJ   **Silliman journal.** Dumaguete city. Silliman univ. 1, jan 1954-.

Sinica; zeitschrift für chinakunde und china forschung. Frankfurt. 1-17, 1926-42. Suppl to **Chinesischer blätter für wissenschaft und kunst.**

Sinica-sonderausgabe. Frankfurt a.m., 1934.

SAR   **Sino-american relations.** Taipei. College of chinese culture. Publ quarterly. 1, spring 1975-.

SIJ   **Sino-indian journal.** Santiniketan, bengal. 1, 1947-.

SIS   **Sino-indian studies.** Santiniketan, bengal. 1, 1944-.

Sino-indica. Calcutta university. Paris. 1, 1927-.

Sinologica. Basel. 1, 1947-.

SAWW   **Sitzungsberichte der akademie der wissenschaften in wien.** *See* Akademie der wissenschaften. Vienna.

Social action. Boston, chicago. 1, 1935-.

SSM   **Social science and medicine.** Oxford. 1, apr 1967-.

Société d'acupuncture. Paris. **Bulletin.** 1, 1950-.

BMSAP | Société d'anthropologie de paris. **Bulletins et mémoires.** 1860-.

Société d'émulation de roubaix. **Mémoires.** 1868-1931.

Société d'ethnographie. **Actes.** See **Ethnographie.**

BSEIS | Société des études indochinoises de saigon. **Bulletin.** 1-71, 1883-1923; n.s. 1, 1926-.

Société de géographie. Paris. **Comptes rendus.** 1882-99. Continued in **Géographie.**

Société de géographie commerciale de bordeaux. **Bulletin.** 1874-1939. Title varies as **Revue de géographie commerciale.**

Société de géographie de l'est. Paris. **Bulletin.** 1-35, 1879-1914.

Société des études japonaises, chinois, tartares et indo-chinois. See Société sinico-japonaise. Paris.

Société finno-ougrienne. See Suomalais-ugrilanen seura.

Société française d'histoire de la médecine. Paris. **Bulletin,** 1902-42. Superseded by **Histoire de la médecine.**

BSAB | Société royale belge d'anthropologie et de préhistoire de bruxelles. **Bulletin.** 1, 1882-.

ASAB | Société royale d'archéologie de bruxelles. **Annales.** 1, 1887-.

Société sinico-japonaise. Paris. 1877 -? as a section of the société d'ethnographie, Paris; also as Société des études japonaises, chinoises, tartares et indo-chinoises and Société sinico-japonaise et océanienne. Sometimes cited as Comité sinico-japonaise. **Annuaire.** 1873-. **Mémoires.** 1-10, 1873-91; n.s. 1-22, 1892-1901? Vol 5-9 of the first ser has title of **Lotus.**

SSCRB | Society for the study of chinese religions. **Bulletin.** Boulder. Univ of colorado. Dept of religious studies. First 3 issues titled SSCR **Newsletter** (1 mar 1976, 2 july 1976, 3 feb 1977) With vol 10 (fall 1982) title changed again, to **Journal of chinese religions,** abbrev **JCR.**

Sociological bulletin. Bombay, delhi. 1, 1952-.

Sources orientales. Publisher's series. Paris. 1, 1959-. Irregularly publ; each vol has its own title.

Southeast asia; an international quarterly. Carbondale. Southern illinois univ. Center for vietnamese studies. 1.1/2, winter-spring 1971.

SEAJT | **South east asia journal of theology.** Singapore. 1, 1959-.

SWJA | **Southwestern journal of anthropology.** Albuquerque. 1, 1945-.

BMFEA | Stockholm. Ostasiatiska samlingarna (Museum of far eastern antiquities) **Bulletin.** 1, 1929-.

Structure et évolution des techniques. See **S.E.T.**

Studi e materiali di storia delle religioni. Rome universati. Rome. 1, 1925-.

SM | **Studia missionalia.** See under Rome.

SS | **Studia serica.** West china union university. Chinese cultural studies research institute. 1, 1940-. See also **Monograph** ser A, no 1, 1947-; B, no 1, 1942-.

Studia taiwanica. Taipei. 1, 1956-. Catalogued under T'ai-wan yen-chiu.

Studien zur frühchinesischen kulturgeschichte. Antwerp. 1-2, 1941-43.

SCR | **Studies in comparative religion.** Bedfont, engl. 1, winter 1967-. Publ quarterly.

Studies on buddhism in japan. International buddhist society. Tokyo. 1-3, 1939-41.

Studio; an illustrated magazine of fine and applied art. London. 1, 1893-. **London Studio.** N.Y. 1931-38, american ed.

Studium generale; zeitschrift für die einheit der wissenschaften zusammenhang ihrer begriftsbildungen und forschungs methoden. Berlin. 1, 1947-.

Sunday at home. London. 1854-1940.

Suomalais-ugrilainen seura. Helsingfors. **Aika kau skirja (Journal)** 1, 1886-.

SCMM   **Survey of China mainland magazines.** See **Selections from china...**

SCMP   **Survey of china mainland press.** HK. American consulate general. 1, nov 1, 1950-.

Symbolon; jahrbuch für symbolforschung. Basel. 1, 1960-.

Synthesis; the undergraduate journal in the history and philosophy of science. Boston. 1.1, winter 1972.

Tamkang journal. See **Tan-chiang hsüeh-pao.**

TR   **Tamkang review.** Taipei. Tamkang college of arts and sciences. Graduate institute of western languages and literature. 1.1, apr 1970-.

Tan-chiang hsüeh-pao. Taipei. 1958-. Engl title **Tamkang journal.**

Technology review. MIT boston. 1, 1899-.

TJR   **Tenri journal of religion.** Research institute for religion. Tenri, japan. 1, 1955-.

TheE&TheW   **The east and the west. A quarterly review for the study of missions.** Westminster, s.w. engl. Publ by Society for the propagation of the faith in foreign parts. 1-25, 1903-27.

Theologische literaturzeitung. Leipzig, berlin. 1, 1876-.

Theosophical forum. N.Y., point loma, calif. 1-70, 1889-95; ser 2, 1, 1929-.

Theosophical path; illustrated monthly. Point loma, calif. 1-45, 1911-1935. Merged into **Theosophical forum.**

THM   **T'ien hsia monthly.** Shanghai. 1-12, 1935-41.

Tōhōgaku ronshu. Tokyo. 1, 1954-.

BMFJ   Tokyo. Maison franco-japonaise. **Bulletin.** 1-15, 1927/29-47; n.s. 1, 1951-. 1-5, titled **Bulletin seri-française.**

TBMRD   Tokyo. Tōyō bunko (oriental library). Research department. **Memoirs.** No. 1, 1926-.

BROMA   Toronto. Royal ontario museum. Art and archaeology division. **Bulletin.** No 1-27, 1923-58. Supersedes the Royal ontario museum of archaeology which publ no 1-23.

TP   **T'oung pao.** Leiden. 1-10, 1890-99; ser 2, 1, 1900-.

TBMRD   Tōyō bunko, **memoirs of the research department.** See under Tokyo.

Tōyō gakuhō. Tokyo. 1, 1911-.

TUAS   **Tōyō university asian studies.** Tokyo. 1, 1961; 2, 1964.

Transactions. See under the name or location of the organization.

Travel. N Y. 1, 1901-. Title varies. Combined with **Holiday** in 1931.

TM   À travers le monde. Paris. 1-20, 1895-1914.

           Tri-quarterly. Evanston, illinois. 1-6, 1958-64; n.s. no 1, 1964-.

           Tribus; veroeffentlichungen des linden-museum. (Stuttgart. Museum für laend- und völkerkunde) Heidelberg. N.f. 1, 1951-. Vol 1 issue as Jahrbuch des linden museum.

TJ   Tsinghua journal of chinese studies. Peking, taipei. 1-12, 1924-37; n.s. 1, 1956-. Supersedes Tsing-hua journal. Peking. 1-4, 1919-? Chinese title, Ch'ing-hua hsüeh-pao.

NC   Twentieth century. London. 1, 1877-. Title varies as follows: 1877-1900 as Nineteenth century; a monthly review; 1901-50 as Nineteenth century and after.

           Unitas. Quarterly review of the arts and sciences. Manila. Univ of santo tomas. 1, 1922-.

           United asia; international magazine of asian affairs. Bombay. 1, 1948-.

QJCA   United States. Library of congress. Quarterly journal of current acquisitions. 1, 1943-.

           United States. National museum. Bulletin. 1, 1875-. Proceedings. 1, 1878-.

           United states. National museum. Smithsonian institution. Annual report of the board of regents. 1, 1846-. From 1884, there are two ann vol, the second of which is Report of the u.s. national museum.

USJPRS   United states joint publications research service.

           Universitas; zeitschrift für wissenschaft, kunst und literatur. Stuttgart. 1, 1946-.

           University of ceylon review. Colombo. 1, 1943-.

JOR   University of madras. Madras. Journal. 1-14, 1928-42. Continued in two sections as follows: A-Humanities. 15-18, 1943-46; B-Science. 15, 1943-. Annals of oriental research. 1, 1936- Vol 1 as Journal of Oriental research.

UPUMB   University of Pennsylvania museum bulletin. See under Pennsylvania. State University. University museum.

VBS   Vajra bodhi sea. Monthly publication of the orthodox buddha dharma in america. San francisco, sino-american buddhist association. 1.1, apr 1970-.

           Variétés sinologiques. Shanghai. 1-66, 1892-1938.

           Verhandlungen. See under the name of the institution, organization, congress, etc.

           Veröffentlichungen aus dem königlichen museum für völkerkunde. See under Berlin, Staatliche museem.

           Visva-bharati bulletin. Calcutta. 1, 1924-.

VBA   Visva-bharati annals. Santiniketan, india. No. 1, 1945-.

VBQ   Visva-bharati quarterly. Calcutta. 1-8, 1923-32; n.s. 1, 1935-.

           Voice of Buddhism. Buddhist missionary society. Kuala lumpur. 1, 1964?-.

           Le voile d'isis. Paris. 1-?, 1890-?, 2e sér, 2, (?) 3e sér, 3, no 1-56, 1910-14.

           Walters art gallery. Baltimore. Journal. 1, 1938-.

           Warburg and courtauld institutes. Journal. See under London. University.

           Welt des orients: wissenschaftliche beiträge zur kunde des morgenländes. Wuppertal. 1, 1947-.

           Die weisse fahne. Pfullingen. 1-16, 1920-35;?-.

Der weltkreis. Berlin. 1-3, 1929-33.

Der wendepunkt im leben und im leiden. Zürich, Leipzig. 1, 1923-. Vol 1 lacks date.

WMM   **Wesleyan Methodist magazine.** See **Methodist magazine.**

West and East. Taipei. 1, 1956-. Also listed under chinese title **Chung mei yüeh-k'an.**

JWCBorder   West china border research society. Chengtu. **Journal.** 1-16, 1922/23-45. 12-16 issued in two series,
ResS   General and natural sciences, A and B respectively.

West china missionary news. Chengtu. 1, 1899-.

WBKKGA   **Wiener beiträge zur kunst- und kulturgeschichte asiens.** Verein der freunde asiatischen kunst und
kultur in wien. Vienna. 1-11, 1926-37?

Wiener völkerkundliche mitteilungen. Vienna. 1, 1953-. Issuing agent varies.

WZKM   **Wiener zeitschrift für die kunde des morgenländes.** Wien. Orientalisches institut. 1, 1887-.
Suspended 1919-23; 1942-47.

Wiener zeitschrift für die kunde sud- und ostasiens und archiv für indische philosophie.
Indologische institut, univeritaet wien. Vienna, 1, 1957-.

Wirkendes wort. Paedagogischen verlag schwann. Duesseldorf. 1, 1966-.

Wissen und leben. See **Neue schweizer rundschau.**

Wissenschaftliche annalen der gesammten heilkunde. Berlin. 1-30, 1825-34. 1-24 (1825-32) as
Litterarische annalen der gesammten heilkunde. Superseded by the **Neue wissenschaftliche. . . .**

Die woche, modern illustrierte zeitschrift. Berlin 1, 1899-.

Worcester, mass. Art museum. **Annual.** 1, 1935/36-.

World mission. London. 1966-.

Worldmission. N Y. 1, 1950-.

World's chinese students' journal. Shanghai. 1-8, 1906-14.

Yana. Zeitschrift für buddhismus und religiöse kultur auf buddhistischen grundlage. München;
utting am ammersee.

Yoga; international journal on the science of yoga. Bulsar, india. 1, 1933-.

Yoga; internationale zeitschrift für wissenschaftliche yoga-forschung. Harburg-wilhelmsburg. 1,
1931-?

Yoga series. Madanapalli, india. 1, 1956-.

YE   **Young East.** Tokyo. 1-8, 1925-41. Superseded by **Young east; Japanese buddhist quarterly.**

Young East. Tokyo. 1-15, 1952-66.

Zalmoxis, revue des études religieuses. Paris. 1, 1938.

Zeitschrift. See also the names or locations of issuing organizations.

Zeitschrift für bauwesen. Berlin. 1-81, 1851-1931.

ZBK   **Zeitschrift für bildende kunst.** Leipzig. 1-65, 1866-1932.

Zeitschrift für buddhismus. Half-title for the following item: **Zeitschrift für buddhismus und vervandt
gebiete.** Munich. 1-9, 1914-31.

Zeitschrift für die historische theologie. Leipzig. 1-45, 1831-75.

ZE   **Zeitschrift für ethnologie.** Berliner gesellschaft für anthropologie, ethnologie und urgeschichte. Berlin. 1, 1869-. May include **Verhandlungen** of the society.

Zeitschrift für geopolitik in gemeinschaft und politik. Bad godesberg, etc. 1, 1924-. 1924-55 as **Zeitschrift für geopolitik.**

Zeitschrift für menschenkunde und zentralblatt für graphologie. Heidelberg, vienna, etc. 1, may 1925-. Title varies. Cited in text as **Zeitschrift für menschenkunde.**

ZMK   **Zeitschrift für missionskunde and religionswissenschaft.** Allgemeiner evangelisch-protestantischen missionsverein. Berlin. 1-54, 1886-1939.

ZMR   **Zeitschrift für missionswissenschaft und religionswissenschaft.** Institut für missionswissenschaftliche forschungen. Münster. 1, 1911-. Title varies.

Zeitschrift für religionspsychologie. Güterslah. 1-11, 1928-37.

Zeitschrift für religions-psychologie. Leipzig. 1-6, 1907-13.

ZRGG   **Zeitschrift für religious- und geistes-geschichte.** Marburg. 1, 1948-.

Zeitschrift für systematische theologie. Berlin. 1, 1923-.

Zeitschrift für theologie und kirche. Tübingen. 1891-1917; 1920-38; 1950-.

Zeitwende; die neue furche. Hamburg, etc. 1, 1925-.

Zinbun. Memoire of the research institute for humanistic studies, kyoto university, kyoto. Publ annually in english, each issue containing usually 1 or 2 art and tsl. Postwar ser, 1, 1957-.

PART ONE

Bibliography
and
General Studies

1. BIBLIOGRAPHY

American theological library association. **Index to religious periodical literature.** Chicago, vol 1 (1953) et seq.

Association for asian studies. **Bibliography of asian studies.** Annual publ; from 1.1 (nov 1941) through 15.4 (aug 1956) incl in **Far eastern quarterly.**

Au, Donna & Sharon Rowe. Bibliography of taoist studies. In **BIS-I** (1977) 123-148.

Barrow, John G. (comp) **A bibliography of bibliographies in religion.** Ann arbor, mich (1955) 489 p. See 4. Non-christian religions b. Buddhism; k. Taoism.

Beautrix, P. **Bibliographie de la littérature prajñāpāramitā.** Bruxelles (1971) ix + 59 p.

Beautrix, P. **Bibliographie du bouddhisme. I. Éditions de textes.** Bruxelles (1970) 210 p.

Beautrix, P. **Bibliographie du bouddhisme zen.** Bruxelles (1969) 114 p.

Beautrix, P. **Bibliographie du bouddhisme zen. Premier supplément.** Bruxelles (ca. 1975) 119 p.

Benz, Ernst & Nambara Minoru (comp) **Das christentum und die nichtchristlichen hochreligionen. Begegnung und auseinandersetzung. Eine internationale bibliographie.** Leiden (1960) See 21-22, 46-51, 62, 79-82, 83-86.

Berkowitz, M.J. & Poon, Eddie K.K. (comp) **Hongkong studies: a bibliography.** Chin univ of hong kong (1969) 137 p.

Bernard-Maître, Henri. Un dossier bibliographique de la fin du xviie siècle sur la question des termes chinois. **RechScRelig** 36 (1949) 25-79.

Bibliographie bouddhique (various ed) Paris (1930-1937) t 1 - 7/8. t 9-20 (1949) t 21-23 (1952) t 23 fasc annexe (1955) t 24-27 (1958) t 28-31 (1961) t 32, Index général des tomes 24-27 et 28-31 (1967)

Centre de documentation du C.N.R.S. Paris. **Bulletin signalétique. Sciences religieuse (revue trimestrielle)** Sep sec on "Religions d'asie" begins with vol 30.1 (1976) In earlier issues see "Science de religions" indexes under "Chine."

Chang, Lucy Gi Ding (comp) Acupuncture: a selected bibliography. **CC** 5.1 (1963) 156-160.

Chesneaux, Jean (ed) **Popular movements and secret societies in China 1840-1950.** Stanford univ (1972) Bibliography of works concerning secret societies, 279-288 (abbrev as **PMSSC**) Orig french ed: **Mouvements populaires et sociétés secrètes en chine aux xixe et xxe siècle,** paris (1970) (abbrev as **MPSSC**) Contents of the two versions are quite different.

Cohen, Alvin P. A bibliography of writings contributory to the study of chinese folk religion. **JAAR** 43.2 (june 1975) 238-265, gloss chin characters . . . "all secondary materials written in english, french, or german"

Cordier, Henri (comp) **Bibliotheca sinica.** Paris (1904-24) 5 vol. Repr taipei (1966).

Critical bibliography of the history of science and its cultural influences. **Isis** (annual) See sec HS 35.2, The far east (to c.1600) Prior to 1967 bibliog appeared in pt 4; since then publ as sep issue, pt 5. Most entries annot.

Demiéville, Paul. **Choix d'études bouddhiques (1929-1970)** Leiden (1973) xli + 497 p, bibliog of author 1920-1971 by Gisele de Jong. Repr in 1 vol of 13 art and 4 rev. Each repr is sep listed in our bibliog.

Demiéville, Paul. **Choix d'études sinologiques (1921-1970)** Leiden (1973) xli + 633 p, bibliog of author 1920-1971 by Gisele de Jong. Repr in 1 vol of many art relating to relig among other subj. Each repr is sep listed in our bibliog.

Diehl, Katherine Smith (comp) **Religions, mythologies, folklore: an annotated bibliography.** New brunswick, n.j. (1956) 2nd ed (1962)

Dobson, W.A.C.H. The religions of china (excepting buddhism) Being chap 2 in Charles J. Adams (ed) **A reader's guide to the great religions,** NY and london (1965) 31-44.

Dobson, W.A.C.H. The religion of china (excepting buddhism) Chap 4 in Charles J. Adams (ed) **A reader's guide to the great religions,** NY & london 2nd rev & enl ed (1977) 90-105. Text is identical in 2nd ed, only a few items being added to listings.

Eberhard, Wolfram. Neuere forschungen zur religion chinas 1920-1932. **ARW** 33 (1936) 304-344. Engl tsl: Studies of chinese religion 1920-1932, in **MSVC** (1971) 335-399.

Edmunds, Albert J. (comp) A buddhist bibliography, based upon the libraries of philadelphia. **JPTS** (1902-03) 1-60. Suppl in **LD** 4 (1904) 147-150, 193-198.

Erbacher, Hermann (comp) **Bibliographie der fest- und gedenkschriften für personlichkeiten aus evangelischer theologie und kirche 1881-1969.** Neustadt an der aisch (1971) See M: Religionswissenschaft 64: Religionsgeschichte: China (no 6334-6339)

Farazza, Armando R. & Mary Ornan. **Anthropological and cross-cultural themes in mental health. An annotated bibliography, 1925-1974.** Univ missouri (1977) 386 p, author & subj indexes; arr by years.

Franke, O. Die religionswissenschaftliche literatur über china seit 1909. **ARW** 18 (1915) 394-479.

Fu, Charles Wei-hsun & Wing-tsit Chan. **Guide to chinese philosophy.** Boston (1978) For various relevant sec consult detailed Contents.

Gard, Richard A. (ed) **Buddhist text information.** NY, institute for advanced studies of world religions. No 1 (nov 1974)-.

Genähr, J. New books on the religions and philosophy of china. **IRM** 3 (1914) 175-178.

Gotō, Kimpei. Studies on chinese religion in postwar japan. **MS** 15.2 (1956) 463-511.

Haas, Hans (comp) **Bibliographie zur frage nach den wechselbeziehungen zwischen buddhismus und christentum.** Berlin (1921) leipzig (1922) 47 p.

Haas, Hans. Neuer literatur über den buddhismus von china und japan. **OZ** 1 (1912-13) 238-245.

Haimes, Norma. Zen buddhism and psychoanalysis—a bibliographic essay. **Psychologia** 15 (1972) 22-30.

Hamilton, Clarence H. (comp) **Buddhism in India, ceylon, china and japan: a reading guide.** Univ Chicago (1931) 107 p.

Hanayama, Shinsho (comp) **Shinsho hanayama bibliography on buddhism.** Commemoration committee for prof. shinsho hanayama's sixty-first birthday (ed) Tokyo (1961)

Harrassowitz, Otto (publishers) **Catalog 512: Buddhism.** Wiesbaden (1971) 48 p.

Held, Hans Ludwig. **Deutsche bibliographie des buddhismus.** München (1916) repr Hildesheim & NY (1973) 190 p.

International bibliography of the history of religions. Bibliographie internationale de l'histoire des religions (various ed) Leiden (1954-1971) vol 1 - 15 (for years 1952-68) vol 20 (for 1973) publ (1979)

Jong, J.W. de. A brief history of buddhist studies in europe and america. **EB** n.s. 7.1 (may 1974) 55-106; 7.2 (oct 1974) 49-82. Re tsl of chin budd texts see esp chap 4, Future perspectives, 70-82.

Kang, Thomas H. Confucian publication in western languages. **Korea Journal** 12.7 (1972) 24-32.

Karpinski, Leszek M. **The religious life of man: guide to basic literature.** Metuchen, n.j. & london (1978) See sec, Chinese religions, 256-274. Entries sel, class, annot.

Kramers, R.P. Religie in china: een selective bibliographie. **China informatie** 3.4 (1969) 4-13.

Kumar, B.K. **China through the ages. A select bibliography 1911-1977.** Delhi (1978) See appropriate sec.

Lagerwey, John. Notes on french sinology and chinese religion. **SSCRB** 4 (oct 1977) 5-9.

Lalou, Marcelle. Onze années de travaux européens sur le bouddhisme (mai 1936-mai 1947) **Muséon** 61 (1948) 245-276.

La Vallée Poussin, Louis de. Notes de bibliographie bouddhique. **MCB** 3 (1934-35) 355-407; 5 (1936-37) 243-304.

Lesh, T. Zen and psychotherapy: a partially annotated bibliography. **Journal of humanistic psychology** 10 (1970) 75-83.

Ling, Scott K. **Bibliography of chinese humanities 1941-1972. Studies on chinese philosophy, religion, history, geography, biography, art, and language and literature.** Taipei (1976) See Philosophy & religion, 91-134; Religion, 106-134.

Lust, John (comp) **Index sinicus.** Cambridge, engl (1964) Periodical literature and collective works publ 1920-1955.

Marceron, Désiré J.-B. (comp) **Bibliographie du taoisme.** Paris (1898-1901) Forms pt 1 and 2 of t 15, Publications du comité sinico-japonais.

March, Arthur C. (comp) **A buddhist bibliography.** London (1935) xi + 257 p. Annual suppl 1 (1936) . . . 5 (1940)

Merkel, R.F. Zur geschichte der erforschung chinesisches religionen. **Studi e materiali di storia delle religioni** 15 (1939) 90-107.

Morgan, Kenneth W. **Asian religions. An introduction to the study of hinduism, buddhism, islam, confucianism and taoism.** N.Y. (1964) 30 p.

Nakamura, Hajime. A survey of mahāyāna buddhism with bibliographic notes. **JIC** 3 (1976) 60-145; 4 (1977) 77-135; 5 (1978) 89-138.

Needham, Joseph, with collaboration of Lu Gwei-djen. **Science and civilization in china.** Vol 5, **Chemistry and chemical technology, part II: spagyrical discovery and invention: magisteries of gold and immortality.** Cambridge univ (1974) Bibliog C, Books and journal articles in western languages, 387-469.

Popenoe, Cris. **Inner development. The yes! bookshop guide.** Washington d.c. (1979) See Chinese philosophy, 215-236; Buddhism, 147-167; Sacred art, 565-573, passim. Annot entries.

Religion of the chinese: a selective bibliography. **SM** 6 (1967) 117-132.

Répertoire générale de sciences religieuses. Bibliographie hors commerce . . . (various ed) Paris, publ annually (1950-68) covering years 1950-1959.

Research institute for humanistic studies. **Annual bibliography of oriental studies.** Kyoto univ. See Annual biblio of oriental studies for 19-- in western languages, under appropriate sec of Table of contents.

Revue bibliographique de sinologie (various ed) Paris (1957-1977) 11 vol covering years 1955-1965.

Reynolds, Frank E. Buddhism. Chap 6 in Charles J. Adams (ed) **A reader's guide to the great religions,** NY & london (1965) 2nd rev & enl ed (1977) See China, 196-206 in 2nd ed only.

Richardson, Ernest Cushing (comp) **An alphabetical subject index and index encyclopaedia to periodical articles on religion 1890-1899.** N.Y. (1907) See China.

Robiou, F. Études récentes sur la première religion des chinois. **Revue des questions historiques** 52 (1892) 217-225.

Sakai, Tadao & Noguchi, Tetsurō. Taoist studies in japan. In **FT** (1979) 269-287.

Sasaki, Ruth Fuller. A bibliography of translations of zen (ch'an) works. **PEW** 10.3/4 (1961) 149-168.

Satyaprakash. **Buddhism: a select bibliography.** New delhi (1976)

Schiffeler, John William. Bibliography of the history of chinese folk medicine. **CC** 16.2 (june 1975) 95-104.

Schloss, Oskar. **Verlags-katalog über die deutschsprachliche buddhistische und verwandte literatur.** München (1924) 110 p, 4 pl.

Schmidt, G. von & T. Thilo. **Katalog chinesisches buddhistischer textfragmente.** In collab with T. Inokuchi. App by A. Fujieda & T. Thilo. Berliner turfan-texte, vi. Vol 1 (1975) 209 p, 50 facs, 34 tabl.

Skinner, G. William (ed) **Modern chinese society: an analytical bibliography.** Vol 1, **Publications in western languages, 1644-1972.** Stanford univ (1974) 880 p. See sec 13, 23, 32.2, 33, 36.3, 43, 63, 65.

Smith, William M. The religions of asia: a bibliographical essay. **Choice** 10.5/6 (jul-aug 1973) 723-744.

Some recent articles on religion in communist china. **CB** 510 (15 june 1958) 30 p.

Soymié, M. and Litsch, F. (comp) Bibliographie du taoisme études dans les langues occidentales. **Études taoistes** [publ in tokyo] 3 (1968) 247-318; 4 (1971) 225-289.

Strickmann, Michel. Bibliographic notes on chinese religious studies. **SSCRB** 3 (feb 1977) 11-19; 4 (oct 1977) 10-19.

Taam, Cheuk-woon. On studies of confucius. **PEW** 3 (1953) 147-165.

Thompson, Laurence G. **Studies of chinese religion: A comprehensive and classified bibliography of publications in english, french, and german through 1970.** With research and editorial assistance of Justine Pinto. Encino & belmont, calif (1976) xlv + 190 double col p, general abbrev, abbrev of publ, details concerning serial sources, index of authors, editors, compilers, translators, photographers and illustrators.

Timmons, Beverly & Joe Kamiya. The psychology and physiology of meditation and related phenomena: a bibliography. **JTP** 2.1 (1970) 41-59.

Timmons, Beverly & Demetri P. Kanellakos. The psychology and physiology of meditation and related phenomena: bibliography ii. **JTP** 6.1 (1974) 32-38.

Topley, Marjorie (comp) Published and unpublished materials on hong kong by overseas affiliated scholars. **JOS** 8.1 (1970) 219-225.

Vanderstappen, Harrie A. (ed) **The t.l. yuan bibliography of western writings on chinese art and archaeology.** London (1975) Covers 1920 through 1965, books and art. See detailed Contents.

Vessie, Patricia Armstrong. **Zen buddhism. A bibliography of books and articles in english** 1892-1975. Ann arbor, mich (1976)

Wickeri, Philip L. Annotated listing of major articles on religion from the chinese press, january 1-june 30, 1980. **CF** 23.3/4 (1980) 174-179.

Wickeri, Philip L. Annotated listing of major articles on religion from the hong kong press, january 1-june 30, 1980. **CF** 23.3/4 (1980) 180-184.

Yoo, Yushin, **Books on buddhism: an annotated subject guide.** Metuchen, n.j. (1976)

Yoo, Yushin. **Buddhism: a subject index to periodical articles in english, 1728-1971.** Metuchen, n.j. (1973) xxii + 162 p, author/subj index, title index.

Yu, David C. Present-day taoist studies. **RSR** 3.4 (oct 1977) 220-239.

Yuan, T.L. (comp) **China in western literature.** Yale univ (1958) 'A continuation of cordier's bibliotheca sinica' for books only, publ 1921-57.

Zeuschner, Robert B. A selected bibliography on ch'an buddhism in china. **JCP** 3.3 (june 1976) 299-311. Publ in western langs and jap.

2.   GENERAL STUDIES
      (See also MODERN RELIGION)

Abel, Karl (tsl) **Arbeiten der kaiserlich russischen gerandschaft zu peking über china, sein volk, seine religion, seine institutionen, sozialen verhältnisse, etc.**

Aus dem russischen nach dem in st. petersburg 1852-57 veröffentlichten original von K.A. und F.A. Mecklenburg. Berlin (1858)

Ansley, Delight. The good ways. N.Y. (1950) See chap 7, The road from china, 129-147.

Archer, John C. Faiths men live by. N.Y. (1934 et seq) See p 67-294.

Ayres, Lew. Altars of the east. N.Y. (1956) 284 p, illus. See chap 3-4.

Aziz-us-Samad, Mrs. Ulfat. The great religions of the world. Lahore (1976) See Confucianism, 91-106; Taoism, 107-123.

B.J. La religion des chinois. La Chine 24 (1922) 1225-1233.

Babel, Henry. Le secret des grande religions. Futurologie de la religion. Neuchatel, suisse (1975) See Les grandes religions de la chine, 79-114.

Bahm, Archie J. The world's living religions: a searching comparison of the faiths of east and west. Southern illinois univ (1971)

Ball, J. Dyer. The celestial and his religions; or the religious aspect in china. Being a series of lectures on the religions of the chinese. HK (1906) xviii + 240 p.

Barber, W.T.A. The chambers of the chinese soul. TheE&TheW (1904) 32-37. On understanding native "faith" of the chin.

Bard, Émile. Tsl fr french H. Twitchell. The chinese at home. London (n.d.c. 1908) See chap 6-8, p 43-69.

Barondes, R. de Rohan. China: lore, legend and lyrics. NY (1960) A mélange.

Barthélemy, le Marquis de. Lettres de chine. 1. La chine religieuse . . . RIC n.s. 15/16 (aout 1911) 136-150.

Barton, George A. The religions of the world. Univ chicago (1917 et seq) See chap 11, The religion of china, 201-222.

Bashford, James W. China. An interpretation. NY and cincinnati (1916) See chap 10, Religious life and struggles, 239-265.

Bauer, Wolfgang. China und die hoffnung auf glück. Paradies, utopien, idealvorstellungen. München (1971) Engl tsl Michael Shaw, China and the search for happiness, ny (1976) 502 p, chron table, notes, bibliog, index.

Berle, A.A. The three religions of china. Bibliotheca sacra 52 (1895) 170-173.

Bernard, Henri. l'Attitude du père matthieu ricci en face des coutumes et rites chinois. RechScRelig 28 (1938) 31-47. "Extrait du livre sur Matthieu ricci et la société chinois de son temps."

Berry, Gerald L. Religions of the world. N.Y. (1947, 1956) See sec 8-9, p 47-53.

Bloom, Alfred. China. The quest for ultimate harmony and the great tranquillity. In W. Richard Comstock (genl ed) Religion and man. An introduction, ny etc (1971) 254-333. Also publ in Robert D. Baird & Alfred Bloom (ed) Indian and far eastern religious traditions, ny (1971) which comprises pt 2 and 3 of foregoing bk, under title, Far eastern religious traditions: china, 142-221.

Bodde, Derk. China's cultural tradition: what and whither? N.Y. etc (1957) See sec B, The world of the supernatural, 20-30; sec G, The world of nature, 31-42.

Bodde, Derk. Dominant ideas. In H.F. MacNair (ed) China. Univ california (1946) 18-28.

Boerschmann, Ernst. Anhang. Einige beispiele für die gegenseitige durchdringung der drei chinesischen religionen. ZE 3/4 (1911) 429-435.

Bönner, Theodor. Vergleichende und kritisierende darstellung der chinesischen philosophie (mit anschluss der chinesischen religionen) Berlin-Steglitz (1909) (Besprochen von A. Forke, MSOS 13 [1910] 350-353)

Bouïnais, Albert M.A. La religion en chine. In author's De hanoi à pékin: notes sur la chine, paris (1892) 267-288.

Braden, Charles S. The world's religions. A short history. N.Y. and nashville (1939) rev ed (1954) See chap 10, Religions of china.

Braunthal, Alfred. Salvation in the perfect society. The eternal quest. Univ massachusetts (1979) See sec II, Salvation from suffering and from rebirth: 5, The way of china, 55-60. Re confucianism and "classical taoism"

Browne, Lewis. This believing world. N.Y. (1926) See p 169-198.

Bunsen, C.C.J. Baron. God in history, or the progress of man's faith in the moral order of the world. Tsl fr german Susanna Winkworth. London (1868) See book 3, chap 5, The religious consciousness of the chinese, or sinism, 243-272.

Burder, William. The history of all religions of the world. N.Y. and springfield, mass (rev ed 1881) See Religious ceremonies and customs of the chinese, 678-700.

Burkhardt, Martha. Chinesische kultstätten und kultgebräuche. Erlenbach-Zürich (1920) 176 p.

Burtt, Edwin A. Man seeks the divine. N.Y. (1957) See chap 5, The native religions of china, 129-152.

Bush, Richard C. **Religion in china.** Niles, ill (1977) 82 p, notes, gloss, bibliog, illus.

Carus, Paul. **Chinese life and customs. Illus by chinese artists.** Chicago (1907) 114 p.

Carus, Paul. The religions of china. **OC** 17.10 (1903) 622-624. Re a picture (reproduced) in kircher's bk on china, showing "the three teachers"

Castillon, J. **Anecdotes chinoises, japonaises, siamoises, tonquinoises, etc.; dans lesquelles on s'est attaché princepalement aux moeurs, usages, coutumes et religions de ces différens peuples de l'asie.** Paris (1774) 740 p. Comp fr works on japan and china, mainly by d'Entrecolles and Du Halde, jesuits.

Cave, Sydney. **An introduction to the study of some living religions of the east.** London (1921, 1947) See p 147-172.

Chan, Wing-tsit et al (comp). **The great asian religions: an anthology.** N.Y. etc (1969) See pt 2, Religions of china, 99-227. Textual excerpts.

Chan, Wing-tsit. The path to wisdom. Chinese philosophy and religion. In Arnold Toynbee (ed) **Half the world. The history and culture of china and japan,** ny etc (1973) 95-130.

Chan, Wing-tsit. Perspectives on religion. **FCR** 26.1 (jan 1976) 24-28.

Chang, Chi-hsien. Religious diversity. **FCR** 22.8 (aug 1972) 16-24.

Chavannes, Édouard. Compte rendu de j.j.m. de groot, **religious system of china. RHR** 37 (1898) 81-89.

Chavannes, Édouard. Compte rendu de r. dvorak, **chinas religionen. RHR** 32 (1895) 303-307; 48 (1903) 71-74.

Chen, Sophia H. What is the spiritual resort of a chinese? **NRJ** 7.3 (1947) 26-40.

Chêng, Tê-k'un. An introduction to chinese civilization. Religion and philosophy of the chinese. **Orient** 1.8 (mar 1951) 28-35.

Chêng, Tê-k'un. **The religious outlook of the chinese.** London, the china society, occasional papers no 9 (1956) 8 p.

Child, L. Maria. **The progress of religious ideas, through successive ages.** N.Y. (1855) See vol 1, chap 3, China, 199-221.

China's five religions. **PT** n.s. 15 (1936) 89-95.

Ching, Julia. The chinese religious sense. **Concilium** 126 (1979) 19-25.

Chitty, J.R. **Things seen in china.** NY (1909) See chap 6, Religious life, 217-252.

Clennell, Walter J. **The historical development of religion in china.** London (2nd ed 1926) 262 p.

Corwin, Charles **East to eden? Religion and the dynamics of social change.** Grand rapids, mich (1972) See chap 2, China, 51-93. ". . . a phenomenological study of man as he appears in the . . . chinese . . . tradition'

Cranston, Ruth. **World faith. The story of the religions of the united nations.** N.Y. (1949) See chap 3, The heavenly ways of the chinese sages, 53-76.

Culbertson, Michael Simpson. **Darkness in the flowery land; or, religious notions and popular superstitions in north china.** NY (1857) 235 p.

Current perspectives in the study of chinese religions. Special double issue symposium in **HR** 17.3/4 (feb-may 1978) 207-434. Art sep listed in our bibliog.

Dammann, Ernst. **Grundriss der religionsgeschichte.** Stuttgart etc (1972) See Chinesische religionen, 58-66.

Danton, George H. **The chinese people.** Boston (1938) See chap 7, Religion, 199-232.

DeKorne, John C. **Chinese altars to the unknown god. An account of the religions of china and the reactions to them of christian missions.** Grand rapids, mich (1926) ix-xiii + 139 p, illus.

Denby, Charles. **China and her people.** Boston (1906) See chap 13, Religion and superstition, 174-190.

Dhavamony, M. Self-understanding of world religions as religion. **Gregorianum** 54.1 (1973) 91-130. See sec, The concept of religion in china, 107-112.

Dietrich. Die religionen chinas. **AMZ** 19 (1892) 419-424.

Dobbins, Frank S. assisted by S. Wells Williams and Isaac Hall. **Error's chains: how forged and broken.** N.Y. (1883) See chap 21-25, p 416-497. Same work publ under title: **Story of the world's worship,** chicago (1901) illus.

Dobson, W.A.C.H. Religion in china. In Geoffrey Parrinder (ed) **Man and his gods: encyclopedia of the world's religions,** feltham, engl (1973)

Doolittle, Justus. **Social life of the chinese . . . with special but not exclusive reference to fuhchau.** NY (1865) 2 vol, xvi + 459, 490 p, illus, index for both vol at end of vol 2. Well over half of this work deals with relig. Sep entries listed in our bibliog for each subj. Abbrev **SLC.**

Doré, Henri. **Manuel des superstitions chinoises.** Shanghai, 2nd ed (1936) 221 p, table alphabétique with chin characters.

Doré, Henri. **Recherches sur les superstitions en chine.** Shanghai (1911-1938) 18 vol. Being **Variétés Sinologiques** no 32, 34, 36, 39, 41-42, 44-46, 48-49, 51, 57, 61-62, 66. Profusely illus. See next item.

Doré, Henri. **Researches into chinese superstitions** (Engl tsl of above). Vol 1 (1914) 2 (1915) 3 (1916) 4 (1917) 5 (1918) 6 (1920) 7 (1922) 8 (1926) tsl M.

Kennelly, s.j. Vol 9 (1931) 10 (1933) tsl D.J. Finn, s.j. Vol. 13 (1938) tsl L.F. McGreal, s.j. Above engl vol all publ shanghai; republ taipei 1966-67. (7 vol remain untsl: 11, 12, 14, 15, 16, 17, 18)

Douglas, Robert K. **Society in China.** London (1901) See chap 26, The religions of china, 394-415.

DuBose, Hampton C. **The dragon, image and demon, or the religions of china: confucianism, buddhism, and taoism. Giving an account of the mythology, idolatry and demonolotry of the chinese.** London (1886) 463 p.

Duyvendak, J.J.L. Henri maspero, mélanges posthumes (etc.) (rev art) **TP** 40 (1951) 372-390.

Dye, James W. & William H. Forthman. **Religions of the world. Selected readings.** NY (1967) See pt II, Buddhism, chap 15-17, p 159-174; pt III, Chinese religion, 181-316—mostly on philos.

Eastman, Roger (ed) **The ways of religion.** NY etc (1975) See chap 3, Wing-tsit Chan (tsl) The platform sutra of the sixth patriarch, 154-159; chap 4, I ching: notes on a chinese classic (mainly fr R. Wilhelm) 175-192; chap 5, Confucianism: the ideal of the true man, 193-240; chap 6, Taoism: the way to do is to be, 241-278.

Eberhard, Wolfram. **Moral and social values of the chinese. Collected essays.** Taipei (1971) 502 p, index. Various art concern relig; see sep listing in our bibliog. Abbrev **MSVC.**

Eder, Matthias. **Chinese religion.** Tokyo (1973) vii + 204 p, bibliog, index. Asian folklore studies monograph no 6.

Eder, Matthias. Chinesische religion. In **Die religion in geschichte und gegenwart. Handwörterbuch für theologie und religionswissenschaft,** Tübingen, dritte anflage (1957) bd 1, s 1655a-1661a.

Eder, Matthias. Die religion der chinesen. In Franz König (ed) **Christus und die religionen der erde. Handbuch der religions-geschichte.** Wien and freiburg (1961) vol 3, 319-391. Same title in **Die grossreligionen des fernen osten,** aschaffenburg (1961) ('Der christ in der welt, eine enzyklopädie,' XVII, Reihe die nichtchristlichen religionen, 7. band, p 5-66)

Edkins, Joseph. **Religion in china.** Boston (1859) rev and expanded ed (1878) 260 p.

Edkins, Joseph. **The religious condition of the chinese: with observations on the prospects of christian conversion among that people.** London (1859) viii + 288 p (2nd ed 1878; 3rd ed 1884; french tsl paris 1882) repr taipei (1974)

Edwards, Dwight W. The syncretic mind in chinese religions. **ChRec** 57 (1926) 400-413.

Eichhorn, W. **Die religionen chinas.** Stuttgart (1973) 420 s, 1 faltkarte. Historical treatment.

Eliade, Mircea. **Histoire des croyances et des idées religieuses. Volume 2, de gautama bouddha au triomphe du christianisme.** Paris (1978) Engl tsl Willard Trask, **A history of religious ideas. Volume 2, from gautama buddha to the triumph of christianity.** Univ chicago (1982) See chap 16, The religions of ancient china, 3-43; also, Present position of studies: problems and progress, critical bibliog, 419-433.

Eliot, Charles. The religion of china. **Quarterly review** 207 (1907) 351-376.

Ellwood, Robert S. jr. **Many peoples, many faiths.** Englewood cliffs, n.j. (1976) See chap 5, Dragon and sun: religions of china and japan; china sec 147-184.

Endres, Franz Carl. **Die grossen religionen asiens; eine einführung in das verständnig ihrer grundlagen.** Zürich (1949) 186 p, pl.

Erkes, Eduard. Chinas religiöse entwicklung im zusammenhang mit seiner geschichte. **OZ** 4.1/2 (1915) 58-66.

Ermoni, V. Les religions de la chine. **Science catholique** 7 (mars 1892)

Escarra, Jean. **China then and now.** Peking (1940) See chap 4, sec Religion and philosophy, 103-130. Orig french ed, **La chine: Passé et présent,** Paris (1937)

Faber, Ernst. **Introduction to a science of chinese religion. A critique of max müller and other authors.** Hong kong and shanghai (1879) xii + 154 p.

Feibleman, James K. **Understanding oriental philosophy. A popular account for the western world.** NY (1976) See pt 2, passim.

Feigl, Hermann. Die religion der chinesen. **Oesterreichische monatsschrift für den orient** 21 (1895) 41-51, 74-84, 101-112; 22 (1896) 1-12.

Fielde, Adele M. **Pagoda Shadows.** Boston (1890) See chap 8-14, p 70-112.

Fitch, Mary F. **Their search for god; ways of worship in the Orient.** N.Y. (1947) 160 p.

Forlong, J.G.R. (ed) **Faiths of man. Encyclopedia of religions.** London (1906) republ NY (1964) See vol 1, China, 403-424.

Fradenburgh, J.N. **Living religions, or, the great religions of the orient, from sacred books and modern customs.** N.Y. (1888) 508 p.

Franke, Herbert. **Sinologie.** Bern (1953) See 7, Religion, brauchtum, folklore, 89-109.

Franke, O. Die chinesen. In Alfred Bertholet and Edvard Lehmann (ed) **Lehrbuch der religionsgeschichte begründet von chantepie de la saussaye [q.v.] vierte, vollständig neuarbeitete auflage** . . . Tübingen (1925) See vol 1, 193-261.

Frazier, Allie M. (ed) **Readings in eastern religious thought.** Vol 3, **Chinese and japanese religions.** Philadelphia (1969) See 1-176, China.

Friess, Horace L. (ed) **Non-christian religions a to z. Based on the work of helmuth von glasenapp: Die nichtchristlichen religionen,** frankfurt-am-main (1957) q.v. N.Y. (1963) See Chinese universism, 52-69.

Fryer, John **Oriental studies. A series of college text-books on subjects connected with china, japan & other eastern lands. Course 1, The philosophies and religions of china.** Shanghai (1900) 141 p.

Genähr, J. Die religion der chinesen. **ZMR** 12 (1897) 79-92.

Giles, Herbert A. **Adversaria sinica.** Leyden (1905-08). See no 1-4, 6. (Rev of no 1 in **BEFEO** 6 [1906] 416-421, and no 3 in **TP 7** [1906] 307-309) Abbrev **AdSin.**

Giles, Herbert A. **The civilization of China.** London (1911) See chap 3, Religion and superstition, 55-78.

Giles, Herbert A. **Confucianism and its rivals.** London (1915) ix + 271 p.

Glasenapp, Helmuth von. **Die fünf grossen religionen.** Düssendorf (1951-52) 2 vol. See vol 1, Die chinesische universismus, 152-221. French tsl Pierre Jundt: **Les cinq grandes religions du monde,** paris (1954) 558 p.

Glasenapp, Helmuth von. **Die grossen religionen der östlichen völker.** Zürich (1957) 48 p.

Gowen, Herbert H. **A history of religion.** Milwaukee, wisc (1934) See chap 14-15, The religions of china. 350-380.

Graham, Dorothy, Three faiths of china. **CW** 122 (mar 1926) 774-781.

Grainger, Adam. **Studies in chinese life.** Chengtu (1921) 151 p, chin char.

Granet, Marcel. l'Esprit de la religion chinoise. **Scientia** 45 (may 1929) 329-337. Repr **ESC** (1953) 251-260.

Granet, Marcel. **La religion des chinois.** Paris (1922) xi + 175 p, repr (1951) Engl tsl Maurice Freedman, **The religion of the chinese people,** ny etc (1975) 200p, intro essay by tsl on Marcel Granet, 1884-1940, sociologist; ed notes, bibliog, index.

Granet, Marcel. **Études sociologiques sur la chine.** Paris (1953) Contains inter alia repr of 5 art, all sep listed in our bibliog. Abbrev **ESC.**

Groot, J.J. M. de. **Religion in china. Universism: a key to the study of taoism and confucianism.** N.Y. and london (1912) xv + 327 p.

Groot, J.J. M. de. **The religion of the chinese.** N.Y. (1910) vii + 230p.

Groot, J.J. M. de. Die religionen der chinesen. In P. von Hinneberg (ed) **Die kultur der gegenwart,** teil 1, abteilung 3, **Die orientalischen religionen,** berlin and leipzig (1906) 162-193.

Groot, J.J. M. de. **The religious system of china.** Leiden (1892-1910) repr taipei (1964) 6 vol. Vol 1-3: Disposal of the dead; vol 4-6: The soul and ancestral worship. (Compte rendu par Éd. Chavannes, **RHR** 37 [1898] 81-89)

Groot, J.J. M. de. **Universismus. Die grundlage d. religion u. ethik, d. staatswesens u. d. wissenschaften chinas.** Berlin (1918) viii + 404 p, 7 tafeln. (P. Pelliot rev in **JA** sér 11, 15/16 [juil/sept 1920] 158-165; E. Schmitt, in **OZ** 6.3/4 [1917-18] 279-289)

Grube Wilhelm. **Religion und kultus der chinesen.** Leipzig (1910) vii + 220 p, 8 pl.

Grützmacher, Richard H. **Primitive und fernöstliche religionen: china und japan.** Leipzig (1937) 49 p.

Gutzlaff, Charles. **China opened** . . . London (1838) Rev Andrew Reed. See chap 15, Religion, 183-247.

Gutzlaff, Charles. **The journal of two voyages along the coast of china in 1831 & 1832** . . . NY (1833) See app essay, Religions of china, 299-314.

Hackmann, Heinrich. China, volk und kultur. Materialien zu einer einführenden vorlesung. **Sinica** 12 (1937) See sec, Die religion, 229-232.

Happel, Julius. Die religion in china. **ZMK** 5 (1890) 129-31, 191-201, 251-259; 6 (1891) 45-52.

Harding, D.E. **Religions of the world.** London (1966) See sec 4, p 51-67.

Hardwick, Charles. **Christ and other masters . . . Part III: Religions of china, america and oceania.** Cambridge (1858) See Religions of china, 272-346.

Hare, William L. **Chinese religion: a historical and literary sketch of ancestor worship, the teachings of kung fu tze and lao tze, and chinese natural philosophy.** London (1907) 62 p.

Harlez, Charles de. La religion en chine. À propos du dernier livre de m. a. réville. **Magasin littéraire et scientifique** (1889) 34 p.

Harlez, Charles Joseph. **La religion et les cérémonies de la china moderne.** Bruxelles (1894)

Harlez, Charles de. The religion of the chinese people. **New world** 2 (1893-94) 646-676.

Harlez, Charles de. Les religions de la chine. **Muséon** 10 (1891-92) 145-176, 275-298, 523-548.

Harlez, Charles de. **Les religions de la chine. Aperçu historique et critique.** Leipzig (1891) 270 p.

Hartman, L.O. **Popular aspects of oriental religions.** N.Y. and cincinnati (1917) See chap 2, Fifty centuries of worship, 39-64, illus snapshots.

Hawkridge, Emma. **The wisdom tree.** Boston (1945) See pt 3, chap 3, Chinese, 403-466, illus.

Headland, Isaac Taylor. Religion. Chap 13 in author's **HLC** (1914) 123-130.

Heiler, F. Die religion der chinesen. In **Die religionen der menschheit im vergangenheit und gegenwart,** stuttgart (1959) 108-134.

Henry, B.C. Feasts, pastimes, and folk-lore. Chap 8 in author's **CD** (1885) 152-172.

Holcombe, Chester. **The real chinaman.** NY (1909) See chap 6-7, p 116-170

Hopfe, Lewis M. **Religions of the world.** Beverly hills, calif & london (1976) 2nd ed (1979) See esp chap 7, Chinese religions, 120-145.

Horton, Walter M. Oriental religion: eastern asia, ii: The chinese national religion; III: Buddhism in china, 74-88. In Henry N. Wieman and Walter M. Horton, **The growth of religion,** chicago and NY (1938)

Hsiao, C. Introduction to spirituality in some chinese traditions. **NEAJT** 12 (mar 1974) 36-47.

Hsu, Francis L.K. **Americans and chinese. Reflections on two cultures and their people.** N.Y. (1953; 2nd ed 1970). See in 2nd ed, chap 9-10.

Hsu, Francis L.K. **Religion, science, and human crisis; a study of china in transition and its implications for the west.** London (1952) x + 142 p, illus.

Hu, Chang-tu et al. **China. Its people, its society, its culture.** New haven, conn (1960) See chap 6, Religion, 110-139.

Hughes, E.R. & K. Hughes. **Religion in china.** London (1950) 151 p.

Humphreys, Christmas. The religion of china. **MW** 18 (1943) 29-33.

Hurd, William. **A new universal history of the religious rites, ceremonies, and customs of the whole world: or, a complete and impartial view of all the religions in the various nations of the universe, both antient and modern, from the creation down to the present time** . . . London, n.d. (ca. 1780?) See The religion of the chinese, 58-66 (Taken from writings of Du Halde and Le Comte)

Hutchinson, John A. **Paths of faith.** N.Y. etc (1969) See chap 8, Chinese religion, 203-258.

Hutchinson, John A. and James A. Martin jr. **Ways of faith. An introduction to religion.** N.Y. (1953) See chap 2, Classical ways of china, 51-82.

Ingalls, Jeremy. Religions of asia in a world community. Part II: Worldviews in china. **Common cause** 3 (dec 1949-jan 1950) 253-261, 317-324.

James, E.O. **Teach yourself history of religions.** London (1956) See chap 4, Religion in china and japan, 89-114.

Jeremias, Alfred. **Allgemeine religions-geschichte.** München (1918) See 4, chap 2, Die religion in china, 170-197.

Johnson, Samuel. **Oriental religions and their relation to universal religion.** Vol. II: **China.** Boston (1877) repr san francisco (1978) 975 p.

Johnston, R.F. **Lion and dragon in northern china.** London (1910) See chap 8, Village customs, festivals and folk-lore, 155-194.

Jurji, Edward J. (ed) **The great religions of the modern world.** Princeton univ (1946) See sec on confucianism and taoism.

Kaltenmark, M. et O. Kaltenmark. Les religions de la chine. In Joseph Chaine et René Grousset (ed) **Littérature religieuse,** paris (1949) 719-815.

Kaltenmark, Maxime. Religions de la chine. In École pratique des hautes études, Ve sec – sciences religieuses, **Problèmes et méthodes d'histoire des religions,** Paris (1968) 53-56.

Kaufman, Walter. **Religions in four dimensions, existential and aesthetic, historical and comparative.** NY (1976) See chap 12, From ceylon to japan, 327-356, illus.

Kenny, P.D. Religion in unknown china. **Quiver** (1901) 508-515.

Kern, Maximilian. **Das licht des ostens: die weltanschauungen des mitteleren und fernen asiens, indien-china-japan, und ihr einfluss auf das religiöse and sittliche leben, auf kunst und wissenschaft dieser länder.** Stuttgart (1922) 597 p, 3 col pl (abbrev as **LO**)

Kesson, John. **The cross and the dragon.** London (1854) See chap 13, Religious influences in china—confucius and his system. Taouism. Buddhism, 169-186.

Kiang, Kang-hu. **Chinese civilization. An introduction to sinology.** Shanghai (1935). See pt 2, chap 15; pt 3, chap 1-4, 6-7, 13-14, 16; pt 4, chap 3.

Kidd, Samuel. **China.** London (1841) See sec e, The three sects, 135-189; sec 6, on popular relig.

Kim, Young Oon. **World religions. Volume 3: faiths of the far east.** NY (1976) See Buddhism, 1-51; Taoism, 87-120; Confucianism, 121-160; brief bibliog for each sec.

Kitagawa, Joseph M. **Religions of the east.** Philadelphia, pa (1960). See chap 2, Chinese religions and the family system, 40-85.

Köster, Hermann. Was ist eigentlich universismus? **Sinologica** 9 (1967) 81-95.

Kraemer, H. **The christian message in a non-christian world.** Grand rapids, mich (1938) 3rd ed (1956) See chap 6, sec on China, 182-191.

Kranz, P. Lichtstrahlen aus den in china herrschenden religion anschauungen. **ZMK** 8 (1893) 10-20, 65-70.

Krause, F.E.A. Die chinesischen religionen. In C. Clemen (ed) **Religionen der erde.** München (1927) 79-94. Engl tsl A.K. Dallas: **Religions of the world; their nature and their history,** NY and chicago (1931) illus; see 78-92.

Latourette, Kenneth Scott. **The chinese; their history and culture.** N.Y. (1934 et seq) 4th rev ed (1964) See vol 2, chap on Religion, with bibliog.

Latourette, Kenneth Scott. **A history of christian missions in china.** NY (1929) See chap 2, The religious background of the chinese, 6-24.

Lavollée, C. Sur la religion et les divinités de la chine. **Illustration** 4 (16 janv 1847) repr in **ROA** sér 2, 3 (1848) 349-352.

Lay, G. Tradescant. **The chinese as they are.** London (1841) See chap 19, Religions of china, 94-101.

Legge, James. A fair and dispassionate discussion of the three doctrines accepted in china. From liu mi, a Buddhist writer. **Trans. ninth ICO.** London vol 2 (1893) 563-582.

Letourneau, Charles. **l'Évolution religieuse dans les diverses races humaines.** Paris (1898) See chap 10, B, La religion de la chine, 270-293.

Lewis, John. **The religions of the world made simple.** NY (1958) rev ed (1968) See chap 6, Buddhism in china and japan, 46-48; chap 7, Confucianism and taoism, 52-58.

Li, Dun-jen. **The essence of chinese civiliza-tion.** Princeton, n.j. etc (1967) See pt 1, Philosophy and religion, passim.

Life Magazine Editorial Staff. Religion in the land of confucius. **Life** 38 (4 apr 1955) 64-84. Mostly illus, partly in col.

Life Magazine Editorial Staff. **The world's great religions.** N.Y. (1957) See The philosophy of china, 71-98; photos, many in col.

Life Magazine Editorial Staff. **The world's great religions. Vol One: Religions of the east.** N.Y. (1955) See: The philosophy of china, 83-110; photos, many in col.

Lin, Yutang. **The chinese way of life.** NY (1959) See, Confucianism, buddhism, and taoism, 82-89. Juvenile level.

Lin, Yutang. **My country and my people.** NY (1935) See chap 4, Ideals of life, 100-132.

Little, Archibald. (rev by Mrs. A. Little) **Gleanings from fifty years in china.** London (1910) See chap 4, Religion and philosophy.

Loewe, Michael. **Ways to paradise. The chinese quest for immortality.** London (1979) 270 p, illus, app, notes. Based on han dynasty relics.

Lohmann, T. Religion im alten und neueren china. **Theologische literaturzeitung** 85 (1960) 805-806.

Lowe, H.Y. **The adventures of wu. The life cycle of a peking man.** Peking, 2 vol (1939-40) Orig publ in **The peking chronicle.** Repr, 2 vol in 1, princeton univ (1983) xxii, 239, 250 p, index, errata. Intro Derk Bodde. See passim.

Lyon, Quinter M. **The great religions.** N.Y. (1957) See pt 4, Oriental religions of man and nature, chap 17-22, p 265-353.

MacGowan, John. **Sidelights on chinese life.** London (1907) illus. See chap 4, Religious forces in china, 65-93.

Maclay, R.S. **Life among the chinese.** NY (1861) See chap 6-7, Religions . . . 87-120.

Malmquist, Göran. Die religionen chinas. In J.P. Asmussen & Jørgen Laessøe heraus in verbindung mit Carston Colpe, **Handbuch des religionsgeschichte,** göttingen, b 3 (1968, 1972) 1-68, illus.

Man, myth and hope. An illustrated encyclopedia of the supernatural. NY (1970) See vol 4, China, 456-465, lavishly illus. See also vol 24, Contents guide and bibliog, 3266 ff. See also Index, China.

Mao, W.E. The religion of the chinese. **CSM** 20 (1925) 12-15.

Martin, W.A.P. The san chiao, or three religions of china. In author's **Lore of cathay,** NY and chicago (1901) repr taipei (1971) 165-204.

Maspero, Henri. **Le taoïsme et les religions chinoises.** Paris (1971) 658 p. préface de Max Kaltenmark. "Ce recueil est basé sur les deux premiers volumes des **Mélanges posthumes sur les religions et l'histoire de la china** édités par Paul Demiéville en 1950 . . ." (cited in our bibliog as **HMRC,** q.v.)

Maspero, Henri. **Les religions chinoises.** (Mélanges posthumes sur les religions et l'histoire de la chine: I) Paris (1950) 225 p. Avant-propos par P. Demiéville. (Includes 3 unpubl and 2 re-issued studies) Abbrev as **HMRC.** Repr in Henri Maspero, **Le taoïsme et les religions chinoises,** paris (1971) q.v.

Masson-Oursel, Paul. La chine. In Maxime Gorce & Raoul Mortier (ed) **Histoire générale des religion,** paris (1944-51) t 4, 448-465.

Matignon, J.J. **La chine hermétique; superstitions, crime et misère (souvenirs de biologie sociale).** . . Paris (nouvelle ed 1936; orig ed Paris 1898, title sans **La chine hermétique**) 374 p, 42 pl.

McCarland, S. Vernon, Grace E. Cairns, & David C. Yu. **Religions of the world.** NY (1969) See pt 5, Religions of east asia, chap 19-24, p 521-708.

Medhurst, W.H. **China: its state and prospects.** London (1840) See chap 8, The religions of china, 181-219.

Mei, Y.P. China: philosophy, religions, and science: sec 9, Philosophy and religion. In **EncyA** (1971, 1975, 1980) vol 6, 551a-559a.

Mémoires concernant l'histoire, les sciences, les arts, les moeurs et les usages des chinois par les missionaires de pékin (amyot, bourgeois, ko. poirot, gaubil) Paris (1776-1814) 16 vol. See passim (abbrev as **MCLC**)

Mensching, Gustav. **Soziologie der grossen religionen.** Bonn (1966) See 2, Soziologie des chinesischen universismus, 42-53.

Menzel. **Die religion der chinesen und die bisherigen missions-versuche in china.** Breslau (1898)

Menzies, Allan. **History of religion.** London (1905) See chap 8, China, 102-121.

Millican, Frank R. (tsl) The religious experience of the chinese people: wang chih-hsin: chung-hua min-tsu-ti tsung-chiao ching-yen. **ChRec** 58.3 (mar 1927) 192-207.

Milloué, Léon de. **Catalogue du musée guimet. Pt. I: Inde, chine et japon. Précédée d'un aperçu sur les religions de l'extrême-orient et suivie d'un index alphabétique es noms des divinités et des principaux termes techniques.** Lyon (1883)

Milne, William C. **Life in china.** London (1858) See Contents, passim.

Moore, George F. **History of religions.** Vol 1: **China, japan** . . . etc. N.Y. (1913) See chap 1-5, China, 3-92.

Morgan, Kenneth W. **Asian religions. An introduction to the study of hinduism, buddhism, islam, confucianism, and taoism.** N.Y. (1964) 30 p.

Moule, Arthur Evans. **The chinese people. A hand book on china.** London (1914) See chap 4-5, p 164-222.

Müller, F. Max. The religions of china. **NC** 48 (1900): 1. Confucianism (sept) 373-384; 2. Taoism (oct) 569-581; 3. Buddhism (nov) 730-742.

Murphy, John. **The origins and history of religions.** Manchester univ (1949) See chap 6 p 327-389.

Murray, Hugh, et al. **An historical and descriptive account of china.** Edinburgh& london (1836) See vol 2, chap 2, Religion of china, 124-159.

Nakamura, Hajime. **Parallel developments. A comparative history of ideas.** Tokyo (1975) xx + 567 p. See passim.

Nevius, John L. **China and the chinese.** NY (1868) See Contents.

Noss, John B. **Man's religions.** NY (1949 et seq; 6th ed 1980) See pt 3, chap 9, Native chinese religion and taoism, 234-264; chap 10, Confucius and confucianism . . . 265-301; incl suggestions for further reading.

Ogilvie, C.L. **Some aspects of chinese life and thought.** Shanghai & peking (n.d.—?1918) See sec, Chinese religions, 69-95.

On the three principal religions in china. **The asiatic journal and monthly register,** 9 (1832) 302-316.

O'Neill, Frederick W.S. **The quest for god in china.** N.Y. and london (1925)

Orelli, Conrad von. **Allgemeine religionsgeschichte.** Bonn (1911) See vol 1, A, Turanische gruppe, 1, Religion der chinesen, 30-89.

Orr, Robert G. **Religion in china.** NY (1980) 144 p, suggestions for further reading, notes, a few photos. See chap 6-9 on "traditional religions."

Overmyer, Daniel L. Rev of D.H. Smith, **Chinese religions,** q.v. **HR** 9 (1969-70) 256-260.

Owen, George. The religions of china. **ChRec** 21.2 (feb 1890) 84-87. "Abridged from the **London missionary chronicle**"

Parker, E.H. **Ancient china simplified.** London (1908) See Contents.

Parker, Edward Harper. **China and religion.** London (1905) xxv + 317, illus. ("Popular ed" 1910)

Parker, E.H. The religion of the chinese. **New century review** 2 (1897) 179-190. Same title in author's **China past and present,** london (1903) bk 3, chap 1, 80-92.

Parker, Edward Harper. **Studies in chinese religion.** London (1910) 308 p, index, photos. ". . . in the main . . . the original studies from which a summary was made and a popular work published, in 1905, called **China and religion.**"

Parrinder, Edward G. **An introduction to asian religions.** London (1957) vi + 138 p. See chap 5, Chinese religion, 87-115.

Parrinder, Geoffrey. **The faiths of mankind. A guide to the world's living religions.** N.Y. (1965) Original title: **The world's living religions,** london (1964) See chap 5, China's three ways, 89-110.

Parrinder, Geoffrey. **Worship in the world's religions.** London (1961) 2nd ed (1974) repr totowa, n.j. (1976) See pt 3, The far east, 117-152.

Parrish, Fred L. **History of religion: the destiny-determining factor in the world's cultures.** N.Y. (1965) See chap 11, The yinyang-tao religion of china (sixth century b.c. and after) 160-179.

Patai, R. Religion in middle eastern, far eastern, and western culture. **SWJA** 10 (1954) 233-254.

Paton, William. **Jesus Christ and the world's religions.** London (1947) See chap 5, The message of christianity to china, 67-81.

Pavie, Théodore. Les trois religions de la chine, leur antagonisme, leur développement et leur influence. **RDM** sér 5, 9/12 (1 fevr 1845)

Peeters, Hermes. **The religions of china. Confucianism, taoism, buddhism, popular belief.** Peking (1941) 64 p. (Lectures delivered at the College of Chinese Studies)

Peisson, J. **Histoire des religions de l'extrême-orient.** Amiens (1888-89). 2 fasc: viii + 53; 53-127.

Pernitzsch, Max G. **Die religionen chinas.** Berlin (1940)

Perzynski, Friedrich. **Von chinas göttern. Reisen in china.** München (1920) 260 s, 80 bildtafeln.

Petit, J.A. La chine philosophique et religieuse depuis l'antiquité jusqua'à l'établissement de la propagation de la foi. **Revue du monde catholique** 28 (juin-sept 1888)

Pfleiderer, Otto. **Religion and historic faiths.** Tsl fr german Daniel A. Huebsch. N.Y. (1907) See chap 5, The chinese religion, 89-102.

Phillips, Edith C. **Peeps into china, or, the missionary's children.** London etc (2nd ed n.d.—pre-1894) See chap 3, The religions of china, 44-68.

Porkert, Manfred. **China—konstanten im wandel. Moderne interpretationen der chinesischen klassik.** Stuttgart (1978) See Religion und philosophie, 31-82.

Price, Frank W. Religion in china. (Abstract) In Cheng Chi-pao (ed) **Symposium on chinese culture.** N.Y. (1964) 38-40.

Puech, H.C. (ed) **Histoire des religions.** Tome I: **Religions antiques. Religions de salut (inde et extrême-orient)** Paris (1970) 1,528 p, illus, cartes.

Radford, Ruby L. **Many paths to god.** Wheaton, ill (1970) See 4, The path of chinese wisdom, taoism and confucianism, 45-57.

Radhakrishnan, Sarvapelli. **India and china. Lectures delivered in china in may 1944.** Bombay (1944)

Rawlinson, Frank. Religion in china — many gods; no god! **MRW** n.s. 25.3 (1912) 177-182.

Rees, J. Lambert. The three religions and their bearing on chinese civilization. **ChRec** 27 (1896) 157-169, 222-231.

Rees, J. Lambert. The three religions of china and their influence on character. **TheE&TheW** 4 (1906) 301-320.

Reichelt, Karl Ludvig. **Meditation and piety in the far east. A religious-psychological study.** Tsl fr norwegian Sverre Holth. N.Y. and london (1954) 171 p.

Reichelt, Karl Ludvig. **Religion in chinese garment.** Tsl fr norwegian Joseph Tetlie. N.Y. and london (1951) 180 p.

Reid, Gilbert. **Glances at china.** London (1892) See chap 4, 5, 14, 25.

Reischauer, August Karl. **The nature and truth of the great religions.** Tokyo (1966) See sec A:VI, The god-concept in chinese religion, 63-75; sec B:5, Chinese religion and the good life, 122-147; sec C:VI, Chinese religion and individual destiny, 171-173.

Religion in china. **ChRec** 33 (1902) Three art: by Stanley Smith, 334-343; I. Genähr, 487-497; Stanley Smith, 610-618.

Religious glimpses of eastern asia. Being **SM** 16 (1967) Five art; four relevant ones are listed under appropriate headings in this bibliog.

A Resident in Peking. **China as it really is.** London (1912) See chap 10, Religions of china, 86-95.

Réville, Albert. **Histoire des religions.** Tome III: **La religion chinoise.** Paris (1889) Sec 1: jusqu'à la page 400; Sec 2: 401-710.

Réville, Albert. La religion chinoise. **Muséon** 12 (1893) 282f.

Réville, Albert. La religion chinoise à propos d'un ouvrage de m. de harlez [i.e. **Les religions de la chine,** q.v.] **RHR** 27.2 (1893) 226.

Ring, George C. **Religions of the far east: their history to the present day.** Milwaukee, wis (1950) x + 350 p, illus.

Ringgren, Helmer & Åke V. Ström. **Religions of mankind today and yesterday.** Ed J. C. G. Greig. Tsl Niels L. Jensen. Philadelphia (1967) Orig swedish ed 3rd ed (1964) Stockholm. See pt 3, sec 2, The far east, 1, China, 390-407.

Rosny, Léon de. **Les religions de l'extrême-orient.** Paris (1886) 36 p.

Rowley, Harold H. **Submission and suffering, and other essays in eastern thought.** Cardiff, univ wales (1951) 170 p, index.

Saint-Thècle, Adrien de. Traité des sectes religieuses chez les chinois et les tonquinois. **JA** sér 1, t 2 (1823) 163-175. Table of contents and brief abstracts tsl into french fr an unpubl latin ms completed in 1750.

Sarkar, B.K. **Chinese religion through hindu eyes. A study in the tendencies of asiatic mentality.** Shanghai (1916) repr delhi (1975) xxxii + 331 p.

Saussaye, P.D. Chantepie de la. **Lehrbuch der religionsgeschichte.** Freiburg (1887) See vol 1, Die chinesen, 232-261. Engl tsl Beatrice

S. Colyer-Ferguson, **Manual of the science of religion,** london and NY (1891) See The chinese, 332-374. French tsl sous la direction de Henri Hubert et Isidore Lévy, **Manuel d'histoire des religions,** paris (1904) See chap 3, Les chinois (traduit par P. Bettelheim) 39-60.

Savage, Katherine. **The story of world religions.** N.Y. (1966) See chap 6, The religions of china, 89-103, illus. Juvenile level.

Scarth, John. **Twelve years in china.** Edinburgh (1860) See chap 8, Religion in china, 74-94.

Schafer, Edward H. **Ancient china.** N.Y. (1967) Through t'ang dynasty. See chap 3-5; many relevant illus.

Schmitt, Erich. **Die chinesen.** No 6 in Alfred Bertholet (ed) **Religionsgeschichtliches lesebuch,** tübingen (1917) 110 p, index.

Schmitt, Erich. "Universismus." **OZ** 6.3/4 (1917-18) 279-289. Re book by J.J.M. de Groot q.v.

Schoeps, Hans-Joachim. **An intelligent person's guide to the religions of mankind.** Tsl fr german Richard & Clara Winston. London (1967) See Religion in china, 181-196.

Schwarz, Henry G. Some random thoughts on religion and religious policy in china. **Ajia kenkyujo kiyo** 7 (1980) 1-39.

Seeger, Elizabeth. **Eastern religions.** NY (1973) See pt 4, The religions of china, 103-155, illus.

Shah, Ikbal Ali. **The spirit of the east. An anthology of the scriptures of the east, with an explanatory introduction.** London (1939) repr (1973) See Quotations from the four books, 36-48; Quotations from "tao teh king" by lao tzu, 49-53.

Sirr, Henry Charles. **China and the chinese.** London (1849) See vol 2, chap 8-9, p 145-185.

Smalley, Frank A. **Chinese philosophy and religion.** London (1947) 42 p, illus.

Smart, Ninian. **The long search.** Boston & Toronto (1977) See chap 8, China, 250-267.

Smart, Ninian. **The religious experience of mankind.** N.Y. (1969) See sec Religions of the far east, 141-190. 2nd rev ed, (1976) See 159-209.

Smith, Arthur H. **Rex christus. An outline.** NY (1904) See chap 2, The religions of china, 44-83, incl bibliog.

Smith, Arthur H. **The uplift of china.** Cincinnati & NY (1907) illus. See chap 4, The strength and weakness of the religions, 83-114.

Smith, D. Howard (ed) China and the far east. Sec in S.G.F. Brandon (genl ed) **A dictionary of comparative religion,** NY (1970) See Synoptic index, Chinese cults and philosophies, 668.

Smith, D. Howard, **Chinese religions.** N.Y. etc (1968) 222 p. Historical treatment.

Smith, Mrs J. Gregory. **From dawn to sunrise: a review, historical and philosophical, of the religious ideas of mankind.** N.Y. (1880) See China and its religions, 180-199.

Smith, Stanley. **China from within, or the story of the chinese crisis.** London (1901) See chap 12, Religion in china, 172-189.

Smith, Stanley. Religion in china. **ChRec** 33 (1902) 334-343. (Extracted from **China from within**) See notice in **JRAS** (1904) 517-523.

Société des Études Japonaises, Chinoises, Tartares et Indo-Chinoises. **Chrestomathie religieuse de l'extrême-orient.** Paris (1887) 52 p.

Söderblom, N. **Die religionen der erde.** Halle a. saale (1905) 65 p.

Soothill, W.E. **A mission in china.** Edinburgh & london (1907) illus. See chap 15-18 for chin relig, 208-270. Amer ed, ny etc (n.d.) entitled **A typical mission in china.**

Soothill, William E. **The three religions of china.** Oxford (1923) repr westport, conn (1973) 271 p.

Soper, Edmund D. **The religions of mankind.** N.Y. and nashville (1921) 3rd rev ed (1951) See chap 8, The religion of china, 160-175.

Speer, Robert E. **The light of the world. A brief comparative study of christianity and non-christian religions.** West medford, mass (1911) See chap 3, Animism, confucianism and taoism, 121-176.

Spiegelberg, Frederic. **Living religions of the world.** Englewood cliffs, n.j. (1956) See chap 9-12, p 179-353.

Stange, H.O.H. Die religion des alten china (in anthropologisches hinsicht) In C.J. Bleeker (ed) **Anthropologie religieuse. l'Homme et sa destinée à la lumière de l'histoire des religions,** leiden (1955)

Stein, Rolf. Les religions de la chine. In **l'Encyclopédie française.** Paris (1957) See sec C, chap 4.

Steininger, H. Religions of china. In C. J. Bleeker & George Widengren (ed) **Historia religionum. Handbook for the history of religion. Volume Two: Religions of the present.** Leiden (1971) 465-515.

Stewart, James L. **Chinese culture and christianity. A review of china's religions and related systems from the christian standpoint.** N.Y. etc (1926) 316 p, bibliog, index.

Stronath, Alexander. A general view of what are regarded by the chinese as objects of worship. **JIA** 2 (1848) 349-352.

Stübe, R. Religion und kultus der chinesen. **Zeitschrift für religions-psychologie** 3 (1910) 346-350.

Tan, Yün-shan. What is chinese religion. **VBQ** n.s. 3 (1937-38) 152-163.

Tao, Pung Fai. Religionsbekenntnisse. Sec 3 in author's **China's geist und kraft,** breslau (1935) 111-121.

The Taoist pope on religion. **OC** 28.11 (nov 1914) 707-709.

Taylor, Charles. **Five years in china.** NY (1860) See Contents.

Thiele, Margaret R. **None but the nightingale. An inroduction to chinese literature.** See chap 7, Some superior men, 73-110.

Thompson, Laurence G. Chinese religion. **EncyB** 15th ed **(Britannica 3)** (1974) **Macropaedia** vol 4, 422a-428a.

Thompson, Laurence G. **Chinese religion: an introduction.** Belmont, calif (1969) 2nd ed, rev & enl, encino & belmont, calif (1975) 3rd ed, further rev & enl, belmont (1979) 163 p, table of chin relig hist, time line of chin relig hist, app, notes, sel readings, gloss, index.

Thompson, Laurence G. (comp & ed) **The chinese way in religion.** Encino & belmont, calif (1973) 241 p. Anthol of readings fr texts and studies.

Thomson, J. **The land and people of china.** London (1876) See chap 8, Religion, 189-215.

Thomson, John Stuart. **The chinese.** NY (1909) See chap 9, Chinese religion and superstition, 363-386.

Ting, W.Y. Konfuzianismus, taoismus und buddhismus. **CDA** (1933) p 24.

Tourchier, Louis. l'Esprit religieux des chinois. **Études** (20 dec 1910) 788-803.

Townley, Susan. **My chinese notebook.** London (1904) See several sec, 90-130.

Tscharner, Eduard Horst von. Ostasien. In **Mensch und gottheit in den religionen.** Herausgegeben von der universität bern. Bern-leipzig (1942) 91-119

Tsukamoto, Zenryū & Makita Tairyō. China: history of religion. **Comité Japonais des sciences historiques** (1960) 324-329.

Underwood, Horace Grant. **The religions of eastern asia.** N.Y. and london (1910) 267 p.

Vail, Albert & Emily M. Vail. **Transforming light. The living heritage of world religions.** NY etc (1970) See chap 7, Lao tzu and confucius, 68-82; Buddhism in china, 83-91.

Van der Sprenkel, O.B. Chinese religion. Rev art on H.H. Gerth's tsl of Max Weber, **The religion of china** (1951) **British journal of sociology** 5 (1954) 272-275.

Variété. **Relations de la chine** (oct 1912) 529-546. Mostly on various popular deities.

Vinson, Julien. **Les religions actuelles.** Paris (1888) See chap 4, Les religions de la chine et du japon, 196-224.

Walshe, W. Gilbert. China. In **HERE** 3, 549-552.

Wei, Francis C.M. Religious beliefs of the ancient chinese and their influence on the national character of the chinese people. **ChRec** 42.6 (june 1911) 319-328; 42.7 (july 1911) 403-415.

Wei, Francis C.M. **The spirit of chinese culture.** N.Y. (1947) 186 p, index.

Whitehead, James D., Yu-ming Shaw & N.J. Girardot (ed) **China and christianity. Historical and future encounters.** Univ notre dame (1979) xv + 293 p. Relevant art listed sep in our bibliog. Abbrev **C&C.**

Wieger, Léon. Articles on the religions of china in A. d'Alès (ed) **Dictionnaire apologetique de la foi catholique,** paris (4th ed 1911)

Wieger, Léon. **Histoire des croyances religieuses et des opinions philosophiques en chine depuis l'origine, jusqu'à nos jours.** Sien-sien (2nd enl ed 1922) 796 p. Engl tsl E.T.C. Werner: **A history of the religious beliefs and philosophical opinions in china from the beginning to the present time.** Hsien-hsien (1927) repr ny (1969) 774 p, illus.

Wieger, Léon. La religion des chinois. In Joseph Huby et al, **Christus. Manuel d'histoire des religions.** Paris (1916) chap 4.

Wieger, Léon. **The religion of china.** London (1909) 32 p.

Wilhelm, Richard. **Die religion und philosophie chinas, aus den originalurkunden übersetzt und herausgegeben.** Tsingtau (1912?) See notice by P. Masson-Oursel in **JA** sér 11, 1 (mars-avril 1913) 491-494.

Wilhelm, Richard. **Die seele chinas.** Berlin (1926) 356 p, illus. Engl tsl John H. Reece: **The soul of china.** N.Y. (1928) 382 p.

Williams, S. Wells. Religion of the chinese. In author's **The middle kingdom.** N.Y. rev ed (1883) repr Taipei (1965) vol 2, 188-274.

Wolf, Arthur P. (ed) **Religion and ritual in chinese society.** Stanford univ (1974) xii + 377 p, refs, char list, index. Art listed sep in our bibliog. Abbrev **RRCS.**

Woog-Garry, Valentine. **Histoire, doctrine et rites des principales religions.** Paris (1959) See sec Les religions d'extrême-orient, 137-156.

Wu, John C.H. **Beyond east and west.** NY (1951) See chap 12, The religions of china, 149-188.

Wyder, H. The religion of the chinese: an interpretation by a western missionary. **QNCCR** 5.2 (1961) 14-23.

Yang, C.K. **Religion in chinese society. A study of contemporary social functions of religion and some of their historical factors.** Univ california (1961) 473 p, notes, bibliog.

Yang, C.K. The role of religion in chinese society. Chap 12 in John Meskill (ed) with assistance of J. Mason Gentzler, **An introduction to chinese civilization,** lexington, mass, toronto, london (1973) 643-674.

Yang, Yung-ch'ing. **China's religious heritage.** N.Y. and nashville, tenn (1943) 196 p.

Yeates, T. The religion of the chinese, without altars, temples, priests, or any proper term to denote the true God. **ChRep** 15 (1846) 203-207.

Yeh, George K.C. & C.P. Fitzgerald. **Introducing china.** London (1948) See chap 9, The chief religions, 48-56.

Yeh, Theodore T.Y. **Confucianism, christianity and china.** N.Y. (1969) 249 p, notes, bibliog.

Zia, N.Z. The common ground of the three chinese religions. **CF** 9.2 (1966) 17-34.

Zur religiösen charakteristik der chinesen. **AMZ** 24 (1897) 283-300.

PART TWO

Chinese Religion
Exclusive of Buddhism

1. TERMINOLOGY

Bernard-Maître, Henri. De la question des termes à la querelle des rites de chine. **NZM** 14 (1958) 178-195, 267-275.

Bernard-Maître, Henri. Un dossier bibliographique de la fin du XVIIIe siècle sur la question des termes chinois. **RechScRelig** 36 (1949) 25-79.

Boone, W.J. Defense of an essay on the proper rendering of the words elohim and theos into the chinese language. **ChRep** 19.7 (july 1850 et seq) 345-385, 409-444, 465-478, 569-618, 625-650. Re "term question"

Boone, William J. An essay on the proper rendering of the words elohim and theos into the chinese language. **ChRep** 17.1 (jan 1848) 17-53, 57-89. Re "term question"

Boone, W.J. Explanation and notes upon art iii, in the july no. of vol. xvii, entitled "a few plain questions," &c. by the writer . . . **ChRep** 18.2 (feb 1849) 97-100. Re "term question"

Bowring, John. Thoughts upon the manner of expressing the word for god in chinese. **ChRep** 18.11 (nov 1849) 600-604. Re "term question"

Brandon, S.G.F.(ed) **A dictionary of comparative religions.** N.Y. (1970) See passim.

Chalmers, John. Tauist words and phrases. In **DV** (1872) vol 2, pt 3, no 7, p 229-237.

Chan, Wing-tsit. Chinese and buddhist religious terminology. In Vergilius Ferm (ed) **Encyclopedia of religion,** N.Y. (1945) passim. Repr as pamphlet, n.y. (1945) 36p.

Chen, Chung-hwan, What does lao-tzu mean by the term "tao"? **TJ** n.s. 4.2 (1964) 150-161.

Chinese terms to denote the deity; note from an impartial reader; views of drs marshman, morrison, milne, and others, communicated in former numbers of the repository. **ChRep** 16.3 (mar 1847) 121-129. Re "term question"

Chinese terms to denote the deity: views of drs morrison, milne, marshman, and others, communicated in former volumes of the chinese repository. **ChRep** 16.2 (feb 1847) 99-102. Re "term question"

A Correspondent at ningpo. Remarks on the words and phrases best suited to express the names of god in chinese. **ChRep** 15.11 (nov 1846 et seq) 568-574, 577-601; 16.1 (jan 1847) 30-34. Re "term question"

Edkins, J. Some brief reasons for not using ling in the sense of spirit. **ChRec** 8.6 (nov-dec 1877) 524-529.

A Few plain questions addressed to those missionaries, who, in their preaching or writing, teach the chinese to worship shang-ti. **ChRep** 17.7 (july 1848) 357-360. Re "term question"

Havret, Henri. **T'ien-tchou 'seigneur du ciel.' A propos d'une stèle bouddhique de tch'eng-tou.** Shanghai (1901) repr nendeln (1975) 30 p. (**Variétés sinologiques** no 19)

Helm, B. Shen and shang-ti. **ChRec** 7.6 (nov-dec 1876) 436-442. Re "term question"

Hutchinson, A.B. Shall t'ien-chü (sic) supersede shang-te (sic) and shin (sic)? **ChRec** 8.2 (mar-apr 1877) 146-152. Re "term question"

Inquirer. Is the shangti of the chinese classics the same being as jehovah of the sacred scriptures? **ChRec** 8.5 (sep-oct 1877) 411-426.

Inquirer. A letter to prof. f. max muller on the sacred books of china, part 1. **ChRec** 11.3 (may-june 1880) 161-186. Critique of legge's tsl of ti and shangti.

An Inquiry respecting the mode of designating the third person of the godhead in chinese. **ChRep** 16.7 (july 1847) 351-356. Re "term question"

Kaltenmark, Max. Ling-pao: note sur un terme du taoïsme religieuse. **MIHEC** 2 (1960) 559-588.

Legge, James. A letter to professor f. max muller. Chiefly on the translation into english of the chinese terms ti and shang ti . . . **ChRec** 12.1 (jan-feb 1881) 35-53. Reply to art by Inquirer q.v.

Legge, James. **The notions of the chinese concerning gods and spirits.** HK (1852) repr taipei (1971) Re proper tsl of basic relig terms.

Letter to the editor of the chinese repository respecting the objects to be had in view in translating elohim and theos. **ChRep** 19.2 (feb 1850) 90-97. Re "term question"

Letter to the repository editor upon the use of the terms shin and shangti. **ChRep** 18.2 (feb 1849) 100-102. Re "term question"

Looker-on. Letter regarding the word used for god in chinese. **ChRep** 19.5 (may 1850) 280-281. Re "term question"

Looker-on. Letter to the editor of the repository upon dr. legge's argument of the word for god in chinese. **ChRep** 19.10 (oct 1850) 524-526. Re "term question"

Maspero, Henri. Le mot ming. **JA** 223 (1933) 249-296. Concludes word was used in sense of "sacred," esp in connection with swearing an oath, as well as in sense of "bright"

Mateer, C.W. The meaning of the word shen. **ChRec** 3.2 (1901) 61-72, 107-116, 220-231, 284-290, 340-352, 447-456, 499-508; 33 (1902) 71-79, 123-132, 186-193, 232-244, 290-298, 343-347, 400-404.

McClatchie, Thos. God. **ChRec** 8.5 (sep-oct 1877) 398-411. Re "term question"

McClatchie, Rev Canon. The term for "spirit" in chinese. **ChRec** 7.2 (mar-apr 1876) 92-99. Mostly re relation of term "ch'i" to several other terms.

Medhurst, W.H. An inquiry into the proper mode of rendering the word god in translating the sacred scriptures into the chinese language. **ChRep** 17.3 (mar 1848 et seq) 105-133, 161-187, 209-242, 265-310, 321-354. Re "term question"

Medhurst, W.H. senior. An inquiry into the proper mode of translating ruach and pneuma, in the chinese version of the scriptures. **ChRep** 19.9 (sep 1850) 478-485. Re "term question"

Medhurst, W.H. Letter to the editor of the repository, accompanied with a translation of a chinese tract upon nourishing the spirit. **ChRep** 19.8 (aug 1850) 445-459. Re "term question"

Dr Medhurst et al. Remarks in favor of shangti and against shen, as the proper term to denote the true god. **ChRep** 16.1 (jan 1847) 34-39. Re "term question"

Medhurst, W.H. Remarks on the notes of 2.2 in a letter addressed to the editor of the chinese repository. **ChRep** 17.9 (sep 1848) 459-462. Re "term question"

Medhurst, W.H. Reply to the essay of dr. boone on the proper rendering of the words elohim and theos into the chinese language . . . **ChRep** 17.9 (sep 1848 et seq) 489-520, 545-574, 601-646. Re "term question"

A Missionary. Thoughts on the term proper to be employed in translating elohim and theos into chinese. **ChRep** 19.4 (apr 1850) 185-206. Re "term question"

Parrinder, Geoffrey. **A dictionary of non-christian religions**. Philadelphia (1971) See passim.

Philo. Animadversions on the philological diversions of philo, by w. h. medhurst, sen., in his inquiry into . . . , examined in a note by philo. **ChRep** 19.9 (sep 1850) 486-491. Re "term question"

Ratchnevsky, Paul (unter mitarbeit von Johann Dill und Doris Heyde) **Historisch-terminologisches wörterbuch der yuan-zeit: medizinwesen.** Berlin (1967) xix + 118 p.

Reichelt, Karl Ludvig. Indigenous religious phrases that may be used to interpret the christian message. **ChRec** 58.2 (feb 1927) 123-126. Phrases fr budd and taoism.

The Religion of the chinese, without altars, temples, priests, or any proper term to denote the true god. **ChRep** 16.4 (apr 1847) 203-207. Re "term question"

Rice, Edward (comp) **Eastern definitions. A short encyclopedia of religions of the orient.** NY (1978) See passim.

Shen, Chien-shih. Tsl Ying, Ts'ien-li. An essay on the primitive meaning of the character kuei. **MS** 2 (1935) 1-20.

On the Signification of the character jin: jin chih nan yen. Communicated for the chinese repository. **ChRep** 15.7 (1846) 329-343. Re jen, for which author's tsl is "humanity"

Smith, D. Howard (ed) China and the far east. Sec in S.G.F. Brandon (genl ed) **A dictionary of comparative religion,** NY (1970) See Synoptic index, chinese cults and philosophies, 668.

Smith, Stanley P. Chinese philosophy and the truth as it is in jesus. **TheE&TheW** 11 (1913) 413-438. ". . . a few definitions of important terms . . ." e.g. shen, kuei, ti.

Some remarks on the chinese terms to express the deity. **ChRep** 7.6 (oct 1838) 314-321. Sel fr **ICG** 3.16 (apr 1821) 97-105; re "term question"

Terms for deity to be used in the chinese version of the bible: the words shangti, tien, and shin examined and illustrated, in a letter to the editor of the chinese repository. **ChRep** 15.6 (june 1846) 311-317. Re "term question'

Ti, Shan Kough. Is it right to call the supreme being 'shangti'? **ChRec** 53.11 (nov 1922) 694-699; 53.12 (dec 1922) 757-762.

Waidtlow, C. The symbol for god in chinese writing. **ChRec** 49.7 (july 1918) 471-472. Fanciful interpretations of several chin char.

Walker. J.E.Too straight is crooked the other way. **ChRec** 8.6 (nov-dec 1877) 519-524. Re "term question"

Watters, T. Tao:—an essay on a word. **ChRec** 4 (1871) 1-4, 33-35, 100-102.

2. ANTIQUITY

Akatsuka, Kiyoshi. An attempt to restore the original state of how "shang-ti" was worshipped in the time of the yin dynasty. Tokyo, **Trans 11th ICO** (1966) 58-60.

Allan, Sarah. Shang foundations of modern chinese folk religion. In **LL&R** (1979) 1-21.

Andersson, Johan Gunnar. On symbolism in the prehistoric painted ceramics of china. **BMFEA** 1 (1929) 65-69.

Banerjee, Anukul Chandra. Religious condition of china prior to the advent of buddhism. **MB** 82.4/5 (apr-may 1974) 196-199.

Bank J. Philosophie sociale, magie et langage graphique dans le hong-fan. **Tel quel** 48/49 (1972) 20-32.

Barnard, Noel. A preliminary study of the ch'u silk manuscript; a new reconstruction of the text. **MS** 17 (1958) 1-11, illus.

Barnard, Noel **Scientific examination of an ancient chinese document as a prelude to decipherment, translation and historical assessment—the ch'u silk manuscript.** Australian national univ (1971) 12 + 56 p, illus, bibliog.

Bilsky, Lester James. **The state religion of ancient china.** Taipei (1975) 2 vol, I. vii-232, II. 233-448, app, notes, gloss, bibliog, illus.

Bishop, Carl W. The worship of earth in ancient china. **JNCBRAS** 64 (1933) 24-43.

Bodde, Derk. **Festivals in classical china. New year and other annual observances during the han dynasty 206 B.C.—A.D.220.** Princeton univ (1975) xvi + 439, chron table, bibliog, index, illus 7 pl.

Boltz, William G. Philological footnotes to the han new year rites. **JAOS** 99.3 (july-sep 1979) 423-439. Rev art on D. Bodde's **Festivals in classical china** (1975) q.v.

Bridgman, E.C. (tsl). Chinese sacrifices, illustrated by quotations from the shu king. **ChRep** 17 (1848) 97-101.

Buckens, F. Les antiquités funéraires du honan central et la conception de l'âme dans la chine primitive. **MCB** 8 (1946-47) 1-101.

Bulling, A. Guttkind. A late shang place of sacrifice and its historical importance. **Expedition** 19.4 (1977) 1-11, illus.

Bunge, Martin L. **The story of religion, from caveman to superman.** Pasadena, calif. (1931) See chap 7, Chinese religion, 52-60.

Chang, Kwang-chih. Evidence for the ritual life in prehistoric china. **ASBIE** 9 (1960) engl summ 269-270.

Chang, Kwang-chih. **Shang civilization.** Yale univ (1980) 417 p, app, bibliog, index, illus. See Index under relevant headings.

Chang, Tsung-tung. **Der kult der shang-dynastie im spiegel der orakel-inschriften. Eine paläographische studie zur religion im archaischen china.** Frankfurt-am-main (1970) vi + 331 p.

Chavannes, Édouard. Le dieu du sol dans l'ancienne religion chinoise. **RHR** 43 (1901) 125-246. A rev version of this study forms Appendice to author's vol, **Le t'ai chan** q.v.

Chavannes, Édouard. La divination par l'écaille de tortue dans la haute antiquité chinoise (d'après un livre de m. lo tchen-yu) **JA** 10e sér, 17 (1911) 127-137.

Chinese sacrifices, illustrated by quotations from the shu king. **ChRep** 17.2 (feb 1848) 97-101.

Chow, Tse-Tsung. The childbirth myth and ancient chinese medicine: a study of aspects of the wu tradition. In **AC:SEC** (1978) 43-89.

Cohen, Alvin P. Coercing the rain deities in ancient china. **HR** 17.3/4 (feb-may 1978) 244-265.

Cornaby, W. Arthur. The supreme as recognized in ancient china. **ChRec** 35.1 (jan 1904) 5-18. Re shang-ti in ancient texts.

Creel, Herrlee Glessner. **The birth of china. A study of the formative period of chinese civilization.** N.Y. (1937) See chap 12, The gods of shang; chap 13, Sacrifice; chap 25, Religion [of chou]

Creel, Herrlee G. **The origins of statecraft in china.** Vol 1, **The western chou empire.** Univ chicago (1970) See app c, The origin of the deity t'ien, 493-506.

Danckert, Werner. Musikgötter und musikmythen altchinas. **ZE** 88 (1963) 1-48.

Day, Clarence Burton. Religious origins in china. **ChRec** 71.5 (may 1940) 295-303. Repr in **PRPCC** (1975) Re shang and chou.

Dittrich, Edith. **Das motiv des tierkampfes in der altchinesischen kunst.** Wiesbaden (1963) 248 s, literaturverzeichnis, anhang, bibl, katalog (119 pl with explanations)

Dohrenwend, Doris J. Jade demonic images from early china. **ArsOr** 10 (1975) 55-78, 20 pl.

Dubs, Homer H. An ancient chinese mystery cult. **HTR** 35 (1942) 221-240.

Dubs, Homer H. The archaic royal jou religion. **TP** 46 (1958) 217-259.

Dung, Hwe Zi. The earliest historical idea of god in china. **ChRec** 62.8 (aug 1931) 486-493; 62.9 (sep 1931) 562-571.

Eberhard, Wolfram. Das astronomische weltbild im alten china. **Die naturwissenschaften** 24.33 (1936) 517-519.

Eberhard, Wolfram. Leben und gedanken des alltagsmenschen in china. **Deutsche-china gesellschaft, mitteilungsblatt** 6 (1978) 2-9.

Eberhard, Wolfram. **Lokalkulturen im alten china.** Leiden (1942) vol 1, passim. Vol 2, **Die lokalkulturen des südens und ostens.** Peiping (1942) "Greatly revised version" of vol 2, engl tsl Alide Eberhard: **The local cultures of south and east china.** Leiden (1968) 520 p, bibliog, index. See passim.

Eberhard, Wolfram. **Sternkunde und weltbild im alten china. Die Sterne** 6 (1932) 129-138:

Eberhard, Wolfram. **Sternkunde und weltbild im alten china.** Taipei (1970) 417 p.

Ecsedy, I. Historical time and mythological history in ancient china. **KT:OS** 2 (1978) 61-66.

Edkins, Joseph. Astrology in ancient china. **ChRev** 14 (1885-86) 345-351.

Eichhorn, Werner. Allgemeine bemerkungen über das religiöse im alten china. **OE** 26.1/2 (1979) 13-21.

Eichhorn, Werner. **Die alte chinesische religion und das staatskultwesen.** Leiden (1976) xvii + 262 s.

Eichhorn, W. Zur religion im ältesten china (shang-zeit) **Wiener zeitschrift für die kunde süd-und ostasiens** 2 (1958) 33-53.

Eliade, Mircea. **Histoire des croyances et des idées religieuses.** Vol 2, **De gautama bouddha au triomphe du christianisme.** Paris (1978) Engl tsl Willard Trask, **A history of religious ideas.** Vol 2, **From gautama buddha to the triumph of christianity.** Univ chicago (1982) See chap 16, The religions of ancient china, 3-43; also, Present position of studies: problems and progress, critical bibliog, 419-433.

Erdberg-Consten, Eleanor von. Ornamente und symbole der altchinesischen bronzen. Stuttgart. **Jahrbuch für asthetik und allgemeine kunstwissenschaft,** 6 (1961) 159-176.

Erkes, E. The god of death in ancient china. **TP** 35 (1940) 185-210.

Erkes, E. A neolithic chinese idol? **AA** 3 (1928) 141-143.

Erkes, Eduard, Der primat des weibes im alten china. **Sinica** 10 (1935) 166-176.

Erkes, E. Die totenbeigaben im alten china. **AA** 6 (1935) 17-36.

Erkes, E. Zum altchinesischen orakelwesen. **TP** 35 (1940) 364-370.

Esbroek, A. van. Les cultes préhistoriques de la chine. **Nouvelle clio** 5 (1953) 195-196.

Everett, John R. **Religion in human experience.** London (1952) See chap 8, Pre-buddhist china, 150-162.

Gibson, H.E. Divination and ritual during the shang and chou dynasties. **CJ** 23 (1935) 22-25.

Giles, Herbert A. **Religions of ancient china.** London (1905) repr folcroft, pa (1976) repr norwood, pa (1977) v + 65 p.

Giles, Lionel. Wizardry in ancient china. **AP** 13 (1942) 484-489.

Granet, Marcel. **La civilization chinoise.** Paris (1929) Engl tsl Kathleen E. Innes and Mabel R. Brailsford: **Chinese civilization.** London and n.y. (1930) repr ny (1974). See esp second pt, Chinese society, passim.

Granet, Marcel. Coutumes matrimoniales de la chine antique. **TP** 13 (1912) 516-588. Repr in **ESC** (1953)

Granet, Marcel. **Danses et légendes de la chine ancienne.** Paris (1926) 2 vol.

Granet, Marcel. Le depôt de l'enfant sur le sol: rites anciens et ordalies mythiques. **RA** (1922) Repr **ESC** (1953) 159-202.

Granet, Marcel. **Fêtes et chansons anciennes de la chine.** Paris (1919) 301 p. Notices: **BEFEO** 19 (1919) 65-75 by H. Maspero; **RHR** 83 (1921) 96-98 by P. Masson-Oursel. Engl tsl E.D. Edwards: **Festivals and songs of ancient china.** N.Y. (1932) 281 p.

Granet, Marcel. Le Langage de la douleur d'après le rituel funéraire de la chine classique. **Journal de psychologie normale et pathologique** 19.2 (fev 1922) 97-118. Repr in **ESC** (1953)

Granet, Marcel. Programme d'études sur l'ancienne religion chinoise. **RHR** 69 (mars-avril 1914) 228-239.

Granet, Marce. La vie et la mort. Croyances et doctrines de l'antiquité chinoise. In **EPHE**, section des sciences religieuses, **Annuaire** 1920-1921 (1920) 1-22. Repr in **ES** (1953)

Grube, W. Die religion der alten chinesen. In **Religions-geschichtliches lesebuch in verbindung,** mit W. Grube. .. K. Geldner . . . et al, Tübingen (1908) 1-69.

Hager, Joseph. **Panthéon chinois, ou, parallèle entre le culte religieux des grecs et celui des chinois. Avec des nouvelles preuves que la chine a été connue des grecs, et que les sérès des auteurs classiques ont été des chinois.** Paris (1806)

Halbwachs, Maurice. Histoires dynastiques et légendes religieuses en chine, d'après un livre récent de m. granet. **RHR** 94 (1926) 1-16. Critique of Granet's **Danses et légendes de la chine ancienne,** q.v.

Harlez, Charles de. Les croyances religieuses des premiers chinois. **MCAM** t 41 (1888) 60 p.

Harlez, Charles de. La religion chinoise dans le tchün-tsiu de kong-tze et dans le tso-tchuen. **TP** 3.3 (1892) 211-237.

Harper, Donald J. The han cosmic board (shih) **EC** 4 (1978-79) 1-10. See further C. Cullen, Some further points on the shih, ibid 6 (1980-81) 31-46; and Harper's The han cosmic board: a response to Christopher Cullen, **ibid** 47-56.

Hentze, Carl. **Bronzegerät Kultbauten; religion im ältesten china der shang-zeit.** Antwerpen (1951) xix + 273 p, 103 pl.

Hentze, Carl. **Chinese tomb figures: a study in the beliefs and folklore of ancient china.** London (1928) repr ny (1974) 112 p.

Hentze, Carl. **Les figurines de la céramique funéraire; matériaux pour l'étude des croyances et du folklore de la chine ancienne.** Dresden (1928) 2 vol, pl.

Hentze, Carl **Frühchinesische bronzen und kultdars-tellungen.** Antwerp (1937) 167 p + portfolio of pl.

Hentze, Carl. **Funde in alt-china; das welterleben im ältesten china.** Göttingen etc (1967) 299 p, 48 pl. See passim. See also rev by Eleanor von Erdberg-Costen in

ZRGG 25.2 (1973) 159-167 and Hentze's rejoinder in **ibid.** 26.3 (1974) 262-265.

Hentze, Carl. Gods and drinking serpents. **HR** 4.2 (1965) 179-208. 57 photo-illus.

Hentze, C. Methodologisches zur untersuchung alchinesischer schriftzeichen. **SinSon** (1934) 34-45, fig.

Hentze, Carl. **Objets rituels, croyances et dieux de la chine antique et de l'amérique.** Antwerp (1936) 122 p.

Hentze, Carl. Das ritual der wiederbelebung durch die "neue haut" (altchina — ocienien — amerika) **Sinologica** 6.2 (1961) 69.82, illus.

Hentze, Carl. **Die sakralbronzen und ihre bedeutung in den früh-chinesischen kulturen.** Antwerpen (1941) 2 vol, pl.

Hentze, C. Die tierverkleidung in erneuerungs- und initiationsmysterien (ältestes china, zircumpazifische kulturen und gross-asien) **Symbolon** 1 (1960) 39-86, illus.

Hentze, Carl. **Tod, auferstehung, weltordnung; das mythische bild im ältesten china, in den grossasiatischen und zirkumpazifischen kulturen.** Zürich (1955) 2 vol.

Hentze, Carl. Zur hirschsymbolik auf den ältesten chinesischen bronzegefässen. In **Asien** (1971) 198-206.

Hentze, Carl & Ch. Kim. Göttergestalten in der ältesten chinesischen schrift. In authors' **Ko- und chi-waffen in china und in amerika,** Antwerpen (1943) 19-54, abb, alte schriftzeichen.

Hentze, Carl and Chewon Kim. **Ko- und Chi-waffen in china und in amerika. Göttergestalten in der ältesten chinesischen schrift.** Antwerpen (1943) 59 p, pl.

Ho, Ping-ti. **The cradle of the east.** Univ chicago & chin univ of HK (1975) See chap 7, Society, religion, thought, 269-339. From prehistory to beginning of chou dyn, ca. 1000 b.c.

Hopkins, E. Washburn. **The history of religions.** N.Y. (1926) See chap 14, Religions of china. Pre-confucian religion, 224-248.

Hopkins, Lionel C. Working the oracle. **NCR** 1 (1919) 111-119, 249-261, pl. Re oracle bones.

Hsu, Cho-yun. The concept of predetermination and fate in the han. **EC** 1 (fall 1975) 51-56.

Huang, Wen-shan. The artistic expression of totems in ancient chinese culture. **ASBIE** 21 (spring 1966) 1-13.

Huang, Wen-shan. The origins of chinese culture: a study of totemism. **Congrès internationale des sciences anthropologiques et ethnographiques Paris (1960)** vol 2 (1963) 139-143.

Huang Wen-shan. Totemism and the origin of chinese philosophy. **ASBIE** 9 (spring 1960) 51-66.

Hulsewé, A.F.P. Watching the vapors; an ancient chinese technique of prognostication. **NachrDGNVO** 125 (1979) 40-49.

Ikeda, Suetoshi. Ancestor worship and nature worship in ancient china — especially the concepts of ti and t'ien. **Proc IX ICHR 1958,** Tokyo (1960) 100-105.

Ingram, J.H. The civilization and religion of the shang dynasty. **CJ** 3 (1925) 473-483, 536-545.

Inquirer. The theocratic nature of the chinese government, and the principles of its administration as stated in the chinese classics. **ChRec** 9.1 (jan-feb 1878) 28-49.

Jacobs, Fang-chih Huang. The origin and development of the concept of filial piety in ancient china. **CC** 14.3 (1973) 25-55.

Jao, Tsung-i. A study of an astrological picture from a changsha tomb of the fighting states period. **JOS** 1 (1954) 69-84.

Ju, I-hsiung. The ancient chinese metaphysical characters through the oracle writing. **Unitas** 42.1 (mar 1969) entire issue, 1-155, illus. See chap 3, The metaphysical concepts in oracle characters, 67-110.

Kaltenmark, Max. Religion de la chine antique. In **HCP:HR** (1970) 927-957.

Kaltenmark, Max & Ngo, van Xuyet. La divination dans la chine ancienne. In André Caquot et Marcel Leibovici (comp) **La divination,** Paris (1968) t 1, 333-356.

Karlgren, Bernhard. Legends and cults in ancient china. **BMFEA** 18 (1946) 199-365 (See rev by W. Eberhard in **AA**, 9)

Karlgren, Bernhard. Some fecundity symbols in ancient china. **BMFEA** 2 (1930) 1-54.

Karlgren, Bernhard. Some ritual objects of prehistoric china. **BMFEA** 14 (1942) 65-69.

Karlgren, Bernhard. Some sacrifices in chou china. **BMFEA** 40 (1968) 1-31.

Keightley, David N. The origin of the ancient chinese city: a comment. **EC** 1 (fall 1975) 63-65. Rev art on L. Vandermeersch's rev of Paul Wheatley, **The pivot of the four quarters** (1971) q.v.

Keightley, David N. Religion and the rise of urbanism. **JAOS** 93.4 (oct-dec 1973) 527-538. Rev art on Paul Wheatley, **The pivot of the four quarters** (1971) q.v.

Keightley, David N. The religious commitment: shang theology and the genesis of chinese political culture. **HR** 17.3/4 (feb-may 1978) 211-225.

Keightley, David N. **Sources of shang history. The oracle-bone inscriptions of bronze age china.** Univ calif (1978) xvii + 281 p, illus, 5 app, tables, 2 bibliog.

Kiang, Chao-yuan. **Le voyage dans la chine ancienne, considéré principalement sous son aspect magique et religieux.** Trad du chin par Fan, Jen. Shanghai (1937) 375 p.

Koeppen, Georg von. Zwei träume aus dem tso-chuan und ihre interpretation. **ZDMG** 119 (1969) 133-156.

Koskikallio, T. The religious motive in the book of poetry (shih ching) **ChRec** 71.12 (dec 1940) 768-780.

Köster, Hermann. Zur religion in der chinesischen vorgeschichte. **MS** 14 (1949-55) 188-214.

Kuan Feng & Lin, Lü-shih. Thought of the yin dynasty and the western chou. **CSP** 2.1-2 (fall-winter 1970-71) 4-53.

Kuan, Feng & Lin, Lü-shih. Development of thought and the birth of nationalist philosophy at the end of the western chou and the beginning of the eastern chou. **CSP** 2.1-2 (fall-winter 1970-71) 54-79.

Kuo, P.C. Folkways in prehistoric china. **THM** 4 (1937) 115-135.

Kurz, H. Mémoire sur l'état politique et religieux de la chine, 2300 ans avant notre ère, selon le chou-king. **Nouv. JA** 5 (1830) 401-436; 6 (1830) 401-451.

Lanciotti, Lionello. On some religious beliefs in ancient china. **E&W** 4.2 (1953) 95-97.

Larre, Claude. Le sens de la transcendance dans la pensée chinoise. **Concilium** 146 (1979) 59-67. Re t'ien in ancient confucianism and taoism.

Laufer, Berthold. Religious and artistic thought in ancient china. **AArch** 6 (1917) 295-310.

Levi, Jean. Le mythe de l'âge d'or et les théories de l'évolution en chine ancienne. **l'Homme** 17.1 (jan-mars 1977) 73-103.

Li, Chi. **Anyang.** Univ washington (1977) See chap 14, Worship of ancestors and other spirits, 247-254.

Li, Hsüan-pe. Ancient chinese society and modern primitive society. National central library, nanking **Philobiblon** 1.2 (1946) 4-25.

Lindell, Kristina. Stories of suicide in ancient china. An essay on chinese morals. **ActaO** 35 (1973) 167-239.

Ling, Shun-sheng. Dog sacrifice in ancient china and the pacific area. **ASBIE** 3 (1957) engl summ 37-40, illus.

Ling, Shun-sheng. Origin of the she in ancient china. **ASBIE** 18(1964) (1964) engl abrmt 36-44.

Ling, Shun-sheng. Turtle sacrifice in ancient china. **ASBIE** 31 (1971) Engl abstract 41-46.

Liu, Mau-tsai. Die traumdeutung im alten china. **AS** 16.1-4 (1963) 35-65.

Loewe, Michael. Water, earth and fire—the symbols of the han dynasty. **NachrDGNVO** 125 (1979) 63-68.

Loewe, Michael. **Ways to paradise. The chinese quest for immortality.** London (1979) 270 p, illus, app, notes. Based on han dynasty relics.

Lou, Dennis Wing-sou. Rain-worship among the ancient chinese and the nahua-maya indians. **ASBIE** 4 (1957) 31-108, illus.

Major, John S. Astrology in the huai-nan-tzu and some related texts. **SSCRB** 8 (fall 1980) 20-31.

Major, John S. Research priorities in the study of ch'u religion. **HR** 17.3/4 (feb-may 1978) 226-243.

Maspero, Henri. **La chine antique.** Paris (1927) rev ed (1955) Engl tsl Frank A. Kierman, jr, **China in antiquity,** univ mass (1978) See Book II, Social and religious life, chap 2-5, 93-168.

McCaffree, Joe E. **Divination and the historical and allegorical sources of the i ching, the chinese classic, or book of changes.** Los angeles (1967) 64 p, illus.

Meacham, William. The importance of archeology in the understanding of certain developmental aspects of chinese religions, with reference to data from hongkong. **CF** 15.4 (winter 1972) 189-209.

Meacham, William. Religion and the origins of shang civilization: notes on a theory of proto-history. **CF** 17.2/3 (1974) 63-74.

Milloué, L. de. La religion primitive de la chine. **CMG** (1907) 141-181.

Morgan, Evan. A case of ritualism. **JNCBRAS** 49 (1918) 128-143. Re usurpation by feudal state of lu of royal prerogative to perform suburban sacrifice to heaven (chiao)

Morgan, Evan. Sacrifices in ancient china. **JNCBRAS** 70 (1939) 30-36.

Morley, Arthur. A study in early chinese religion. **NCR** 1 (may 1919) 176-208; sec 2: (july 1919) 262-281; sec 3: (aug 1919) 372-384.

Mortier, F. Du sens primitif de l'antiquité et la célèbre figure divinatoire des taoistes chinois et japonais (sien t'ien) **BSAB** 59 (1948) 150-160.

Mullie, J. Les formules du serment dans le tso-tchouen. **TP** 38 (1948) 43-74.

Munsterberg, Hugo. An anthropomorphic deity from ancient china. **OA** 3.4 (1951) 147-152, illus.

Needham, Joseph. The cosmology of early china. In Carmen Blacker & Michael Loewe (ed) **Ancient cosmologies,** london (1975) 87-109.

Owen, G. The ancient cult of the chinese as found in the shu-ching. **JPOS** 1.5 (1887) 203-224.

Paper, Jordan. The meaning of the "t'ao-t'ieh." **HR** 18.1 (aug 1978) 18-41.

Parker, E.H. Ancient chinese spiritualism. **AR** 19 (1923) 117-123.

Parrish, Fred L. **History of religion: the destiny-determining factor in the world's cultures.** N.Y. (1965) See chap 4 (B) In china: in the pre-confucian period (before the sixth century b.c.) 46-54.

Pichon, Jean-Charles. **Les cycles du retour éternel.** Paris (1963) See t 2, p 157-184.

Plath, J.H. **Die religion und der cultus der alten chinesen.** Abth. 1: **Die religion der alten chinesen.** München (1862) 108 p, 23 illus. Abth 2: **Der cultus der alten chinesen.** München (1863) 136 p. **Chinesische texte** (f. vol 2) München (1864) 46 pl.

R., S.C.B. The tuang [sic] fang sacrificial table. **BMMA** 19 (1924) 141-144, illus.

Die religion der alten chinesen. **OstL** 7.27 (1893) 423-426.

Robiou. F. Études récentes sur la première religion des chinois. **Revue des questions historiques** 25 (1892) 217-225.

Ross, John **The original religion of china.** Edinburgh and london (1909) 327 p.

Rotours, Robert des. La religion dans la chine antique. In Maurice Brillant and René Aigrain (ed) **Histoire des religions.** Paris (1953) t 2, 7-83.

Rousselle, Erwin. Konfuzius und das archaische weltbild der chinesischen frühzeit. **Saeculum** 5 (1954) 1-33.

Rowley, H.H. **Prophecy and religion in ancient china and israel.** Univ london (1956) 154 p.

Rydh, H. Seasonal fertility rites and the death cult in scandinavia and china. **BMFEA** 3 (1931) 69-98.

Schafer, Edward H. Ritual exposure in ancient china. **HJAS** 14 (1951) 130-184.

Schilling, Werner. **Einst konfuzius heute mao tse-tung. Die mao-faszination und ihre hintergrunde.** Weilheim/oberbayern (1971) 329 p, anmerkungen, literaturverzeichnis, zur transkription chinesischer namen, abkürzungen, personenverzeichnis.

Schindler, Bruno. **Das priestertum im alten china.** Leipzig (1919)

Schindler, Bruno. On the travel, wayside and wind offerings in ancient china. **AM** 1 (1924) 624-656.

Schwartz, Benjamin. Speculations on the beginnings of chinese thought. **EC** 2 (fall 1976) 47-50.

Schwartz, Benjamin. Transcendence in ancient china. **Daedalus** (spring 1975) 57-68.

Seiwert, Hubert. Mythologie im chinesischen altertum. **ZMR** 62.3 (juli 1978) 203-208.

Seiwert, Hubert. Orakelwesen im ältestern china: shang und westliche chou-dynastie. **ZMR** 64.3 (juli 1980) 208-236, engl summ 236.

Shih, C.C. [Ching-ch'eng] Notes on a phrase in the tso chuan: 'The great affairs of a state are sacrifice and war.' **CC** 2.3 (1959) 31-47.

Shih, J. Mediation in chinese religion. **SM** 21 (1972) 113-126. Re the li in ancient china.

Sjöholm, Gunnar. The boundaries between religion and culture with a reference to the interpretation of ancient chinese religion. **CF** 13.4 (1970) 5-20.

Sjfohelm, Gunnar. Les limites entre la religion et la culture à l'occasion de l'interprétation de la religion antique. In Sven S. Hartman (ed) **Syncretism: based on papers read at the symposium on cultural contact, meeting of religions, syncretism, held at abo on the 8th-10th of september 1966,** Stockholm (1969) 110-127.

Smith, D.H. Chinese religion in the shang dynasty. **Numen** 8 (1961) 142-150.

Smith, D.H. Divine kingship in ancient china. **Numen** 4 (1957) 171-203.

Smith, David Howard. Religious developments in ancient china prior to confucius. **JRLB** 44 (1962) 432-454.

Söderblom, Nathan. **Das werden de gottesglaubens. Untersuchungen über die angänge der religion.** Deutsche bearbeitung, herausgegeben von Rudolf Stübe. Leipzig (1916) See 6, Chinesischen schang-ti [Notice by Bruno Schindler in **OZ** 4 (1916) 322-326]

T'ang, Chün-i. Cosmologies in ancient chinese philosophy. **CSP** 5.1 (fall 1973) 4-47.

Tiele, C.P. **Outlines of the history of religion to the spread of the universal religions.** Tsl fr dutch J. Estlin Carpenter. Preface (1877) 5th ed london (1892) See chap 2, Religion among the chinese, 25-38.

Tung Tso-pin. **An interpretation of the ancient chinese civilization.** Taipei (1952) See esp sec 3, Religious beliefs, 18-21; repr in **CWayRel** (1973) 1-6.

Vandermeersch, Léon. De la tortue et l'achillée. In J.P. Vernant (ed) **Divination et rationalité,** Paris (1974) 29-51.

Vandermeersch, Léon. Religions de la chine. **AnnEPHE** 88 (1979-80) 137-142. Re archaic traditions acc to confucianism.

Vandermeersch, Léon. **Wangdao ou la voie royale. Recherches sur l'esprit des institutions de la chine archaïque. Tome 1, Structures cultuelles et structures familiales.** Paris (1977) 358 p. **Tome 2, Structures politiques, les rites.** Paris (1980) 603 p, tables, index. See Table générale des matières.

Waidtlow, C. Ancient religions of china. **NCR** 4 (1922) 283-297, 373-387.

Waidtlow, C. The identity of the ancient religions of china and scandinavia. **ChRec** 51.8 (aug 1920) 558-563; 51.9 (sep 1920) 623-628.

Wales, H.G. Quaritch. **The mountain of god. A study in early religion and kingship.** London (1953) See chap 2, China, 32-55.

Warneck, Johann. Die urreligion chinas. **AMZ** 38 (1911) 393-413.

Wei Hwei-lin. Categories of totemism in ancient china. **ASBIE** 25 (1968) 25-34.

Weygandt, J.W.H. **Ritualfragmente zum schädelopfer in altchina.** Nurtingen (1953) 21 p, illus.

Wheatley, Paul. **The pivot of the four quarters. A preliminary enquiry into the origins and character of the ancient chinese city.** Chicago (1971) xix + 602 p, fig, maps, notes, gloss, index. See esp pt 2, The early chinese city in comparative perspective, esp chap 5, The ancient chinese city as a cosmo-magical symbol, 411-476.

Wilhelm, Hellmut. On the oracle recorded in tso-chuan, hsi 4 (656 b.c.) **JAOS** 9.4 (oct-dec 1971) 504-505.

Wilhelm, Hellmut. Schriften und fragmente zur entwicklung der staatsreligion theorie in der chou zeit. **MS** 12 (1947) 41-96.

Wilhelm, Hellmut. Der sinn des geschehens nach dem buch der wandlung. **EJ** 26 (1957) 351-386.

Ymaizoumi, M. Des croyances et des superstitions des chinois avant confucius. Tsl M. Tomii. **CPOL 1878,** t 2, lyon (1880) 56-61.

Ymaizoumi, M. Du culte des ancêtres en chine sous la dynastie de tcheou, **CPOL 1878,** t 2, lyon (1880) 68-79.

Yuan, Te-hsing. Tsl Earl Wieman. The world of totems. **Echo,** pt 1, 4.11 (dec 1974) 26-41, illus; pt 2, 5.1 (jan 1975) 36-53, illus.

3. MYTHOLOGY

Arlington, L.C. Chinese mythology. **ChRev** 25 (1900-01) 178-180.

Balfour, F.H. The peach and its legends. In author's **Chinese scrapbook** (1887) 145-148.

Ball, J. Dyer. Scraps from chinese mythology. **ChRev** 9 (1880-81) 195-212; 11 (1882-83) 69-86, 203-217, 282-297, 382-390; 12 (1883-84) 188-193, 324-331, 402-407; 13 (1884-85) 75-85.

Basset, B.E. Lecture on chinese mythology. **JWCBorderResS** 5 (1932) 92-101.

Bauer, Wolfgang. Der herr vom gelben stein (huang shih kung): wandlung einer chinesischer legenden figur. **OE** 3 (1956) 137-152, table.

Bazin (aîné) Notice du chan-haï-king, cosmographie fabuleuse attribuée au grand yu. **JA** sér 3, t 8 (nov 1839) 337-382.

Beauclair, Inez de. Appendix: comment: the place of the sun myth in the evaluation of chinese mythology. **ASBIE** 13 (1962) 123-132, bibliog.

Belpaire, B. Le folklore de la fondre en chine sous la dynastie des t'ang. **Muséon** 52 (1939) 163-172.

Birch, Cyril. **Chinese myths and fantasies, retold by cyril birch.** London (1961) 200 p. illus.

Bodde, Derk. Myths of ancient china. In Samuel N. Kramer (ed) **Mythologies of the ancient world,** n.y. (1961) 367-408. Repr in Chang Chun-shu (ed) **The making of modern china,** englewood cliffs, nj (1975) 15-37; also repr **ECC** (1981) 45-84.

Brandauer, Frederick P. The hsi-yu pu as an example of myth-making in chinese fiction. **TR** 6.1 (apr 1975) 99-120.

Buschan, G. Tiergötter und fabeltiere bei den völkern des antike und des ostasiatischen kulturkreises. **Ciba zeitschrift** 8.86 (1942) 3005-3010.

Bush, Susan, Thundermonsters and wind spirits in early sixth century china and the epitaph tablet of lady yüan. **BMFA** 72 (1974) 25-55, illus.

Campbell, Joseph. **The masks of god: oriental mythology.** N.Y. (1962) See pt 3, chap 7, Chinese mythology, 371-460.

Chalmers, John. Chinese mythology. **ChRev** 14 (1885-86) 33-36.

Chan Ping-leung. An interpretation of two ancient chinese myths. **TJ** n.s. 7.2 (aug 1969) 206-232, engl summ.

Chang, Kwang-chih. Changing relationships of man and animal in shang and chou myths and art. **ASBIE** 16 (1963) 133-146, illus; repr in **EarlyCC** (1976) 174-196.

Chang, Kwang-chih. The chinese creation myths: a study in method. **ASBIE** 8 (1959) engl summ 77-79.

Chang, Kwang-chih. A classification of shang and chou myths. **ASBIE** 14 (1962) engl abrmt 75-94; repr in **EarlyCC** (1976) 149-173.

Charpentier, Léon. La mythologie populaire chez les chinois. **NR** (1 dec 1900) 359-372.

Chow, Tse-tsung. The childbirth myth and ancient chinese medicine: a study of aspects of the wu tradition. In **AC:SEC** (1978) 43-89.

Christie, Anthony. **Chinese mythology.** Feltham, middlesex, engl (1968) 141 p, illus.

Clerke, E.M. Dragon myths of the east. **AQR** 4 (1887) 98-117.

Couchoud, Paul Louis (ed) **Mythologie asiatique illustrée.** Paris (1928) x + 431 p, illus.

Coyajee, Jehangir Cooverjee. **Cults and legends of ancient iran and china.** Bombay (1936) 308 p.

Duyvendak, J.J.L. The mythico-ritual pattern in chinese civilization. **Proceedings 7th ICHR** (1951) 137-138.

Dyson, Verne. **Forgotten tales of ancient china.** Shanghai (1927) xiii + 384 p, illus.

Eberhard, Wolfram. **Lokalkulturen im alten china.** Leiden (1942) vol 1, passim. Vol 2, **Die lokalkulturen des südens und ostens.** Peiping (1942) "Greatly expanded version" of vol 2, engl tsl Alide Eberhard: **The local cultures of south and east china.** Leiden (1968) 520 p, bibliog, index. See passim.

Ecsedy, I. Historical time and mythological history in ancient china. **KT:OS** 2 (1978) 61-66.

Eichhorn, Werner. Wang chia's shih-i-chi. **ZDMG** 102, n.s. 27 (1952) 130-142. "... dieser aus mythen, legenden und tatsachen kompilierten mirakel-historie."

Erkes, E. Chinesisch-amerikanische mythenparallelen. **TP** 24 (1926) 32-53. (See further E. von Zach: Einige bemerkungen zu Erkes's ... **TP** 24 (1926) 382-383; Erkes: Zu E. von Zach's Bemerkungen ... **TP** 25 (1928) 94-98.

Erkes, E. Eine p'an-ku-mythe der hsia-zeit? **TP** 36 (1942) 159-173.

Erkes, Eduard, Der pfau in religion und folklore. **JSMVL** 10 (1926-51 sic) 67-73.

Erkes, E. Spuren chinesischer weltschöpfungsmythen. **TP** 28 (1931) 355-368.

Erkes, Eduard. Spuren einer kosmogonischen mythe bei laotse. **AA** 8 (1940) 16-38.

Erkes, Eduard. Ein taoistische schöpfungsgeschichte für kinder. **CDA** (1932) 14-15.

Faust Ulrich. **Mythologien und religionen des ostens bei johann gottfried herder.** Münster (1977) See d. China, 1. Religion und mythologie in den 'ideen' (1787 und 1785) 174-181; Adrastea vierter band (1802) 181-186.

Feng, Han-yi and Shryock, J.K. Chinese mythology and dr. ferguson. **JAOS** 53 (1933) 53-65. (Criticism of ferguson's Chinese mythology q.v.)

Ferguson, John C. Chinese mythology. In John A. MacCulloch (ed) **The mythology of all races,** vol 8: **Chinese, japanese.** Boston (1928) 3-203. See further author's rebuttal of Feng and Shryock's criticism, item above: Chinese mythology: a reply. **JAOS** 54 (1934) 85-87.

Forke, A. Mu wang und die königin von saba. **MSOS** 7 (1904) 117-172.

Forke, A. Se wang mu. **MSOS** 9 (1906) 409-417.

Franke, Herbert. Indogermanische mythenparallelen zu einem chinesischen text der han zeit. In **MMDFL** (1963) 243-249.

Gates, Jean. Model emperors of the golden age in chinese lore. **JAOS** 56 (1936) 51-76.

Gieseler, G. Le mythe du dragon en chine. **RA** 5e sér, 6 (1917) 104-170.

Giles, Herbert A. Who was si wang mu? In author's **AdSin,** shanghai (1905) 1-19.

Girardot, Norman J. Myth and meaning in the tao te ching: chapters 25 and 42. **HR** 16 (1977) 294-328.

Girardot, Norman J. The problem of creation mythology in the study of chinese religion. **HR** 15.4 (may 1976) 289-318.

Goodall, John A. **Heaven and earth. Album leaves from a ming encyclopedia.** Boulder, colo (1979) sel fr san-ts'ai t'u-hui. Tsl by Graham Hutt. See passim.

Grube, Wilhelm. **Taoistischer schöpfungsmythen nach dem sên-sien-kien, I.1.** Berlin (1896) 13 p.

Harlez, Charles de. **Shĕn-siĕn-shu. Le livre des esprits et des immortels. Essai de mythologie chinoise d'après les textes originaux.** Bruxelles (1892) 492 p. Not a tsl — chin title apparently made up by author.

Hentze, Carl. **Funde in alt-china; das welterleben im ältesten china.** Göttingen etc (1967) 299 p, 48 pl. See passim. See also rev by Eleanor von Erdberg-Costen in **ZRGG** 25.2 (1973) 159-167 and Hentze's rejoinder in **ibid** 26.3 (1974) 262-265.

Hentze, Carl. **Tod, auferstehung, weltordnung; das mythische bild im ältesten china, in den grossasi-atischen und zirkumpazifischen kulturen.** Zürich (1955) 2 vol.

Hu, Nien-yi. Myths and legends of ancient china. **CL** 1 (jan 1978) 96-102.

Humphreys, H. The horn of the unicorn. **Antiquity** 27 (1953) 15-19.

Izushi, Yoshihiko. A study of origin of the ch'i-lin and the feng-huang. **TBMRD** 9 (1937) 79-109.

James, E.O. **Creation and cosmology. A historical and comparative inquiry.** Leiden (1969) See chap 3, India and the far east.

Kaltenmark, Max, La naissance du monde en chine. In **La naissance du monde** ('Sources orientales' t 1) Paris (1959) 453-468.

Kim, Chewon. Han dynasty mythology and the korean legend of tan gun. **ACASA** 3 (1948-49) 43-48.

Kingsmill, T.W. Siwangmu and k'wenlun. **JNCBRAS** 37 (1906) 185-190.

Kingsmill, T.W. Some myths of the shiking. **JNCBRAS** 31 (1896) 182-192.

Koppers, W. Der hund in der mythologie der zirkumpazifischen volker. **Wiener beiträge zur kulturgeschichte und linguistik** 1 (1930) 359-399. See rev by Paul Pelliot, **TP** 28 (1931) 431-470.

Krieg, Claus W. **Chinesische mythen und legenden.** Zürich (1946) 298 p, illus.

Kühnert, J. Entst. d. welt u. d. wesen d. menschen n. chin. anschauung. **Ausland** 66 (1893) 150-154.

Lacouperie, Terrien de. Le coco du roi de yueh et l'arbre aux enfants. Note de mythologie populaire en extrême-orient. **Trans ninth ICO, London 1892.** Vol 2 (1893) 897-905.

Lacouperie, Terrien de. On the ancient history of glass and coal and the legend of nü-kwa's coloured stones in china. **TP** 2 (1891) 234-243.

Laufer, Berthold. Columbus and cathay, and the meaning of america to the orientalist. **JAOS** 51 (1931) 87-103. Re mythol and relig resemblances.

Lee, André. **Légendes chinoises.** Pékin (1937) 124 p, illus.

Levi, Jean. Le mythe de l'âge d'or et les théories de l'évolution en chine ancienne. **l'Homme** 17.1 (jan-mars 1977) 73-103.

Ling, Jui-tang. The goddess of the moon. **CJ** 2 (1924) 497-502.

Ling, Shun-sheng. Kun lun chiu and hsi wang mu. **ASBIE** 22 (1966) engl abrmt 253-255.

Littleton, L.A. Chinese mythology in san francisco. **OM** 2nd ser 1 (june 1883) 612-617.

Liu, C.H. On the dog-ancestor myth in asia. **SS** 1 (1941) 277-314.

Loewe, Michael. **Ways to paradise. The chinese quest for immortality.** London (1979) 270 p, illus, app, notes. Based on han dyn relics.

MacKenzie, Donald A. **Myths of china and japan.** London (1923) 404 p.

Major, John S. Myth, cosmology, and the origins of chinese science. **JCP** 5.1 (mar 1978) 1-20.

Maspero, Henri. Légendes mythologiques dans le chou-king. **JA** 204 (1924) 1-100.

Maspero, Henri. The mythology of modern china. In J. Hackin et al, **Asiatic mythology.** N.Y. (n.d.) 252-384, illus. Tsl fr french, **Mythologie asiatique illustrée**, paris (1928) by F.M. Atkinson.

Mercatante, Anthony S. **Good and evil: mythology and folklore.** NY (1978) See chap 14, Chinese mythology and folklore, 127-135.

Miao, D.F. The moon in chinese legend. **CJ** 19 (1933) 112-114.

Moor, de **Essai sur les légendes chinoises concernant fo-hi, kong-kong, niuva, shin-nong et tchi-yeou. Précédé d'un coup d'oeil sur la religion primitive des chinois et sur l'introduction du christianisme en chine.** Paris (?) (1901) 58 p.

Morrison, John R. **Mythology of the various races and religions of china.** Publ in china (?) (ca. 1830) 100 drawings by chin artists.

München-Helfen, Otto. Der schuss auf die sonnen. **WZKM** (1937) 75-95.

Münke, Wolfgang. **Die klassische chinesische mythologie.** Stuttgart (1976) 389 p, index. Ency coverage alphabetically arr, with long intro. Rev by H. Seiwert in **ZMR** 62.3 (1978) 203-208.

A series on Mythological characters of archaic times in **ChRep:** Portrait of Pwanku, among the chinese, the reputed progenitor of the human family, 11 (1842) 46-47, illus. Portrait of the three sovereigns, the immediate successors of pwanku, among the chinese the reputed progenitor of the human family, **ibid** 110-113, illus. Portrait of fuhi, the first of the five sovereigns, whose reign commenced two thousand eight hundred and fifty-two years before christ, **ibid** 173-176, illus. Portrait of shinnung, or the blazing emperor, the second of the five sovereigns, with brief notices of his life, **ibid** 322-324, illus. Portrait of wang ti, the third of the five emperors, with notices of his life and character, **ibid** 386-388, illus. Portrait of shauhau, the fourth of the five ancient sovereigns, with remarks on chinese historical writing, **ibid** 452-453, illus. Portrait of chuenhiu, one of the most ancient sovereigns of china, **ibid** 616-617, illus. Portrait of the emperor ku kausin, classed among the five emperors of china, **ibid** 12 (1843) 75-77, illus.

O'Neill, John. **The night of the gods. An inquiry into cosmic and cosmogonic mythology and symbolism.**

London, vol 1 (1893) 581 p, vol 2 (1897) Notices in **TP** 4.5 (1893) 444-452, 8 (1897) 231-232; nécrologie in **ibid** 6.1 (1895) 77-78.

Ou-I-Tai. Chinese mythology. In Felix Guiran (ed) **New larousse encyclopedia of mythology,** tsl fr french Richard Aldington and Delano Ames. London, n.y. etc (1959) new ed (1968) 379-402, illus.

Perry, John W. **Lord of the four quarters. Myths of the royal father.** N.Y. (1966) See 5, The far east: china, 204-218 ('. . . we find in china the source and leading exponent of the sacral kingship.')

Plaks, Andrew H. **Archetype and allegory in the dream of the red chamber.** Princeton univ (1976) See esp chap 1, Archetype and mythology in chinese literature, 11-26; chap 2, The marriage of nü-kua and fu-hsi, 27-42.

Ragne, Beatrix von. The moon-palace; some iconographical remarks. **OA** n.s. 22.2 (summer 1976) 189-191, illus.

Riddel, W.H. Concerning unicorns. **Antiquity** 19 (1945) 194-202.

Rosenkranz, Gerhard. Das all und der mensch im chinesischen mythos. In **Festgabe für hans schomerus zum 65. geburtstag am 20.3.1967,** karlsruhe-durlach (1967) 42-47.

Rousselle, Erwin. Dragon and mare, figures of primordial chinese mythology. In **The mystic vision: papers from the eranos yearbooks.** Princeton univ (1968) 103-119 (For german orig see following item)

Rousselle, E. Drahe und stute; gestalten der mythischen welt chinesischer urzeit. **EJ** 2 (1934) 11-33; **CDA** (1935) 6-17 (For engl version, see item above)

Rousselle, Erwin. Die frau in gesellschaft und mythos der chinesen. **NachrDGNVO** 49 (1939) 12-24; 50 (1939) 10-17. Same title in **Sinica** 16 (1941) 130-151, pl.

Rousselle, Erwin. Die toteninsel. **Sinica** 16 (1941) 266-273.

Sanders, Tao Tao (text) Johnny Pan (illus) **Dragons, gods and spirits from chinese mythology.** NY etc (1980) 132 double-col p, sources, index.

Schafer, Edward H. **Pacing the void. T'ang approaches to the stars.** Univ calif (1977) 352 p. illus, app, notes, bibliog, gloss, index.

Schiffeler, John William. Chinese folk medicine. A study of the shan-hai ching. **AsFS** 39.2 (1980) 41-83.

Schiffeler, John William. **Legendary creatures of the shan hai ching.** Taipei (1977) xiv + 148 p, index, bibliog. Brief excerpts with illus.

Schmitt, G. Der "göttliche jäter" als erfinder des pfanzenanbaus (le devin sarchur, inventeur de l'agriculture) **Abhandlungen und berichte des staatlichen museums für völkerkunde dresden** (Berlin) 37 (1979) 139-168. Re shen-nung.

Seiwert, Hubert. Mythologie im chinesischen altertum. **ZMR** 62.3 (juli 1978) 203-208.

Sinensis. Chinese mythology. **ChRec** 3 (1870-71) 197-201, 234-239, 299-303, 310-315, 347-353; 4 (1871-72) 19-23, 46-48, 93-96, 130-132, 192-195, 217-222.

Soymié, M. China: the struggle for power. In Pierre Grimal (ed) **Larousse world mythology** tsl fr french **Mythologies de la méditerranée au gange et Mythologies des steppes, des iles et des forêts** (1963) by Patricia Beardsworth, london, n.y. etc (1965) 271-292, illus.

Sproul, Barbara C. **Primal myths. Creating the world.** NY etc (1979) See, Five myths of china and japan, 199-210.

Stein, Rolf A. La légende du foyer dans le monde chinois. In **Échanges et communications,** LaHaye (1970) t 2, 1280-1305.

Sun Zuoyun. Tsl Suzanne Cahill. An analysis of the western han murals in the luoyang tomb of bo qianqiu. **Chinese studies in archeology** 1.2 (fall 1979) 44-78.

Tan, J.M. **Légendes chinoises.** Louvain (1929) 126 p.

Tu, John Er-wei. The moon-mythical character of the god yu-huang. In **ExHum** (1976) 501-510.

Vallerey, Gisèle. **Contes et légendes de chine.** Paris (1936 and 1946) 254 p, illus.

Werner, E.T.C. **A dictionary of chinese mythology.** Shanghai (1932) repr n.y. (1961) 627 p, bibliog.

Werner, E.T.C. **Myths and legends of china.** London (1922) 454 p, gloss, index, illus.

Wilhelm, Hellmut. Chinese mythology. **EncyB 3** (1974) **Macropaedia** vol 4, 410b-415a.

Yen, Alsace. Shang-ssu festival and its myths in china and japan. **AsFS** 34.2 (1975) 45-86. Re purification rite.

Yetts, W. Perceval. The chinese isles of the blest. **Folk-lore** 30 (mar 1919) 35-62.

Yuan, Te-hsing. Dragons. Part 1: dragon tales. **Echo** 6.1 (july 1976) 45-56, illus.

Yuan, Te-hsing. Tsl Earl Wieman. The world of totems. **Echo,** pt 1, 4.11 (dec 1974) 26-41, illus; pt 2, 5.1 (jan 1975) 36-53, illus.

4. ART AND SYMBOLISM

Alexander, Mary and Frances. **A handbook on chinese art symbols.** Photos by Dewey G. Mears. Austin, texas (1958) 77 p, illus, bibliog.

Andersson, J.G. Hunting magic in the animal style. **BMFEA** 4 (1932) 221-320.

Andersson, J.G. On symbolism in the prehistoric painted ceramics of china. **BMFEA** 1 (1929) 65-69.

Art in the worship of the east. **FCR** 23.3 (mar 1973) 35-46. Photo-story re implements used in temple worship.

Ayrton, W.E. and John Perry. Sur les miroirs magiques du japon. **ACP** 5e sér, 20 (1880) 110-142.

Ayscough, Florence. The symbolism of the forbidden city, peking. **JNCBRAS** 61 (1930) 111-126.

Balfour, F.H. The peach and its legends. In author's **Chinese scrapbook** (1887) 145-148.

Ball, Katherine M. **Decorative motives of oriental art.** London & NY (1927) 286 p, 673 illus. See passim.

Banks, Michael. Religion and art in the northern wei dynasty. **AofA** 10.4 (july-aug 1980) 68-74, illus. Re ming-ch'i and budd sculpture.

Baruch, Jacques. Introduction à la symbolique chinoise. A propos de "yin" et "yang." **MEO** 1.4 (1971) 277-285.

Behrsing, S. Tou-mu, eine chinesische himmelsgöttin. **OZ** 27 (1941) 173-176.

Beltran, A. **Symbolism of oriental religious art.** Los angeles (1953) 122 p, illus.

Boerschmann, Ernst. **Die baukunst und religiöse kultur der chinesen.** Vol 1: **P'u t'o shan.** Berlin (1911) 203 p, 33 pl, fig.

Boerschmann, Ernt. **Die baukunst und religiöse kultur der chinesen.** Vol 2: **Gedächtnistempel; tzé tang.** Berlin (1914) xxiv + 288 p, illus.

Boerschmann, Ernst. K'uei-sing-türme und fengshui-säulen. **AM** 2 (1925) 503-530.

Böttger, Walter. Chinesische drachengewändet aus dem fundus des leipzig museums für völkerkunde. **JSMVL** 29 (1973) 163-190, mit 1 farbtafel, 13 abbildungen auf tafel 1-16, und 6 figuren im text.

Brace, A. Unifying symbolism of chinese religions. **JWCBorderResS** 3 (1926-29) 154-155.

Brewster, D. Accounts of a curious chinese mirror, which reflects from its polished face the figures embossed upon its back. **Philosophical magazine** 1 (1832) 438-441.

Brodrick, A.H. The flight of the phoenix. **AR** 36 (1940) 758-772.

Bulling, A. **The decoration of mirrors of the han period. A chronology.** Ascona (1960) 116 p, bibliog, index, 81 pl.

Bulling, A. The decoration of some mirrors of the chin and han periods. **AA** 18 (1955) 20-45.

Bulling, A. Guttkind. The guide of souls picture in the western han tomb in ma-wang-tui near ch'ang-sha. **OA** n.s. 20.2 (summer 1974) 158-173, illus.

Bulling, A. Die kunst der totenspiele in der östlichen han-zeit. **OE** 3 (1956) 28-56, illus.

Bulling, A. **The meaning of china's most ancient art; an interpretation of pottery patterns from kansu (ma ch'ang and panshan) and their development in the shang, chou, and han periods.** Leiden (1952) xx + 150 p, illus.

Bulling, A. Neolithic symbols and the purpose of art in china. **BM** 82/83 (1943) 91-101.

Bulling, A. Three popular motives in the art of the eastern han period. The lifting of the tripod. The crossing of a bridge. Divinities. **AAA** 20 (1966/67) 25-53, illus.

Bush, Susan. Thundermonsters and wind spirits in early sixth century china and the epitaph tablet of lady yüan. **BMFA** 72 (1974) 25-55, illus.

Cameron, Nigel. China's mythological beasts. **EH** 17.11 (nov 1978) 29-31, illus.

Cameron, Nigel, text and photos. A chinese bestiary. **Orientations** 10.10 (oct 1979) 38-42, illus col photos.

Cammann, Schuyler. Chinese mirrors and chinese civilization. **Archaeology** 2.3 (sept 1949) 114-120.

Cammann, Schuyler. Cosmic symbolism of the dragon robes of the ch'ing dynasty. In **A&T** (1947) 125-129.

Cammann, Schuyler. Imperial dragon robes of the later ch'ing dynasty. **OA** 3 (1950) 7-16.

Cammann, Schuyler. The lion and grape patterns on chinese bronze mirrors. **AA** 16 (1953) 265-291.

Cammann, Schuyler. The magic square of three in old chinese philosophy and religion. **HR** 1 (1961) 37-80.

Cammann, Schuyler. A ming dynasty pantheon painting. **ACASA** 18 (1964) 38-46, illus.

Cammann, Schuyler. Ming festival symbols. **ACASA** 7 (1953) 66-70, illus. Re symbols on ming dyn court costumes.

Cammann, Schuyler. Old chinese magic squares. **Sinologica** 7 (1962) 14-53.

Cammann, Schuyler. On the decoration of modern temples in taiwan and hongkong. **JAOS** 88.4 (1968) 785-790. Reaction to W. Eberhard's art, Topics and moral values in chinese temple decorations, q.v.

Cammann, Schuyler. Origins of the court and official robes of the ch'ing dynasty. **AA** 12 (1949) 189-201.

Cammann, Schuyler. A rare t'ang mirror. **AQ** 9 (1946) 93-113.

Cammann, Schuyler. A robe of the ch'ien-lung emperor. **Journal of the walters art gallery** 10 (1947) 9-20.

Cammann, Schuyler. Significant patterns on chinese bronze mirrors. **ACASA** 9 (1955) 43-62.

Cammann, Schuyler. The symbolism in chinese mirror patterns. **JISOA** 9 (1952-53) 45-63.

Cammann, Schuyler. The symbolism of the cloud collar motif. **AB** 33 (1951) 1-9.

Cammann, Schuyler. The 'TLV' pattern on cosmic mirrors of the han dynasty. **JAOS** 68.4 (1948) 159-167.

Cammann, Schuyler. Types of symbols in chinese art. In **SCT** (1953) 195-231.

Carus, Paul. Kwan yin pictures and their artists. **OC** 27 (1913) 683.

Casey, E.T. Two chinese imperial robes. **EB** 26.3 (1938) 3-6.

Chang, Kwang-chih. Changing relationships of man and animal in shang and chou myths and art. **ASBIE** 16 (1963) 133-146, illus; repr in **EarlyCC** (1976) 174-196.

Chao, D. The snake in chinese belief. Calcutta, **Folklore** 19.6 (1978) 159-168.

Chavannes, Édouard. De l'expression des voeux dans l'art populaire chinois. **JA** sér 9, t 18 (sep-oct 1901) repr as book under same title, paris (1922) Tsl Elaine Spaulding Atwood, **Five happinesses; symbolism in chinese art,** ny and tokyo (1973) 152 p.

Chavannes, Édouard. **La sculpture sur pierre en chine en temps des deux dynasties han.** Paris (1893) 88 p, illus.

Cheng, F.-k. & W.-s. Shen. **A brief history of chinese mortuary objects.** Peking, Yenching Journal of Chinese Studies Monograph Series No. 1 (1933).

Chêng, Tê-k'un.Ch'ih yü: the god of war in han art. **OA** 4.2 (summer 1958) 45-54.

Chêng, Tê-k'un. Yin-yang wu-hsing and han art, **HJAS** 20 (1957) 162-186.

Chou, Fong. A dragon-boat regatta. **BMMA** ser 2, 26.9 (may 1968) 389-398, illus. Re handscroll by yüan dyn artist wang cheng-p'eng.

Chou, Tzu-ch'iang. Chinese phoenix and the bird of paradise: a new identification of the ancient chinese phoenix. **ASBIE** 24 (1967) engl summ 117-122 + 12 p pl.

Clutton-Brock, A. Chinese and european religious art. **BM** 20 (1922) 197-200, illus.

Cohn, William. Chinese wall-paintings. **BM** 82/83 (1943) 168-174. A general discussion.

Cohn, W. The deities of the four cardinal points in chinese art. **TOCS** 18 (1940-41) 61-75.

Combaz, G. Masques et dragons en asie. **MCB** 7 (1939-45) 1-138.

Conrady, August. **Das älteste document zur chinesischen kunstgeschichte, t'ien-wen.** Leipzig (1931) vii + 266 p.

Conrady, G. Les huit immortels taoïstes dans l'art chinois pa-hien. **BSAB** 65 (1954) 167-170.

Coomaraswamy, Ananda K. What is common to indian and chinese art? **SCR** 7.2 (spring 1973) 75-91.

Cooper, J.C. **An illustrated encylopaedia of traditional symbols.** London (1978) 208 p, illus, gloss, bibliog. See passim.

Cooper, J.C. The symbolism of the taoist garden. **SCR** 11.4 (autumn 1977) 224-234.

Coral-Rémusat, Gilberte de. Animaux fantastique de l'indochine, de l'insulinde et de la chine. **BEFEO** 36 (1936) 427-435.

Croissant, Doris. Funktion und wanddekor der opferschreine von wu liang tz'u. Typologische und ikonographische untersuchen. **MS** 23 (1964) 88-162, pl.

Demiéville, Paul. La montagne dans l'art littéraire chinois. **FA** 20 (1965) 7-32, pl.

Dietz, E. Another branch of chinese painting. **Parnassus** 2.6 (1930) 35. On taoist paper scrolls.

Dieulafoy, Marcel. Les piliers funéraires et les lions de ya tcheou. **CRAIBL** (1910) 362-377.

Dittrich, Edith. **Das motiv des tierkampfes in der altchinesischen kunst.** Wiesbaden (1963) 248 p, literaturverzeichnis, anhang, bibl katalog (119 pl with explanations)

Dohrenwend, Doris J. Jade demonic images from early china. **ArsOr** 10 (1975) 55-78, 20 pl.

Dubs, Homer H. Hill censers. In **SSBKD** (1959) 259-264.

Dye, D.S. Symbolism of the designs. **JWCBorderResS** 2 (1924-25) 74-76.

Dye, Daniel S. **The yin yang dance of life and basic patterns, as seen in west china between december 1908 and april 1949.** Penfield downs, pa (1950) 26 p, illus.

Eberhard, Wolfram. Topics and moral values in chinese temple decorations. **JAOS** 87.1 (1967) 22-32. Further see Eberhard's Rejoinder to schuyler camman, **JAOS** 88.4 (1968) 790-792.

Ecke, Gustav. Zur architektur der gedächtnishalle. (Contribution to the study of sculpture and architecture—

Der grabtempel des kang ping, aufgenommen von p. szongott) **MS** 5 (1940) 467-478.

Edkins, Joseph. **Ancient symbolism among the chinese.** London and shanghai (1889) 26 p.

Edkins, Joseph. The ju-i, or, sceptre of good fortune. **EA** 3 (1904) 238-240.

Edmunds, W. **Pointers and clues to the subjects of chinese and japanese art.** London (1934) 706 p, illus.

Éléments de décoration chinoise; motifs décoratifs relevés dans les temples et yamens. Pékin (1931) 60 col pl.

Eliasberg, Danielle. **Imagerie populaire chinoise du nouvel an.** ArtsAs t 35 (1978) entire issue, 131 p, col pl.

Erdberg-Consten, Eleanor von. Die architektur taiwans; ein beitrag zur geschichte der chinesen baukunst. **R-WAW** Vorträge G189 (1973) 71 p, illus b-&-w and col photos.

Erdberg-Consten, Eleanor von. Ornamente und symbole der altchinesischen bronzen. **Jahrbuch für asthetik und allgemeine kunstwissenschaft,** Stuttgart, 6 (1961) 159-176.

Erdberg-Consten, Eleanor von. A statue of lao tzu in the po-yün-kuan. **MS** 7 (1942) 235-241.

Erdberg-Consten, Eleanor von. A terminology of chinese bronze decoration. **MS** 16 (1957) 287-314; 17 (1958) 208-254; 19 (1959) 245-293; illus.

Erkes, Eduard. A chinese bronze landscape. **Sinologica** 3 (1953) 190-192, illus. Represents shen-nung and a taoist saint (?)

Erkes, Eduard. Der chinese und das tier. **Sinologica** 1 (1948) 273-291.

Erkes, E. Idols in pre-buddhist china. **AA** 3 (1928) 5-12, illus.

Erkes, E. Der ikonographische charakter einiger chou-bronzen. (I. Der tiger, II. Die eule nachtrag zu "die eule") **AA** 6 (1936-37) 111-117; 7 (1937) 92-108; 8 (1940) 49.

Erkes, Eduard. Der pfau in religion und folklore. **JSMVL** 10 (1926-51 sic) 67-73.

Erkes, E. Some remarks on karlgren's "fecundity symbols in ancient china." **BMFEA** 3 (1931) 63-68.

Exposition d'iconographie populaire: images rituelles du nouvel an. Peking, Centre franco-chinois d'études sinologiques (1942) Unillus catalogue of exhibition of july 1942.

Fairbank, Wilma. The offering shrines of 'wu liang tz'u.' **HJAS** 6 (1941) 1-36, 10 fig. Repr in author's **Adventures in retrieval,** harvard univ (1972) 41-86.

Fairbank, Wilma. A structural key to han mural art. **HJAS** 7 (1942) 52-88, illus. Comparison of offering shrines of chu wei at chin hsiang with hsiao-t'ang shan and wu liang tz'u shrines. Repr in author's **Adventures in retrieval,** harvard univ (1972) 87-140.

Ferguson, John C. Decorations of chinese bronzes. An interpretation. **JNCBRAS** 72 (1946) 1-6.

Ferguson, John C. Religious art in china. **THM** 1 (1935) 239-247.

Fernald, Helen E. Some chinese grave figures. **MJ** 17 (1926) 75-93.

Finsterbusch, Käte. Han-zeitliche symbole. In **SSM/FHF** (1979) 231-244, illus.

Fisher, Robert E. Tibetan art and the chinese tradition. **AofA** 5.6 (nov-dec 1975) 42-49, illus.

Fong, Mary H. A probable second "chung k'uei" by emperor shun-chih of the ch'ing dynasty. **OA** n.s. 23.4 (winter 1977) 423-437. Re a painting at occidental college, los angeles.

Fontein, Jan. Chinese art. In **EncyWA** (1959-68) 3, 466a-577a. Chron by periods, and within each period by kind of art. See pasim, also relevant illus in sec at end of vol.

Friend, Robert. Traditional new year pictures mirror the changes in china. **EH** 17.4 (apr 1978) 34-37, illus.

Fu, Tien-chun. The sculptured maidens of the tsin temple. **CL** 4 (apr (1962) 92-98, illus. A sung dyn temple to yi chiang in taiyuan.

Gieseler, G. Le mythe du dragon en chine. **RA** 5e sér, 6 (1917) 104-170.

Gieseler, G. Les symboles de jade dans le taoisme. **RHR** 105 (1932) 158-181.

Goette, J. Jade and man in life and death. **THM** 3 (1936) 34-44.

Goidsenhoven, J.P. van. Le symbolisme dans la céramique chinoise. **BSAS** 40 (1940) 78-97, illus.

Goodall, John A. **Heaven and earth. Album leaves from a ming encyclopedia.** Boulder, colo (1979) 192 p, illus. Tsl Graham Hutt. Sel fr san-ts'ai t'u-hui. See passim.

Govi, M. Les miroirs magiques des chinois. Tsl fr italian M. Pomonti. **ACP** 5e sér, 20 (1880) 99-105.

Govi, M. Nouvelles expériences sur les miroirs chinois. Tsl fr italian M. Pomonti. **ACP** 5e sér, 20 (1880) 106-110.

The graphic art of chinese folklore. Taipei, National museum of history, republic of china (1977) 101 p, repr of col prints, notes in chin and engl. Sel fr collection at museum; all are prints relating to pop relig.

Gray, Basil. A great taoist painting. **OA** 11 (1965) 85-94, illus. On yen pien hsiang — "metamorphoses of heavenly being."

Gynz-Rekowski, Georg v. Die psyche des menschen in der europäischen und chinesischen kunst. In **ATOW** (1967) 245-258.

Hall, Ardelia R. The early significance of chinese mirrors. **JAOS** 55 (1935) 182-189.

Hall Ardelia R. The wu ti mirrors. **OZ** 20 (1934) 16-23, pl.

Hansford, S. Howard. The disposition of ritual jades in royal burials of the chou dynasty. **JRAS** (1949) 138-142.

Hartman, Joan M. Chinese tomb sculpture. The collection of mr and mrs ezekiel schloss. **OA** n.s. 15.1 (winter 1969) 286-292, illus.

Hartman, Joan M. An interesting han jade in the los angeles county museum of art. **AA** 36 (1974) 55-64, illus.

Hartner, Willy. Studien zur symbolik der frühchinesischen bronzen. **Paideuma** 3.6/7 (1949) 279-290.

Hayes, L. Newton. **The chinese dragon.** Shanghai (1922) xvi + 66 p, illus.

Heidenreich, Robert. Beobachtungen zum stadtplan von peking. **NachrDGNVO** 81 (1957) 32-37. Re symbolism.

Hentze, Carl. Altchinesische kultbilder und ihre ausstrahlungen. **Sinologica** 8 (1965) 137-155, illus.

Hentze, Carl. Antithetische t'ao-t'ieh motive. **IPEK** 23 (1970-73) 118-137, illus.

Hentze, Carl. Die bedeutung des inschrift si tse sun. **Sinologica** 4 (1954-56) 156-165, illus. Re bronze inscription.

Hentze, Carl. **Chinese tomb figures. A study in the beliefs and folklore of ancient china.** London (1928) xii + 105 p, illus.

Hentze, Carl. Comment il faut lire l'iconographie d'un vase en bronze chinois de la période chang. **Conferenze tenute all'Is. M.E.O.** (1952) 49-108.

Hentze, Carl. Le culte de l'ours ou du tigre et le t'ao-tie. **Zalmoxis** 1 (1938) 50-68, illus.

Hentze, Carl. Discussions à propos d'un livre récent. (Reply to Erkes' rev of Hentze's book, **Les figurines de la céramique funéraire) AA** 3 (1928) 47-66, illus.

Hentze, Carl. **Funde in alt china: das welterleben im ältesten china.** Göttingen etc (1967) 299 p, 48 pl. See passim. See also rev by Eleanor von Erdberg-Costen in **ZRGG** 25.2 (1973) and Hentze's rejoinder in **ibid** 26.3 (1974) 262-265.

Hentze, Carl. Gods and drinking serpents. **HR** 4 (1965) 179-208, pl.

Hentze, Carl. Die göttin mit dem haus auf dem kopf. **Antaios** 7 (1965) 47-67, illus.

Hentze, Carl. **Das haus als weltort der seele. Ein beitrag zur seelensymbolik in china.** Stuttgart (1961) 179 p, illus.

Hentze, Carl. Les jades archaïques en chine. **AA** 3 (1928) 199-216; 4 (1930-32) 35-40. See P. Pelliot, Lettre ouverte à m. carl hentze, **RAA** 6 (1929-30) 103-122, 196; see further W.P. Yetts, A propos de la lettre ouverte, **ibid** 191.

Hentze, Carl. Methodologisches zur untersuchung altchinesischer schriftzeichen. **SinSon** (1934) 34-45, fig.

Hentze, Carl. Mythologische bildsymbole im alten china. **Studium generale** 6 (1953) 264-277.

Hentze, Carl. Die regenbogenschlange: alt-china und alt-amerika. **Anthropos** 61 (1966) 258-266, illus.

Hentze, Carl. Schamanenkronen zur han-zeit in korea. **OZ** n.f. 9 (1933) 156-163, illus, bibliog.

Hentze, Carl. Le symbolisme des oiseaux dans la chine ancienne. **Sinologica** 5.2 (1957) 65-92; 5.3 (1958) 129-149, illus.

Hentze, Carl. Die tierverkleidung in erneuerungs- und initiationsmysterien (ältestes china, zircumpazifische kulturen und gross-asien) **Symbolon** 1 (1960) 39-86, illus.

Hentze, Carl. Die wanderung der tiere um die heiligen berg. **Symbolon** 4 (1964) 9-104, pl.

Hentze, Carl. Zur hirschsymbolik auf den ältesten chinesischen bronzegefässen. In **Asien** (1971) 198-206, illus.

Hentze, Carl. Zur ursprünglichen bedeutung des chinesischen zeichens t'ou-kopf. **Anthropos** 45 (1950) 801-820, illus.

Hermand, L. l'Art symbolique en chine. **RC** (juil 1907) 141-169.

Hirth, Friedrich. Chinese metallic mirrors with notes on some ancient specimens of the musée guimet, paris. In **BAV** n.y. (1907) 208-256.

Hodous, Lewis, The dragon. **JNCBRAS** 48 (1917) 29-41.

Hollis, H.C. Cranes and serpents. **BCMA** 25 (1938) 147-151.

Hopkins, L.C. The dragon terrestrial and the dragon celestial. A study of the lung and the ch'en. **JRAS** (1931) 791-806; (1932) 91-97.

Hopkins, L.C. Where the rainbow ends. An introduction to the dragon terrestrial and the dragon celestial. **JRAS** (1931) 603-612.

Hornblower, G.D. Early dragon-forms. **Man** 33 (1933) 79-87. See author's Additional notes on early dragon-forms, **ibid** 36 (1936) 22-24.

Howey, M. Oldfield. **The encircled serpent. A study of serpent symbolism in all countries and ages.** N.Y. (1955) See chap 26, Chinese serpent lore, 253-266.

Huang Wen-shan. The artistic expression of totems in ancient chinese culture. **ASBIE** 21 (1966) 1-13.

Huggins, M.I. Cicada, tortoise, dove, hare, deer and crane in chinese symbolism. **Nature magazine** 41 (1948) 93-96, 108, illus.

Huntington, Harriet E. Symbolism of chinese snuff bottles. **AofA** 4.2 (mar-apr 1974) 42-47, illus.

In the presence of the dragon throne. **Orientations** 11.2 (feb 1980) 37-42, illus col-photos. Re Asia house gallery (ny) exhibit of ch'ing court costumes and their symbolism.

Ito, C. Architecture (Chinese). In **HERE** 1 (1908) 693-696.

Izushi, Yoshihiko. A study of the origin of the ch'i-lin and the feng-huang. **TBMRD** 9 (1937) 79-109, illus.

James, Jean M. A provisional iconology of western han funerary art. **OA** n.s. 25.3 (autumn 1979) 347-357, illus. Paintings, murals, banners.

Kaler, Grace. Chinese symbolism: the crane. **Hobbies** 71.12 (1967) 50. Chinese symbolism: the phoenix. **Ibid** 71.11 (1967) 50-57.

Kaler, Grace. Portrait in bronze: kuan ti, chinese god of war. **Hobbies** 72.1 (1967) 50, 47.

Kaltenmark, Max. Miroirs magiques. In **MSPD** t 2 (1974) 151-166. Re mirrors in taoism.

M.K. (Max Kaltenmark) and M.S. (Michel Strickmann) Symbolisme traditionelle et religions populaires. **EVF** (1968) 4, Chine sec 5, 362a-365c.

Karlgren, Bernhard. Some fecundity symbols in ancient china. **BMFEA** 2 (1930) 1-54 + 6 p pl.

Kleinman, Arthur. The symbolic context of chinese medicine. **AJCM** 3.2 (1975) 103-124.

Komor, Mathias. Chinese roof-figures. **THM** 2 (1936) 355-359.

Körner, Brunhild. Die brautkrone der chinesen. **Baessler archiv** 6 (1958) 81-98.

Köster, Hermann. **Symbolik des chinesischen universismus.** Stuttgart (1958) 104 p, kart.

Kung, Hsien-lan (ed) **The life of confucius. Reproduced from a book entitled sheng chi t'u, being rubbings from the stone "tablets of the holy shrine."** Shanghai (n.d.)

Kuo, Li-cheng. Chinese funerary arts. **Echo** 3.7 (july-aug 1973) 34-41, illus col-photos. Re ming-ch'i.

Laing, Ellen Johnston. Neo-taoism and the "seven sages of the bamboo grove" in chinese painting. **AA** 36.1/2 (1974) 5-54, illus.

Laufer, Berthold. **Chinese pottery of the han dynasty.** Leiden (1909) repr tokyo and vermont (1962) illus. See esp chap 4, sec Tazzas or sacrificial vessels; sec Hill-censers; sec Hill-jars. Rev by Ed. Chavannes in **TP** 11 (1910) 300 et seq.

Laufer, Berthold. **The diamond. A study in chinese and hellenistic folk-lore.** Chicago (1915) 75 p.

Laufer, Berthold. **Jade. A study in chinese archaeology and religion.** Chicago (1912); repr south pasadena, calif (1946) repr ny (1974) 370 p, illus.

Lee, Sherman E. Kleinkunst: two early chinese wood sculptures. **AAA** 20 (1966-67) 66-68, illus. Re a kuan-yin and a taoist fig.

Lees, G.F. On the symbolism of jade. **Apollo** 29 (1939) 70-75.

Legeza, I.L. Art and tao. **Apollo** 95 #126 (aug 1972)

Legeza, Laszlo Ireneus. **Art and tao; an exhibition of taoist symbolism in chinese art, gulbenkian museum, summer-autumn, 1972.** Durham (1972) 25 p.

Legeza, Laszlo. Chinese taoist arts. **AofA** 7.6 (nov-dec 1977) 32-37.

Legeza, I.L. On the grammar of taoist popular art and symbolism: the problem of talismanic graphs. In Margaret Medley (ed) **Chinese painting and the decorative style. A colloquy held 23-25 June 1975.** Univ london (n.d.) 148-162, 3 p pl.

Legeza, Laszlo. **Tao magic. The chinese art of the occult.** London & ny (1975) Text 7-30, pl 31-128, brief note on the tao-tsang (taoist canon) and brief bibliog.

Legeza, Laszlo. Taoist colour symbolism in ming and ch'ing ceramics. **AofA** 9.5 (sept-oct 1979) 84-90, illus.

Lessing, Ferdinand. Über die symbolsprache in der chinesischen kunst. **Sinica** 9 (1934) 121-155, 217-231, 237-269; 10 (1935) 31-42.

Lion Lucien. **Les ivoires religieux et médicaux chinois d'après la collection lucien lion.** Texte de Henri Maspero, René Grousset, Lucien Lion. Paris (1939) 96 p, pl.

Loeb, J. Chinese landscape painting as religious art. **Vassar journal of undergraduate studies** 8 (1934) 1-16, illus.

Loehr, Max. **Chinese art: symbols and images.** Wellesley, mass (1967) 63 p, illus.

Loewe, Michael. Man and beast; the hybrid in early chinese art and literature. **Numen** 25.2 (aug 1978) 97-117, illus.

Loewe, Michael. Water, earth and fire — the symbols of the han dynasty. **NachrDGNVO** 125 (1979) 63-68.

Loewe, Michael. **Ways to paradise. The chinese quest for immortality.** London (1979) 270 p, illus, app, notes. Based on han dyn relics.

Loewenstein, Prince John. **Swastika and yin-yang.** London (1942) 28 p, illus.

Lotus. **Echo** 4.8 (sep 1974) 45-49, 55-56, illus.

Lovelock, B. Dragon robes. **EW** 6.8 (1952) 34-35.

Marin J. The chinese dragon — a myth and an emblem. **AP** 23 (1952) 103-115.

Markbreiter, Stephen. The temple of heaven in peking. **AofA** 2.3 (may-june 1972) 9-12, illus. General description.

Maryon, Herbert. A note on magic mirrors. **ACASA** 17 (1963) 26-28.

Maspero, Henri. Les ivoires chinois et l'iconographie de chine. Text by Maspero from the Lucien Lion volume q.v.; repr in author's **Les religions chinoises,** paris (1950) 229-239 (**Mélanges posthumes sur les religions et l'histoire de la chine,** t 1)

McFarlane, Sewell S. Stone figures in china. **Geographical journal** 22 (aug 1903) 210-211.

Meister, W. Eine datierte taoistische bronzeplastik. **OZ** 21 (1935) 93-95.

Miao, D.F. Some chinese paintings of deities. **CJ** 19.1 (july 1933) 6-8, 1 illus. Re chung-k'uei, t'ien-kuan, sung-tze-kuan-yin.

Millard, R.A. A taoist figure dated 607 a.d. **AA** 20 (1957) 45-49.

Milloué, Léon de. **Catalogue du musée guimet. Pt I: Inde, chine et japon. Précédé d'un aperçu sur les religions de l'extrême-orient et suivie d'un index alphabétique des noms des divinités et des principaux termes techniques.** Lyon (1883)

Mirrors, Japanese: brief notices. Atkinson, R.W. **Nature** 16 (1877) 62; Darbishire, R.D. **ibid** 142-143; Thompson, Sylvanus P. **ibid** 163; Parnell, J. **ibid** 227-228; T.C.A. **ibid** 31 (1884-85) 264.

Moore, Albert C. **Iconography of religions: an introduction.** Philadelphia (1977) See chap 6, Religions of east asia . . . China, 170-180.

Morgan, Harry T. **Chinese symbolism.** Los angeles (ca. 1941) 16 p, illus.

Morgan, Harry T. **Chinese symbolism and its associated beliefs.** Los angeles (1945) 20 p, illus.

Morgan, Harry T. **Chinese symbols and superstitions.** South pasadena, calif (1942) 192 p, illus, bibliog, index.

Munsterberg, Hugo. An anthropomorphic deity from ancient china. **OA** 3.4 (1951) 147-152, illus.

Munsterberg, Hugo. The symbolism of the four directions in chinese art. **AQ** 14 (1951) 33-44.

Musée Guimet. See various catalogues, from 1880—.

Nachbaur, A. (ed) **Les images populaires chinoises.** Pekin (1926) 181 p, illus.

Nance, F.N. Chinese symbolism. **CJ** 20 (1934) 5-24.

Nott, Charles Stanley. **Chinese culture in the arts.** N.Y,. (1946) xx + 134, illus.

Nott, S.C. **Chinese jade symbolism.** St augustine, fla (1941) 26 p, illus.

Nott, S.C. **Chinese jade throughout the ages.** London (1936) 2nd ed tokyo and rutland, vt (1962) 193 p, illus.

Nott, Charles Stanley. **Chinese jades in the stanley charles nott collection . . . exhaustively reviewing the symbolic ritualistic appurtenances of chinese jades and their various sacrificial usages . . .** St. augustine, fla. (1942) xvi + 536 p, 118 pl.

Nott, S.C. **The symbolic importance of chinese jade.** St. augustine, fla (1941) 20p.

Nott, S.C. **Voices from the flowery kingdom . . . incorporating a complete survey of the numerous emblematic forces . . .** NY (1947) 278 p, illus.

Paper, Jordan. The meaning of the "t'ao-t'ieh." **HR** 18.1 (aug 1978) 18-41.

Pelliot, Paul. Lettre ouverte à m. carl hentze. **RAA** 6 (1929-30) 103-122, 196. See Hentze item, Les jades archaïques en chine.

Pelliot, Paul. Les plaques de l'empereur du ciel. **BMFEA** 4 (1932) 115-116.

Penniman, T.K. and Cohn, W. A steatite figure of the k'ang hsi period in the pitt rivers museum, oxford (god of longevity) **Man** 45 (1945) 73-74.

Perzynski, Friedrich. **Von chinas göttern. Reisen in china.** München (1920) 260 s, 80 bildtafeln.

Petterson, Richard. The native arts of taiwan. **Claremont quarterly** 11.3 (1964) 49-58, 12 p of photos.

Pichon, Jean-Charles. **Les cycles du retour éternel.** Paris (1963) See t 2, p 157-184.

Plumer, James M. The chinese bronze mirrors: two instruments in one. **AQ** 7 (1944) 91-108.

Pommeranz-Liedtke, Gerhard. Bilder für jedes neue jahr. Zur wandlung des chinesischen neujahrbildes. **ZBK** 1 (1955)

Pommeranz-Liedtke, Gerhard. **Chinesische neujahrsbilder.** Dresden (1961) 202 p, illus, bibliog.

Pontynen, Arthur. Buddhism and taoism in chinese sculpture, a curious evolution in religious motif. **FMB** 49.6 (june 1978) 16-21.

Pontynen, Arthur. The deification of laozi in chinese art and history. **OA** 26.2 (summer 1980) 192-200, illus.

Pontynen, Arthur. The dual nature of laozi in chinese history and art. **OA** 26.3 (autumn 1980) 308-313, illus.

Porkert, M. Farbenemblamatik in china. **Antaios** 4 (1962-63) 154-167.

Priest, Alan. The exhibition of chinese court robes and accessories. **BMMA** 26 (1931) 283-288.

Priest, Alan. 'Li chung receives a mandate.' (Sung painting) **BMMA** 34 (1939) 254-257.

Priest, Alan. A note on kuan ti. **BMMA** n.s. 25 (1930) 271-272.

Priest, Alan. The owl in shang and chou bronzes. **BMMA** 33 (1938) 235-240.

Prinsep, James. Note on the magic mirrors of japan. **JRASB** 1 (1832) 242-245.

Prints to welcome the new year. **Echo** 3.1 (jan 1973) 38-43, illus b-&-w and col. A special chinese new year issue.

Prunner, Gernot. **Papiergötter aus china.** Hamburg (1973) 85 p, illus, bibliog.

Przyluski, J. Dragon chinois et naga indien. **MS** 3 (1938) 602-610.

R., S.C.B. The tuang [sic] fang sacrificial table. **BMMA** 19 (1924) 141-144, illus.

Ragne, Beatrix von. The moon-palace; some iconographical remarks. **OA** n.s. 22.2 (summer 1976) 189-191, illus.

Ranasinghe, Alex. The chinese dragon, its significance and the chinese response to it. **APQCSA** 4.3 (winter 1972) 33-41.

Rawson, Philip & Laszlo Legeza. **Tao. The chinese philosophy of time and change.** London (1973) 128 p, illus 129 b-&-w and col pl.

Riboud, Krishna. Some remarks on the face-covers (fu-mien) discovered in the tombs of astana. **OA** n.s. 23.4 (winter 1977) 438-454. Re chin burials of six dyn period in tombs of turfan area.

Riddel, W.H. Tiger and dragon. **Antiquity** 19 (1945) 27-31.

Roberts, L. Chinese ancestral portraits. **Parnassus** 9.1 (1937) 28.

Rogers, Millard. A taoist figure dated 607 a.d. **AA** 20.1 (1957) 45-49, pl.

Rosenzweig, Daphne Lange. Stalking the persian dragon: chinese prototypes for the miniature representations. **KdeO** 12.1/2 (1978-79) 150-176, illus.

Ross, D. A comparative study of religion and symbolism among buddhists, adherents of popular religion, protestants and catholics in taiwan. Ottowa, **Kerygma** 14 (1980) 101-116.

Rotours, Robert des. Le culte des cinq dragons sous la dynastie des t'ang (618-907) In **MSPD** t 1 (1966) 261-280, 3 pl.

Rudolph, Conrad. The wu family shrines. **JAC** 4 (spring 1980) 21-47.

Rychterová, Eva. Commemorative ancestor portraits. **NO** 4 (1965) 176-177, illus.

Rydh, Hannah. Symbolism in mortuary ceramics. **BMFEA** 1 (1929) 71-120, 11 pl, 62 fig.

Salmony, Alfred. **Antler and tongue: an essay on ancient chinese symbolism and its implications.** Ascona (1954) 39 p, illus. See rev by Heine-Geldern, **AA** 18 (1955) 85-90.

Salmony, Alfred. The cicada in ancient chinese art. **Connoisseur** 91 (mar 1933) 174-179, illus.

Salmony, Alfred. The magic bell and the golden fruit in ancient chinese art. In **A&T** (1947) 105-109.

Salmony, Alfred. Note on the iconography of the shang period. **RAA** 11 (1937) 102-104.

Salmony, Alfred. The owl as ornament in archaic chinese bronzes. **Parnassus** 6.2 (1934) 23-25.

Salmony, Alfred. A problem in the iconography of three early bird vessels. **ACASA** 1 (1945-46) 53-65.

Salmony, Alfred. The third early chinese owl with snake legs. **AA** 14 (1951) 277-282.

Salmony, Alfred. The three governors of taoism, an unusual chinese bronze sculpture. **GBA** 6e sér, 25 (1944) 315-317.

Salmony, Alfred. With antler and tongue. **AA** 21.1 (1958) 29-36, illus.

Saussure, Léopold de. Le cycle des douze animaux et le

symbolisme cosmique des chinois. **JA** sér 11, 15/16, t 196/197 (1920) 55-58, fig.

Saussure, Léopold de. La tortue et le serpent. **TP** sér 2, 18/19 (1918-19) 247-248, fig.

Schafer, Edward H. A t'ang taoist mirror. **EC** 4 (1978-79) 56-59.

Schiffeler, John William. The yang-wu: a cultural transformation. **CC** 13.3 (sep 1972) 35-42. Re the "sun-crow"

Schloss, Ezekiel. **Ming-ch'i.** NY (1975) 13 p, 100 illus. Catalog of exhib at katonah gallery, ny, 1975.

Schultze, O. Der religiöse einfluss auf die chinesische kunst. **Mitt. geogr. comm. ges.** (1906) 1-11.

Schuster, C.A. A comparative study of motives in western chinese folk embroideries. **MS** 2 (1936-37) 21-80.

Schuster, C. A prehistoric symbol in modern chinese folk art. **Man** 36 (1936) 201-203.

Segalen, Victor, Gilbert de Voisins & Jean Lartigue. **L'Art funéraire à l'époque des hans.** Paris (1935) 304 p, 121 fig. Material fr Mission archéol en chine, 1914; this is vol 1.

Sewell, Jack V. Notes on cast-iron figure sculptures of china; consideration of a recently acquired head. Art instit of chicago **Museum studies** 3 (1968) 7-20, illus. "Head of a deity, perhap sheng mu." Other sculptures also illus.

Simmons, P. A chinese imperial robe. **BMMA** 24 (1929) 134-135.

Soon, Tan Tek. The chinese tree of life. **Monist** 10 (july 1900) 625.

Soothill, William E. **The hall of light; a study of early chinese kingship.** Ed Lady Hosie and G.F. Hudson. London (1951) xxii + 289, illus.

Soper, Alexander C. The dome of heaven in asia. **AB** 29 (1947) 225-248.

Sowerby, Arthur de Carle. Animals in chinese art. **CJ** 24.4 (apr 1936) 188-201, illus photos.

Sowerby, Arthur de Carle. Animals in the myths, legends and fairy tales of china. **CJ** 31.1 (july 1939) 10-21, illus photos.

Sowerby, Arthur de Carle. The flora of chinese art. **CJ** 26.6 (june 1937) 310-320, illus.

Sowerby, Arthur de Carle. Legendary figures in chinese art. Kuan yin, the goddess of mercy. **CJ** 14.1 (jan 1931) 3-4, illus.

Sowerby, Arthur de Carle. Legendary figures in chinese art. Kuan yü, the god of war. **CJ** 15.1 (july 1931) 4, frontispiece illus.

Sowerby, Arthur de Carle. Legendary figures in chinese art. K'uei hsing, the distributor of literary degrees. **CJ** 15.2 (aug 1931) 57-58, illus.

Sowerby, Arthur de Carle. Legendary figures in chinese art. Pa hsien, the eight immortals. **CJ** 14.2 (feb 1931) 53-55, illus.

Sowerby, Arthur de Carle. Legendary figures in chinese art. Shou hsing, the god of longevity. **CJ** 14.3 (mar 1931) 109-110, illus.

Sowerby, Arthur de Carle. Legendary figures in chinese art. Ts'ai shen, the god of wealth. **CJ** 14.5 (may 1931) 210-211.

Sowerby, Arthur de Carle. The owl in chinese art. **CJ** 25.1 (july 1936) 8-12.

Sowerby, Arthur de Carle. Reptiles, fishes and invertebrates in chinese art. **CJ** 25.5 (nov 1936) 251-259, illus.

Sowerby, Arthur de Carle. Rocks, mountains and water in chinese art. **CJ** 27.2 (aug 1937) 58-63, illus.

Soymié, Michel. La lune dans les religions chinoises. In **La lune: mythes et rites** ('Sources orientales' 5) paris (1962) 289-321.

Stein, Rolf A. Architecture et pensée religieuse en extrême-orient. **ArtsAs** 4.3 (1957) 163-186, illus.

Stein, Rolf. Jardins en miniature d'extrême-orient. **BEFEO** 42 (1942) 1-104, 5 pl.

Stevens, Keith G. Soul images and gods of the boat people. **AofA** 7.6 (1977) 52-61, illus b-&-w and col. photos. Boat people of hk.

Sullivan, Michael. The magic mountain. **Asian review** 51 (1955) 300-310.

Sun, Zuoyun. Tsl Suzanne Cahill. An analysis of the western han murals in the luoyang tomb of bo qianqiu. **Chinese studies in archeology** 1.2 (fall 1979) 44-78.

Sung, Yu. Paintings of taoist and buddhist legends. **Echo** 2.5 (may 1972) 37-43, illus. Re some paintings in national palace museum, taipei.

Temple carvings and sculptures in ancient style. **FCR** 22.11 (nov 1972) 33-44. Photo-story re carvings at a temple in sanhsia, taiwan (outskirts of taipei)

Thilo, Thomas. **Klassische chinesische baukunst: strukturprinzipien und funktion.** Vienna (1977) 252 s, taf, anhang, karte. See passim for budd and taoist architecture.

Thompson, Laurence G. Efficacy and afficacy in chinese religion. **SSCRB** 6 (fall 1978) 31-49.

Thompson, Laurence G. Taiwanese temple arts and cultural integrity. **SSCRB** 8 (fall 1980) 70-78.

Thorpe, W.A. Creatures of the chinese zodiac. **Apollo** 11 (1930) 108-113, illus.

Till, Barry. Some observations on stone winged chimeras at ancient chinese tomb sites. **AA** 42 (1980) 261-281.

Tomb jades of the chou period. **BMMA** 19 (1924) 121-123.

Tomita, Kojirō. A chinese sacrificial stone house of the sixth century a.d. **BMFA** 40 (1942) 98-110. Re gravegoods.

Tomita, Kojirō and A. Kaiming Chiu. Portraits of wu ch'üan-chieh (1269-1350) taoist pope in yüan dynasty. **BMFA** 44 (1946) 88-95.

Tredwell, Winifred Reed. **Chinese art motives interpreted.** N.Y. and london (1915) xiii + 110 p, illus.

Trubner, Henry. A stone demon from hsiang-t'ang shan. **Annual, royal ontario museum** (1961) 73-74.

Visser, M. W. de. **The dragon in china and japan.** Amsterdam (1913) xii + 242 p.

Vuilleumier, B. **The art of silk weaving in china; symbolism of chinese imperial robes.** London (1939) 45 p, illus.

Vuilleumier, B. Tissus et tapisseries de soie dans la chine ancienne. Technique et symbolisme. **Revue de l'art ancien et moderne** 69 (1936) 197-216.

Vuilleumier, B. Vêtements rituels impériaux chinois et chasuble des premiers mandchous. **Revue de l'art ancien et moderne** 71 (1937) 243-245.

Wang, C.S. Birds and chinese tradition. **CJ** 21.6 (dec 1934) 308-311, illus. Symbolic meanings of a few birds.

Wang, Sung-hsing. Taiwanese architecture and the super-natural. In **RRCS** (1974) 183-192.

Ward, Barbara E. Not merely players: drama, art and ritual in traditional china. **Man** 14.1 (mar 1979) 18-39.

Waterbury, Florance, **Bird deities in china.** Ascona (1952) 191 p, bibliog, index. See rev by J. LeRoy Davidson, **AB** 36.3 (1954) 233-235.

Waterbury, Florance. An early chinese ritual vessel. **Worcester art museum annual** 4 (1941) 73-76. See rev by J. LeRoy Davidson, **AB** 25.3 (1943) 281-284.

Waterbury, Florance. **Early chinese symbols and litera-ture: vestiges and speculations, with particular reference to the ritual bronzes of the shang dynasty.** NY (1942) 164 p, pl.

Waterbury, Florance. The nedzu ho: chinese ritual vessels of the ho type. In **A&T** (1947) 110-115.

Waterbury, Florance. Speculations on the significance of a ho in the freer gallery. **AA** 15 (1952) 114-124.

Waterbury, Florance. The tiger and agriculture. **AA** 10.1 (1947) 55-56. Reply to a rev of her book **Early chinese symbols and literature,** q.v. by J. LeRoy Davidson in **AB** 25 (sept 1943)

Watson, William. A grave guardian from ch'angsha. **BMQ** 17.3 (1952) 52-56.

Weber, Charles D. The spirit path in chinese funerary practice. **OA** n.s. 24.2 (summer 1978) 168-178, illus. Re stone fig at tombs.

Wenley, A.G. **The grand empress dowager wen ming and the northern wei necropolis at fang shan.** Freer gallery. **Occasional papers** 1.1 (1947) 22 p, 7 pl.

Wenley, Archibald. The po-shan hsiang-lu. **ACASA** 3 (1948-49) 5-12.

Wheat, William T. Temple roof decorations. **Echo** 5.9 (oct 1975) 17-27, illus.

White, William C. **Chinese temple frescoes. A study of three wall-paintings of the thirteenth century.** Univ toronto (1940) xvii + 230 p, illus. (Contains 2 pts: 1 — general intro, 11 chaps; 2 — the 3 frescoes ('the paradise of maitreya,' 'the lord of the northern dipper,' 'the lord of the southern dipper')

White, William C. The lord of the northern dipper. **BROMA** 13 (1945) 32 p, illus. See item above.

White, William C. The lord of the southern dipper. **BROMA** 14 (1946) 32 p, illus. See author's book, above.

Whitlock, H.P. Chinese design: basic symbolic patterns of chinese art. **NH** 39 (1937) 49-57, illus.

Whitlock, H.P. Familiar symbols in jade; the key to the understanding of the exquisite taoist designs of this art lies in the delightful lore of old china. **NH** 46 (1940) 6-15, illus.

Whitlock, H.P. Gods and immortals in jade. **NH** 46 (1940) 152-159, illus.

Whitlock, H.P. Jade, the mythology and symbolism expressed in the carvings of the jewel of heaven. **NH** 32 (1932) 497-507, illus.

Wilhelm II, German emperor. **Die chinesische monade; ihre geschichte und ihre dichtung.** Leipzig (1934) 66 p, illus.

Williams, C.A.S. **Outlines of chinese symbolism and art motives.** Shanghai, 2nd rev ed (1932) repr as **Enclyclopedia of . . .,** N.Y. (1960) 467 p, illus.

Wiou, Frida. **Les symboles de la chine.** Paris (1970) 208 p, illus, bibliog.

Wong, K.C. The court robe and diadem of the ancient emperor of china. **CJ** 5 (1926) 281-286.

Woodblock prints for the new year. **FCR** 25.2 (feb 1975) 29-32, col-photos.

Wright, Arthur F. The cosmology of the chinese city. In **CLIC** (1977) 33-73.

Yetts, W.P. A propos de la lettre ouverte à m. carl hentze. **RAA** 6 (1929-30) 191. Re P. Pelliot's Lettre, **ibid** 103-122, 196.

Yetts, W.P. Chinese tomb jade. **Folk-lore** 33 (1922) 319-321.

Yetts, W. Perceval. Notes on flower symbolism in china. **JRAS** (1941) 1-21, illus.

Yetts, W.P. Pictures of a chinese immortal. **BM** 39 (1921) 113-121.

Yetts, W. Perceval. **Symbolism in chinese art.** Leyden (1912) 28 p, illus.

Yin, Teng-kuo. Tsl Robert Christensen. Scrolls and prints of chung kuei. **Echo** 6.7 (sep 1977) 28-35, 54, illus. Special issue on chung k'uei.

Yuan, Te-hsing. Tsl Earl Wieman. The world of totems. **Echo** , pt 1 4.11 (dec 1974) 26-41, illus; pt 2 5.1 (jan 1975) 36-53, illus.

5. RELIGION AND HISTORY (See also SECTS AND SECRET SOCIETIES)

Allen, C.F.R. (tsl) Proclamation against idol processions. In **DV** Vol 2, pt 3, no 61, p 516-518.

Allen, H.J. The connexion between taoism, confucianism and buddhism in early days. **Trans third ICHR,** oxford (1908) vol 1, 115-119.

Bauer, Wolfgang. **Das bild in der weissage-literatur-chinas. Prophetische texte im politischen leben vom buch der wandlung bis zu mao tse-tung.** München (1973) 74 s.

Bauer, Wolfgang. **China und die hoffnung auf glück. Paradies, utopien, idealvorstellungen.** München (1971) Tsl Michael Shaw, **China and the search for happiness,** ny (1976) 502 p, chron table, notes, bibliog, index. See rev art by Vitali Rubin, **TP** 59 (1973) 68-78.

Bielenstein, Hans. An interpretation of the portents in the ts'ien-han-shu. **BMFEA** 22 (1950) 127-143, diagr.

Boardman, Eugene P. Millenary aspects of the taiping rebellion, 1851-64. In Sylvia L. Thrupp (ed) **Millenial dreams in action: essays in comparative study,** the hague (1962) 70-79.

Bünger, Karl. Die rechtsidee in der chinesischen geschichte. **Saeculum** (1952) 192-217.

Bünger, Karl. Religiöse bindungen im chinesischen recht. In K. Bünger and Hermann Trimborn (ed) **Religiöse bindungen in frühen und in orientalischen rechten,** wiesbaden (1952) 58-69.

Chan, Hok-lam. Chang chung and his prophecy: the transmission of the legend of an early ming taoist. **OE** 20.1 (june 1973) 65-102.

Chan, Hok-lam. Liu ping-chung (1216-74), a buddhist-taoist statesman at the court of khubilai khan. **TP** 53.1/3 (1967) 98-146.

Chan, Hok-lam. Die prophezeiung des liu chi (1311-1375) Ihre entstehung und ihre umwandlung im heutigen china. **Saeculum** 25.4 (1974) 338-365. Übers aus dem englischen von Karl-Theo Humbach (fr engl version given at 29th ICO, Paris 1973)

Chan, Hok-lam. The rise of ming t'ai-tsu (1369-88): facts and fictions in early ming official historiography. **JAOS** 95.4 (oct-dec 1975) 679-715, chin gloss. Deals in part with omens, legends, myths in establishing founder's credentials, particularly taoistic elements.

Chan, Wing-tsit. The historic chinese contribution to religious pluralism and world community. In E.J. Jurji (ed) **Religious pluralism and world community. Interfaith and intercultural communication,** leiden (1969)

Chang, Hao. **Liang ch'i-ch'ao and intellectual transition in china, 1890-1907.** Harvard univ (1971) See Index under budd; relig.

Chavannes, Édouard. Inscriptions et pièces de chancellerie chinoises de l'époque mongole. **TP** 5 (1904) 366-404. Document dealing with controversy betw buddhists and taoists under the mongols.

Ch'en, Kenneth K.S. Buddhist-taoist mixtures in the pa-shih-i-hua t'u. **HJAS** 9 (1945) 1-12.

Ch'en, Kenneth K.S. Inscribed stelae during the wei, chin, and nan-ch'ao. In **StAs** (1975) 75-84.

Chia, Chung-yao. The church-state conflict in the t'ang dynasty. In E-tu Zen Sun and John DeFrancis (ed and tsl) **Chinese social history. Translations of selected studies,** washington, d.c. (1956) 197-206. Largely fr Ennin's **journal.**

Chung, David. The han-san-wei-i (three religions are one) principle in far eastern societies. **TransKBRAS** 38 (oct 1961) 95-118.

Collis, Maurice. **The first holy one.** N.Y. (1948) 280 p, illus, index. On confucius and confucianism until triumph of confucianism in former han dynasty.

Coulborn, Rushton. The state and religion: iran, india and china. **CSSH** 1 (1958) 44-57.

Creel, H.G. **Religion as a political sanction in ancient china.** Far eastern leaflet (dec 1941)

Demiéville, Paul. La situation religieuse en chine au temps de marco polo. In **Oriente poliana,** rome (1957) 193-234.

Dien, Albert E. Yen chih-t'ui (531-591+): a buddho-confucian. In **CP** (1962) 43-64.

Dubs, Homer H. The attitude of han kao-tzu to confucianism. **JAOS** 57 (1937) 172-180.

Dubs, Homer H. The custom of mourning to the third year. Chap 11, app 1 in Dubs (tsl) **The history of the former han dynasty by pan ku,** vol 3, baltimore, md (1955) 40-42.

Dubs, Homer H. The sacred field. Chap 4, app 2 in Dubs (tsl) **The history of the former han dynasty by pan ku,** vol 1, baltimore, md (1938) 281-283. Re field personally plowed by emperor to open agricultural season.

Dubs, Homer H. The victory of han confucianism. **JAOS** 58 (1938) 435-449. Same title in Dubs (tsl) **The history of the former han dynasty by pan ku,** baltimore, md, vol 2 (1944) chap 9, app 2, p 341-353.

Dunstheimer, G.H. Religion officielle, religion populaire et sociétés secrètes en chine depuis les han. In **EncyP:HR** 3, (1976) 371-448, bibliog.

Ecsedy, I. Historical time and mythological history in ancient china. **KT:OS** 2 (1978) 61-66.

Edkins, Joseph. **The early spread of religious ideas especially in the far east.** Oxford (1893) 144 p.

Edkins, Joseph. The introduction of astrology into china. **ChRev** 15 (1886-87) 126-128.

Edkins, Joseph. Religious persecution in china. **ChRec** 15.6 (nov-dec 1884) 433-444.

Edwards, E.D. **Chinese prose literature of the t'ang period, a.d. 618-906.** London, 2 vol (1937-38) repr ny (1974) See vol 1, chap 5, Religion—magic and magical practices, 49-59; vol 2 passim.

Edwards, E.D. Some aspects of the conflicts of religion in china during the six dynasties and t'ang periods. **BSOAS** 7.3 (1933-35) 799-808.

Eichhorn, Werner. Der aufstand der zauberin t'ang sai-êhr im jahre 1420. **OE** 1 (1954) 11-25.

Eichhorn, Werner, Bemerkungen zum aufstand des chang chio und zum staate des chang lu. **MIOF** 3.2 (1955) 291-327.

Eichhorn, Werner. Description of the rebellion of sun ên and earlier taoist rebellions. **MIOF** 2 (1954) 325-352.

Eichhorn, Werner. Nachträgliche bemerkungen zum aufstand des sun ên. **MIOF** 2 (1954) 463-476.

Enjoy, Paul d'. De la législation chinoise à l'égard des congregations religieuse. **BMSAP** 5e sér, 5 (1904) 154-157.

Erkes, Eduard. China's religiöse entwicklung in zusammenhang mit seiner geschichte. **OZ** 4.1/2 (1915) 58-66.

Fisher, Carney T. The great ritual controversy in the age of ming shih-tsung. **SSCRB** 7 (fall 1979) 71-87.

Franke, O. Der konfuzianismus zwischen han- und sui-zeit. **SinSon** (1934) 1-11.

Franke, Wolfgang. Some remarks on lin chao-en (1517-1598) **OE** 20.2 (1973) 161-173.

Franke, Wolfgang. Some remarks on the "three-in-one doctrine" and its manifestations in singapore and malaysia. **OE** 19 (1972) 121-130. Incl tsl of 2 inscriptions and ten photo pl.

Genähr, J. "Sectarianism and religious persecution in china." **ChRec** 36.3 (mar 1905) 131-137; 36.4 (apr 1905) 169-175. Rev art on the work by J.J.M. de Groot, q.v.

Gernet, Jacques. Christian and chinese world views in the fourteenth century. **Diogenes** 105 (spring 1979) 93-115.

Gernet, Jacques. **La vie quotidienne en chine à la veille de l'invasion mongole 1250-1276.** Paris (1959) Engl tsl H.M. Wright: **Daily life in china on the eve of the mongol invasion 1250-1276.** See chap 5, The seasons and the universe: The seasons and days of the year — festivals — religion (p 179-218) The 3rd sec of this chap repr in **TC** (1970) 161-179.

Groot, J.J.M. de. Is there religious liberty in china? **MSOS** 5 (1902) 103-151.

Groot, J.J.M. de **Sectarianism and religious persecution in china.** Leiden (1901) repr Taipei (1963) repr shannon, ireland & ny (1974) 2 vol, 595 p, index.

Harlez, Charles de. La religion des insurgés tchang-mao. **TP** 9.5 (1898) 397-401.

Harlez, Charles de. Le tien fu hia fan tchao shu, livre religieux des tai-ping. **TP** 10.3 (1899) 307-318.

Harrison, James P. **The communists and chinese peasant rebellions. A study in the rewriting of history.** NY (1969) See pt 2, Communist analysis of the chinese peasant rebellions: chap 7, Religious attitudes, 165-189.

Ho, Yun-yi. Ritual aspects of the founding of the ming dynasty 1368-1398. **SSCRB** 7 (fall 1979) 58-70.

Hu, Schi. Tsl W. Franke. Der ursprung der ju und ihre beziehung zu konfuzius und lao-dsi. **SinSon** (1936) 1-42.

Hu, Shih. Religion and philosophy in chinese history. In Sophia H. Chen Zen (ed) **Symposium on chinese culture,** shanghai (1931) 31-58.

Hughes, E.R. Chinese religion in the third century b.c. **AR** 31 (1935) 721-733.

Hummel, Siegbert. **Zum buddhistischen weltbild.** Leipzig (1948)

Itano, Chōhachi. The t'u-ch'an prophetic books and the establishment of confucianism. **TBMRD**, pt 1, 34 (1976) 47-111; pt 2, 36 (1978) 85-107.

Kaltenmark, Max. Religion et politique dans la chine de ts'in et des han. **Diogène** 34 (avr-juin 1961) 18-46.

Kandel, Barbara. **Taiping jing. The origin and transmission of the 'scripture on general welfare'—the history of an unofficial text.** Hamburg, **MDGNVO** 75 (1979) 111 p.

Kao, Chü-hsün. The ching lu shen shrines of han sword worship in hsiung-nu religion. **Central asiatic journal** 5 (1960) 221-232.

Kimura, Eiichi. The new confucianism and taoism in china and japan from the fourth to the thirteenth centuries. **CHM** 5 (1960) 801-829.

Lai, Whalen. Toward a periodization of chinese religion. **SSCRB** 8 (fall 1980) 79-90.

Laufer, Berthold. Religiöse toleranz in china. **Globus** 86 (1904) 219-220.

Lay, W.T. (tsl) Another proclamation against idolatrous processions. **Missionary recorder** 1 (1867) 55-56. Chin text and tsl of proclamation by viceroy wu of fukien, 21 apr 1867.

Levenson, Joseph R. Confucian and taiping "heaven": the political implications of clashing religious concepts. **CSSH** 4 (1962) 436-453.

Levy, Howard S. The bifurcation of the yellow turbans in later han. **Oriens** 13-14 (1960-61) 251-255.

Levy, Howard S. Yellow turban religion and rebellion at the end of han. **JAOS** 76 (1956) 214-227.

Lewy, Guenter. Heterodoxy and rebellion in traditional china. Chap 3 in author's **R&Rev** (1974) 57-69.

Lewy, Guenter. Religion and revolution and the major traditions—confucianism. In chap 2 of author's **R&Rev** (1974) 14-25.

Liu, James T.C. How did a neo-confucian school become the state orthodoxy? **PEW** 23.4 (oct 1973) 483-506.

Liu, James T.C. The sung emperors and the ming-t'ang or hall of enlightenment. In Françoise Aubin (ed) **Études song: sung studies in memoriam étienne balazs,** the hague (1973) sér 2, Civilisation, vol 1, 45-58.

Liu, Ts'un-yan. Lin chao-ên (1517-1598) the master of the three teachings. **TP** 53 (1967) 253-278. Repr **LTY:SP** (1976)

Liu, Ts'un-yan. Lu hsi-hsing: a confucian scholar, taoist priest and buddhist devotee of the sixteenth century. **AS** 18/19 (1965) 115-142; repr **LTY:SP** (1976)

Liu, Ts'un-yan. The penetration of taoism into the ming neo-confucianist elite. **TP** 57.1/4 (1971) 31-102; repr **LTY:SP** (1976)

Loewe, Michael. The case of witchcraft in 91 b.c.; its historical setting and effect on han dynastic history. **AM** 15.2 (1970) 159-196. Same title as chap 2 in author's **CCHC** (1974)

Loewe, Michael. K'uang heng and the reform of religious practices (31 b.c.) **AM** 17.1 (1971) 1-27. Same title as chap 5 in author's **CCHC** (1974)

I.M. (Ilse Martin) Der taoistische einfluss im zeitgeist der wei- und chin-epoche, von sun te-hsüan. Deutschland institut, peking **Sinologische arbeiten** 3 (1945) 177-183. In sec, Inhalt sangaten der chinesischen sinologischen arbeiten in chang-te hsüeh-chih 6.1 und 2.

Maspero, Henri. Le ming-t'ang et la crise religieuse chinoise avant les han. **MCB** 9 (1948-51) 1-71.

Maspero, Henri. La religion chinoise dans son dévellopement historique. In author's **HMRC** (1950) 15-138.

Maspero, Henri. La société et la religion des chinois anciens et celles des tai modernes. In author's **HMRC** (1950) 139-194.

M'Clatchie, M.T. The chinese on the plain of shinar, or a connection established between the chinese and all other nations through their theology. **JRAS** 16 (1856) 368-435.

Meacham. William. Religion and the origins of shang civilization: notes on a theory of proto-history. **CF** 17.2/3 (1974) 63-74.

Mears, W.P. The religious history of china. **CMI** 47, n.s. 20 (1895) 321-334.

Medhurst, Dr. (tsl) The book of religious precepts of the t'haeping dynasty. **NCH** 147 (14 may 1853)

Michaud, Paul. The yellow turbans. **MS** 17 (1958) 47-127, bibliog.

Milne, W.C. The rebellion of the yellow caps, compiled from the history of the three states. **ChRep** 10 (1841) 98-103.

Miyakawa, Hisayuki. Legate kao p'ien and a taoist magician lü yung-chih in the time of huang ch'ao's rebellion. **ActA** 27 (1974) 75-99.

Morgan, Evan. A case of ritualism. **JNCBRAS** 49 (1918) 128-143. Re usurpation by feudal state of lu of royal prerogative to perform suburban sacrifice to heaven (chiao)

Naquin, Susan. **Millenarian rebellion in china. The eight trigrams uprising of 1813.** Yale univ (1976) 384 p, maps, 3 app, notes, sel bibliog, gloss-index.

Ngo, Van Xuyet. **Divination, magie et politique dans la chine ancienne. Essai suivi de la traduction des "biographies des magiciens" tirées de l'histoire des hans posterieurs.'** Paris (1976) 264 p. App, Les arts ésoteriques du "fang-chou lie-tchouan." Annexes re chronol, bibliog, index of chin char, map.

Ogel, Bahaeddin. Religious tolerance in the medieval chinese administration. **ACQ** 5.1 (spring 1977) 125-127. Re tolerance of islam in yüan and early ming.

Overmyer, Daniel L. Boatmen and buddhas: the lo chiao in ming dynasty china. **HR** 17.3/4 (feb-may 1978) 284-302.

Overmyer, Daniel L. Dualism and conflict in chinese popular religion. In **T&T** (1980) 153-184.

Overmyer, Daniel L. Folk-buddhist religion: creation and eschatology in medieval china. **HR** 12.1 (aug 1972) 42-70.

Pak, Hyobom. **China and the west. Myths and realities in history.** Leiden (1974) viii + 120 p. ". . . interacting forces of religion and politics."

Parsons, James B. Overtones of religion and superstition in the rebellion of chang hsien-chung. **Sinologica** 4.3 (1955) 170-177.

Paul, Diana. Empress wu and the historians: a tyrant and saint of classical china. In **UW** (1980) 191-206.

Peeters, Jan. **Eine stimme aus der sung-zeit über die heterodoxie: lun-yü, II, 16.** Breslau (1938) 83 p.

Perry, Elizabeth J. Worshipers and warriors: white lotus influence on the nian rebellion. **Modern china** 2.1 (jan 1976) 4-22.

Prisco, Salvatore, III. The vegetarian society and the huashan ku-t'ien massacre of 1895. **Asian forum** 3.1 (jan-mar 1971) 1-13.

Rachewiltz, Igor de. The hsi-yu lu by yeh-lü ch'u'ts'ai. **MS** 21 (1962) 1-128. See for controversy betw buddhism and taoism in yuan dynasty.

Rachewiltz, Igor de. Yeh-lü ch'u'ts'ai (1189-1243): buddhist idealist and confucian statesman. In **CP** (1962) 189-216.

Religionen und religionspolitik im alten und neuen china. **China-analysen** 9 (july/aug 1970) 46-96.

Rotours, Robert de. Le culte des cinq dragons sous la dynastie des t'ang (618-907) In **MSPD** t 1 (1966) 261-280, 3 pl.

Rule, Paul A. Jesuit and confucian? Chinese religion in the journals of matteo ricci, s.j., 1583-1610. **JRH** 5 (1968) 105-124.

Sargent, Galen E. Les débats personnels de tchou hi en matière de méthodologie . **JA** 243 (1955) 213-228.

Schiffeler, John William. An essay on the traditional concept of soul in chinese society,. **CC** 17.2 (june 1976) 51-56.

Shapiro, Sheldon. Morality and religious reformations. **CSSH** 18 (1976) 438-457. Incl chin comparisons.

Sivin, Nathan. On the word "taoist" as a source of perplexity. With special reference to the relations of science and religion in traditional china. **HR** 17.3/4 (feb-may 1978) 303-330.

Smith, D. Howard. Conflicting ideas of salvation in a.d. fifth century china. In Eric J. Sharpe & John R. Hinnells

(ed) **Man and his salvation; studies in memory of s.g.f. brandon,** manchester univ (1973) 291-303.

Stein, Rolf A. Remarques sur les mouvements du taoïisme politico-religieux au IIe siècle ap. j.-c. **TP** 50.1/3 (1963) 1-78.

Strickmann, Michel. The mao shan revelations: taoism and the aristocracy. **TP** 63.1 (1977) 1-64.

T'ang Chün-i. The formation of confucius' position in chinese history and culture. **ChFor** 1.1 (jan 1974) 1-48.

Taylor, Romeyn. Ming t'ai tsu and the gods of the wells and moats. **Ming studies** 4 (spring 1977) 31-49.

Topley, Marjorie. Chinese religion and rural cohesion in the nineteenth century. **JHKBRAS** 8 (1968) 9-43.

Tsai, Wen-hui. Historical personalities in chinese folk religion: a functional interpretation. In **LL&R** (1979) 23-42.

Ubelhör, Monika. Geistesströmungen der späten ming-zeit, die als wirken der jesuiten in china begünstigten. **Saeculum** 23.2 (1972) 172-185.

Vandermeersch, Léon. **Wangdao ou la voie royale. Recherches sur l'esprit des institutions de la chine archaïque. Tome 1, Structures cultuelles et structures familiales.** Paris (1977) 358 p. **Tome 2, Structures politiques, les rites.** Paris (1980) 603 p, tables, index. See Table générale des matières.

Vandier-Nicolas, Nicole. Les échanges entre le bouddhisme et le taoïsme des han aux t'ang. In **AC** t 1 (1959) 166-170.

Waidtlow, C. The imperial religions of ch'in and han. **ChRec** 58 (1927) 565-571, 698-703.

Waidtlow, C. The religion of emperor wu of the han. **ChRec** 55 (1924) 361-366, 460-464, 527-529.

Waidtlow, C. The religion of the first emperor (ch'in shih huang) **ChRec** 57 (1926) 413-416, 487-490.

Waley, Arthur. The heavenly horses of ferghana: a new view that the chinese expeditions of 102 b.c. had a magico-religious significance. **History today** 5 (feb 1955) 95-103, illus.

Waley, Arthur. History and religion. **PEW** 5 (1955-56) 75-78.

Wallacker, Benjamin E. Han confucianism and confucius in han. In **AC:SEC** (1978) 215-228.

Walshe, W.G. Religious toleration in china. **CR** 85 (mar 1904) 442-447. On persecutions of buddhism.

Watters, T. (tsl) Discourse on heresy by a chinese emperor. **ChRec** 4.9 (feb 1872) 225-227. The emperor is yung cheng, 1727.

Weber-Schäfer, Peter. **Oikumene und imperium. Studien zur zivil-theologie des chinesischen kaiserreichs.** München (1968) 317 p. Historical through period of han wu-ti.

Werner. E.T.C. The origin of the chinese priesthood. **JNCBRAS** 59 (1928) 188-199.

Wills, John E. jr. State ceremony in late imperial china: notes for a framework for discussion. **SSCRB** 7 (fall 1979) 46-57.

Woodin, S.F. (tsl) A proclamation against certain idolatrous practices. **Missionary recorder** 1 (1867) 22-23. Chin text and tsl of proclamation by viceroy tso of fukien, 5 mar 1865.

Wright, Arthur F. The formation of sui ideology. In **CTI** (1957) 71-104.

Wright, H.K. The religious element in the tso chuan. **JNCBRAS** 48 (1917) 171-188.

Wright, Harrison K. Religious persecution in china: a historical study of the relations between church and state. **ChRec** 52 (1921) 233-249, 341-354, 397-411.

Young, C. Walter. The isles of the blessed. An historical myth. **CJ** 8.4 (apr 1928) 171-175. Re ch'in-shih-huang's search for immortality.

6. RELIGIOUS THOUGHT

A.L. Chinese notions as to the moment of death. **ChRev** 10 (1881-82) 431.

Antonini, P. Personne de l'éternel d'après la doctrine des chinois. **Compte rendu du congrès scientifique international des catholiques,** paris, t 1 (1897) 115-133.

Ball, J. Dyer. **The chinese at home.** NY etc (1912) See chap 25, What john chinaman believes, 331-341.

Bauer, Wolfgang. **China und die hoffnung auf glück. Paradies, utopien, idealvorstellungen.** München (1971) Tsl Michael Shaw, **China and the search for happiness,** ny (1976) 502 p, chron table, notes, bibliog, index. See rev art by Vitali Rubin, **TP** 59 (1973) 68-78.

Berling, Judith A. **The syncretic religion of lin chao-en.** Columbia univ (1980) 360 p, app, notes, gloss, sel bibliog.

Bertholet, R. l'Astrobiologie et l'état chinois. (l'Astrobiologie et la pensée d'asie: essai sur les origines des sciences et des théories morales II-III) **RMM** 40 (1933) 41-64, 457-479.

Bodde, Derk. The chinese view of immortality: its expression by chu hsi and its relationship to buddhist thought. **RofR** 6 (1942) 369-383. Repr **ECC** (1981) 316-330.

Bodde, Derk. Dominant ideas. In H.F. MacNair (ed) **China,** univ calif (1946) 18-28.

Bodde, Derk. Evidence for 'laws of nature' in chinese thought. **HJAS** 20 (1957) 709-727.

Brandon, S.G.F. **The judgment of the dead. The idea of life after death in the major religions.** N.Y. (1967) See chap 9, The judgment of the dead bureaucratically organized, 178-188.

Bruce, J.P. The theistic import of the sung philosophy. **JNCBRAS** 49 (1918) 111-127.

Buckens, F. Les antiquités funéraires du honan central et la conception de l'âme dans la chine primitive. **MCB** 8 (1946-47) 1-101.

Capra, Fritjof. **The tao of physics. An exploration of the parallels between modern physics and eastern mysticism.** Berkeley, calif (1975) 330 p, notes, bibliog, index. See esp chap 7, Chinese thought, 101-112; chap 8, Taoism, 113-120; see also passim.

Carroll, Thomas D. Some cyclical characteristics of chinese astrology. **JCS** 3 (1963) 4-21.

Castiglioni, Arturo. Tsl fr italian V. Gianturco. **Adventures of the mind.** NY (1946) See chap 10, Chinese magic of numbers and letters, 123-231.

Chalmers, John. Chinese natural theology. **ChRev** 5 (1876-77) 271-281.

Chan, Wing-tsit. Chu hsi's appraisal of lao tzu. **PEW** 25.2 (apr 1975) 131-144. Same title in **MS/CA** (1977) 5-9.

Chan, Wing-tsit. The individual in chinese religions. In Charles A. Moore (ed) with assistance of Aldyth V. Morris, **The status of the individual in east and west,** univ hawaii (1968) 181-198.

Chan, Wing-tsit. The neo-confucian solution of the problem of evil. **ASBIHP** 28 (1957) 773-791.

Chan, Wing-tsit. **A source book in chinese philosophy.** Princeton univ (1963) xxv + 856 p, chron of dynasties, chron of philosophers, app On translating certain chinese philosophical terms, bibliog, gloss of chin characters, index. For religious thought see passim (table of contents as well as index give good indications)

Chan, Wing-tsit. Wang yang-ming's criticism of buddhism. In **WPDMD** (1968) 31-37.

Chang, Aloysius. A christian interpretation of the god-concept in tao te ching. **CC** 15.1 (mar 1974) 16-28.

Chang, Aloysius. Does confucian jen mean christian love? **World mission** 24.4 (winter 1973-74) 50-56.

Chang, Aloysius. Fan chen and his "treatise on the destruction of the soul" **CC** 14.4 (dec 1973) 1-8.

Chang, Carsun. Buddhism as a stimulus to neo-confucianism. **OE** 2.2 (1955) 157-166.

Chao, Paul. Human nature and the concept of sin in confucianism and christianity. **CC** 16.2 (june 1975) 45-62.

Chao, T.C. Present-day religious thought and life in china. In **CToday,** 2nd ser, london (1926) 33-49.

Chau, Yick-fu. Religious thought in ancient china. Tsl fr chin F.P. Brandauer. **CF** 10.1 (1967) 20-33; 10.2 (1967) 20-33.

Chaudhuri, H. The concept of brahman in hindu philosophy (with a sec on brahman, tao and t'ai-chi) **PEW** 4 (1954) 47-66.

Chen, Ellen Marie. Tao as the great mother and the influence of motherly love in the shaping of chinese philosophy. **HR** 14.1 (aug 1974) 51-64.

Ch'en, Kenneth. The buddhist contributions to neo-confucianism and taoism. In **TC** 155-160. Excerpt from author's **Buddhism in china: a historical survey** q.v. 471-476.

Chêng, Tê-k'un. Yin-yang, wu-hsing and han art. **HJAS** 20 (1957) 162-186.

Chiang, Liu. The religious ideas of tan shu-tung (t'an ssu-t'ung). **ChRec** 58.12 (dec 1927) 773-775. Rev art on chap 1 of t'an's jen hsüeh.

Chinese theology. **ChRep** 2.7 (nov 1833) 310-312. Re ideas of confucius and mencius.

Chung, David. The han-san-wei-i (three religions are one) principle in far eastern societies. **TransKBRAS** 38 (oct 1961) 95-118.

Cobb, John B. jr. Post-conference reflections on yin and yang. **JCP** 6.4 (dec 1979) 421-426.

Cohen, Alvin P. Avenging ghosts and moral judgment in ancient chinese historiography: three examples from shih-chi. In **LL&R** (1979) 97-108.

Coomaraswamy, Ananda K. What is common to indian and chinese art? **SCR** 7.2 (spring 1973) 75-91.

Cornaby, W. Arthur. The supreme as recognized in ancient china. **ChRec** 35.1 (jan 1904) 5-18. Re shang-ti in ancient texts.

Courant, Maurice. Sur le prétendu monothéisme des anciens chinois. **RHR** 41 (1900) 1-21.

Creel, Herrlee Glessner. **Sinism: a study of the evolution of the chinese world-view.** Chicago (1929) vii + 127 p.

Creel, H.G. Sinism — a clarification. **JHI** 10 (1949) 135-140.

Crofoot, J.W. The chinese idea of sin. **ChRec** 42.10 (oct 1911) 561-571.

Cua, Antonio S. Dimensions of li (propriety): reflections on an aspect of hsun tzu's ethics. **PEW** 29.4 (oct 1979) 373-394.

Danto, Arthur C. **Mysticism and morality: oriental thought and moral philosophy.** NY and london (1972) See chap 6, Conforming to the way, 101-120. Re the tao of lao tzu, chuang tzu, confucius.

Darroch, J. The etymology of the character for sin. **ChRec** 42.10 (oct 1911) 571-577.

Demiéville, Paul. Une descente aux enfers sous les t'ang: la biographie de houang che-k'iang. In **Études d'histoire et de littérature chinoises offertes au professeur jaroslav prusek,** paris (1976) 71-84.

Dictionary of the history of ideas. Studies of selected pivotal ideas. Phillip P. Wiener, ed-in-chief. NY (1968, 1973) See vol 5, Index, china, 55.

Donner, Neal. The mahāyānization of the chinese dhyāna tradition. **EB** 10.2 (oct 1977) 49-64.

Drake, F.S. The contribution of chinese religious thought. **ChRec** 72 (sept-oct 1941) 496-505, 537-545.

Dubs, Homer H. Theism and naturalism in ancient chinese philosophy. **PEW** 9 (1959-60) 163-172.

Dung Hwe Zi. The earliest historical idea of god in china. **ChRec** 62.8 (aug 1931) 486-493; 62.9 (sept 1931) 562-571.

Duperray, E. La survie dans la tradition religieuse chinoise. **Bulletin de la société saint-jean-baptiste** 8.7 (1968)

Durme, J. van. **La notion primitive de 'dieu' en chine.** Bruges (1927) 16 p.

Eberhard, Wolfram. Das astronomische weltbild im alten china. **Die naturwissenschaften** 24.33 (1936) 517-519.

Eberhard, Wolfram. **Beiträge zur kosmologischen spekulation der chinesen der han-zeit.** Berlin (1933) 100 p, diagr. Constitutes an art in **Baessler archiv** 16.1.

Eberhard, Wolfram. Fatalism in the life of the common man in noncommunist china. **Anthropological quarterly** 39 (1966) 148-160. Repr in author's **MSVC** (1971)

Eberhard, Wolfram. Fate in traditional chinese life. **Asian student** 13 (29 may 1965) 5-6.

Eberhard, Wolfram. **Guilt and sin in traditional china.** Univ california (1967) 141 p, gloss, bibliog, index.

Eberhard, Wolfram. Leben und gedanken des alltags-menschen in china. **Deutsche-china gesellschaft, mitteilungsblatt** 6 (1978) 2-9.

Eberhard, Wolfram. Sternkunde und weltbild im alten china. **Die sterne** 6 (1932) 129-138.

Eberhard, Wolfram. **Sternkunde und weltbild im alten china.** Taipei (1970) 417 p.

Eliade, Mircea. **Histoire des croyances et des idées religieuses. Vol 2, de gautama bouddha au triomphe du christianisme.** Paris (1978) Engl tsl Willard Trask, **A history of religious ideas. Vol 2, from gautama buddha to the triumph of christianity.** Univ chicago (1982) See chap 16, The religions of ancient china, 3-43; also, Present position of studies: problems and progress, critical bibliog, 419-433.

Eliade Mircea. **The sacred and the profane. The nature of religion** (German ed 1957) engl tsl Willard Trask, n.y. (1959) See sec Desacralization of nature (151-155) using 'miniature gardens' as example.

Erdberg-Consten, Eleanor von. Time and space in chinese cosmology. **Philippine quarterly of culture and society** 162 (1973) 120-131.

Erkes, Eduard. Ssu er pu wang [death without annihilation] **AM** 3.2 (1953) 156-161.

Erkes, E. Die totenbeigaben im alten china. **AA** 6 (1936-37) 17-36.

Forke, A. Chinesische und indianische philosophie. **ZDMG** 98 (1944) 195-237. Compares certain concepts: 1. Tao = brahaman, das absolute; 2. Wu-wei = nivrtti, passivität; 3. Wei-hsin lun = māyā, idealismus; 4. Chinesische anklänge an sāmkhya und yoga.

Forke, Alfred. Das unsterblichkeitsproblem in der chinesischen philosophie. **FF** 11 (1935) 114-115.

Forke, A. **The world-conception of the chinese.** London (1925) xiv + 300.

Franke, Wolfgang. Some remarks on lin chao-en (1517-1598) **OE** 20.2 (1973) 161-173.

Franke, Wolfgang. Some remarks on the "three-in-one doctrine" and its manifestations in singapore and malaysia. **OE** 19 (1972) 121-130; incl tsl of 2 inscriptions and 10 photo pl.

Frazier, Allie M. (ed) **Readings in eastern religious thought. Vol 3, Chinese and japanese religions.** Philadelphia (1969) See 1-176 for china.

Fu, Charles Wei-hsun. Morality or beyond: the neo-confucian confrontation with mahayana buddhism. **PEW** 23.3 (july 1973) 375-396.

C.G. l'Homme et l'univers. **EUF** (1968) vol 4, see Chine, sec 1, 263c-266c.

Galpin, Francis W. Notes concerning the chinese belief of evil spirits. **ChRec** 5.1 (jan-feb 1874) 42-50.

Girardot, Norman J. Chaotic "order" (hun-tun) and benevolent "disorder" (luan) in the chuang tzu. **PEW** 28.3 (july 1978) 300-321.

Girardot, Norman J. Myth and meaning in the tao te ching: chapters 25 and 42. **HR** 16 (1977) 294-328.

Girardot, Norman J. "Returning to the beginning" and the arts of mr. hun-tun in the chuang tzu. **JCP** 5 (1978) 21-69.

Glüer, Winfried. Salvation today—chinese interpretations. **CF** 16.1 (1973) 33-46.

Graham, D.C. Chinese yinyang and fengshui conceptions. **ChRec** 67.1 (jan 1936) 34-38; 67.3 (mar 1936) 166-172.

Graham, D.C. Mysterious potency in the chinese religion. **ChRec** 60 (1929) 235-237.

Granet, Marcel. **La pensée chinoise.** Paris (1934) xxiii + 611 p, bibliog, index.

Granet, Marcel. Tsl Rodney Needham. Right and left in china. In Rodney Needham (ed) **Right and left; essays on the dual symbolic classification,** univ chicago (1973) 43-58. Tsl fr **ESC** (1953) La droite et la gauche en chine, 261-278.

Granet, Marcel. La vie et la mort. Croyances et doctrines de l'antiquité chinoise. **AnnEPHE, sec des sciences religieuses (1920-21)** (1920) 1-22. Repr **ESC** (1953) 203-220.

Grava, Arnold. Tao: an age-old concept in its modern perspectives. **PEW** 13 (1963) 235-249.

Grison, P. Formes et formules traditionelles, VIII. La voie du ciel. **FA** 106 (1955) 507-513.

Groot, J.J.M.de, **The religious system of china.** Leiden (1892-1910) Repr taipei (1964) 6 vol. 1-3: Disposal of the dead; 4-6: The soul and ancestral worship. Compte rendu par Éd. Chavannes, **RHR** 37 (1898) 81-89.

Gynz-Rekowski, Georg v. Die psyche des menschen in der europäischen und chinesischen kunst. In **ATOW** (1967) 245-258.

Hackmann, Heinrich F. **Chinesische philosophie.** München (1927) 406 p.

Harlez, Charles de. **Essai d'anthropologie chinoise.** N.p. (?Bruxelles) n.d. (?1895) Re basic relig ideas of the chin.

Harper, Donald J. The han cosmic board (shih) **EC** 4 (1978-79) 1-10. See further C. Cullen, Some further points on the shih, **ibid** 6 (1980-81) 31-46; and Harper's The han cosmic board: a response to Christopher Cullen, **ibid** 47-56.

Harrell, Stevan. The concept of "soul" in chinese folk religion. **JAS** 38.3 (may 1979) 519-528.

Harrell, C. Stevan. When a ghost becomes a god. In **RRCS** (1974) 193-206.

Hay, Eldon R. Religion and the death of god: hsün tzu and rubenstein. **SEAJT** 11 (spring 1970) 83-93.

Hoare, J.C. **God and man in the chinese classics, a short study of confucian theology.** Ningpo (1895) 52 p. Same title in **ChRec** 26 (1895) 201-210, 260-270.

Hodous, Lewis. Chinese conceptions of paradise. **ChRec** 45.6 (june 1914) 358-371.

Hodous, Lewis. Mo-ti and christianity. **IRM** 13 (apr 1924) 258-266.

Hoffheimer, Daniel J. Science and symbolism in chinese astronomy. **Synthesis; the undergraduate journal in the history and philosophy of science** 1.4 (1973) 24-34.

Hsiang, Paul S. God in ancient china. **Worldmission** 7 (1956) 224-232.

Hsiang, Paul S. The humanism in the religious thought of ancient china. **CC** 10 (sept 1969) 13-21.

Hsiao, Paul Shih-yi. Der chinesische mensch in philosophisch-religiöser sicht. In **ATOW** (1967) 223-235.

Hsin, Kwan-chue. Tao—the source of creativity. **ACQ** 7.4 (winter 1979) 27-36.

Hsu, Cho-yun. The concept of predetermination and fate in the han. **EC** 1 (fall 1975) 51-56.

Hsu, Dau-lin. Crime and cosmic order. **HJAS** 30 (1970) 111-125.

Hsu, Sung-peng. Lao tzu's conception of evil. **PEW** 26.3 (1976) 301-316.

Hsu, Sung-peng. Lao tzu's conception of ultimate reality: a comparative study. **IPQ** 16.2 (june 1976) 197-217.

Hu, Shih. The concept of immortality in chinese thought. **Harvard divinity school bulletin** (1946) 23-43.

Hu, Shih. The natural law in the chinese tradition. In **NLIP** 5 (1953) 119-153.

Huang, Siu-chi. The moral point of view of chang tsai. **PEW** 21.2 (apr 1971) 145-156.

Hudson, W.H. Gods and demons: some current chinese conceptions. **ChRec** 51.8 (aug 1920) 550-556.

Ikeda, Suetoshi. Die eigentliche chinesische religion und yin-yang gedanke. **JRelSt** 38.3 (1965)

Ideda, Suetoshi. The origin and development of the wu-hsing (five elements) idea: a preliminary essay. **E&W** n.s. 16.3/4 (1966) 297-309.

Izutsu, Toshihiko. The i ching mandala and confucian metaphysics. **EJ** 1976 (1980) 363-404. Re I ching, ho-t'u, lo-shu, t'ai-chi-t'u.

James, E.O. **Creation and cosmology. A historical and comparative inquiry.** Leiden (1969) See chap 3, India and the far east.

James, F. Huberty. The theism of china. **New world** 6 (1897) 307-323. Same title in **ChRec** 28 (1897) 481-487, 516-524.

Jochim, Christian. Ethical analysis of an ancient debate: moists versus confucians. **JRE** 8.1 (1980) 135-147.

Johnson, W.S. A chinese view of immortality. **HJ** 36 (1937-38) 287-292. Re Hu Shih and his "social immortality"

Ju, I-hsiung. The ancient chinese metaphysical characters through the oracle writing. **UNITAS** 42.1 (mar 1969) entire issue, 1-155, illus. See chap 3, The metaphysical concepts in oracle characters, 67-110.

Katō, Jōken. **Religion and thought in ancient china.** Cambridge (1953) 44 p.

Katō, Jōken. Religion and thought in ancient china. **JSR:LPH** 8 (1957) 17-19.

Kim, Ha Tai. Transcendence without and within: the concept of t'ien in confucianism. **International journal for philosophy of religion** 3.3 (fall 1972) 146-160.

Kimura, Eiichi. Taoism and chinese thought. **ActaA** 27 (1974) 1-18.

Kuan, Feng & Lin, Lü-shih. Development of thought and the birth of materialistic philosophy at the end of the western chou and the beginning of the eastern chou. **CSP** 2.1-2 (fall-winter 1970-71) 54-79.

Kuan, Feng & Lin, Lü-shih. Thought of the yin dynasty and the western chou. **CSP** 2.1-2 (fall-winter 1970-71) 4-53.

Kühnert, J. Entst. d. welt u.d. wesen d. menschen n. china anschauung. **Ausland** 66 (1893) 150-154.

Lacy, Carleton. Ethical values in chinese monism. **ChRec** 62.1 (jan 1931) 29-32.

Lambert, William W, Leigh M. Triandit & Margery Wolf. Some correlates of beliefs in the malevolence and benevolence of supernatural beings: a cross-societal study. **Journal of abnormal and social psychology** 58 (1959) 162-169.

Lamont, H.G. (tsl) An early ninth century debate on heaven: liu tsung-yüan's t'ien shuo and liu yü-hsi's t'ien lun. **AM** 18.2 (1973) 181-208; 19.1 (1974) 37-85.

Larre, Claude. Le sens de la transcendance dans la pensée chinoise. **Concilium** 146 (1979) 59-67. Re t'ien in ancient confucianism and taoism.

Laufer, Berthold. Religious and artistic thought in ancient china. **AArch** 6 (1917) 295-310.

Lee, Jung Young. Yin-yang way of thinking: a possible way for ecumenical theology. **IRM** 60 (july 1971) 363-370.

Legge, James. **The notions of the chinese concerning god and spirits.** Hong kong (1852) repr taipei (1971) Re proper tsl of basic religious terms.

Lemaître, Solange. **Le mystère de la mort dans les religions d'asie.** Paris (1943) xi + 151 p.

Liebenthal, Walter. The immortality of the soul in chinese thought. **MN** 8 (1952) 327-397.

Liebenthal, W. On trends in chinese thought. In **SJV** (1954) 262-278.

Liu, Shu-hsien. Theism from a chinese perspective. **PEW** 28.4 (oct 1978) 413-418.

Liu, Ts'un-yan. Lu hsi-hsing: a confucian scholar, taoist priest and buddhist devotee of the sixteenth century. **AS** 18/19 (1965) 115-142; repr in **LTY:SP** (1976)

Loewe, Michael. **Ways to paradise. The chinese quest for immortality.** London (1979) 270 p, illus, app, notes. Based on han dyn relics.

Lu, Martin. The confucian view of immortality and its cultural implications. Singapore, **Review of southeast asian studies** 7 (1977) 47-59.

Lübke, A. **Der himmel der chinesen.** Leipzig (1931) 141 p.

MacGowan, John. **Sidelights on chinese life.** London (1907) illus. See chap 10, Hades, or the land of shadows, 201-223.

Machle, Edward J. Hsün tzu as a religious philosopher. **PEW** 26.4 (1976) 443-461.

Maclagan, Patrick J. **Chinese religious ideas: a christian valuation.** London (1926) 238 p.

Mahdihassan, S. Indian and chinese cosmic elements. **AJCM** 7.4 (1979) 316-323.

Mahdihassan, S.The term chhi: its past and present significance. **CME&W** 6.4 (1978) 272-276.

Major, John S. Myth, cosmology, and the origins of chinese science. **JCP** 5.1 (mar 1978) 1-20.

Martin, W.A.P. The speculative philosophy of the chinese. **American journal of theology** 1 (1897) 289-297.

McClelland, Hardin T. Religion and philosophy in ancient china. **OC** 36 (1922) 35-49, 102-115, 174-187. Brief sketch, more on philosophy than relig; despite title, goes through chu hsi.

M'Clatchie, M.T. The chinese on the plain of shinar, or a connection between the chinese and all other nations through their theology. **JRAS** 16 (1856) 368-435.

M'Clatchie, Thomas. **Confucian cosmogony. A translation of section forty-nine of the 'complete works' of the philosopher choo-foo-tze,, with explanatory notes.** Shanghai (1874) xviii + 161 p, incl chin text.

Mew, James. **Traditional aspects of hell (ancient and modern)** London (1903) repr ann arbor, mich (1971) See, Buddhist hell, esp 43-102. Incl H.A. Giles tsl of yü li ch'ao chuan, with illus.

Moreau, J. La pensée de l'asie et l'astrobiologie d'après m. rené berthelot. **RMM** 48 (1941) 48-73.

Morgan, Evan. Destiny, fate. **JNCBRAS** 51 (1920) 25-44.

Morgan, Evan. An inquiry into the meaning of the term shang-ti. **ChRec** 72.3 (mar 1941) 134-138.

Nakamura, Hajime. **Parallel developments. A comparative history of ideas.** Tokyo (1975) xx + 567 p. On chin relig see passim.

Needham, Joseph. The cosmology of early china. In Carmen Blacker and Michael Loewe (ed) **Ancient cosmologies,** london (1975) 87-109.

Neville, Robert. From nothing to being: the notion of creation in chinese and western thought. **PEW** 30.1 (jan 1980) 21-34.

Notices of chinese cosmogony: formation of the visible universe, heaven, earth, the sun, moon, stars, man, beasts &c., selected from the complete works of chu hi of the sung dynasty. **ChRep** 18.7 (july 1849) 342-347.

Overmyer, Daniel L. China. Chap 6 in Frederick H. Holck (ed) **Death and eastern thought,** nashville & ny (1974) 198-225.

Overmyer, Daniel L. Dualism and conflict in chinese popular religion. In **T&T** (1980) 153-184.

Overmyer, Daniel L. Folk-buddhist religion: creation and eschatology in medieval china. **HR** 12.1 (aug 1972) 42-70.

Paper, Jordan D. The early development of chinese cosmology. **CC** 15.2 (june 1974) 15-25. Re wu-hsing and yin yang.

Parrinder, Geoffrey. **Sex in the world's religions.** Oxford univ (1980) See chap 5, Chinese yin and yang, 77-102.

Pauthier, G. **Lettre inédite du p. prémare sur le monothéisme des chinois** . . . Paris (1861) 54 p.

Pelliot, Paul. Die jenseitsvorstellung der chinesen. **Eranos** 7 (1939) 61-82.

Podgorski, Frank. Reading the holy books of china. **JD** 3.3 (july-sep 1978) 309-317. Re ancient confucian and taoist classics.

Pott, William S. A. Further observations on the confucian god-idea. **ChRec** 50.12 (dec 1919) 825-833. See Y.Y. Tsu, The confucian god-idea, **Ibid** 50.5 (may 1919) 294-306.

Raguin, Yves. Mediation dans le bouddhisme et le taoïsme. **SM** 21 (1972) 77-92.

Ranasinghe, Alex. The chinese dragon, its significance and the chinese response to it. **ABQCSA** 4.3 (winter 1972) 33-43. A genl discussion of chin relig ideas.

Rawlinson, Frank J. **Chinese ideas of the supreme being.** Shanghai (1927) 57 p.

Rawlinson, Frank. Some chinese ideas of the supreme being. **ChRec** 57.11 (nov 1926) 796-812.

Rawlinson, Frank. Some chinese ideas of god. **ChRec** 50.7 (july 1919) 461-468; 50.8 (aug 1919) 545-552; 50.9 (sep 1919) 613-621.

Rawlinson, Frank. A prevalent chinese theory of the universe. **ChRec** 57.9 (sep 1926) 644-658. Viz, it is an "ethical universe"

Reischauer, August Karl. **The nature and truth of the great religions.** Tokyo (1966) See sec A:VI, The god-concept in chinese religion, 63-75; sec B:V, Chinese religion and the good life, 122-147; sec C:VI, Chinese religion and individual destiny, 171-173.

Réveillère, le contre-admiral. Philosophie de la religion chinoise. **Revue d'europe** 9 (mars 1902) 194-197; **RIC** 5, no 187 (19 mai 1902) 448-449.

Ross, John. Chinese classical theology. **ChRec** 33.9 (1902) 436-438.

Ross, John (tsl) Shang-ti. **ChRec** 25.3 (mar 1894) 123-129. Tsl of an essay by "the chief taoist priest of manchuria"

Rousselle, E. Konfuzius und das archaische weltbild der chinesischen frühzeit. **Saeculum** 5 (1954) 1-33.

Rowley, H.H. The chinese philosopher mo ti. **JRLB** 31 (1948) 241-276. For "religious elements" see 271-276.

Ruyer, R. Dieu-personne et dieu-tao. **RMM** 52 (1947) 141-157.

Saint Ina, Marie de. China's contribution to the spiritual foundation of humanity. **IPQ** 6.3 (sept 1966) 445-454. Mostly on i-ching theory.

Saso, Michael. What is the ho-t'u? **HR** 17.3/4 (feb-may 1978) 399-416.

Saussure, Léopold de. La cosmologie religieuse en chine, dans l'iran et chez les prophètes hébreux. **Actes du CIHR, 1923,** paris (1925)

Saussure, L. de. Le système cosmologique sino-iranien. **JA** 202 (1923) 235-297.

Schafer, Edward H. **Pacing the void. T'ang approaches to the stars.** Univ calif (1977) 352 p, illus, app, notes, bibliog, gloss, index.

Schiffeler, John William. The traditional concept of soul in chinese philosophy. **CC** 17.2 (june 1976) 51-56.

Schindler, Bruno. The development of chinese conceptions of supreme beings. **AMHAV** (1923) 298-366.

Schmidt, P. Persian dualism in the far east. In **OSCEP** (1933) 405-406.

Schwartz, Benjamin. Speculations on the beginnings of chinese thought. **EC** 2 (fall 1976) 47-50.

Schwartz, Benjamin. Transcendence in ancient china. **Daedalus** (spring 1975) 57-68.

Seidel, Anna. Buying one's way to heaven: the celestial treasury in chinese religions. **HR** 17.3/4 (feb-may 1978) 419-431. Rev art on Hou Ching-lang, **Monnaies d'offrande et la notion de trésorerie dans la religion chinoise** q.v.

Shih, Joseph. The ancient chinese cosmogony. **SM** 18 (1969) 111-130.

Shih, Joseph. God and man in early taoism. In **Religions; fundamental themes for a dialogic understanding.** Rome (1970)

Shih, J. Mediation in chinese religion. **SM** 21 (1972) 77-92. Mostly concerned with the li.

Shih, Joseph. The notions of god in the ancient chinese religion. **Numen** 16 (1969) 99-138.

Shih, Joseph. The tao: its essence, its dynamism, and its fitness as a vehicle of christian rvelation. **SM** 15 (1966) 117f.

Shih, Joseph. The two theological schools in the late chou china (722-221 b.c.) **SM** 16 'Religious glimpses of eastern asia' (1967) 9-35.

Shih, Vincent Y.C. A critique of motzu's religious views and related concepts. In Hong kong univ dept chin, **Symposium on chinese studies . . .** Hong kong (1968) vol 3, 1-17.

Simbriger, Heinrich. Betrachtungen über yang und yin. **Antaios** 7 (1965) 126-148.

Sjöholm, Gunnar. Observations on the chinese ideas of fate. In Helmer Ringgren (ed) **Fatalistic beliefs in religion, folklore and literature,** stockholm (1967) 126-132.

Smith, D. Howard. Chinese concepts of the soul. **Numen** 5 (1958) 165-179.

Smith, D. Howard. Conflicting ideas of salvation in a.d. fifth century china. In Eric J. Sharpe & John R. Hinnells (ed) **Man and his salvation; studies in memory of s.f.g. brandon,** manchester univ (1973) 291-303.

Smith, D. Howard. Saviour gods in chinese religion. In **SG** (1963) 174-190.

Smith, Huston. Transcendence in traditional china. **RS** 2 (1967) 185-196.

Smith, Wilfred C. **The faith of other men.** Toronto (1962) n.y. (1963) See chap 5, The chinese, 67-80.

The soul of an idol. **Our missions** 12 (1905) 30.

Steininger, Hans. Der heilige herrscher, sein tao und sein praktisches tun. In **SJFAW** (1956) 170-177.

Strausz und D.V. von Torney. **Der altchinesische monotheismus.** Heidelberg (1885)

Suzuki, Daisetz T. Zen buddhism on immortality: an extract from the hekiganshu. **EB** 3 (1924-25) 213-223.

T'ang Chün-i. Cosmologies in ancient chinese philosophy. **CSP** 5.1 (fall 1973) 4-47.

Taylor, Rodney L. Religion and utilitarianism: mo tzu on spirits and funerals. **PEW** 29.3 (july 1979) 337-346.

The Ten courts of hades. **Echo** 4.7 (july-aug 1974) 37-51, 60, illus.

Thompson, Laurence G. Objectifying divine power: some chinese modes. In Spencer J. Palmer (ed) **Deity and death,** brigham young univ (1978) 135-145.

Tien, Antoine Tcheu-kang. **l'Idée de dieu dans les huit premiers classiques chinois. Ses noms, son existence et sa nature étudiée à la lumière des découvertes archéologiques.** Fribourg (1942) 224 p.

Tong, P.K.K. Study of thematic differences between eastern and western religious thought. **Journal of ecumenical studies** 10 (spring 1973) 337-360.

Tscharner, E.H. von. Leben und tod im denken der grossen chinesischen weisen. **MSGFOK** 6 (1944) 69-95.

Tschen, Yuan. Johann adam schall von bell und der bonze mu tschen-wen. **MS** 5 (1940) 316-328.

Tsu, Y.Y. The confucian god-idea. **ChRec** 50.5 (may 1919) 294-306.

Tsu, Y.Y. The chinese idea of worship. **ChRec** 45.10 (oct 1914) 615-625.

Tu, Wei-ming. The confucian perception of adulthood. **Daedalus** 105.2 (apr 1976) 109-123; repr in **H&SC** (1979) 35-56.

Tu, Wei-ming. The creative tension between jen and li. **PEW** 18.1/2 (jan-apr 1968) 29-39; repr in **H&SC** (1979 5-16.

Tu, Wei-ming. Hsiung shih-li's quest for authentic existence. In Charlotte Furth (ed) **The limits of change: essays on conservative alternatives in republican china,** harvard univ (1976) 242-275, 366-400; repr in **H&SC** (1979) 219-256.

Tu, Wei-ming. **Humanity and self-cultivation: essays in confucian thought.** Berkeley, calif (1979) xxii + 364 p, gloss, sel bibliog, index. Essays sep listed in our bibliog. Abbrev **H&SC.**

Tu, Wei-ming. An inquiry into wang yang-ming's four sentence teaching. **EB** n.s. 7.2 (oct 1974) 32-48; repr in **H&SC** (1979) 162-178.

Tu-Wei-ming. Li as a process of humanization. **PEW** 22.2 (apr 1972) 187-201; repr in **H&SC** (1979) 17-34.

Tu, Wei-ming. Mind and human nature. **JAS** 30.3 (may 1971) 642-647; repr in **H&SC** (1979) 111-118. Rev art on Mou Tsung-san's work on neo-confucian thought.

Tu, Wei-ming. On the mencian perception of moral self-development. **Monist** 66.1 (jan 1978) 72-81; repr in **H&SC** (1979) 57-68.

Tu, Wei-ming. Reconstituting the confucian tradition. **JAS** 33.3 (may 1974) 441-454; repr in **H&SC** (1979) 119-137. Rev art on Ch'ien Mu's book on chu hsi.

Tu-Wei-ming. Subjectivity and ontological reality: an interpretation of wang yang-ming's mode of thinking. **PEW** 23.1/2 (jan-apr 1973) 187-205; repr in **H&SC** (1979) 138-161.

Tu, Wei-ming. Transformational thinking as philosophy. **PEW** 24 (jan-apr 1976) 75-80; repr in **H&SC** (1979) 179-185. Rev art on Ronald Dimberg, **The sage and society.**

Tu, Wei-ming. The unity of knowing and acting: from a neo-confucian perspective. In T.M.P. Mahadevan (ed) **Philosophy: theory and practice,** madras (1970) 190-205; repr in **H&SC** (1979) 83-101.

Tu, Wei-ming. Yen yüan: from inner experience to lived concreteness. In W.T. de Bary (ed) **The unfolding of neo-confucianism,** columbia univ (1975) 511-541; repr in **H&SC** (1979) 186-215.

Tucci, G. The demoniacal in the far east. **E&W** 4 (1953) 3-11.

Ubelhör, Monika. Geistesströmungen der späten ming-zeit, die als wirken der jesuiten in china begünstigten. **Saeculum** 23.2 (1972) 172-185.

Vandier-Nicolas, Nicole. Le jugement des morts en chine. In **Le jugement des morts,** paris (1961) 231-254. 'Sources orientales' no. 4.

Vale, J. The chinese idea of salvation. **ChRec** 46.4 (apr 1915) 211-220.

Vandermeersch, Léon. La conception chinoise des rites. Aix-marseille, **Cahiers linguistique d'orientalisme et de slavistique** 8 (july 1976) 75-86.

Vandermeersch, Léon. **Wangdao ou la voie royale. Recherches sur l'esprit des insitutions de la chine archaïque. Tome 1, Structures cultuelles et structures familiales.** Paris (1977) 358 p. **Tome 2, Structures politiques, les rites.** Paris (1980) 603 p, tables, index. See Table générale des matières.

Veith, Ilza. Psychiatric thought in chinese medicine. **JHMAS** 10.3 (july 1955) 261-268.

Voskamp, C.J. Die animistischen vorstellung im volks-glauben der chinesen. **Religion und geisteskult** 7 (1913) 207-212.

J.W. Die ansichten der chinesen über die seelen-wanderung. **OstL** 13 (1899) 341-342.

Wallace, Westwood. Religious elements in the writings of motse. **ChRec**. 62.9 (sep 1931) 557-561.

Wei, Tat. Confucius and the i-ching. In Finley P. Dunne, jr (ed) **The world religions speak on 'the relevance of religion in the modern world',** the hague (1970) 64-71.

Werner, E.T.C. **The chinese idea of the second self.** Shanghai (1932) 49 p.

Werner, E.T.C. Rebuttal notes on chinese religion and dynastic tombs. **JNCBRAS** 56 (1925) 134-148. Rebuttal of F. Ayscough's critical comment in her Cult of the ch'eng huang lao yeh, **JNCBRAS** 55 (1924)

White, Hugh W. **Demonism verified and analyzed.** Shanghai (1922)

Wienpahl, Paul. Spinoza and wang yang-ming. **RS** 5 (1969) 1927.

Wilhelm, Hellmut. A note on sun ch'o and his yü-tao-lun. **SIS** 5.3/4 Liebenthal festschrift (1957) 261-271.

Wilhelm, Hellmut. Wanderungen des geistes. **EJ** 33 (1964) 177-200. Examples fr literature and the yi ching.

Wilhelm, Richard. Chinesische schicksalsbeherrschung. **CBWK** 1.3 (1926) 88-103.

Wilhelm, Richard. **Der mensch und das sein.** Jena (1931) 338 s. Re-issued as **Wandlung und dauer. Die weisheit des i ging,** düsseldorf-köln (1956) See passim.

Wilhelm, Richard. Tod und erneuerung nach der ostasiatischen welt-auffassung. **CDA** (1929-30) 49-69. Engl tsl Jane A. Pratt, Death and renewal. **Spring** (1962) 20-44; also tsl Irene Eber, Death and renewal, in Eber's tsl, **Lectures on the i ching. Constancy and change,** princeton univ (1979) 135-165.

Winance, Eleuthère. A forgotten chinese thinker: mo tzu. **IPQ** 1.4 (dec 1969) 593-619. Emphasizes religious aspects of his thought.

Wu, Joseph S. Some humanistic characteristics of chinese religious thought. **RS** 5 (1969) 99-103.

Yang, C.K. The functional relation between confucian thought and chinese religion. In **CTI** (1957) 269-290.

Yang, Thaddeus. Tsl Fr McGlade. The chinese philosopher and st. thomas aquinas. **Worldmission** 3.1 (spring 1952) 40-51.

Yao Shan-yu. The cosmological and anthropological philosophy of tung chung-shu. **JNCBRAS** 73 (1948) 40-68.

Yearley, Lee H. Mencius on human nature: the forms of his religious thought. **JAAR** 43.2 (june 1975) 187-198.

Yearley, Lee H. Toward a typology of religious thought: a chinese example. **JR** 55.4 (oct 1975) 426-443.

Yeh, E.K. The chinese mind and human freedom. **IJSP** 18 (1972) 132-136.

Young, John D. The cosmological gulf between china and the west. **CF** 23.2 (1980) 102-108.

Yü, Ying-shih. Life and immortality in the mind of han china. **HJAS** 25 (1964-65) 80-122.

7. CONFUCIUS AND CONFUCIANISM
(For entries concerning the politically motivated anti-Confucian campaign in the 1970s, see also Section 37: in Peoples Republic)

Allen, Herbert J. The connexion between taoism, confucianism and buddhism in early days. **Trans 3rd ICHR**, oxford (1908) vol 1, 115-119.

Amberley, Viscount. **An analysis of religious belief.** London (1876) See vol 1, pt 2: Means of communication downwards. V. Holy persons. Sec 1. Confucius.

Ancient dance honoring the sage. **Vista** [Taipei] 4 (1975) 14-20.

Arlington, Lewis Charles. **Some remarks on the worship offered confucius in the confucian temple.** Peiping (1935) 8 + 20 p, pl. China chronicle 10.

Armstrong, Alexander. **Shantung (china): a general outline of the geography and history . . . and notes of a journey to the tomb of confucius.** Shanghai (1891). See sec 3, The burial place of confucius, 181-186.

Ashmore, William. A moral problem solved by confucian-ism. **ChRec** 2.10 (mar 1870) 282-285.

Ashmore, William. The ideal man of confucius. **ChRec** 3.4 (sep 1870) 89-92.

Atkins, Gaius G. and Charles S. Braden. **Procession of the gods.** N.Y. and london (1930 et seq) 3rd rev ed (1948) See chap 11, Confucianism and the religion of heaven, 325-361.

Aziz-us-Samad, Mrs. Ulfat. **The great religions of the world.** Lahore (1976) See Confucianism, 91-106.

Bach, Marcus. **Had you been born in another faith.** Englewood cliffs, n.j. (1961) See chap 4, Had you been born a confucianist, 63-82.

Bahm, Archie J. **The world's living religions.** Southern illinois univ (1964) See pt 2, Religions of china and japan; confucianism, p 175-198.

Baker, Dwight Condo. Gates of the sages. A pilgrimage in the land of lu (south shantung) **CJ** 4.1 (jan 1926) 23-30, photos.

Baker, N. Confucianism. In J.N.D. Anderson (ed) **The world's religions,** london (1950)

Balazs, Étienne. Confucius. In **AC** t 1 (1959) 142-145.

Baldwin, S.L. Confucianism. In **DR** (1884) 378-419.

Ballou, Robert O. et al (ed) **The bible of the world.** N.Y. (1939) See sec Confucianist scriptures, 379-467.

Bauer, Wolfgang. **China und die hoffnung auf glück. Paradies, utopien, idealvorstellungen.** München (1971) Tsl Michael Shaw, **China and the search for happiness,** ny (1976) 502 p, chron table, notes, bibliog, index. See rev art by Vitali Rubin, **TP** 59 (1973) 68-78.

Beach, Harlan P. The ethics of confucianism. In E. Hershey Sneath (ed) **The evolution of ethics as revealed in the great religions,** yale univ (1927) 39-74.

Bergen, P.D. The sages of shantung. In Robert C. Forsyth (ed) **Shantung, the sacred province of china,** shanghai (1912) 9-23. Re confucius.

Bergeron, Marie-Ina. La mystique de confucius. In **EMM** (1975) 181-194.

Biallas, Franz Xaver. **Konfuzius und sein kult. Ein beitrag zur kulturgeschichte chinas und ein führer zur heimatsstadt des konfuzius.** Peking (1928) 130 p, illus, plans.

Bieg, Lutz. Die geistigen kräfte des alten china: der konfuzianismus. In Eduard J.M. Kroker (ed) **China: auf dem weg zur "grossen harmonie"** stuttgart (1974) 12-28.

Bishop, Carl W. Shantung: china's holy land. **UPUMB** 12.2 (june 1921) 85-115.

Bonsall, Bramwell S. **Confucianism and Taoism.** London (1934) 127 p.

Braden, Charles S. **Jesus compared. Jesus and other great founders of religions.** Englewood cliffs, n.j. (1957) See Jesus and confucius, 108-131.

Braden, Charles S. (comp) **The scriptures of mankind: an introduction.** N.Y. (1952) See chap 9, The sacred literature of the chinese: Confucian, 236-273.

Bradley, David G. **A guide to the world's religions.** Englewood cliffs, n.j. (1963) See chap 15, Confucianism, 141-149.

Brou, Alexandre. Bulletin des missions chine: le défaite de confucius. **Études** (20 nov 1917) 493-506.

Brou, Alexandre. La nouvelle chine et le culte de confucius. **RC** (janv-avril 1918) 3-15, illus.

Brown, Brian. **The story of confucius, his life and sayings.** Philadelphia (1927) 265 p, pl.

Brown, David A. **A guide to religions.** London (1975) See chap 9, Two chinese religions, 89-103. Re confucianism and taoism.

Browne, Lewis (comp) **The world's great scriptures. An anthology of the sacred books of the ten principal religions.** N.Y. (1946) See sec The scriptures of confucianism, 209-291.

Burrell, David J. **The religions of the world.** Philadelphia (1902) See chap 8, Confucianism, 231-262.

Burrows, Millar. **Founders of the great religions. Being personal sketches of lao-tse, confucius, buddha, jesus, etc.** London and n.y. (1931) 243 p.

Burtt, Edwin A. **Man seeks the divine.** N.Y. (1957) See chap 6, Confucianism, 153-184.

Carus, Paul. Ceremony celebrated under the chinese republic in honor of confucius. **OC** 32.3 (mar 1918) 155-172, illus.

Cauvin, le Dr. Excursion au tai-chann et au tombeau de confucius. **RGI** 9 (août-sept-nov 1884) 10 (janv — nov 1885) 12 (janv 1887)

Cavin, Albert. **Le confucianisme.** Paris (1968) 295 p, illus.

Chai, Ch'u & Winberg Chai. Confucianism and taoism. In **RS&P** (1973) 180-194.

Champion, Selwyn G. and Dorothy Short (comp) **Readings from world religions.** Boston (1951) See chap 7, Confucianism, 126-144.

Chan, Wing-tsit. Chinese and western interpretations of jen (humanity) **JCP** 2 (1974-75) 107-129.

Chan, Wing-tsit. Chu hsi's appraisal of lao tzu. In **MS/CA** (1977) 5-9.

Chan, Wing-tsit. Confucianism. In Vergilius Ferm (ed) **Religion in the twentieth century,** paterson, n.j. (1948) 95-111. Paperbk ed (1965) entitled **Living schools of religion.**

Chan, Wing-tsit. Confucianism. **EncyB** 3 (1974) **Macropaedia** vol 6, 305a-310b.

Chan, Wing-tsit. The orderly realm of the chinese sages. In **Great religions of the world,** National geographic society (1971) 1922-129, illus. See also 2 p of texts fr analects et al, 167-168.

Chang, Chi-yun. Tsl Wen-yen Tsao. Confucius' contribution to world civilization. **CC** 15.3 (sep 1974) 1-8.

Chang, Chi-yun. Tsl Orient Lee. Confucius' philosophy of life. **CC** 21.3 (sep 1980) 1-38. Chap 2 of author's **Confucianism: a modern interpretation.**

Chang, Chi-yun. Tsl Orient Lee. The great confucius. **CC** 21.2 (june 1980) 1-56. Chap 1 of author's **Confucianism: a modern interpretation.**

Chang, Ch'i-yun. **A life of confucius.** Tsl fr chin Shih, Chao-yin. Taipei (1954) 113 p.

Chang, Chi-yun. A life of confucius. **CC** 16.2 (june 1975) 13-36.

Chang, Chi-yun. Ralph waldo emerson and confucius. **SAR** 1.3 (1975) 54-60.

Chang, Chi-yun. A system of cardinal values for ideal personality and ideal society: confucianism as a world religion. **CC** 21.3 (sep 1980) 39-70.

Chang, Hsin-hai. The essentials of confucian wisdom. **HJ** 26 (1927-28) 410-426.

Chang, Joseph. Confucius était-il agnostique ou croyant? **Mission bulletin** 6 (1954) 421-426, 547-551.

Chao, Paul. Human nature and the concept of sin in confucianism and christianity. **CC** 16.2 (june 1975) 45-62.

Chao, T.C. Christianity and confucianism. **IRM** 17 (oct 1928) 588-600.

Chen, Pin. Confucius the man. **FCR** 28.9 (sep 1978) 22-28.

Cheng, Ching-yi. Tsl J. Leighton Stuart. Translation of protest against the movement in favor of making confucianism a state religion. **ChRec** 44.11 (nov 1913) 687-692.

Cheng, Chung-ying. Dialectic of confucian morality and metaphysics of man. **PEW** 21.2 (apr 1971) 111-123.

Cheng, Chung-ying. On yi as a universal principle of specific application in confucian morality. **PEW** 22.3 (july 1972) 261-280.

Cheng, Chung-ying. Religious reality and religious understanding in confucianism and neo-confucianism. **IPQ** 13.1 (mar 1973) 33-62.

Cheng, Chung-ying. Theory and practice in confucianism. **JCP** 1.2 (mar 1974) 179-198.

Cheng, F.T. Confucianity (sic) and the individual. **CC** 15.2 (june 1974) 4-14.

Cheng, T'ien-hsi. Confucius. The man and his teachings. **AR** (jan 1950)

Chi, Lin. Anti-confucian struggles of peasant insurgents. **CL** 7 (july 1974) 86-92.

Chiang, Tien. The struggle between the confucian and legalists in the history of chinese literature and art. **CL** 7 (july 1975) 94-102.

Ching, Julia. Confucianism: a critical re-assessment of the heritage. **IPQ** 15.1 (mar 1975) 3-33.

Ching, Julia. Confucianism: a philosophy of man. In **C&C** (1979) 8-34.

Ching, Julia. **Confucianism and christianity: a comparative study.** Tokyo etc (1977) xxvi + 234 p, notes, bibliog, index.

Ching, Julia. Confucius and his modern critics: 1916 to the present. **PFEH** 10 (1974) 117-146.

Ching, Julia. Hyphenated christianity. **CN** 16.3 (summer 1978) 33-36. Incl some discussion of "what is confucianism?"

Ching, Julia. The problem of god in confucianism. **IPQ** 17.1 (mar 1977) 3-32.

Ching, Julia. The problem of self-transcendence in confucianism and christianity—prayer, meditation, mysticism, cult. **CF** 19.2 (1976) 81-97.

Ching, Julia. Truth and ideology: the confucian way (tao) and its transmission (tao-t'ung) **JHI** 36.3 (july-sep 1974) 371-388.

Ching, Julia. Will confucianism survive? A critical re-assessment of the heritage. **CF** 18.4 (1975) 197-218.

Chiu, Koon-noi. The religious elements in the teaching of confucius. **CSPSR** 12 (1928) 237-250; 431-450.

Chou, Chung-i. The common points in the opinion of chinese buddhists and confucianists. **West and East** 14 (apr 1969) 8-10.

Clarke, James F. **Ten great religions.** Boston and n.y. (1871) See chap 2, Confucius and the chinese, or the prose of asia, 32-76.

Clopin, Camille. Comparaison entre lao-tse, pythagore et confucius. Résultats définitifs pour la chine des deux doctrines examinées par m. milloué dans une conférence au musée guimet. **La géographie** 27.3 (1920) 60 p.

Cohen, Maurice. Confucius and socrates. **JCP** 3.2 (mar 1976) 159-168.

Cole, A. Confucianism today. **Christianity today** 4.6 (21 dec 1959) 16-18, 25.

Confucianism. In Henry O. Dwight, H. Allen Tapper jr, and Edwin M. Bliss (ed) **The encyclopedia of missions,** n.y. and london (2nd ed 1910) 188-193.

Confucianism: religion and ethics. A special issue of **PEW** 21.2 (apr 1971) Art sep listed in our bibliog.

Confucius. In Larousse, **Grande dictionnaire universel,** paris (préface 1865) t 4, p 919-921.

Confucius' reactionary ideas about music. **CL** 8 (aug 1974) 94-98.

Contag, Victoria. **Konfuzianische bildung und bildwelt.** Zürich and stuttgart (1964) xxxi + 296 p, 20 bildtafeln.

Cordier, Henri. Le confucianisme et le shinto. **Revue du clergé français** (1 fev 1911) 257-273.

Cordier, Henri. Confucius. In **La grande encyclopédie,** paris (n.d.) t 12, p 397-399.

Couchod, Paul. Tsl fr french Frances Rumsay. **Japanese impressions with a note on confucius.** London (1921) See Confucius, 131-155; mostly re visit by author to ch'ü-fu.

Couchoud, Paul Louis (tsl) **Une visite au tombeau de confucius avec une note de lin tcheu et une préface de lou tseng-tsiang . . ..** Pékin (1920) 38p, text français et chin.

Creel, H.G. Confucius. **EncyB 3** (1974) **Macropaedia** vol 6, 310b-312a.

Creel, Herrlee G. **Confucius, the man and the myth.** N.Y. (1949) 363 p, app, notes, refs, bibliog, map, index.

Creel, H.G. Was confucius agnostic? **TP** 29 (1932) 55-99.

Criticism of lin piao and confucius. **CL** 6 (june 1974) 86-106.

Crow, Carl. **Master kung. The story of confucius.** N.Y. and london (1938) 346 p, illus, end-paper map.

Cua, Antonio S. The concept of paradigmatic individuals in the ethics of confucius. **Inquiry** 14.1/2 (1971) 41-55. Repr in Arne Naess & Alastair Hannay (ed) **Invitation to chinese philosophy,** oslo etc (1972) 41-55.

Cua, Antonio S. Confucian vision and experience of the world. **PEW** 25.3 (july 1975) 319-333. See also his A reply to munitz, **ibid,** 353-355.

Cua, Antonio S. **Dimensions of moral creativity. Paradigms, principles, and ideals.** Penn state univ (1977) 180 p. See chap 4, The excursion to confucian ethics, 50-65; chap 5, Confucian paradigmatic individuals, 66-78.

Cua, Antonio S. Practical causation and confucian ethics. **PEW** 25.1 (jan 1975) 1-10.

Cua, Antonia S. Reflections on the structure of confucian ethics. **PEW** 21.2 (apr 1971) 125-140.

Dawson, Christopher. **Enquiries into religion and culture.** N.Y. (1934) See pt 2, chap The mystery of china, 128-138.

Dawson, Christopher. The rise of the world religions: confucius and the tao. In James Oliver & Christina Scott (ed) **Religion and world history; selections from the works of christopher dawson,** ny (1975) 54-67.

DeBary, William T. Confucianism. In Johnson E. Fairchild (ed) **Basic beliefs. The religious philosophies of mankind,** n.y. (1959) 92-113.

Delius, Rudolf von. **Kungfutse, seine persönlichkeit und seine lehre.** Leipzig (1930) 66 p.

Doré, Henri. Le confucéisme sous la republic. **La chine** 28 (1922) 1533-1543; 29 (1922) 1559-1571.

Doré, Henri. Le confucéisme sous la république, 1911-1922. **NCR** 4 (1922) 298-319.

Doré, Henri. Le culte de confucius sous la république chinoise (1911-1922) **Études** (20 août 1922) 433-448.

Douglas, Robert K. **Confucianism and taoism.** London (?) (1879)

Dow, Tsung-i. Creativity as the self-realization of man's potential—the supreme value of man: marxian and confucian. **Dialectics and Humanism. The polish philosophical quarterly** 5.4 (1978) 33-41.

DuBose, Hampden C. **The dragon, image and demon, or the religions of china: confucianism, buddhism, and taoism. Giving an account of the mythology, idolatry and demonolotry of the chinese.** London (1886) 463 p.

Dubs, Homer H. The confucian attitude to the worship of ancestors. **ChRec** 58.8 (aug 1927) 498-505.

Dubs, Homer H. Confucianism and superstition. **ChRec** 57.4 (apr 1926) 247-253; 57.5 (may 1926) 333-340.

Dubs, Homer H. The date of confucius' birth. **AM** 1.2 (1950) 139-146.

Dubs, Homer H. The political career of confucius. **JAOS** 66.4 (oct-dec 1946) 273-282.

Dubs, Homer H. The attitude of han kao-tzu to confucianism. **JAOS** 57 (1937) 172-180.

Dvorak, Rudolf. **Darstellungen aus dem gediete der nichtchristlichen religionsgeschichte** (12 bd), **Chinas religionen.** Erste teil: **Confucius und seine lehre.** Münster (1895) vii + 244 p. Rev by Éd. Chavannes in **RHR** 32 (1895) 303-307; **ibid** 48 (1903) 71-74.

E. (R. Étiemble?) Confucius et confucianisme. **EVF** (1968) vol 4, 873c-881c.

Eakin, Frank. **Revaluing scripture.** N.Y. (1928) See chap 16, The king and shu (confucian) 172-188.

Eastman, Max. **Seven kinds of goodness.** N.Y. (1967) See 2, The teacher of growth: confucius, 31-42.

Eberhard, Wolfram. Konfuzius als revolutionär und sittenkritiker. **Der weltkreis** 3 (1933) 1-7. Engl tsl in author's **MSVC** (1971) Confucius as a revolutionist and a critic of morals, 401-411.

The Editors. Confucius. **EncyB** 3 (1974) **Macropaedia** vol 4, 1108a-1109b.

Edkins, Joseph. A visit to the city of confucius. **JNCBRAS** n.s. 8 (1874) 79-92.

Edmunds, Charles K. Shantung: china's holy land. **NGM** 36.3 (sept 1919) 231-252.

Edwards, E.D. **Confucius.** London and glasgow (1940) xii + 146 p.

Étiemble, René. **Confucius.** Paris (1958) viii + 314.

Étiemble, René. Confucius et la chine contemporaine. **Évidences** (1954) 13-18.

Faber, Ernst. **Confucianism.** Shanghai (1895) 12 p. See same title in **CMH** (1896) 1-11; see also author's **China in the light of history** (tsl fr german E.M.H.) Shanghai (1897) app.

Faber, Ernst. Confucianism. **ChRec** 33.4 (apr 1902) 159-175.

Faber, Ernst. Notes on taoism and confucianism. **ChRec** 33.6 (june 1902) 271-276.

Faucett, Lawrence. **Six great teachers of morality.** Tokyo (1958) See chap 7, Seeking confucius in his sayings, 395-489, illus.

Faucett, Lawrence W. **The united nations and moral philosophy.** San marcos, calif (1968) See chap 3, China, confucius, and world peace, 15-27.

Faurot, Albert. The oldest birthday party. **SJ** 2 (1975) 166-172. Birthday of confucius as celebrated in taiwan, korea, and japan.

Feibleman, James K. **Understanding oriental philosophy. A popular account for the western world.** NY (1976) See pt 2, Confucius, 88-96; other chap passim.

Feng, Yu-lan. On confucius. **CSP** 9.3/4 (spring-summer 1978) 3-135.

J.C.F. (John C. Ferguson) Restoration of confucius. **CJ** 22.3 (mar 1935) 102. Nationalist govt decrees ranks and titles.

Fielde, Adele M. **A corner of cathay.** NY (1894) See sec, Confucius and his teachings, 166-213.

Finegan, Jack. **The archeology of world religions.** Princeton univ (1952) vol 2: **Buddhism, confucianism, taoism,** 234-599, illus.

Fingarette, Herbert. Comments on charles fu's discussion of confucius: the secular as sacred. **PEW** 28.2 (apr 1978) 223-226.

Fingarette, Herbert. **Confucius: the secular as sacred.** NY etc (1972) 84 p, notes, bibliog. See rev art by Henry Rosemont, **PEW** 26.4 (oct 1976) 463-478.

Fingarette, Herbert. Human community as holy rite: an interpretation of confucius' analects., **HTR** 59.1 (1966) 53-67. Repr in author's **On responsibilty,** ny (1967)

Fingarette, Herbert. The problem of the holy in the analects. **PEW** 29.2 (apr 1979) 129-140.

Ford, Eddy L. **A comparison of confucian and christian ideals.** Foochow (192 ?) 54 p.

Forlong, J.G.R. **Short studies in the science of comparative religions embracing all the religions of asia.** London (1897) chap 6, Confucius and his faith.

Franck, Harry A. **Wandering in northern china.** NY & london (1923) See chap 15, Rambles in the province of confucius, illus photos.

Franke, O. Der geschichtliche konfuzius. **ZDMG** 79 (1925) 163-191.

Franke, O. Der konfuzianismus zwischen han- und sui-zeit. **SinSon** (1934) 1-11.

Franke, O. Die religiöse und politische bedeutung des konfuzianismus in vergangenheit und gegenwart. **Zeitschrift für systematische theologie** 8 (1931) 579-588.

Frost, S.E., jr (ed) **The sacred writings of the world's great religions.** N.Y.(?) (1943) See chap 4, Confucianism, 91-118.

Fu, Charles Wei-hsun. Confucianism and taoism. Chap 12 in Isma'īl Rāgī al Farūqī & David E. Sopher (ed) **Historical atlas of the religions of the world,** ny & london (1974) 109-125, bibliog, illus, map.

Fu, Charles Wei-hsun. Fingarette and munro on early confucianism: a methodological examination. **PEW** 28.2 (apr 1978) 181-198. See also Fingarette's Comments . . . **ibid,** 223-226.

Fu, Yunlung. Tsl William A. Wycoff. Studies on confucius. **CSP** 12.2 (winter 1980-81) 25-51.

Gaer, Joseph. **How the great religions began..** N.Y. (1929) rev ed (1956) See bk 2, pt 1, Confucianism, the teachings of a great sage, 113-145.

Gaer, Joseph (comp) **The wisdom of the living religions.** N.Y. (1956) See pt 3. The sayings of confucianism, 93-114.

Gen, Lewis. What legge thinks of confucius. **EH** 1.12 (june 1961) 44-46.

Giles, Herbert A. **Confucianism and its rivals.** London (1915) ix + 271 p.

Giles, Herbert A. Le confucianisme au XIXe siècle. **Chine et sibérie** (dec 1900) 536-540, 555-559. Tsl fr **North-american review** 171 (july-dec 1900) 359-374. See also same title in engl: Confucianism in the nineteenth century, in, various authors, **Great religions of the world,** n.y. and london (1901) 3-30.

Giles, Lionel. Introduction to confucianism. In Selwyn G. Champion (ed) **The eleven religions and their proverbial lore. A comparative study,** n.y. (1954) 68-74 (the 'proverbial lore' on p 75-91)

Glüer, Winfried. Contemporary confucianism. **CF** 13.1 (spring 1970) 17-33.

Glüer, Winfried. Salvation today—chinese interpretations. **CF** 16.1 (1973) 33-46. Genl considerations; confucianism; budd.

Gobien, Charles le. Éclaircissement sur les honneurs que les chinois rendent à confucius et aux morts. In author's **Affaires de la chine,** paris (1700) vol 3, 217-332.

Graham, A.C. Confucianism. In **ZCE** (1959) 365-384.

Granet, Marcel. Confucius (551-479). In Sebastien Charlety (ed) **Les grandes figures,** paris (1939) 35-40.

Grant, G.M. **Religions of the world in relation to christianity.** London (1894) chap 3, Confucianism; chap 4, Sources of the strength and weakness of confucianism.

Gray, John Henry. **China.** William G. Gregor (ed) London (1878) illus sketches. See vol 1, chap 4, Religion—confucianism, 66-142.

Grimm, Tilemann. Meister kung; zur geschichte der wirkungen des konfuzius. **R-WAW** Vorträge G216 (1976) 44 p, 4 pl portraits.

Gripenoven, Jeanne. **Confucius et son temps.** Neuchâtel, etc (1955) 116 p.

Groot, J.J.M. de. **Religion in china. Universism: a key to the study of taoism and confucianism.** N.Y. and london (1912) (see also author's **Universismus...**)

Grützmacher, Richard H. **Konfuzius, buddha, zarathustra, muhammed.** Leipzig (1921) 92 p.

Guénon, René. Taoism and confucianism. **SCR** 6.4 (autumn 1972) 239-250.

Gundry, D.W. **Religions. A preliminary historical and theological study.** London and n.y. (1958) See 5, The monistic religions, confucianism, 78-84.

Haas, Hans. **Lao-tsze und konfuzius. Einleitung in ihr spruchgut.** Leipzig (1920) 60 p.

Haas, Hans. **Das spruchgut k'ung-tsze's und lao-tsze's in gedanklicher zusammenordnung.** Leipzig (1920) 244 p.

Hakeda, Yoshito S. (tsl) **Kūkai, major works; translated, with an account of his life and a study of his thought.** Columbia univ (1972) See, "The argument of kimo (confucianist)" 103-114.

Hansen, Chad. Freedom and moral responsibility in confucian ethics. **PEW** 22.2 (apr 1972) 169-186.

Hardon, John A. **Religions of the orient. A christian view.** Loyola univ (1970) See Confucianism, 77-106.

Hardon, John A. **Religions of the world.** N.Y. (1963) chap 6, Confucianism, 156-192.

Hardwick, Charles. **Christ and other masters.** Cambridge (1858) See Confucianism, 278-306.

Hart, Virgil Chittendon. **The temple and the sage.** Toronto (1891) 12 p, illus.

Hattori, U. Confucius' conviction of his heavenly mission. **HJAS** 1 (1935) 96-108.

Henry, B.C. Confucius and confucianism. Chap 4 in author's **CD** (1885) 62-79.

Herod, F.G. **World religions.** ?London (1970) niles, ill (1975) See chap 3, Confucianism, 33-36; chap 4, The tao, 37-39.

Herzer, Rudolf. Konfuzius in der volksrepublik. **ZDMG** 119.2 (1970) 302-331.

Hessel, R.A.E. Calvin versus confucius: a sociological inquiry. **Japan christian quarterly** 26 (july 1960) 175-179.

Hesse-Wartegg, Ernst von. China's 'holy land.' A visit to the tomb of confucius. With pictures from photgraphs taken by the author. **Century illustrated magazine** 60 (1900) 803-819.

Hesse-Wartegg, Ernst von. Zum grabe des confucius. In **Schantung** (1898) 168-175.

Hesse-Wartegg, Ernst von. Die vaterstadt des confucius. In **Schantung** (1898) 176-188.

Hindery, R. Ethics and esthetics in asian traditions: confucianism, a paradigm for western religious and social change. Philadelphia, **Journal of ecumenical studies** 15.2 (1978) 227-242.

Hirth, Friedrich. Confucius and the chinese. In J. Herman Randall, and J.L. Gardner Smith (ed) **The unity of religions,** n.y. (1910) 13-28. .

Hoang, Tzu-yue. Lao-tseu, khong-tseu, mo-tseu. (Étude comparative sur les philosophies) **Annales de l'université de lyon** (1925) 37 p.

Hodous, Lewis. Confucianism. In Edward J. Jurji (ed) **The great religions of the modern world,** princeton univ (1946) 1-23.

Hopfe, Lewis M. **Religions of the world.** Beverly hills, calif & london (1976) See chap 7, sec Confucianism, 135-145.

Hopkins, E. Washburn. **The history of religions.** N.Y. (1926) See chap 15, Confucius, lao-tse, taoism, 249-274.

Hisang, Paul S. Confucianism, raw material for christianity. **Worldmission** 5 (1955) 320-331.

Hsiao, Ching-fen. An introduction to spirituality in some chinese traditions. **NEAJT** 12 (mar 1974) 36-47. Mostly on confucianism and neo-confucianism.

Hsiao, Paul S. Y. Dschündz, das menschenideal der chinesen. **ZMR** 39 (1955) 269-283.

Hsieh, Tehyi. **Konfuzius. Eine einführung in das leben und werken des weisen und eine auswahl seiner gespräche und gedanken.** Übers von Ilse Kramer. Zürich (1954) 78 p.

Hsü, Dau-lin. The myth of the "five human relations" of confucius. **MS** 29 (1970-71) 27-37.

Hsüan, Mo. The chinese communists' evaluation of confucius and the political aims of their all-out campaign to "criticize confucius" **CSP** 7.3 (spring 1976) 4-39.

Hu, Schï. Tsl fr chin W. Franke. Der ursprung der ju und ihre beziehung zu konfuzius und lao-dsï. **SinSon** (1936) 1-42.

Hu, Shih (tsl) On observing the birthday of confucius. **ChRec** 66.3 (mar 1935) 153-158. Tsl fr tu-li p'ing-lun 9 sep 1934; a diatribe against the observance.

Huang, Thomas Y. Current anti-confucius movement in communist china. **CC** 16.4 (dec 1975) 9-24.

Hubbard, Elbert. **Little journeys to the homes of great teachers,** vol 22.2 (feb 1908) Confucius.

Hughes, E.R. Confucianist sacrifice and religious education. **ChRec** 62.7 (july 1931) 407-414.

Hume, Robert E. **The world's living religions. With special reference to their sacred scriptures and in comparison with christianity.** N.Y. (1924) rev ed (1959) See pt, Religions originating in east asia (china, japan): 6. Confucianism.

Hwang, Philip Ho. A new interpretation of confucius. **PEW** 30.1 (jan 1980) 45-56.

Itano, Chōhachi. The t'u-ch'an prophetic books and the establishment of confucianism. **TBMRD** 34 (1976) 47-111; 36 (1978) 85-107.

Jan, Yün-hua. Tsung-mi's questions regarding the confucian absolute. **PEW** 30.4 (oct 1980) 495-504.

Jin, Jingfang. Tsl William A. Wycoff. On the question of methodology in the study of confucius. **CSP** 12.2 (winter 1980-81) 68-75.

Joblin, Kingsley J. The humanistic faith of confucius. **CC** 12.3 (sep 1971) 1-8.

Johnston, Reginald F. **Confucianism and modern china.** London (1934) n.y. (1935) 272 p, illus.

Joos, G. Konfuzius und lao-tse. In **Geistige reiche und religiöse fragen der gegenwart** (1940) 14-24.

Jurji, Edward J. **The christian interpretation of religion. Christianity in its human and creative relationships with the world's cultures and faiths.** N.Y., (1952) See chap 8, The religion of humanism: confucianism, 172-191.

Kaizuka, Shigeki. **Confucius.** Tsl fr jap Geoffrey Bownas. London and n.y. (1956) 192 p, chron tables, maps, index.

Kaltenmark, Max. Le confucianisme. In **AC** t 1 (1959) 146-150.

Kaltenmark, Max. Confucius et ses disciples dans les textes non confucianistes. **RHR** 151.1 (jan-mars 1937) 134-136.

Kang, Thomas H. Confucian publication in western languages. **Korea Journal** 12.7 (1972) 24-32.

Kelen, Betty. **Confucius in life and legend.** NY (1971) 160 p, bibliog.

Kellett, E.E. **A short history of religions.** N.Y. (1934) See p 428-443.

Kemp, E.G. The home of confucius, küfow. Chap 7 in author's **FC** (1909) 53-65.

Kern, M. Konfuzianismus und taoismus. In **LO** (1922) 325-350.

Kim, Ha Tai. Transcendence without and within: the concept of t'ien in confucianism. **International journal for philosophy of religion** 3.3 (fall 1972) 146-160.

Kim, Young Oon. **World religions. Volume 3: Faiths of the far east.** NY (1976) See Confucianism, 121-160, brief bibliog.

Kimura, Eiichi. The new confucianism and taoism in china and japan from the fourth to the thirteenth centuries a.d. **CHM** 5 (1959-60) 801-829.

Klügmann, Karl. Aus dem religiösen leben der chinesen Am grabe der konfuzius. Auf dem taishan. **Geist des ostens** 1 (1913) 284-295.

Koo, Bon Myung. Thorough comparative studies on the morality of confucius and socrates. Seoul, **Journal of east and west studies** 4.2 (1975) 3-25.

Koung-tsee, philosophe. In **MCLC** t 3 (1778) 41-43.

Kramers, R.P. Der konfuzianismus als religion. Versuche zur neubelebung eines konfuzianischen glaubens. **AS** 18/19 (1965) 143-166.

Kranz, Pastor. Some of professor j. legge's criticisms on confucianism. **ChRec** 29 (1898) 273-282, 341-345, 380-388, 440-445.

Krause, Friedrich E.A. **Ju-tao-fo. . . Die religiösen und philosophischen systeme ostasiens.** München (1924) 588p.

Ku, Hung-ming. **The spirit of the chinese people.** Peking (1915) See essay of title name, 1-73. Mostly on confucianism as chin substitute for relig. German tsl, **Der geist des chinesischen volkes,** jena (1924) see 41-106.

Kuan, Feng & Lin, Lü-shih. Third discussion on confucius. **CSP** 2.4 (summer 1971) 246-263.

K'ung, Hsien-lan (ed) **The life of confucius. Reproduced from a book entitled sheng chi t'u, being rubbings from the stone 'tablets of the holy shrine.'** Shanghai (n.d.) Cp Lair and Wang (tsl) **An illustrated life of confucius.**

Kung, Teh-cheng. The life and thought of confucius. **ACQ** 3.4 (winter 1975) 20-26.

Kung, Te-cheng. Rites—but more than ritual. **FCR** 23.5 (may 1973) 20-23. Confucius on the li.

Kupperman, Joel J. Confucius and the nature of religious ethics. **PEW** 21.2 (apr 1971) 189-194.

Lai, Whalen, Reflections on "esoteric confucianism" **HR** 17.1 (aug 1977) 89-99. Rev art on Lo Meng-tse, **Le paradoxal destin politique de confucius,** paris (1972) Lo's bk written in chin with french title.

Lair, H.P. and Wang, L.C. (tsl) **An illustrated life of confucius, from tablets in the temple at chufu, shantung, china.** n.p. (n.d.) repr taipei (1972) 113 p. Cp K'ung, Hsien-lan (ed) **The life of confucius . . .**

Lancashire, Douglas. Confucianism in the twentieth century. In **China and its place in the world,** auckland (1967) 26-42.

Laughlin, J.H. A day with confucius. **ChRec** 25.7 (july 1894) 311-314. A visit to ch'ü-fu. Apparently repr fr **Church at home and abroad.**

Lee, H.T. Is confucianism a religion? **CSM** 21 (1926) 52.57.

Lee, Shao-chang. The attitude of confucius toward religion. **NRJ** 8 (july 1947) 43-50.

Lee, Tsung-ying. Confucius and his times. **EH** 13.3 (1974) 2-6.

Lee, W.J. Heaven, earth and confucius. **FCR** 19 (sept 1969) 10-14.

Lefeuvre, J. Confucianism and scientific humanism in modern china. **JCS** 5 (1967) 63-76.

Legge, James. **Christianity and confucianism compared in their teaching of the whole duty of man.** London (?) (1884) 36 p.

Legge, James. **Confucianism in relation to christianity.** Shanghai and london (1877) 12 p.

Legge, James. Confucius. **EncyB** 9th ed (1882) vol 6, 258b-265a.

Legge, James. Confucius. In **EncyB,** 11th ed (1910-11) vol 6, p 907-912.

Legge, James. Confucius the sage, and the religion of china. In **RSW** (1889 et seq) 61-75.

Legge, James. Imperial confucianism. **ChRev** 6.3 (nov-dec 1877) 147-158; 6.4 (jan-feb 1878) 223-235; 6.5 (mar-apr 1878) 299-310; 6.6 (may-june 1878) 363-374.

Legge, James. **The life and teachings of confucius.** Philadelphia (1867)

Legge, James. **The religions of china. Confucianism and taoism described and compared with christianity.** London (1880) repr folcroft, pa (1976) norwood, pa (1977) 310 p.

Legge, James, and Anon. Confucius. **EncyB** 14th ed (1929) vol 6, 236b-239b.

Leslie, Daniel. **Confucius.** Paris (1962) 224 p.

Lessing, Ferdinand D. Bodhisattva confucius. **Oriens** 10.1 (1957) 110-113.

Levenson, Joseph. The place of confucius in communist china. **CQ** 12 (oct-dec 1962) 1-18. repr in Albert Feuerwerker (ed) **History in communist china,,** MIT (1968) 56-73.

Lewis, John. **The religions of the world made simple.** NY (1958) rev ed (1968) See chap 7, Confucianism and taoism, 52-58.

Lewy, Guenter. Religion and revolution and the major traditions—confucianism. In chap 2 of author's **R&Rev** (1974) 14-25.

Liang, Si-ing. **La rencontre et le conflit entre les idées des missionaires chrétiens et les idées des chinois en chine depuis la fin de la dynastie des ming.** Paris (1940) 159 p.

Life and times of confucius; notices of his ancestors, and of the time, place and circumstances of his birth. Selected from the annals and genealogy of the sage, and other chinese works. **ChRep** 18.7 (july 1849) 337-342.

Lillico, S. The tomb of confucius. **CJ** 21 (1934) 221-224.

Lim, Boon Keng. The confucian way of thinking of the world and god. Prepared for publ and annot David A. Wilson. **AR** ser 4, 7 (apr 1919) 168-178.

Lin, Chih-hao. Lu hsun, a great fighter against confucianism. **CL** 4 (apr 1974) 81-88.

Lin, Tien-min. Is chinese communism incompatible with confucius? **RH** 10.1 (winter 1976) 26-30.

Lin, Timothy Tien-min. The concept of man in confucianism and christianity. **NEAJT** 14 (mar 1975) 20-24.

Lin, Timothy Tian-min. The confucian concept of jen and the christian concept of love. **CF** 15.3 (autumn 1972) 162-172.

Lin, Yu-sheng. The evolution of the pre-confucian meaning of jen and the confucian concept of moral autonomy. **MS** 31 (1974-75) 172-204.

Liu, Kang-sheng. Confucius' universal standard. **FCR** 22.9 (sep 1972) 16-27. Incl tsl of bits of chung-yung by Ku Hung-ming.

Liu, Kang-sheng. He loved men and learning. **FCR** 21.9 (sep 1971) 19-22.

Liu, Kang-sheng. Why mao hates confucius. **FCR** 23.11 (nov 1973) 16-20.

Liu, Shu-hsien.The confucian approach to the problem of transcendence and immanence. **PEW** 22.1 (jan 1972) 45-52.

Liu, Shu-hsien. A philosophic analysis of the confucian approach to ethics. **PEW** 22.4 (oct 1972) 417-425.

Liu, Shu-hsien. The religious import of confucian philosophy: its traditional outlook and contemporary significance. **PEW** 21.2 (apr 1971) 157-175.

Liu, Ts'un-yan. Lu hsi-hsing: a confucian scholar, taoist priest and buddhist devotee of the sixteenth century. **AS** 18/19 (1965) 115-142. Repr in **LTY:SP** (1976)

Liu, Wu-chi. **Confucius. His life and times.** N.Y. (1955) repr westport, conn (1972) xv + 189 p.

Lo, Hsiang-lin. An inquiry into the doctrinal system of confucius from the lun-yü. **CSP** 8.1 (fall 1976) 57-76.

Lo, R.Y. The basic philosophy of confucius and its later development. **ChRec** 54.1 (jan 1923) 14-21.

Lo, Stanislaus Kuang. The meeting of christianity and confucianism. **ACQ** 5.1 (spring 1977) 36-40.

Lou, Tseng-tsiang (Dom Celestine) **The ways of confucius and of christ.** Engl tsl Michael Derrick, london (1948) 140 p, illus. German tsl Kaspar Hürlimann, **Konfuzianer und christ,** luzera (1947) 219 p, illus.

Louie, Kam. **Critiques of confucius in contemporary china.** HK (1980) 186 p.

Lu, Martin. The confucian view of immortality and its cultural implications. Singapore **Review of southeast asian studies** 7 (1977) 47-59.

Lyall, Leslie. Confucius. In Norman Anderson (ed) **The world's religions,** grand rapids, mich (1950) 4th ed "completely rev" (1975) 219-227.

Lyon, D. Willard (ed) **Religious values in confucianism. A source book of facts and opinions.** N.Y. and london (1927) 42 p.

Lyon, David Willard. Will confucianism be a force to be reckoned with in the coming days in china? **ChRec** 59.2 (feb 1928) 73-88.

MacGillivray, D. Confucianism weighed in english balances. **ChRec** 34.7 (july 1903) 329-340.

Maclagan, P.J. Position and prospects of confucianism in china. **IRM** 3 (apr 1914) 225-242.

Mahood, G.H. Socrates and confucius: moral agents or moral philosophers? **PEW** 21.2 (apr 1971) 177-188.

Malebranche, Nicolas [1628-1715] **Entretien d'un philosoph chrétien et d'un philosoph chinois, suivi de l'avis au lecteur.** Avec une introduction et des notes par A. LeMoine. Marseille (1936) 11 + 119 p.

Martin, Alfred W. **Great religious teachers of the east.** N.Y. (1911) See chap 4, Confucius and lao-tze, 105-148.

Martin, Alfred W. (comp) **Seven great bibles.** N.Y. (1930) See chap 4, The bible of confucianism, 123-153.

Martin, Bernard & Shui, Chien-tung. **Makers of china— confucius to mao.** NY and oxford (1972) See, Confucius, 3-11.

Masdoosi, Ahmad Abdullah al. **Living religions of the world. A socio-political study.** Tsl fr urdu Zafar Ishaq Ansari. Karachi (1962) See chap 10, Confucianism, 214-257.

Matgioi (A. de Pourvoirville) **La chine des lettrés . . . leur religion . . .** Paris (1910)

McCartee, D.B. On a chinese tablet illustrating the religious opinions of the literary class. **JAOS** 9.2 (1851) lxi.

Mei, Chih-chun. Confucius' continuing influence. **FCR** 20.9 (sep 1970) 13-18.

Mei, Y.P. Confucius. **EncyA** (1971) vol 7, 540-543.

Mei, Y.P. Confucius. **EncyA** (1975) vol 7, 540a-543a.

Mei, Y.P. Confucianism. **EncyB 3** (1974) **Macropaedia** vol 4, 1091b-1099b.

Messing, Otto. Confuzianismus. **ZE** 46 (1914) 754-772, fig.

Morton, W. Scott. The confucian concept of man: the original formulation. **PEW** 21.1 (jan 1971) 69-77.

Mou, Tseng-san. Confucianism as a religion. **QNCCR** 4.2 (july 1960) 1-12.

Moule, A.C. Confucianism, or the religion of the chinese. **TheE&TheW** 21 (1923) 269-277.

Müller, F. Max. The religions of china. Confucianism. **NC** 48 (sept 1900) 373-384.

Noss, John B. **Man's religions.** N.Y. (1949 et seq) 3rd rev ed (1963) See pt 3, chap 10, Confucius and confucianism: a study in optimistic humanism, 369-427.

Notice of the chi-shing pien nien-shi ki, or annals and genealogy of the most holy sage, with a translation of the preface of the editor k'ung chau-hwan, a member of the confucian family. **ChRep** 18.5 (may 1849) 254-259.

M.C.P. Confucianism in its practical bearings upon the spread of christianity in china. **ChRec** 12.3 (may-june 1881) 218-224.

Pak, Hyobom. **China and the west. Myths and realities in history.** Leiden (1974) viii + 120 p ". . . interacting forces of religion and politics"

Paper, Jordan. Confucianism in the post-han era. **CC** 16.2 (june 1975) 37-44.

Parker, E.H. Laocius and confucius as rival moralists. **AR** 20 (1924) 698-704; 21 (1925) 129-146.

Parrinder, E.G. **What world religions teach.** London etc (1963) See chap 8, Confucius and the social order, 72-79.

Peake, Cyrus H. China revives confucianism. **OC** 50 (1936) 24-31.

Peeters, Hermes. **The religions of china. Confucianism, taoism, buddhism, popular belief.** Peking (1941) 64 p.

Peisson, Z. Le confucianisme. **RR** 2 (1890)

Perrot, Albert. Le retour offensif de la vieille chine. Le confucianisme redevenu religion d'état. **Études** (20 mai 1914) 461-480; (juil 1914) 425-438, fig.

Pham-Quynh. Consideration sur l'humanisme confucéen. **FA** 87 t 9 (août 1959) 643-647.

Planchat, Edmond. Le tombeau de confucius. **Le temps** (lundi 13 dec 1897)

Podgorski, Frank. Reading the holy books of china. **JD** 3.3 (july-sep 1978) 309-317. Re ancient confucian and taoist classics.

Politella, Joseph. **Taoism and confucianism.** Iowa city (1967) 167 p.

The position and prospects of confucianism in china. **Chinese review** 1 (apr 1914) 50-51.

Pott, William S.A. Further observations on the confucian god-idea. **ChRec** 50.12 (dec 1919) 825-833. See Y.Y. Tsu, The confucian god-idea, **ibid**, 50.5 (may 1919) 294-306.

Potter, Charles F. **The great religious leaders.** N.Y. (1958) Rev ed of **The story of religion**, n.y. (1929) See chap 6, Confucius. . . The apostle of morality (including lao-tse of the divine way) 141-164.

Provine, Robert C. The sacrifice to confucius in korea and its music. **TransKBRAS** 50 (1975) 43-69, illus.

Pulleyblank, E.G. Confucianism, history of. **EncyB 3** (1974) **Macropaedia** vol 4, 1099b-1103b.

La question du confucianisme et le gouvernement de pékin. **BAF** 16 (oct-dec 1916) 175-176.

Reid, Gilbert. **A christian's appreciation of other faiths.** Chicago and london (1921) See lecture on his apprecia- tion of confucianism. . . 11-49.

Rhee, S.N. Fear god and honor your father and mother; two injunctions in the book of proverbs and the confucian classics. **Encounter** 26 (spring 1965) 207-214.

Richard, Timothy. Modern confucianism. Chap 14 in author's **CbyM** (1907) 232-245.

Rosemont, Henry jr. Confucius, the secular as sacred. **PEW** 26.4 (oct 1976) 463-478. Rev art on Fingarette's bk of same title q.v.

Rosemont, Henry jr. Notes from a confucian perspective: which human acts are moral acts? **IPQ** 16.1 (mar 1976) 49-61.

Rosenkranz. Gerhard. **Der heilige in den chinesischen klassikern; eine untersuchung über die erlöser- erwartung in konfuzianismus und taoismus.** Leipzig (1935) vii + 188 p.

Ross, Floyd H. and Tynette Wilson Hills. **Questions that matter most, asked by the world's religions.** Boston (1954) See sec 3, Chinese religions, chap 11, Confucianism. Paperbk title: **The great religions by which men live.**

Ross, John. Our attitude towards confucianism. **ChRec** 18.1 (1887) 1-11.

Ross, John. Religion of confucius. **Chinese review** 1 (july 1914) 125-133.

Rotours, Robert des. Confucianisme et christianisme. **Sinologica** 1 (1948) 231-245.

Rousselle, E. Konfuzius und das archaische weltbild der chinesischen frühzeit. **Saeculum** 5 (1954) 1-33.

Roy, A.T. Attacks upon confucianism in the 1911-1927 period. **CCJ** 4.1 (1964) 10-26.

Roy, A.T. Attacks upon confucianism in the 1911-1927 period.: (2) and (3) From a taoist lawyer: wu yu. **CCJ** 4 (1965) 149-163; 5 (1965) 69-78.

Roy, A.T. The background of the confucian dilemma in the period 1927-47. **CCJ** 9.2 (may 1970) 182-201.

Roy, A.T. Confucian thought in the nineteen-thirties: ch'en li-fu—part I: his theory of the universe and of the significance of man. **CCJ** 7.1 (nov 1967) 72-89.

Roy, A.T. Confucian thought in the nineteen-thirties: ch'en li-fu—part II: application of his theory to social, cultural, and political questions. **CCJ** 8.1 (nov 1968) 63-92.

Roy, A.T. Confucianism and social change. **CCJ** 3 (nov 1963) 88-104.

Roy, A.T. Liberal re-evaluation of confucianism in the 1911-1927 period. **CCJ** 6.1 (nov 1966) 79-100.

Roy, A.T. Notes on the inner struggle in ch'ing confucianism. **CCJ** 10.1/2 (oct 1971) 48-63.

Rubin, Vitali. The end of confucianism? **TP** 59 (1973) 68-78. Rev art on W. Bauer's **China und die hoffnung auf glück** q.v.

Rygaloff, Alexis. **Confucius.** Paris (1946) xii + 125 p.

Saint-Denys, le Marquis d'Hervey. Mémoire sur les doctrines religieuses de confucius et de l'école des lettrés. **MAIBL** t 32, 2e partie (1887) Publ sep paris (1887) 23 p.

Saint-Ina, [Marie de] Confucius: witness to being. **IPQ** 3.4 (dec 1963) 537-553.

Saitschick, Robert. Kungfutse, der 'meister' der religion chinas. **Hochland** 9 (1912) 15-38.

Schilling, Werner. **Einst konfuzius heute mao tse-tung. Die mao-faszination und ihre hintergründe.** Weiheim/Oberbayern (1971) 329 s, anmerkungen, literatur-verzeichnis, zur transkription chinesischer namen, abkürzungen, personenverzeichnis.

Schmidt, Charles. The 'wen miao,' commonly styled 'the confucian temple' in shanghai. **MDGNVO** (1877) 11-12, photo.

Schmitt, Erich. **Konfuzius; sein leben und seine lehre.** Berlin (1926) 216 p, pl.

Schneider, Laurence A. (tsl) A translation of ku chieh-kang's essay 'The confucius of the spring and autumn era and the confucius of the han era.' **PTP** (1965) 105-147.

Schütz, Ludwig Harald. **Die hohe lehre des confucius.** Frankfurt am main (1909) 64 p, illus, chin texts.

Selected articles criticizing lin piao and confucius. 2. Peking (1975) 229 p.

Semenoff, Marc. **Confucius, sa vie, ses pensées, sa doctrine.** Paris (1951) 157 p, fig.

Sherley-Price, Lionel D. **Confucius and christ; a christian estimate of confucius.** Westminster, engl (1951) 248 p, illus.

Shih, J. Mediation in chinese religion. **SM** 21 (1972) 77-92. Mostly re the li.

Shih, Joseph. The place of confucianism in the history of chinese religion. **Gregorianum** 51 (1970) 485-508.

Shryock, J.K. Confucianism. In H.F. MacNair (ed) **China,** univ california (1946) 245-253.

Sih, Paul K.T. Will confucian thought survive in the modern age? **CC** 17.2 (june 1976) 27-30.

Sims, Bennett B. **Confucius.** N.Y. (1968) 139 p, illus, map.

Smart, Ninian. **The religious experience of mankind.** N.Y. (1969) See chap 4, Chinese and japanese religious experience; sec, Confucianism and taoism, 141-190.

Smith, Arthur H. Confucianism. In **The message of the world's religions,** n.y. (1898) Chap 3, 41-64. Repr fr **Outlook.**

Smith, Carl T. Radical theology and the confucian tradition. **CF** 10.4 (1967) 20-33.

Smith, D. Howard. **Confucius.** NY (1973) 240 p, map, notes, bibliog, table of principal events, table of dyn, index.

Smith, D.H. Ethical standards in world religions. **ET** 85 (apr 1974) 201-205.

Smith, Huston. **The religions of man.** N.Y. (1958) See chap 4, Confucianism, 142-174.

Smith, Ruth (ed) **The tree of life. Selections from the literature of the world's religions.** NY (1942) See sec, From the confucianist religion, 157-188.

Soulié, Charles George de Morant. **La vie de confucius (kong tse)** Paris (1929) 213 p.

Spencer, Sidney. **Mysticism in world religion.** N.Y. (1963) london (1966) See sec 4, Taoist and confucianist mysticism, confucianism, 113-122.

Sprenkel, O. van der. Confucius: six variations. In Wang, Gung-wu (ed) **Self and biography: essays on the individual and society in asia,** sydney univ (1975) 99-122.

Staiger, Brunhild. **Das konfuzius-bild im kommunistischen china; die neubewertung von konfuzius in der chinesisch-marxistische gesichtsschreibung.** Wiesbaden (1969) 143 p.

Stanley, Charles A. jr. T'ai shan and the tomb of confucius. **EA** 4 (1905) 301-309.

Starr, Frederick. **Confucianism; ethics, philosophy, religion.** N.Y. (1930) ix + 250, illus.

Storrs, Christopher. **Many creeds, one cross.** N.Y. (1945) See chap 5, Confucius and humanism, 101-126.

Stroup, Herbert. **Founders of living religions.** Philadelphia (1974) See chap 6, Confucius and confucianism, 126-153.

Stübe, R. **Das zeitalter des confucius.** Tübingen (1913) 54 p.

Suryadinata, Leo. Confucianism in indonesia: past and present. **Southeast asia; an international quarterly** 3.3 (spring 1974) 881-903.

Suzuki, Teitaro. Confucius. **OC** 13.11 (nov 1899) 644-649, frontispiece portrait of confucius.

"The systems of buddha and confucius compared," extracted from the **ICG**, no 5, août 1818 (p 149-157) **ChRep** 2 (1833-34) 265 f.

Taam, Cheuk-woon. On studies of confucius. **PEW** 3 (1953) 147-165.

Takeuchi, Teruo. A study of the meaning of jen advocated by confucius. **ActaA** 9 (1965) 57-77.

T'ang, Chun-i. Confucianism and chinese religions. In Moses Jung, Swami Nikhilanda and Herbert W. Schneider (ed) **Relations among religions today. A handbook of policies and principles,** leiden (1963), Chap 2.

T'ang, Chun-i. The development of ideas of spiritual value in chinese philosophy. In **PCEW** (1962) 227-235. Repr in **TC** (1970) 137-146, as: Spiritual values in confucian philosophy.

T'ang, Chün-i. The formation of confucius' position in chinese history and culture. **ChFor** 1.1 (jan 1974) 1-48.

T'ang, Chün-i. Religious beliefs and modern chinese culture. Part II: The religious spirit of confucianism. **CSP** 5.1 (fall 1973) 48-85.

Tao, Hsi-sheng. The ethical program of social organization of confucianism. **ChFor** 2.1 (jan 1975) 21-40.

Thomas, Henry and Dana Lee. **Living biographies of religious leaders.** N.Y. (1942) See chap on Confucius, 57-68.

Thompson, Laurence G. Confucianism as a way of ultimate transformation. In **East/West cultures. Religious motivations for behavior: a colloquium,** santa barbara, calif (1978) 1-38.

Thornberry, Mike. The encounter of christianity and confucianism: how modern confucianism views the encounter. **SEAJT** 10 (1968) 47-62.

Throop, Montgomery Hunt. Proverbs and the analects. A comparison of their teachings, moral and religious. **ChRec** 60.5 (may 1929) 323-330; 60.6 (june 1929) 371-378.

Tong, Lik Kuen. Confucian jen and platonic eros: a comparative study. **CC** 14.3 (sep 1973) 1-8.

Too-yu. The systems of foe and confucius compared, translated from the chinese. **ICG** no 5 (1818) 149-157.

Topley, Marjorie. Is confucius dead? **FEER** 58 (21 dec 1967) 561-563.

Trivière, Léon. La campagne contre le confucianisme en chine. **Études** (jan 1974) 805-829.

Trood, S.M.E. **The religions of mankind. An introductory survey.** London (1929) See chap 7, The native religions of china and japan—confucianism, 93-105.

Tsao, Wen-yen. Confucianism and religious tolerance. **CC** 9.2 (1968) 51-54.

Tsao, Wen-yen. The timeless wisdom of confucius. **CC** 15.3 (sep 1974) 17-24.

Tschepe, A. **Heiligtümer des konfuzianismus im k'ü-fu und tschouhien.** Jentschou-fu (1906) viii + 132 p, 63 illus, 3 maps. Notices in **JNCBRAS** 39 (1908) 189-194; **AQR** ser 3,25 (apr 1908) 399-400.

Tschepe, A. The tomb of the holy yen-fu-tse. **FE** 1 (1906) 113-118.

Tschepe, A. Voyage au pays de confucius et de ses disciples. **RC** (avr 1910) 533-540, fig.

Tsu, Y.Y. The confucian god-idea. In **CToday** 2 (1926) 58-73.

Tu, Wei-ming. The confucian perception of adulthood. **Daedalus** 105.2 (apr 1976) 109-123; repr in **H&SC** (1979) 35-56.

Tu, Wei-ming. Confucianism: symbol and substance in recent times. **ATS** 1.1 (apr 1976) 42-66; repr in **H&SC** (1979) 257-296.

Tu, Wei-ming. The creative tension between jen and li. **PEW** 18.1/2 (jan-apr 1968) 29-39; repr in **H&SC** (1979) 5-16.

Tu, Wei-ming. **Humanity and self-cultivation: essays in confucian thought.** Berkeley, calif (1979) xxii + 364 p, gloss, sel bibliog, index. Essays sep listed in our bibliog. Abbrev **H&SC.**

Tu, Wei-ming. Li as a process of humanization. **PEW** 22.2 (apr 1972) 187-201; repr in **H&SC** (1979) 17-34.

Tu, Wei-ming. On the mencian perception of moral self-development. **Monist** 61.1 (jan 1978) 72-81; repr in **H&SC** (1979) 57-68.

Tu, Wei-ming. On the spiritual development of confucius' personality. **SyY:T&W** 11.3 (sep 1973) 29-37.

Tu, Wei-ming. Yen yüan: from inner experience to lived concreteness. In W.T.de Bary (ed) **The unfolding of neo-confucianism,** columbia univ (1975) 511-541; repr in **H&SC** (1979) 186-215.

Turnbull, Grace H. (comp) **Tongues of fire. A bible of sacred scriptures of the pagan world.** N.Y. (1929) See The confucian canon, 121-156.

Uno, Seiichi. Reflections on asian culture—on confucianism. **ACQ** 1.1 (fall 1973) 35-38.

Unschald, Paul U. Confucianism. In **EBio** (1978) vol 1, 200a-204b.

Valbert, G. Confucius et la morale chinoise. **RDM** 150 (1898) 673-684.

Van Buskirk, William R. **The saviors of mankind.** N.Y. (1929) See chap 2, Confucius, 25-61.

Vandermeersch, Léon. **Wangdao ou la voie royale. Recherches sur l'esprit des institutions de la chine archaïque.** T1, **Structures cultuelles et structures familiales.** Paris (1977) 358 p. T2, **Structures politiques, les rites.** Paris (1980) 603 p, tables, index. See, Table générale des matières.

Voss, Carl Hermann. **Living religions of the world: our search for meaning.** Cleveland (1968) See Confucianism and taoism: the will of heaven, 71-86.

W. Sketch of the life of confucius, the chinese moralist. **ChRep** 11.9 (aug 1842) 411-425.

Waddell, N.A. (tsl) A selection from the ts'ai ken t'an ('vegetable-root discourses') **EB** 2.2 (nov 1919) 88-98.

Wallacker, Benjamin E. Han confucianism and confucius in han. In **AC:SEC** (1978) 215-228.

Wang, Ching-wei. Confucius and modern society. **ChRec** 65.11 (nov 1934) 683-689.

Watts, Harold H. **The modern reader's guide to religions.** N.Y. (1964) See chap 19, Chinese and japanese religion, confucianism, 538-554.

Weber, Max. **Konfuzianismus und taoismus.** Tübingen (1922) (Author's Gesammelte aufsätze zur religions-soziologie, 1) Engl tsl Hans H. Gerth: **The religion of china: confucianism and taoism.** Glencoe, ill. (1951) london (1952) xi + 308 p.

Wei, Tat. Confucius and the i-ching. In Finley P. Dunne, jr (ed) **The world religions speak on 'the relevance of religion in the modern world,'** the hague (1970) 64-71.

Wen, Chun. Confucius' reactionary views on literature and art. **CL** 10 (oct 1974) 111-118.

Widgery, Alban G. **Living religions and modern thought.** N.Y. (1936) See chap 5, Confucianism and shinto, 108-134.

Wilhelm, Richard. In der heimat des konfuzius, eine reiseerrinnerung. **CBWK** 1.1 (1925) 26-42.

Wilhelm, Richard. **Kung-tse, leben und werk.** Stuttgart (1925) 210 p.

Wilhelm, Richard. **K'ungtse und der konfuzianismus.** Berlin and leipzig (1928) 104 p. Engl tsl George H. and Annina P. Danton: **Confucius and confucianism.** N.Y. and london (1931) x + 181 p.

Williams, David Rhys. **World religions and the hope for peace.** Boston (1951) See chap 1, The reasonableness of confucius, 3-13.

Williams, E.T. Confucianism and the new china. **HTR** 9.3 (1916) 258-285.

Williams, E.T. Confucius and his teaching. Chap 11 in author's **CYT,** 223-248.

Wu, Ching-hsiung (John C.H. Wu) The thought of confucius and chinese culture. **CSP** 8.1 (fall 1976) 77-88.

Wu, John C. H. Confucian humanism and the modern world. **CC** 15.3 (sep 1974) 9-16.

Wu, John C.H. The real confucius. The china academy, **Bulletin of the institute of pacific research** 1 (mar 1967) 77-89.

Wu, L.C. Engl tsl Z. S. Zia. Christianity in the light of confucian thought. **ChRec** 62.1 (jan 1931) 21-29.

Wu, S. Confucianism and its significance to christianity in china. **CF** 12.1 (1969) 4-23.

Yang, Liang-kung. The confucian school's outlook on spiritual beings. **ACQ** 5.3 (autumn 1977) 1-7.

Yang, Ming-che. Confucianism. **FCR** 17 (apr 1967) 22-28.

Yang, Ming-che. Confucianism vs tao and buddha. **FCR** 19 (jan 1969) 21-29.

Yeh, George K.C. **The confucian conception of jen.** London (1943) 14 p. **China society occasional papers,** n.s. 3.

Yeh, George & C.P. Fitzgerald. **Introducing china.** London (1948) See chap 8, Teachings of confucius, 43-47.

Yeh, Theodore T.Y. **Confucianism, christianity and china.** N.Y. (1969) 249 p, notes, bibliog.

Yen, Ching-hwang. The confucian revival movement in singapore and malaysia, 1899-1911. **JSEAS** 7.1 (mar 1976) 33-57.

Yen, Joseph C. Y. Christianity and confucianism: a brief survey of their central idea. Taipei, **Soochow journal of humanities** 2 (mar 1977) 158-164.

Yetts, Walter Perceval. **The legend of confucius.** London (1943) **China society occasional papers,** n.s. 5.

Yoon, Hong-key. The analysis of korean geomancy tales. **AsFS** 34.1 (1975) 21-34.

Youn, Laurent Eulsu. **Confucius, sa vie, son oeuvre, sa doctrine.** Paris (1943) 126 p.

Young, Conrad Chun-shih. Name taboo and confucianism. An anthropological view. **ASBIE** 30.2 (autumn 1970) 111-120.

Young, John D. An early confucian attack on christianity: yang kuang-hsien and his pu-te-i. **JCUHK** 3.1 (dec 1975) 156-186.

Young, John D. 'Original confucianism' versus neo-confucianism: matteo ricci's chinese writings. In **MS/CA** (1977) 371-377.

Yu, Chin-sei. The quest for sagehood in confucius. Seoul, **Korea Journal** 17.9 (sep 1977) 33-41.

Yu, Pung Kwang. Confucianism. In **WPR** vol 1 (1893) 374-439.

Zaehner, R.C. **Concordant discord. The interdependence of faiths.** Oxford univ (1970) See chap 12, The way of man, 237-257.

Zia, Rosina C. The conception of "sage" in lao-tze and chuang-tze as distinguished from confucianism. **CCJ** 5 (may 1966) 150-157.

Zia, Z.K. The confucian civilization. The confucian theory of moral and religious education and its bearing on the future civilization of china. **ChRec** 54.10 (oct 1923) 575-583; 54.11 (nov 1923) 648-656; 54.12 (dec 1923) 721-729; 55 (1924) 16-24, 95-103, 160-167, 230-233.

Zia, Z.K. Confucius. **ChRec** 61.3 (mar 1930) 164-168. Brief note on some leading ideas of confucius about relig.

8. NEO-CONFUCIAN RELIGIOUS THOUGHT & PRAXIS

Berling, Judith A. Paths of convergence: interactions of inner alchemy taoism and neo-confucianism. **JCP** 6.2 (june 1979) 123-147.

Berling, Judith A. **The syncretic religion of lin chao-en.** Columbia univ (1980) 360 p, app, notes, gloss, sel bibliog.

Berthrong, John. "Suddenly deluded thoughts arise." **SSCRB** 8 (fall 1980) 32-55. Re Mou tsung-san on neo-confucianism and t'ang budd philos.

Bocking, Brian. Neo-confucian spirituality and the samurai ethic. **Religion** 10 (spring 1980) 1-15.

Chan, Wing-tsit. Chu hsi's appraisal of lao tzu. **PEW** 25.2 (apr 1975) 131-144. Same title in **MS/CA** (1977) 5-9.

Cheng, Chung-ying. Religious reality and religious understanding in confucianism and neo-confucianism. **IPQ** 13.1 (mar 1973) 33-62.

Cheng, Chung-ying. Theory and practice in confucianism. **JCP** 1 (1973-74) 179-198.

Ch'ien, Anne Meller. Hu chü-jen's (1434-84) self-cultivation as ritual and reverence in everyday life. **JCP** 6.2 (june 1979) 183-210.

Ch'ien, Anne. Meditation and ritual in neo-confucian tradition. **JD** 2.2 (apr 1977) 173-188.

Ching, Julia. Beyond good and evil. The culmination of the thought of wang yang-ming (1472-1529) **Numen** 22.2 (aug 1973) 125-134.

Ching, Julia. Chu hsi's theory of human nature. **Humanitas** 15.1 (feb 1979) 77-100. Incl relig aspects.

Ching, Julia. **Confucianism and christianity: a comparative study.** Tokyo etc (1977) xxvi + 234 p, notes, bibliog, index.

Ching, Julia. The problem of god in confucianism. **IPQ** 17.1 (mar 1977) 3-22.

Ching, Julia. Some notes on the "wang yang-ming controversy." **JOSA** 9 (1972-73) 14-20.

Ching, Julia. **To acquire wisdom. The way of wang yang-ming.** Columbia univ (1976) See esp chap 6, The culmination: wu-shan, wu-ô, 146-187.

Ching, Julia. Truth and ideology: the confucian way (tao) and its transmission (tao-t'ung) **JHI** 36.3 (july-sept 1974) 371-388.

Fu, Charles Wei Hsun. Morality or beyond: the neo-confucian confrontation with mahayana buddhism. **PEW** 23.3 (july 1973) 375-396.

Graf, Olaf. **Tao und jen, sein und sollen im sungchinesischen monismus.** Wiesbaden (1970) xii + 429 s, gloss chin terms, bibliog, index to names, general index. See rev by H.R. Schlette, **ZMR** 57.1 (1973) 60-64.

Hsiao, Ching-fen. An introduction to spirituality in some chinese traditions. **NEAJT** 12 (mar 1974) 36-47. Mostly on confucianism and neo-confucianism.

Huang, Siu-chi. The moral point of view of chang tsai. **PEW** 21.2 (apr 1971) 145-156.

Izutsu, Toshihiko. The temporal and a-temporal dimensions of reality in confucian metaphysics. **EJ 1974** (1977) 411-447. Re neo-confucian thought and spiritual cultivation.

Jiang, Paul Yun-ming. Ch'en pai-sha (1428-1500) in the development of neo-confucianism. **JOSA** 6 (1968-69) 65-81.

Kim, Ha Tai. The religious dimension of neo-confucianism. **PEW** 27.3 (july 1977) 337-348.

Kramers, Robert. The sense of predicament in neo-confucian thought as a topic for christian reflection. **CF** 21.3 (1978) 107-114.

Liu, James T.C. How did a neo-confucian school become the state orthodoxy? **PEW** 23.4 (oct 1973) 483-506.

Liu, Ts'un-yan. The penetration of taoism into the ming neo-confucianist elite. **TP** 57.1/4 (1971) 31-102.

Mungello, David E. The reconciliation of neo-confucianism with christianity in the writings of joseph de prémare, s.j. **PEW** 26.4 (oct 1976) 389-410.

Notices of chinese cosmogony: formation of the visible universe, heaven, earth, the sun, moon, stars, man, beasts, &c., selected from the complete works of chu hi of the sung dynasty. **ChRep** 18.7 (july 1849) 342-347.

Rule, Paul A. The confucian interpretation of the jesuits. **PFEH** 6 (sept 1972) 1-61.

Shih, Vincent Yu-chung. The mind and the moral order. **MCB** 10 (1952-55) 347-364.

Smith, D. Howard. **Confucius.** NY (1973) 240 p. See chap 7, The revival of confucianism in the sung dynasty, 142-157.

Taylor, Rodney L. The centered self: religious auto-biography in the neo-confucian tradition. **HR** 17.3/4 (feb-may 1978) 266-283.

Taylor, Rodney Leon. **The cultivation of sagehood as a religious goal in neo-confucianism. A study of selected writings of kao p'an-lung, 1562-1626.** Missoula, montana (1978) x + 215 p, bibliog.

Taylor, Rodney L. Meditation in ming neo-orthodoxy: kao p'an-lung's writings on quiet-sitting. **JCP** 6 (1979) 149-182.

Taylor, Rodney L. Neo-confucianism, sagehood and the religious dimension. In **AR-HR** (1974) 9-32.

Taylor, Rodney L. Neo-confucianism, sagehood and the religious dimension. **JCP** 2 (1975) 389-415.

Thompson, Laurence G. Confucianism as a way of ultimate transformation. In **East/West cultures. Religious motivations for behavior: a colloquium,** santa barbara, calif (1978) 1-38.

Tu, Wei-ming. **Humanity and self-cultivation: essays in confucian thought.** Berkeley, calif (1979) xxii + 364 p, gloss, sel bibliog, index. Essays sep listed in our bibliog. Abbrev **H&SC.**

Tu-Wei-ming. "Inner experience": the basis of creativity in neo-confucian thinking. In Christian F. Murck (ed) **Artists and traditions: uses of the past in chinese culture,** princeton univ (1976) 9-15; repr in **H&SC** (1979) 102-110.

Tu, Wei-ming. An inquiry into wang yang-ming's four-sentence teaching. **EB** n.s. 7.2 (oct 1974) 32-48; repr in **H&SC** (1979) 162-178.

Tu, Wei-ming. Mind and human nature. **JAS** 30.3 (may 1971) 642-647; repr in **H&SC** (1979) 111-118. Rev art on Mou tsung-san's ideas.

Tu, Wei-ming. The neo-confucian concept of man. **PEW** 21.1 (jan 1971) 79-87; repr in **H&SC** (1979) 71-82.

Tu, Wei-ming. Neo-confucian ontology, a preliminary questioning. **JCP** 7.2 (june 1980) 93-114.

Tu, Wei-ming. **Neo-confucian thought in action. Wang yang-ming's youth (1472-1509)** Univ california (1976) 222 p, notes, bibliog, gloss, index.

Tu, Wei-ming. Reconstituting the confucian tradition. **JAS** 33.3 (may 1974) 441-454; repr in **H&SC** (1979) 119-137. Rev art on Ch'ien mu book on chu hsi.

Tu, Wei-ming. Subjectivity and ontological reality: an interpretation of wang yang-ming's mode of thinking. **PEW** 23.1/2 (jan-apr 1973) 187-205; repr in **H&SC** (1979) 138-161.

Tu, Wei-ming. Ultimate self-transformation as a communal act: comments on modes of self-cultivation in traditional china. **JCP** 6.2 (june 1979) 237-246.

Tu, Wei-ming. The unity of knowing and acting: from a neo-confucian perspective. In T.M.P. Mahadevan (ed) **Philosophy: theory and practice,** madras (1970) 190-205; repr in **H&SC** (1979) 83-101.

Wienpahl, Paul. Spinoza and wang yang-ming. **RS** 5 (1969) 19-27. Comparisons intended, among other things, "to make mysticism clearer."

Wienpahl, Paul. Wang yang-ming and meditation. **JCP** 1 (1973-74) 199-227.

Wittenborn, Allen. Tao and jen: the moral dimensions of chu hsi's philosophy. **ACQ** 7.4 (winter 1979) 1-13.

Young, John D. 'Original confucianism' versus neo-confucianism: matteo ricci's chinese writings. In **MS/CA** (1977) 371-377.

Zaehner, R.C. **Concordant discord. The interdependence of faiths.** Oxford univ (1970) See chap 13, The proud synthesis, 258-278.

9. ETHICS AND MORALS

(See also Sec. 7, **Confucius and Confucianism;** Sec. 8, **Neo-Confucian Religious Thought & Praxis**)

Almeder, Robert. The harmony of confucian and taoist moral attitudes. **JCP** 7.1 (mar 1980) 51-54.

Ashmore, William. A moral problem solved by confucianism. **ChRec** 2.10 (mar 1870) 282-285.

Bach, Marcus. **Major religions of the world.** N.Y. and nashville (1959) See chap 6, Confucianism and taoism—religion of good ethics, 74-84.

Baudens, G. Les doctrines morales de la chine. (extrait de la **china review.** Compte rendu analytique) **Revue maritime et coloniale** 41 (1874) 392-395.

Beach, Harlan P. The ethics of confucianism. In E. Hershey Sneath (ed) **The evolution of ethics as revealed in the great religions,** yale univ (1927) 39-74.

Bertholet, René. l'Astrobiologie et les moralistes chinois. **RMM** 40.4 (1933) 457-479.

Cernada, E.C. & G. Cernada. Ethical judgments about induced abortion. **ASBIE** 41 (spring 1976) 47-59.

Cernada, George P. **Basic beliefs about a new human life and ethical judgment: family planning field workers in taiwan.** Univ massachusetts, international area studies programs, occ papers ser no 5 (1979) 46 p.

Chan, Wing-tsit. The individual in chinese religions. In **SIEW** (1968) 181-198. Repr in **CM** (1967) 31-76.

Chan, Wing-tsit. K'ang yu-wei and the confucian doctrine of humanity (jen) In Jung-pang Lo (ed) **K'ang yu-wei: a biography and a symposium,** tucson, ariz. (1967) 355-374.

Chang, Aloysius. How christian are the chinese: are age old indigenous values predisposing them to christian morality? **Worldmission** 24.3 (fall 1973) 46-50.

Chang, C. Essai d'une adaptation des exercises spirituels à l'âme chinoise. **SM** 6 (1950-51) 199-219.

Chang, Tsung-tung. Chinesische moralphilosophien, gestern und heute. **Schopenhauer jahrbuch** 60 (1979) 83-106, bibliog.

Chavannes, Édouard. Les prix de vertu en chine. **CRAIBL** (1904) 667-691.

Chavannes, Édouard. De quelques idées morales des chinois. **BAF** (avr-juin 1917) 85-88. Idem: **Revue franco-étrangère** (juil-sept 1917) 230-235.

Cheng, Chung-ying. Dialectic of confucian morality and metaphysics of man. **PEW** 21.2 (apr 1971) 111-123.

Cheng, Chung-ying. On yi as a universal principle of specific application in confucian morality. **PEW** 22.3 (july 1972) 269-280.

Chien, Wen-hsien. The confucian ethics. **The world's chinese students' journal** 6.7 (nov 1912) 95-98.

Chih, Hung. Chinese daily life as a locus for ethics. **Concilium** 126 (1979) 33-41.

Chinese tables of merits and errors. **JIA** n.s.2 (1858) 210-220. ". . . stated to be extracted from a chinese work called kung-kwo-kih, i.e. 'merits and errors scrutinized'. . ." Extracted from **ICG** (1821)

Ching, Julia. Beyond good and evil. The culmination of the thought of wang yang-ming (1472-1529) **Numen** 22.2 (aug 1973) 125-134.

Ching, Julia. Chinese ethics and kant. **PEW** 28.2 (apr 1978) 161-172.

Chow, Bonaventura Shan-mou. **Ethica confucii.** Kohn (1957) 136 p.

Cohen, Alvin P. Avenging ghosts and moral judgment in ancient chinese historiography: three examples from shih-chi. In **LL&R** (1979) 97-108.

Confucianism: religion and ethics. A special issue of **PEW** 21.2 (apr 1971) Art sep listed in our bibliog.

Cua, A.S. Chinese moral vision, responsive agency, and factual beliefs. **JCP** 7.1 (mar 1980) 3-36.

Cua, Antonio S. The concept of paradigmatic individuals in the ethics of confucius. **Inquiry** 14.1/2 (1971) 41-55. Repr in Arne Naess & Alastair Hannay (ed) **Invitation to chinese philosophy,** oslo etc (1972) 41-55.

Cua, Antonio S. Dimensions of li (propriety): reflections on an aspect of hsun tzu's ethics. **PEW** 29.4 (oct 1979) 373-394.

Cua, Antonio S. **Dimensions of moral creativity. Paradigms, principles, and ideals.** Penn state univ (1977) 180 p. See chap 4, The excursion to confucian ethics, 50-65; chap 5, Confucian paradigmatic individuals, 66-78.

Cua, A.S. Practical causation and confucian ethics. **PEW** 25.1 (jan 1975) 1-10.

Cua, Antonio S. Reflections on the structure of confucian ethics. **PEW** 21.2 (apr 1971) 125-140.

Cua, A.S. Tasks of confucian ethics. **JCP** 6.1 (mar 1979) 55-67.

David, Alexandra, La morale chinoise. **Les documents du progrès** Paris (?1913) See also author's Chinesische moral. **Dokumente des fortschritte,** Berlin 7.8 (1914) 216-219.

Doolittle, Justus. Meritorius and charitable practices. Chap 6 and 7 in author's **SLC** vol 2 (1865) 164-196.

Dubs, Homer H. Chinese religious education. **ChRec** 55.5 (may 1924) 285-290. Re hsiu shen, ethical readers, until recently used in govt schools.

Eberhard, Wolfram. **Moral and social values of the chinese. Collected essays.** Taipei (1971) Pertinent art, all publ before 1970, are individually listed in our bibliog (Abbrev **MSVC**)

Eckardt, André. Die ethischen grundbegriffe bei laotse. **PJGG** 59.2 (1949) 200-207.

Edkins, Joseph. Ancient chinese thought, political and religious. **JNCBRAS** 31 (1896-97) 166-181.

Endres, Franz C. **Ethik des alltags.** Zürich, leipzig (1939) 135 p, pl.

Farjenel, Fernand. **La morale chinoise, fondement des sociétés d'extrême-orient.** Paris (1906) 258 p.

Faucett, Lawrence. **Six great teachers of morality.** Tokyo (1958) See chap 7, Seeking confucius in his sayings, 395-489, illus.

Faucett, Lawrence W. **The united nations and moral philosophy.** San marcos, calif (1968) See chap 3, China, confucius, and world peace, 15-27.

Faust, Ulrich. **Mythologien und religionen des ostens bei johann gottfried herder.** Münster (1977) See, D. China, 1. Religion und mythologie in den 'ideen' (1787 und 1785) 174-181; Adrastea vierter band (1802) 181-186.

Forke, Alfred. Unbewusste und passive moral der taoisten. In **Handbuch der philosophie,** münchen (d?) abt 5, c 165-171.

Franke, O. (tsl) **Kêng tschi t'u. Ackerbau und seidengewinnung in china; ein kaiserliches lehr- and mahn-buch.** Hamburg (1913) mit 102 taf, 57 illus in text. See, Einleitung: Ackerbau und seidengewinnung als ethische und religionsbildende elemente, 3-38.

Galpin, F. Notes on the ethical and christian value of chinese religious tracts and books. **ChRec** 12 (1881) 202-217.

Genähr, J. Conscience in the chinese classics. **ChRec** 42.10 (oct 1911) 577-584.

Haenisch, Erich. Die heiligung des vater- und fürstennamens in china; ihre ethische begründung und ihre bedeutung in leben und schriftum. **Berichte über die verhandlungen der philologisch-historischen klasse der sächsischen akademie der wissenschaften zu leipzig** 84.4 (1932) 1-20.

Hang, Thaddeus T'ui-chieh. Jen experience and jen philosophy. **JAAR** 42.1 (mar 1974) 53-65.

Hansen, Chad. Freedom and moral responsibility in confucian ethics. **PEW** 22.2 (apr 1972) 169-186.

Henke, Frederick G. Moral development of the chinese. **PS** (july 1915) 78-89.

Horning, Emma (tsl and analysis) Ts'ao ta ku's "precepts for women" (i.e. the "nü chieh" of pan chao) **ChRec** 66.6 (june 1935) 356-363.

Horning, Emma (tsl) Family instructions by empress jen hsia wen (wife of ming emp ch'eng tsu) **ChRec** 64.1 (jan 1933) 42-47; 64.2 (feb 1933) 100-110.

Hsiang, Paul S. The humanism in the religious thought of ancient china. **CC** 10.3 (1969) 13-21.

Hsieh Yu-wei. The status of the individual in chinese ethics. In **SIEW** (1968) Repr in **CM** (1967) 307-322.

Hsu, Jing & Tseng Wen-shing. Family relations in classic chinese opera. **IJSP** 20 (1974) 159-172.

Hsü, Pao-chien. Ethical realism in neo-confucian thought. Columbia univ thesis (n.d. ca. 1924) N.Y. and peking (1933) 165 p, illus.

Huang, Joe C. Ideology and confucian ethics in the characterization of bad women in socialist literature. In **Deviance** (1977) 37-51.

Huang, Siu-chi. The moral point of view of chang tsai. **PEW** 21.2 (apr 1971) 145-156.

Hummel, Arthur W. Some basic moral principles in chinese culture. In Ruth Nanda Ashen (ed) **Moral principles of action,** ny (1952)

Hunt, Arnold D. & Robert B. Crotty. **Ethics of world religions.** Minneapolis (1978) See Confucianism, 127-146.

Jochim, Christian. Ethical analysis of an ancient debate: moists versus confucians. **JRE** 8.1 (1980) 135-147.

Jung, Hwa Yol. Jen: an existential and phenomenological problem of intersubjectivity. **PEW** 16.3/4 (1966) 169-188.

Kao, John J. & Frederick F. Kao. Medical ethics, history of: sec 4, Contemporary china. In **EBio** (1978) vol 3, 917a-922a.

Keënyun yewheo shetee or odes for children in rhyme, on various subjects, in thirty-four stanzas. **ChRep** 4 (oct 1835) 287-291. Moralistic verse for children.

Kiang, Kang-hu. The religious basis of everyday chinese life. **AP** 2 (1931) 200-203.

Ku, Cheng-kang. The moral concept in chinese culture. **ACQ** 1.1 (fall 1973) 10-13.

Ku, Hung-ming. The religion of a gentleman in china. **CSM** 17 (1922) 676-679.

Kupperman, Joel J. Confucius and the nature of religious ethics. **PEW** 21.2 (apr 1971) 189-194.

Kupperman, Joel J. The supra-moral in chinese ethics. **JCP** 1.2 (mar 1974) 153-160.

Lacy, Carleton. Ethical values in chinese monism. **ChRec** 62.1 (jan 1931) 29-32.

Lee, T.H. The chinese idea of righteousness. **ChRec** 44.9 (sept 1913) 531-542.

Lee, Teng Hwee. The chinese idea of righteousness. **National review** 13 (may 1913) 459-460, 484-485.

Lin, Yu-sheng. The evolution of the pre-confucian meaning of jen and the confucian concept of moral autonomy. **MS** 31 (1974-75) 172-204.

Lindell, Kristina. Stories of suicide in ancient china. An essay on chinese morals. **ActaO** 35 (1973) 167-239.

Liu, Shu-hsien. A philosophic analysis of the confucian approach to ethics. **PEW** 22.4 (oct 1972) 417-425.

Liu, Ts'un-yan. Yüan huang and his "four admonitions." **JOSA** 1/2 (1967) 108-132. Repr **LTY:SPC** (1976).

Mahood, G.H. Socrates and confucius: moral agents or moral philosophers? **PEW** 21.2 (apr 1971) 177-188.

Martin, W.A.P. The ethical philosophy of the chinese. In author's **The lore of cathay,** n.y. (1901) repr taipei (1971) 205-233.

Morton, W.Scott. The confucian concept of man: the original formulation. **PEW** 21.1 (jan 1971) 69-77.

Nakamura, Hajime. The influence of confucian ethics on the chinese translations of buddhist sutras. **SIS** 5.3/4 (1957) 156-170.

Nakamura, Keijiro. The history and spirit of chinese ethics. **International journal of ethics** 8 (1897-98) 86-100.

Nivison, David S. Communist ethics and chinese tradition. **JAS** 16 (1956) 51-74.

Oehler, W. Sind die chinesen uns als volk moralisch überlegen? **EMM** n.s. vol 66 (feb 1922) 48-52.

Park, Pong Bae. Confucian moral philosophy of harmony. **NEAJT** 9 (sept 1972) 1-12.

Parker, E.H. Laocius and confucius as rival moralists. **AR** 20 (1924) 698-704; 21 (1925) 129-146.

Pike, E. Royston. **Ethics of the great religions.** London (1948) See chap 13, Confucianism, 215-228; chap 14, Taoism, 229-235.

Pohlman, W.J. (tsl) A confucian tract, exhorting mankind always to preserve their celestial principles and the good hearts. **ChRep** 15 (1846) 377-385, chin text and tsl.

Pott, William S.A. An approach to the study of confucian ethics. **NCR** 2 (1920) 448-455.

Pott, William S.A. The 'natural' basis of confucian ethics. **NCR** 3 (1921) 192-197.

Rawlinson, Frank J. **Chinese ethical ideals; a brief study of the ethical values in china's literary, social and religious life.** Shanghai (1934) x + 128 p.

Rawlinson, Frank. The chinese idea of truth. **ChRec** 43.12 (dec 1912) 706-713. ". . . from the point of view of the ethical idea of veracity."

Rawlinson, Frank. Chinese ideas of personality. **ChRec** 62.9 (sept 1931) 571-575. Re ethics.

Rawlinson, Frank J. The chinese sense of evil. **ChRec** 63.7 (july 1932) 428-434.

Rawlinson, Frank. The ethical values of micius. **ChRec** 63.2 (feb 1932) 93-102.

Rawlinson, Frank. The golden rule in china. **ChRec** 57.10 (oct 1926) 720-734.

Rawlinson, Frank. A prevalent chinese theory of the universe. **ChRec** 57.9 (sept 1926) 644-658. Viz., an "ethical universe."

Rawlinson, Frank. Religion and ethics in china. **ChRec** 64.9 (sept 1933) 561-569.

Reynolds, Frank E. Death: sec 2, Eastern thought. In **EBio** (1978) vol 2, 229b-235b, passim.

Robinson, David A. From confucian gentleman—to the new chinese 'political' man. In John Robert Nelson (ed) **No man is alien,** leiden (1971) chap 8, 149-161.

Rosemont, Henry, jr. Notes from a confucian perspective: which human acts are moral acts? **IPQ** 16.1 (mar 1976) 49-61.

Rotermund, W. **Die ethik lao-tse's mit besonderer bezugnahme auf die buddhistische moral.** Gotha (1874) 26 p.

Rowley, H.H. The chinese sages and the golden rule. **JRLB** 24 (1940) 321-352. Deals with lao tzu, confucius, mo tzu.

Rudd, H.F. **Chinese moral sentiments before confucius: a study in the origin of ethical valuations.** Shanghai (1916?) 220 p.

Schaefer, Thomas E. Perennial wisdom and the sayings of mencius. **IPQ** 3.3 (sept 1963) 428-444. On universality of moral wisdom.

Schultz, J.P. Riciprocity in confucian and rabbinic ethics. **JRE** 2 (spring 1974) 143-150.

Shapiro, Sheldon, Morality and religious reformations. **CSSH** 18 (1976) 438-457. Incl chin comparisons.

Sheffield, D.Z. The ethics of christianity and of confucianism compared. **ChRec** 17 (1886) 365-379.

Shu, Seyuan. **Une conception du bien moral.** Paris (1941) 128 p.

Smith, D.H. Ethical standards in world religions. **ET** 85 (apr 1974) 201-205.

Su, Jyun-hsyong. Menschenliebe und rechtschaftenheit im chinesischen rechtsleben. **Kairos** 9 (1967) 185-189.

Suppaner-Stanzel, Irene. Die ethischen ziele des taoismus und des existenzialismus. In festschrift: **Der mensch als persönlichkeit und als problem,** münchen (1963) 106-126.

Takeuchi, Teruo. A study in the meaning of jên advocated by confucius. **ActaA** 9 (1965) 57-77.

Tao, Hsi-sheng. The ethical program of social organization of confucianism. **ChFor** 2.1 (jan 1975) 21-40.

Tompkinson, Leonard. **Mysticism, ethics and service in chinese thought.** London (1956) 24 p.

Touan, Tchang-yuan. **La grande doctrine morale de dieu.** Trad en français par le colonel Tang-che. Pékin (1918) 97 p.

Tscharner, E.H. von. La pensée "métaphysique" et ethique de lao-tse. **Scientia** 72 (1942) 29-36.

Tu, Wei-ming. The neo-confucian concept of man. **PEW** 21.1 (jan 1971) 79-87; repr in **H&SC** (1979) 71-82.

Tu, Wei-ming. On the mencian perception of moral self-development. **Monist** 61.1 (jan 1978) 72-81; repr in **H&SC** (1979) 57-68.

Two sources of morality: polarization of moral standards; factions; clans. **CNA** 864 (10 dec 1971) 1-7.

Unschuld, Paul U. Confucianism. In **EBio** (1978) vol 1, 200a-204b.

Unschuld, Paul U. Medical ethics, history of: sec 3, Prerepublican china. In **EBio** (1978) vol 3, 911a-917a.

Unschuld, Paul U. **Medical ethics in imperial china. A study in historical anthropology.** Univ california (1979) 141 p, gloss, bibliog, index.

Valbert, G. Confucius et la morale chinoise. **RDM** 150 (1898) 673-684.

Whitehead, Raymond L. Enmity and ethics in the chinese revolution. **CF** 13.2 (summer 1970) 17-44.

Whitehead, Raymond L. Love and animosity in the ethic of mao. **CF** 17.2-3 (1974) 119-135.

Whitehead, Raymond L. Love and struggle in mao's ethic. **Christian century** 91.3 (23 jan 1974) 75-77.

Wickieri, Philip L. Morality and party reform: a problem in chinese ideology. **CF** 23.3/4 (1980) 141-149.

Wieger, Léon. **Moeurs et usages populaires.** Ho-kien-fu (1905) 548 p. Engl tsl L. Davrout: **Moral tenets and customs in china.** Texts in chin. Ho-kien-fu (1913) 604 p, illus.

Wittenborn, Allen. Tao and jen: the moral dimension of chu hsi's philosophy. **ACQ** 7.4 (winter 1979) 1-13.

Wu, Pei-yi. Self-examination and confession of sins in traditional china. **HJAS** 39.1 (june 1979) 5-38.

Yang, C.K. The functional relationship between confucian thought and chinese religion. In **CTI** (1957) 269-290.

Zenker, Ernst Victor. **Soziale moral in china und japan.** München, leipzig (1914) 42 p.

10. FILIALITY

Allan, C. Wilfrid. Chinese picture tracts. **EA** 5 (1906)

Bellah, Robert N. Father and son in christianity and confucianism. **Psychoanalytic review** 52 (1965) 92-114. Repr in author's collection: **Beyond belief: essays on religion in a post-traditional world,** n.y. (1970) 76-99.

Carus, Paul. Filial piety in china. **OC** 16.12 (dec 1902) 754-764, illus.

Chen, Joseph. Les doctrines chrétienne et confucéene de la piété filiale. **Laval théologique et philosophique** 19 (1963) 335-349.

Ch'en Kenneth. Filial piety in chinese buddhism. **HJAS** 28 (1968) 81-97.

Cordier, Henri. Bulletin critique des religions de la chine-(la piété filiale en chine) **RHR** 3.2 (1881) 218-227.

Cordier, Henry. La piété filiale et le culte des ancêtres en chine. **CMG** 35 (1910) 67-101. Also in **Bibliothèque de vulgarisation des BVAMG** 35 (1910)

Doolittle, Justus. Chinese anecdotes: filial and dutiful children. 3rd sec of chap 18 in author's **SLC** vol 1 (1865) 452-459.

Faber, Ernst. A critique of the chinese notions and practice of filial piety. **ChRec** 9 (1878) 329-343, 401-418; 10 (1879) 1-18, 83-96, 163-174, 243-253, 323-329, 416-428; 11 (1880) 1-12.

Giles, Herbert A. What is filial piety? In author's **AdSin** 1 (1905) 20-25.

Ho, Sai Ming. The chinese concept of filial piety. **SEAJT** 3.2 (oct 1961) 53-58.

Ho, Y.F. & L.Y. Lee. Authoritarianism and attitude toward filial piety in chinese teachers. **Journal of social psychology** 92 (1974) 305-306. Significant correlation found.

Hoogers, Joseph. Théorie et pratique de la piété filiale chez les chinois. **Anthropos** 5 (1910) 1-15, 688-702, illus.

Hsiao, Harry Hsin-o. Concepts of hsiao (filial piety) in the classic of poetry and the classic of documents. **Journal of the institute of chinese studies of the chinese university of hong kong** 10.2 (1979) 425-443.

Hsiao, Henry Hsin-i. Problems concerning tseng tzu's role in the promotion of filial pietism. **CC** 19.1 (mar 1978) 7-18.

Hsieh Yu-wei. Filial piety and chinese society. In **PCEW** (1962) 411-427. Repr in **CM** (1967) 167-187.

Hsu, Francis L.K. **Clan, caste and club.** Princeton univ (1963) 335 p.

Jacobs, Fang-chih Huang. The origin and development of the concept of filial piety in ancient china. **CC** 14.3 (sept 1973) 25-55.

Koehn, Alfred (tsl) **Piété filiale en chine.** Peking (1943) 24 p. Engl ed: **Filial devotion in china.** Peking (1944) Tsl of Kuo, Chü-ching, **Erh-shih-ssu hsiao.**

Lin, Timothy Tien-min. Confucian filial piety and christian ethics. **NEAJT** 8 (mar 1972) 43-48.

Lord, E.C. Filial piety among the chinese, its character and influence. **ChRec** 14.4 (july-aug 1883) 289-301.

MacGillivray, Donald. The twenty-four paragons of filial piety. **ChRec** 31.8 (aug 1900) 392-402.

Ming, H.S. Chinese concepts of filial piety. **SEAJT** 3 (oct 1961) 53-58.

A Resident in Peking. **China as it really is.** London (1912) See chap 4, Ancestor worship and filial piety, 25-30.

Sachse, H. (tsl) Twenty-four examples of filial piety. **FE** 1 (1906) 181-186.

Stolberg, Baron. Filial affection as taught and practised by the chinese. **CW** 9 (1869) 416-421.

Than, Ba Tho (tsl) La piété filiale. Préceptes de la morale confucéene. **BSEIS** sér 1 (1908) 67-81. French tsl of stories of 24 paragons of filiality.

Thiersant, Dabry de. **La piété filiale en chine.** Paris (1877) 226 p.

Tsaou-ngo temple. **ChRec** 3.8 (jan 1871) 206-207. Temple near hangchou whose chief deity is a girl noted for filiality.

Urhsheih-sze heaou, or twenty-four examples of filial piety. **ChRep** 6.3 (july 1837) 130-142. Tsl.

What is filial piety? **JNCBRAS** 20 (1885) 115-144.

Williams, E.T. Confucianism in the home. Chap 12 in author's **CYT**, 249-262.

11. DEATH & ANCESTRAL CULT
(See also Sec. 12, **Feng-shui**)

Addison, James Thayer. **Chinese ancestor worship. A Study of its meaning and its relations with christianity.** n.p. (1925) 85 p.

Addison, James T. Chinese ancestor worship and protestant christianity. **JR** 5.2 (1925) 140-149.

Addison, James Thayer. The meaning of chinese ancestor worship. **ChRec** 55.9 (sept 1924) 592-599, biblio of wk in engl.

Addison, J.T. The modern chinese cult of ancestors. **JR** 4 (1924) 492-503.

Ahern, Emily M. Affines and the rituals of worship. In **RRCS** (1974) 279-308.

Aijmer, Göran. Ancestors in the spring. The qingming festival in central china. **JHKBRAS** 18 (1978) 59-82.

Aijmer, Göran. A structural approach to chinese ancestor worship. **BTLVK** 124.1 (1968) 91-98.

Amélineau, E. Les coutumes funéraires de l'égypte ancienne comparées avec celles de la chine. **Études critique et d'histoire par les membres de la section des sciences religieuses de l'école des hautes études.** Paris (1906) 2e sér, 1-34.

Ancestral worship. **ChRev** 7 (1878-79) 290-301, 355-364.

Arlington, L.C. The ceremony of disintering in china. **ChRev** 25.4 (1901) 176-178.

Baker, Hugh D. Burial, geomancy and ancestor worship. In **ASONT** (1965) 36-39.

Baker, Hugh D.R. **Chinese family and kinship.** Columbia univ (1979) See chap 4, Ancestor worship, 71-106; Ancestor worship in contemporary china, 206-211; app 2, Feng-shui fighting, 219-225.

Beyerhaus, Peter. The christian approach to ancestor worship. **Ministry** 6.4 (july 1966) 137-145.

Bidens. Mourning etiquette. **ChRev** 7 (1878-79) 351-352.

Blodget, H. Ancestral worship in the shu king. **JPOS** 3.2 (1892)

Boerschmann, Ernst. **Die baukunst und religiöse kultur der chinesen.** Vol 2; **Gedächtnistempel; tzé tang.** Berlin (1914) xxiv + 288 p, illus.

Bouïnais, Lt.-Col. et A. Paulus. **Le culte des morts dans le céleste empire et l'annam comparé au culte des ancêtres dans l'antiquité occidentale.** Paris (1893) xxxiii × 267 p.

Burial societies. **ChRev** 13 (1884-85) 429-430.

Butcher, Charles H. Notes on the funeral rites performed at the obsequies of takee. **JNCBRAS** 2 (1865) 173-176.

Chao, P. The mourning ritual within the chinese kinship system. **CC** 13.2 (june 1972) 49-71.

Chen, Chi-lu. Ancestral worship associations of the taiwan chinese. In **MS/CA** (1977) 53-58.

Chen, Chung-min. Ancestor worship and clan organization in a rural village of taiwan. **ASBIE** 23 (1967) engl abrmt 21-24.

Cheng, F.-k & W.-s. Shen. **A brief history of chinese mortuary objects.** Peking (1933) Yenching journal of chinese studies monograph series no 1. See rev by W. Eberhard, **AA** 6 (1935) 147-148.

Chikusa, Tatsuo. Succession to ancestral sacrifices and adoption of heirs to the sacrifices: as seen from an inquiry into customary institutions in manchuria. In **CFL&SC** (1978) 151-175.

Chinese ancestral worship and its significance. **Biblical world** 7 (1896) 290-291.

Chow, Lien-hwa. The problem of funeral rites. **Practical anthropology** 11.5 (sept-oct 1964) 226-228.

Comber, Leon. **Chinese ancestor worship in malaya.** Singapore (1956) 41 p, 20 pl, chin index, bibliog.

Cordier, Henri. La piété filiale et le culte des ancêtres en chine. **CMG** 35 (1910) 67-101. Also publ in **BVAMG** 35 (1910)

Crémazy, L. Le culte des ancêtres en chine et dans l'annam. **RIC** 107 (1900) 1066-1068; 108 (1900) 1088-1089.

Davia, Jacques. La mort et les chinois. **TM** 5 (1899) 150-151.

Dehergne, Joseph. Les tablettes dans le culte des ancêtres en chine confucéene. **RechScRelig** 66.2 (1978) 201-214.

Denby, Charles. **China and her people.** Boston (1906) See chap 15, Disposal of the dead, 197-202.

Doolittle, Justus. Ancestral tablets and ancestral halls. Chap 8 in author's **SLC** vol 1 (1865) 217-235.

Doolittle, Justus. Death, mourning, and burial. Chap 6 and 7 in author's **SLC** vol 1 (1865) 168-216.

Douglas, Robert K. **Society in china.** London (1901) See chap 12, Funeral rites, 219-227.

Dubs, Homer H. The confucian attitude to the worship of ancestors. **ChRec** 58.8 (aug 1927) 498-505.

Dubs, Homer H. The custom of mourning to the third year. Chap 11, app 1, in Dubs (tsl) **The history of the former han dynasty by pan ku,** vol 3, baltimore (1955) 40-42.

Eatwell, W. On chinese burials. **Journal of the anthropological institute of great britain and ireland** 1.2 (1871) 207-208.

Edkins, Joseph. Literature of ancestral worship in china. **Academy** 28 (1885) 186-187.

Eigner, J. The significance of ancestor worship in china. **CJ** 26 (1937) 125-127.

Erkes, E. Ahnenbilder und buddhistische skulpturen aus altchina. **JSMVL** 5 (1913) 26-32, illus. Notice by Ed. Chavannes, **TP** (1914) 291-297.

Erkes, Eduard. Der schamanistische ursprung des chinesischen ahnenkultus. **Sinologica** 2 (1950) 253-262.

Erkes, E. Zum problem des chinesischen ahnenbildes. **AA** 8 (1945) 105-106; also in **Sinologica** 3 (1953) 240-241.

Faber, E. Seventeen paragraphs on ancestral worship. **Records of shanghai missionary conference** (1890)

Fabre, A. Avril au pays des aïeux. In **CCS** vol 8 (1935) Ancestor worship and burial practices re ch'ing ming, specifically in shun-te, kuangtung.

Farjenel, F. Du culte des ancêtres en chine. **JA** sér 10, t 2 (1903) 85-96.

Farjenel, Fernand. Quelques particularités du culte des ancêtres en chine. **JA** 10e sér, 1 (1903) 85-86.

Farjenel, Fernand (tsl) Rites funéraires chinois; les funérailles impériales et celles des gen du peuple. Louvain (ca 1904) 63 p Offprint fr **Le Muséon.**

Fernald, Helen E. Some chinese grave figures. **MJ** 17 (1926) 75-93.

Ferro, G. Vigna dal. l'Etiquette où la mort: moeurs d'extrême-orient. **TM** 4 (1898) 366-367.

Fielde, Adele M. **A corner of cathay.** NY (1894) See Mortuary customs, 49-70; mostly re swatow.

Freedman, Maurice. Ancestor worship: two facets of the chinese case. In **SOERF** (1967) 85-103.

Freedman, Maurice. **Chinese lineage and society: fukien and kwangtung.** Univ london (1966) See esp chap 5, Geomancy and ancestor worship, 118-154, incl photo.

Freedman, Maurice. **Lineage organization in south-eastern china.** London school of economics (1958) See chap 5, 10, 11.

Freedman, Maurice. Ritual aspects of chinese kinship and marriage. In **FKCS** (1970) 163-187.

Fung, Yu-lan. The confucianist theory of mourning, sacrificial and wedding rites. **CSPSR** 15 (1931) 335-345.

Galpin, F. China's tribute to the dead. **JMGS** 11 (1895) 209-216.

Gautier, Judith. **Les peuples étranges.** Paris (1879) See pt 2, sec Cérémonies funèbre, 210-220.

Gieseler, G. Le jade dans le culte et les rites funéraires en chine sous les dynasties tcheou et han. **RA** 5 sér, 4 (1916) 61-128, illus.

Gobien, Charles le. Éclaircissement sur les honneurs que les chinois rendent à confucius et aux morts. In author's **Affaires de la chine,** paris (1700) t 3, 217-332.

Gordon-Cumming, C.F. The offerings of the dead. Chap 16, vol 1, of author's **WinC** (1886) 277-321.

Granet, Marcel. Le langage de la douleur d'après le rituel funéraire de la chine classique. **Journal de psychologie normale et pathologique** 19.2 (fev 1922) 97-118; repr in **ESC** (1953)

Groot, J.J.M.de. The demise of an amoy gentleman. **ChRev** 19.5 (1891) 281-284.

Groot, J.J.M.de. **The religious system of china.** Leiden (1892-1910) repr taipei (1964) 6 vol. 1-3: Disposal of the dead; 4-6: The soul and ancestral worship. Compte rendu par Éd. Chavannes, **RHR** 37 (1898) 81-89.

Guimbretière, P. Les chinois et leurs morts. **RC** (janv 1906) 37-42.

Hardy, J. and C. Lenormand. l'Importance et l'agencement des tombeaux chinois. **TM** 12 (1906) 409-412, illus.

Harrell, C. Stevan. The ancestors at home: domestic worship in a land-poor taiwanese village. In **Ancestors** (1976) 373-385.

Headland, Isaac Taylor. Funeral ceremonies and ancestor worship. Chap 16-17 in author's **HLC** (1914) 147-160.

Henry, B.C. Ancestral worship and geomancy. Chap 7 in author's **CD** (1885) 123-151.

Hoogers, Joseph. Au sujet des sacrifices et offrandes chinoises pour les morts. **Anthropos** 4.2 (mars-avr 1909) 526.

Hsu, Francis L.K. **Clan, caste and club.** Princeton univ (1963)

Hu, Hsien-chin. **The common descent group in china and its function.** N.Y. (1948) See chap 2, Ancestor veneration, 31-40, illus., and passim.

Hwang, Bernard. Ancestor cult today. **Missiology** 5.3 (july 1977) 339-365.

Ikeda, Suetoshi. Ancestor worship and nature worship in ancient china—especially the concepts of ti and t'ien. **Proc IX ICHR 1958,** Tokyo (1960) 100-105.

J. Rites performed for the dead. **ChRev** 9 (1880-81) 397. See further D.G., same title, in **ibid** 10 (1881-82) 145-146.

James, T.W. Douglas. The christian approach to ancestor worship. **ChRec** 56.11 (nov 1925) 729-733.

Kalff, L. **Der totenkult in südschantung, ein beitrag zur volkskunde des landes.** Yenchowfu (1932) viii + 109 p, illus, diagr.

Kranz, P. The teaching of the chinese classics on ancestral worship. **ChRec** 35 (1904) 237-245.

Kuo, Li-cheng. Chinese funerary arts. **Echo** 3.7 (july-aug 1973) 34-41, illus col photos. Re ming ch'i.

Laufer, Berthold. The development of ancestral images in china. **Journal of religious psychology** 6 (1913) 111-123. Abrmt in W.A. Lessa and E.Z. Vogt (ed) **Reader in comparative religion,** evanston, ill. and white plains, n.y. (1958) 404-409.

Lecomte, Louis Daniel (1655-1728) **Réponse à la lettre de messieurs des missions étrangères, au pape, sur les cérémonies chinoises.** N.p., n.d. 396 p.

Leong, Y.K. and L.K. Tao. **Village and town life in china.** London (1915) See The ancestral hall, 22-31.

Li, Chi. **Anyang.** Univ washington (1977) See chap 14, Worship of ancestors and other spirits, 247-254.

Li, Yih-yuan. Chinese geomancy and ancestor worship: a further discussion. In **Ancestors** (1976) 329-338.

Ling, Shun-sheng. Ancestral tablet and genital symbolism in ancient china. **ASBIE** 8 (1959) engl summ 39-46 + 14 p pl.

Ling, Shun-sheng. Origin of the ancestral temple in china. **ASBIE** 7 (1959) engl summ 177-184 + 6 p pl.

Liu, David & James Hayes. Royal asiatic society—visit to the tang family graves on saturday, 11th december, 1976. **JHKBRAS** 17 (1977) 179-185, pl 45-53 end of vol.

Loi, Michelle. La vie et la mort en chine contemporaine. **Ethno-psychologie** 27.1 (mar 1972) 79-101.

Lynn, Jermyn Chi-hung. **Social life of the chinese.** Peking-Tientsin (1928) See chap 9, Funerals. Re peking.

MacGowan, John. Ancestor worship. Chap 7 in author's **L&S** (1909) 71-86.

Mariage des morts au chan-si. **TM** 5 (1899) 191.

Martin, Ernest. Le culte des ancêtres, le culte des morts et le culte des funérailles chez les chinois. **Journal d'hygiène** 17 (1891) 313-320, 325-332.

Martin, Ernest. Les sépultures dans l'extrême-orient. **Revue scientifique** 31 (9 dec 1893) 753-756.

Martin, W.A.P. How shall we deal with the worship of ancestors. **ChRec** 33.3 (mar 1902) 117-119.

Martin, W.A.P. The worship of ancestors. How shall we deal with it? **ChRec** 35 (1904) 301-308.

Martin, W.A.P. The worship of ancestors in china. In author's **Hanlin papers,** london and shanghai (1880) repr in author's **The Lore of Cathay,** n.y. (1901) repr taipei (1971) 264-278.

Matignon, J.J. Un enterrement à pékin. In author's **l'Orient lointain. . .,** paris (?) (d?) 127-151.

Matignon, J.J. Les morts qui gouvernent. (A propos de l'immobilisme de la chine) **Archives d'anthropologie criminelle** 15 (1900) 457-484. See also author's **Superstitions, crime et misère. . .,** paris (1898) 337-374.

Matignon, J.J. Les préliminaires de l'enterrement en chine. **Bulletin société de géographie commerciale de bordeaux** 38e ann (1912) 244-249, illus.

Mayers, W.F. On the stone figures at chinese tombs and the offerings of living sacrifices. **JNCBRAS** 12 (1878) 1-17.

Mecquenem, J. de. Le faire-part de décès du général wou lou-tchen. **BAAFC** (janv 1914) 36-44, fig.

Mei, Y.P. Ancestor-worship: origin and value. **CSM** 21.6 (1926) 19-25.

Milloué, L. de. Culte et cérémonies en honneur des morts dans l'extrême-orient. **CMG** (1899-1900 et 1900-1901) 135-159.

Mitchell-Innes, Norman G. Birth, marriage and death rites of the chinese. **FLJ** 5 (1887) 221-245.

Moese, Wolfgang. Ancestor worship and ceremonies. In **CRWMS** (1979) 364-385, illus.

Moroto, Sojun. The idea of ancestor in chinese classics. In **RSJ** (1959) 192-201.

Moule, Arthur E. Ancestral worship. Chap 7 in author's **NC&O** (1891) 193-222.

Munn, William. Ancestor-worship: its origins and results. **Church missionary review** 71 (dec 1920) 319-328.

Nelson, H.G.H. Ancestor worship and burial practices. In **RRCS** (1974) 251-278.

Nitschkowsky. Der chinesische ahnenkultus. **AMZ** 22 (1895) 289-301, 360-374, 385-391.

Noël, Alexandre. **Conformité des cérémonies chinoises avec l'idolatrie grecque et romaine; pour servir de confirmation à l'apologie des dominicains mission-aires de la chine . . .** Cologne (1700) 9 letters individually paginated.

Otake, Emiko. Two categories of chinese ancestors as determined by their malevolence. **AsFS** 39.1 (1980) 21-31.

Pacifique-Marie, P. d'Aingreville. Funérailles païennes en chine. **MC** 36 (1904) 406-408, 417-419, 429-431, 442-444.

Pakenham-Walsh, W.S. Memorials to the dead and their relation to christian practice. **ChRec** 41.4 (apr 1910) 264-268.

Paléologue, Maurice. Sépultures chinoises. **RDM** 3e période, sér 9, t 83 (15 oct 1887) 918-932.

Parker, E.H. Animals at funerals. **ChRev** 17 (1888-89) 114.

Parker, E.H. Animals in funeral processions. **ChRev** 14 (1885-86) 171.

Parker, E.H. Funeral rites. **ChRev** 14 (1885-86) 225.

Parker, E.H. Phraseology of mourning. **ChRev** 15 (1886-87) 188.

Pasternak, Burton. Chinese tale-telling tombs. **Ethnology** 12.3 (july 1973) 259-273. ". . . relationship betw grave composition and tomb sacrifices on the one hand, and lineage segmentation, lineage trusts, and the nature of the relationship betw living and dead members of the descent group on the other . . . based on data collected on three hakka descent groups in meinung county, southwestern taiwan."

Pitcher, P.W. Chinese 'ancestral worship.' **MRW** n.s. 7 (1894) 81-86.

Poore, Major R. Ancestral worship in china and 'family worth-ship' in england, as a practical basis of efficient state administration. **IAQR** ser 2,8 (july 1894) 141-149. See also Eugène Simon, 'Une imitation . . .' in **La reforme soziale** 25/26 (1893) 304-321.

Poseck, Helena von. Chinese customs connected with birth, marriages, deaths . . . III. Death and burial. **EA** 4 (1905) 24-32.

Potter, Jack M. Wind, water, bones and souls: the religious world of the cantonese peasant. **JOS** 8.1 (1970) 139-153. Repr in **C Way Rel** (1973) Study of ping shan, new territories, hong kong.

Present-day attitude towards ancestor worship. A symposium. **ChRec** 59.4 (apr 1928) 228-232.

Price, P.F. The worship of ancestors. **ChRec** 33 (1902) 253-255.

Pruitt, Ida. **Old madame yin. A memoir of peking life, 1926-1938.** Stanford univ (1979) See chap 13 for description of woman's burial clothes.

Ravary, P. Les tablettes des ancêtres et leurs registres de la famille en chine. **ER** 18e ann, 5e sér, 6 (1874) 762-768.

Reynolds, Frank E. Death: sec 2, Eastern thought. In **EBio** (1978) vol 2, 229b-235b, passim.

A resident in peking. **China as it really is.** London (1912) See chap 4, Ancestor worship and filial piety, 25-30.

Roberts, L. Chinese ancestral portraits. **Parnassus** 9.1 (1937) 28.

Rudolph, Conrad. The wu family shrines. **JAC** 4 (spring 1980) 21-47.

Rychterová, Eva. Commemorative ancestor portraits. **NO** 4 (1965) 176-177, illus.

Schalek, Alice. Chinesische sterbesitten. **Welt auf reisen** 14 (1914) 57-60.

Schloss, Ezekiel. **Ming-ch'i.** NY (1975) 13 p, 100 illus. Catalog of exhib at katonah gallery, ny, 1975.

Scott, A.C. Costumes of the chinese (Female mourning costume) **Orient** 2.2 (1951) 29.

Segalen, Victor, Gilbert de Voisins & Jean Lartigue. **l'Art funéraire à l'époque des hans.** Paris (1935) 304 p, 121 fig. Mission archéol en chine 1914, t 1.

Serebrennikov, J.J. Funeral money in china. **CJ** 18 (1933) 191-193.

Shih, C.C. A study of ancestor worship in ancient china. In **SW** (1964) 179-190.

Spiegel, H. Die architektur der gräber. **WBKKA** 7 (1932-33) 66-87.

Stanley, C.A. Ancestral worship. **ChRec** 33 (1902) 268-270.

Stevens, Keith. Ancestral images. **JHKBRAS** 18 (1978) 200-202. Suppl to author's art, Altar images . . . in **ibid** 41-48. Tsl of brief sec in Liu Wen-san, Taiwan tsung-chiao yi-shu (taiwanese religious art)

Stover, Leon E. **The cultural ecology of chinese civilization. Peasants and elites in the last of the agrarian states.** NY (1974) See chap 13, Funerals and ancestors, 201-214.

Tavernier, E. Le culte des ancêtres. **BSEIS** n.s. 1 (1926) 133-173.

Tchang, Mathias. **Tombeau des liang, famille siao, lère partie: siao choen-tche.** Shanghai (1912) xiii + 108 p, illus (Variétés sinologiques no 33)

Thiel, Joseph. Doppelsprüche auf den torsäulen der grahaine. **Sinologica** 6 (1959) 25-56, 6 pl.

Thiele, Peter. Chinesische totenbräuche in nordtaiwan. **ZE** 100 (1975) 99-114.

Thompson, Laurence G. Funeral rites in taiwan. In author's **CWayRel** (1973) 160-169.

Tiberi, Fortunato. Der ahnenkult in china nach den kanonischen schriften. **AL** 27 (1963) 283-475.

Tombs of ancestors. **ChRep** 1.12 (apr 1833) 499-503.

Topley, Marjorie. Chinese rites for the repose of the soul. **JMBRAS** 25 (1952) 149-160.

Torrance, Thomas. Burial customs in sz-chuan. **JNCBRAS** 41 (1910) 57-75, illus.

Vandermeersch, Léon. **Wangdao ou la voie royale. Recherches sur l'esprit des institutions de la chine archaïque.** T 1, Structures cultuelles et structures

familiales. Paris (1977) 358 p, T 2, **Structures politiques, les rites.** Paris (1980) 603 p, tables, index. See Table générale des matières.

Volpert, A. Gräber und steinskulpturen der alten chinesen. **Anthropos** 3 (1908) 14-18, illus.

W, Dr J. Totenkult in china. **Asien** 6? (dez 1906) 40-41.

Walker, J.E. Ancestral worship **ChRec** 34 (1903) 199.

Walshe, W.G. Some chinese funeral customs. **JNCBRAS** 35 (1903-04) 26-64.

Waong, P.L. Les tablettes des ancêtres. **BUA** 3e sér, 2 (1941) 243-280.

Weber, Charles D. The spirit path in chinese funerary practice. **OA** n.s. 24.2 (summer 1978) 168-178, illus. Re stone fig at tombs.

Wei, Louis Tsing-sing. Das begräbnis im chinesischen konfuzianismus. **Concilium** 4 (feb 1968) 142-143.

Werner, E.T.C. Reform in chinese mourning rites. **NCR** 2 (1920) 223-247.

Wilhelm, Richard. Das altechinesische ahnenopfer. **Sinica** 5 (1930) 150-151.

Wilhelm [Richard]. Totenbräuche in schantung. **MDGNVO** 11.1 (1906) 33-45. See also R. Wilhelm, same title, in **ZMK** 23 (1908) 78-88, illus.

Williams, S. Wells. The worship of ancestors among the chinese: a notice of the . . . kia li tieh-shih tsih-ching or collection of forms and cards used in family ceremonies. **ChRep** 18 (1849) 361-384.

Wilson, B.D. Chinese burial customs in hong kong. **JHKBRAS** 1 (1960-61) 115-123.

Wimsatt, Genevieve. Chinese funerals. Chap 9 in author's **GC** (1927) 131-144.

Wolf, Arthur P. Aspects of ancestor worship in northern taiwan. In **Ancestors** (1976) 339-364.

Wolf, Arthur P. Chinese kinship and mourning dress. In **FKCS** (1970) 189-208.

Wolf, Arthur P. Gods, ghosts, and ancestors. In **RRCS** (1974) 131-182.

Wong, Yu-yui. 'The filial mourning head-dress society' in the villages of chang-i, shantung. Institute of pacific relations, research staff of secretariat (comp & tsl) **Agrarian china; selected source materials from chinese authors.** Univ of chicago (n.d—preface 1938) 204-207.

Worshiping at the tombs. **ChRep** 1.5 (sept 1832) 201-203.

Yang, Kun. **Recherches sur le culte des ancêtres comme principe ordonnateur de la famille chinoise; la succession au culte, la succession au patrimoine.** Univ lyon (1934) 174 p.

Yates, M.T. **Ancestral worship.** Shanghai (1877) 48 p.

Yates, M.T. Ancestral worship and fung-shuy. **ChRec** 1.3 (july 868) 23-28, 37-43.

Ymaizoumi, M. Du culte des ancêtres en chine sous la dynastie de tcheou. **CPOL** t 2, lyon (1880) 68-79.

Young, Conrad Chun-shih. Name taboo and confucianism. An anthropological view. **ASBIE** 30.2 (autumn 1970) 111-120.

Yuan, L.Z. **Through a moon gate.** Shanghai (1938) See chap 3, On to the next world, 67-86.

12. FENG-SHUI
(See also Sec. 11: **Death and the Ancestral Cult**)

Aijmer, Göran. Being caught by a fishnet: on fengshui in southeastern china. **JHKBRAS** 8 (1968) 74-81.

Anderson, E.N. & Marja L. Feng-shui: ideology and ecology. In joint authors' collection, **Mountains and waters: essays on the cultural ecology of south coastal china,** taipei (1973) 127-146.

Baker, Hugh D.R. Burial, geomancy and ancestor worship. In **ASONT** (1965) 36-39.

Baker, Hugh D.R. **Chinese family and kinship.** Columbia univ (1979) See app 2, Feng-shui fighting, 219-225 (tsl fr a chin bk publ 1963)

Ball, J. Dyer. **The chinese at home.** NY etc (1912) See chap 4, Wind and water, or "fung-shui," 32-44.

Bas, Rene Q. Wind, water and wealth. **Orientations** 1.8 (aug 1970) 46-47, 1 illus.

Boerschmann, E. K'ueising türme und fengshuisäulen. **AM** 2 (1925) 503-530.

Boxer, B. Space, change and feng-shui in tsuen wan's urbanization. **JAAS** 3 (1968) 226-240.

Chinese pagodas, their supposed influence on the productions of the soil, the prosperity of the people, and the government of the elements; with notices of the lions of canton. **ChRep** 6 (1837-38) 189-192.

Danielli, M. The geomancer in china, with some reference to geomancy as observed in madasgascar. **Folk-lore** 63 (1952) 204-226.

Dukes, Edwin J. Feng-shui. In **HERE** vol 5 (1914) 833-835.

Dukes, Edwin J. Feng-shui: the biggest of all bugbears. Chap 8 in author's **ELC** (1885) 175-190.

Edkins, Joseph. Fengshui. **ChRec** 4 (1871-72) 274-277, 291-298, 316-320. Repr **Shanghai budget** (27 apr, 15 june, 6 and 13 july 1872)

Eitel, Ernest J. **Feng-shui: or, the rudiments of natural science in china.** London (1873) 84 p. repr cokaygne (1973) bristol, engl (1979). French tsl L. de Milloué, **AMG** 1 (1880) 203-253.

Feng-shui. **Cornhill magazine** (mar 1874)

Feuchtwang, Stephan D.R. **An anthropological analyis of chinese geomancy.** Vientianne (1974) 263 p, 2 app, list of wks cited, fig.

Fisher, Tom Feng shui: the occult science of geomancy. **Echo** 2.10 (nov 1972) 15-19, 54-55, illus photos.

Freedman, Maurice. Ancestor worship: two facets of the chinese case. **SOERF** (1967) 85-103.

Freedman, Maurice. **Chinese lineage and society: fukien and kwangtung.** Univ london (1966) See esp chap 5: Geomancy and ancestor worship, 118-154, incl photos.

Freedman, Maurice. Geomancy. **Proceedings of the royal anthropological institute of great britain and ireland for 1968,** 5-15. Presidential address.

Freedman, Maurice. A report on social research in the new territories of hongkong 1963. **JHKBRAS** 16 (1976) See 218-236 on 'fung shui.' Posthumous publ.

Gordon-Cumming, C.F. Feng-shui. Chap 18, vol 1 in author's **WinC** (1886) 331-355.

Grout, G.C.W. Ceremonies of propitiation carried out in connection with road works in the new territories in 1960. **JHKBRAS** 11 (1971) 204-209.

Hayes, James W. Geomancy and the village. In **TICHK** (1967) 22-30.

Hayes, James. Local reactions to the disturbance of 'fung shui' on tsing yi island, hong kong, september 1977-march 1978., **JHKBRAS** 19 (1979) 213-216, 3 pl.

Hayes, James. Local reactions to the disturbance of 'fung shui' on tsingyi island, hong kong, march 1978-december 1980. **JHKBRAS** 20 (1980) 155-156.

Hayes, James W. Movement of villages on lantau island for fung shui reasons. **JHKBRAS** 3 (1963) 143-144.

Hayes, James W. Removal of villages for fung shui reasons. Another example from lantau island, hong kong. **JHKBRAS** 9 (1969) 156-158.

Hubrig. Fung schui oder chinesische geomantie. **Verhandlungen berlin gesellschaft für anthropologie ethnologie und urgeschichte** (1879) 34-43.

Kamm, John Thomas. Field notes on the social history of fung-shui of kam tin. **JHKBRAS** 17 (1977) See The fung-shui of kam tin, 215-216.

Lapicque, P.A. Le fin du 'fong chouei' ou la disparition des esprits des eaux et des airs. **RIC** n.s. 16 (sept 1911) 299-301.

Li, Yih-yuan. Chinese geomancy and ancestor worship: a further discussion. In **Ancestors** (1976) 329-338.

Lip, Evelyn. **Chinese geomancy.** Singapore (1979) 126 p, copiously illus col drawings and diagrams, chin char.

Lung, Daniel. Fungshui, an intrinsic way of environmental design. Illustrated by the case of kat hing wai in the new territories of hong kong. **JHKBRAS** 20 (1980) 81-92.

MacGowan, John. Fêngshui. Chap 8 in author's **L&S** (1909) 87-98.

March, Andrew L. An appreciation of chinese geomancy. **JAS** 27.2 (1968) 253-268, bibliog.

Meyer, Jeffrey F. Feng-shui of the chinese city. **HR** 18.2 (nov 1978) 138-155.

Morgan, Carole. A short glossary of geomantic terms. **JHKBRAS** 20 (1980) 209-214.

P'eng, Tso-chih. Chinesischer stadtbau unter besonderer berücksichtigung der stadt peking. **NachrDGNVO** 89/90 (1961) 5-80, fig.

Pennick, Nigel. **East asian geomancy.** Cambridge (1975) 1 + 14 p, illus, plans.

Peterson, Mark A. Chinese geomancy. **Asia; journal of the society for asian studies, brigham young university** 4 (mar 1971) 25-36.

Porter, L.C. Feng shui or how the chinese keep in tune with nature. **ChRec** 51.12 (dec 1920) 837-850.

Potter, Jack. Wind, water, bones and souls: the religious world of the cantonese peasant [Ping shan, new territories of hong kong] **JOS** 8.1 (1970) 139-153. Repr in **CWayRel** (1973)

Regnault, Jules. Rôle du foung-choei et de la sorcellerie dans la vie privée et publique des jaunes. **Revue politique et parlementaire** (10 nov 1905) 353-373. (Étude extr. en grande partie d'un rapport présenté par le dr regnault au congrès colonial de 1905, sous le titre: Hystérie, hypnose et sorcellerie en chine et en indo-chine)

Rousselle, E. Zum system der kaiserlichen grabanlagen. **Sinica** 7 (1932) 155-160.

Shen, D.C. "Fung shui" woodlands. **JHKBRAS** 14 (1974) 188-189. Repr fr **Wildlife conservation newsletter** 14 (oct 1971) publ by Agriculture, forestry and fisheries dept, hongkong govt.

Sinensis. Chinese mythology: on the chinese geomancy known as feng shui. **ChRec** 4 (1872) 19-23, 46-48, 93-96, 130-132, 217-222.

Strauch, Judith. A tun fu ceremony in tai po district, 1981: ritual as a demarcator of community. **JHKBRAS** 20 (1980) 147-153. The term tun fu is not in dictionaries.

Stringer, H. Fengshui. **CJ** 3.6 (june 1925) 305-307.

Turner, F.S. Feng-shui. **Cornhill magazine** 29 (1874) 337-348.

Yates, M.T. Ancestral worship and fung-shuy. **ChRec** 1.3 (1868) 23 et seq, 37-43.

Yoon, Hong-key. The analysis of korean geomancy tales. **AsFS** 34.1 (1975) 21-34.

Yoon, Hong-key. **Geomantic relationships between culture and nature in korea.** Taipei (1976) 1xx + 279 p, app, bibliog, maps, illus.

13. STATE & RELIGION

Amicus. The worship of confucius. **ICG** 11 (1820) 254-256.

Arlington, Lewis C. **Some remarks on the worship offered confucius in the confucian temple.** Peiping (1935) 8, 20p, pl.

Arlington, L.C. & William Lewisohn. **In search of peking.** Peking (1935) See Contents, for various temples.

Ayscough, Florence. The chinese cult of ch'eng huang lao yeh. **JNCBRAS** 55 (1924) 131-155.

Ayscough, Florence. The symbolism of the forbidden city, peking. **JNCBRAS** 61 (1930) 111-126.

Bechert, Heinz. Staatsreligion in den buddhistischen ländern. **IAF** 2.2 (apr 1971) See sec 3, China, 174-175.

Biallas, Franz Xaver. **Konfuzius und sein kult.** Peking and leipzig (1928) 130 p, literaturnachweis, anmerkungen, abbildungen, karten.

Bilsky, Lester James. **The state religion of ancient china.** Taipei, 2 vol (1975) vol 1, viii + 232 p; vol 2, 233-448, app, notes, gloss, bibliog.

Blodget, Henry. Prayers of the emperor for snow and rain. **ChRec** 15.4 (july-aug 1884) 249-253.

Blodget, Henry. The worship of heaven and earth by the emperor of china. **JAOS** 20 (1899) 58-69.

Borch, A. von. The imperial tombs west of peking. **EA** 1 (sept 1902) 181-191.

Bouillard, G. Environs de peking. iv. Tombeaux proprement dit. **La chine** 16 (1922) 569-578.

Bouillard, G. Le temple de la terre. **La chine** 34 (1923) 53-66.

Bouillard, G. Le temple de l'agriculture. **La chine** 33 (1922) 1833-1850.

Bouillard, G. Tombeaux des ming. **La chine** (all 1922) 19: 789-800; 20: 865-879; 21: 975-994; 22: 1051-1062.

Bouillard, G. Les tombeaux des ts'ing. **La chine** (all 1922) 23: 1137-1154; 24: 1187-1203; 25: 1273-1284.

Bouillard, G. **Tombeaux impériaux** (ming et ts'ing) Peking (1931) 225 p.

Bouillard, G. and Vaudescal. Les sépultures impériales des ming (che-san ling) **BEFEO** 20.3 (1920) 1-128, 44 pl Rev in **TP** 21 (1922) 57-66 by Paul Pelliot.

Bourne, Frederick S.A. Notes of a journey to the imperial mausolea, east of peking. **Proceedings of the royal geographical society** n.s. 5 (1883) 23-31.

Brandt, M. von. **Die chinesische philosophie und der staats-confucianismus.** Stuttgart (1898) 121 p.

Bredon, Juliet. **Peking.** Shanghai etc (1922) See Contents, for various temples.

Brodrick, A.H. The sacrifices of the son of heaven. **AR** 36 (1940) 118-128.

Bünger, Karl. **Studien über religion und staat in china.** Tübingen (1949) vii + 179 p.

Chavannes, Édouard. Traité sur les sacrifices fong et chan de se ma t'sien. **JPOS** 3.1 (1890) xxxi + 95.

Cheng, Ching-yi. Tsl J. Leighton Stuart. Translation of protest against the movement in favor of making confucianism a state religion. **ChRec** 44.11 (mar 1913) 687-692.

Combaz, Gilbert. Les sépultures impériales de la chine. **ASAB** 21 (1907) 381-462.

Combaz, Gilbert. Les temples impériaux de la chine. **ASAB** 26 (1912) 223-323.

Coulborn, Rushton. The state and religion: iran, india, and china. **CSSH** 1.1 (1958) 44-57.

Creel, Herrlee Glessner. **The birth of china. A study of the formative period of chinese civilization.** N.Y. (1937) See chap 28, The decree of heaven, 367-380.

Creel, Herrlee Glessner. **The origins of statecraft in china.** Vol 1: **The western chou empire.** Univ chicago (1970) See chap 5, The mandate of heaven, 81-100.

Dard, Émile. Au tombeau des mings. **Revue hebdomadaire** ann 18 (25 juin 1910) 512-520.

Demiéville, P. Notes d'archéologie chinoise. 1. l'Inscriptions de yun-kang; 2. le bouddha du k'o chan; 3.

les tombeaux des song meridioneaux. **BEFEO** 25.3/4 (1925) 449-468.

Devéria, Gabriel. Sépultures impériales de la dynastie ta ts'ing. **TP** 3 (1892) 418-421.

Doolittle, Justus. Interior view of peking. Chap 19 in author's **SLC** vol 2 (1865) 438-463.

Doolittle, Justus. The state religion. Chap 14 in author's **SLC** vol 1 (1865) 353-375.

Dubs, Homer H. The sacred field. Chap 4, app 2, in Dubs (tsl) **The history of the former han dynasty by pan ku,** vol 1, baltimore (1938) 281-283. Re field personally ploughed by emperor to open planting season.

Dubs, Homer H. The victory of han confucianism. **JAOS** 58 (1938) 435-449. Rev version of this art in Dubs (tsl) **The history of the former han dynasty by pan ku,** baltimore, md (1944) vol 2, app 2, 435-449.

Dunstheimer, G.H. Religion officielle, religion populaire et sociétés secrètes en chine depuis les han. In **EncyP:HR** (1976) 371-448, bibliog.

E(dkins), J(oseph) The chinese altar of burnt offerings. **OC** 14.12 (dec 1900) 752-755.

Edkins, Joseph. The hall of light [ming t'ang] **ChRev** 15 (1886-87) 165-167.

Edkins, Joseph. **Religion in china.** Boston (1859; rev and enl ed 1878) See chap 2, Imperial worship.

Eichhorn, Werner. **Die alte chinesische religion und das staatskultwesen.** Leiden (1976) xvii + 262 s.

Eichhorn, Werner. Die wiedereinrichtung der staatsreligion im anfang der sung-zeit. **MS** 23 (1964) 205-263.

Eisenstadt. S.N. Religious organizations and political process in centralized empires. **JAS** 21.3 (1962) 271-294.

Ellwood, Robert S. jr. **The feast of kingship.** Sophia univ, tokyo (1973) See, for china, chap 1, sec 4, 19-26.

Fabre, Maurice. **Pékin, ses palais, ses temples et ses environs, guide historique et descriptif.** Tien-tsin (ca.1937) xv + 347 p, illus. Illustré par Y.Darcy; compositions originales de J. Malval.

Farjenel, Fernand (tsl) Le culte impérial en chine. **JA** 10e sér, 8 (1906) 491-516. ('le sacrifice au grand dieu du ciel'; tsl fr ta ch'ing hui-tien)

Farjenel, F. (tsl) **Rites funéraires chinois; les funérailles impériales et celles des gens du peuple.** Louvain (ca. 1904) 63 p. Offprint from **Le muséon.**

Farquhar, David M. Emperor as bodhisattva in the governance of the ch'ing empire. **HJAS** 38.1 (1978) 5-34.

Favier, A. **Peking.** Lille (1900) See esp chap 16 and 17 for temples.

Ferguson, John C. The t'ai miao of peking. **THM** 6 (1938) 185-190.

Fischer, Emil S. A journey to the tung ling and a visit to the desecrated eastern mausolea of the ta tsing dynasty, in 1929. **JNCBRAS** 61 (1930) 20-39.

Fischer, Emil S. T'ai miao, a description of the supreme hall of sacrifices of the forbidden city. **JNCBRAS** 64 (1933) 72-76.

Fisher, Carney T. The great ritual controversy in the age of ming shih-tsung. **SSCRB** 7 (fall 1979) 71-87.

Fonssagrives, Eugène. **Si-ling. Étude sur les tombeaux de l'ouest de la dynastie des ts'ing.** Paris (1907) 180 p (**AMG** 31, pt 1)

Forrest, R.J. The ming tombs near nanking. **NCH** 571 (6 july 1861)

Franke, O. **Studien zur geschichte des konfuzianischen dogmas und der chinesischen staatsreligion; das problem des tsch'un-ts'iu und tung tschung-schu's tsch'un-ts'iu fan lu.** Hamburg (1920) 329 p.

Funérailles de l'impératrice orientale de la chine. **MC** 14 (1882) 52-54.

Gausseron, Bernard H. Les tombeaux des ming. **Monde moderne** 74 (fév 1901) 225-228.

Gingell, W.R. (tsl) Chinese state mourning. **Siam repository** 2 (1870) 185-187.

Gordon-Cumming, C.F. The temple of heaven. Chap 32, vol 2, of author's **WinC** (1886) 164-190.

Grantham, Alexandra E. **The ming tombs.** Peking (1926) 21 p, illus.

Grantham, Alexandra E. **The temple of heaven: a short study.** Peking (n.d.) 40p.

Groot, J.J.M. de. **The religious system of china.** Leiden (1892-1910) repr taipei (1964) 6 vol. On ming imperial tombs see 3, 1177-1282; on ch'ing imperial tombs see 3, 1282-1373.

Hackenbroich, H. Die totengefolge der chinesischen kaiser. **Deutscher forschungsdienst** 52 (1958) 2-3.

Happel, Julius. **Die altchinesische reichsreligion vom standpunkte der vergleigenden religionsgeschichte.** Leipzig (1882) 46 p. French tsl in **RHR** 4.6 (1881) 257-298.

Happer, Andrew P. A visit to peking. **ChRec** 10.1 (jan-feb 1879) 23-47. Sep publ as **A visit to peking, with some notices of the imperial worship at the altars of heaven, earth, sun, moon and the gods of the grain and land,** shanghai (1879) 27 p.

Happer, Andrew P. The worship of heaven by the chinese emperor. **MRW** n.s. 7 (1894) 86-89.

Harlez, Ch. de (tsl) **Tà ts'iñg tsí lì . . . La religion et les cérémonies impériales de la chine moderne d'après le cérémonial et les décrets officiels.** Bruxelles (1893) 556 pp.

Heidenreich, Robert. Beobachtungen zum stadtplan von peking. **NachrDGNVO** 81 (1957) 32-37. Re symbolism.

Heigl, Ferdinand. **Die religion und kultur chinas.** Berlin (1900) 678 p. See teil 1, Die reichsreligion von china.

Herder, A.E. von. Einiges über die dung ling und die si ling. **Sinica** 7 (1932) 149-155.

Herzer, Rudolf. Der streit über das 'grosse ritual': eine hofkontroverse der frühen chia-ching-zeit (1522-1566) **OE** 19.1/2 (dec 1972) 65-83.

Herzer, Rudolf. **Zur frage der ungesetzlichen opfer yin szu und ungesetzlichen errichtefen kultstätten yin-tz'u.** Hamburg (1963) 94 p.

Ho, Yun-yi. Ritual aspects of the founding of the ming dynasty 1368-1398. **SSCRB** 7 (fall 1979) 58-70.

Hodous, L. The sacrifice to heaven. **ChRec** 46.8 (aug 1915) 484-492; 46.10 (oct 1915) 600-606; 46.12 (dec 1915) 764-774, illus, fig.

Hsiao, Kung-ch'üan. **Rural china: imperial control in the nineteenth century.** Univ washington (1960) See 220-229, Tz'u-ssu: local sacrifices; 229-235, Heretical sects.

Hu, Shih. The establishment of confucianism as a state religion during the han dynasty. **JNCBRAS** 60 (1929) 20-41.

Huang, K'uei-yen and John K. Shryock (tsl) A collection of chinese prayers. Translated with notes. **JAOS** 49 (1929) 128-155. From a book used by officials in anhui.

Hubert, Ch. Les si-ling ou tombeaux de l'ouest. **Bulletin société géographie de l'est** 33 (1912) 16-37.

Hubert, Ch. Les tombeaux des ming. **Bulletin société de géographie de l'est** 32 (1911) 107-115, plan.

Idols presented to the emperor of china, on his birth-day. **ICG** no 3 (1818) 54-55.

Imbault-Huart, Camille. Les tombeaux des ming près de peking. **TP** 4 (1893) 391-401, 3 photos.

Imbault-Huart, Camille. Une visite au temple de confucius à changhai. **JA** 7e sér, 16 (1880) 533-538.

The Imperial sacrifices. **Echo** 4.11 (dec 1974) 12-21, 49, illus.

Inquirer [Happer, A.P.] The state religion of china. **ChRec** 12.3 (1881) 149-192.

Inquirer. The theocratic nature of the chinese government, and the principles of its administration as stated in the chinese classics. **ChRec** 9.1 (jan-feb 1878) 28-49.

Jochim, Christian. The imperial audience ceremonies of the ch'ing dynasty. **SSCRB** 7 (fall 1979) 88-103.

K. Das ming-grab bei nanking. **OstL** 13 (1899) 536.

Kobayashi, T. Some political aspects of the problem of confucian state religion. **JOSA** 7.1/2 (dec 1970) 46-69.

Kopetsky, Elma E. Two fu on sacrifices by yang hsiung: the fu on kan-ch'üan and the fu on ho-tung. **JOS** 10.2 (july 1972) 85-118. Tsl with intro.

Krause, F.E.A. Zum konfuzianischen dogma und der chinesischen staatsreligion. **ARW** 21 (1922) 212-218.

Legge, James. Imperial confucianism. **ChRev** 6.3 (1877) 147-158; 6.4 (1878) 223-235; 6.5 (1878) 299-310; 6.6 (1878) 363-374.

Ling, Shun-sheng. A comparative study of the ancient chinese feng and shan [sacrifices] and the ziggurats of mesopotamia. **ASBIE** 19 (1965) engl abrmt 39-51 + 10 p pl.

Ling, Shun-sheng. The sacred enclosures and stepped pyramidal platforms of peiping. **ASBIE** 16 (1963) engl abrmt 83-100, pl.

Ling, Shun-sheng. The sacred places of chin and han periods. **ASBIE** 18 (1964) engl abrmt 136-142.

Liu, James T.C. How did a neo-confucian school become the state orthodoxy? **PEW** 23.4 (oct 1973) 483-506.

Liu, James T.C. The sung emperors and the ming-t'ang or hall of enlightenment. In Françoise Aubin (ed) **Études song: sung studies in memoriam étienne balazs,** the hague (1973) ser 2, Civilisation, t 1, 45-58.

Liu, James T.C. Two forms of worshipping the heaven in sung china. **ASBIE** 18 (1964) engl summ 50f.

Lyall, A.C. Official polytheism in china. **NC** 28 (1890) 89-107.

Lyall, Alfred C. **Asiatic studies religious and social.** London (1882) 306 p. See chap 6, relations between the state and religion in china. French tsl: **Études sur les moeurs religieuses et sociales de l'extrême-orient.** Paris (1907)

J.M. Mourning days at the court of peking. **ChRev** 15 (1886-87) 181-182.

Markbreiter, Stephen. The temple of heaven in peking. **AofA** 2.3 (may-june 1972) 9-12, illus. General descr.

Martin, E. Les funérailles d'une impératrice de chine. **RE** 1 (1882) 230-234.

Meech, Samuel E. The imperial worship at the altar of heaven. **ChRec** 47.2 (feb 1916) 112-117.

Messing, Otto. Über die chinesische staatsreligion und ihren kultus. **ZE** 43.2 (1911) 348-375.

Meyer, Jeffrey F. **Peking as a sacred city.** Taipei (1976) 225 p, map, illus, bibliog.

Meynard, A. Sacrifice to heaven and earth. **Asia** 28 (1928) 799-803.

Montuclat. Une visite aux tombeaux des ming. **La chine** (1921) 398-402.

Morgan, Evan. A case of ritualism. **JNCBRAS** 49 (1918) 128-143. When feudal state of lu usurped royal prerogative to perform suburban sacrifice to heaven (chiao)

Morrison, Robert. The state religion of china . . . **ChRep** 3 (1834) 49; repr **The cycle** (3 dec 1870)

Moule, G.E. Notes on the ting-chi or half-yearly sacrifice to confucius. **JNCBRAS** 33 (1900-01) 37-73 (as misprinted; actually 120-156) photos, drawings, plans, musical score.

Parker, E.H. Side lights on chinese religious ideas. **Gentleman's magazine** 282 (1897) 593-603.

P'eng, Tso-chih. Chinesischer stadtbau unter besonderer berücksichtigung der stadt peking. **NachrDGNVO** 89/90 (1961) 5-80, fig.

Perrot, Albert. Le retour offensif de la vieille chine. Le confucianisme redevenu religion d'état. **Études** 139 (20 mai 1914) 461-480; 140 (juil 1914) 425-438, fig.

Perry, John W. **Lord of the four quarters. Myths of the royal father.** N.Y. (1966) See chap 5, The far east: china, 204-218. '. . . we find in china the source and leading exponent of the sacral kingship.'

Playfair, G.M.H. Days of official mourning in china. **ChRev** 17 (1888-89) 47-48.

A Prayer for rain, written by his imperial majesty taou-kwang and offered up on the 28th day of the sixth month of the 12th year of his reign,—july 24th, 1832. **ChRep** 1.6 (oct 1832) 236-239.

Price, Julius J. The chinese state religion. **OC** 38 (1924) 252-256.

Promulgation of the calendar. **Echo** 4.11 (dec 1974) 22-24, 50-51, illus. Re Imperial almanac.

Ransdorp, R. Official and popular religion in the chinese empire. In Pieter H. Vrijhof & Jacques Waardenburg (ed) **Official and popular religion. Analysis of a theme for religious studies**, the hague (1979) 387-426.

Rousselle, Erwin. Zum system der kaiserlichen grabanlagen. **Sinica** 7 (1932) 155-160.

Schlegel, G. Ming graves. **TP** 2e sér, 2 (1901) 162.

Schnupftabackdose. Worship of the emperor's tablet. **ChRev** 8 (1879-80) 61.

Schüler, Wilhelm. Die gründung des "amtes zur regelung der riten" in peking. **OR** 9.1 (2 jan 1928) 15-17.

Schüler, W. Die kultushandlungen der heutigen chinesischen staatsreligion. **ZMK** 26 (1911) 84-87.

Shryock, John K. **The origin and development of the state cult of confucius.** N.Y. and london (1932) 298 p. app, bibliog, index.

Smith, D.H. Divine kingship in ancient china. **Numen** 4 (1957) 171-203.

Soothill, William E. **The hall of light; a study of early chinese kingship.** Ed Lady Hosie and G.F. Hudson. London (1951) xxii + 289 p, illus.

Soothill, William E. Kingship in china. **JNCBRAS** 61 (1930) 92-99.

State ceremonial in late imperial china: a symposium. **SSCRB** 7 (fall 1979) 46-103. Four art sep listed in our bibliog.

The State religion of china: objects of the governmental worship; the ministers or priests, and the preparation required for their service; sacrifices, offerings and ceremonies; and penalties for informality. **ChRep** 3.2 (june 1834) 49-53.

Steininger, Hans. Der heilige herrscher, sein tao und sein praktisches tun. In **SJFAW** (1956) 170-177.

Stokes, John The temple of heaven. **EH** 17.9 (sept 1978) 23-29, illus.

Stuhr, P.F. **Die chinesische reichsreligion und die systeme der indischen philosophie in ihrem verhältsnisz zu offenbarungslehren mit rücksicht auf die anwichten von windischmann, schmitt und ritter, betrachtet von P.F. Stuhr.** Berlin (1835) vi + 109 p.

Swann, Peter C. **Chinese monumental art.** N.Y. (1963) See sec, The tombs of the ming emperors, 212-227 (pl 119-125) Chinese architecture. Peking and the forbidden city, 228-259 (pl 126-140) Photos Claude Arthaud and François Hébert-Stevens.

Tamura, Zitsuzo and Yukio Kubayashi. Tombs and murals of ch'ing-ling. Liao imperial mausoleums of the 11th century a.d. in eastern mongolia. **Japan quarterly** 1 (1954) 34-45.

Taylor, Romeyn. Ming t'ai-tsu and the gods of the walls and moats. **Ming studies** 4 (spring 1977) 31-49.

Tran-Ham-Tan. Étude sur le van-mieu [wen miao] de ha-noi (temple de la littérature) **BEFEO** 45 (1951) 89-117, planche.

Vandermeersch, Léon. **Wangdao ou la voie royale. Recherches sur l'esprit des institutions de la chine** archaïque. T 1, **Structures cultuelles et structures familiales.** Paris (1977) 358 p. T 2, **Structures politiques, les rites.** Paris (1980) 603 p, tables, index. See Table générale des matières.

Waidtlow, C. The imperial religions of ch'in and han. **ChRec** 58 (1927) 565-571, 698-703.

Waidtlow, C. The religion of emperor wu of the han. **ChRec** 55 (1924) 361-366, 460-464, 527-529.

Waidtlow, C. The religion of the first emperor. **ChRec** 57 (1926) 413-416, 487-490.

Wang, Kuo-wei. Jonny Hefter (tsl) Ming-t'ang-miao-ch'in-t'ung-k'ao. Aufschluss über die halle der lichten kraft, ming t'ang, über die ahnentempel miao, sowie über die wohn palaste ch'in. **OZ** n.f. (1931) 17-35, 70-86.

Wang Ngen-jong. Cérémonial de la cour et coutumes du peuple de pékin. **BAAFC** 2.2 (avr 1910) 105-138; 2.3 (juil 1910) 215-237; 2.4 (oct 1910) 347-368; 3.2 (avr 1911) 134-155; 3.3 (juil 1911) 66-84.

Watters, Thomas. **A guide to the tablets in a temple of confucius.** Shanghai (1879) 259 p.

Weber-Schäfer, Peter. **Oikumene und imperium. Studien zur ziviltheologie des chinesischen kaiserreichs.** München (1968) 317 p. Historical study through period of han wu-ti.

Wenley, A.G. **The grand empress dowager wen ming and the northern wei necropolis at fang shan.** Freer gallery. **Occasional papers** vol 1.1 (1947) 22 p, 7 pl.

Werner, E.T.C. Rebuttal notes on chinese religion and dynastic tombs. **JNCBRAS** 56 (1925) 134-148.

Wiethoff, Bodo. Der staatliche ma-tsu kult. **ZDMG** 116.2 (1966) 311-357, illus.

Wilhelm, Hellmut. Schriften und fragmente zur entwicklung der staatsreligion theorie in der chou zeit. **MS** 12 (1947) 41-96.

Williams, E.T. Agricultural rites in the religion of old china. **JNCBRAS** 67 (1936) 25-49.

Williams, E.T. Confucianism as a state religion. Chap 13 in author's **CYT,** 263-288.

Williams, E.T. The state religion of china during the manchu dynasty. **JNCBRAS** 44 (1913) 11-45.

Williams, E.T. The worship of lei tsu, patron saint of silk workers. **JNCBRAS** 66 (1935) 1-14.

Williams, E.T. Worshipping imperial ancestors in peking. **JNCBRAS** 70 (1939) 46-65.

Wills, John E. jr. State ceremony in late imperial china: notes for a framework for discussion. **SSCRB** 7 (fall 1979) 46-57.

Yabao, Presciano (photos) Lovely, mystic navel of china. **Orientations** 3.6 (june 1972) 24-31, col photos and brief text. Re altar of heaven, peking.

14. TAOISM—GENERAL
(See also Sec. 15: **Lao Tzu & Tao Te Ching**)

Ampère J.J. La troisième religion de la chine, lao-tseu. **RDM** 4e sér, 31 (15 août 1842) 521-539.

Aziz-us-Samad, Mrs. Ulfat. **The great religions of the world.** Lahore (1976) See Taoism, 107-123.

Bahm, Archie J. **The world's living religions.** Southern illinois univ (1964) See pt 2, Religions of china and japan; Taoism, p 151-174.

Balfour, Frederic H. Taoism. In **RSW** (1889 et seq) 76-91.

Bancroft, Anne. **Religions of the east.** NY (1974) See Taoism, 181-208.

Block, Marguerite. Taoism. In Johnson E. Fairchild (ed) **Basic beliefs. The religious philosophies of mankind,** n.y. (1959) 114-134.

Blofeld, John. **Beyond the gods. Buddhist and taoist mysticism.** London & NY (1974) 164 p, gloss.

Blofeld, John. **The secret and sublime. Taoist mysteries and magic.** London (1973) 217 p.

Blofeld, John. **Taoism. The road to immortality.** Boulder, colo (1978) 195 p, illus, app: tables pertaining to the wu hsing five activities (science)

Bonsall, Bramwell S. **Confucianism and taoism.** London (1934) 127 p.

The Book of Tao. A brief outline of the esoteric schools of buddhism and tao in china. Adyar (1933) 24 p.

Bradley, David G. **A guide to the world's religion.** Englewood cliffs, n.j. (1963) See chap 14, Taoism, 134-140.

Brémond, René. **La sagesse chinoise selon le tao. Pensées choisies et traduites** . . . Paris (1955) 208 p.

Brown, David. A. **A guide to religions.** London (1975) See chap 9, Two chinese religions, 89-103.

Burtt, Edwin A. **Man seeks the divine.** N.Y. (1957) See chap 7, Taoism, 185-201.

Capra, Fritjof. **The tao of physics. An exploration of the parallels between modern physics and eastern mysticism.** Berkeley, calif (1975) 330 p, notes, bibliog, index. See esp chap 7,Chinese thought, 101-112; chap 8, Taoism, 113-120; but also passim.

Carus, Paul. Taoism and buddhism. **OC** 20 (1906) 654-667, illus.

Chai, Ch'u & Winberg Chai. Confucianism and taoism. In **RS&P** (1973) 180-194.

Chalmers, John. Tauism. **ChRev** 1.4 (1873) 209-220.

Chan, Wing-tsit. Taoism. **EncyB** (1960) vol 21, 796f.

Chan, Wing-tsit. Taoism. In **EncyB 3** (1974) **Macropaedia** vol 21, 677b-681a.

Chan, Wing-tsit. Taoism. In **EncyA** (1975) vol 26, 276-277.

Chen, Lucy H. (Ch'en Hsiu-mei) Spirit calling. In author's collection, **Spirit calling; tales about taiwan,** taipei (1962) 73-87. Fictional account of summoning sick person's spirit by taoist priest.

Cooper, J.C. **Taoism. The way of the mystic.** NY (1972) 128 p, index.

Cordier, Henri. Taoism. **Catholic encyclopédie.** n.p. (n.d.) 446-448.

Couling, C.E. The oldest dress and the newest; or taoism in modern dress. **HJ** 22 (1924) 245-259.

Creel, H.G. What is taoism? **JAOS** 76.3 (1956) 139-152. Repr in author's collection: **What is taoism and other studies in chinese cultural history,** univ chicago (1970) 1-24.

Day, Clarence B. A unique buddhist-taoist union prayer conference. **ChRec** 56.6 (june 1925) 366-369. Conference held at monastery near Hangchou for soldiers who died in world war and for victims of tokyo-yokohama earthquake.

Dobbins, Frank S. Assisted by S. Wells Williams and Isaac Hall. **Error's chains: how forged and broken.** N.Y. (1883) Same work publ under title, **Story of the world's worship,** chicago (1901) See chap 21-22, 416-444, illus.

La Doctrine des tao-sse en chine. **Actes de la société d'ethnographie** 3 (1863) 229f.

Douglas, Robert K. **Confucianism and taoism.** London (1879)

DuBose, Hampden C. **The dragon, image and demon, or the religions of china: confucianism, buddhism, and taoism. Giving an account of the mythology, idolatry and demonolotry of the chinese.** London (1886) 463 p.

Dubs, Homer H. Taoism. In H.F. MacNair (ed) **China,** univ california (1946) 266-289.

Duyvendak, J.J.L. Henri maspero, **mélanges posthumes** . . . **TP** 40 (1951) 372-390 (Rev)

Dvořák, Rudolf. **Darstellungen aus dem gebiete der nichtchristlichen religionsgeschichte** (12 Bd): **Chinas religionen.** Zweiter teil: **Lao tsï und seine lehre.** Münster (1903) viii + 216 p.

Eichhorn, W. Taoism. In **ZCE** (1959) 385-401.

Erkes, E. Eine taoistische schöpfungsgeschichte für kinder. **CDA** (1932) 14-15.

l'Esprit des races jaune—le taoisme et les sociétés secrètes chinoises. Paris (1897) 32 p.

Étiemble, René. Le mythe taoïste en france au XXe siècle. **FA** 17 (1960-61) 1834-1843.

Étiemble, René. Le vision taoïste. **Nouvelle revue française** n.s. 13 (août 1965) 357-366.

Faber, E. Notes on taoism and confucianism. **ChRec** 33.6 (june 1902) 271-276.

Faber, Ernst. **Der taoismus** (1884)

Faber, Martin, et al. Taoism. **CMH** (1896) 23-31.

Fielde, Adele M. **A corner of cathay.** NY (1894) See sec, The tauists and their magic arts, 214-256.

Finegan, Jack. **The archeology of world religions.** Princeton uni (1952) Vol 2: **Buddhism, confucianism, taoism,** 234-599, illus.

Forlong, J.G.R. **Short studies in the science of comparative religions embracing all the religions of asia.** London (1897) chap 5, Laotsze and tao-ism.

Franck, A. Le taoisme et son fondateur. **Bulletin de la société d'ethnographie** 6 (1892) 5-59.

Fu, Charles Wei-hsun. Confucianism and taoism. Chap 12 in Isma'īl Rāgī al Farūqī & David E. Sopher (ed) **Historical atlas of the religions of the world,** ny & london (1974) 109-125, bibliog, illus, map.

Gaer, Joseph. **How the great religions began.** N.Y. (1929) rev ed (1956) See bk 2, pt 2, Taoism, the religion few can understand, 149-175.

Gauchet, L. Contribution à l'étude du taoisme. **BUA** 3e sér, 9 (1948) 1-38.

Giles, Herbert A. **China and the chinese.** NY (1902) See lecture 5, Taoism, 141-174.

Giles, Lionel. Introduction to taoism. In Selwyn G. Champion (ed) **The eleven religions and their proverbial lore. A comparative study,** n.y. (1945) 272-277 (the 'proberbial lore' is on 278-287)

Girardot, Norman J. Part of the way: four studies on taoism. **HR** 11.2 (1972) 318-337. Rev art on Creel, **What is taoism?** Kaltenmark, **Lao tzu and taoism;** Schipper, **l'Empereur wou des han . . .'** Izutsu, **The key philosophical concepts in sufism and taoism** qqv.

Girardot, Norman J. Taoism. In **EBio** (1978) vol 4, 1631a-1638a.

Goullart, Peter. **The monastery of jade mountain.** London (1961) 189 p, illus. French tsl (1971)

Groot, J.J.M. de. **Religion in china. Universism: a key to the study of taoism and confucianism** (see also author's **Universismus. . .**) N.Y. and london (1912)

Grosier, l'Abbé. De la religion des chinois-sect des tao-sée. In author's **Description générale de la chine,** paris (1785) 2e pt chap 2.

Grube, W. Vorläufiges verzeichnis einer taoistischen bildersammlung. **Mitteilungen aus der ethnologischen abteilung der königlichen museen zu berlin** 1.1 (1885) 16-38.

Guénon, René. Taoism and confucianism. **SCR** 6.4 (autumn 1972) 239-250.

Gulik, R.H. van. The mango trick in china: an essay on taoist magic. **TASJ** ser 3, 3 (1954) 117-175.

Gundry, D.W. **Religions. A preliminary historical and theological study.** London and n.y. (1958) See 5, The monistic religion: Taoism, 75-78.

Hackmann, Heinrich. China, religionen taoismus. **Jahresberichte der geschichtswissenschaft** 34 (1911)

Hackman, Heinrich. Ein chinesisches urteil über den taoismus von lung hu shan und shang ch'ing. **AO** 7 (1929) 293-304.

Hail, William J. Taoism. In Vergilius Ferm (ed) **Religion in the twentieth century,** paterson, n.j. (1948) 81-93. Paperbk ed (1965) entitled **Living schools of religion.**

Hardon, John A. **Religions of the world.** N.Y. (1963) chap 7: Taoism, 193-203.

Hardwick, Charles. **Christ and other masters.** Cambridge (1858) See sec 2, Tao-ism or the school of the fixed way, 307-321.

Hart, Virgil C. Taoism. In **DR** (1884) 285-339.

Henry, B.C. Taoism. Chap 6 in author's **CD** (1885) 100-122.

Herbert, Edward (pseud for Kenney, Edward H.) **A taoist notebook.** London (1955) 80 p.

Herod, F.G. **World religions.** ?London (1970) niles, ill (1975) See chap 4, Tao, 37-39; chap 3, confucianism, 33-36.

Hodous, Lewis, Taoism. In **EncyB** 14th ed (1929) vol 21, 797a-b.

Hodous, Lewis. Taoism. In Edward J. Jurji (ed) **The great religions of the modern world,** princeton univ (1946) 24-43.

Hopfe, Lewis M. **Religions of the world.** Beverly hills, calif & london (1976) See chap 7, sec Taoism, 124-135.

Hopkins, E. Washburn. **The history of religions.** N.Y. (1926) See chap 15, Confucius, lao-tse, taoism, 249-274.

Hsü Ti-shan. Taoism. In W.L. Hare (ed) **Religions of the empire,** london (?) (1920) 245-271.

James F. Huberty, Taoism. **ChRec** 28.12 (dec 1897) 584-587.

Hume, Robert E. **The world's living religions. With special reference to their sacred scriptures and in comparison with christianity.** N.Y. (1924) rev ed (1959) See pt, Religions originating in east asia (china, japan): 7. Taoism.

Inglis, James W. Taoism from the christian standpoint. **ChRec** 46.10 (oct 1915) 595-599.

Jurji, Edward J. **The christian interpretation of religion. Christianity in its human and creeative relationships with the world's cultures and faiths.** N.Y. (1952) See chap 9, Mysticism and effortless spontaneity: taoism, 192-198.

Kaltenmark, Maxime. **Lao tseu et le taoïsme.** Paris (1965) Engl tsl Roger Greaves: **Lao tzu and taoism.** Stanford univ (1969) In latter see chap 5, The taoist religion, 107-143.

Kaltenmark, Max. Le maître spirituel dans la chine ancienne. **Hermès** 4 (1967, no spécial: le maître spirituel dans les grandes traditions d'occident et d'orient) 219-225.

Kaltenmark, Max. La mystique taoïste. In **La mystique et les mystiques,** paris (1965) 649-667.

Kaltenmark, Max. Le taoïsme. In **AC** t 1 (1959) 151-160.

Kaltenmark, Max. Le taoïsme religieux. In **HCP:HR** (1970) 1216-1248.

Kandel, Barbara. A visit to the china taoist association. **SSCRB** 8 (fall 1980) 1-4. Peking 24 july 1980.

Kern, M. Konfuzianismus und taoismus. **LO** (1922) 325-350.

Kim, Young Oon. **World religions.** Vol 3: **Faiths of the far east.** NY (1976) See Taoism, 87-120, brief bibliog.

Kimura, Eiichi. Taoism and chinese thought. **ActaA** 27 (1974) 1-18.

King, Winston L. The way of tao and the path to nirvana. In **SA** (1963) 121-135.

Klaproth, Julius H. von. De la religion des tao-szu en chine. **Nouvelles annales des voyages** 2 (1833) 129.

Krause, Friedrich E.A. **Ju-tao-fo . . . Die religiösen und philosophischen systeme ostasiens.** München (1924) 588 p.

Krone, Rudolf. Der taoismus in china. **Berichte des rheinischen missionsgesellschaft** 7 (1857) 102-111; 8 (1857) 114-119.

Legeza, Laszlo. Chinese taoist art. **AofA** 7.6 (1977) 32-37, ill b-&-w & col photos.

Legge, James. **The religions of china. Confucianism and taoism described and compared with christianity.** London (1880) repr folcroft, pa (1976) norwood, pa (1977) 310 p.

Lewis, John. **The religions of the world made simple.** NY (1958) rev ed (1968) See chap 6, Buddhism in china and japan, 46-48; chap 7, Confucianism and taoism, 52-58.

Li, Dun J. (tsl) Taoist religion. Chap 4 in tsl's anthology, **The essence of chinese civilization,** princeton etc (1967) 49-68. Tsl of sel pieces.

Lin, T.C. The taoist in every chinese. **THM** 11 (1940-41) 211-225.

Liu, Da. **The tao and chinese culture.** NY (1979) 168 p, index.

Macintosh, Charles Henry. **Tao.** Chicago (1926)

Maclagan, P.J. Taoism. In **HERE** 12, 197-202.

Masdoosi, Ahmad Abdullah al. **Living religions of the world. A sociopolitical study.** Tsl fr urdu Zafar Ishaq Ansari. Karachi (1962) See chap 6, Taoism, 142-146.

Maspero, Henri. **Le taoïsme.** Paris (1950) 268 p. (**HMRC** t 2) Entire work repr in Maspero, **Le Taoïsme et les religions chinoises,** paris (1971) q.v.

Maspero, Henri. **Le taoïsme et les religions chinoises.** Préface de Max Kaltenmark. Paris (1971) 658 p. "Ce recueil est basé sur les deux premiers volumes des **Mélanges posthumes sur les religions et d'histoire de la chine** (abbrev **HMRC** in our bibliog) édités par Paul Demiéville, en 1950 . . . "

Matgioï [A. de Pourvoirville] Le taoïsme contemporain: sa hiérarchie, son enseignement, son rôle. **MCSJ** 19 (1889) 179-218.

Mead, G.R.S. **Quests old and new. (Taoism, buddhism, christianity . . .)** (1913)

Mears, W.P. The philosophy, ethics, and religion of taoism. Chiefly as developed by chwang-tsze. (A comparative sketch) **CR** 19.4 (1875-76) 225-242.

Miyahara, Mimpei. Taoism, the popular religion of china. **Contemporary japan** 9 (1940) 1140-1153.

Mortier, F. Le taoisme et ses variations doctrinales. **BSAB** 65 (1954) 161-166.

Moule, Arthur E. Buddhism and taoism as they affect chinese life. Chap 6 in author's **NC&O** (1891) 163-192.

Müller, F. Max. The religions of china. 2: Taoism. **NC** 48 (oct 1900) 569-581.

Murphy, Gardner and Lois B. Murphy. Taoism. In authors' **Asian psychology,** n.y. and london (1968) 155-168.

Nguyen, Duy-Can. The role of taoism in today's society. **CC** 11.3 (sept 1970) 54-58.

Noss, John B. **Man's religions.** N.Y. (1949 et seq) 3rd rev ed (1963) See pt 3, chap 9, Chinese religion and the taoists, 327-368.

Pang Tzu-yau. Notes on popular taoism. **CF** 7.4 (1963) 9-16.

Parker, E.H. Taoism. **IAQR** ser 3, 22 (oct 1906) 311-333.

Parker, E.H. The taoist religion. **Dublin review** 133 (july-oct 1903) 128-162. Repr london (1904) 35 p, bibliog.

Pauthier, G. **Mémoire sur l'origine et la propagation de la doctrine du tao, fondée par lao-tseu; traduit du chinois, et accompagné d'un commentaire tiré des livres sanskrits et du tao-de-king de lao-tseu** ... Paris (1831) 79 p. See further exchange of correspondence on this work betw author, J. Klaproth et al, **JA** 7 and 8.

Peeters, Hermes. **The religions of china. Confucianism, taoism, buddhism, popular belief.** Peking (1941) 64 p.

Peyraube, Alain. Trois études sur les religions chinoises. **ASSR** 35 (jan-juin 1973) 151-157. Rev art on Doré, **Manuel des superstitions chinoises;** Gulik, **La vie sexuelle dans la chine ancienne;** Maspero, **Le taoïsme et les religions chinoises** qqv.

Politella, Joseph. **Taoism and confucianism.** Iowa city (1967) 167 p.

Préau, André. **La fleur d'or et le taoïsme sans tao.** Paris (1931) 62 p. 2 art orig in **Le voile d'isis** (fév et avr 1931)

Rao, K.Bhaskara. **Taoism and buddhism.** Vijayawata (n.d., Foreword 1971) vi + 86 p.

Rawson, Philip & Laszlo Legeza. **Tao. The chinese philosophy of time and change.** London (1973) 128 p, profusely illus.

Reid, Gilbert. **A christian's appreciation of other faiths.** Chicago and london (1921) See lectures 1 and 2 on his appreciations of confucianism and taoism, 11-49.

Richard, Timothy. Taoism, prize essay. Chap 15 in author's **CbyM** (1907) 246-264.

Rosenkranz, Gerhard. **Der heilige in den chinesischen klassikern; eine untersuchung über die erlöser-** **erwartung in konfuzianismus und taoismus.** Leipzig (1935) vii + 188 p.

Rosny, Léon de. **Le taoisme.** Paris (1892) xxvi + 179 p.

Rosny, Léon de. Le tao-sséime. In author's **Variétés orientales, historiques, géographiques, scientifiques, bibliographiques et littéraires,** paris, 3e éd (1872) 171-176.

Ross, Floyd H. and Tynette Wilson Hills. **Questions that matter most, asked by the world's religions.** Boston (1954) See sec 3, Chinese religions; chap 10, taoism ... Paperbk title; **The great religions by which men live.**

Rousselle, Erwin. Der lebendige taoismus in heutigen china. **Sinica** 8 (1933) 122-131.

K.M.S. (Kristofer M. Schipper) Taoïsme. In **EUF** (1968) vol 15, 738b-744a; **ibid** (1973) vol 15, 738-744.

Sakai, Tadao & Noguchi Tetsurō. Taoist studies in japan. In **FT** (1979) 269-287.

Saso, Michael R. The taoist tradition in taiwan. **CQ** 41 (jan-mar 1970) 83-102.

Saso, Michael. **The teachings of taoist master chuang.** Yale univ (1978) 317 p, notes, bibliog, index and chin char, illus, fig.

Saso, Michael & David W. Chappell (ed) **Buddhist and taoist studies I.** Univ hawaii (1977) 162 p, bibliog of taoist studies, gloss with chin char, index, illus. Four essays on taoism, one on buddhism; listed sep in our bibliog. Abbrev **BTS-I.**

Seidel, Anna. Taoism. **EncyB 3** (1974) **Macropaedia** vol 17, 1034b-1044b.

Sivin, N. Report on the third international conference on taoist studies. **SSCRB** 7 (fall 1979) 1-23.

Smart, Ninian. **The religious experience of mankind.** N.Y. (1969) See chap 4, Chinese and japanese religious experience; sec, Confucianism and taoism, 141-190.

Smith, D.H. Learning from other faiths. V. Taoism. **ET** 83 (july 1972) 292-296.

Smith, D. Howard (comp & tsl) **The wisdom of the taoists.** NY (1980) 90 p. Mostly fr lao tzu and chuang tzu.

Smith, Huston. **The religions of man.** N.Y. (1958) chap 5, taoism, 175-192.

Smith, Ruth (ed) **The tree of life. Selections from the literature of the world's religion.** NY (1942) See sec, From the taoist religion, 189-212.

Spencer, Sidney. **Mysticism in world religion.** N.Y. (1963) london (1966) See 4, Taoist and confucianist mysticism, i. Taoism, 97-133.

Stein, Rolf A. Un exemple de relations entre taoïsme et religion populaire. In **Fukui hakase festschrift: Tōyō bunka ronshū,** ?Tokyo (1969) 79-90.

Strickmann, Michel. History, anthropology, and chinese religion. **HJAS** 40.1 (1980) 201-248. Rev art on Michael Saso, **The teachings of taoist master chuang.** q.v.

Taoism. Special issue of **ActaA** 27 (1974) Art sep listed in our bibliog.

Taoism. In Henry O. Dwight, H. Allen Tapper jr, and Edwin M. Bliss (ed) **Enclopaedia of missions,** N.Y. and london, 2nd ed (1910) 724-729.

Taoism. A prize essay. In **WPR** (1893) vol 2, 1355-1358.

The taoist pope on religion. **OC** 28.11 (nov 1914) 707-709.

The taou sect of china. **Asiatic journal** ser 2, 5 (1831) 97-104.

Trood, S.M.E. **The religions of mankind. An introductory survey.** London (1929) See chap 8 . . . Taoism and shinto, 106-122.

Tsumaki, Naoyoshi. Dōkyō no kenkyū, études sur le taoïsme. **Tōyō Gakuhō** 1.1, 1-56; 1.2, 20-51; 2.1 58-75.

Vandier-Nicolas, N. Pensée chinoise et taoïsme. **AS** 4 (1950) 64-89.

Vandier-Nicolas, Nicole. **Le taoïsme.** Paris (1965)

Van Over, Raymond. **Chinese mystics.** NY etc (1973) xxx + 183 p. Sel fr taoist and budd texts.

Van Over, Raymond. **Taoist tales.** NY etc (1973) 250 p.

Voss, Carl Hermann. **Living religions of the world: our search for meaning.** Cleveland (1968) See Confucianism and taoism: the will of heaven, 71-86.

Waddell, N.A. (tsl) A selection from the ts'ai ken t'an ('vegetable-root discourses') **EB** 2.2 (nov 1919) 88-98.

Walshe, W. Gilbert. Chinese mysticism. In **HERE** 9, 87-89.

Watts, Harold H. **The modern reader's guide to religions.** N.Y. (1964) See chap 19, Chinese and japanese religion: taoism, 554-565.

Weber, Max. **Konfuzianismus und taoismus.** Tübingen (1922) (Author's Gesammelte aufsätze zur religions-soziologie, 1) Engl tsl Hans H. Gerth: **The religion of china: confucianism and taoism.** Glencoe, ill. (1951); london (1952) xi + 308 p.

Welch, Holmes, **The parting of the way. Lao tzu and the taoist movement.** Boston and london (1957); slightly rev ed (1965) 204 p, app, bibliog, index.

Welch, Holmes & Anna Seidel (ed) **Facets of taoism. Essays in chinese religion.** Yale univ (1979) 302 p, intro, index. Contributions by 10 scholars, listed sep in our bibliog. Abbrev **FT.**

Wilhelm, Richard. **Lao-tse und der taoismus.** (1925) repr stuttgart (1948) 164 p.

Williams, E.T. Taoism. Chap 15 in author's **CYT** (1928) 316-338.

Winter, H.J.J. Science, buddhism and taoism. **AP** 21 (may 1950) 206-208.

Yang, Ju-chou. **Taoism through the ages.** N.p. (?taipei) n.d. 327 p, bibliog, index.

Yang, Ming-che. Confucianism vs. tao and buddha. **FCR** (jan 1969) 21-29.

Yang, Ming-che. Taoism. **FCR** 17 (july 1967) 20-26.

Yewdale, M.S. The wisdom of tao. **AP** 21 (1950) 365-368.

Yu, David C. Present-day taoist studies. **RSR** 3.4 (oct 1977) 220-239.

Zaehner, R.C. **Concordant discord. The interdependence of faiths.** Oxford univ (1970) See chap 11, The way of heaven and earth, 214-236.

Zia, Rosina C. The conception of "sage" in lao-tze and chuang-tze as distinguished from confucianism. **CCJ** 5 (may 1966) 150-157.

Zürcher, Erik. Buddhist influence on early taoism. **TP** 66.1/3 (1980) 84-147.

15. LAO TZU & TAO TE CHING*
(See also Sec 14: **Taoism—General**)

Abel-Rémusat, J.P. Mémoire sur la vie et les opinions de lao-teu, philosophe chinois du VIe siècle avant notre ère. **MAIBL** 7 (1820) 1-54. See also Extrait d'un mémoire . . . **JA** 3 (1823) 1-15.

Affinités des doctrines de lao-tse et du bouddha. Date incontestable de l'existence de lao-tse. Un savant prétend que lao-tse était un philosophe japonais. In **EM** (d?) t 26, 343 f.

Alexander, Edwin. The mountain and the valley, a comparative study of grace in the old testament and tao te ching. **CC** 20.3 (sept 1979) 71-84.

Alexander, G.G. Tao-ism. What lao-tze meant by tao. **IAQR** 3rd ser, 4 (1897) 387-396.

*No attempt is made to list the constantly increasing number of translations of the text (see our remarks in Foreword).

Amberley, John Russell, Viscount. **An analysis of religious belief.** London (1876) See vol 1, pt 2, Means of communication downwards. V. Holy persons. Sec 2, Lao-tse.

Anderson, A.E. The tao te king. A chinese mysticism. Univ calif, **University chronicle** 22 (1920) 395-402.

Baumann, C. Reflections prompted by lao-tse; a psychological approach. **Bulletin de la société suisse des amis de l'extrême-orient** 8 (1946) 49-62.

Beky, Gellert. **Die welt des tao.** Freiburg & München (1972) 253 p, bibliog.

Benton, Richard P. Tennyson and lao tzu. **PEW** 13.2 (1962) 233-240.

Besse, J. (tsl) **Lao-tseu, notice historique (tirée des mémoires historiques de sse-ma-tsien)** Paris (1909) 167 p.

Bisson, T.A. Lao-tsu and the tao te ching. **CJ** 15 (1931) 120-127.

Bodde, Derk. Further remarks on the identification of lao tzu. **JAOS** 64 (1944) 24-27.

Bodde, Derk. The new identification of lao tzu proposed by professor dubs. **JAOS** 62 (1942) 8-13.

Bodde, Derk. Two new translations of lao tzu. **JAOS** 74 (1954) 211-217. Repr **ECC** (1981) 388-394.

Borel, H. **Lao tzu's tao and wu-wei.** N.Y. (1919) thetford, vt. (1939) 139 p.

Borel, Henri. **The rhythm of life. Based on the philosophy of lao-tse.** Tsl fr dutch M.E. Reynolds. London (1921?) 89 p. Rev ed of author's **Wu wei** q.v.

Borel, Henri. **Wu wei. A phantasy based on the philosophy of lao tse.** Tsl fr dutch Meredith Ianson. London (1904 and 1907) vii + 69 p.

Braden, Charles S. **Jesus compared. Jesus and other great founders of religions.** Englewood cliffs, n.j. (1957) See Jesus and lao-tzu, 132-146.

Brecht, B. **Legende von der entstehung des buches taoteking auf dem weg des laotse in die emigration.** Zürich (1960)

Bucke, Richard M. Von komischen bewusstein: li-r=laotse. **Yoga** 5 (1958) 284-288.

Burrows, Millar. **Founders of the great religions. Being personal sketches of lao-tse, confucius, buddha, jesus, etc.** London and n.y. (1935) 243 p.

Carus, Paul. The authenticity of the tao-teh-king. **The monist** 11.3 (1900)

Chamberlain, Ida Hoyt. 'Magic writing' from ear to the east series. **China monthly** 2 (nov 1941) 9-12, 17-21. Account of recording music of tao-teh ching as chanted by priests.

Chan, Wing-tsit. Chu hsi's appraisal of lao tzu. **PEW** 25.2 (apr 1975) 131-144. Same title in **MS/CA** (1977) 5-9.

Chan, Wing-tsit. Lao-tzu. In **EncyB** (1972) vol 13, 714b-715a.

Chan, Wing-tsit. The orderly realm of the chinese sages. In National Geographic Soc, **Great religions of the world** (1971) 122-129, illus.

Chang, Constant C.C. Lao-tze's theory of yiu and wu—being and non-being in taoism. **CC** 20.1 (mar 1979) 9-14.

Chang, Constant C.C. The monoism (sic) of taoism. **FCR** 22.3 (mar 1972) 31-34. Same title in **CC** 14.3 (sept 1973) 9-16.

Chavannes, Édouard. Lao-tseu. In **GE** (d?) t 21, 938-939.

Chen, Chung-hwan. What does lao-tzu mean by the term "tao"? **TJ** n.s. 4.2 (1964) 150-161.

Chen, Ellen Marie. Is there a doctrine of physical immortality in the tao te ching? **HR** 12.3 (feb 1973) 231-249.

Chen, Ellen Marie. The origin and development of being (yu) from non-being (wu) according to the tao te ching. **IPQ** 13.3 (sept 1973) 403-417.

Chen, Ellen Marie. Tao as the great mother and the influence of motherly love in the shaping of chinese philosophy. **HR** 14.1 (aug 1974) 51-64.

Cheney, Sheldon. **Men who have walked with god.** N.Y. (1956) See 1, The golden age and the mystic poet lao-tse, 1-37.

Chiu, Moses. **Kritische betrachtung über lau-tsze und seine lehre.** Berlin (1911) 83 p.

Clopin, Camille. Comparaison entre lao-tse, pythagore et confucius. Résultats définitifs pour la chine des deux doctrines examinées par m. de milloué dans une conférence au musée guimet. **La géographie** 27.3 (1898) 285f.

Cook, Earl F. The mysticism of lao-tze. **OC** 33.7 (july 1919) 441-448.

Cordier, Henri Lao tseu. **BVAMG,** t 36. Paris (1911) 31-68.

Cornaby, W. Arthur. Lao tzu redivivus. **ChRec** 37 (1906) 67-74, 124-131.

Dahm, Annemarie. Welterkenntnis und lebensdeutung bei lao dsi. **Yoga** 6 (1961) 17-25; 7 (1961) 1-14; 8 (1961) 8-13.

Délétie, Henri. 'Tao te king' et son interpretation. **Rencontre orient-occident** 5 (jan-déc 1963-64) 9-12; (jan-juin 1965) 11-15; (july-sept 1965) 12-14.

Dubs, Homer H. The date and circumstances of the philosopher lao-dz. **JAOS** 61 (1941) 215-221.

Dubs, Homer H. The identification of lao-tse. A reply to professor bodde. **JAOS** 62 (1942) 300-304.

Eckardt, André. Die ethischen grundbegriffe bei laotse. **PJGG** 59.2 (1949) 200-207.

Eckardt, André. Der gottesbegriff bei laotse. **PJGG** 58.2 (1948) 88-99; 58.3 (1948) 211-218.

Eckardt, André. Laotse und die philosophie des ostens. **Universitas** 12 (1957) 355-362.

Eckstein, Baron d'. Le livre de la voie et de la vertu... trad ... par stanislas julien. **JA** sér 3, t 14 (août-sep 1842) 283-318, 399-442. Rev art, with samkhya comparisons.

Edkins, Joseph. The tau te ching. **ChRev** 13 (1884-85) 10-19.

Elwald, Oscar. **Laotse.** München (1928) 86 p.

Engler, Friedrich. Laotse, sein leben und seine persönlichkeit. **Das edel leben, zeitschrift für praktische philosophie** 12.11 (1963) 14-17.

Erdberg-Consten, Eleanor von. A statue of lao tzu in the po-yün-kuan. **MS** 7 (1942) 235-241.

Erkes, Eduard. Kumārajīvas laotse kommentar. **ZMR** 50 (1935) 49-53.

Erkes, Eduard. Ein märchenmotiv bei laotse. **Sinologica** 3 (1953) 100-105.

Erkes, Eduard. Spuren einer kosmogonischen mythe bei laotse. **AA** 8 (1940) 16-38.

Étiemble, René. En relisant lao-tseu. **Nouvelle revue française** n.s. 15 (mar 1967) 457-476.

Feibleman, James K. **Understanding oriental philosophy. A popular account for the western world.** NY (1976) See pt 2, chap 19, Laotse and the tao, 107-113.

Folberth, Otto. **Meister eckhart und laotse. Ein vergleich zweier mystiker.** Mainz (1925) 119 p.

Forke, A. Waley's tao-tê king. **ZDMG** 95 (1941) 36-45.

Gabelentz, Georg von der. The life and teachings of lao-tse. **ChRev** 17 (1888-89) 189-198. Tsl fr **Allgemeine real-encyclopädie der wissenschaft und kunst,** 2, sec xlii (1889)

Gaer, Joseph (comp) **The wisdom of the living religions.** N.Y. (1956) See pt 9, The sayings of taoism, 259-274.

Giles, Herbert A. Lao Tzû and the tao tê king. In author's **Ad Sin** 3 (1906) 58-78.

Giles, Herbert A. The remains of lao tzû. **ChRev** 14 (1885-86) 231-280; 355-356. Separate work by same title, hong kong (1886) 50 p in 2 col; only in part identical with above art. See further various criticisms and rebuttals in later issues of **ChRev**; esp A critical notice of the Remains of lao tsze, retranslated, **ibid** 16 (1887-88) 195-214.

Girardot, Norman J. Myth and meaning in the tao te ching: chapters 25 and 42. **HR** 16 (1977) 294-328.

Griffith, Gwilym Oswald. **Interpreters of reality; a comment on heracleitus, lao tse and the christian faith.** London (1946) 106 p.

Guimet. E. Lao-tzeu et le brâhmanisme. **Actes** 2e **CIHR,** Bâle (1904) 16 p.

Haas, Hans. **Lao tsze und konfuzius. Einleitung in ihr spruchgut.** Leipzig (1920) 60 p.

Haas, Hans. **Das spruchgut k'ung-tsze's und lao-tsze's in gedanklicher zusammenordnung.** Leipzig (1920) 244 p.

Haas, Hans. **Weisheitworte des lao-tsze.** Leipzig (1920) 36 p.

Han fei's criticism and transformation of the thought of "lao tzu." **SPRCM** 837 (8 sept 75) 29-35.

Harlez, Charles de. Lao-tze, le premier philosophe chinois ou un prédécesseur de schelling au VIe siècle avant notre ère. **MCAM** t 37 (1884) Sep publ, bruxelles (1885) 32 p.

Heiler, F. Weltabkehr und weltrückkehr ausserchristlicher mystiker. 1. teil: laotse und bhagavadgita. **Eine heilige kirche** 22 (1941) 181-213.

Hesse, J. Laotze, ein vorchristlicher wahrheitszeuge. **Basler missionsstudien** 44 (1914) 64 p.

Hoang, Tzu-yue. Lao-tseu, khong-tseu, mo-tseu. (Étude comparative sur les philosophies) **Annales de l'université de lyon** (1925) 37 p.

Holzmann, Ferdinand. **Kleines laotse brevier. Zur stärkung und erleuchtung des herzens in der bedrängnis des tages zusammengestellt aus dem tao-te-king.** Heidelberg (1948) 8 p.

Homann, R. Die laozi-diskussion in der volksrepublic china nach den funden von ma-wang-dui. **AS** 30 (1976) 79-113, bibliog.

Hsiao, Paul. Laotse und die technik. **Die katholischen missionen** 75 (1956) 72-74.

Hsiung, Pin-ming. Non-quietist laotse. **Cina** 8 (1963) 39-41.

Hsu, Sung-peng. Lao tzu's conception of evil. **PEW** 26.3 (1976) 301-316.

Hsu, Sung-peng. Lao tzu's conception of ultimate reality: a comparative study. **IPQ** 16.2 (june 1976) 197-218. Comparisons esp with hinduism, budd, christianity.

Hu Schï. W. Franke (tsl) Der ursprung der ju und ihre beziehung zu konfuzius und lao-dsï. **SinSon** (1936) 1-42.

Hu, Shih. A criticism of some recent methods in dating lao tzu. Tsl Homer H. Dubs. **HJAS** 2 (1937) 373-397.

Hummel, Siegbert. **Zum ontologischen problem des dauismus (taoismus). Untersuchen an lau dsi, kap. 1 und 2.** Leipzig (1948) 45 p.

Hundhauser, Vincenz. **Lau dse: das tao als weltgesetz und vorbild.** Peking (1948) 83 p.

Hurvitz, Leon. A recent japanese study of lao-tzu: kimura eiichi's rōshi no shin-kenkyū. **MS** 20 (1961) 311-367.

Izutsu, Toshihiko. **A comparative study of the key philosophical concepts of sufism and taoism; ibn 'arabi and lao-tzu, chuang-tzu.** Tokyo, 2 vol (1967) index of chin words and phrases. Publ Keio gijuku daigaku, Keio instit of cultural & linguistic studies.

Jan, Yün-hua. Problems of tao and tao te ching. **Numen** 22.3 (dec 1975) 208-234.

Jan, Yün-hua. The silk manuscripts on taoism. **TP** 63.1 (1977) 65-84.

Jan, Yün-hua. Tao yüan or tao: the origin. **JCP** 7.3 (sept 1980) 195-204. Tsl fr silk ms, han tomb no 3, ma-wang-tui; incl reconstructed chin text.

Jang, Ching-schun. **Das chinesische philosoph lau-dze und seine lehre.** Übers von Gerhard Kahlenbach. [Ost] berlin (1955) 136 p.

Joos, G. Konfuzius und lao-tse. In **Geistige reiche und religiöse fragen der gegenwart** (1940) 14-24.

Kaltenmark, Max. Lao-tseu. In **Dictionnaire bio-graphique des auteurs,** paris (1964) t 2, 61-63.

Kaltenmark, Max. Lao-tseu dans la religion taoiste. École pratique des hautes études, section des sciences religieuses, **Annuaire 1958-1959,** p 63f.

Kaltenmark, Max. **Lao tseu et le taoisme.** Paris (1965) Engl tsl Roger Greaves: **Lao tzu and taoism.** Stanford univ (1969) 158 p, bibliog.

Kaltenmark, Max. Lao-tzu. In **EncyB 3** (1974) **Macropaedia** vol 10, 679b-680b.

Karlgren, Bernhard. Notes on lao-tse. **BMFEA** 47 (1975) 1-18.

Kimura, Eiichi. A new study on lao-tzu. **Philosophical studies in japan** 1 (1959) 85-104.

Kingsmill, T.W. Notes on the tao teh king. **JNCBRAS** n.s. 31.2 (1896) 206-209.

Kramers, R.P. Die lao-tsû—diskussionen in der chinesischen volksrepublik. **AS** 22 (1968) 31-67.

Krebsová, Berta. Lao-tzu—the old master. **NO** 1.6 (dec 1960) 10-11.

Lanczkowski, Günter. Neutestamentliche parallelen zu láo-tsés tao-te-king. In **Gott und die götter. Festgabe für emil fischer zum 60. geburstag,** berlin (1958) 7-15.

Lao-tseu. In Larousse, **Grande dictionnaire universel,** paris (préface 1865) t 10, 177-178.

La Légende des taosséistes sur lao-tse. In **EM** (d?) t 26, p 171.

Legge, James. Lao-tsze. In **EncyB** 9th ed (1882) vol 14, 295a-298a.

Legge, James. Lao-tsze. In **EncyB** 11th ed (1920-11) vol 16, 191-194.

Legge, James. Lao-tse. In **EncyB** 14th ed (1929) vol 13, 712b-714a.

Lie, Hwa-sun. **Der begriff skandalon im neuen testament und der wieder-kehrgedanke bei laotse.** Bern & frankfurt (1973) 252 p.

Liebenthal, Walter. Lord atman in the lao-tzu. **MS** 27 (1968) 374-380.

Lin Yutang. A note on lao-tse. **EW** 3/4 (1949) 18f.

Lin, Yutang. The wisdom of lao-tse. **AP** 20 (1949) 2-5.

Lüth, Paul E.H. Weltgeheimnis und weltgefühl bei lao tse. In **Schule der freiheit, Uchtdorf im Pommern,** vol 9 (1941-42) 306-312.

Magee, John B. **Religion and modern man. A study of the religious meaning of being human.** NY etc (1967) See chap 6, Taoism and the tao te ching, 83-97.

Martin, Alfred W. **Great religious teachers of the east.** N.Y. (1911) See chap 4, Confucius and lao-tze, 105-148.

Martin, Alfred W. (comp) **Seven great bibles.** N.Y. (1930) See chap 5, An older contemporary of confucius and his book; —lao-tze and the tao teh-king.

Martin, Bernard & Shui, Chien-tung. **Makers of china—confucius to mao.** NY & Oxford (1972) See Lao tzu, 15-17.

Maspero, Henri. Études sur le taoisme. Le saint et la vie mystique chez lao-tseu et tchouang-tseu. **Bulletin de l'association française des amis de l'orient** 3 (1922) 69-89. Repr in author's **Le taoisme,** paris (1950) 225-242.

Maurer, Herrymon. **The old fellow.** N.Y. (1943) 296 p.

Medhurst, C. Spurgeon. The tao teh king. An apprecia-tion. **ChRec** 30 (nov 1899) 540-551. (2) —. An analysis. **Ibid** 31 (jan 1900) 20-33.

Medhurst, C. Spurgeon. **The tao teh king. A short study in comparative religion.** Chicago (1905) xix + 134 p.

Mémoires concernant l'histoire, les sciences, les arts, les moeurs, les usages etc. des chinoise; par les missionaires de pékin. See t 3, paris (1778) Lao tsee, 38-41 (abbrev as **MCLC**)

Möller, N. De la métaphysique de lao-tseu. **Revue catholique** 4 (1849-50)

Müller, F.M. Die lehre des lao-tse. **Die woche** 44.3 (nov 1900)

Neef, Hans. **Die im tao-tsang erhaltenen kommentare zu tao-tê-ching kapitel vi.** Bochum (1938)

Noguier, A. **Lao-tse, un philosophe chinois du Viéme siècle avant notre ère.** Montauban (1906) 79 p.

Opitz, Peter-Joachim. **Lao-tzu. Die ordnungsspek-ulation in tao-tê-ching.** München (1967) 202 p.

Osk, Ewald. **Lao-tse.** München (1928)

Osk, Ewald. **Von laotse bis tolstoi.** Berlin (1927)

Pachow, W. Laotzû and gautama buddha: an inquiry into the authenticity of laotzu's mission to india. In **PFV** (1966) 293-303. Repr **ChBudd** (1980)

Paravey, Charles-Hippolyte de. Explication du texte de lao-tseu sur la trinité. Le tao-te-king considéré non comme un livre historique mais comme un traité de philosophie. **APC** 4e sér, t 8 (1841) 246-258.

Parker, E.H. Laocius and confucius as rival moralists **AR** 20 (1924) 698-704; 21 (1925) 129-146.

Parker, E.H. The tau teh king remains. **ChRev** 14 (1885-86) 323-333.

Parrinder, E.G. **What world religions teach.** London etc (1963) See chap 9, Lao tse and the way.

Pauthier, Georges. **Mémoire sur l'origine et la propa-gation de la doctrine du tao, fondée par lao-tseu; traduit du chinois et accompagné d'un commentaire tiré des livres sanscrits et du tao-te-king de lao-tseu, etab-lissant la conformité de certaines opinions philo-sophiques de la chine et de l'inde; orné d'un dessein chinois; suivi de deux oupanishads des vedas, avec le texte sanscrit et persan.** Paris (1831) 79 p. See critical rev by Anon [Stanislas Julien?] in **Nouveau JA** 7 (1831) 465-493; see further Pauthier's rebuttal in **ibid** 8 (1831) 129-158.

Pelliot, Paul. Autour d'une traduction sanscrite du tao tö king. **TP** n.s. 13 (1912) 351-430.

Podgorski, Frank. Reading the holy books of china. **JD** 3.3 (july-sept 1978) 309-317. Re ancient confucian and taoist classics.

Pontynen, Arthur. The deification of laozi in chinese history and art. **OA** 26.2 (summer 1980) 192-200, illus.

Pontynen, Arthur. The dual nature of laozi in chinese history and art. **OA** 26.3 (autumn 1980) 308-313, illus.

Potter, Charles Francis. **The greal religious leaders.** N.Y. (1958) Rev ed of **The story of religion,** n.y. (1929) See chap 6, Confucius . . . (including lao-tse of the divine way) 141-164.

Reid, Gilbert. Taoism, an appreciation. **OC** 32.10 (oct 1918) 613-626. Mostly on lao tzu.

Roberts, Moss. The metaphysical polemics of the tao te ching: an attempt to integrate the ethics and metaphysics of lao tzu. **JAOS** 95.1 (jan-mar 1975) 36-42.

Robinet, Isabelle. **Les commentaires du tao tö king jusqu'au VIIe siècle.** Paris (1977) 333 p.

Rosny, Léon de. La philosophie du tao-teh king, leçon faite à l'école pratique des hautes-études. **Mémoires société des études japonaises** (janv 1887) 5-24.

Rosny, Léon de. **Le taoïsme.** Paris (1892) xxxvi + 179 p.

Rosny, Léon de. La texte du tao-teh-king et son histoire. Bibliothèque de l'ecole des hautes etudes,**Sciences religieuses,** t 1 (1889) 323-340.

Rotermund, W. **Die ethik lao-tse's mit besonderer bezugnahme auf die buddhistische moral.** Gotha (1874) 26 s.

Rousselle, Erwin. Lao-dsïs gang durch seele, geschichte und welt. Versuch einer deutung. **CDA** (1935) 24-41; also in **EJ** 3 (1935) 179-205.

Rousselle, Erwin. Lau-dsï und sein buch. (Über die tiergöttin, zu lao-tse, kap. 6) **Sinica** 16 (1941) 120-129.

Saitschick, Robert. Lao-tse. **Der wendepunkt im leben und im leiden** 13 (1936) 70-76.

Saitschick, Robert. **Schöpfer lebenswerte von laotse bis jésus.** Zürich (1945)

Schmidt, K.O. Künder des lichtes, III. Laotse. **Zu freien ufern** 13 (1963) 452-455.

Schulz, Bernard. Legende von der entstehung des buches tao te king auf dem weg des laotse in die emigration. **Wirkendes wort** 7 (dec 1956) 81-86.

Smith, Carl T. A heideggerian interpretation of the way of lao tzu. **CF** 10.2 (1967) 5-19.

Stroup, Herbert. **Founders of living religions.** Philadelphia (1974) See chap 5, Lao-tzu and taoism, 107-125.

Stübe, R. **Lao-tse. Seine persönlichkeit und seine lehre.** Tübingen (1912) 32 p.

Le Tao-teh-king. Identité des methodes de lao-tse et du bouddha. Commentaire bouddhique du tao-teh-king. Lao-tse sous le nom de lauthu. **CISE,** paris (1881) 765-771.

Thiel, Joseph. Der begriff des tao im tao-te-ching. **Sinologica** 12 (1972) 30-108.

Trêve, Jacques. **l'Enseignement de lao-tsu.** Tunis (1934) 7 p.

Tröltsch, Charlotte Freifrau von. **Lao-tse; die bisher unbekannte lebensgeschichte des chinesischen weisen und sein wirken; aufgenommen durch besondere begabung eines dazu berufenen.** München (1935) 345 p.

Tscharner, E.H. von. Laotse und das innere licht. **Die weisse fahne** 28 (1955) 68-71.

Tscharner. E.H. von. La pensée "métaphysique" et éthique de lao-tse. **Scientia** 72 (1942) 29-36.

Turnbull, Grace H. (comp) **Tongues of fire. A bible of sacred scriptures of the pagan world.** N.Y. (1929) See The book of lao-tzu, 157-166.

Ular, Alexandre. Lao-tse le nietzschéen. A propos du livre de la voie et la ligne droite. **Revue blanche** 27 (1902) 161-167.

Van Buskirk, William R. **The saviors of mankind.** N.Y. (1929) See chap 1, Lao-tze, 1-24.

Watters, Thomas. **Lao-tzu. A study in chinese philosophy.** Hong kong (1870) 114 p. Most of this appeared first in **ChRec** 1 (1868) 31-32, 57-61, 82-86, 106-109, 128-132, 154-160, 209-214. The present book added 2 chap: 8, Lao tzu and confucius; 9, conclusion.

Weddingen. **La théodicée de lao-tze.** Louvain (1885)

Wilhelm, Richard. Laotse, der verborgene weise. **Sinica** 3 (1928) 26-31.

Wilhelm, Richard (übers und erläut) **Laotse. Tao te king.** Jena (1921) xxxii + 113 s. Re-issued düsseldorf/köln (1950)

Williams, David Rhys. **World religions and the hope for peace.** Boston (1951) See chap 3, Lao-tse and the inner life, 22-32.

Wu, John C. H. Who was lao tzu? **CC** 15.2 (june 1974) 1-3.

Yang, Ching-schun. **Der chinesische philosoph laudse und seine lehre.** Tsl fr russian G. Kahlenbach. Berlin (1955) 136 p.

Yewdale, M.S. Understanding the chinese through the tao teh king. **AP** 5 (1934) 582-584.

Ymaizoumi, M. Étude de m. ymaizoumi, sur le livre de la vertu et de la voie. **CPOL** t 2, lyon (1880) 82-88.

16. OTHER TAOISTS TEXTS—THE CANON

Abel-Rémusat, J.P. (tsl) **Le livre des récompenses et des peines.** paris (1816) new ed (1939) (T'ai shang kan ying p'ien)

Andersen, Poul (tsl) **The method of holding the three ones. A taoistic manual of meditation of the fourth century a.d.** London & malmö (1979) 66 p. + chin text of Chin-ch'üeh ti-chün san-yüan-chen-yi ching.

Balfour, F.H. (tsl) The book of purity and rest. **ChRev** 9 (1880-81) 83-85 (Ch'ing ching ching)

Balfour, Frederic Henry (tsl)The book of recompences [sic] **ChRev** 8 (1879-80) 341-352 (T'ai shang kan ying p'ien)

Balfour, Frederic H. The "su shu" or book of plain words. **ChRev** 9.3 (1880-81) 162-167.

Balfour, Frederic Henry (tsl)The 't'ai-hsi' king; or the respiration of the embryo. **ChRev** 9 (1880-81) 224-226 (T'ai hsi ching)

Balfour, Frederic Henry (tsl) **Taoist texts, ethical, political and speculative.** London and shanghai (1884) 118 p (Tao teh ching, Yin fu ching, T'ai hsi ching, Hsin yin ching, Ta t'ung ching, Ch'ih wen tung, Ch'ing ching ching, Hung lieh chuan ti yi tuan, Su shu, Kan ying p'ien)

Balfour, F.H. (tsl) Three brief essays. **ChRev** 9 (1880-81) 380-382 (Hsin yin ching, Ta t'ung ching, Ch'ih wen tung)

Balfour, Frederic Henry (tsl) The 'Yin-fu classic; or, clue to the unseen.' **ChRev** 10 (1881-82) 44-54.

Ballou, Robert O. et al (ed) **The bible of the world.** N.Y. (1939) See sec, Taoist scriptures, 471-558.

Barrett, T.H. On the transmission of the shen tzu and the yang-sheng yao-chi,. **JRAS** (1980 no 2) 168-176. Rev art on Paul M. Thompson, **The shen tzu fragments,** oxford univ (1979) Second text is taoist.

Bauer, Wolfgang (übers) Ko hung's rede über 'die kunst des innehaltens.' In **Asien** (1971) 1-22. Re pao-p'u-tzu wai-p'ien 49A.

Beck, B.J. Mansvelt. The date of the taiping ching. **TP** 66.4/5 (1980) 149-182.

Belpaire, B. Note sur un traité taoïste. **Muséon** 59 (1946) 655-659.

Braden, Charles S. (comp) **The scriptures of mankind: an introduction.** N.Y. (1952) See chap 9, The sacred literature of the chinese . . . taoist, 273-290.

Browne, Lewis (comp) **The world's great scriptures. An anthology of the sacred books of the ten principal religions.** N.Y. (1946) See sec, The scriptures of taoism, 295-358.

Champion, Selwyn G. and Dorothy Short, (comp) **Readings from world religions.** Boston (1951) See chap 6, Taoism, 103-125.

Chavannes, Édouard and Paul Pelliot. Au sujet du canon taoistes. Un traité manichéen retrouvé en chine, traduit et annoté . . . **JA** (1911) 499-617; (1913) 99-199; 261-394, 325-329.

Dschi, Hiän-lin. Lieh tzu and buddhist sutras; a note on the author of lieh-tzu and the date of its composition. **SS** 9.1 (1950) 18-32. Tsl fr chin Chou, Ju-ch'ang.

Eichhorn, Werner. T'ai-p'ing und t'ai-p'ing religion. **MIOF** 5 (1957) 113-140. Re expression t'ai-p'ing, with tsl of 2 taoist texts.

Erkes, E. (tsl, ed, annot) The chao-yin-shi. 'Calling back the hidden scholar' by huai-nan-tzu. **AM** 1 (1924) 119-124.

Erkes, E. Der druck des taoistischen kanon. **Gutenberg jahrbuch** (1935) 326-327.

Frost, S E. jr. (ed) **The sacred writings of the world's great religions.** N.Y. (1943) See 3, Taoism, 79-90.

Gabelentz, Georg von der. Ueber das taoistische werk wên-tsi. **Berichte der k. sächs. ges. d. wiss phil.-hist. cl.** 39 (1887) 434-442.

Gaer, Joseph. **The wisdom of the living religions.** London (1958) chap 9, The sayings of taoism, 227-239.

Gauchet, L Contribution à l'étude du taoisme. **BUA** 3e sér, 9 (1948) 1-38.

Gauchet, L. En marge du 'canon taoiste.' **BUA** 2e sér, 36 (1937) 1-29.

Gauchet, L. Un livre taoïque, le cheng-shen king, sur la génération des esprits dans l'homme. **BUA** 3e sér, 10 (1949) 63-72.

Gauchet, L. Le tou-jen king des taoïstes, son texte primitif et sa date probable. **BUA** 3e sér, 2 (1941) 511-534.

Gauchet, L. A travers le canon taoïque: quelques synonymes du tao. **BUA** 3e sér, 3 (1942) 303-319.

Giles, Lionel A t'ang manuscript of the sou shên chi . . . **NCR** 3 (1921) 378-385, 460-468. See also W.P. Yetts, **ibid** 65.

Girardot, Norman J. Chaotic ''order'' (hun-tun) and benevolent ''disorder'' (luan) in the chuang tzu. **PEW** 28.3 (july 1978) 299-322.

Graham, David C. (tsl) Bridge for becoming immortals, taoist. A translation. **ChRec** 63 (1932) 171-177, 226-237, 301-307, 372-382.

Harlez, Charles de. Le gan-shih-tang . . ou lampe de la salle obscure. **Actes onzième ICO** Paris (1897) 2e sec 37-48.

Harlez, Charles de (tsl) Ko-hiuen. Shang-ts'ing-tsing king, ou le livre de la pureté et du repos constant. Textes taoistes traduits des originaux chinois et commentés. **AMG** 20 (1891) 75-82.

Harlez, Charles de. La lampe de la salle obscure (gan-shih-tang). Traité de morale taoïste. La piété filiale, l'infanticide, le respect du ciel, les biens de la fortune. **RHR** 27 (1893) 294-314.

Harlez, Charles de. Le livre du principe lumineux et du principe passif shang thsing tsing king. **MCAM** 37 (1885)

Harlez, Charles de (tsl) **Textes tâoïstes traduits des originaux chinois et commentés.** Paris (1891) 391 p. (Préface; lao tze et le tao-te-king; ko-hiuen; wen-tze; han-fei-tze; hoei-nan-tze; tchuang-tze; lie-tze; hoang-ti nei-king; tchang-tze).

Homann, R. (tsl) **Pai wen p'ien, or the hundred questions. A dialogue between two taoists on the macrocosmic and microcosmic system of correspondences.** Leiden (1976) x + 109 p.

Huebotter, Franz (tsl) **Classic on the conformity of yin. Schrift von konformität der yin.** Tsingtao (1936) 12 p.

Julien, Stanislas (tsl) **Le livre des récompenses et des peines, en chinois et en francais; accompagné de quatre cents légendes, anecdotes et histoires, qui font connaître les doctrines les croyances, et les moeurs de la secte des tao-ssé.** Paris (1835) 531 p.

Julien, Stanislas (tsl) La visite du dieu du foyer à iu-kong **ROA** 2e sér, 16 (1854) 267-276. Previously publ in author's **Livre des récompenses et des peines** q.v. and in french ed of Sir John F. Davis: **Chine,** paris (1857) t 2.

Kaltenmark, Max. Au sujet du houang-t'ing king. **AnnEPHE,** (1967-68) 80-81.

Kaltenmark, Max. The ideology of the t'ai-p'ing ching. In **FT** (1979) 19-52.

Kaltenmark, Max (tsl) **Le lie-sien tchouan . . . Biographies légendaires des immortels taoiste de l'antiquité.** Pékin (1953) 204 p.

Kandel, Barbara. **Taiping jing. The origin and transmission of the 'scripture on general welfare' — the history of an unofficial text.** Hamburg, **MDGNVO** 75 (1979) 111 p.

Kandel, Barbara. **Wen tzu: ein beitrag zur problematik und zum verständnis eines taoistischen textes.** Bern (1974) 362 s.

Legge, James. **The sacred books of china. The texts of taoism.** London (1891) 2 vol. F. Max Müller, ed. Sacred books of the east; vol 39 (pt 1) The tao teh king; the writings of kwang-sze [chuang-tzu] books 1-17; vol. 40 (pt 2) The writings of kwang-sze, books 18-33; the thâi-shang tractate of actions and their retributions; app 1-8 (Later repr as 2 vol in 1)

Liou, Tse Houa (tsl) **Lu yen. Le secret de la fleur d'or [par lu tsou]. Suivi du lire de la conscience et de la vie.** Paris (1969) 143 p, illus.

Liu, Hua-yang. Hui ming king. Das buch vom bewusstein und leben. **CBWK** 1.3 (1926) 104-114, 122-123.

Liu, Ts'un-yan. The composition and historical value of the tao-tsang. In **ESCH** (1973) 104-119.

Loon, Piet van der. A taoist collection of the fourteenth century. In **SSM/FHF** (1979) 401-406.

Lu, K'uan-yü (Charles Luk) tsl. **Taoist yoga. Alchemy and immortality. A translation, with introduction and notes, of the secrets of cultivating essential nature and eternal life (hsin ming fa chueh ming chih) by the taoist master chao pi ch'en, born 1860).** London (1970) 206 p, illus.

Morgan, Evan. The operations and manifestations of the tao exemplified in history or the tao confirmed by history. 12th essay in huai nan tzû. **JNCBRAS** 52 (1921) 1-39.

Ni, Hua-ching (tsl & comm) **The complete works of lao tzu. Tao teh ching and hua hu ching.** Malibu and los angeles (1979) 219 p.

Ōfuchi, Ninji. The formation of the taoist canon. In **FT** (1979) 253-268.

Paravey, M. de. Explication du texte de lao-tseu sur la trinité. **APC** 4e sér, 8 (?1909)

Pelliot, Paul. Les premières éditions du canon bouddhique et du canon taoïque. In **Les débuts de l'imprimerie en chine,** paris (1953) **Oeuvres posthumes de paul pelliot,** 4, 88-93.

Pen tsi king (livre du termes originel). Ouvrage taoiste inédit du VIIe siècle. Manuscrits retrouvés à touen-houang reproduits en facsimilés. Introduction par Wu Chi-yü. Paris (1960) Mission paul pelliot, documents conservés à la bibliothèque nationale, 53 p + 208 facs.

Pfizmaier, A. Chinesische begründungen der taolehre. **SAWW** 111 (1885) bd 2, heft 5, s 801-867. Separately publ wien (1886) 69 p (T'ang text: tao yen nei wai mi chüeh ch'üan shu—ch'uan tao chi by lü yen)

Pfizmaier, A. Ueber einige gegenstände des taoglaubens. **SAWW** 79; separately publ wien (1875) (T'ang text: Tao yen nei wai mi chüeh ch'üan shu by lü yen)

Philastre, P.L.F. Exégèse chinoise. **AMG** 1 (1880) 255-318. Tsl of Yin fu ching.

Podgorski, Frank. Reading the holy books of china. **JD** 3.3 (july-sept 1978) 309-317. Re ancient confucian and taoist classics.

Robinet, Isabelle. Introduction au kieou-tchen tchong-king. **SSCRB** 7 (fall 1979) 24-45.

Robinet, Isabelle. Randonnées extatiques des taoïstes dans les astres. **MS** 32 (1976) 159-273.

Rosny, Léon de (tsl) Le livre de la récompense des bienfaits secrets. **ROA** 2e sér, 16 (1854) 202-207; et **APC** t 53.

Saso, Michael. A guide to the chuang-lin hsü tao-tsang. **JCS** 16-17 (1979) 9-28.

Saso, Michael. **The teachings of taoist master chuang.** Yale univ (1978) 317 p, notes, bibliog, index and chin char, illus, fig.

Schipper, Kristofer. Le calendrier de jade—note sur le laozi zhongjing. **NachrDGNVO** 125 (1979) 75-80.

Schipper, K.M. **Concordance du houang-t'ing king, nei-king et wai-king.** Paris (1975) 11 + 6 + 9 + 333 p.

Schipper, Kristofer (ed) **Concordance du pao-p'ou-tseu nei-p'ien.** Paris (1965) xxxvii + 755 p.

Schipper, K.M. **Concordance du tao-tsang. Titres des ouvrages.** Paris (1975) iii + 28 + 6 + 219 p.

Schubert, Renate. Das erste kapitel des pao-p'u-tzu wai-p'ien. **ZDMG** 119.2 (1970) 278-301.

Shastri, H.P. Hindu ideas and taoist texts. **AP** 10 (1939) 294-297.

Stein, Rolf A. Textes taoïstes relatifs à la transmission des livres rélevés. **ACF** 68e ann (1968) 453-457.

Steininger, Hans. Der heilige herrscher — sein tao und sein praktische tun (kuan yin tze traktat) In **Sino-japonica** (1956) 170-177.

Strickmann, Michel. The longest taoist scripture. **HR** 17.3/4 (feb-may 1978) 331-354.

Strickman, Michel. The mao shan revelations; taoism and the aristocracy. **TP** 63.1 (1977) 1-64.

Strickmann, Michel. Taoist literature. In **EncyB 3** (1974) **Macropaedia** vol 17, 1051a-1055a.

Ting, Simon. **The mysticism of chuang tzu.** Univ philippines (1975) 252 p. Repr fr **Philippines social sciences & humanities review** 40 (mar-june 1975)

Tonn, W. (tsl) The book of eternal purity and rest. **CJ** 31 (1939) 112-117.

Wieger, Léon, **Taoïsme. T. 1: Bibliographie générale. I. Le canon (patrologie) II. Les index officiels et privés.** Ho-kien-fou (1911) 336 p.

Wieger, Léon. **Taoïsme. T. 2: Les pères du système taoïste, lao, tzeu lie-tzeu, tchoang tzeu. Texte revu sur les anciennes éditions taoïstes, traduit d'après les commentaires et la tradition taoïstes.** Ho-kien-fou (1913) 521 p, Repr paris (1950)

Wilhelm, Richard. Dschuang dsï, der mystiker, **Sinica** 3 (1928) 73-80.

Wilhelm, Richard (tsl) **Das geheimnis der goldenen blüte, ein chinesisches lebensbuch.** München (1929) enl ed zürich and leipzig (1939) Engl tsl Cary F. Baynes: **The**

secret of the golden flower; a chinese book of life.
London (1931) enl ed n.y. (1962) repr ny (1975)
Foreword and comm C.G. Jung (T'ai yi chin hua tsung
chih; enl ed also has part of second text: hui ming ching)

Yao, Tao-chung. The historical value of the ch'üan-chen
sources in the tao-tsang. **Sung studies newsletter** 13
(1977) 67-76.

Yoshioka, Yoshitoyo. Historical study of taoist scriptures.
JSR:LPH 8 (1957) 99-101.

17. TAOIST THEORY
(See also Sec 4: **Art & Symbolism**)

Bagchi, P.C.The chinese mysticism. **CalR** 49 (1933)
66-69.

Bauer, Wolfgang. Ko hung's rede über 'die kunst des
innehaltens.' In **Asien** (1971) 1-22. Re pao-p'u-tzu
wai-p'ien 49A.

Berthier, Brigitte. Le miroir brisé ou le taoïste et son
ombre. **l'Homme** 19.3/4 (juil-déc 1979) 205-222. Re
taoism and femininity.

Carmody, Denise Lardner. Taoist reflections on feminism.
Religion in life 46.1 (summer 1977) 234-244.

Chang, Chung-yüan. The concept of tao in chinese
culture. **RofR** 17 (1952-53) 115-132.

Chang, Chung-yüan. **Creativity and taoism.** N.Y. (1963)
241 p, illus. See esp chap 2-4.

Chang, Chung-yüan. Creativity as process in taoism. **EJ**
25 (1956) 391-415.

Chang, Chung-yüan. Purification and taoism. **Proc 11th
ICHR** vol 2, leiden (1968) 139-140 (abstract)

Chang, Chung-yüan. Tao and the sympathy of all things.
EJ 24 (1955) 407-432.

Chang, Chung-yüan. Tao as inner experience. **ZRGG**
10.1 (1958) 15-23.

Chang, Tsung-tung. The origin of early taoist thought. In
MS/CA (1977) 37-44.

Chen, Chung-hwan. What does lao-tzu mean by the term
"tao"? **TJ** n.s. 4.2 (1964) 150-161.

Cooper, J.C. The symbolism of the taoist garden. **SCR**
11.4 (autumn 1977) 224-234.

Davis, Tenney L. The dualistic cosmogony of huai-nan-tzu
and its relation to the background of chinese and
european alchemy. **Isis** 25 (1936) 327-340.

Desai, Santosh. Taoism: its essential principles and
reflection in poetry and painting. **CC** 7.4 (dec 1966)
54-64.

Doub, William. Mountains in early taoism. In M.C. Tobias
& H. Drasdo (ed) **The mountain spirit,** woodstock, ny
(1979) 129-135.

Eichhorn, Werner. Die dauistische spekulation im zweiten
kapitel des dschuang dsi. **Sinica** 17 (1942) 140-162.

Eichhorn, Werner. T'ai-p'ing und t'ai-p'ing religion.
MIOF 5 (1957) 113-140. Re expression 't'ai-p'ing,' with
tsl of 2 taoist texts.

Erkes, Eduard. Ein taoistische schöpfungsgeschichte für
kinder. **CDA** (1932) 14f.

Erkes, Eduard. Das weltbild des huai-nan-tze. Ein beitrag
zur ethnographie und kultgurgeschichte des alten china.
OZ 5.1/4 (1917) 27-32.

Fitch, Robert F. A study of a taoist hell. **ChRec** 45.10
(1914) 603-606.

Forke, Alfred. **Chinesische mystik.** Berlin (1922) 32 p.

Fukunaga, Mitsuji. 'No-mind' in chuang-tzu and in ch'an
buddhism. **Zinbun** 12 (1969) 9-45.

Gillard, Jean-Louis. **Métaphysique taoïste et
acuponcture chinoise.** Bordeaux (1968) 51 p.

Girardot, Norman J. Chaotic "order" (hun-tun) and
benevolent "disorder" (luan) in the chuang tzu. **PEW** 28.3
(july 1978) 300-321.

Girardot, Norman J. "Returning to the beginning" and the
arts of mr. hun-tun in the chuang tzu. **JCP** 5 (1978) 21-69.

Girardot, Norman J. Taoism. In **EBio** (1978)
1631a-1638a, bibliog.

Grube, Wilhelm. **Taoistischer schöpfungsmythen nach
dem sen-sien-kien, I.1.** Berlin (1896) 13 p.

Hall, David L. Process and anarchy: a taoist vision of
creativity. **PEW** 28.3 (july 1978) 271-286.

Homann, R. (tsl) **Pai wen p'ien, or the hundred
questions. A dialogue between two taoists on the
macrocosmic and microcosmic system of correspondences.** Leiden (1976) x + 109 p.

Hou, Ching-lang. The chinese belief in baleful stars. In **FT**
(1979) 193-228.

Hsiao, Paul S. Y. Schuld als spaltung vom tao. **Proc 11th
ICHR** vol 2, leiden (1968) 141-142 (abstract)

Hsin, Kwan-chue. Tao—the source of creativity. **ACQ** 7.4
(winter 1979) 27-36.

Hsu, Sung-peng. Han-shan te-ch'ing: a buddhist interpretation of taoism. **JCP** 2 (1974-75) 417-427.

Hsu, Sung-peng. Lao tzu's conception of ultimate reality:
a comparative study. **IPQ** 16.2 (june 1976) 197-217.

Hummel, Siegbert. **Zum ontologischen problem des dauismus (taoismus) untersuchungen an lao dsï, kapitel 1 und 42.** Leipzig (1948) 45 p.

Izutsu, Toshihiko. The absolute and the perfect man in taoism. **EJ** 36, zürich (1968) 379-441.

Izutsu, Toshihiko. **A comparative study of the key philosophical concepts of sufism and taoism; ibn 'arabi and lao-tzu, chuang-tzu.** Tokyo, 2 vols (1967) index of chin words and phrases. Publ Keio gijuku daigaku, keio instit of culture and linguistic studies.

Kaltenmark, Max. The ideology of the t'ai-p'ing ching. In **FT** (1979) 19-52.

Kroker, Eduard Josef M. **Die realitäts idee bei chuang chou. 3 parabeln, ein meditation.** St. augustine/siegburg (1969) 31 p.

Lee, Hsing-tsun. A new look at taoism and buddhism. **ACQ** 4.4 (winter 1976) 117-156.

Legeza, I.L. On the grammar of taoist popular art and symbolism: the problem of talismanic graphs. In Margaret Medley (ed) **Chinese painting and the decorative style. A colloquy held 23-25 june 1975,** univ london (n.d.) 148-162, 3 p pl.

Lin, Robert K. The concept of naturalness in taoism and ch'an (zen) **ACQ** 3.4 (winter 1975) 37-51.

Linssen, R. **l'Éveil suprême. Base théoretique et pratique du bouddhisme ch'an du zen du taoïsme et des enseignements de krishnamurti.** Bruxelles (1970) 160 p.

Möller, N. De la métaphysique de lao-tseu. **Revue catholique** 4 (1849-50).

Morgan, Evan. An ancient chinese philosopher's view on the perfect life (huai-nan tzu) **AR** 21 (1925) 449-464.

Morgan, Evan. The cosmic spirit. Its nature, operations and influence. **JNCBRAS** 62 (1931) 153-171.

Morgan, Evan. The taoist superman. **JNCBRAS** 54 (1923) 229-245. Repr in author's anthol, **A new mind and other essays,** shanghai (1930) 28-47.

Murakami, Yoshimi. Affirmation of desire in taoism. **ActaA** 27 (1974) 57-74.

Murakami, Yoshimi. 'Nature' in lao-chuang thought and 'no-mind' in ch'an buddhism.**KGUAS** 14 (1965) 15-31.

Ni, Hua-ching. **Tao—the subtle universal law and the integral way of life.** Los angeles (1979) 165 p.

Ni, Hua-ching. **The taoist inner view of the universe and the immortal realm.** Los angeles (1979) 218 p.

Ōfuchi, Ninji. On the ku ling-pao-ching. **ActaA** 27 (1974) 33-56.

Paravey, Charles-Hippolyte de. Explication du texte de lao-tseu sur la trinité. Le tao-te-king considéré non comme un livre historique mais comme un traité de philosophie. **APC** 4e sér, 8 (1841) 246-258.

Reid, G.P. Revolution as taught by taoism. **International journal of ethics** 35 (1924-25) 289-295.

Robinet, Isabelle. Randonnées extatiques des taoïstes dans les astres. **MS** 32 (1976) 159-273.

Rousselle, Erwin. Seelische führung im lebenden taoismus. **EJ** 1 (1933) 135-199.Same title in **CDA** (1934) 21-44.

Rousselle, Erwin. **Zur seelischen führung im taoismus.** Darmstadt (1962) Repr of 3 art, without chin characters.

Saso, Michael. Buddhist and taoist notions of transcendence: a study in philosophical contrast. In **BTS-I** (1977) 3-22.

Saso, Michael. **The teachings of taoist master chuang.** Yale univ (1978) 317 p, notes, bibliog, index and chin char, illus, fig.

Saso, Michael. What is the ho-t'u? **HR** 17.3/4 (feb-may 1978) 399-416.

Schafer, Edward H. Li po's star power. **SSCRB** 6 (fall 1978) 5-15.

Schafer, Edward H. **Pacing the void. T'ang approaches to the stars.** Univ california (1977) 352 p, illus, app, notes, bibliog, gloss, index.

Schafer, Edward H. A t'ang taoist mirror. **EC** 4 (1978-79) 56-59.

Schipper, K.M. Autour des visions dans le taoïsme. **Nouvelles de l'institut catholique de paris** 1 (1977) 161-170.

Shih, Joseph. God and man in early taoism. In **Religions; fundamental themes for a dialogistic understanding,** rome (1970).

Shih, J. The tao: its essence, its dynamism, and its fitness as a vehicle of christian revelation. **SM** 15 (1966) 117-133.

Smart, Ninian. Logos doctrine and eastern beliefs. **ET** 78 (mar 1967) 168-171. Discusses hinduism, budd, taoism.

Smith, Huston. Tao now: an ecological testament. In Ian G. Barbour (ed) **Earth might be fair. Reflections on ethics, religion, and ecology,** englewood cliffs, n.j. (1972) 62-81.

Solomon, Bernard S. Meditation on two concepts of reality: biblical and taoist. **Tri-quarterly** no 8 (winter 1967) 125-131.

Suppaner-Stanzel, Irene. Die ethischen ziele des taoismus und des existenzialismus. In festschrift: **Der mensch als persönlichkeit und als problem,** münchen (1963) 106-126.

Thiel, Joseph. Der begriff des tao im tao-te-ching. **Sinologica** 12 (1972) 30-108.

Ting, Simon. **The mysticism of chuang tzu.** Univ philippines (1975) 252 p. Repr fr **Philippines social sciences and humanities review** 40 (mar-june 1975)

Tomonobu, A. Imamichi. Das seinsproblem in der philosophie des ostasiatischen altertums. Konfutse und tschuang tschou. **Jahrbuch für psychologie und psychotherapie** 6 (1958) 54-64.

Tscharner, E.H. von. La pensée "métaphysique" et éthique de lao-tse. **Scientia** 72 (1942) 29-36.

Vichert, Clarence G. Fundamental principles in chinese boxing. **JWCBorderResS** 7 (1935) 43-46.

Wang, Tch'ang-tche. Le mysticisme de tchoang-tse. **BUA** 3e sér, 2.3 (1941) 382-402.

Wilhelm, Richard. Dschuang dsï, der mystiker. **Sinica** 3 (1928) 73-80.

Woo, Kang. An exposition of the tao theory of chuang tze. **Atti del XII, congresso internazionale di filosofia,** 239-245.

Yen, Ling-fen. Problem of being and non-being in the taoist philosophy. **ACQ** 6.4 (winter 1978) 17-24.

Yip, Wai-lim. The taoist aesthetic: wu-yen tu-hua, the unspeaking, self-generating, self-conditioning, self-transforming, self-complete nature. In William Tay, Ying-hsiung Chou & Heh-hsiang Yuan (ed) **China & the west: comparative literature studies,** chin univ of hk (1980) 17-32.

Zenker, E.V. Der taoismus der frühzeit. Die alt-und gemeinchinesische weltanschauung. **SAWW** 222 (1945) 1-56.

18. TAOIST LITURGY & RITUAL

Goullart, Peter. **The monastery of jade mountain.** London (1961) See chap 9, Exorcism. 83-90.

Hou, Ching – lang. The chinese belief in baleful stars. In **FT** (1979) 193-228.

Jordan, David K. The chiaw of shigaang(taiwan): an essay in folk interpretation. **AsFS** 35.2 (1967) 81-107.

Kaltenmark, Max. Miroirs magiques. In **MSPD** t 2 (1974) 151-166.

Keupers, John. A description of the fa-ch'ang ritual as practiced by the lü shan taoists of northern taiwan. In **BTS-I** (1977) 79-94.

Legeza, Laszlo. Chinese taoist arts. **AofA** 7.6 (nov-dec 1977) 32-37.

Legeza, Ireneus L. On the grammar of taoist graphic art and symbolism: the problem of talismanic graphics. In Margaret Medley (ed) **Chinese painting and the decorative style,** univ london (1976) 148-165.

McCreery, John L. The parting of the ways: a study of innovation in ritual. **ASBIE** 46 (autumn 1978) 121-137. Re individual differences in ritual as performed by taoists in taiwan.

Pang, Duane. The p'u-tu ritual. In **BTS-I** (1977) 95-122.

Pas, Julian F. Symbolism of the new light. Further researches into taoist liturgy: suggested by a comparison between the taoist fen-teng ritual and the christian consecration of the easter candle. **JHKBRAS** 20 (1980) 93-115.

Rebirth of kuanhsi's tai ho temple. **Echo** 2.10 (nov 1972) 23-31, illus.

Robinet, Isabelle. Randonnées extatiques des taoïstes dans les astres. **MS** 32 (1976) 159-273.

Saso, Michael. Lu shan, ling shan, and mao shan: taoist fraternities and rivalries in north taiwan. **ASBIE** 34 (autumn 1972) 119-147.

Saso, Michael. On the ritual meditation of orthodox heavenly master sect. **JCS** 8 (1971) 1-19.

Saso, Michael. On the ritual use of the yellow court canon. **JCS** 9 (1972) 1-20.

Saso, Michael. Orthodoxy and heterodoxy in taoist ritual. In **RRCS** (1974) 325-336.

Saso, Michael. Orthodoxy in the taoist tradition. In **AR-HR** (1974) 1-8.

Saso, Michael. **Taoism and the rite of cosmic renewal.** Washington state univ (1972) 120 p, notes, bibliog, illus.

Saso, Michael. **The teachings of taoist master chuang.** Yale univ (1978) 317 p, notes, bibliog, index and chin char, illus, fig.

Schipper, K.M. **Le fen-teng. Rituel taoïste.** Paris (1975) intro material 1-32, refs to sources in tao-tsang 33-38, notes 39-42, text in printed form, photos, text in callig facsimile, descr acc to author's notes taken at chiao in su-ts'o, taiwan, 26 mar 1967.

Schipper, K.M. The written memorial in taoist ceremonies. In **RRCS** (1974) 309-324.

Stein, Rolf A. Les cultes populaires dans le taoïsme organisé. **ACF** 70e ann (1970) 437-443.

Stein, Rolf A. Les fêtes de cuisine de taoïsme religieux. **ACF** 71e ann (1971) 431-440.

Stein, Rolf A. Spéculations mystiques et thèmes relatifs aux "cuisines" du taoïsme. **ACF** 72e ann (1972) 489-499.

Wolf, Arthur P. (ed) **Religion and ritual in chinese society.** Stanford univ (1974) xii + 377p. Art sep listed in our bibliog. Abbrev **RRCS.**

Wu, Linda. The biggest festival of them all. **Echo** 4.1 (jan 1974) 29-44, illus. Re various chiao in different parts of taiwan.

19. TAOISM & HISTORY

Allen, Herbert J. The connexion between taoism, confucianism and buddhism in early days. **Trans. 3rd ICHR,** oxford (1908) vol 1, 115-119.

Allen, Herbert J. Similarity between buddhism and early taoism. **ChRev** 15 (1886-87) 96-99.

Amiot, P. Lettre du p. amiot, Peking, 16 oct 1787. **MCLC** 15 (1791) 208-392.

Bazin, Antoine P.L. Recherches sur l'origine, l'histoire et au constitution des ordres religieux dans l'empire chinois. **JA** 5e sér, 8 (août 1856) 105-174.

Belpaire, Bruno. Le taoisme et li t'ai-po. **MCB** 1 (1931-32) 1-14.

Brecht, B. **Legende von der entstehung des buches taoteking auf dem weg des laotse in die emigration.** Zürich (1960)

Chan, Hok-lam. Chang chung and his prophecy: the transmission of the legend of an early ming taoist. **OE** 20.1 (june 1973) 65-102.

Chan, Hok-lam. Liu pin-chung (1216-1274), a buddhist-taoist statesman at the court of khubilai khan. **TP** 53.1/3 (1967) 98-146.

Chavannes, Édouard. Inscriptions et pièces de chancellerie chinoises de l'époque mongole. **TP** 5 (1904) 366-404. Documents dealing with controvery betw buddhists and taoists.

Ch'en, Kenneth. The buddhist contributions to neo-confucianim and taoism. In **TC** (1970) 155-160. Excerpt from author's **Buddhism in china: a historical survey** q.v. 471-476.

Ch'en Kenneth K.S. Buddhist-taoist mixtures in the pa-shih-i-hua t'u. **HJAS** 9 (1945-47) 1-12.

Ch'en, Kenneth. Neo-taoism and the prajñā school during the wei and chin dynasties. **CC** 1 (oct 1957) 33-46, bibliog.

Cibot, Fr. Notice du cong-fou des bonzes tao-sée. **MCLC** 4 (1779) 441-451, illus.

Conrady, A. Die anfänge des taoismus. **Sinica** 3 (1928) 124-133.

Couling, C.E. The oldest dress and the newest, or taoism in modern china. **HJ** 22 (1924) 245-259.

Couling, C. The patriarch lu, reputed founder of the chih tan chiao. **JNCBRAS** 58 (1927) 157-171.

Creel, H.G. On two aspects of early taoism. In **SJV** (1954) 43-53. Repr in author's collection: **What is taoism and other studies in chinese cultural history,** univ chicago (1970) 37-47.

Doub, Wiliam. Mountains in early taoism. In M.C. Tobias & H. Drasdo (ed) **The mountain spirit,** woodstock, ny (1979) 129-135.

Durrant, Stephen W. The theme of family conflict in early taoist biography. Albuquerque, **Selected papers in asian studies,** western conference, assoc for asian studies, vol 2 (1977) 2-8.

Duyvendak, J.J.L. Le taoisme sous les t'ang **Actes 21e ICO,** paris (1949) 272.

Edkins, Joseph. Foreign origin of taoism. **ChRev** 19.6 (1890-91) 397-399.

Edkins, Joseph. Phases in the development of taoism. **JNCBRAS** 5 (1855) 83-99.

Edkins, J. Religious persecution in china. **ChRec** 15.6 (nov-dec 1884) 433-444. Brief historical survey.

Edkins, Joseph. Steps in the growth of early taoism. **ChRec** 15 (1884) 176-190.

Edkins, Joseph. Taoism in ts'in and han dynasties. **ChRec** 15 (1884) 335-350.

Eichhorn, W. Bemerkungen zum aufstand des chang chio und zum staate des chang lu. **MIOF** 3 (1955) 291-327.

Eichhorn, Werner. Bemerkung zur einführung des zölibats für taoisten. **RSO** 30 (1955) 297-301.

Eichhorn, W. (tsl) **Ch'ing-yuan t'iao fa shih lei. Beitrag zur rechtlichen stellung des buddhismus und taoismus in sung-staat. Übersetzung der sektion taoismus und buddhismus aus dem ch'ing-yuan t'iao-fa shih-lei (ch. 50 und 51) Mit original text in faksimile.** Leiden (1968) 178 p.

Eichhorn, W. Description of the rebellion of sun ên and earlier taoist rebellions. **MIOF** 2 (1954) 325-352.

Eichhorn, Werner. Nachträgliche bemerkungen zum aufstande des sun ên. **MIOF** 2 (1954) 463-476.

Erkes, E. Die anfänge des taoismus. **Sinica** 3 (1928) 124-133.

Erkes, E. Ueber den heutigen taoismus und seine literatur. **Litterae orientales** 53 (1933) 1-5.

Faber, Ernst. The historical characteristics of taoism. **ChRev** 13 (1884-85) 231-247. A propos F.H. Balfour's **Taoist texts** q.v.

Franke, Herbert. Bemerkungen zum volkstümlichen taoismus der ming-zeit. **OE** 24.1/2 (dez 1977) 205-215.

Franke, Otto. Ein dokument zur geistesgeschichte der han-zeit. **SAWW** (1924) 56-78.

Franke, O. Taoismus und buddhismus zur zeit der trennung von nord und süd. **Sinica** 9 (1934) 89-113.

Fukui, Kōjun. Fundamental problems regarding the schools of religious taoism. In **RSJ** (1959) 451-459.

Granet, Marcel. Remarques sur le taoïsme ancien. **AM** 2 (1925) 146-151. Repr **ESC** (1953) 243-249.

Groot, J.J.M. de. On the origin of the taoist church. **Trans 3rd ICHR**, vol 1, oxford (1908) 138-149.

Hackmann, H. Ein chinesisches urteil über den taoismus von lung hu shan und shang ch'ing. **AO** 7 (1929) 293-304.

Hart, V.C. The heavenly teachers. **ChRec** 10 (1879) 445-453. Author's report of his visit to lung-hu shan and interview with 61st chang t'ien-shih.

Imbault-huart, Camille. La légende du premier pape des taoistes èt l'histoire de la famille pontificale de tchang. **JA** 8e sér, 4 (nov-dec 1884) 389-461.

Jan, Yün-hua. The silk manuscripts on taoism. **TP** 63.1 (1977) 65-84.

Kaltenmark, Max. Recherches sur l'histoire du taoisme religieux. École pratique des hautes études, section des sciences religieux, **Annuaire** (1959-60) 53f.

Kaltenmark, Max. Religion et politique dans la chine des ts'in et des han. **Diogène** 34 (1961) 18-46.

Kimura, Eiichi. The new confucianism and taoism in china and japan from the fourth to the thirteenth centuries a.d. **CHM** 5 (1959-60) 801-829.

Klaproth, J.H. et M.G. Pauthier: Mémoire sur l'origine et la propagation de la doctrine du tao, fondée par lao-tseu . . . **JA** sér 2, t 7 (1831) 465-493. Rev art on Pauthier's bk publ Paris 1831. See further Pauthier's Lettre à m. le rédacteur, **ibid** t 8 (1831) with reply to him fr Commission du **JA** and a letter of Klaproth to Commission, **ibid** 129-131; further, letter to ed by Klaproth counter-rebutting Pauthier, **ibid** 220-238, and a second letter to ed, 414-439.

Kopsch, H. The master of heaven. In **DV** vol 2, pt iii, 226-229.

Kroll, Paul W. Szu-ma ch'eng-chen in t'ang verse. **SSCRB** 6 (fall 1978) 16-30.

Kubo, Noritada. Prolegomena on the study of the controversies between buddhists and taoists in the yüan period. **TBMRD** 26 (1968) 39-61.

Lai, Whalen. Toward a periodization of the taoist religion. **HR** 16.1 (aug 1976) 75-85. Rev art on Yoshioka Yoshitoyo's history of taoism (in jap)

Laing, Ellen Johnston. Neo-taoism and the "seven sages of the bamboo grove" in chinese painting. **AA** 36.1/2 (1974) 5-54, illus.

Levy, Howard S. The bifurcation of the yellow turbans in later han. **Oriens** 13-14 (1960-61) 251-255.

Levy, Howard S. Yellow turban religion and rebellion at the end of han. **JAOS** 76 (1956) 214-227.

Link, Arthur E. Cheng-wu lun: the rectification of unjustified criticism. **OE** 8.2 (dec 1961) 136-165.

Liu, Ts'un-yan. Lu hsi-hsing: a confucian scholar, taoist priest and buddhist devotee of the sixteenth century. **AS** 18/19 (1965) 115-142; repr **LTY:SP** (1976)

Liu, Ts'un-yan. The penetration of taoism into the ming neo-confucianist elite. **TP** 57.1/4 (1971) 31-102; repr **LTY:SP** (1976).

Liu, Ts'un-yan. **Selected papers from the hall of harmonious wind.** Leiden (1976) ix + 452 p. All but one are repr, mostly on history of taoism. Repr art sep listed in our bibliog. Abbrev **LTY:SP.**

Liu, Ts'un-yan. The taoists' knowledge of tuberculosis in the twelfth century. **TP** 57.5 (1971) 285-301; repr **LTY:SP.**

I(lse) M(artin) Der taoistische einfluss im zeitgeist der wei- und chin- epoche, von sun te-hsüan. **Sinologische arbeiten** 3 (1945) 177-183. In sec, Inhalt sangaten des chinesischen sinologischen arbeiten in chung-te hsüeh-chih 6.1 und 2. Publ by Deutschland institut, peking.

Mather, Richard B. K'ou ch'ien-chih and the taoist theocracy at the northern wei court 425-451. In **FT** (1979) 103-122.

Mead, G.R.S. An historical note on taoism. In W.L. Hare (ed) **Religions of the empire,** london (1925) 243-244.

Michaud,Paul. The yellow turbans. **MS** 17 (1958) 47-127, bibliog.

Milne, W.C. The rebellion of the yellow caps, compiled from the history of the three states. **ChRep** 10 (1841) 98-103.

Miyakawa, Hisayuki. Legate kao p'ien and a taoist magician lü yung-chih in the time of huang ch'ao's rebellion. **ActaA** 27 (1974) 75-99.

Miyakawa, Hisayuki. Local cults around mount lu at the time of sun en's rebellion. In **FT** (1979) 83-102.

Morrison, Robert. Account of the sect tao-szu, from "The rise and progress of the three sects." In author's **Horae sinicae,** london (1812) **Idem in Uhr-chih-tsze-teen-se-yin-pe-keaou, being a parallel dictionary between the two intended dictionaries by the rev. robert morrison and antonio montucci, 11.d, together with morrison's horae sinicae, a new edition,** london (1817) 167-170.

Pachow, W. Laotzû and gautama buddha; an enquiry into the authenticity of laotzû's mission to india. In **PFV** Colombo (1966) 293-303. Repr **ChBudd** (1980)

Pauthier, Georges. **Mémoire sur l'origine et la propagation de la doctrine du tao, fondée par lao-tseu; traduit du chinois et accompagné d'un commentaire tiré des livres sanscrits et du tao-te-king de lao-tseu, etablissant la conformité de certaines opinions philosophiques de la chine et de l'inde; orné d'un dessein chinois; suivi de deux oupanishads des vedas, avec la texte sanscrit et persan.** Paris (1831) 79 p. See critical rev by Anon (Stanislas Julien?) in **NouvJA** 7 (1831) 465-493. See further Pauthier's rebuttal in **ibid** 8 (1831) 129-158.

Pauthier, M. Relation du voyage de k'hiéou, surnomme tchang-tch'un (long printemps), à l'ouest de la chine, au commencement du XIIIe siècle de notre ère. **JA** 6e sér, 9/10 (1867) 39-86.

Pelliot, Paul. Les mo-ni et le houa-hou-king. **BEFEO** 3 (1903) 318-327.

Pelliot, Paul. Les premières éditions du canon bouddhique et du canon taoïque. In **Les débuts de l'imprimerie en chine,** paris (1953) **Oeuvres posthumes de paul pelliot,** 4, 88-93.

Rosny, Léon de. Les origines du taoisme. **RHR** 22 (1890) 161f.

Saso, Michael. Red-head and black-head: the classification of the taoists of taiwan according to the documents of the 61st heavenly master. **ASBIE** 30 (aug 1970)

Saso, Michael. **The teachings of taoist master chuang.** Yale univ (1978) 317 p, notes, bibliog, index and chin char, illus, fig.

Schafer, Edward H. The capeline cantos; verses on the divine loves of taoist priestesses. **AS** 32.1 (1978) 5-65.

Schafer, Edward H. **Mao shan in t'ang times.** Boulder, colo (1980) 72 p, notes, diagram. SSCR monograph No. 1.

Schafer, Edward H. The restoration of the shrine of wei hua-ts'un at lin-ch'uan in the eighth century. **JOS** 15.2 (1977) 124-137. Re female immortal who revealed scriptures to yang hsi on mao shan.

Schipper, Kristofer. **l'Empereur wou des han dans le légende taoïste; han wou-ti nei tchouan.** Paris (1965) 132 + ix p, index. Incl chin text.

Seidel, Anna K. **La divinisation de lao tseu dans le taoisme des han.** Paris (1969) 171 p, facs chin texts, bibliog, index.

Seidel, Anna K. The image of the perfect ruler in early taoist messianism: lao-tzu and li hung. **HR** 9.2/3 (nov-feb 1969-70) 216-247.

Seidel, Anna Der kaiser und sein ratgeber; lao tzu und der taoismus der han-zeit. **Saeculum** 29 (1978) 18-50.

Seidel, Anna. Das neue testament des tao; lao tzu und die entstehung der taoistischen religion am ende der han-zeit. **Saeculum** 29 (1978) 147-172.

Sivin, Nathan. On the word "taoist" as a source of perplexity. With special reference to the relations of science and religion in traditional china. **HR** 17.3/4 (feb-may 1978) 303-330.

Sivin, Nathan. Shen kua. In **Dictionary of scientific research,** ny (1975) vol 12, 259-292.

Sivin, Nathan & Chaoying Fang. Wang hsi-shan. In **Dictionary of ming biography,** columbia univ (1976) vol 2, 1379-1382.

Stein, R.A. Un exemple de relations entre taoïsme et religion populaire. In **Fukui hakase festschrift: Tōyō bunka ronshū,** ?Tokyo (1969) 79-90.

Stein, Rolf A. Quelques aspects des paroisses taoïstes. **ACF** 69e ann (1969) 466-471.

Stein, Rolf A. Religious taoism and popular religion from the second to the seventh centuries. In **FT** (1979) 53-82.

Stein, R.A. Remarques sur les mouvements du taoïsme politico-religieux au IIe siècle ap. j.-c. **TP** 50 (1963) 1-78.

Strickmann, Michel. The mao shan revelations. Taoism and the aristocracy. **TP** 63.1 (1977) 1-64.

Strickmann, Michel. Taoism, history of. In **EncyB 3** (1974) **Macropaedia** vol 17, 1044b-1050b.

Strickmann, Michel. A taoist confirmation of liang wu ti's suppression of taoism. **JAOS** 98.4 (oct-dec 1978) 467-474.

Ten Broek, Janet Rinaker and Yiu Tung. A taoist inscription of the yuan dynasty: the tao-chia pei. **TP** 40 (1950-51) 60-122. Tablet in the tung-yüeh miao, peking.

Thiel, Joseph. Der streit der buddhisten und taoisten zur mongolzeit. **MS** 20 (1961) 1-81.

Waley, Arthur (tsl) **The travels of an alchemist: the journey of the taoist, ch'ang-ch'un ... from china to the hindukush at the summons of chingiz khan, recorded by his disciple, li chih-ch'ang.** London (1931) xi + 166 p, map. Repr westport, conn (1976), taipei (1978)

Ware, James R. The wei shu and the sui shu on taoism. **JAOS** 53 (1933) 215-250; 54 (1934) 290-294.

Welch, Holmes. The chang t'ien shih and taoism in china. **JOS** 4 (1957-58) 188-212.

Welch, Holmes. Syncretism in the early taoist movement. Harvard univ **Papers on china,** 10 (1956) 1-54.

Wieger, Léon. **The evolution of taoist doctrines.** Engl tsl Lydia G. Robinson, from author's **Taoïsme, t.1** q.v. under Taoist Texts. Chicago (1913)

Wieger, L. **Taoïsme. Tome 1 — Bibliographie générale. I. Le canon (patrologie) 2. Les index officiels et privés.** Ho-kien-fou (1911) 336 p.

Wilhelm, Richard. On the sources of chinese taoism. **JNCBRAS** 45 (1914) 1-12.

Wong, Shiu-hon. The cult of chang san-feng. **JOS** 17.1/2 (1979) 10-53.

Yao, Tao-chung. Ch'üan-chen taoism and yüan drama. **JCLTA** (feb 1980) 44-56.

Yao, Tao-chung. The historical value of the ch'üan-chen sources in the tao-tsang. **Sung studies newsletter** 13 (1977) 67-76.

Zenker, E.V. Der taoismus des frühzeit. Die altund gemeinchinesische weltanschauung. **SAWW** 222.2 (1943) 1-56.

Zürcher, Erik. Buddhist influence on early taoism. **TP** 66.1/3 (1980) 84-147.

20. TAOIST IMMORTALS

Bas, Rene Q. Photos by Arthur Kan. The eight immortals of the taoist cosmos. **Orientations** 10.7 (july 1979) 50-57, illus col-photos.

Bauer, Wolfgang. Der herr vom gelben stein (chuang shih kung); wandlungen einer chinesischer legendenfigur. **OE** 3 (1956) 137-152.

Broman, Sven. Eight immortals crossing the sea. **BMFEA** 50 (1978) 25-48. Re chin shadow play in coll of ethnol museum of sweden, stockholm. Tsl of libretto with comm, index of chin char, illus, facs of text.

Chao, Ching-shen. Tsl Earl Wieman. An analysis of the eight immortals in literature. **Echo** 5.2/3 (feb-mar 1975) 72-86, 93, illus col pl & b-&-w woodcuts.

Conrady, G. Les huit immortels taoïstes dans l'art chinois. Pa hien. **BSAB** 65 (1954) 167-170.

Couling, C.E. The patriarch lu, reputed founder of the chin tan chiao. **JNCBRAS** 58 (1927) 157-171.

DeWoskin, Kenneth (tsl) In search of the supernatural— selections from the sou-shen chi. **Renditions** 7 (spring 1977) 103-114.

Diez, E. Dauistische unsterbliche. **Sinica** 16 (1941) 48-53.

Edkins, Joseph. The eight genii. **EA** 2.3 (1903) 284-287.

Eichhorn, Werner. Eine erzählung aus dem wenchien hou-lu. **OE** 2 (1955) 167-174.

Eight immortals. **Echo** 5.2/3 (feb-mar 1975) Entire double issue devoted to this subj. Art sep listed in our bibliog.

The Eight immortals. **Echo** 5.2/3 (feb-mar 1975) 4-12. Mostly col illus of various depictions.

Giles, Lionel (tsl) **A gallery of chinese immortals.** London (1948) 127 p.

Grady, Diane, "with special thanks to Kuo Li-cheng" Legends of the eight immortals. **Echo** 5.2/3 (feb-mar 1975) 24-71, profusely illus col pl.

Grube, W. (tsl) Taoistischer schöpfungsmythus nach dem sēn-siēn-kién. In **Festschrift für adolf bastien auf seimem 70. geburstag 26 jani 1896,** berlin (1896) p 445-458.

Gützlaff, C. A general account of the gods and genii; in 22 vol. From a correspondent. **ChRep** 7 (1839) 505 et seq. (re shen hsien t'ung chien)

Hall, Manly P. **The adepts in the eastern esoteric tradition.** Los angeles (1957) 113 p, illus. Taoist, confucian, budd.

Holzman, Donald. A chinese conception of the hero. **Diogenes** 36 (1961) 33-51. Re juan ch'i (210-263 a.d.) and his 'biography of master great man' — a taoist immortal.

Jacquet, E. Légende de yĕ sou, selon le chin siĕn thoung kian [shen hsien t'ung chien] **NouvJA** 7 (1831) 223-228.

Kaltenmark, Max (tsl) **Le lie-sien tchouan: biographies légendaires.** Peking (1953) 204 p.

Kaltenmark, Max. Un procédé de vol magique dans le taoïsme. **SF** (1972) 5-13.

Kroll, Paul W. Szu-ma ch'eng-chen in t'ang verse. **SSCRB** 6 (fall 1978) 16-30.

Lai, T'ien-ch'ang. **The eight immortals.** HK (1972) 90 p, illus, gloss.

Laloy, Louis. **Légendes des immortels (d'après les auteurs chinois)** Paris (1922) 108 p.

Ling, Peter C. The eight immortals of the taoist religion. **JNCBRAS** 49 (1918) 53-75.

Morgan, Evan. The taoist superman. **JNCBRAS** 54 (1923) 229-245.

Parry, D. The eight immortals. **EW** 7.1 (1953) 26-27.

Pavie, Théodore. Yu-ki le magicien, légende chinoise. **RDM** (15 mars 1851) 1129-1144.

Pfizmaier, August. Die lebensverlängerungen der männer des weges (tao shih) **SAWW** 68 (1871) 641f, 652f, 665f, 679f, 695f.

Porkert, Manfred. **Biographie d'un taoïste légendaire: tcheou tseu-yang.** Paris (1979) 169 p.

Robinet, Isabelle. Metamorphosis and deliverance from the corpse in taoism. **HR** 19.1 (aug 1979) 37-70.

Robinet, Isabelle. Randonnées extatiques des taoïstes dans les astres. **MS** 32 (1976) 159-273.

Schafer, Edward H. The restoration of the shrine of wei hua-ts'un at lin-ch'uan in the eighth century. **JOS** 15.2 (1977) 124-137. Re female immortal who revealed scriptures to yang hsi on mao shan.

Schafer, Edward H. Three divine women of south china. **ChLit** 1 (1979) 31-42.

Schipper, Kristofer. Religions de la chine. **AnnEPHE** 88 (1979-80) 129-136. Re taoist hagiography.

Seidel, Anna K. **La divinisation de lao tseu dans le taoïsme des han.** Paris (1969) 171 p, facs chin texts, bibliog, index.

Seidel, Anna. A taoist immortal of the ming dynasty: chang san-feng. In **SSMT** (1970) 483-531.

Sowerby, A. de C. S. Legendary figures in chinese art. Pa hsien, the eight immortals. **CJ** 14.2 (feb 1931) 53-55, illus.

Tien, Tsung. The eight immortals. **Orient** 3.1 (1952) 50-52.

Wimsatt, Genevieve. The eight immortals greet you. Chap 7 in author's **GC** (1927) 101-116.

Wong, Shiu-hon. The cult of chang san-feng. **JOS** 17.1/2 (1979) 10-53.

Yang, Richard F.S. A study of the origin of the legend of the eight immortals. **OE** 5.1 (1958) 1-22.

Yao Tao-chung. Ch'üan-chen taoism and yüan drama. **JCLTA** 10.1 (feb 1980) 44-56.

Yarger, Rosie. The eight immortals. **Samadhi** (jan-feb 1974) 6-10.

Yen, Yuan-shu (tsl) Yellow millet dream. A yuan dynasty play by ma chih-yuan. **Echo** 5.2/3 (feb-mar 1975) 13-23, 94. Re the 8 immortals.

Yetts, W. Perceval. The chinese isles of the blessed. **Folk-lore** 30 (mar 1919) 35-62.

Yetts, W. Perceval. The eight immortals. **JRAS** (oct 1916) 773-807, illus.

Yetts, W.P. Eight immortals. **Arts & decoration** 48 (june 1938) 22-24, illus.

Yetts, W. Perceval. More notes on the eight immortals. **JRAS** (1922) 397-426.

Yetts, W.P. Pictures of a chinese immortal. **BM** 39 (1921) 113-121.

Yetts, W. Perceval. Taoist tales. **NCR** 1 (mar 1919) 11-18, pl; (may 1919) 169-175. See further, same title, — A rejoinder, **ibid** 3 (feb 1921) 65-68.

Young, C. Walter. The isles of the blessed. An historical myth. **CJ** 8.4 (apr 1928) 171-175. Re search for immortality of ch'in shih-huang.

21. TAOIST PANTHEON & CULTS

Chavannes, Édouard. Le jet des dragons. **Mémoires concernant l'asie orientale** 3 (1919) 53-220, illus pl and reproductions of rubbings and texts.

Edkins, Joseph. Place of hwang-ti in early taoism. **ChRev** 15.4 (1886-87) 233-239.

Edkins, Joseph. A sketch of the tauist mythology in its modern form. **JNCBRAS** 1.3 (dec 1859) 45-49.

Edkins, Joseph. Titles of tauist gods. **ChRev** 24.4 (1895-96) 199.

Fêng, Han-chi. The origin of yü huang. **HJAS** 1 (1936) 242-250.

Fitch, R.F. A study of a taoist hell. **ChRec** 45.10 (oct 1914) 603-606, photos.

Gauchet, L. Recherches sur la triade taoïque. **BUA** 3e sér, 10 (1949) 326-366.

Kubo, Noritada. Taoist belief in okinawa with special emphasis on the kitchen god belief. **ActaA** 27 (1974) 100-115.

Maspero, Henri. Les dieux taoistes: comment on communique avec eux. **CRAIBL** (1937) 362-374.

Maspero, Henri. Le panthéon taoiste avant les t'ang. **JA** (1936) 483.

Mortier, F. De sens primitif de l'antiquité et la célèbre figure divinatoire des taoistes chinois et japonais (sien t'ien) **BSAB** 59 (1948) 150-160.

Mueller, Herbert. Über das taoistische pantheon des chinesen, seine grundlagen und seine historische entwicklung. **ZE** 3-4 (1911) 393-428.

Natsume Ikken. Various phases of revelation in taoism. **TJR** 1 (mar 1955) 53-65, fig.

Soymié, Michel. Biography de chan tao-k'ai. **MIHEC** 1 (1957) 415-422. Patron saint of lo-fou shan.

22. TAOIST SECTS, PRIESTS, MONACHISM

Balfour, Frederic H. (1) Taoist hermits. In author's **Leaves from my chinese scrapbook,** london (1887) 135-139. (2) A taoist patriarch. In **ibid,** 140-144.

Bertolucci, Guiliano. Reminiscences of the mao-shan. **E&W** 24.3/4 (sept-dec 1974) 403-415, illus. Re author's brief visit during summer 1947.

Bourne, F.S. **The lo-fu mountains; an excursion.** Shanghai (1895)

Drake, F.S. The taoists of lao-shan. **ChRec** 65 (1934) 238-245, 308-318.

Eichhorn, Werner. Bemerkung zur einführung des zölibats für taoisten. **RSO** 30 (1955) 297-301.

Erkes, Eduard. Die anfänge des dauistischen mönchtums. **Sinica** 11 (1936) 36-46.

Goullart, Peter. **The monastery of jade mountain.** London (1961) 189 p, photo illus. French tsl (1971)

Hackmann, H. **Die dreihundert mönchsgebote des chinesischen taoismus.** Amsterdam (1931) 60 p + 24 p chin text.

Hackmann, Heinrich. Die mönchsregeln des klöstertaoismus. **OZ** 8 (1919-20) 142-170.

Hegel, Robert. A day in the life of a taoist priest. **Echo** 1.10 (nov 1971) 34-38, 53-55, illus.

Irving, E.A. A visit to the buddhist and tao-ist monasteries on the lo fau shan. **BIM** 157 (mar 1895) 453-467.

F. R. Popular theology in china. **ChRec** 54.5 (may 1923) 277-278. Re visit to a taoist temple in chefoo.

Saso, Michael. Lu shan, ling shan, and mao shan: taoist fraternities and rivalries in north taiwan. **ASBIE** 34 (autumn 1972) 119-147.

Saso, Michael. On the ritual meditation of orthodox heavenly master sect. **JCS** 8 (1971) 1-19.

Saso, Michael. Orthodoxy in the taoist tradition. In **AR-HR** (1974) 1-8.

Saso, Michael. Red-head and black-head: the classification of the taoists of taiwan according to the documents of the 61st generation heavenly master. **ASBIE** 30 (1972) 69-82.

Saso, Michael. **The teachings of taoist master chuang.** Yale univ (1978) 317 p, notes, bibliog, index and chin char, illus, fig.

Schafer, Edward H. The capeline cantos; verses on the divine loves of taoist priestesses. **AS** 32.1 (1978) 5-65.

Schafer, Edward H. **Mao shan in t'ang times.** Boulder, colo (1980) 72 p, notes, diagram. SSCR monograph no 1.

Schmitt, Erich. Taoistische klöster im licht des universismus. **MSOS** 19 (1916) 76-104.

Schüler, Wilhelm. Aus einem taoistischen kloster. **ZMK** 24 (1909) 265-269.

Yoshioka, Yoshitoyo. Taoist monastic life. In **FT** (1979) 229-252.

23. TAOIST YOGA & ALCHEMY*

Amiot, J.J.M. Extrait d'une lettre . . . **MCLC** 15 (1791) v.

Amiot, J.J.M. Extrait d'une lettre sur la secte des tao-sée. **MCLC** 15 (1791) 208-259.

Andersen, Poul (tsl) **The method of holding the three ones. A taoist manual of meditation of the fourth century a.d.** London & malmö (1979) 66 p + chin text of chin-ch'üeh ti-chün san-yüan-chen-yi ching.

Anderson, Mary. The quest for immortality and long life. **Echo** 4.5 (may 1974) 41-46, 56, illus.

Balfour, Frederic (tsl) The "t'ai-hsi" king or the respiration of the embryo. **ChRev** 9 (1880) 224-226. Taoist text, Hsiu-chen pi-lu.

Barnes, W.H. The apparatus, preparations and methods of the ancient chinese alchemists. **JCE** 11 (1934) 655f.

Barnes, W.H. Chinese influence on western alchemy. **Nature** 135 (1935) 824f.

Barnes, W.H. Diagrams of chinese alchemical apparatus. **JCE** 13 (1936) 453.

Barnes, W.H. Possible references to chinese alchemy in the -4th or -3rd century. **CJ** 23 (1935) 75-79.

Barnes, W.H. and H.B. Yuan. T'ao the recluse (452-536 a.d.); chinese alchemist. **Ambix** 2 (1946) 138-147.

Belpaire, B. Note sur un traité taoiste. **Muséon** 59 (1946) 655.

Bergeron, Marie-Ina. La mystique taoïste. In **EMM** (1975) 195-242.

* The exhaustive bibliography in this field is Joseph Needham, **Science and Civilization in China,** vol 5, pt 2, cambridge univ (1974) bibliog C, 387-469.

Berling, Judith A. Paths of convergence: interactions of inner alchemy taoism and neo-confucianism. **JCP** 6.2 (june 1979) 123-147.

Beurdeley, M. (ed) **The clouds and the rain; the art of love in china.** With contributions by K. Schipper on taoism and sexuality and other materials. London (1969)

Biroen, H. Taoismus: praktische system der wandlung und sublimation. **Yoga** 7.6 (1960) 27-31.

Blofeld, John. **Beyond the gods. Buddhist and taoist mysticism.** London & ny (1974) 164 p, gloss.

Blofeld, John **Gateway to wisdom. Taoist and buddhist contemplative and healing yogas adapted for western students of the way.** Boulder, colo (1980) See pt 1, Taoist theory and practice, 11-87.

Boehmer, Thomas. Taoist alchemy: a sympathetic approach through symbols. In **BTS-I** (1977) 55-78.

Bonmarchand, G. (tsl) Les notes de li yi-chan (yi-chan tsa tsouan) traduit du chinois; étude de littérature comparée. **BMFJ** n.s. 4.3 (1955) 1-84.

Chang, Chung-yüan. An introduction to taoist yoga. **RofR** 21 (1956) 131-148. Repr in **CWayRel** (1973) 63-76.

Chatley, Herbert. Alchemy in china. **National review** 14 (25 oct 1913) 456-457.

Chattopadhyaya, D. Needham on tantrism and taoism. **New age** 6.1 (1957) 43; 7.1 (1958) 32.

Ch'en, Kuo-fu and Tenney L. Davis (tsl) Inner chapters of pao-p'u-tzu. **PAAAS** 74.10 (dec 1941) 297f. Tsl chap 8 and 11; precis of remainder.

Chikashige, Masumi. **Alchemy and other chemical achievements of the ancient orient.** Engl tsl Nobuji Sasaki. Tokyo (1936) vii + 102 p, illus, pl. Repr ny (1974) under title, **Oriental alchemy.**

Chou, Hsiang-kung. Taoismus and yoga. **Vivos voco: die weisse fahne ruft die legenden** 35 (1962) 156-158.

Chou, I-liang. Tantrism in china. **HJAS** 8 (1945) 241f.

Cibot, P.M. Notice sur le cong-fu, exercice superstitieux des taoche pour guérir le corps de ses infirmités et obtenir pour l'âme une certain immortalité. **MCLC** 4 (1779) 441-448.

Clasper, Paul. Jungian psychology, taoism and christian faith. **CF** 21.1 (1978) 36-52. Re jung's ideas as presented in R. Wilhelm's tsl, **The secret of the golden flower** q.v.

Coudert, Allison. **Alchemy: the philosopher's stone.** Boulder, colo (1980) See chap 7, The chinese elixir addicts, 161-191.

Cowdry, E.V. Taoist ideas of anatomy. **AMH** 3 (1921) 301-309.

Coyaji, J.C. Some shahnamah legends and their chinese parallels. **JRASB** n.s. 24 (1928) 177f.

Coyaji, J.C. The shahnamah and the fêng shên yen i. **JRASB** n.s. 26 (1930) 491f.

Daumas, M. La naissance et le développement de la chimie en chine. **S.E.T.; Structure et évolution des techniques** 6 (1949) 11f.

Davis, Tenney L. The chinese beginnings of alchemy. **Endeavour** 2 (1943) 154 f.

Davis, Tenney L. The dualistic cosmogony of huainan-tzu and its relation to the background of chinese and european alchemy. **Isis** 25 (1936) 327-40.

Davis, Tenney L. Huang ti, legendary founder of alchemy. **JCE** 11 (1934) 635f.

Davis Tenney L. The identity of chinese and european alchemical theory. **Journal of unified science** 9 (1929) 7f.

Davis, Tenney L. Ko hung (pao p'u tzu), chinese alchemist of the 4th century a.d. **JCE** 11 (1934) 517 f.

Davis, Tenney L. Liu an, prince of huai-nan. **JCE** 12 (1935) 1f.

Davis, Tenney L. The problem of the origins of alchemy. **Scientific monthly** 43 (1936) 551f.

Davis, Tenney L. Wei po-yang, father of alchemy. **JCE** 12 (1935) 51f.

Davis, Tenney L. and Chao Yün-ts'ung (tsl) An alchemical poem by kao hsiang-hsien. **Isis** 30 (1939) 236f.

Davis, Tenney L. and Chao Yun-ts'ung. Chang po-tuan, chinese alchemist of the 11th century a.d. **JCE** 16 (1939) 53f.

Davis, Tenney L. and Chao Yün-ts'ung (tsl) Chang po-tuan of t'ien-t'ai; his wu chen p'ien (essay on the understanding of the truth); a contribution to the study of chinese alchemy. **PAAAS** 73 (1940) 97f.

Davis, Tenney L. and Chao Yün-ts'ung. A fifteenth-century chinese encyclopaedia of alchemy. **PAAAS** 73 (1940) 391f.

Davis, Tenney L. & Chao Yün-ts'ung (tsl) The four-hundred word chin tan of chang po-tuan. **PAAAS** 73 (1940) 371f.

Davis, Tenney L. and Chao Yün-ts'ung. The secret papers in the jade box of ch'ing-hua. **PAAAS** 73 (1940) 385f.

Davis, Tenney L. and Chao Yün-ts'ung. Shih hsing-lin, disciple of chang po-tuan and hsieh tao-kuang, disciple of shih hsing-lin. **PAAAS** 73 (1940) 381f.

Davis, Tenney L. and Chao Yün-ts'ung (tsl) Three alchemical poems by chang po-tuan. **PAAAS** 73 (1940) 377f.

Davis, Tenney L. and Ch'en Kuo-fu. Shang yang tzu, taoist writer and commentator on alchemy. **HJAS** 7 (1942) 126f.

Davis, Tenney L. and Nakaseko Rokuro. The jofuku [hsü shen] shrine at shingu; a monument of earliest alchemy. **Nucleus** 15.3 (1937) 60-67.

Davis, Tenney L. and Nakaseko Rokuro. The tomb of jofuku [hsü fu] or joshi [hsü shih]; the earliest alchemist of historical record. **Ambix** 1 (1937) 109, illus; **JCE** (1947) 415.

Davis, Tenney L. and Wu Lu-ch'iang. The advice of wei po-yang to the worker in alchemy. **Nucleus** 8 (1931) 115-117; repr in **Double bond** 8 (1935) 13.

Davis, Tenney L. and Wu Lu-ch'iang. Chinese alchemy. **Scientific monthly** 31 (1930) 225f.

Davis, Tenney L. and Wu Lu-ch'iang. Ko hung on the gold medicine. **JCE** 9 (1932) 103-105.

Davis, Tenney L. and Wu Lu-ch'iang. Ko hung on the yellow and the white. **JCE** 13 (1936) 215-218.

Davis, Tenney L. and Wu Lu-ch'iang. The pill of immortality. **Technology review** 33 (1931) 383f.

Davis, Tenney L. and Wu Lu-ch'iang. T'ao hung-ch'ing. **JCE** 9.5 (may 1932) 859-862.

Dubs, Homer H. The beginnings of alchemy. **Isis** 38.1/2 (1947) 62-86.

Dubs, Homer H. The origin of alchemy. **Ambix** 9 (1961) 23-36.

Dudgeon, J. "Kung-fu," or medical gymnastics. **JPOS** 3.3 (1893); 3.4 (1895) 341f.

Dudgeon, John. **The beverages of the chinese; kung-fu or tauist medical gymnastics.** Tientsin (1895) illus. Repr & ed by William R. Berk, under title **Chinese healing arts; internal kung-fu,** culver city, calif (1979) 209 p, illus.

Eliade, Mircea. Alchemy and science in china. **HR** 10 (1970) 178-182. Rev art on N. Sivin's **Chinese alchemy** . . q.v.

Eliade, Mircea. The forge and the crucible: a postscript. **HR** 8.1 (1968) 74-88.

Eliade, Mircea. **Forgerons et alchimistes.** Paris (1956) Engl tsl Stephen Corrin: **The forge and the crucible,** london (1962) See chap 11, Chinese alchemy, 109-126.

Eliade, Mircea. The myth of alchemy. **Parabola** 3.3 (aug 1978) 6-23.

Erkes, Eduard. Die taoistische meditation und ihre bedeutung für das chinesische geistesleben. **Psyche** 2.3 (1948-49) 371-379.

Feifel, E. (tsl) Pao-p'u-tzu nei-p'ien, translated and edited. **MS** 6 (1941) 113-311; 9 (1944) 1-33; 11 (1946) 1-32.

Feng, Chia-lo and H.B. Collier. A sung-dynasty alchemical treatise; the "outline of alchemical preparations" [tan fang chien yuan] by tuku t'ao. **JWCBorderResS** 9 (1937) 199f.

Filliozat, J. Taoïsme et yoga. **Dan viêt nam** 3 (1949) 113-120.

Filliozat, J. Taoïsme et yoga. **JA** 257.1/2 (1969) 41-87.

Forke, A. Ko hung der philosoph und alchymist. **Archiv für die geschichte der philosophie** 41 (1932) 115f. See author's **Geschichte d. mittelälterlichen chinesischen philosophie,** hamburg (1934) 204f.

Fukui, Kōjun. A study of chou-i ts'an-t'ung-ch'i. **ActaA** 27 (1974) 19-32.

Girardot, Norman J. Rev of J. Needham, **Science and civilization in china,** vol 5 pt 2: **Spagyrical discovery and invention: magisteries of gold and immortality** (1974) q.v. **JCP** 5 (1978) 85-91.

Grison, Pierre. The golden flower and its fruit. **SCR** 2.3 (summer 1968) 141-146.

Gruman, Gerald J. **A history of ideas about the pro- longation of life. The evolution of prolongevity hypothesis to 1800.** Philadelphia (1966) See 4, Taoist prolongevitism in theory, 28-37; Taoist prolongevitism in practice, 37-49; The alchemists; chinese alchemy, 51-56.

Gulik, R.H. van. Indian and chinese sexual mysticism. App 1 in author's **Sexual life in ancient china,** q.v. 339-359.

Gulik, R.H. van. **Sexual life in ancient china.** Leiden (1961) 392 p. See passim.

Hakeda, Yoshito S. (tsl) **Kūkai, major works; translated, with an account of his life and a study of his thought.** Columbia univ (1972) See "The argument of kyobu (taoist)," 114-120.

Hiordthal, T. Chinesische alchimie. In Paul Diergart (ed) **Beiträge aus der geschichte der chemie,** leipzig und wien (1909) 215-224. See comm by Éd. Chavannes in **TP** 2e sér, 10 (1909) 389.

Ho, Peng-yoke. Alchemy in ming china. **Actes XIIe Congrès Intl. Hist. Sci. 1968** (1971) 3a, 119-123.

Ho, Peng Yoke. Alchemy on (sic) stones and minerals in chinese pharmacopaeias. **CCJ** 7.2 (may 1968) 155-170.

Ho, Peng Yoke & Beda Lim. Ts'ui fang, a forgotten 11th-century chinese alchemist. **Japanese studies in the history of science** 11 (1972) 101-112.

Ho, Peng Yoke, Goh Thean Chye & Beda Lim. Lu yu, the poet-alchemist. Canberra, australian national univ occ paper no 13, faculty of asian studies (1972) 51 p. Re "poet's alchemical beliefs and activities . . ."

Ho, Peng Yoke, Goh Thean Chye & David Parker. Po chü-i's poems on immortality. **HGAS** 34 (1974) 163-186.

Ho, Peng-yoke & Yu Wang-luen. Physical immortality in the early nineteenth-century novel ching-hua-yüan. **OE** 21.1 (june 1974) 33-51.

Ho, Ping-yü and Ch'en T'ieh-fan. On the dating of the shun-yang lü chen-jen yao shih chih, a taoist pharmaceutical and alchemical manual. **JOS** 9 (1971) 181f.

Ho, Ping-yü and Joseph Needham. Elixir poisoning in medieval china. **Janus** 48 (1959) 221-251.

Ho, Ping-yü and Joseph Needham. The laboratory equipment of the early medieval chinese alchemist. **Ambix** 7 (1959) 57-115.

Ho, Ping-yü and Joseph Needham. Theories of categories in early medieval chinese alchemy. **Journal of the warburg and courtauld institutes** 22 (1959) 173-210.

Ho, Ping-yü and Ts'ao T'ien-ch'in. An early medieval chinese alchemical text on aqueous solutions. **Ambix** 7 (1959) 122-158.

Homann, Rolf (tsl & annot) **Pai wen p'ien or the hundred questions; a dialogue between two taoists on the macrocosmic and microcosmic system of correspondences.** Leiden (1976) x + 109 p.

Huang, Tzu-ch'ing. Über die alte chinesische alchemie und chemie. **Wissenchaftliche annalen** 6 (1957) 721f.

Huang, Wen-shan. On longevity. **ASBIE** 46 (autumn 1978) 139-150. Comparisons of taoist and non-chin theories.

Johnson, Obed S. **A study of chinese alchemy.** Shanghai (1928) xi + 156 p.

Jung, C.G. **Alchemical studies.** Engl tsl R.F.C. Hull. London (1968) Collected works vol 8. See "European commentary"on the t'ai-i chin hua tsung chih, 1055; "Interpretation of the visions of zosimos," 57-108.

Kaltenmark, Max. Au sujet du houang-t'ing king. **AnnEPHE** (1967-68) 80-81.

Kaltenmark, Max. Hygiène et mystique en chine. **Bulletin de la société d'acuponcture** 33.3 (1959) 21-30.

Kaltenmark, Max. Ling-pao: note sur un terme du taoisme religieux. **MIHEC** 2 (1960) 559-588.

Kaltenmark, Max & K.M. Schipper. Religions de la chine. **AnnEPHE** 87 (1978-79) 109-117. Re mao shan taoism and yang-sheng (nurturing life)

Kao, John J. Chinese alchemy: confluence and transformation. **CME&W** (1977) 233-240.

Lê-Hu'o'ng (tsl fr chin) **Tao-yin. Lien-tao ch'ang-sheng fa. (Guide de la méthode de longue vie par la pratique du tao.** Bruxelle (1972) viii + 19 p, 32 croquis in-texte.

Liu, Ts'un-yan. Lu hsi-hsing and his commentaries on the ts'an-t'ung ch'i. **TJ** 7.1 (1968) 71-98. Repr **LTY:SP** (1976

Liu, Ts'un-yan. Taoist self-cultivation in ming thought. In **SSMT** (1970) 291-330.

Lo, L.C. (übers) Liu hua-yang; hui ming ching, das buch von bewusstein und leben. **CBWK** 3.1 (1926) 104-114, fig.

Loewe, Michael. Chinese alchemy. **History of science** 9 (1970) 90-93. Rev art on N. Sivin, **Chinese alchemy . . .** q.v.

Lu, Gwei-djen. The inner elixir (nei-tan): chinese physiological alchemy. In Mikuláš Teich & Robert Young (ed) **Changing perspectives in the history of science; essays in honour of joseph needham,** london (1973) 68-84.

Lu, K'uan-yü (Charles Luk) **The secrets of chinese meditation. Self-cultivation by mind control as taught in the ch'an, mahâyâna and taoist schools in china.** London (1964) 240 p, gloss, index, illus. German tsl H.-U. Rieker, **Geheimnisse der chinesischen meditation,** zürich & stuttgart (1967) 296 s.

Lu, K'uan-yü (Charles Luk) **Taoist yoga. Alchemy and immortality. A translation, with introduction and notes, of the secrets of cultivating essential nature and eternal life (hsin ming fa chueh ming chih) by the taoist master chao pi ch'en, born 1860.** London (1970) 206 p, gloss, index, illus.

Mahdihassan, S. Alchemy a child of chinese dualism as illustrated by its symbolism. **IQB** 8 (1959) 15 f.

Mahdihassan, S. Alchemy and its chinese origin as revealed by its etymology, doctrines and symbols. **IQB** (1966) 22-58.

Mahdihassan, S. Alchemy and its connection with astrology, pharmacy, magic and metallurgy. **Janus** 46 (1956) 81-103.

Mahdihassan, S. Alchemy in its proper setting, with jinn, sufi, and suffa as loan-words from the chinese. **IQB** 7 (1959) 1f.

Mahdihassan, S. Alchemy in the light of jung's psychology and of dualism. **Pakistan philosophical journal** 5 (1962)95f.

Mahdihassan, S. Chemistry a product of chinese culture. **Pakistan journal of science.** 9 (1957) 26f.

Mahdihassan, S. Chinese alchemy in the light of its fundamental terms. **AJCM** 8.4 (1980) 307-312.

Mahdihassan, S. The chinese origin of alchemy. **United asia** (India) 5.4 (1953) 241-244.

Mahdihassan, S. The chinese origin of the word chemistry. **Current science** 15 (1946) 136f. Another probable origin of the word chemistry from the chinese. **Ibid.,** 234.

Mahdihassan, S. Der chino-arabische ursprung des wortes chemikalie. **Pharmazeutische industrie** 23 (1961) 515f.

Mahdihassan, S. A comparative study of greek and chinese alchemy. **AJCM** 7.2 (1979) 171-181.

Mahdihassan, S. The early history of alchemy. **Journal of the university of bombay** 29 (1960) 173 f.

Mahdihassan, S. The genesis of alchemy. **Indian journal of the history of medicine** 5.2 (1960) 41f.

Mahdihassan, S. Das hermetische siegel in china. **Pharmazeutische industrie** 22 (1960) 92f.

Mahdihassan, S. Landmarks in the history of alchemy. **Scientia** 57 (1963) 1f.

Mahdihassan, S. The soma of the aryans and the chih of the chinese. **May and baker pharmaceutical bulletin** 21.3 (1972) 30f.

Mahdihassan, S. A triple approach to the problem of the origin of alchemy. **Scientia** 60 (1966) 444-455.

Martin, W.A.P. Alchemy in china. Abstract in **JAOS** 9 (1871) xlvi; **ChRev** 7 (1879) 242; repr in author's **Hanlin papers,** london and n.y. (1880) vol 1, p. 221, and **The lore of cathay,** n.y. and chicago (1901) p 44f.

Maspero, H. Les procédés de 'nourrir le principe vital' dans la religion taoiste ancienne. **JA** 229 (1937) 177-252, 353-430.

Maspero, H. Les dieux taoistes; comment on communique avec eux. **CRAIBL** (1937) 362-374.

Masson-Oursel, Paul. Tao et yoga. In **AC** t 1 (1959) 160-162.

McGowan, D.J. The movement cure in china (taoist medical gymnastics) **Chinese imperial customs, medical report series** 29 (1885) 42f.

Mély, F. de. l'Alchimie chez les chinois et l'alchemie grecque. **JA** ser 9 t 6 (1895) 314-340.

Mortier, F. Les procédés taoistes en chine pour la prolongation de la vie humaine. **BSAB** 45 (1930) 118-129.

Needham, Joseph. The elixir concept and chemical medicine in east and west. **JCUHK** 2.1 (june 1974) 242-265.

Needham, Joseph. The refiner's fire; the enigma of alchemy in east and west. A lecture given in london (1971) but apparently not publ in engl; french tsl, somewhat modified, Artisans et alchimistes en chine et dans le monde héllénistique, **La pensée** 152.3 (1970)

Needham, Joseph, with collab of Lu, Gwei-djen. **Science and civilization in china.** Vol 5, **Chemistry and chemical technology.** Pt 2, **Spagyrical discovery and invention: magisteries of gold and immortality.** Cambridge univ (1974) xxxii + 510 p, illus, 3 bibliog, general index.

Needham, Joseph, with collab of Ho Ping-yü & Lu Gwei-djen. **Science and civilization in china.** Vol 5, **Chemistry and chemical technology.** Pt 3, **Spagyrical discovery and invention: historical survey, from cinnabar elixirs to synthetic insulin.** Cambridge univ (1976) xxv + 481 p, illus, 3 bibliog, general index.

Ni, Hua-ching. **The taoist inner view of the universe and the immortal realm.** Los Angeles (1979) 218 p.

Odier, Daniel & Marc de Smedt. **Les mystiques orientales.** ?Paris (1972) See Le taoisme, 56-74.

Pálos, István. **Atem und meditation. Moderne chinesische atemtherapie als vorschule der medication. Theorie, praxit, originaltexte.**

Partington, J.R. An ancient chinese treatise on alchemy [ts'an t'ung ch'i of wei po-yang] **Nature** 136 (1935) 287f.

Partington, J.R. Chinese alchemy (a) **Nature** 119 (1927) 11; (b) **Ibid,** 120 (1927) 878; (c) **Ibid,** 128 (1931) 1074.

Partington, J.R. The relationship between chinese and arabic alchemy. **Nature** 120 (1928) 158f.

Pelliot, Paul. Notes sur quelques artistes des six dynasties et des t'ang. **TP** 22 (1923) 214f.

Pfizmaier, A. Die taolehre von den wahren menschen und den unsterblichen. **SAWW** 63 (1869) 217-280.

Pokora, T. An important crossroad of chinese thought. (Includes discussion of yogistic trends in ancient taoism) **ArchOr** 29 (1961) 64f.

Préau, André. **La fleur d'or et le taoïsme sans tao.** Paris (1931) 62 p ('Réunit deux articles parus en février et avril 1931 dans la revue **La voile d'isis**')

Read, Bernard. Chinese alchemy. **Nature** 120 (1927) 877.

Robinet, Isabelle. Randonnées extatiques des taoïstes dans les astres. **MS** 32 (1976) 159-273.

Roi, J. and Ou Yun-joei. Le taoïsme et les plantes d'immortalité. **BUA** 3e sér, 2 (1941) 535-546.

Rousselle, Erwin. Seelische führung im lebenden taoismus. **EJ** 1 (1933) repr of author's orig publ in **CDA** 21 (1934) together with his Ne ging tu, "die tafel des inneren gewebes," ein taoistisches meditationsbild mit beschriftung, orig publ in **Sinica** 8 (1933) 207-216. Engl version of all three papers, entitled Spiritual guidance in contemporary taoism, in Joseph Campbell (ed) **Spiritual disciplines; papers from the eranos yearbooks,** ny (1960) 59-101, illus. See further author's **Zur seelischen führung im taoismus; ausgewählte aufsätze,** darmstadt (1962)

Rousselle, E. Die typen der meditation in china. **CDA** (1932) 20-46.

Saso, Michael. On the ritual meditation of orthodox heavenly master sect. **JCS** 8 (1971) 1-19.

Saso, Michael. On the ritual use of the yellow court canon. **JCS** 9 (1972) 1-20.

Saso, Michael. The taoists who did not die. **Afrasian** (student journal, london institute of oriental and african studies) 3 (1970) 13f.

Saso, Michael. **The teachings of taoist master chuang.** Yale univ (1978) 317 p, notes, bibliog, index and chin char, illus, fig.

Scaligero, Massimo. Tao and grail: the search of earthly immortality. **E&W** 8 (1957) 67-72.

Schafer, Edward H. The jade woman of greatest mystery. **HR** 17.3/4 (feb-may 1978) 387-398.

Schafer, Edward H. The stove god and the alchemists. In **StAs** (1975) 261-266.

Schipper, K.M. (tsl) **l'Empereur wou des han dans la légende taoiste; le 'han wou-ti-nei-tchouan.'** Paris (1965) 132 + ix p, index, chin text.

Schipper, Kristofer. The taoist body. **HR** 17.3/4 (feb-may 1978) 355-386.

Seidel, Anna. **La divinisation de lao tseu dans le taoisme des han.** Paris (1969) 169 p, app, facs, bibliog, index.

Seidel, Anna, A taoist immortal of the ming dynasty: chang san-feng. In **SSMT** (1970) 483-526.

Sivin, Nathan. **Chinese alchemy: preliminary studies.** Harvard univ (1968) 339 p, app, index. Mainly a study of sun ssu-mo's tan ching yao chüeh, with critical ed of text.

Sivin, Nathan. Chinese alchemy as a science. In **NCELYY** (1970) 35-50.

Sivin, Nathan. On the pao p'u tzu nei p'ien and the life of ko hung (283-343 a.d.) **Isis** 60 (1969) 388-391. Reply to rev by Pierre Huard & Ming Wong of J.R. Ware's **Alchemy, medicine & religion . . .** q.v. Includes Sivin's tsl of discussion on ko hung's dates by William Hung.

Sivin, Nathan. On the reconstruction of chinese alchemy. **Japanese studies in the history of science** 6 (1967) 60f.

Spooner, Roy C. Chang tao-ling, the first taoist pope. **JCE** 15 (1938) 503f.

Spooner, Roy C. Chinese alchemy. **JWCBorderResS** 12 (1940) 82.

Spooner, Roy C. and C.H. Wang. The divine nine-turn tan-sha method, a chinese alchemical recipe. **Isis** 28 (1948) 235-242.

Stadelmann, Heinrich. Biologie des laotse. **Zeitschrift für menschenkunde** 12 (1935) 207-225.

Stein, O. References to alchemy in buddhist scriptures. **BSOAS** 7 (1933) 263.

Stein, Rolf A. Conceptions relatives à la nourriture (chine) **ACF** 73e ann (1973) 457-463.

Stein, Rolf A. l'Habitat, le monde et le corps humain en extrême-orient et en haute-asie. **JA** 245 (1957) 37-74.

Stein, Rolf A. Spéculations mystiques et thèmes relatifs aux "cuisines" [ch'u] du taoisme. **ACF** 72 (1972) 489f.

Steininger, Hans. **Hauch- und körperseele und der dämon bei kuan-yin-tze. Untersuchungen zur chinesischen psychologie und ontologie.** Leipzig (1953) 93 p.

Strickmann, M. Notes on mushroom cults in ancient china. Rijksuniversiteit gent, gand (1966) (Paper to the 4e journée des orientalistes belge, brussels, 1966)

Strickmann, Michel. On the alchemy of t'ao hung-ching. In **FT** (1979) 123-192.

Swanson, Jerry. A 3rd-century taoist treatise on the nourishment of life: hsi k'ang and his yang-sheng lun. In Richard Tursman (ed) **Studies in philosophy and the history of science: essays in honor of max fisch,** coronado (1970) 139-158.

Ting, Simon. **The mysticism of chuang tzu.** Univ philippines (1975) 252 p. Repr fr **Philippines social sciences and humanities review** 40 (mar-june 1975)

Ts'ao, T'ien-ch'in, Ho Ping-yü and Joseph Needham. An early medieval chinese alchemical text on aqueous solutions. **Ambix** 7 (1959) 122-158.

Waley, Arthur. Notes on chinese alchemy. **BSOAS** 6.1 (1930-32) 1-24.

Waley, Arthur. References to alchemy in buddhist scriptures. **BSOAS** 6.4 (1932) 1102-1103.

Waley, Arthur (tsl) **The travels of an alchemist; the journey of the taoist, ch'ang-ch'un . . . from china to the hindukush at the summons of chinghiz khan, recorded by his disciple, li chih-ch'ang.** London (1931) x + 166 p, p, map. Repr westport, conn (1976) taipei (1978)

Ware, J.R. (tsl) **Alchemy, medicine, and religion in the china of a.d. 320. The nei p'ien of ko hung (pao-p'u tzu)** M.I.T. (1966) 388 p.

Wasson, R.G. **Soma. The divine mushroom of immortality.** Harcourt brace johanovich; printed in italy (1968) See chap 13, The marvelous herb [ling chih] 77-92, pl.

Wilhelm, Hellmut. Eine chou-inschrift über atemtechnik. **MS** 13 (1948) 385-388.

Wilhelm, Richard (tsl) **Das geheimnis der goldenen blüte, ein chinesisches lebensbuch.** München (1929) enl ed zürich & leipzig (1939) Engl tsl Cary F. Baynes, **The secret of the golden flower; a chinese book of life.** London (1931) enl ed ny (1962) repr ny (1975) Foreword and comm C.G. Jung. Chin orig is t'ai yi chin hua tsung chih; enl ed also incl pt of another text, hui ming ching. Illus.

Wilson, W.J. (ed) Alchemy in china. **Ciba symposia** 2.7 (1940) 594-624, bibliog.

Wu, Lu-ch'iang and Tenney L. Davis. An ancient chinese alchemical classic, ko hung on the gold medicine and on the yellow and the white. The fourth and sixteenth chapters of pao-p'u-tsu. **PAAAS** 70.6 (1935) 221-241.

Wu, Lu-ch'iang and Tenney L. Davis. An ancient chinese treatise on alchemy entitled ts'an t'ung ch'i written by wei po-yang about 142 a.d. **Isis** 18.2 (1932) 210-289.

Wu, Lu-ch'iang and Tenney L. Davis. (tsl) Translation of ko hung's biography in the lie-hsien-chuan. **JCE** (1934) 517-520.

Yewdale, M.S. The therapeutic power of taoism. **AP** 7 (1936) 271-274.

24. MEDITATION — GENERAL

Blofeld, John. **Beyond the gods. Buddhist and taoist mysticism.** London & ny (1974) 164 p, gloss.

Ch'ien, Anne. Meditation and ritual in neo-confucian tradition. **JD** 2.2 (apr 1977) 173-188.

Dumoulin, H. La mystique de l'orient et de l'occident. **BUA** 3e sér, 5 (1944) 152-202.

Lu, K'uan-yü (Charles Luk) **The secrets of chinese meditation. Self-cultivation by mind control as taught in the ch'an, mahāyāna and taoist schools in china.** London (1964) 240 p, gloss, index, illus. German tsl H.-U. Rieker, **Geheimnisse der chinesischen meditation.** zürich & stuttgart (1967) 296 s.

Rousselle, Erwin. Die typen der meditation in china. **CDA** (1932) 20-46.

Taylor, Rodney L. Meditation in neo-confucian orthodoxy: kao p'an-lung's writings on quiet-sitting. **JCP** 6 (1979) 149-182.

Tu, Wei-ming. Ultimate self-transformation as a communal act: comments on modes of self-cultivation in traditional china. **JCP** 6.2 (june 1979) 237-246.

Wienpahl, Paul. Wang yang-ming and meditation. **JCP** 1.2 (mar 1974) 199-227.

Wilhelm, Hellmut. Eine chou-inschrift über atemtechnik. **MS** 13 (1948) 385-388.

25. POPULAR RELIGION & "SUPERSTITIONS" — GENERAL

Ahern, Emily M. The power and pollution of chinese women. **WCS** 1975) 193-214.

Allan, Sarah. Shang foundations of modern chinese folk religion. In **LL&R** (1979) 1-21.

Allan, Sarah & Alvin P. Cohen (ed) **Legend, lore, and religion in china. Essays in honor of wolfram eberhard on his seventieth birthday.** San francisco (1979) Art sep listed in our bibliog. Abbrev **LL&R.**

Anderson, E.N. & Marja L. Oh lovely appearance of death: the deformation of folk religion. In authors' **Fishing in troubled waters; research on the chinese fishing industry in west malaysia,** taipei (1977) 165-189.

The Bondage of fear, as illustrated among the chinese. **ChRec** 30.12 (dec 1899) 590-598. Re superstitions.

Bone, Charles. Chinese superstitions. **WMM** 120 (1897) 363-371.

Bredon, Juliet. Hell 'à la chinoise.' The several wards of the taoist inferno. **Asia** 25 (1925) 138-141.

Bryson, Mrs. M.I. **Home-life in china.** NY (n.d. — late 19th century?) See, pt 1, chap 9, Idolatry and superstitions, 151-177. Juvenile level.

Chao, D. The snake in chinese belief. Calcutta, **Folklore** 19.6 (1978) 159-168.

A chapter of folklore. **JNCBRAS** 49 (1918) Four art listed in this bibliog sep by author: H.L. Harding, Lewis Hodous, James Hutson, H.A. Ottewill.

Clarke, G.W. (tsl) The yü-li or precious records. **JNCBRAS** 28.2 (1893) 233-400. Deals with hells and punishments.

Cohen, Alvin P. A chinese temple keeper talks about chinese folk religion. **AsFS** 36.1 (1977) 1-17.

Cornaby, W.A. Christian suggestions in chinese superstitions. **ChRec** 41.4 (apr 1910) 257-264. Mostly explaining "superstitions."

Davaranne, Theodor. **Chinas volksreligion; dargestellt nach einer rundfrage und verglichen mit den grundlehren des laotze, konfuzius und buddha.** Tübingen (1924) 48 p.

Day, Clarence Burton. **Chinese peasant cults. Being a study of chinese paper gods.** Shanghai (1940) repr taipei (1969) 243 p, bibliog, app 1 thru 10, lists of ma-chang (paper gods) illus.

Day, Clarence B. **Popular religion in pre-communist china.** Taipei & san francisco (1975) vii + 102 p. Repr of various art publ pre-1949, all listed sep in our bibliog.

Doolittle, Justus. Charms and omens. Chap 13 in author's **SLC** vol 2 (1865) 307-330.

Doolittle, Justus. Singular and popular superstitions. Chap 4 in author's **SLC** vol 2 (1865) 91-133.

Doré, Henri. **Recherches sur les superstitions en chine.** Shanghai (1911-1938) 18 vol. Being **Variétés sinologiques** no 32, 34, 36, 39, 41-42, 44-46, 48-49, 51, 57, 61-62, 66. Profusely illus. See next item.

Doré, Henri. **Researches into chinese superstitions** (eng tsl of above) Vol 1 (1914) 2 (1915) 3 (1916) 4 (1917) 5 (1918) 6 (1920) 7 (1922) 8 (1926) tsl M. Kennelly, s.j. Vol 9 (1931) 10 (1933) tsl D.J. Finn, s.j. Vol 13 (1938) tsl L.F. McGreal, s.j. Above engl vol all publ shanghai, repr taipei 1966-67. Seven vol remain untsl: 11, 12, 14, 15, 16, 17, 18.

Doré, Henri. Superstitions chinoises pour les enfants. **RC** (oct 1911) 247-253, fig.

Dunstheimer, G.H. Religion officielle, religion populaire et sociétés secrètes en chine depuis les han. In **EncyP:HR** 3 (1976) 371-448, bibliog.

Edwards, E.D. **Chinese prose literature of the t'ang dynasty, a.d. 618-906.** London, 2 vol (1937-38) repr ny (1974) See, vol 1, chap 5, Religion—magic and magical practices, 49-59; vol 2, passim.

Elwin, Arthur. Chinese superstitions. **ChRec** 21.7 (July 1890) 314-320.

Fielde, Adele M. **A corner of cathay.** NY (1894) See sec, Sundry superstitions, 139-151. Mostly re swatow.

Giles, Herbert A. **The civilization of china.** London (1911) See chap 3, Religion and superstition, 55-78.

Giles, Herbert A. (tsl) **Strange stories from a chinese studio.** Shanghai etc 4th rev ed (1926) Tsl of liao chai chih yi. See app 1, on purgatory.

The Graphic art of chinese folklore. Taipei, national museum of history, republic of china (1977) 101 p reproductions col prints, notes in chin and engl. Sel fr coll at museum, all prints relating to pop relig.

Grube, Wilhelm. Die chinesische volksreligion und ihre beeinflussung durch den buddhismus. **Globus** 63 (1893) 297-303.

Grube, W. Sammlung chinesischer volksgötter aus amoy. **Ethnologisches notizblatt** 1.2 (1895) 27-33.

Harrell, Stevan. The concept of "soul" in chinese folk religion. **JAS** 38.3 (may 1979) 519-528.

Harrell, Stevan. Modes of belief in chinese folk religion. **JSSR** 16.1 (mar 1977) 55-65.

Harvey, E.D. **The mind of china.** Yale univ (1933) x + 321 p. See passim.

Headland, Isaac Taylor. Chinese superstitions. Chap 28 in author's **HLC** (1914) 257-268.

Hefter, J. Über das regenbittopfer. **Zeitschrift für geopolitik** 62 (1930) 337-338.

Hodous, Lewis. Folk religion. In H.F. MacNair (ed) **China,** univ california (1946) 231-244.

Hodous, Lewis. **Folkways in china.** London (1929) 248 p, illus. Mostly on foochow. Repr ny (1973)

Hodous, Lewis. The kite festival in foochow. **JNCBRAS** 49 (1918) 76-81. Art no 1 under heading: A chapter of folklore.

Horning, Emma. Values in rural chinese religion. **ChRec** 61 (1930) 39-42. 168-175, 234-238, 299-307, 775-781.

Hou, Ching-lang. The chinese belief in baleful stars. In **FT** (1979) 193-228.

Hou, Ching-lang. **Monnaies d'offrande et la notion de trésorerie dans la religion chinoise.** Paris (1975) 238 p, notes, bibliog, chin texts, pl, index, tipped-in samples of spirit money.

Hwang, Teh-shih. One of the characteristics of taiwan folk religion. **JCS** 16-17 (1979) 63-68. The characteristic: "personalization" of nature spirits.

M.K. (Max Kaltenmark) and M.S. (Michel Strickmann) Symbolisme traditionnel et religions populaires. **EUF** (1968) vol 4, see Chine, sec 5, 362a-365c.

Kermadec, H. de. La religion populaire chinoise actuelle. **Rythmes du monde** 10.2 (1962) 13-36.

Körner, Brunhild. **Die religiöse welt der bäuerin in nord-china.** Stockholm (1959) 86 p, 12 pl.

Leong, Y.K. and L.K. Tao. **Village and town life in china.** London (1915) See The village temple, 32-39.

Little, Mrs. Archibald. Superstitions. Chap 11 in author's **IntC** (ca. 1900) 145-157.

Mansfield, M.T. Chinese superstitions. **FLJ** 5 (1887) 127-129.

Maspero, Henri. The mythology of modern china. In J. Hackin et al, **Asiatic mythology.** Tsl fr french F.M. Atkinson. N.Y. (n.d.) 252-384, illus.

Meacham, William. The importance of archaeology in the understanding of certain developmental aspects of chinese religion, with reference to data from hong kong. **CF** 15.4 (1972) 189-209. Re "popular religious practices"

Moese, Wolfgang. Temples and religion. In **CRWMS** (1979) 303-363.

Moule, Arthur E. Superstitions. Chap 8 in author's **NC&O** (1891) 223-239.

Nicouleau, M. Superstitions chinoises. **MC** (15 déc 1911) 595-597, fig (22 déc 1911) 610-611.

Oehler, W. Der buddhismus als volksreligion im heutigen china. **EMM** 55 (1911) 308-317.

Oehler, W. Die religion in chinesischen volksleben. In **LO** (1922) 411-454.

Overmyer, Daniel L. Dualism and conflict in chinese popular religion. In **T&T** (1980) 153-184.

Overmyer, Daniel L. Folk-buddhist religion: creation and eschatology in medieval china. **HR** 12.1 (aug 1972) 42-70.

Overmyer, Daniel L. **Folk buddhist religion. Dissenting sects in late traditional china.** Harvard univ (1976) xi + 295 p, notes, bibliog, gloss, index.

Parker, Albert George. A study of the religious beliefs and practices of the common people of china. **ChRec** 53.8 (aug 1922) 503-512; 53.9 (sept 1922) 575-585.

Parker, A.P. Some notes on the history of folk-lore of old shanghai. **JNCBRAS** 47 (1916) 85-102.

Peeters, Hermes. **The religions of china. Confucianism, taoism, buddhism, popular belief.** Peking (1941) 64 p.

Peyraube, Alain. Trois études sur les religions chinoises. **ASSR** 35 (jan-juin 1973) 151-157. Rev art on Doré, **Manuel des superstitions chinoises**; Gulik, **La vie sexuelle dans la chine ancienne**; Maspero, **Le taoïsme et les religions chinoises** qqv.

Pommeranz-Liedtke, Gerhard. Bilder für jedes neue jahr. Zur wandlung des chinesischen neujahrbildes. **ZBK** 1 (1955)

Pommeranz-Liedtke, Gerhard. **Chinesische neujahrsbilder.** Dresden (1961) 202 p, biblog, pl.

Ransdorp, R. Official and popular religion in the chinese empire. In Pieter H. Vrijhof & Jacques Waardenburg (ed) **Official and popular religion. Analysis of a theme for religious studies,** the hague (1979) 387-426.

Ringgren, Helmer and Ake Ström. **Die religionen der völker. Grundriss der allgemeinen religions-geschichte.** Stuttgart (1959) Tsl fr swedish Inga Ringgren and C.M. Schröder. See pt 4, Die ostasiatischen schriftkulturen: die chinesen, 419-436.

Schlegel, Gustave. Der todtenvogel bei den chinesen. **IAE** 11 (1898) 86-87.

Seidel, Anna. Buying one's way to heaven: the celestial treasury in chinese religions. **HR** 17.3/4 (feb-may 1978) 419-431. Rev art on Hou Ching-lang, **Monnaies d'offrande** . . . q.v.

Smith, Arthur H. **Village life in china. A study in sociology.** N.Y. (1899) See chap 11, Village temples and religious societies, 136-140; chap 12, Cooperation in religious observances, 141-145.

Stein, Rolf A. Un exemple de relations entre taoïsme et religion populaire. In **Fukui hakase festschrift: tōyō bunka ronshū,** ?Tokyo (1969) 79-90.

Stevens, Keith G. Under altars (hsia-t'an) **JHKBRAS** 17 (1977) 85-100, pl 20-31 at end of vol.

Stewart-Lockhart, J.H. Chinese folk-lore. **Folk-lore** 1 (1890) 359-368.

Stover, Leon E. **The cultural ecology of chinese civili-zation. Peasants and elites in the last of the agrarian states.** NY (1974) See chap 8, The kitchen god, 122-132.

Tang, Mei-chun. **Urban chinese families. An anthropo-logical field study in taipei city, taiwan.** National taiwan univ (1978) See passim.

Thoms, P.P. (tsl) Prohibitions addressed to chinese converts of the romish faith . . . with notes illustrating the customs of the country. **ChRep** 20.2 (feb 1851) 85-94. Extracted fr **ICG**.

Topley, Marjorie. Paper charms, and prayer sheets as adjuncts to chinese worship. **JMBRAS** 26 (1953) 63-80, illus.

Ts'ai, Wen-hui. Historical personalities in chinese folk religion. **SyY:T&W** 11.1 (may 1973) 34-46.

The Twilight of china's gods. HK (1958) 14 p.

Vale, Joshua. **Chinese superstitions.** Shanghai (1904) 27 p, london (1906) 48 p.

Vandier-Nicolas, N. Le jugement des morts en chine. In **Le jugement des morts,** paris (1961) 231-254 ('Sources orientales' no 4)

Vleeschower, E. de. K'iyu [ch'i yü, praying for rain] **FS** 2 (1943) 39-50.

Willoughby-Meade, Gerald. **Chinese ghouls and goblins.** London (1928) xv + 431 p, illus.

Wolf, Arthur P. Gods, ghosts, and ancestors. In **RRCS** (1974) 131-182.

Wolf, Arthur P. (ed) **Religion and ritual in chinese society.** Stanford univ (1974) xii + 377 p. Individual art sep listed in our bibliog. Abbrev **RRCS**.

Wright, A.R. Some chinese folk-lore. **Folk-lore** 14 (1903) 292-298.

Yu, David C. Chinese folk religion. **HR** 12.4 (may 1973) 378-387. Rev art on repr of books by Groot and Doré in taipei.

Yuan, L.Z. **Through a moon gate.** Shanghai (1938) See chap 6, The gods and the devils, 121-142.

26. LOCAL STUDIES — MAINLAND

Aijmer, Göran. Ancestors in the spring. The qingming festival in central China. **JHKBRAS** 18 (1978) 59-82.

Aijmer, Göran. **The dragon boat festival in the hunan and hupeh plains, central china: a study in the ceremonialism of the transplantation of rice.** Stockholm (1964) 135 p, bibliog.

Anderson, Eugene N. The boat people of south china. **Anthropos** 65 (1970) 248-256.

Anderson, E.N. &Marja L.Homage to the locality: religion in the agricultural landscape. In **CE** (1973) 147-166.

Bodde, Derk (tsl) **Annual customs and festivals in peking, as recorded in the yen-ching sui-shih-chi by tun li-ch'en.** Peiping (1936) repr univ hong kong (1965) with new intro and corr; xxii + 147, 6 app, bibliog, index, illus, end-paper plan of peking.

Bone, C. The religious festivals of the cantonese. **ChRec** 20 (1889) 367-371, 391-403.

Bouillard, G. Calendrier chinois et européen à l'usage des residents de peking. **La chine** (all following 1922) 10: 69-76; 12: 282-284; 14: 453-460; 16: 603-608; 18: 721-723; 20: 881-882; 22: 1081-1086; 24: 1205-1209; 26: 1353-1356; 28: 1529-1532; 29: 1583-1586.

Bouillard, G. Usages et coutumes à pékin durant la (1) 2e lune, **La chine** 35 (1923) 117-136; (2) 3e lune: 37 (1923) 249-264; (3) 4e lune: 38 (1923) 299-311; (4) 5e lune: 18 (1922) 703-720; (5) 6e lune: 39 (1923) 391-405; (6) 7e lune: 40 (1923) 469-479; (7) 8e lune: 26 (1922) 1335-1355; (8) 9e lune: 29 (1922) 1573-1582; (9) 10e lune: 30 (1922) 1639-1651; (10) 11e lune: 32 (1922) 1791-1796.

Box, Ernest. Shanghai folk-lore. (1) **JNCBRAS** 34 (1901-02) 101-135 (2) **Ibid** 36 (1905) 130-156.

Brown, Frederick R. **Religion in tientsin.** Shanghai (1908) 62 p.

Brown, Frederick R. Superstitions common in kiangsi province. **NCR** 4.6 (1922) 493-504.

Brown, H.G. What the gods say in west china. **JWCBorderResS** 3 (1926-29) 134-150.

Chao, Wei-pang. The dragon-boat race in wu-ling, hunan. **FS** 2 (1943) 1-18.

Chao, Wei-pang. Games at the mid-autumnal festival in kuangtung. **FS** 3.1 (1944) 1-16.

Chiang, Liu. Religion in foochow. **ChRec** 66.2 (feb 1935) 89-94.

Coffin, Edna, et al. Religion. In Far eastern and russian institute, univ washington (comp) **A regional handbook on northwest china. HRAF** 1 (1956) 324-363.

Cordier, G. Croyances populaires au yunnan. **RIC** (juin 1909) 597-601. Same title in **La chine** 36 (1923) 203-208.

Culbertson, M. Simpson. **Darkness in the flowery land; or religious notions and popular superstitions in north china.** N.Y. (1857) 235 p.

Daudin, P. Deux amulettes du yunnan. **BSEIS** n.s. 21 (1946) 35-40.

Day, C.B. Shanghai invites the god of wealth. **CJ** 8 (1928) 289-294. Repr in **PRPCC** (1975)

Dols, J. Fêtes et usages pendant le courant d'une année dans la province de kan-sou (chine) **AL** 1 (1937) 203-274.

Doolittle, Justus. **Social life of the chinese . . . with special but not exclusive reference to fuhchau.** NY, 2 vo (1865) vol 1, xvi + 459 p, vol 2, 490 p, illus, index for both vol at end of vol 2. Well over half of this work deals with relig. Sep entries for various subj listed in our bibliog. Abbrev **SLC.**

Doré, Henri. **Manuel des superstitions chinoises.** Chang-hai [shanghai] 2e ed (1936) 221 p.

Drake, F.S. Religion in a manchurian city. **ChRec** 66.2 (feb 1935) 104-111; 66.3 (mar 1935) 161-170

Eastlake, F.Warrington, Cantonese superstitions about infants. **ChRev** 9 (1880-81) 301-306.

Eberhard, Wolfram. **The local cultures of south and east china.** Leiden (1968) 520 p. Tsl fr german Alide Eberhard. "A greatly revised version of the second volume of my **Lokalkulturen im alten china** in english translation." See passim.

Eberhard, Wolfram. **Studies in chinese folklore and related essays.** Indiana univ and the hague (1970) 329 p, notes, bibliog, index, illus. All but 3 studies are republ, and most are tsl fr german William Templer. See pt 1: Essays on the folklore of chekiang, china.

Eberhard, Wolfram. The supernatural in chinese folktales from chekiang. In Wayland D. Hand (ed) **Humaniora . . . essays honoring archer taylor . . .** Locust valley, n.y. and gluckstadt (1960) 335-341.

Eberhard, Wolfram. Zur volkskunde von chèkiang. **ZE** 67 (1935) 248-265.

Edgar, J.H. Notes on litholatry on the western frontiers of china. **CJ** 4 (1926) 105-110.

Edgar, J.H. The sin bearer, a note on comparative religion. **JWCBorderResS** 3 (1926-29) p 151.

Eitel, E.J. The religion of the hakkas, **NQ** 1.12 (dec 1867) 161-163; 2.10 (oct 1868) 145-147; 2.11 (nov 1868) 167-169; 3.1 (jan 1869) 1-3.

Ethnographische beiträge aus der ch'ing hai provinz, zusammengest. von ch'ing hai missionären anlassl. des 75. jahrgen jubiläums der gesellschaft des göttlichen wortes. Catholic univ of peking (1952) [publ in japan] 354 p, 10 pl.

Ewer, F.H. Some account of festivals in canton. **ChRec** 3.7 (dec 1870) 185-188.

Ewer, F.H. and J. Doolittle. Native fete and natal days observed at canton and foochow. In **DV** 2, pt 3, no 30.

Fabre, A. Avril au pays des aïeux. **CCS** vol 8 (1935) Ancestor worship and burial practices re ch'ing ming, specifically in shun-tè, kuangtung.

Faulder, H. Croyier. The temples of shanghai. **CJ** 30.6 (june 1939) 340-345.

Fèng, Han-yi and John K. Shryock. Marriage customs in the vicinity of i-ch'ang. **HJAS** 13 (1950) 362-430.

Freedman, Maurice. **Chinese lineage and society: fukien and kwangtung.** Univ london (1966) See esp chap 5, Geomancy and ancestor worship, 118-154, incl photos.

Frick, Johann. How blood is used in magic and medicine in ch'inghai province. **Anthropos** 46 (1951) 964-979. Tsl fr german J.E. Mertz.

Frick, Johann. Magic remedies used on sick children in the western valley of sining. **Anthropos** 46 (1951) 175-186. german orig in **ibid** 45 (1950) 787-800.

Frick, Johannes. Die regenprozession in lungsi, nordwest china. In **Festschrift paul schebesta zum 75. geburstag,** vienna-mödling (1963) 385-400.

Frick, J. Der traum und seine deutung bei den chinesen in ch'inghai. **Anthropos** 49 (1954) 311-313.

Gamble, Sidney D. **North china villages. Social, political, and economic activities before 1933.** Univ california (1963) See 119-125 on community religion; 239-262 on history of a specific clan.

Gamble, Sidney D. **Ting hsien: a north china rural community.** Stanford univ (1954) See part 5, Social and religious activities, esp chap 17, Festivals and customs, and chap 18, Religion, 371-421.

Graham, David Crockett. **Folk religion in southwest china.** Washington, d.c. (1961) 246 p, bibliog, index, illus. Folk religion in ssuch'uan.

Graham, David C. Notes on the primitive religion of the chinese in szechuan. **JWCBorderResS** 1 (1922-23) 53-55.

Graham, David C. **Religion in szechuan province china.** Washington, d.c. (1928) 83 p, 25 pl.

Graham, David C. Religion of the chinese in szechwan. **ChRec** 66.6 (june 1935) 363-369; 66.7 (july 1935) 421-428; 66.8 (aug 1935) 484-490; 66.9 (sept 1935) 547-555.

Graham, David C. Some strange customs in szechwan province (1) the 'human chicken' (2) human sacrifices in west china (3) uprisings of the boxers or red lantern society. **JWCBorderResS** 8 (1936) 141-144.

Graham, D.C. Strange gods in west china. **ChRec** 57.10 (oct 1926) 693-698.

Graham, David C. The temples of suifu. **ChRec** 61 (1930) 108-120.

Graham, David C. Tree gods in szechwan province. **JWCBorderResS** 8 (1936) 59-61, 2 photos.

Groot, J.J.M. de. **Les fêtes annuellement célébrées à emoui (amoy). Étude concernant la religion populaire des chinois.** (Being **AMG** 11 and 12) Paris (1886) repr taipei (1977) 2 vol. Tsl fr dutch C.G. Chavannes.

Grootaers, Willem A. The hagiography of the chinese god chen-wu. (The transmission of rural traditions in chahar) **FS** 11 (1952) 139-182.

Grootaers, Willem A. The hutu god of wan-ch'uan (chahar) **SS** 7 (1948) 41-53.

Grootaers, W.A. Rural temples around hsuan-hua (south chahar), their iconography and their history. **FS** 10 (1951) 1-116.

Grootaers, W.A. Les temples villageois de la région au sud de tat'ong (chansi nord), leurs inscriptions et leur histoire. **FS** 4 (1945) 161-212.

Grootaers, W.A., Li Shih-yu and Chang Chi-wen. Temples and history of wanch'üan (chahar). The geographical method applied to folklore. **MS** 13 (1948) 209-316.

Grube, Wilhelm. Pekinger todtengebräuche. **JPOS** 4 (1898) 79-142.

Grube W. Sammlung chinesischer volksgötter aus amoy. **Ethnologisches notizblatt** 1.2 (1895) 27-33.

Gutzlaff, Charles. Temple of teen how [t'ien hou] at meichow. **ChRep** 2 (1834) 563-565.

Hankey, Rosalie. Ghosts and shamanism in kwangtung. **CFQ** 2 (1943) 303-308.

Harding, H.L. On a method of divination practised at foochow. **JNCBRAS** 49 (1918) 82-85. Art no 2 under heading, A chapter of folklore.

Headland, Isaac T. Religion in peking. In **WPR** (1893) vol 2, 1019-1023.

Herrmann, F. Zur volkskunde der hakka in kuang-tung. **Sinica** 12 (1937) 18-38.

Hodous, Lewis. **Folkways in china.** London (1929) 248 p, illus. Mostly on foochow.

Hodous, Lewis, The great summer festival of china as observed in foochow: a study in popular religion. **JNCBRAS** 43 (1912) 69-80.

Hodous, Lewis. The reception of spring as observed in foochow, china. **JAOS** 42 (1922) 53-58.

Hsu, Francis L.K. **Magic and science in western yunnan.** N.Y. (1943) 53 p.

Hsu, Francis L.K. **Religion, science and human crisis.** London (1952) 142 p. West town, yunnan.

Hsu, Francis L.K. **Under the ancestors' shadow. Chinese culture and personality.** Columbia univ (1948) re-issued stanford univ (1967) with new chap. Re west town, yunnan. See 'The world of spirits,' 136-143; 'Man's relation with spiritual worlds,' 144-154.

James, F.H. North-china sects. **ChRec** 30 (1899) 74-76.

Johnston, R.F. **Lion and dragon in northern china.** London (1910) See chap 8-17, for religion in territory of weihaiwei, 155-425.

Körner, Brunhild. Nan-lao-ch'üan, eine flutsage aus westchina, und ihre auswirkung auf örtliches brauchtum. **Ethnos** 15.1/2 (jan-mar 1950) 46-56.

Körner, Brunhild. **Die reliöse welt der bäuerin in nordchina.** Stockholm (1959) 86 p, 12 pl.

Kulp, Daniel Harrison, II. **Country life in south china. The sociology of familism. Vol 1, Phenix village, kwangtung, china.** Columbia univ (1925) repr taipei (1966) See esp chap 10, Religion and the spiritual community, 284-314.

Laprairie, Père. Les religions du seutchouan. **Revue nationale chinoise** 41, no 134 (fev 1941) 125-142.

Leung, A.K. Peiping's happy new year. **NGM** 70 (1936) 749-792.

Li, Wei-tsu. On the cult of the four sacred animals (szu ta men) in the neighborhood of peking. **FS** 7 (1948) 1-94 (fox, weasel, hedgehog, snake)

Liu, Carl H.F. A study of the religions of hsichow (yünnan) **ChRec** 72.5 (may 1941) 235-243; 72.6 (june 1941) 302-308; 72.7 (july 1941) 378-389; 72.8 (aug 1941) 431-441.

Liu, Chiang. Fukien folkways and religion. **ChRec** 64 (1933) 701-713. See also same title in **ACSS** (1957) 20-35.

Liu, Chiang. Religion, funeral rites, sacrifices and festivals in kirin. **ChRec** 65 (1934) 227-238. See also same title in **ACSS** (1958-59) 8-20.

Liu, Mau-tsai. Der niang-niang kult in der mandschurei. **OE** 19.1/2 (dec 1972) 109-119.

Lowe, H.Y. **The adventures of wu. The life cycle of a peking man.** Peking, 2 vol (1939-40) Orig publ in **The peking chronicle.** Repr 2 vol in 1, princeton univ (1983) xxii, 239, 250 p, index, errata. See passim. Intro Derk Bodde.

Lutschewitz, W. Die religiösen sekten in nordchina, mit besonderer berücksichtigung d. sekten in shantung. **OstL** (1905) 1: 203-207, 247-251, 291-293, 337-340.

Macintyre, John. Roadside religion in manchuria. **JNCBRAS** n.s. 21.1 (1886) 43-66.

Maclagan, P.J. Folk-lore. Account of some customs observed in the first moon in the village of yü-lu-hsiang, ch'ao-chou-fu, chieh-yang hsien. **ChRev** 23 (1894-95) 120.

Martin, Ilse. Frühlingsdoppelsprüche (ch'un-lien) von 1942 an pekinger haustüren. **FS** 2 (1943) 89-174.

Murray, A. Jowett. Religion in the villages of north china. **Religion** 16 (july 1936) 18-25.

Ng, Yong-sang. Fa-ti, land of flowers. Canton's new year pilgrimage to its garden suburb. **CJ** 20 (1934) 184-186.

Ng, Yong-sang. The temple of no sorrows. A cantonese santa claus story. **CJ** 19 (1933) 280-284.

Oberle, A. Der hundertkopfdämon im volksglauben des westtales und des chinesisch-tibetanischen kontakt-gebietes im osttale von kuei-te in der provinz ch'ing-hai. In **Ethnographische beiträge aus der ch'inghai province (china)** Peking (1952) 222-233.

Osgood, Cornelius. **Village life in old china. A community study of kao yao, yunnan.** N.Y. (1963) Field work done 1938. See chap 18, Death and funerals, 288-300; chap 19, The shaman performs, 301-317; chap 20, Religious ideas, 320-327; chap 21 The ceremonial year, 328-345.

Palen, Lewis S. A guest of the empress of heaven. At home with gods and beggars in an ancient temple in manchuria. **Asia** 29 (1929) 50-53, 74-75, illus photos.

Parker, A.P. Some notes on the history of folk-lore of old shanghai. **JNCBRAS** 47 (1916) 85-102.

Porter, Henry D. A modern shantung prophet. **ChRec** 18 (1887) 12-21.

Potter, Jack M. Cantonese shamanism. In **RRCS** (1974) 207-232.

Potter, Jack M. Wind, water, bones and souls: the religious world of the cantonese peasant [ping shan, new territories of hong kong] **JOS** 8.1 (1970) 139-153. Repr in **CWayRel** (1973) 218-230.

Religion. In Stanford univ china project (comp) **East China, HRAF** 1 (1956) 344-387.

Religion. In Stanford univ china project (comp) **North china, HRAF** 1 (1956) 318-366.

Religion. In Stanford univ china project (comp) **Southwest china, HRAF** 1 (1956) 321-377.

Ross, John. Superstitions of manchuria. **ChRec** 8.6 (nov-dec 1877) 516-519.

Sadler, J. Chinese customs, and superstitions; or, what they do at amoy. **ChRev** 22 (1893-94) 755-758.

Schafer, Edward H. **Mao shan in t'ang times.** Boulder, colo (1980) 72 p, notes, diagram. SSCR monograph no 1.

Schroeder, D. Das herbstdankopfer der t'ujen im sining-gebiet, nordwestchina. **Anthropos** 37-40 (1942-45) 867-873.

Shryock, John K. **The temples of anking and their cults. A study of modern chinese religion.** Paris (1931) 203 p, app, bibliog, index, illus.

Social and religious life (in fukien) Chap 4 in **Fukien. A study of a province of china,** by the "Anti-cobweb club," Shanghai (1925) 23-33.

Sowerby, A. de C. A monster procession in shanghai [kuan-yin] **CJ** 21 (1934) 6-7.

Spring festival in shanghai. **FEER** 51 (3 mar 1966) 413-415, illus.

Stenz, Georg M. **Beiträge zur volkskunde süd-schantungs.** Leipzig (1907) 1116 p. Herausgegeben und eingeleitet von A. Conrady.

Swallow, Robert W. **Sidelights on peking life.** Peking (1927) xviii + 135 p, illus.

Tang, Peter S.H. Religion. In Far eastern and russian institute, univ washington (comp) **A regional handbook on northeast china, HRAF** 1 (1956) 227-243.

Thiel, Joseph. Der erdgeist-tempel als weiterent-wicklung des alten eralters. (Aus eigener feldforschung in süd-shantung) **Sinologica** 5.3 (1958) 150-155, illus 10 photos.

Treudley, Mary Bosworth. **The men and women of chung ho ch'ang.** Taipei (1972) See chap 9, Health and sanitation, 173-184; chap 11, The religion of the community, 204-238.

Trippner, J. Der wandernde medizingott. **Anthropos** 46 (1951) 801-807. In ch'ing-hai.

Volpert, Ant. Volksgebräuche bei der neujahrsfeier in ost-schantung (china) **Anthropos** 12-13 (1917-18) 1118-1119.

Wang, Lan. Tsl Margaret Mar. Chinese new year and its age-old customs. **Echo** 1.1 (jan 1971) 29-33, illus. Memories of tientsin.

Wen, Chung-i. The water gods and the dragon boats in south china. **ASBIE** 11 (1961) engl summ 121-124, 6 pl.

Wimsatt, G.B. Peking gate gods. **AArch** 26 (1928) 127-133.

Wong, C.M. The ancient customs of cantonese marriage. **ACSS** (1960-61) 60-65.

Woon, Yuen-fong. Social organization and ceremonial life of two multi-surname villages in hoi-p'ing county, south china, 1911-1949. **JHKBRAS** 17 (1977) 101-111.

27. DEITIES AND IMAGES — GENERAL

Amicus. Demons. **ICG** 5 (1818) 144-145.

Baity, Philip C. The genesis of gods in taiwanese folk religion: a preliminary analysis. In **AR-HR** (1974) 33-47.

Baity, Philip C. The ranking of gods in chinese folk religion. **AsFS** 36.2 (1977) 75-84.

Baity, Philip C. **Religion in a chinese town.** Taipei (1975) 307 p, gloss, ref cited, 2 maps. The town is tanshui, taiwan.

Buck, Samuel (pseud) The chinese spirit world. **Orient** 2.1 (1951) 31-34; 2.2 (1951) 21-24; 2.3 (1951) 31-34; 2.4 (1951) 22-25; 2.5 (1951) 26-28; 2.6 (1952) 32-35; 2.7 (1952) 39-42; 2.8 (1952) 31-33; 2.9 (1952) 31-34; 2.10 (1952) 28-30, 32; 2.11 (1952) 51-54; 2.12 (1952) 48-51.

Cèntre franco-chinois d'études sinologiques. **Exposition d'iconographie populaire: images rituelles du nouvel an.** Pekin (1942) xi + 238 p.

Day, Clarence Burton. **Chinese peasant cults. Being a study of chinese paper gods.** Shanghai (1940) 243 p, bibliog, app 1-10, index, illus. Repr taipei (1969)

Day, C.B. Paper gods for sale. **CJ** 7 (1927) 277-284. Repr in **PRPCC** (1975)

Dean, J.A. Consecrated images of china. **CJ** 21 (1934) 150-161.

Doolittle, Justus. Popular gods and goddesses. Chap 10 and 11 in author's **SLC** vol 1 (1865) 255-293.

Erkes, E. Gestaltwandel der götter in china. **FF** 21-22 (1947) 261-266.

Erkes, E. Idols in pre-buddhist china. **AA** 3 (1928) 5-12, illus.

Frei, G. Zum chinesischen gottesbegriff. **NZM** 1 (1945) 221-228.

Graham, David C. Image worship in china. **ChRec** 60 (1929) 513-514.

Graham, D.C. Strange gods in west china. **ChRec** 57.10 (oct 1926) 693-698.

Gray, John Henry. Ed William G. Gregor. **China.** London (1878) See vol 1, chap 5, Popular gods and goddesses, 143-165, illus sketches.

Greeley, Alexandra. Photos by Arthur Kan. Paper gods of old china. **Orientations** 9.6 (june 1978) 37-46, illus col photos of ma-chang.

Harrell, Stevan. When a ghost becomes a god. In **RRCS** (1974) 193-206.

Haydon, A. Eustace. **Biography of the gods.** N.Y. (1941) See chap 7, The gods of china, 166-198; see also chap 6, Buddhas and bodhisattvas, 126-165, passim.

Hayes, L. Newton. Gods of the chinese. **JNCBRAS** 55 (1924) 84-104.

Knodt, E. **Chinesische götter.** Berlin (1916)

Kuo, Li-cheng. Tsl Linda Lee. Paper gods. **Echo** 4.1 (jan 1974) 20-27, illus.

Lanjuinais, J.D. Notice du panthéon-chinois du docteur hager. **Moniteur** (1807)

Maclagen, P.J. Demons and spirits (chinese) In **HERE** 4, 576-578.

Mong, Lee Siow. Chinese polytheism. **ACSS** (1962-63) 15-17.

Montell, G. The idol factory of peking. **Ethnos** 19 (1954) 143-156.

Perzynski, F. Von chinas göttern. **Neue orient** 6 (1920) 192-196.

Perzynski, Friedrich. **Von china's göttern.** München (1920) 261 p, 80 pl.

Prunner, Gernot. **Papiergötter aus china.** Hamburg (1973) 85 p, 16 pl, text fig. Fr hamburgisches museum für völkerkunde.

Simmons, E.Z. Idols and spirits. **ChRec** 19.11 (nov 1888) 500-507.

The Soul of an idol. **Our missions** (1905) 30.

Stevens, Keith. Altar images from hunan and kiangsi. **JHKBRAS** 18 (1978) 41-48, illus b-&-w photos.

Stevens, Keith G. The craft of god carving in singapore. **JHKBRAS** 14 (1974) 68-75.

Thompson Laurence G. Objectifying divine power: some chinese modes. In Spencer J. Palmer (ed) **Deity & death,** brigham young univ (1978) 135-145.

28. SPECIFIC DEITIES AND CULTS

Adolph, Paul E. Shen nung, ancient pharmacologist and agriculturalist. **CJ** 24.2 (feb 1936) 68-72, illus map and photos.

Alexéiev, Basil M. **The chinese gods of wealth.** London (1928) 36 p, 24 pl.

Anderson, Eugene N. jr. The happy heavenly bureaucracy. Supernaturals and the hong kong boat people. In author's **ESCBP** (1972) 11-19.

Anderson, Mary M. Kuan yin: goddess of mercy. **Echo** 3.9 (oct 1973) 28-32, 55-56, illus col photos.

Ayscough, Florence. The chinese cult of ch'eng huang lao yeh. **JNCBRAS** 55 (1924) 131-155.

Bedford, O.H. Kuan yü, china's god of war. **CJ** 27 (1937) 127-130.

Behrsing, S. Tou-mu, eine chinesische himmelsgöttin. **OZ** 27 (1941) 173-176.

Blodget, Henry. The worship of the earth in china. **MRW** n.s. 10 (1897) 519-521. Same title in **ChRec** 25.12 (dec 1894) 563-566.

Blofeld, John. **Compassion yoga: the mystical cult of kuan yin.** London (1977) Alternative title: **Bodhisattva of compassion; the mystical tradition of kuan yin.** Boulder, colo (1978) 158 p, app, gloss, illus.

Bridgman, J.G. (tsl) Mythological account of some chinese deities, chiefly those connected with the elements. Translated from the siú shinki [sou shen chi] **ChRep** 19 (1850) 312-317.

Buck, Samuel (pseud) Gods and goddesses of navigation. **Orient** (apr 1952) 25-27.

Buck, Samuel (pseud) Why chinese women worship kwan yin. **Orient** 2.8 (1952) 18-20, 22.

Chamberlayne, John H. The chinese earth-shrine. **Numen** 13 (oct 1966) 164-182.

Chamberlayne, John H. The development of kuan yin, chinese goddess of mercy. **Numen** 9 (1962) 45-62.

Chan, Ping-leung. Chinese popular water-god legends and the hsi yu chi. In **Essays in chinese studies presented to professor lo hsiang-lin,** univ hong kong (1970) 299-317.

Chavannes, Édouard. Le jet des dragons. **Mémoires concernant l'asie orientale** 3. Paris (1919) 53-220, pl + reproductions of rubbings and texts.

Chavannes, Édouard. **Le t'ai chan. Essai de monographie d'un culte chinoise. Appendice: Le dieu du sol dans la chine antique.** Paris (1910) repr taipei (1970) 591 p, maps, pl, index.

Chen, Ying-chieh. She calls the winds and cures the sick. **FCR** 22.6 (june 1972) 19-22, illus photos. Re Matsu.

Chêng, Tê-K'un. Ch'ih yü: the god of war in han art. **OA** 4.2 (summer 1958) 45-54.

The Chinese new year. **Echo** 3.1 (jan 1973) 12-24, illus col and b-&-w photos. This is special issue on The chinese new year.

Chiu, Kun-liang. Tsl Robert Christensen. The city god's own theatrical troupe. **Echo** 6.1 (july 1976) 13-24, illus col photos.

Chung Kuei. **Echo** 6.7 (sept 1977) A special issue on this subject.

Cohen, Alvin P. Fiscal remarks on some folk religion temples in taiwan. **MS** 32 (1976) 85-158.

Collins, Valerie. Pilgrimage to peikang. **Echo** 1.5 (may 1971) 27-32, illus. Pilgrimage to matsu shrine.

Creel, Herrlee G. **The origins of statecraft in china.** Vol 1, **The western chou empire.** Univ chicago (1970) See app C, The origin of the deity t'ien, 493-506.

Day, Clarence B. Contemporary chinese cults. **FEQ** 6 (1947) 294-299.

Day, Clarence B. The cult of the hearth. **CJ** 10 (1929) 6-11. Repr in **PRPCC** (1975)

Day, Clarence B. Kuan-yin: goddess of mercy. **CJ** 10 (1929) 288-295. Repr in **PRPCC** (1975)

Day, Clarence B. Shanghai invites the god of wealth. **CJ** 8 (1928) 289-294. Repr in **PRPCC** (1975)

Day, Clarence B. Studying the kitchen god. **ChRec** 57 (1926) 791-796.

Drake, F.S. The tao yüan, a new religious and spirit-ualistic movement. **ChRec** 54 (mar 1923) 133-144.

Dudbridge, Glen. **The legend of miao-shan.** London (1978) 128 p, app, works cited, index. See rev by Anna Seidel, **JAS** 38.4 (aug 1979) 770f.

Dudgeon, John H. Medical divinities. In **DV** vol 2, pt 3, no 26, 318-319.

Dudgeon, John H. The worship of the moon. **ChRec** 13.2 (mar-apr 1882) 129-134.

Eastlake, F. Warrington. Equine deities. **TASJ** 11 (1883) 260-285.

Edgar, J.H. Notes on litholatry on the western frontiers of china. **CJ** 4 (1926) 105-110.

Edkins, Joseph. Account of kwan-ti, the god of war. **NCH** no 313 and 314, (26 july and 2 aug 1856) Repr in **Shanghai miscellany** (1857) no paging.

Edkins, Joseph. Place of hwang ti in early tauism. **ChRev** 15 (1886-87) 233-239.

Edkins, Joseph. Titles of tauist gods. **ChRev** 24.4 (1895-96) 199.

Edkins, Joseph. The use of the term . . . yu-hwang, addressed to mathetes. **ChRec** 25 (feb 1894) 91-92.

Edkins, Joseph. Worship of the god of fire. **ChRev** 18.2 (1889-90) 124-125.

Eitel, E.J. On dragon-worship. **NQ** 3.3 (mar 1869) 34-36.

Eliasberg, Danielle. **Le roman du pourfendeur de démons.** Paris (1976) 425 p, 1 pl. Re chung k'uei.

Erkes, E. Zum problem der weiblichen kuanyin. **AA** 9 (1946) 316-320, illus.

Esbroek, A. van. Les cultes préhistoriques de la chine. **Nouvelle Clio** 5 (1953) 195-196.

K.F. Die chinesische totencult. **OstL** 7.25 (1893) 548-549.

Fêng, H.Y. The origin of yü huang. **HJAS** 1 (1936) 242-250.

Feuchtwang, Stephan. School-temple and city-god. In **CLIC** (1977) 581-608.

Fielde, Adele M. **Pagoda shadows.** Boston (1890) See chap 13, The stone princess and her train, 102-107. Re Matsu.

Fisher, Tom. The peikang pai pai. **Echo** 3.3 (mar 1973) 21-25, illus col photos. Re Matsu festival.

Fong, Mary H. A probable second "chung k'uei" by emperor shun-chih of the ch'ing dynasty. **OA** n.s. 23.4 (winter 1977) 423-437. Re a painting at occidental college, los angeles.

D.G. The kitchen-god. **ChRev** 7 (1878-79) 418-422; 8 (1879-80) 388-390.

Goddess of mercy. **Orientations** 1.12 (dec 1970) 46, 1 illus. Re kuan yin.

Graham, David C. Original vows of the kitchen god. **ChRec** 61 (1930) 781-788; 62 (1931) 41-50, 110-116.

Graham, David C. Tree gods in szechwan province. **JWCBorderResS** 8 (1936) 59-61.

Groot, J.J.M. de. The idol kwoh sing wang. **ChRev** 7 (1878-79) 91-98.

Groot, J.J.M. de. Two gods of literature and a god of barbers. **ChRev** 9 (1880-81) 188-190.

Grootaers, Willem A. The hagiography of the chinese god chen-wu. (The transmission of rural traditions in chahar) **FS** 11 (1952) 139-182.

Grootaers, Willem A. The hutu god of wan-ch'üan (chahar) **SS** 7 (1948) 41-53.

Gutzlaff, Charles. Temple of teen how [t'ien hou] at meichow. **ChRep** 2 (1834) 563-565.

Hart, H.H. Kuan yin, the goddess of mercy. **AP** 11 (1940) 527-529.

Hegel, Robert. For the glory of kuan ti. **Echo** 2.6 (june 1972) 28-35, illus. Re festival at tahsi, taiwan.

Hegel, Robert. The seventh and eighth lords: china's divine bodyguards. **Echo** 1.7 (july-aug 1971) 14-19, illus.

Hodous, Lewis. The chinese church of the five religions. **JR** 4 (1924) 71-76.

Hodous, Lewis. The god of war. **ChRec** 44 (1913) 479-486.

Hodous, Lewis. The pearly emperor. **ChRec** 50.11 (nov 1919) 749-759.

Hommel, R.P. The idols of the thieves. **CJ** 10 (1929) 57-58.

Hosie, Lady. **Two gentlemen of china.** London (1929) See chap 26, Lares et penates, 286-299. Generalities on household gods and beliefs.

Hou, Ching-lang. The chinese belief in baleful stars. In **FT** (1979) 193-228.

Hsu, Shin-yi. The traditional ecology of the locust cult in traditional china. **Annals of the association of american geographers** 59.4 (dec 1969) 731-752.

Hudspeth, W.H. Tree worship. **CJ** 7 (1927) 206-208.

Huizenga, Lee S. Lü tsu and his relation to other medicine gods. **CMJ** 58 (1940) 275-283.

Hummel, Siegbert. Guan-yin in der unterwelt. **Sinologica** 2 (1950) 291-293, pl.

Hutson, James. Chia shen, the domestic altar. **JNCBRAS** 49 (1918) 93-100. Art 4 under heading: A chapter of folklore.

Johnston, R.F. The cult of military heroes in china. **NCR** 3 (feb 1921) 41-64; 3 (apr 1921) 79-91.

Kao, Chü-hsün. The ching lu shen shrines of han sword worship in hsiung-nu religion. **Central asiatic journal** 5 (1960) 221-232.

Koehn, Alfred. **Harbingers of happiness, the door gods of china.** Peiping (1948) 38 p, illus. Same title in **MN** 10 (1954) 81-106.

Lacouperie, Terrien de. The kitchen-god of china. **BOR** 8 (1895) 25-38.

Lacouperie, Terrien de. The silk goddess of china and her legend. **BOR** 4.12 (1890) 270-290; 5.1 (1891) 5-10.

Lecourt, H. Le dieu de l'âtre. **La chine** 70 (1924) 781-788.

Lee, Pi-cheng [Lü Pi-ch'eng] **Kwan yin's saving power; some remarkable examples of response to appeals for aid, made known to kwan yin by his devotees.** Oxford (1932) 39 p.

Lee, Tao. Ten celebrated physicians and their temple. **CMJ** 58 (1940) 267-274.

Lenz, Frank B. The house of longevity. **ChRec** 51 (1920) 170-176. Title ref to temple near nanchang, kiangsi, dedicated to a deified magistrate.

Li, Wei-tsu. On the cult of the four sacred animals (szu ta men) in the neighborhood of peking. **FS** 7 (1948) 1-94 (fox, weasel, hedgehog, snake)

Lin, Heng-tao. Tsl Tom McHugh. Door gods. **Echo** 6.3 (nov 1976) 12-20, 32, illus b-&-w and col photos.

Ling, Shun-sheng. The sacred places of chin and han periods. **ASBIE** 18 (1964) engl abrmt 136-142.

Liu, Chi-wan. The belief and practice of the wen-shen cult in south china and formosa. **PIAHA** (1963?) 715-722.

Liu, Chi-wan. Tsl Earl Wieman. Taiwan's plague gods. Part I: legends. **Echo** 6.6 (june 1977) 26-33, 50-51, illus.

Liu, Chi-wan. The temple of the gods of epidemics in taiwan. **ASBIE** 22 (1966) 93-95.

Liu, Mau-tsai. Der niang-niang kult in der mandschurei. **OE** 19.1/2 (dec 1972) 109-119.

Loewe, Michael. **Ways to paradise. The chinese quest for immortality.** London (1979) 270 p, illus, app, notes. Based on han dyn silk painting, TLV bronze mirrors, and representations of hsi wang mu.

Lou, Dennis Wing-sou. Rain worship among the ancient chinese and the nahua and maya indians **ASBIE** 4 (1957) 31-108.

Lyon, David N. Life and writings of the god of literature (wen ti ch'üan shu) **ChRec** 20 (1889) 411-420, 439-449.

MacGowan, John. The temple of the emperor of the city. Chap 10 in author's **L&S** (1909) 111-124. Re ch'eng-huang.

Maspero, Henri. The mythology of modern china. In J. Hackin et al, **Asiatic mythology,** n.y. (n.d.) 252-384, illus. Tsl fr french F.M. Atkinson.

Mayers, William F. On wen-ch'ang, the god of literature: his history and worship. **JNCBRAS** n.s. 6 (1869/70) 31-44.

McCartee, D.B. (tsl) Translation of an inscription upon a stone tablet commemorating the repairs upon the ch'eng hwang miau or temple of the tutelary deity of the city . . . in the department of lai-chôu, in the province of shantung, a.d. 1752. **JNCBRAS** 6 (1869-70) 173-177.

M'Clatchie, T. Phallic worship. **ChRev** 4 (1875-76) 257-261.

Miao, D.F. Ho ho, the gods of marriage. **CJ** 16 (1932) 112-114.

Miao, D.F. Some chinese paintings of deities. **CJ** 19.1 (july 1933) 6-8, 1 illus. Re Chung k'uei, t'ien kuan, sung tze kuan yin.

Mortier, F. Le dragon chinois, son culte et ses fêtes. **BSAB** 62 (1951) 136-140.

Mythological account of hiuen-tien shang-ti, the high ruler of the sombre heavens, with notices of the worship of shang ti among the chinese. **ChRep** 18.2 (feb 1849) 102-109. Fr sau shin ki (sou shen chi)

Mythological account of some chinese deities, chiefly those connected with the elements, translated from the siu shin ki (sou shen chi) **ChRep** 19.6 (june 1850) 312-317.

Nachbaur, Albert & Wâng Ngen Jông. **Les images populaires chinoises. Mîn kiên tchi t'oû siáng.** Pékin (1926) 92 1 col illus, 96 pieces (35 mounted col, 10folding col, 43 (3 col, 2 fold col) in 3 pockets. Sel of paper gate-gods, tui-tzu, w intro and explanations.

Nagel, August. Die sieben schwestern. **OstL** 25.46 (17 nov 1911) 425-426.

Ng, Yong-sang, Lung mu, the dragon mother. The story of the west river's own guardian angel. **CJ** 21.1 (july 1936) 18-20.

Ottewill, H.A. Note on the tu t'ien hui . . . held at chinkiang on the 31st may, 1917. **JNCBRAS** 49 (1918) 86-92. Art 3 under heading, A chapter of folklore.

Owen, G. Animal worship among the chinese. **ChRec** 18 (1887) 249-255, 334-346.

Parker, E.H. Medical deities. **ChRev** 17 (1888-89) 115.

Parker, E.H. Saints of literature. **ChRev** 15 (1886-87) 183-184.

Petrie, James B. Gods of healing. **Orientations** 3.12 (dec 1972) 49-50, 1 illus.

Petrie, James. Tu ti kung. **Echo** 2.9 (oct 1972) 38-42, 56, illus.

Pfizmaier, A. Ueber die schriften des kaisers des wen-tschang. **SAWW** 73 (1873) 329-384. Also publ sep, wien (1873) 58 p.

Power, Eileen. The little god. In E.R. Hughes (ed) **China body and soul,** london (1938) 107-115. Exposing a local god to sun to obtain rain, in peking area.

Priest, Alan. A note on kuan ti. **BMMA** 25 (1930) 271-272.

Roberts, John M., Chien Chiao & Triloki N. Pandey. Meaningful god sets from a chinese personal pantheon and a hindu personal pantheon. **Ethnology** 14.2 (apr 1975) 121-148. A technical quantitative study.

Rostovtzeff, M. I. Le dieu équestre dans la russe méridionale, en indo-scythie et en chine. **Seminarium kondakovianum** 1 (1927) 141-146.

Rotours, Robert des. Le culte des cinq dragon sous la dynastie des t'ang (618-907) In **MSPD** t 1 (1966) 261-280, 3 pl.

Rousselle, Erwin. Die krieger des neuen jahres. **Sinica** 17 (1942) 251-259

Rousselle, Erwin. Der kult der buddhistischen madonna kuan-yin. **NachrDGNVO** no 68 (1944) 17-23.

Rydh, H. Seasonal fertility rites and the death cult in scandinavia and china. **BMFEA** 3 (1931) 69-93.

Schafer, Edward H. **Pacing the void. T'ang approaches to the stars.** Univ california (1977) 352 p, illus, app, notes, bibliog, gloss, index.

Schafer, Edward H. The stove god and the alchemists. In **StAs** (1975) 261-266.

Schipper, Kristofer. Démonologie chinoise. In **Génies, anges et démons,** Paris (1971) 403-429. Sources orientales t 8. Coverage is limited to fukienese coast and taiwan.

Schlegel, G. Ma-tsu-po . . . koan-yin with the horsehead . . . **TP** 9.5 (1898) 402-406.

Schultze, O. Der chines. drache u.s. vereheung. **EMM** (1891) 13-27.

Seaman, Gary. **Temple organization in a chinese village.** Taipei (1978) 173 p, bibliog, char list, chronol, 2 maps. Re spirit-writing cult.

The seven lucky gods. **Orient** 2.8 (1952) 29-30.

S[huck] J.L. (tsl) Sketch of kwanyin, the chinese goddess of mercy. Translated from the sow shin ke [sou shen chi] **ChRep** 10 (1841) 185-191.

S[huck] J.L. (tsl) Sketch of teën fe [t'ien fei] or matsoo po, the goddess of chinese seamen. Translated from the sow shin ke [sou shen chi] **ChRep** 10 (1841) 84-87.

S[huck] J.L. (tsl) sketch of yuhwang shangte, one of the highest deities of chinese mythology. Translated from the sow shin ke [sou shen chi] **ChRep** 10 (1841) 305-309.

Smith, D. Howard. Saviour gods in chinese religion. In **SG** (1963) 174-190.

Smith, G. Elliott. Dragons and rain gods. **JRLB** 5 (1918-20) 317-380.

Sowerby, A. de C.S. Legendary figures in chinese art. Kuan yin, the goddess of mercy. **CJ** 14.1 (jan 1931) 3-4, illus.

Sowerby, A. de C.S. Legendary figures in chinese art. Kuan yü, the god of war. **CJ** 15.1 (july 1931) 4, frontisp, illus.

Sowerby, A. de C.S. Legendary figures in chinese art. K'uei hsing, the distributor of literary degrees. **CJ** 15.2 (aug 1931) 57-58, illus.

Sowerby, A. de C.S. Legendary figures in chinese art. Shou hsing, the god of longevity. **CJ** 14.3 (mar 1931) 109-110, illus.

Sowerby, A. de C.S. Legendary figures in chinese art. Ts'ai shen, the god of wealth. **CJ** 14.5 (may 1931) 210-211.

Spruyt, Dr. Les génies gardiens des portes. **Chine et sibérie** 2 (mai 1901) 193-195.

Stein, Rolf A. Un exemple de relations entre taoïsme et religion populaire. In **Fukui hakase festschrift: Tōyō bunka ronshū,** ?Tokyo (1969) 79-90.

Stevens, K.G. Chief marshall t'ien, patron of the stage, of musicians and wrestlers—east and south east china. **JHKBRAS** 15 (1975) 303-310.

Stevens, Keith. Chinese preserved monks. **JHKBRAS** 16 (1976) 292-297, bibliog, 2 photos. Cases cited of budd, taoists, and non-monks as well.

Steven, Keith. Three chinese deities: variations on a theme. (With special reference to overseas chinese communities in south east asia) **JHKBRAS** 12 (1972) 169-195. The deities are t'ai sui, fa chu kung and cheng ho.

Stevens, Keith. The immortal fan (cantonese: fan sin) **JHKBRAS** 18 (1978) 198-199.

Stevens, Keith. The saintly guo (sheng gong) **JHKBRAS** 18 (1978) 193-198.

Stevens, Keith. Under altars (hsia-t'an) **JHKBRAS** 17 (1977) 85-100, pl 20-31 at end of vol.

Sung, Lung-fei. Two examples of the pilgrimage activities in taiwan. **ASBIE** 31 (1971) engl summ 129-133, 20 p pl. Re pilgrimages to matsu temples.

Sung, Shi. Tsl Earl Wieman. On the road to peikang. **Echo** 3.3 (mar 1973) 26-33, 55-56, illus col-photos. Re Matsu.

Suzuki, D.T. The kuan-yin cult in china. **EB** 6 (1935) 339-353.

Tay, C.N. Kuan-yin: the cult of half asia. **HR** 16.2 (nov 1976) 147-177.

The temple of the supreme ruler, near sung wong toi, kowloon. **JHKBRAS** 19 (1979) 202-204.

Thiel, P.I. Der erdgeist-tempel als weiterentwicklung des alten erdalters. (Aus eigener feldforschung in süd-shantung) **Sinologica** 5.3 (1958) 150-155, 10 photos.

Thompson, Laurence G. The cult of matsú. In author's **CWayRel** (1973) 196-201.

Thompson, Laurence G. Yu ying kung: the cult of bereaved spirits in taiwan. In **StAs** (1975) 267-277.

Tran-Ham-Tan. Étude sur le van-mien [wen-miao] de ha-noi (temple de la littérature) **BEFEO** 45 (1951) 89-117, planche.

Trippner, J. Der wandernde medizingott. **Anthropos** 46 (1951) 801-807.

Tsai, Wen-hui. Historical personalities in chinese folk religion: a functional interpretation. In **LL&R** (1979) 23-42.

Tu, John Er-wei. The moon-mythical character of the god yu-huang. In **ExHum** (1976) 501-510.

Volpert, P.A. Tsch'öng huang [ch'eng huang] **Anthropos** 5.5/6 (sept-dec 1910) 991-1026.

Wen, Chung-i. The water gods and the dragon-boats in south china. **ASBIE** 11 (1961) engl summ 121-124, 6 pl.

Werner, E.T.C. Chinese composite deities. **JNCBRAS** 54 (1923) 250-267.

Wieman, Earl. The gods of nankunshen. **Echo** 3.6 (june 1973) 16-25, 54, illus.

Wiethoff, Bodo. Der staatliche ma-tsu kult. **ZDMG** 116.2 (1966) 311-357.

Williams, E.T. The worship of lei tsu, patron saint of silk workers. **JNCBRAS** 66 (1935) 1-14.

Williams, S. Wells. Mythological account of hiuen-tien shangti, the high ruler of the sombre heavens, with notices of the worship of shangti among the chinese. **ChRep** 18 (1849) 102 et seq.

Wimsatt, G.B. Peking gate gods. **AArch** 26 (1928) 127-133.

Wong, K. Chimin. Hua t'o, the god of surgery. **CMJ** 41 (1927)

Wright, A.R. Chinese tree-worship and trial by ordeal. **Folk-lore** 22 (1911) 233-234.

Wright, A.R. Tree worship in china. **Folklore** 17 (1906) 190.

Wu, Linda. Home, grand auntie, let's go home! **Echo** 4.4 (apr 1974) 19-38, 49-56, illus. Pilgrimage to peikang matsu shrine.

Wu, Ping-chung. Matsu, goddess of the sea. **Echo** 1.1 (jan 1971) 12-17, illus.

Wu ti. Die kriegsgott d. chinesen. **OstL** 13 (1899) 50.

Yeh, Sui Yen. Ma chu—the goddess of sailors. **ACSS** (1964-67) 35-38, 2 photos.

29. RELIGIOUS CALENDAR— FESTIVALS—CUSTOMS

Adam, Maurice. **Us et coutumes de la région de pékin d'après le je sia sieou wen k'ao, ch. 146-147-148.** Pékin (1930) viii + 48 p, pl.

Aijmer, Göran. Ancestors in the spring. The qingming festival in central china. **JHKBRAS** 18 (1978) 59-82.

Aijmer, Göran. **The dragon boat festival in the hunan and hupeh plains, central china; a study in the ceremonialism of the transplantation of rice.** Stockholm (1964) 135 p, bibliog.

Allen, G.W. New year decorations in china. **Discovery** 3 (1922) 188-190.

Anderson, E.N. jr. The changing tastes of the gods: chinese temple fairs in malaysia. **AsFS** 36.1 (1977) 19-30.

Anderson, Mary & Kuo Li-cheng. Tung chih. **Echo** 4.11 (dec 1974) 5-11, illus.

Bateson, Joseph H. Festivals and fasts (chinese) In **HERE** 5, p 843.

Beatty, John. Chinese new year and the lion dance. **Papers in anthropology,** univ oklahoma, 15.2 (fall 1974) 102-116.

Bell of antermony. Fêtes données à la cour à l'occasion de la nouvelle année, 1721. **La chine** 12 (1922) 215-220.

Best wishes for the new year of the horse. **FCR** 28.1 (jan 1978) col photo pic story.

Bitton, W. Nelson. Some chinese feasts and the christian attitude towards them. **ChRec** 41.4 (apr 1910) 269-281.

Blake, C. Fred. Death and abuse in marriage laments: the curse of chinese brides. **AsFS** 37.1 (1978) 13-33.

Bodde, Derk. **Annual customs and festivals in peking, as recorded in the yen-ching sui-shih-chi by tun li-ch'en.** Peiping (1936) repr univ hong kong (1965) xxii + 147, 6 app, bibliog, index, illus.

Bodde, Derk. **Festivals in classical china. New year and other annual observances during the han dynasty 206 b.c.-a.d.220.** Princeton univ (1975) xvi + 439 p, chronol table, bibliog, index, illus 7 pl.

Boltz, William G. Philological footnotes to the han new year rites. **JAOS** 99.3 (july-sept 1979) 423-439. Rev art on Bodde's **Festivals in classical china** q.v.

Bone, C. The chinese moon festival. **EA** 5 (1906) 29-32.

Bone, C. The religious festivals of the cantonese. **ChRec** 20 (1889) 367-371, 391-393.

Bouillard, G. Calendrier chinois et européen à l'usage des residents de pékin. **La chine** (all 1922) 10: 69-76; 12: 282-284; 14: 453-460; 16: 603-608; 18: 721-723; 20: 881-882; 22: 1081-1086; 24: 1205-1209; 26: 1353-1356; 28: 1529-1532; 29: 1583-1586.

Bouillard, G. La nouvelle année chinoise, usages et coutumes. **La chine** 11 (1922) 127-181.

Bouillard, G. Les pèlerinages de la première quinzaine de la première lune. **La chine** 12 (15 fev 1922) 193-213.

Bouillard, G. Usages et coutumes à pékin durant la (1) 2e lune. **La chine** 35 (1923) 117-136; (2) 3e lune: 37 (1923) 249-264; (4) 4e lune: 38 (1923) 229-311; (5) 5e lune: 18 (1922) 703-720; (6) 6e lune: 39 (1923) 391-405; (7) 7e lune: 40 (1923) 469-479; (8) 8e lune: 26 (1922) 1335-1355; (9) 9e lune: 29 (1922) 1573-1582; (10) 10e lune: 30 (1922) 1639-1651; (11) 11e lune: 32 (1922) 1791-1796.

Bredon, Juliet. **Chinese new year festivals: a picturesque monograph of the rites, ceremonies and observances in relation thereto.** Shanghai (1930) 29 p.

Bredon, Juliet and Igor Mitrophanow. **The moon year. A record of chinese customs and festivals.** Shanghai (1927) 508 p, bibliog, chart, index, illus.

Bryson, Mrs M. I. **Home-life in china.** NY (n.d.—late 19th century?) See Pt 1, chap 8, Chinese festivals and holidays, 132-150. Juvenile level.

Buck, Samuel (pseud) (a series in **Orient**) The chinese first moon — new year, 1.7 (feb 1951) 22-24; The chinese second moon — earth spirits, 1.8 (mar 1951) 22-24; The chinese third moon – ch'ing ming, 1.9 (apr 1951) 22-24; The chinese fourth moon — buddhism, 1.10 (may 1951) 17-19; The chinese fifth moon — dragon boat festival, 1.11 (june 1951) 20-22; The chinese sixth moon — china's methuselah, 1.12 (july 1951) 17-20; The chinese eighth moon — mid-autumn, 1.2 (sept 1950) 18-20; The chinese ninth moon — the double ninth, 1.2 (sept 1950) 20-23; The chinese tenth moon, 1.4 (nov 1950) 20-22; The chinese eleventh moon —astrological influences, 1.5 (dec 1950) 20-22; The chinese twelfth moon — oracles, 1.6 (jan 1951) 20-22.

Buck, Samuel (pseud) Origin of the dragon boat. **Orient** 2.11 (1952) 37-40.

Burkhardt, Valentine R. **Chinese creeds and customs.** Hong kong. Vol 1 (1953) 181 p; vol 2 (1955) 201 p; vol 3 (1958) 164 p; each vol with index, illus.

Carleton, Mary Sing-Gieo. **Chinese festivals.** N.p. (n.d.) 31 p, illus.

Cêntre franco-chinois d'études sinologiques. **Exposition d'iconographie populaire: images rituelles du nouvel an.** Pekin (1942) xi + 238 p.

Chao, Wei-pang. The dragon-boat race in wu-ling, hunan. **FS** 2 (1943) 1-18.

Chao, Wei-pang. Games at the mid-autumnal festival in kuangtung. **FS** 3.1 (1944) 1-16.

Charpentier, Léon. Les fêtes du nouvel an et du renouveau en chine. **NR** n.s. 8 (1901) 161-176.

Chen, Tsu-lung. Note on the wedding ceremonies and customs observed in tun-huang in the second half of the ninth century. **E&W** n.s. 22.3/4 (sept-dec 1972) 313-327.

Cheng, Alfred (tsl) The year of the tiger. Translated from the chinese farmers' almanac. **Echo** 4.1 (jan 1974) 45-47, 61-68, illus.

Cheng, Homer Hui-ming. **Chinese religious festivals in singapore.** Singapore, china society annùal publication (1949).

Ch'i hsi festival. **Echo** 4.8 (sept 1974) Special issue on this festival.

Chinese customs and superstitions. **EA** 4 (1905) 298-300. See further same title in **ibid,** 5 (1906) 99-100.

Chinese farmers' almanac—daily instructions. A series in **Echo**: 3.1 (jan 1973) 26-33; 3.3 (mar 1973) 12-14; 3.8 (sept 1973) 12-14; 3.9 (oct 1973) 9-11; 3.10 (nov 1973) 9-11; 3.11 (dec 1973) 11-13; 4.1 (jan 1974) 5-7; 4.2 (feb 1974) 9-11; 4.3 (mar 1974) 11-13; 4.4 (apr 1974) 9-11; 4.5 (may 1974) 7-9; 4.7 (july-aug 1974) 7-9; Enter the year of the dragon, tsl fr chinese farmers' almanac by Melinda Liu, 5.10 (nov 1975) 9-11, 47-52, illus.

Chinese new year—solar and lunar. **FCR** 21.1 (jan 1971) 35-42. Picture story.

Das Chinesische neujahr und seine feier. **OstL** 18 (1904) 267-269.

Chu, Liang-cheng. New year and gods **FCR** 11.2 (1961) 13-16.

Cormack, Annie. **Chinese birthday, wedding, funeral, and other customs.** Peking (1922) 220 p, pl. enl ed (1923) and (1927) 3rd ed repr taipei (1974)

Cormack, Annie. **Chinese births, weddings and deaths.** Peking (1923) 35 p, pl.

Cormack, Annie. **Everyday customs in china.** Edinburgh and london (1935) 264 p, illus.

Daudin,P. Coutumes du nouvel an chinois. **FA** 6 (1950) 864-867.

Davis, A.R. The double ninth festival in chinese poetry: a study of variations upon a theme. In **Wen-lin** (1968) 45-64.

Day, Clarence B. The new year ceremonials of chow-wang-miao. **CJ** 32 (1940) 6-12. Repr **PRPCC** (1975)

Dols, J. Fêtes et usages pendant le courant d'une année dans la province de kan-sou (chine) **AL** 1 (1937) 203-274.

Doolittle, Justus. Bethrothal and marriage. Chap 2 and 3 in author's **SLC** vol 1 (1865) 41-91.

Doolittle, Justus. Established annual customs and festivals. Chap 1, 2, and 3 of author's **SLC** vol 2 (1865) 13-90.

Doré, Henri. **Manuel des superstitions chinoises.** Shanghai, 2e ed (1936) 221 p.

Dukes, Edwin J. The chinese new year. Chap 4 in author's **ELC** (1885) 84-100.

Dymond, F.J. The feast of the seventh moon. **EA** 2.4 (dec 1903) 376-378.

Eberhard, Wolfram. Auspicious marriages. **Sociologus** 13.1 (1963) 49-53. Repr in **SCFRE** (1970) 201-207.

Eberhard, Wolfram. **Chinese festivals.** N.Y. (1952) new ed taipei (1972) 152 p, illus.

Eberhard, Wolfram. Chinesische volkskalendar und buddhistischer tripitaka. **OL** 40.6 (1937) 346-349.

Eder, Matthias. Spielgeräte und spiele im chinesischen neujahrsbrauchtum, mit aufzeigung magischer bedeutungen. **FS** 6.1 (1947) 1-207.

Eigner, J. Celebrating the ancient dragon boat festival. **CJ** 27 (1937) 8-10.

Eitel, E.J. (comp) **Eastern religious kalendar for . . . 1882.** Hong kong (1881)

Elegant, Robert (text) & Brian Brake (photos) Text: Men, gods and spirits; picture essay: Buns for the spirits. In Elegant, Brake, & Editors of Time-Life Books, **Hong Kong,** amsterdam (1977) 95-127.

Ewer, F.H. and J. Doolittle. Native fete and natal days observed at canton and foochow. In **DV** vol 2, pt 3, no 30.

Fabre. A. Avril au pays des aïeux. **CCS** 8 (1935) Ancestor worship and burial practices at ch'ing ming, specifically in shun-te, kuangtung.

Fêng, Han-yi and J.K. Shryock. Marriage customs in the vicinity of i-ch'ang. **HJAS** 13 (1950) 362-430.

Festivals and pai pais. **Echo** 6.5 (feb 1977) 70.

For man's humanity to man. **FCR** 28.7 (july 1978) col photo pic story on dragon-boats and races.

Friend, Robert. Traditional new year pictures mirror the changes in china. **EH** 17.4 (apr 1978) 34-37, illus.

Goodwin, P. Dragon boat festival. **GM** 33 (1961) 479-485.

Graham, Dorothy. The first day of the first moon [in peking] **CW** 122 (jan 1926) 487-492.

Grainger, A. Permanent values in chinese festivals. **ChRec** 49.11 (nov 1918) 732-736.

Granet, Marcel. Coutumes matrimoniales de la chine antique. **TP** 13 (1912) 416-588; repr **ESC** (1953)

Gray, John Henry. Ed William G. Gregor. **China.** London (1878) See vol 1, chap 11, Festivals, 278-328, illus sketches.

Groot, J.J.M. de. **Les fêtes annuellement célébrées à émoui (amoy) Étude concernant la religion populaire des chinois.** Being **AMG** 1 and 2, paris (1886) 2 vol. Tsl fr dutch C.G. Chavannes.

Hegel, Robert. Dragon boat festival. **Echo** 1.5 (may 1971) 42-44, 49, illus.

Hell, H. (E. de T.) Une fête chinoise. **RIC** 14 (dec 1910) 607-609.

Highbaugh, Irma. **Family life in west china.** N.Y,. (1948) xi + 240 p.

Hodous, Lewis. The ch'ing ming festival. **JNCBRAS** 46 (1915) 58-60.

Hodous, Lewis. The feast of cold food. **NCR** 4 (1922) 470-473.

Hodous, Lewis. **Folkways in china.** London (1929) 248 p, illus, list of works consulted, list of chin names, index.

Hodous, Lewis. The great summer festival of china as observed in foochow: a study in popular religion. **JNCBRAS** 43 (1912) 69-80.

Hodous, Lewis. The kite festival in foochow. **JNCBRAS** 49 (1918) 76-81. Being art 1 under heading, A chapter of folklore.

Hodous, Lewis. The reception of spring observed in foochow, china. **JAOS** 42 (1922) 53-58.

Hooyman and Vogelaar. Relation abrégée du tien-bing, vulgairement appelé la fête de morts, chez les chinois de batavia. **JA** 2 (1823) 236-243. Tirée des **Mémoires de la société de batavia** 6 (1792) et trad du hollandais.

Hoy, William. Native festivals of the california chinese. **Western folklore** 7 (1948) 240-250.

Hummel, Margaret G. **Fun and festival from china.** N.Y. (1948) 48 p, illus.

Imbault-huart, Camille. La fête de la miautomne et du lapin lunaire. **JA** 8e sér, 5 (jan 1885) 71-73.

Imbault-Huart, Camille. Origine de la fête du double-neuf. **JA** 8e sér, 3 (jan 1884)

Imbert, Henri. **Poésies chinoises sur les fêtes annuelles.** Pekin (1924) 34 p, illus.

Jones, E.E. The attitude of the chinese church toward non-christian festivals. **ChRec** 47.3 (mar 1916) 161-169.

Langlois, Jack. Festival of the lonely ghosts. **Echo** 3.7 (july-aug 1973) 16-21, illus.

Lanöe, F. Tsing ming. **La chine** 65 (1924) 313-314.

Lay, G. Tradescant. **The chinese as they are.** London (1841) See chap 21, Festivities and processions, 192-203.

Lee, Jon. Some chinese customs and beliefs in california. **CFQ** 2 (1943) 191-204.

Leung, A.K. Peiping's happy new year. **NGM** 70 (1936) 749-792.

Lin Yueh-hwa. **The golden wing. A sociological study of chinese familism.** London (1948) repr westport, conn. (1974) On betrothal and wedding see chap 4, 36-48; on major festivals see loc. cit.

Liu, Chiang. The mid-autumn festival. **ACSS** (1956) 2-8.

Liu, Chiang. Religion, funeral rites, sacrifices and festivals in kirin. **ChRec** 65 (1934) 227-238. Same title in **ACSS** (1958-59) 8-20.

Lo, Dorothy and Leon Comber. **Chinese festivals in malaya.** Singapore (1958) 66 p, bibliog, indexes, illus.

Lum, Peter. **Great day in china: the holiday moon.** London and n.y. (1964) 32 p, illus.

Lunar new year festival. **CN** 9.2 (spring 1971) 23.

Maclagan, P.J. Folk-lore. Account of some customs observed in the first moon in the village of yü-lu-hsiang, ch'ao-chou-fu, chieh-yang-hsien. **ChRev** 23 (1894-95) 120.

Marriage beyond the grave. **CJ** 35.2 (aug 1941) 45-46.

Martin, Ilse. Frühlingsdoppelsprüche . . . von 1942 an pekinger haustüren. **FS** 2 (1943) 89-174.

McOmber, Douglas. Considering the festival of the fifth day of the fifth month. **Journal of the society for asian studies** 3 (apr 1970) 17-29.

Montuclat. l'Année du rat. **La chine** 58 (1924) 147-156.

Morgan, Carole. **Le tableau du boeuf du printemps. Étude d'une page de l'almanach chinois.** Paris (1980) 292 p, 17 fig, croquis.

Morgan, Harry T. **Chinese festivals.** Los angeles (1941) 16 p, illus.

Mori, S. The festivals of the 15th of the first month in the chinese calendar. **Journal of the oriental society of kyoto** 22 (1954) 168-180.

Nagel, August. Die sieben schwestern. **OstL** 25.46 (17 nov 1911) 425-426.

Ng, Yong-sang. Fa-ti, land of flowers. Canton's new year pilgrimage to its garden suburb. **CJ** 20 (1934) 184-186.

Ottewill, H.A. Notes on the tu t'ien hui, held at chinkiang on the 31st may 1917. **JNCBRAS** 49 (1918) 86-92.

Otto, P. Some notes on chinese festivals and their observances. **EA** 2 (1903) 81-94.

Parish, William L. & Martin King Whyte. The annual cycle of festivals, chap 14 in authors' **VFCC** (1978) 273-297.

Prints to welcome the new year. **Echo** 3.1 (jan 1973) 38-43, illus.

Richard, Timothy. **Calendar of the gods in china.** Shanghai (1916) 37 p.

Rousselle, Erwin. Chinesische neujahrsbräuche. **Sinica** 12 (1937) 1-17.

Rousselle, Erwin. Die krieger als torwache des neuen jahres. **Sinica** 17 (1942) 251-259.

Saso, Michael. Chinese new year's customs in taiwan. **JCS** 4 (1964) 37-52.

Saso, Michael. **Taiwan feasts and customs. A handbook of the principal feasts and customs of the lunar calendar on taiwan.** Hsinchu (1965) 95 p.

Schlegel, G. La fête de fouler le feu célébrée en chine et par les chinois à java, le treize du troisième mois, anniversaire du 'grand dieu protecteur de la vie' (pao chîng [sheng] ta ti) **IAE** 9 (1896) 193-195, 1 pl.

Schröder, Dominik. Ying-hsi, die bewillkommnung der freude. **Anthropos** 41/44.1/3 (1946-49) 185-192.

Schwarz, Ernst. Das drachenbootfest und die "neun lieder." **Wissenschaftliche zeitschrift der humbolt-universität zu berlin, gesellschafts-und sprachwissenschaftliche reihe** 16 (1967) 443-452.

Scidmore, E.R. The moon's birthday. **Asia** 21 (1921) 251-254, 262, 264.

Shen, Ting-su. The chinese new year. **FCR** 11.2 (1961) 5-12.

Smith, Arthur H. The new year in china. **OC** 14.1 (jan 1900) 43-45. Extract fr author's **Village life in china** (1899)

Sowerby, Arthur de C. The chinese lunar calendar. **CJ** 12.1 (jan 1930) 2-4; 12.2 (feb 1930) 61-64; 12.3 (mar 1930) 128; 12.4 (apr 1930) 179-180; 12.6 (june 1930) 316-317; 13.1 (july 1930) 3-4; 13.2 (aug 1930) 54; 13.3 (sept 1930) 103; 13.5 (nov 1930) 243-244; 13.6 (dec 1930) 291-292.

Sowerby, Arthur de C. The chinese yuletide. **CJ** 7.6 (dec 1927) 271-273. Compares aspects of christmas and chin new yr, 1 col illus.

Sowerby, Arthur de C. Crossing the year. **CJ** 3 (1925) 53-57.

Sowerby, Arthur de C. The dragon boat festival. **CJ** 20 (1934) 305-306.

Splitter, Henry W. The chinese feast of lanterns. **JAFL** 63 (oct-dec 1950) 438-443.

Spring festival in shanghai. **FEER** 51 (3 mar 1966) 413-415, illus.

Stuart, J. Leighton. A glance at chinese worshippers. **MRW** n.s. 4 (1891) 531-533.

Sun, Chan-ko. The spring festival. **PC** 5 (1953) 19-20

Sung, H.C. Der 7.7 — ein chinesischer festag. **Sinologica** 3.1 (1951) 50-51.

Sung, Shi. Ch'ing-ming. **Echo** 1.3 (mar 1971) 33-37, illus.

Sung, Shi. Tsl Robert Hegel. The day they launched the floating lanterns. **Echo** 2.7 (july-aug 1972) 30-35, 53-54, illus col photos. Re festival of 7th month 15th day in chupei, near hsinchu.

Superstitions and customs of the chinese. **JIA** n.s. 2 (1888) 349-363.

Swallow, Robert W. **Sidelights on peking life.** Peking (1927) xviii + 135 p. illus.

Tao, Frank. The spring festival. **China magazine** 18 (feb 1948) 29-32.

Thompson, Laurence G. P'eng-hu in mid-ch'ing times according to the p'eng-hu chi lüeh of hu chien-wei. **MS** 30 (1972-73) 166-219. For festival calendar see 196-202.

Tien, Tsung. A diabolical almanac (new type almanac) **Orient** 3.8 (1953) 22-23.

Tien, Tsung. The year of the dragon. **Orient** 2.7 (1952) 24-26.

Tien, Tsung. Year of the water snake. **Orient** 3.7 (1953) 18-19, 36.

Tonn, W.Y. Chinese new year. **CJ** 34 (1941) 6-8.

Tuan wu. **Echo** 4.6 (june 1974) Special issue devoted almost entirely to this festival, illus.

Volpert, Ant. Volksgebräuche bei der neujahrsfeier in ost-schantung (china) **Anthropos** 12-13 (1917-18) 1118-1119.

Wang, Chin-hsing. Lantern festival. **Echo** 1.2 (feb 1971) 33-37, illus.

Wang, Lan. Tsl Margaret Mar. Chinese new year and its age-old customs. **Echo** 1.1 (jan 1971) 29-33, illus.

Wei, T.F. Chinese festivals. **CJ** 34 (1941) 106-111.

Wen, Ch'ung-i. The water gods and the dragon-boats in south china. **ASBIE** 11 (1961) engl summ 121-124, 6 pl.

Williams, E.T. The calendar and its festivals. Chap 10 in author's **CYT** (1928) 205-222.

Wolfers, M. Spring festivals in china. **CR** 169 (may 1946) 299-302.

Wong, C.S. **A cycle of chinese festivities.** Singapore (1967) xv + 204 p, notes, bibliog, index, illus.

Worcester, G.R.F. The origin and observance of the dragon boat festival in china. **Mariner's mirror** 42 (1956) 127-131, illus.

Wu, Linda. Race of the dragons. **Echo** 5.6 (june 1975) 7-17. Picture-essay, some pic in col. Re Tuan-wu rivalry betw 2 villages in ilan.

Yao, Meng-chia & Lincoln Kaye. Grappling with the ghosts. **Echo** 6.2 (oct 1976) 13-18, 60, illus. Re chung-yüan festival, as it was observed in taiwan in past, and is observed in hengchun today.

Yen, Alsace. Shang-ssu festival and its myths in china and japan. **AsFS** 34.2 (1975) 45-86. Purification rite.

Young, W. The feast of lanterns at padang (sumatra) **ChRev** 9 (1880-81) 320-321.

Yu, Feng. New year pictures. **PC** 5 (1953) 12-14.

30. TEMPLES AND MOUNTAINS

Allen, C.F.R. (tsl) Fifty-six temple oracles or stanzas. From a tauist temple at foochow. In **DV** vol 2, pt 3, no 58, p 507-512.

Allen, C.F.R. (tsl) Twenty-eight temple oracles or stanzas. From a temple at foochow. In **DV** vol 2, pt 3, no 57, p 504-507.

Alley, Rewi. I-shing and its sacred caves. **CJ** 26.3 (mar 1937) 131-137, illus photos. On lake t'ai-hu near wusih.

Alley, Rewi & R. Lapwood. The sacred mountains of china: heng shan, the taoist stronghold of the north. **CJ** 22.4 (apr 1935) 175-181, illus maps, photos.

Alley, Rewi. Some temples in the western hills [near peking] **EH** 3.9, 27-30, illus.

Alley, Rewi. Sung shan, the central peak [hunan] **EH** 4.7 (1965) 33-36, illus.

Andersson, John Gunnar. **The dragon and the foreign devils.** Boston (1928) See chap 9, The land of temples, 101-112.

Ayscough, Florence. Shrines of history. Peak of the east — t'ai shan. **JNCBRAS** 48 (1917) 57-70.

Baker, Dwight C. **T'ai shan. An account of the sacred eastern peak of china.** Shanghai (1925) repr taipei (1971) xx + 225 p, app, index, map, illus.

Beanlands, Canon. Worship in a chinese joss-house. **TheE&TheW** 2 (1904) 293-305.

Bergen, Paul D. A visit to t'ai shan. **ChRec** 19.12 (dec 1888) 541-546.

Bertolucci, Guiliano. Reminiscences of the mao-shan. **E&W** 24.3/4 (sept-dec 1974) 403-415, illus. Re his visit in summer 1947.

Bouillard, Georges. **Pékin et ses environs, cinquième série, le temple de la terre, les temples du soleil et de la lune, le temple de l'agriculture.** Peking (1923) [44 p] repr fr **la chine** 33, 34.

Bouillard, Georges. **Pékin et ses environs, huitième série, les temples autour du hsiang shan: tien t'ai sze, wo fo sze.** Peking (1924) repr fr **la chine** 48, 49, 51.

Bouillard, Georges. **Pékin et ses environs, première série, le yang shan et ses temples.** Peking (1921) [44p] repr fr **la chine** 3-6.

Bouillard, Georges. **Pékin et ses environs, quatorzième série, environs sud-ouest: she king shan, yün kiü sze, tung yu sze, si yü sze.** Peking (1924) [74 p] repr fr **la chine** (1923)

Bouillard, Georges. **Péking et ses environs, quatrième série, le temple du ciel.** Peking (1923) [100 p] repr fr **la chine** 27, 28, 31.

Bouillard, Georges. **Péking et ses environs, quinzième série, environs sud-ouest: tien k'ai shan, ku shan, shang fang shan, tow shuai sze et les grottes de yün shui t'ung.** Peking (1924) [54 p] repr fr **la chine** 56-59.

Bouillard, Georges. **Pékin et ses environs, sixième série, le temple de pi yün sze.** Peking (1923) [22 p] repr fr **la chine** 44.

Bourne, F.S.A. **The lo-fou mountains: an excursion.** Hong kong (1895) 48 p.

Braekhus, K. & H.D. Dixon. Over anhuei mountains. **CJ** 27.6 (dec 1937) 296-301, illus photos. From hangchow to chiu hua shan via t'ien mu shan and huang shan.

Bretschneider, Emil. Celebrated mountains of china. **JNCBRAS** 16 (1882) 223-228.

Brim, John A. Village alliance temples in hong kong. In **RRCS** (1974) 93-104.

Cammann, Schuyler. On the decoration of modern temples in taiwan and hongkong. **JAOS** 88.4 (1968) 785-790. Criticism of W. Eberhard: Topics and moral values in chinese temple decorations q.v.

Cauvin, Dr. Excursion au tai-chann et au tombeau de confucius. **RGI** (août-nov 1884; janv-nov 1885; janv 1887)

Chambers, William. **Designs of chinese buildings.** London (1757) Facsimile repr farnborough, engl (1969) See: Of the temples of the chinese, 1-5; Of the towers [taa = t'a, or pagodas] 5-6; pl 1-5.

Chavannes, Édouard. **Le t'ai chan. Essai de mono-graphie d'un culte chinois. Appendice: Le dieu du sol dans la chine antique.** Paris (1910) repr taipei (1970) 591 p, maps, pl, index.

Cohen, Alvin P. A chinese temple keeper talks about chinese folk religion. **AsFS** 36.1 (1977) 1-17.

Comber, Leon. **Chinese temples in singapore.** Singapore (1958) 110 p, illus.

Cooper, R.F. **Welcome to hong kong temples.** HK (1977) 95 p, illus col photos and drawings. Guide to 9 temples.

Day, Clarence B. The new year ceremonials of chow-wang-miao. **CJ** 32 (1940) 6-12. Repr **PRPCC** (1975)

Demiéville, Paul. La montagne dans l'art littéraire chinois. **FA** 20 (1965-66) 7-32, pl.

Doub, William. Mountains in early taoism. In M.C. Tobias & H. Drasdo (ed) **The mountain spirit,** woodstock, ny (1979) 129-135.

Drake, F.S. The taoists of lao-shan. **ChRec** 65 (1934) 238-245; 308-318.

Dunlap, Eva Wyman. The chin shan tsui temple: peitaiho. **JNCBRAS** 71 (1940) 67-71.

Eberhard, Wolfram. Chinesische volksliteratur in chinesischen volkstempeln. In Giorgios A. Megas (ed) **IV intl congress for folk-narrative research in athens, lectures and reports,** athens (1965) 100-104. Rev engl tsl in **SCFRE** (1970) 183-189.

Eberhard, Wolfram. Temple-building activities in medieval and modern china — an experimental study. **MS** 23 (1964) 264-318. Repr in author's **MSVC,** taipei (1971)

Eberhard, Wolfram. Topics and moral values in chinese temple decorations. **JAOS** 87 (1967) 22-32. Repr in author's **MSVC,** taipei (1971) See above item by Schuyler Cammann: On the decoration of modern temples in taiwan and hongkong, which is a criticism of Eberhard's art; and further, Eberhard's rejoinder in **JAOS** 88.4 (1968) 790-792.

Edkins, Joseph. T'ai shan, the legendary centre of tauist belief in a future state. **ChRev** 18 (1889-90) 61-62.

S.v.F. The bells of mokanshan. **FE** 1 (1906) 187-192.

Farley, Hugh W. The sacred mountains of china: nan yu shan, hunan's sacred taoist peak. **CJ** 23.4 (oct 1935) 213-219, illus photos. Nanyü shan, i.e. heng shan, 75 mi south of changsha.

Faulder, H. Croyier. The temples of shanghai. **CJ** 30.6 (june 1939) 340-345, 12 illus.

Feuchtwang, Stephan. City temples in taipei under three regimes. In Mark Elvin & G. William Skinner (ed) **The chinese city between two worlds,** stanford univ (1974) 263-301.

Fisher, Tom. Trances, converts, and cures. **Echo** 2.6 (june 1972) 38-42, illus col photos. Re cures at mother earth temple—ti mu miao—puli, taiwan.

Frey, H. **Les temples égyptiens primitifs identifiés avec les temples actuels chinois.** Paris (1909)

Fu, Tien-chun. The sculptured maidens of the tsin temple. **CL** 4 (apr 1962) 92-98, illus. A sung dyn temple to yi chiang in taiyüan.

Geil, William E. **The sacred 5 of china.** London (1926) xix + 355 p, photos, index. Re sacred mts.

Goodrich, Anne Swann. **The peking temple of the eastern peak. The tung-yüeh miao in peking and its lore. MS** monograph, nagoya (1964) 326 p, app, bibliog, 20 pl.

Gordon-Cumming, C.F. Temple theatres. In author's **WinC** (1886) vol 1, chap 15, 270-276.

Graham, David C. The temples of suifu. **ChRec** 61 (feb 1930) 108-120.

Grootaers, W.A. Rural temples around hsüan-hua (south chahar), their iconography and their history. **FS** 10 (1951) 1-116.

Grootaers, W.A. Les temples villageois de la région au sud de tat'ong (chansi nord), leurs inscriptions et leur histoire. **FS** 4 (1945) 161-212.

Grootaers, W.A., Li Shih-yü and Chang Chi-wen. Temples and history of wanch'üan (chahar). The geographical method applied to folklore. **MS** 13 (1948) 209-316.

Gutzlaff, Charles. Temple of teen how [t'ien hou] at meichow. **ChRep** 2 (1834) 563-565.

Happer, A.P. Visit to two celebrated peking temples. **ChRec** 12 (1881) 363-372.

Hayes, James W. Chinese temples in the local setting. In **TICHK** (1967) 86-95.

Hayes, James W. A list of temples in the southern district of the new territories and new kow-loon, 1899-1967. In **TICHK** (1967) 96-98.

Hayes, James. Royal asiatic society—visit to tai mo shan, 3rd april 1976. Historical and general note. **JHKBRAS** 17 (1977) 168-179.

Hers, Joseph. The sacred mountains of china: huang shan and how to get there. **CJ** 22.6 (june 1935) 311-316, photos. In southeast anhui; orig a taoist center.

Hers, Joseph. The sacred mountains of china: sung shan the deserted. **CJ** 24.2 (feb 1936) 76-82, photos.

Huang, Chun-ming. Tsl Earl Wieman & Rick Johnston. The temple of the thousand steps. **Echo** 3.5 (may 1973) 34-42, illus. Re Chih-nan kung in mucha, taipei.

Huang, Yung-sung, as told to Linda Wu. A man and the mountain. **Echo** 3.10 (nov 1973) 40-46, 59-60, illus col photos. Re a temple on wuchih-shan, taiwan.

Hubbard, Gilbert E. **The temples of the western hills [near peking].** Peking and tientsin (1923) 76 p, illus.

Hubbard, G.E. The pilgrims of taishan. **CJ** 3.6 (june 1925) 322-330, illus photos.

Hudson, B.W. Mokanshan [chekiang] **EA** 4 (1905) 285-297.

Ildephonse, Dom Prior. A visit to the t'ai shan. **BCUP** 6 (1931) 98-118.

Imbault-Huart, Camille. Une visite au temple de confucius à changhai. **JA** 7e sér, 16 (oct-déc 1880) 533-538.

Irving, E.A. A visit to the buddhist and tao-ist monasteries on the lo fau shan. **BIM** 157 (mar 1895) 453-467.

Kemp, E.G. The sacred shrine of tai shan. Chap 6 in author's **FC** (1909) 45-52.

Klügmann, Karl. Aus dem religiösen leben der chinese. Am grabe des konfuzius. Auf dem taishan. **Geist des ostens** 1 (1913) 284-295.

Krone, R. Der lofau-berg . . . in china. **Petermanns geographische mitteilungen** (1864) 283-292.

Kupfer, Carl F. Kiu hua shan, or, the nine-lotus-flower mountain. **EA** 4 (1905) 45-56.

Kupfer, Carl F. **Sacred places in china.** Cincinnati, ohio (1911) 111 p. Five of the 7 papers orig publ in **EA.**

Lapwood, R. & Rewi Allen. Hua shan, the sacred mountain of shensi. **CJ** 19.5 (nov 1933) 240-246, illus maps and photos.

Lee, Tao. Ten celebrated physicians and their temple. **CMJ** 58 (1940) 267-274.

Lenz, Frank B. The house of longevity. **ChRec** 51 (1920) 170-176. Title ref to temple near nanchang, kiangsi, dedicated to a deified magistrate.

Leprince-Ringuet, M.F. En chine. Ascension de la montagne sainte de t'aè-houa-chan. **Annuaire club alpin français** 27 (1900) 356-382, illus.

Li, Chien-wu. Tsl Gladys Yang. Climbing mount taishan in the rain. **CL** 7 (1963) 84-89.

Liu, Chi-wan. The temple of the gods of epidemics in taiwan. **ASBIE** 22 (1966) engl summ 93-95.

Loomis, A.W. Our heathen temples. **OM** 1 (nov 1868) 453-461. Re chin temples in san francisco.

Lu, Hung-nien. A visit to yunglokung. **EH** 1.9 (1961) 29-31. Taoist hermitage in juichang hsien, shansi.

Markbreiter, Stephen. The temple of heaven in peking. **AofA** 2.3 (may-june 1972) 9-12, illus. General descr.

Masters, Frederic J. Pagan temples in san francisco. **The californian** 2 (nov 1892) 727-741.

Mateer, Calvin W. T'ai san (sic)—its temples and worship. **ChRec** 10 (1879) 361-369, 403-415.

McCartee, D.B. (tsl). Translation of an inscription upon a stone tablet commemorating the repairs upon the ch'eng hwang miau or temple of the tutelary deity of the city . . . in the department of lai-chôu, in the province of shantung, a.d. 1752. **JNCBRAS** 6 (1869-70) 173 et seq.

Morrison, Mrs. H.M. In the holy places of hua shan: a dance; a legend; and an offering. **Illustrated london news** 211 (30 aug 1947) 247-249, illus.

Moule, A.C. Le t'ai chan par prof. éd. chavannes. (Note de m. chavannes) **TP** (1911) 425-429.

Moule, A.C. T'ai shan. **JNCBRAS** 43 (1912) 3-31, pl.

Mullikin, Mary Augusta, Tai shan, sacred mountain of the east. **NGM** 87.6 (june 1945) 699-719, illus.

Mullikin, Mary Augusta & Anna M. Hotchkis. **The nine sacred mountains of china.** HK (1973) xx + 156 p, illus b-&-w & col; endpaper maps.

Moese, Wolfgang. Temples and religion. In **CRWMS** (1979) 303-363.

Morrison, Hedda, foreword and 111 photos. Wolfgang Eberhard, introduction and taoist musings. **Hua shan. The taoist sacred mountain in west china; its scenery, monasteries and monks.** HK (1973) xxv + 135 p, b-&-w pl, bibliog, endpaper maps.

Myers, John T. **A chinese spirit-medium temple in kwun tong; a preliminary report.** Chinese univ hk (1974) 57 p.

O'Hara, Albert R. A factual survey of taipei's temples and their functions. **JSS** 17 (1967) 323-337. Repr in author's collection; **RCCS** (1971)

Preston, John (tsl) Tablet mottoes from temples. Collected at foochow. In **DV** vol 2, pt 3, no 12, p 258-262.

Rebirth of kuanhsi's tai-ho temple. **Echo** 2.10 (nov 1972) 23-31, illus b-&-w & col photos.

Roussel, Romain. **Les pèlerinages à travers les siècles.** Paris (1954) See Bouddhistes . . . Taoïstes.

Savage-Landor, A. Henry. A journey to the sacred mountain of siao-outai-shan, in china. **Fortnightly review** (sept 1894) 393-409. Repr in **Eclectic magazine** 123 (july-dec 1894) 596 et seq. Also repr in **Littel's living age** 203 (oct-dec 1894) 143 et seq.

Savidge, Joyce. **This is hong kong: temples.** HK (1977) 122 p, addresses of temples, index, illus col photos. Genl info re chin relig and guide to 12 temples.

Scarborough, W. Notes of a visit to the famous wu-tang shan. **ChRec** 5 (1874) 77-82.

Schipper, Kristofer. Les pèlerinages en chine: montagnes et pistes. In **Les pèlerinages,** paris (1960) 303-342 ('Sources orientales,' 3).

Schmidt, Charles. The 'wen miao,' commonly styled 'the confucian temple' in shanghai. (?) **MDGNVO** (1877) 11-12, photo.

Shryock, John K. **The temples of anking and their cults. A study of modern chinese religion.** Paris (1931) repr ny (1973) 203 p, app, bibliog, index, illus.

Siu, Anthony K.K. Distribution of temples on lantau island as recorded in 1979. **JHKBRAS** 20 (1980) 136-139.

Smith, Carl T. Notes on chinese temples in hong kong. **JHKBRAS** 13 (1973) 133-139.

Sowerby, Arthur de C. China's sacred mountains. **CJ** 22.2 (feb 1935) 64-65.

Soymié, Michel. Le lo-feou chan. Étude de géographie religieuse. **BEFEO** 48.1 (1956) 1-139, app, bibliog, index, illus, map.

Stanley, Charles A. jr. T'ai shan and the tomb of confucius. **EA** 4 (1905) 301-309.

Stone, Albert H. & J. Hammond Reed. **Historic lushan: the kuling mountains.** Hankow (1921) 106 p, 76 pl, folding map. See Contents.

Sullivan, Michael. The magic mountain. **AR** 50 (1955) 300-310.

T'ai shan: the sacred mountain of shantung. In Robert C. Forsyth (comp & ed) **Shantung, the sacred province of china,** shanghai (1912) 55-71.

Temple carvings and sculptures in ancient style. **FCR** 22.11 (nov 1972) 33-44. Photo-pic story re carvings at a temple in sanhsia, outskirts of taipei.

Temples (of manka) **Echo** 5.4/5 (apr/may 1975) 18-27, 80-82, col photos.

Temples (of taiwan) **Echo** 5.8 (sept 1975) 40-52, col and b-&-w photos.

Thiel, P.I. Der erdgeist-tempel als weiterentwicklung des alten erdalters. (Aus eigener feldforschung in süd-shantung) **Sinologica** 5.3 (1958) 150-155, 10 photos.

Thompson, Laurence G. P'eng-hu in mid-ch'ing times according to the p'eng-hu chi lüeh of hu chien-wei. **MS** 30 (1972-73) 166-219. For local temples see 193-196.

Topley, Marjorie and James Hayes. Notes on shrines and temples of tai ping shan street area. In **TICHK** (1967) 123-141.

Tran-Ham-Tan. Étude sur le van-mieu [wen-miao] de ha-noi (temple de la littérature) **BEFEO** 45 (1951) 89-117, planche.

Tsaou-ngo temple. **ChRec** 3.8 (jan 1871) 206-207. Temple near hangchow, dedicated to a girl noted for filiality.

Tschepe, A. The hsin-fu-sze temple [kiangsu] **FE** 1 (1906) 238-240.

Tschepe, A. **Der t'ai-schan und seine kulturstätten.** Jentschoufu (1906) 124 p, 35 illus. Notice in **JNCBRAS** 40 (1909) 119-122.

Wales, H.G. Quaritch. The sacred mountain in the old asiatic religion. **JRAS** (1953) 23-30.

Williams, George B. & Daniel D. Wong & Brenda L. Wong. The chinese temples of northern california. In **The life, influence and the role of the chinese in the united states, 1776-1960,** publ by the chinese historical society of america, san francisco (1976) 293-296.

Woodbridge, Samuel I. Kuling. **EA** 2 (1903) 327-336. [in kiangsi].

Yao, Ruth. Temples of taiwan. **FCR** 14.4 (apr 1964) 13-20, illus.

The Yeang-tai mountains and spirit-writing in china. **BIM** 93 (apr 1863) 499-520.

Zacher, J. Die tempelanlagen am südabhang des richtho-fengebirges, erläutert am beispiel von yen-hu-chai-tzu. **FS** 8 (1949) 270-276.

31. RITES AND CEREMONIES

Ahern, Emily M. Affines and the rituals of worship. In **RRCS** (1974) 279-308.

Ahern, Emily M. The problem of efficacy: strong and weak illocutionary acts. **Man** 14.1 (mar 1979) 1-17.

Aijmer, Göran. **The dragon boat festival in the hunan and hupeh plains, central china; a study in the cere-monialism of the transplantation of rice.** Stockholm (1964) 135 p, bibliog.

Alexandre, Noël. **Conformité des cérémonies chinoises avec l'idolatrie grecque et romaine.** Cologne (1700)

Ancient dance honoring the sage. Taipei, **Vista** 4 (1975) 14-20.

Arlington, L.C. The ceremony of disintering in china. **ChRev** 25.4 (1901) 176-178.

Armstrong, E.A. Chinese bull ritual and its affinities. **Folk-lore** 56 (1945) 200-207.

Bennett, Miss M.I. [Procession to propitiate evil spirits] **CMI** 56 (1905) 58.

Bernard-Maître, Henri. Chinois (rites) **Catholicisme hier, aujourd'hui, demain** 2 (1949) col 1059-1063. Same title in **Dictionnaire d'histoire et géographie ecclésiatiques** t 12 (1953) 731-741.

Bernard-Maître, Henri. La correspondance becker-brucker sur la question des rites chinois (1885-1907) **RechScRelig** 54 (1966) 415-425.

Bernard-Maître, Henri. De la question des termes à la querelle des rites de chine. **NZM** 14 (1958) 178-195, 267-275.

Bishop, Carl W. The ritual bull-fight. **CJ** 3 (1925) 630-637.

Brucker, Joseph. Chinois (rites) **Dictionnaire de théologie catholique** 2.2 (1932) col 2363-2391.

Chiang, Liu. Religion, funeral rites, sacrifices and festivals in kirin. **ChRec** 65 (1934) 227-238. Same title in **ACSS** (1958-59) 8-20.

"A Chinese Pastor." Tsl by Anon. On sacrificial offerings. **ChRec** 8.6 (nov-dec 1877) 489-498. Discussion of traditional sacrifices and their rationale.

Chinese sacrifices, illustrated by quotations from the shúking. **ChRep** 17.2 (feb 1848) 97-101.

Cohen, Alvin P. Coercing the rain deities in ancient china. **HR** 17.3/4 (feb-may 1978) 244-265.

Dols, J. l'Usage du sang dans les cérémonies chinoises. **BSAB** 54 (1939) 123-128.

Duyvendak, J.J.L. The mythico-ritual pattern in chinese civilization. **Proc. 7th ICHR, amsterdam 1950** (1951) 137-138.

Eichhorn, W. Über die abergläubischen gebräuche im kreise ting. **Sinica-sonderausgabe forke festschrift** 1 (1937) 43-52.

Farjenal, F. (tsl) **Rites funéraires chinois, les funérailles impériales et celles des gens du peuple.** Louvain (ca 1904) 63 p offpr fr **Le muséon.**

Faurot, Albert. The oldest birthday party. **SJ** 2 (1975) 166-172.

Feuchtwang, Stephan. Domestic and communal worship in taiwan. In **RRCS** (1974) 105-130.

Freedman, Maurice. Ritual aspects of kinship and marriage. In **FKCS** (1970) 163-188.

Frick, Johannes. Die regensprozession in lungsi (nordwest china) In **Festschrift paul schebesta zum 75. geburstag,** wien-mödling (1963) 385-400.

Frick, Johannes, Wiederversöhnung der verletzten ergeister. (Ein brauch im chinesischttibetischen grenzgebiet) **Wiener völkerkundliche mitteilungen** 2 (1954) 39-43.

Fried, Martha Nemes & Morton Fried. **Transitions. Four rituals in eight cultures.** NY & london (1980) Re major rites of passage. See Index, People's republic of china; Taiwan.

Gibson, H.E. Divination and ritual during the shang and chou dynasties. **CJ** 23 (1935) 22-25.

Graham, David C. **The ancient caves of szechuan province, china.** Washington, d.c. (1932) 29 p, illus. Burial customs.

Grout, G.C.W. Ceremonies of propitiation carried out in connection with road works in the new territories in 1960. **JHKBRAS** 11 (1971) 204-209.

Headland, Isaac Taylor. Family and marriage ceremonies. Chap 14-15 in author's **HLC** (1914) 131-146.

Hentze, Carl. Das ritual der wiederbelebung durch die "neue haut" (altchina-ocienien-amerika) **Sinologica** 6.2 (1961) 69-82, illus.

Ho, Ku-li. Fire walking in hsinchuang. **Echo** 2.1 (jan 1972) 18-24, illus.

Hou, Ching-lang. **Monnaies d'offrande et la notion de trésorerie dans la religion chinoise.** Paris (1975) 238 p, notes, bibliog, chin texts, pl, index, tipped-in samples of spirit money.

Hughes, E.R. Confucianist sacrifice and religious education. **ChRec** 62.7 (july 1931) 407-414.

J. Rites performed for the dead. **ChRev** 9 (1880-81) 397. See also D.G., same title, **ibid** 10 (1881-82) 145-146.

Johnston, R.F. Worship (chinese) In **HERE** 12, p 759.

Jordan, David K. Two forms of spirit marriage in rural taiwan. **BTLVK** 127.1 (1971) 181-189.

Kaltenmark, Max. Les danses sacrées en chine. In **Les danses sacrées,** 'Sources orientales' 6, paris (1963) 411-450.

Kaye, Lincoln. Scaling the ladder of swords. **Echo** 6.3 (nov 1976) 40-47, b-&-w & col photos. Exorcism by tung chi (shaman) at a small temple in luchou, northern taiwan.

Klaproth, Julius H. Über religiöse zeremonien der chinesen. **Asiatisches magazin** 2 (1802) 76-78.

Ku Ya-ting. Beating the spring ox. **Echo** 5.1 (Jan 1975) 10-13, illus.

Kung, Te-cheng. Rite—but more than ritual. **FCR** 23.5 (may 1973) 20-23.

Kuo, Li-cheng. Tsl Linda Yee. House building hexes. **Echo** 3.11 (dec 1973) 40-46, 54.

Lanöe, F. La danse des diables au temple de hei seu. **La chine** 15 (1 avr 1922) 557-558.

Lavollée, C. Prières chinoises. **ROA** 6 (1849) 100-104.

Lin, Yueh-hwa. **The golden wing. A sociological study of chinese familism.** London (1948) repr westport, conn (1974) On death and its rituals see chap 10, 103-112.

Ling, Shun-sheng. Turtle sacrifice in ancient china. **ASBIE** 31 (1971) engl summ 41-46, illus.

Lynn, Jermyn Chi-hung. **Social life of the chinese.** Peking-tientsin (1928) See chap 8, Marriages, 109-130. Re Peking customs.

Mayers, W.F. On the stone figures at chinese tombs and the offering of living sacrifices. **JNCBRAS** 12 (1878) 1-17.

Milloué, L. de. Cultes et cérémonies en honneur des morts dans l'extrême-orient. **CMG** (1899-1900 et 1900-01) 135-149.

Mitchell-Innes, Norman G. Birth, marriage, and death rites of the chinese. **FLJ** 5 (1887) 221-245.

Mollard, Sidney G. jr. Confucius and music. **EWCR** 3.3 (feb 1967) 31-39.

Morgan, Evan. A case of ritualism. **JNCBRAS** 49 (1918) 128-143. When feudal state of lu usurped royal prerogative to perform suburban sacrifice to heaven (chiao)

Morisse, Lucien. Les éclipses et les rites chinois. **Asie française.** 2.17 (août 1902) 367-372.

Newell, William H. The sociology of ritual in early china. **Sociological bulletin** 6 (1957) 1-13.

Palatre, Père. Une procession païenne en chine. **MC** 2 (1869) 386-387, 395-397, 405-406. Cortège de se-siang-kong.

Parish, William L. & Martin King Whyte. Life-cycle ceremonies and ritual life. Chap 13 in authors' **VFCC** (1978) 248-272.

Parker, E.H. Funeral rites. **ChRev** 14 (1885-86) 225.

Pfizmaier, A. Die lösung der leichname und schwerter. Ein beitrag zur kenntniss des taoglauben. **SAWW** 64 (1870) 25-92; also publ sep, wien (1870) 70 p.

Practical lessons in sacrificial rites, given at the public literary hall in the department of kwangchow, by two professors from the board of rites in peking, under the direction of the commissioner of territory and finance. **ChRep** 6.5 (sept 1837) 253-255.

A Prayer for rain, written by his imperial majesty taou-kwang and offered up on the 28th day of the sixth month of the 12th year of his reign—july 24th, 1832. **ChRep** 1.6 (oct 1832) 236-239. Tsl and comm.

Propitiating evil spirits. **Annual report of the church missionary society,** london (1905) 351.

Rouleau, Francis A. Chinese rites controversy. In **New catholic encyclopedia** (1967) vol 3 611-617.

Rydh. H. Seasonal fertility rites and the death cult in scandinavia and china. **BMFEA** 3 (1931) 69-93.

Sampson, Theos. Burial in china. **NQ** 2 (1868) 109-111.

Schafer, Edward H. Ritual exposure in ancient china. **HJAS** 14 (1951) 130-184.

Schmeltz, J.D.E. Das pflugfest in china. **IAE** 11 (1898) 72-81.

Schüler, W. Ein tempeleinweihungsfest in china. **ZMK** 21 (1906) 110-115.

Seidel, Anna. Buying one's way to heaven: the celestial treasury in chinese religions. **HR** 17.3/4 (feb-may 1978) 419-431. Rev art on Hou Ching-lang, **Monnaies d'offrande** . . . q.v.

Smedt, L. de. Le mariage en chine. In **Semaine d'ethnologie religieuse: Ve session, luxembourge, 16-22 sept 1929,** paris (1931) 154-168.

Strauch, Judith. A tun fu ceremony in tai po district, 1981: ritual as a demarcator of community. **JHKBRAS** 20 (1980) 147-153. The term tun fu is not in dictionaries.

L.T.T. A perspicuous form of prayer, returning thanks to heaven in fulfillment of vows, táh t'ien chau yuen wan sú. **ChRep** 17.7 (july 1848) 365-366.

Thiel, J. Stellvertretende gelübdeerfüllung. **FS** 1 (1942) 28-32.

Thompson, Laurence G. Funeral rites in taiwan. In author's **CWayRel** (1973) 160-169.

Torrance, Thomas. Burial customs in sz-chuan. **JNCBRAS** 41 (1910)

Tran-Ham-Tan. Étude sur le van-mieu [wen-miao] de ha-noi (temple de la littérature) **BEFEO** 45 (1951) 89-117, planche.

Tsu, Y.Y. The chinese idea of worship. **ChRec** 45.10 (oct 1914) 615-625.

Vandermeersch, Léon. La conception chinoise des rites. **Cahiers linguistique d'orientalisme et de slavistique** 8 (july 1976) 75-86.

Vandermeersch, Léon. **Wangdao ou la voie royale. Recherches sur l'esprit des insitutions de la chine archaïque.** T 1, **Structures cultuelles et familialles,** Paris (1977) 358 p. T 2, **Structures politiques, les rites,** Paris (1980) 603 p, tables, index. See Table générale des matières.

Vleeschower, E. de. K'i yu (Rain ceremony) **FS** 2 (1943) 39-50.

Volpert, A. Chinesische volksgebräuche beim t'chi jü, regenbitten. **Anthropos** 12-13 (1917-18) 144-151.

Werner, E.T.C. Reform in chinese mourning rites. **NCR** 2 (1920) 223-247.

Wolf, Arthur P. Chinese kinship and mourning dress. In **FKCS** (1970) 189-208.

32. DIVINATION

Arlington, L.C. Chinese versus western chiromancy. **CJ** 7 (1927) 67-76, 170-175, 228-235; 8 (1928) 67-76.

Balfour, F.H. A chinese 'planchette' seance. **ChRev** 9 (1880-81) 362-370.

Balfour, F.H. Portents. In author's **Leaves from my chinese scrapbook** (1887) 158-162.

Baruch, Jacques. l'Interpretation des présages dans la chine ancienne. **MEO** 1.2 (1971) 17-132.

Bauer, Wolfgang. **Das bild in der weissage-literatur- chinas. Prophetische texte im politischen leben vom buch der wandlung bis zu mao tse-tung.** München (1973) 74 s. See rev in **NachrDGNVO** 121/122 (1977) 165-168.

Bauer, Wolfgang. Chinese glyphomancy (ch'ai-tzu) and its uses in present-day taiwan. In **LL&R** (1979) 71-96.

Bauer, Wolfgang. Zur textgeschichte des t'ui-pei-t'u, eines chinesischen "nostradamus." **OE** 20.1 (1973) 7-26.

Bielenstein, Hans. An interpretation of the portents in the ts'ien-han-shu. **BMFEA** 22 (1950) 127-143, diagr.

Brown, H.G. What the gods say in west china. **JWCBorderResS** 3 (1926-29) 134-150.

Buck, Samuel (pseud) Chinese fortune telling. **Orient** 2.10 (1952) 39-42.

Chao, Wei-pang. The chinese science of fate-calculation. **FS** 5 (1946) 279-315.

Chao, Wei-pang. The origin and growth of the fu chi [planchette] **FS** 1 (1942) 9-27.

Chavannes, Édouard. La divination par l'écaille de tortue dans la haute antiquité chinoise (d'après un livre de m. lo tchen-yu) **JA** 10e sér, 17 (1911) 127-137.

Chen, Shih-chuan. How to form a hexagram and consult the i ching. **JAOS** 92.2 (1972) 237-249.

Chen, Ying-chieh. Your fortune in numbers. **FCR** 23.10 (oct 1973) 14-17. Re numerology.

Chen, Victor. What's in a fortune? **FCR** 28.7 (july 1978) 25-28. Re physiognomy.

Cohen, Alvin P. An example of word-divination in the tarng shu. **PTP** 11 (dec 1968) 68-75.

Cordier, Georges. (tsl) La divination chinoise: clef des songes. **RIC** n.s. 12 (oct 1909) 1033-1041; n.s. 12 (nov 1909) 1135-1140; n.s. 12 (dec 1909) 1241-1243; n.s. 16 (dec 1911) 638-653; n.s. 17 (mai 1912) 484-491.

Delsol, Paula. Tsl fr french Peter & Tanya Leslie. **Chinese astrology.** NY (1972) 320 p, bibliog, index.

Divination in china. **ICG** no 12 (1820) 318-320.

Doolittle, Justus. Fortune telling. Chap 14 in author's **SLC** vol 2 (1865) 331-348.

Edkins, Joseph. Astrology in ancient china. **ChRev** 14 (1885-86) 345-351.

Edkins, Joseph. The introduction of astrology into china. **ChRev** 15 (1886-87) 126-128.

Fortunes of the snake year. Translated from the chinese farmers' almanac. **Echo** 6.5 (feb 1977) 31-36, 70-71.

Frick, J. Der traum und seine deutung bei den chinesen in ch'inghai. **Anthropos** 49 (1954) 311-313.

Gibson, H.E. Divination and ritual during the shang and chou dynasties. **CJ** 23 (1935) 22-25.

Giles, Herbert A. Mesmerism, planchette and spiritualism in china. **Fraser's magazine** ser 2, 19 (feb 1879) 238-245.

Giles, Herbert A. Palmistry in china. **Nineteenth century and after** (dec 1904) 985-988.

Giles, Herbert A. Phrenology, physiognomy and palmistry. In author's **AdSin** no 6 (1908) 178-184.

Gray, John Henry. Astrologers and fortune-tellers. Vol 2, chap 17 of author's **China** (ed William G. Gregor) london (1878) 1-42.

Groot, J.J.M. de. On chinese divination by dissecting written characters. **TP** 1 (1890) 239-247.

Harding, H.L. On a method of divination practised at foochow. **JNCBRAS** 49 (1918) 82-85. Art 2 under heading, a chapter of folklore.

Harlez, C. de. **Miscellanées chinois. 1—Le rêve dans les croyances chinoises.** Bruxelles (d?) 22p.

Harper, Donald J. The han cosmic board (shih) **EC** 4 (1978-79) 1-10. See further C. Cullen, Some further points on the shih, **ibid** 6 (1980-81) 31-46; further, Harper's The han cosmic board: a response to christopher cullen, **ibid** 47-56.

Hirsh, Charles. La mystique du yi-king. In **EMM** (1975) 169-180.

Hixon, Lex. Coming home. **The experience of enlightenment in sacred traditions.** Garden city, ny (1978) See chap 4, Ten seasons of enlightenment; zen ox-herding, 77-108; chap 9, Conversation with an ancient chinese sage: the oracle text of the i ching, 180-204.

Ho Ku-li (tsl and ed) Your personality and horoscope according to a chinese almanac. **Echo** 2.2 (feb 1972) 15-19, 53-56.

Hopkins, Lionel C. Working the oracle [re oracle bones] **NCR** (1919) 111-119, 249-261, pl.

Hsu, Jin. Counseling in the chinese temple: a psychological study of divination by chien drawing. In **CBS** (1976) 210-221.

Hulsewé, A.F.P. Watching the vapors; an ancient chinese technique of prognostication. **NachrDGNVO** 125 (1979) 40-49.

Keightley, David N. **Sources of shang history. The oracle-bone inscriptions of bronze age china.** Univ california (1978) xvii + 281 p, illus, 5 app, tables, 2 bibliog.

Koeppen, Georg von. Zwei träume aus dem tso-chuan und ihre interpretation. **ZDMG** 119 (1969) 133-156.

Ku, Ya-ting. Beating the spring ox. **Echo** 5.1 (jan 1975) 10-13, illus.

Kwan, L.H. Divination with the i ching. **SF** (1972) 15-26.

Lee, Charles L. (pseud for Yen P'u-sheng) tsl and annot. **The great prophecies of china, by li chung-feng [602-670] and yuan tien-kang.** N.Y. (1950) 64 p.

Lessa, William A. Chinese body divination. In **FRWVSP** (1968) 85-96.

Lessa, William A. **Chinese body divination. Its forms, affinities, and functions.** Los angeles (1968) 220 p, bibliog, index, illus.

Liu, Mau-tsai. Die traumdeutung im alten china. **AS** 16.1-4 (1963) 35-65.

Lum, Chung Park. **Chinese fortune telling.** N.Y. (1930) 15 p, illus.

Macgowan, D.J. Table-moving and spiritual manifestations in china. **NCH** 196 (29 apr 1854) repr **Shanghae almanac for 1855 and Miscellany;** also repr in **China mail** 484 (25 may 1854)

MacGowan, John. The spokesman of the gods. Chap 9 in author's **L&S** (1909) 99-110. Re mediums.

Major, John S. Astrology in the huai-nan-tzu and some related texts. **SSCRB** 8 (fall 1980) 20-31.

Mark, Lindy Li. Orthography, riddles, divination and word magic: an exploration in folklore and culture. In **LL&R** (1979) 43-69.

McCaffree, Joe E. **Divination and the historical and allegorical sources of the i ching, the chinese classic, or book of changes.** Los angeles (1967) 64 p, illus.

Mégroz, R.L. Dream interpretation, chinese—greek—islamic. **AP** 6 (1935) 28-31.

Milloué, L. de. l'Astrologie et les différentes formes de la divination dans l'inde, en chine et au tibet. **CMG** (1899-1900 et 1900-01) 179-205.

Miyazaki, Ichisada. Le développement de l'idée de divination en chine. In **MSPD**, t 1 (1966) 161-166. Re yi ching divination.

Moebius, P. Die grundlagen der chinesischen divinations-lehren. **OZ** 17 (1931) 215-218.

Mortier, F. Les animaux dans la divination et la médecine populaire chinoise. **BSAB** 51 (1936) 268-275.

Mortier, F. Du sens primitif de l'antiquité et la célèbre figure divinatoire des taoistes chinois et japonais (sien t'ien) **BSAB** 59 (1948) 150-160.

L. M. N. Modes of consulting the oracles. **ChRev** 7 (1878-79) 134.

Nakayama, Shigeru. Characteristics of chinese astrology. **Isis** 57 (winter 1966) 442-454.

Natsume, Ikken. Various phases of revelation in taoism. **TJR** 1 (mar 1955) 53-65, fig.

Ngo, Van Xuyet. **Divination, magie et politique dans la chine ancienne. Essai suivi de la traduction des "biographies des magiciens" tirées de 'l'histoire des han postérieurs.'** Paris (1976) 264 p, app, Les arts ésotériques du "fang-chou lie tchouan"; annexes re chronol, bibliog, index chin char, map. See rev by Michael Loewe in **EC** 4 (1978-79) 75-77.

Ohlinger, Franklin. Studies in chinese dreamlore. **EA** 4 (1905) 381-389; 5 (1906) 381-389; 5 (1906) 16-28, 256-267.

Parker, A.P. The chinese almanac. **ChRec** 19.2 (feb 1888) 61-74.

Parker, A.P. Review of the imperial guide to astrology . . . hieh ki pien fang shú. **ChRec** 19 (1888) 493-499, 547-554.

Promulgation of the calendar. **Echo** 4.11 (dec 1974) 22-24, 50-51, illus. Re imperial almanac.

Przyluski, Jean. La divination par l'aiguille flottante et par l'araignée dans la chine méridionale. **TP** n.s. 15 (1914) 214-224.

Schafer, Edward H. The auspices of t'ang. **JAOS** 83 (1963) 197-225. Re " . . . birds richly endowed with mana . . . the birds of auspices,'' with many illus passages fr t'ang lit.

Schafer, Edward H. Li kang: a rhapsody on the banyan tree. **Orient** 6 (1953) 344-353.

Schafer, Edward H. **Pacing the void. T'ang approaches to the stars.** Univ california (1977) 352 p, illus, app, notes, bibliog, gloss, index.

Seiwert, Hubert. Orakelwesen in ältestern china: shang- und westliche chou-dynastie. **ZMR** 64.3 (juli 1980) 208-236, engl summ 236.

Soymié, Michel. Les songes et leur interpretation en chine. In **Les songes et leur interpretation,** paris (1959) 275-305 ('Sources orientales' 2).

The Stars and your future. **Echo** 3.1 (jan 1973) 44-56, illus. Re lunar years acc to zodiacal animals.

Stein, Rolf A. Un exemple de relations entre taoïsme et religion populaire. In **Fukui hakase festschrift: tōyō bunka ronshū,** ?Tokyo (1969) 79-90.

Stiassny, M. Quelques formes de la divination des chinois. **Archives suisses d'anthropologie générale** 12 (1946) 159-163.

Stirling, W.G. Chinese divining blocks and the 'pat kwa' or eight-sided diagram with text figures. **JMBRAS** 2 (1924) 72-73.

Ting, Su. Fortune telling. **Asia** 3 (1953) 428-437.

Towl, Diane Grady. Selecting a spouse—chinese style. **Echo** 3.8 (sept 1973) 26-29, 56-58, illus. Re horoscopic compatability.

Tsai, Wen-hui. A study of divination in chinese temples in taiwan. **SyY:T&W** 6.2 (july 1968) 19-22.

Tseung, F.I. Some aspects of fortune-telling in hong kong. In **TICHK** (1967) 60-72.

Vandermeersch, Léon. De la tortue à l'achillée. In J.P. Vernant (ed) **Divination et rationalité,** paris (1974) 29-51. Re oracle bone divination.

Vandermeersch, Léon. **Wangdao ou la voie royale. Recherches sur l'esprit des institutions de la chine archaïque.** T 1, **Structures cultuelles et structures familiales.** Paris (1977) 358 p, T 2, **Structures politiques, les rites.** Paris (1980) 603 p, tables, index. See Table générale des matières.

What will the rabbit bring you? Your horoscope according to the chinese farmers almanac. **Echo** 5.1 (jan 1975) 14-21, 55-56. Re horoscope of the zodiacal years.

Wilhelm, Hellmut. On the oracle recorded in tso-chuan, hsi 4 (656 b.c.) **JAOS** 9.4 (oct-dec 1971) 504-505.

Wilhelm, Hellmut. Der sinn des geschehens nach dem buch der wandlung. **EJ** 26 (1957) 351-386.

Wimsatt, Genevieve. Fortune telling. Chap 14 in author's **GC** (1927) 197-214.

33. SHAMANISM AND MEDIUMS

Chow, Tse-tsung. The childbirth myth and ancient chinese medicine: a study of aspects of the wu tradition. In **AC:SEC** (1978) 43-89.

Dunstheimer, G.G.H. Deux études sur les religions chinoises. **ASR** 4 (juil-déc 1957) 133-142. Rev art on Vincent Y.C. Shih, Some chinese rebel ideologies, **TP** 44.1/3, 150-226, and Alan J.A. Elliott's **Chinese spirit medum cults** (1955) q.v.

Eitel, E.J. Spirit-rapping in china. **NQ** 1.12 (dec 1867) 164-165.

Eliade, Mircea. **Le chamanisme et les techniques archaïques de l'extase.** Paris (1951) Engl tsl Willard R. Trask: **Shamanism; archaic techniques of ecstacy.** Princeton univ (1964) bibliog, index. For china, see index.

Eliade, Mircea. Einführende betrachtungen über den schamanismus. **Paideuma** 5 (1951) 87-97.

Eliade, Mircea. Le problème de chamanisme. **RHR** 131 (1946) 5-52.

Eliade, Mircea. Smiths, shamans and mystagogues. **E&W** 6 (1955) 206-215.

Elliott, Alan J.A. **Chinese spirit-medium cults in singapore.** London school of economics and political science (1955) 179 p, illus.

Enjoy, Paul d'. Le spiritisme en chine. **BMSAP** 5e sér, 7 (1906) 87-100.

Erkes, E. The god of death in ancient china. **TP** 35 (1940) 185-210.

Erkes, E. Mystik und schamanismus. **AA** 8 (1945) 197-215.

Erkes, Eduard. Der schamanistische ursprung des chinesischen ahnenkultus. **Sinologica** 2 (1950) 253-262.

Giles, Herbert A. Mesmerism, planchette and spiritualism in china. **Fraser's magazine** ser 2, 19 (feb 1879) 238-245.

Goltz, Freiherrn von der. Zauberei und hexenkünste, spiritismus und schamanismus in china. **MDGNVO** bd 6, heft 51 (1893) 1-50.

Grootaers, Willem A. Une séance de spiritisme dans une religion secrète à péking en 1948. **MCB** 9 (1948-51) 92-98.

Hankey, Rosalie. Ghosts and shamanism in kwangtung. **CFQ** 2 (1943) 303-308.

Harvey, E.D. Shamanism in china. In **Studies in the science of society presented to a. g. keller** (1937) 247-266.

Hegel, Robert. Of men possessed and speaking gods. **Echo** 1.3 (mar 1971) 16-23, illus. Re t'ung-chi mediums in taiwan.

Hentze, Carl. Le culte de l'ours et du tigre et le t'ao-t'ié. **Zalmoxis** 1 (1938) 50-68.

Hentze, Carl. Eine schamanen-darstellung auf einem han-relief. **AM** n.s. 1.1 (1944) 74-77.

Hentze, Carl. Eine schamanentracht in ihrer bedeutung für die altchinesische kunst und religion. **Jahrbuch für prähistorische ethnographische kunst** 20 (1960-63) 55-61.

Hentze, Carl. Schamanenkronen zur han-zeit in korea. **OZ** n.f. 9 (1933) 156-163, illus, bibliog.

Hentze, Carl. Zur ursprünglichen bedeutung des chinesischen zeichens t'ou = kopf. **Anthropos** 45 (1950) 801-820.

Hopkins, L.C. The bearskin, another pictographic reconnaissance from primitive prophylactice to present-day panache: a chinese epigraphic puzzle. **JRAS** (1943) 110-117.

Hopkins, L.C. The shaman or chinese wu: his inspired dancing and versatile character. **JRAS** (1945) 3-16.

Hopkins, L.C. The shaman or wu. A study in graphic camouflage. **NCR** 2 (1920) 423-439.

Kagan, Richard C. (ed & tsl) The chinese approach to shamanism. **CSA** 12.4 (summer 1980) 3-135 (entire issue) Intro, 3-30; tsl, 31-125; bibliog, 126-135.

König, H. Schamane und medizinmann. **Ciba zeitschrift** 4.38 (1936) 1294-1301.

Körner, Theo. Das zurückrufen der seele in kuei-chou. **Ethnos** 3.4/5 (july-sept 1938) 108-112.

Kremsmayer, Heimo. Schamanismus und seelenvorstellung im alten china. **AV** 9 (1954) 66-78.

Lanciotti, Lionello. Sword casting and related legends in china. **E&W** (1) 6.2 (july 1955) 106-114; (2) 6.4 (jan 1956) 316-322.

Laufer, Berthold. Origin of the word shaman. **American anthropologist** n.s. 19.3 (1917) 361-371.

Li, Y.Y. Shamanism in taiwan: an anthropological inquiry. In **CBS** (1976) 179-188.

Metzger, Emil. Zauber und zauberjungen bei den chinesen. **Globus** 42.7 (feb 1882) 110-12; 42.8 (feb 1882) 119-121.

Minnaert, P. Le chamanisme. **BSAB** 51 (1936) 216-234.

Minnaert, P. Magie ou thaumaturgie et chamanisme. **BSAB** 48 (1933) 19-34.

Mironov, N.D. and S.M. Shirokogoroff. S'ramanashaman (Etymology of the word 'shaman') **JNCBRAS** 55 (1924) 105-130.

Myers, John T. **A chinese spirit-medium temple in kwun tong: a preliminary report.** Chin univ hong kong (1974) 57 p.

Myers, John T. A hong kong spirit-medium temple. **JHKBRAS** 15 (1975) 16-27, 4 pl.

Neill, Peter. The dish saint, the skeptic, and the ghost. **Echo** 3.4 (apr 1973) 26-40, 56. Re a seance.

Parker, E.H. Ancient chinese spiritualism. **AR** 19 (jan 1923) 117-123.

Pimpaneau, Jacques. Chinese medium cults and creativity in literature. In **China society 25th anniversary journal,** china soc of singapore, (1975) 30-35.

Potter, Jack M. Cantonese shamanism. In **RRCS** (1974) 207-232.

Rock, J.F. Contribution to the shamanism of the tibetan-chinese borderland. **Anthropos** 54.5/6 (1959) 796-816, 4 pl.

Rosner, Erhard. Schamanistische züge der chinesischen volkmedizin: zur bewertung unorthodoxer heilmethoden im traditionellen china. **Medizinhistorisches journal** 9 (1974) 41-48.

Schang, Tscheng-tsu. **Der schamanismus in china: eine untersuchung zur geschichte der chinesischen 'wu'.** Hamburg (1934) 83 p.

Seaman, Gary. In the presence of authority: hierarchical roles in chinese spirit medium cults. In **NABCC** (1980) 61-74.

Suzuki, Mitsuo. The shamanistic element in taiwanese folk religion. In **ExHum** (1976) 253-260.

Tam, Janet L. Singapore trance men. **Orientations** 8.6 (june 1977) 4-5. Re spirit mediums.

Thiel, Jos. Schamanismus im alten china. **Sinologica** 10.2/3 (1968) 149-204.

Tseng. W.S. Psychiatric study of shamanism in taiwan. **AGP** 26 (1972) 561-565.

Vichert, C.G. A study of the growth of a legend. **JWCBorderResS** 8 (1936) 173-174.

Waley, Arthur. **The nine songs. A study of shamanism in ancient china.** London (1955) 64 p, index.

Yap, P.M. The possession syndrome: a comparison of hong kong and french findings. **BJP** 106 (1960) 114-137.

34. MAGIC — SORCERY

Andersson, J.G. Hunting magic in the animal style. **BMFEA** 4 (1932) 221-320.

Bank, J. Philosophie sociale, magie et langage graphique dans le hong-fan. **Tel quel** 48/49 (1972) 20-32.

Black, W.H. On chinese charms. **Journal of the ethnological society.** n.s. 1 (1868-69) 38-39.

Blanchard, Raphael and Bui Van Quy. Sur une collection d'amulettes chinoises. **Revue anthropologique** 28 (mai-juin 1918) 131-172 fig (dessins de mlle Gilberte Zaborowska)

Bodde, Derk. The chinese cosmic magic known as watching for the ethers. In **SSBKD** (1959) 14-35. Repr **ECC** (1981) 351-372.

Bodde, Derk. Sexual sympathetic magic in han china. **HR** 3 (1964) 292-299. Repr **ECC** (1981) 373-380.

Böttger, Walter. Jagdmagie im alten china. In **SJFAW** (1956) 9-14.

Brace, A.J. Spirits and magic in chinese religion. **JWCBorderResS** 5 (1932) 133-148.

Cammann, Schuyler. Magical and medicinal woods in old chinese carvings. **JAFL** 74, no 292 (apr-june 1961) 116-125.

Castiglione, Arturo. Tsl fr italian V. Gianturco. **Adventures of the mind.** NY (1946) See chap 10, Chinese magic of numbers and letters, 123-131.

Charpentier, Léon. La magie chez les chinois. **NR** n.s. 9 (1901) 523-536.

Chatley, Herbert. Magical practice in china. **JNCBRAS** 48 (1917) 16-28.

Ch'en, Hsiang-ch'un. Examples of charm against epidemics with short explanations. **FS** 1 (1942) 37-54, 15 cuts of charms.

Chochod, Louis. **Occultisme et magie en extrême-orient: inde, indochine, chine.** Paris (1949) 404 p, illus.

Comber, Leon. **Chinese magic and superstitions in malaya.** Singapore (1957) 80 p, illus.

Daudin, P. Deux amulettes du yunnan. **BSEIS** n.s. 21 (1946) 35-40.

Day, Clarence B. Celestial insurance limited (popular charms) **Asia** 33 (1933) 113-115.

Dember, H. Ostasiatische zaubespiegel. **OZ** 19 (1933) 203-207.

Dubs, Homer H. The kang-mao amulets. Chap 99, app 3 in Dubs (tsl) **The history of the former han dynasty by pan ku,** vol 3, baltimore (1955) 537-543.

Dunstheimer, G.G. Religion et magie dans le mouvement de boxeurs d'après les textes chinois. **TP** 47.3/5 (1959) 322-267.

Eberhard, Wolfram. Chinesischer bauzauber. **ZE** 71 (1940) 87-99. See rev engl tsl in **SCFRE** (1970) 49-65.

Eder, Matthias. Spielgeräte und spiele im chinesischen neujahrsbrauchtum, mit aufzeigung magischer bedeutungen. **FS** 6.1 (1947) 1-207.

Edwards, E.D. **Chinese prose literature of the t'ang dynasty, a.d. 618-906.** London, 2 vol (1937-38) repr ny (1974) See vol 1, chap 5, Religion—magic and magical practices, 49-59; vol 2, passim.

Elwin, Arthur. A strange scene. **ChRec** 12.1 (jan-feb 1881) 16-19. On exorcism.

Fêng, Han-yi and John K. Shryock. The black magic in china known as ku. **JAOS** 55 (1935) 1-30.

Fischer, C. Chuan-chou. Die magie der umkreisung. **AA** 4 (1930-32) 213-220.

Frick, J. How blood is used in magic and medicine in ch'inghai provice. Tsl fr german James E. Mertz. **Anthropos** 46 (1951) 964-979.

Frick, J. Magic remedies used on sick children in the western valley of sining. Tsl James E. Mertz. **Anthropos** 46 (1951) 175-186. German orig in **ibid** 45 (1950) 787-800.

Giles, Lionel. Wizardry in ancient china. **AP** 13 (1942) 484-489.

Gillis, I.V. Magic writings in modern china. **OC** 49 (1935) 125-128. Re spirit writings on planchette.

Goltz, Freiherrn von der. Zauberei und hexenkünste, spiritismus und schamanismus in china. **MDGNVO** bd 6, heft 51 (1893) 1-50.

Groot, J.J.M.de. **The religious system of china.** Leiden (1892-1910) repr taipei (1964) 6 vol. 1-3: Disposal of the dead; 4-6 The soul and ancestor worship. See passim, esp vol 4-6.

Gulik, R.H. van The mango trick in china: an essay on taoist magic. **TASJ** ser 3, 3 (1954) 117-175.

Henry, Victor. **La magie dans l'inde antique.** Paris (1909) x1 + 286 p.

Herrmann, F. Chinesischer schutz und gluckszauber. **Sinica-Sonderausgabe** (1935) 24-28.

Hsu, Francis L.K. **Magic and science in western yunnan.** N.Y. (1943) 53 p.

Hsu, Francis L.K. **Religion, science and human crisis.** London (1952) 142 p.

Jellison, E.R. Superstitions of the chinese. **ChRec** 24.8 (aug 1893) 373-379. Mostly re foxes.

Johnston, R.F. Magic (chinese) In **HERE** 8, p 259.

Julien, Stanislas. Notice sur les miroirs magiques des chinois et leur fabrication . . . **Comptes rendus de l'académie des science** 24 (1847) 999-1009.

Kaltenmark, Max. Un procédé de vol magique dans le taoïsme. **SF** (1972) 5-13.

Kiang, Chao-yuan. **Le voyage dans la chine ancienne, considéré principalement sous son aspect magique et religieux.** Shanghai (1937) 375 p. Trad du chin par Fan, Jen.

Kuo, Li-cheng. Tsl Susan Converse. Chu yo ko: healing with charms. **Echo** 4.10 (nov 1974) 45-53, illus.

Kuo, Li-cheng. Tsl Linda Yee. The doll behind every mystic. **Echo** 4.7 (july-aug 1974) 15-18, illus. Re camphor-willow god, chang liu shen; incl author's retelling of a story fr liao-chai chih yi.

Kuo, Li-cheng. Tsl Linda Yee. House building hexes. **Echo** 3.11 (dec 1973) 40-46, 54.

Kuo, Li-cheng. Tsl Scott Satterfield. Peopling the sorcerer's stable. **Echo** 5.6 (june 1975) 18-20, illus. Tales of the black magic called tsao-ch'u "making animals."

Legeza, Laszlo. **Tao magic. The chinese art of the occult.** London & ny (1975) Text. 7-30, pl. 31-128; brief note on the tao-tsang and brief bibliog, 128.

Loewe, Michael. The case of witchcraft in 91 b.c.: its historical setting and effect on han dynastic history. **AM** 15.2 (1970) 159-196. Same title as chap 2 in author's **CCHC** (1974)

Manabe, Shunsho. The expression of elimination of devils in the iconographic texts of the t'ang period and its background. **JIBS** 15.2 (mar 1967) 907-914, illus.

Minnaert, P. Magie ou thaumaturgie et chamanisme. **BSAB** 48 (1933) 19-34.

Morgan, Harry T. **Chinese astrology.** Los angeles (ca. 1945) 20 p, illus.

Morrison, John Robert. Some account of charms, and felicitous appendages worn about the person, or hung up in houses, &c., used by the chinese. **Trans RAS** 3 (1833) 285-290; **ChRep** 14 (1845) 229-234.

Mortier, Florent. La magie en chine. **BSAB** 47 (1932) 353-360.

Nevius, John L. **Demon possession and allied themes.** Chicago etc (1886) 494 p, indexes. Mostly chin cases, with some others for comparison.

Ngo, Van Xuyet. **Divination, magie et politique dans la chine ancienne. Essai suivi de la traduction des "biographies des magiciens" tirées de 'l'histoire des han postérieurs.'** Paris (1976) 264 p; app, Les arts ésotériques du "fang-shu lie-tchouan"; annexes re chronol, bibliog, index chin char, map. See rev by Michael Loewe in **EC** 4 (1978-79) 75-77.

Palatre, le père. La magie et le nénuphar blanc au kiangnan. **MC** 10 (1878) 434-441, 446-450, 458-465.

Preston, John. Charms and spells in use amongst the chinese. **ChRev** 2.3 (nov-dec 1873) 164-169.

Regnault, Jules. Rôle du foung-choei et de la sorcellerie dans la vie privée et publique des jaunes. **Revue politique et parlementaire** (10 nov 1905) 353-373. Étude extr. en grande partie d'un rapport présenté par le dr. regnault au congrès colonial de 1905, sous le titre: Hystérie, hypnose et sorcellerie en chine et en indo-chine.

Schafer, Edward H. A t'ang taoist mirror. **EC** 4 (1978-79) 56-59.

Shah, Idries. **Oriental magic.** NY (1973) See chap 17, The occult in china, 149-172.

Soulié, Charles G. **Sciences occult en chine. Le main.** Paris (1932) 136 p, illus.

Stirling, W.G. Chinese exorcists. **JMBRAS** 2 (1924) 41-47.

Tao, Pung-fai. Blick auf die welt der mystik und des aberglaubens in china. **OR** 16.4 (16 feb 1935) 105-108; 16.5 (1 märz 1935) 129-133.

Thiel, Josef. (Aufnahmen von Matthias Eder) Stellvertretende [t'i shen] gelübdeerfüllung. **FS** 1 (1942) 28-36, 6 photos.

Topley, Marjorie. Paper charms and prayer sheets as adjuncts to chinese worship. **JMBRAS** 26.1 (1953) 63-80.

Trying to tempt back the soul of an unconscious invalid. **Annual report of the church missionary society,** london (1906) 319.

Vichert, C.G. A study of the growth of a legend. **JWCBorderResS** 8 (1936) 173-174.

Waley, Arthur. Magical use of phallic representations. Its late survival in china and japan. **BMFEA** 3 (1931) 61-62. A propos B. Karlgren: Some fecundity symbols in ancient chin, **ibid** 2 (1930)

Watters, Thomas. Chinese notions about pigeons and doves. **JNCBRAS** 4 (1867) 225-242. Re magical uses.

Williams, E.T. Witchcraft in the chinese penal code. **JNCBRAS** 38 (1907) 61-96.

35. HEALTH, DISEASE, HEALING & RELIGION

Ahern, Emily M. Sacred and secular medicine in a taiwan village: a study of cosmological disorders. In **MCC** (1975) 91-113. Same title in **CHAS** (1978) 17-39.

Anderson, E.N. & Marja L. Folk medicine in rural hong kong. In **CE** (1973) 121-126.

Arlington, L.C. The mystic art of pulse feeling in china. **CJ** 7 (1927) 67-76, 170-175, 228-235; 8 (1928) 67-76.

Bazin. Notice historique sur le collège médical de peking, d'après le taï-thsing hoei-tien. **JA** sér 5, t 8 (1856) 393-427.

Beau, Georges. **La médecine chinoise.** Paris (1965) 190 p, illus.

Bowers, John Z. Chinese traditional medicine. **Asia** 5 (spring 1966) 62-69.

Breitenstein, H. **Gerichtliche medezin der chinesen von wang-in-hoai.** Nach der holländischen übers des herrn C.P.M. de Grys. Leipzig (1908)

Bridgman, R.F. La médecine dans la chine antique. **MCB** 10 (1955)

Cammann, Schuyler. Magic and medicinal wood in old chinese carvings. **JAFL** 74.292 (apr-june 1961) 116-125.

Cernada, E.C. & G. Cernada. Ethical judgments about induced abortion. **ASBIE** 41 (spring 1976) 47-59.

Chai, Ch'u & Winberg Chai. Confucianism and taoism. In **RS&P** (1973) 180-194.

Chamfrault, A. **Traité de médecine chinoise. . . d'après les textes chinois anciens et modernes.** Angoulème, coquemart (1964) 986 p, diagr.

Chang, Chen-yun. **The history and methods of physical diagnosis in classical chinese medicine.** Tsl Ronald Chen. N.Y. (1969) 72 p, illus.

Cheng, Jay Chi Cheong. Psychiatry in traditional chinese medicine. **Canadian psychiatric association journal** 15.4 (aug 1970) 399-401.

Chiang, Sheng. Exorcism in a modern setting. **Echo** 6.7 (sept 1977) 25-27, illus. Re "dance of chung kuei."

Chinese medicine. **Lancet** 182 (1912) 1006-1007.

Choa, Gerald. Chinese traditional medicine and contemporary hong kong. In **TICHK** (1967) 31-35.

Chow, Tse-tsung. The childbirth myth and ancient chinese medicine: a study of aspects of the wu tradition. In **AC:SEC** (1978) 43-89.

Cowdry, E.V. Taoist ideas of anatomy. **AMH** 3 (1921) 301-309.

Criqui, Fernand. **La médecine chinoise.** Monte-carlo (1967) 96 p, illus.

Dai, Bingham. Zen and psychotherapy. In **RS&P** (1973) 132-141, bibliog.

Diagnostic des médecins chinois. **RC** (1921) 509-513, fig.

Doolittle, Justus. Superstitious treatment of disease. Chap 5 in author's **SLC** vol 1 (1865) 142-167.

Dudgeon, John. **The beverages of the chinese; kung-fu or tauist medical gymnastics.** Tientsin (1895) illus. Repr & ed by William R. Berk, under title **Chinese healing arts; internal kung-fu,** culver city, calif (1979) 209 p, illus.

Dudgeon, J. Chinese arts of healing. **ChRec** 2.6 (nov 1869) 163-167, 2.7 (dec 1869) 183-186, 2.10 (mar 1870) 267-271, 2.11 (apr 1870) 293-298, 2.12 (may 1870) 332-339; 3.2 (july 1870) 40-44, 3.4 (sept 1870) 99-103, 3.5 (oct 1870) 120-125; 4.11 (apr 1872) 281-284.

Dudgeon, J. The great medical college at peking. **ChRec** 2.9 (feb 1870) 237-241.

Dudgeon, John. Kung-fu, or medical gymnastics. **JPOS** 3.3 (1893); 3.4 (1895)

Dudgeon, John. Medical divinities. In **DV**, vol 2, pt 3, no 26, 318-319.

Dudgeon, J. On the disgusting nature of chinese medicines. **ChRec** 2.10 (mar 1870) 285-287.

Epstein, Perle. **Oriental mystics and magicians.** NY (1975) See chap, China, 63-84, illus.

Filliozat, Jean. La médecine indienne et l'expansion bouddhique en extrême-orient. **JA** 224 (1934) 301-311.

Fisher, Tom. Trances, converts, and cures. **Echo** 2.6 (june 1972) 38-42, col photos. Cures at mother earth temple—ti mu miao—in puli.

Frick, Johann. How blood is used in magic and medicine in ch'inghai province. Tsl fr german James E. Mertz. **Anthropos** 46 (1951) 964-979.

Frick, Johann. Magic remedies used on sick children in the western valley of sining. Tsl James E. Mertz. **Anthropos** 46 (1951) 175-186. German orig in **ibid** 45 (1950) 787-800.

Gallin, Bernard. Comments on contemporary socio-cultural studies of medicine in chinese societies. In **MCC** (1975) 273-280. Same title in **CHAS** (1978) 173-181.

Gillard, Jean-Louis. **Métaphysique taoïste et acu-oncture chinoise.** Bordeaux (1968) 51 p.

Girardot, Norman J. Taoism. In **EBio** (1978) 1631a-1638a, bibliog.

Gould-Martin, Katherine. Hot cold clean poison and dirt: chinese folk medical categories. **SSM** 12B.1 (jan 1978) 39-46.

Gould-Martin, Katherine. Medical systems in a taiwanese village: ong-ia-kong, the plague god as modern physician. In **MCC** (1975) 115-141. Same title (minus first phrase) in **CHAS** (1978) 41-67.

Gruenhagen. Die grundlagen der chinesischen medizin. **Janus** 13 (1908) 1-14, 121-137, 191-205, 268-278, 328-337.

Guillemet, Dr. La médecine et les médecins en chine. **Annales d'hygiène et de médecine coloniales** 15 (1912) 152-175, 234-254.

Hackmann, Heinrich. Aus die heilsmethode des budd-hismus. **ZMK** 17 (1902) 360-367.

Haimes, Norma. Zen buddhism and psychoanalysis—a bibliographic essay. **Psychologia** 15 (1972) 22-30.

Hall, Manly Palmer. The fabulous story of jade. **Philosophical research society journal** (winter 1960) 42-45, illus. Re jade as a miraculous substance and as used in medicine.

Hall, Manly P. **The medicine of the sun and moon. The philosophic principles behind the chinese concept of healing.** Los angeles (1972) 32 p, illus.

Harlez, Charles de (tsl) Le livre de hoang-ti (hoang-ti nei king) Textes taoistes traduits des originaux chinois et commentés. **AMG** 20 (1891) 343-368.

Hartner, Willy. Heilkunde im alten china. **Sinica** 16 (1941) 217-265; 17 (1942) 266-328.

Hoeppli, R. Malaria in chinese medicine. **Sinologica** 4 (1954-56) 91-101, illus.

Holbrook, Bruce. Chinese psycho-social medicine. Doctor and tang-ki: an inter-cultural analysis. **ASBIE** 37(spring 1974) 85-110.

Holbrook, Bruce. Ethnoscience and chinese medicine, genuine and spurious. **ASBIE** 43 (spring 1977) 129-180.

Hsiao, Paul Shih-yi. Der chinesische mensch in philo-sophisch-religiöser sicht. In **ATOW** (1967) 223-235.

Hsieh, E.T. A review of ancient chinese anatomy. **Anatomical record** 20 (1921)

Hsu, Francis L.K. **Religion, science and human crisis.** London (1952) 142 p, illus.

Huard, Pierre and Wong Ming. Évolution de la matière médicale chinoise. **Janus** 47 (1958) 3-67.

Huard, Pierre and Wong Ming. Quelques aspects de la doctrine classique de la médecine chinoise. **Biologie médicale** 46 (1957) 3-119.

Huard, Pierre & M. Wong. Structure de la médecine chinoise. **BSEIS** sér 2, t 4 (1957) 299-376. See esp sec 17, Gérontologie et gérontoprophylaxie (re yoga and alchemy)

Huebotter, Franz. **Die chinesische medizin zu beginn des xx jahrbunherts und ihr historisches entwicklungsgang.** Leipzig (1929)

Huebotter, Franz. **Zwei berühmte chinesische ärzte des altertums, chouen-yü i . . . und hoa t'ouo . . .** Tokyo (1927) 48 p.

Huizenga, Lee S. Lü tsu and his relation to other medicine gods. **CMJ** 58 (1940) 275-283.

Hume, Edward H. **The chinese way in medicine.** Baltimore (1940) ref, index, illus. See esp lecture 1, The universe and man in chinese medicine.

Hume, Edward H. The square kettle. **BIHM** 2 (1934) 547-557 (On one of the three isles of the immortals)

Kaltenmark, Max. Hygiène et mystique en chine. **Bulletin de la société d'acuponcture** 33.3 (1959) 21-30.

Kao, John J. & Frederick F. Kao. Medical ethics, history of: sec 4, Contemporary china. In **EBio** (1978) vol 3, 917a-922a.

Kendall, Carlton. Magic herbs. The story of chinese medicine. **CJ** 16.6 (june 1932) 319-327.

Kervyn, Joseph. **Médecine chinoise. Choses vues.** Bruxelles (1947) 15 p.

Kleinman, Arthur. Medical and psychiatric anthropology and the study of traditional forms of medicine in modern chinese culture. **ASBIE** 39 (spring 1975) 107-123.

Kleinman, Arthur. **Patients and healers in the context of culture. An exploration of the borderland between anthropology, medicine, and psychiatry.** Univ california (1980) See passim. Based largely on author's field experience in taiwan.

Kleinman, Arthur. Social, cultural and historical themes in the study of medicine in chinese societies: problems and prospects for the comparative study of medicine and psychiatry. In **MCC** (1975) 645-658.

Kleinman, Arthur. The symbolic context of chinese medicine. **AJCM** 3.2 (1975) 103-124.

Kleinman, Arthur & Lilias H. Sung. Why do indigenous practitioners successfully heal? **SSM** 13B.1 (jan 1979) 7ff. Study of patients treated by shamans (tang-ki)

Kleinman, Arthur et al (ed) **Culture and healing in asian societies: anthropological, psychiatric and public health studies.** Cambridge, mass (1978) 462 p. Several art sep listed in our bibliog. Abbrev **CHAS.**

Kleinman, Arthur et al (ed) **Medicine in chinese cultures: comparative studies of health care in chinese and other societies.** Washington d.c. (1975) Art sep listed in our bibliog. Abbrev **MCC.**

Kuo, Li-cheng. Tsl Susan Converse. Chu yo ko: healing with charms. **Echo** 4.10 (nov 1974) 45-53, illus.

Laird, P.J. [Exorcism of an evil spirit as a cure in china] **CMI** 57.(1906) 540.

Lebra, W.P. (ed) **Culture-bound syndromes, ethnopsychiatry, and alternate therapies.** Univ hawaii (1976) Art sep listed in our bibliog. Abbrev **CBS.**

Lee, T'ao. Achievements of chinese medicine in the sui (589-617 a.d.) and t'ang (618-907 a.d.) dynasties. **CMJ** 71 (1953) 301-320.

Lee, T'ao. Medical ethics in ancient china. **CMJ** 61.2 (apr-june 1943) 123-131.

Lee, T'ao. Ten celebrated physicians and their temple. **CMJ** 58 (1940) 267-274.

Lesh, T. Zen and psychotherapy: a partially annotated bibliography. **Journal of humanistic psychology** 10 (1970) 75-83.

Li, Huan-hsin. Chinese medicine. **CC** 10.1 (1969) 67-79.

Liétord. Le pèlerin bouddhiste chinois i-tsing et la médecine de l'inde au IIIe siècle. **Bulletin de la société française d'histoire de la médecine** 1 (1903) 472-487.

Lion, Lucien. **Les ivoires religieux et médicaux chinois d'après la collection lucien lion. Texte de henri maspero, rené grousset, lucien lion.** Paris (1939) 96 p, pl.

Liu, Ts'un-yan. The taoists' knowledge of tuberculosis in the twelfth century. **TP** 57.5 (1971) 285-301. Repr in **LTY:SP** (1976)

Mackay, George L. Ignorant and superstitious methods of curing disease in north formosa. **ChRec** 24.11 (nov 1892) 524-529.

Mar, Peter G. The use of precious stones in ancient medicine. II. Some natural gem-stones used in chinese medicine. **CJ** 34.5 (may 1941) 220-232.

Martinie, J.A. Essai sur la médecine chinoise. Saigon, **Education** 1 (1948) 15-23.

Martinie, Jean. La médecine chinoise. **FA** 4 (fevr 1949) 549-569.

La Médecine chinoise. **TM** 6 (1900) 397-398.

Milne, Dave. Chinese medicine—ancient remedies for a modern world. **Echo** 1.4 (apr 1971) 36-41.

Morse, William R. **Chinese medicine.** N.Y. (1934) xxiii + 185 p, illus.

Morse, W.R. A memorandum on the chinese procedure of acupuncture. **JWCBorderResS** 5 (1932) 153-196, illus.

Morse, W.R. The practices and principles of chinese medicine. **JWCBorderResS** 3 (1926-1929) 82-104, charts.

Mortier, F. Les animaux dans la divination et la médecine populaire chinoise. **BSAB** 51 (1936) 268-275.

Nakayama, T. **Acupuncture et médecine chinoise vérifées au japon.** Paris (1934) 90 p, illus.

Needham, Joseph and Lu Gwei-djen. Hygiene and preventive medicine in ancient china. **JHMAS** 17 (1962) 429-478.

Nevius, John L. **Demon possession and allied themes.** Chicago etc (1896) 494 p, indexes. Mostly chin cases, with some others for comparison.

Nguyen-Van-Quan. **Acuponcture chinoise pratique; sur quelques recherches touchant la médecine traditionnelle sino-japonaise.** Paris (1936) 126 p. illus.

Oshawa, Georg. **Lehrbriefe der fernöstlichen philosophie und medizin in theorie und praxis.** Übers von Winifried Eggert. Heidelberg (1958) 22 p.

Otsuka, Yasuo. Chinese traditional medicine in japan. In **AMS** (1976) 322-339.

Otto, Johann H. **Das dau, tao, in der chinesischen heilkunst.** Hamburg (1954) 10 p.

Palmer, John Williamson. John chinaman, m.d. **Atlantic monthly** 21 (mar 1868) 257-268. Repr in Louise Desaulniers (ed) **Looking back at tomorrow; twelve decades of insights from the atlantic,** n.p. (1978) 27-41.

Pálos, István. **Atem und meditation. Moderne chinesische atemtherapie als vorschule der meditation. Theorie. Praxis. Originaltexte.** Weilheim (1968) 225 p, illus.

Pálos, István. **Chinesische heilkunst. Rückbesinnung auf eine grosse traditon.** Aus dem ungarischen in deutsche übertragen von Wilhelm Kronfuss. München (1966) 205 p, illus. Engl tsl [unnamed]: Stephan Palos, **The chinese art of healing,** london (1971) 237 p, illus.

Parker, E.H. Medical deities. **ChRev** 17 (1888-89) 115.

Porkert, Manfred. Die energetische terminologie in den chinesischen medizinklassikern. **Sinologica** 8 (1965) 184-210.

Porkert, Manfred. The intellectual and social impulses behind the evolution of traditional chinese medicine. In **AMS** (1976) 63-76.

Rall, Jutta. Über das ch'ao-shih chu-ping yüan-hou lun, ein werk der chinesischen medizin aus dem 7 jahrhundert. **OE** 14 (1967) 143-178, tables.

Rall, Jutta. Uber die wärmekrankheiten. **OE** 9 (1962) 139-153. Tsl of ch'ao yüan-fang: chu-ping yüan-hou lun, On the origins and symptoms of diseases, 610 a.d.; modern ed peking (1955)

Rall, Jutta. **Die vier grossen medizinschulen der mongolenzeit. Stand und entwicklung der chinesischen medizin in der chin und yüan zeit.** Wiesbaden (1970) 114 p.

Read, Bernard E. Ancient chinese medicine and its modern interpretation. **THM** 8 (1939) 221-234, illus.

Rosner, Erhard. Medizinisches gedankengut in der chinesischen 'kameralistischen' literatur. In **Asien** (1971) 494-501.

Rosner, Erhard. Schamanistische züge der chinesischen volkmedizin: zur bewertung unorthodoxer heilmethoden im traditionellen china. **Medizin-historisches journal** 9 (1974) 41-48.

Schiffeler, John William. Chinese folk medicine. A study of the shan-hai ching. **AsFS** 39.2 (1980) 41-83.

Schiffeler, John William. The origin of chinese folk medicine. **CC** 16.4 (dec 1975) 85-101. Same title in **AsFS** 35.1 (1976) 17-35.

Sen, Satiranjan. Two medical texts in chinese translation [in tripitaka] **VBA** 1 (1945) 70-95.

Sivin, Nathan A. A seventh-century chinese medical case history. **BHM** 41 (1967) 76-78, illus.

Smith, Carl T. Notes on tung wah hospital, hong kong. **JHKBRAS** 16 (1976) See 'Religious aspects of tung wah,' 269-272.

Soulié, George de Morant. **l'Acuponcture chinoise.** Paris (1939-41) 2 t, illus. See further same title, paris (1957) 1,000 p, illus.

Soulié, George de Morant. **Précis de la vraie acuponcture chinoise. Doctrine, diagnostic, thérapeutique.** Paris (1936) 6e éd, 199 p, illus; (1947) éd, 201 p, illus; (1964) éd, 209 p, pl, figs.

Topley, Marjorie. Chinese traditional etiology and methods of cure in hong kong. In **AMS** (1976) 243-265.

Topley, Marjorie. Chinese traditional ideas and the treatment of disease: two examples from hong kong. **Man** n.s. 5 (1970) 421-437.

Topley, Marjorie. Cosmic antagonisms: a mother-child syndrome. In **RRCS** (1974) 233-250.

Trippner, P.J. Der wandernde medizingott. **Anthropos** 46 (1951) 801-807. Re ch'inghai.

Tschen, Yin-ko. Buddhistischer in den biographien von tsan tschung und hua to im san guo dschï. **TJ** 6 (1930) 17-20.

Tseng, W.S. Folk psychotherapy in taiwan. In **CBS** (1976) 164-178.

Tseng, W.S. Psychiatric study of shamanism in taiwan. **AGP** 26 (1972) 561-565.

Tseng, Wen-shing. Traditional and modern psychiatric care in taiwan. In **MCC** (1975) 177-194.

Unschuld, Paul. Concepts of illness in ancient china: the case of demonological medicine. **Journal of medicine and pharmacy** 5.2 (1980) 117-132.

Unschuld, Paul. Medical ethics, history of: sec 3, Pre-republican china. In **EBio** (1978) vol 3, 911a-917a.

Unschuld, Paul Ulrich. **Medizin und ethic. Social-konflikte im china des kaiserzeit.** Wiesbaden (1975) viii + 98 s.

Unschuld, Paul U. **Medical ethics in imperial china. A study in historical anthropology.** Univ california (1979) 141 p, gloss, bibliog, index.

Unschuld, Paul Ulrich. **Die praxis des traditionellen chinesischen heilsysteme: unter einschluss der pharmazie dargestellt an den heutigen stand auf taiwan.** Wiesbaden (1973) viii + 182 s, illus.

Veith, Ilza. Psychiatric thought in chinese medicine. **JHMAS** 10.3 (july 1955) 261-268.

Veith, Ilza. Some philosophical concepts of early chinese medicine. Basavangudi, bangalore, Indian institute of culture, **Transactions** 4 (dec 1950) 15 p.

Veith, Ilza. The supernatural in far eastern concepts of mental disease. **BHM** 37.2 (1963) 139-158.

Veith, Ilza. **The yellow emperor's classic of internal medicine.** Univ california (1949) new [but not rev] ed (1966) 260 p, illus. See esp Introduction, passim.

Wieger, Leon. La médecine chinoise. Historique. **Bulletin médical franco-chinois, pékin** 1 (1920) 1-3.

Wong, K. Chimin. Chinese medical superstition. **National medical journal** 2 (1916)

Wong, K. Chimin. Hua t'o, the god of surgery. **CMJ** 41 (1927)

Wong, K. Chimin and Wu Lien-teh. **History of chinese medicine.** Tientsin (1932) 2nd ed shanghai (1936) xxviii + 906 p, illus.

Wu, Agnes Chen-chung & Yu-hei Hu. Many ways to health: a study of 2,000 rural and urban taiwan families. **AJCM** 8.4 (1980) 313-330.

Yap, P.M. The possession syndrome: a comparison of hong kong and french findings. **BJP** 106 (1960) 114-137.

Yewdale, M.S. The therapeutic power of taoism. **AP** 7 (1936) 271-274.

Zimmerman, Werner and Leung Tit-sang. **Chinesische weisheit und heilkunst.** München (1954) 51 p, illus.

Zwaan, J.P. Kleiweg de. **Völkerkundliches und geschichtliches über die heilkunde der china und japaner mit bes. berücksichtigung holländscher einflüssen.** Haarlem (1917) 656 p, illus.

36. RELIGION IN FOLKLORE, TRACT, LITERATURE & DRAMA
(See also **Taoist Immortals**)

Abel-Rémusat, J.P. (tsl) **Le livre des récompenses et des peines, ouvrage taoiste traduit du chinois avec des notes et des éclaircissements.** Paris (1816) 79 p, repr paris (1939) 113 p.

Alexander, Edwin. China's "three ways" as reflected in dream of the red chamber. **CC** 17.1 (mar 1976) 145-157.

W.G.B. (tsl) A discourse on bad luck. Translated from the cantonese colloquial. **ChRec** 21.3 (mar 1890) 112-118.

W.G.B. (tsl) How a man's life was lengthened. (A translation from a cantonese colloquial) **ChRec** 24.1 (jan 1891) 12-14. It was lengthened by spirits.

Barondes, R. de Rohan. **China: lore, legend & lyrics.** NY (1960) See passim. A melange.

Basset, R. Contes et légendes de l'extrême-orient. **RE** 1 (1920) 60-61.

Bauer, Wolfgang. **China und die hoffnung auf glück. Paradies, utopien, idealvorstellung.** München (1971) 703 s. zeittafel, anmerkungen, literaturverzeichnis, chin zeichenglossar. See rev by Vitali Rubin in **TP** 59 (1973) 68-78. Engl tsl by Michael Shaw, **China and the Search for happiness,** ny (1976) 502 p.

Bazin (aîné) Notice du chan-haï-king, cosmographie fabuleuse attribuée au grand yu. **JA** sér 3, t 8 (nov 1839) 337-382.

Beck, L. Adams. Chinese pilgrim's progress. **HJ** 20 (1921) 5-19. Contents derived from T. Richards' tsl A mission to heaven.

Belpaire, Bruno. Le taoisme et li t'ai-po. **MCB** 1 (1931-32) 1-14.

Bischoff, Friedrich A. Hsiao hung's wheel of birth and death. **ChLit** 2.2 (july 1980) 249-257. Re a 20th century novel with "strong budd flavor."

Bodde, Derk. Again some chinese tales of the super-natural. Further remarks on kan pao and his sou-shen chi. **JAOS** 62.4 (1942) 293-299.

Bodde, Derk. Some chinese tales of the supernatural. Kan pao and his sou-shen chi. **HJAS** 6 (1941-42) 338-357. Repr **ECC** (1981) 331-350.

Brandauer, Frederick P. The hsi-yu pu as an example of myth-making in chinese fiction. **TR** 6.1 (apr 1975) 99-120.

Brewster, Paul G. Some parallels between the fêng-shên-yen-i and the shah-nameh and the possible influence of the former upon the persian epics. **AsFS** 31.1 (1972) 115-122. Notes briefly parallels of several legends, and the "fungus of immortality."

Broman, Sven. Eight immortals crossing the sea. **BMFEA** 50 (1978) 25-48. Re chin shadow play in coll of ethno-graphical museum of sweden, stockholm. Tsl of libretto, with comm, index of chin char, illus, facs of text.

Brown, William. From sutra to pien-wen: a study of sudatta erects a monastery and the hsiang-mo pien-wen. Appendix, Sudatta erects a monastery (tsl) **TR** 9.1 (apr 1978) 67-101.

Chan, Ping-leung. Chinese popular water-god legends and the hsi yu chi. In **Essays in chinese studies presented to professor lo hsiang-lin,** univ hong kong (1970) 299-317.

Chang, Ching-erh. The structure and theme of the hsi-yu chi. **TR** 11.2 (winter 1980) 169-188.

Chang, Fu-jui. Le yi kien tche et la société des song. **JA** 256 (1968) 55-93. Text is "un recueil de contes relatifs à des évenements supernaturels."

Chen, Lucy H. (Ch'en Hsiu-mei) Spirit calling. In author's collection, **Spirit calling; tales about taiwan,** taipei (1962) 73-87. Fictional account of calling sick person's spirit by taoist priest.

Chesneaux, Jean. De la modernité du shui-hu-chuan. Pensée, religion et philosophie. In Françoise Aubin (ed) **Études song: in memoriam étienne balazs,** paris (1973) 25-44.

Chiang, Alpha C. Religion, proverbs, and economic mentality. **American journal of economics and sociology** 20.3 (apr 1961) 253-264.

Chiu, Kun-liang. Tsl Robert Christensen. The city god's own theatrical troupe. **Echo** 6.1 (july 1976) 13-24, col photos.

Chiu, Kuen-liang. Tsl Earl Wieman. Dance of chung kuei. **Echo** 6.7 (sept 1977) 17-24, illus.

The Chung kuei plays. **Echo** 6.7 (sept 1977) 3-7, 42, illus.

Chung kuei, the demon slayer: literature: the legends. **Echo** 6.7 (sept 1977) 13-16, illus.

Clayton, George A. Where the river-god lies buried. A chinese nature study. **EA** 3 (1904) 87-91.

Cohen, Alvin P. Avenging ghosts and moral judgment in ancient chinese historiography: three examples from shih-chi. In **LL&R** (1979) 97-108.

A Confucian tract, exhorting mankind always to preserve their celestial principles and their good hearts. **ChRep** 15.8 (aug 1846) 377-385, with chin text.

Cornaby, W. Arthur. Sir diamond, the demon\vanquisher **WMM** 122 (1899) 260-266. Same title in **EA** 4 (1905) 227-236.

Cornaby W. Arthur. Theology and eschatology of the chinese novel. **ChRec** 51 (1920) 166-170, 254-265, 331-342.

A Correspondent. Review of the shin seën tung keën,—a general account of the gods and genii; in 22 vols. **ChRep** 7.10 (feb 1839) 505-525; 7.11 (mar 1839) 553-568.

Davis, A.R. The double-ninth festival in chinese poetry: a study of variations upon a theme. In **Wen-lin** (1968) 45-64.

Demiéville, Paul. La montagne dans l'art littéraire chinois. **FA** 20 (1965-66) 7-32, pl.

Dennys, N.B. The folklore of china. **ChRev** 3.5—5.2 (mar-apr 1875—sept-oct 1876) Sep publ as **The folklore of china,** hong kong (1876) 156 p, repr detroit (1971) ny (1972)

DeWoskin, Kenneth (tsl) In search of the supernatural—selections from the sou-shen chi. **Renditions** 7 (spring 1977) 103-114.

Dien, Albert E. The yan-hun chih (accounts of ghosts with grievances): a sixth-century collection of stories). In **Wen-lin** (1968) 211-228.

Dudbridge, Glen. **The legend of miao-shan.** London (1978) 128 p, app, works cited, index. See Anna Seidel rev in **JAS** 38.4 (aug 1979) 770f.

Duyvendak, J.J.L. A chinese 'divina commedia.' **TP** 41 (1952) 255-316. On Lo Mao-teng: San-pao ta-chien hsia hsi-yang chi (1597) a fictitious and fantastic account of the voyages of cheng ho.

Eberhard, Wolfram. Orakel und theater in china. **AS** 18/19 (1965) 11-30.

Eberhard, Wolfram. Chinesische volksliteratur in chinesischen volkstempeln. In **IV Intl congress for folk-narrative research in athens, lectures and reports,** Georgios A. Megas (ed) athens (1965) 100-105. Rev engl tsl in **SCFRE** (1970) 97-112.

Eberhard, Wolfram. **Erzählungsgut aus südost-china.** Berlin (1966)

Eberhard, Wolfram. **Studies in chinese folklore and related essays.** Indiana univ and the hague (1970) 329 p, notes, bibliog, index, illus. All but 2 are republ, and most are tsl fr german William Templer. See pt 1, Essays on the folklore of chêkiang, china, 17-144; pt 2, Essays on the folklore of china, 145-230. (Abbrev **SCFRE**)

Eberhard, Wolfram. **Studies in taiwanese folktales.** Taipei (1970) 193 p.

Eberhard, Wolfram. A study of ghost stories from taiwan and san francisco. **AsFS** 33.2 (1971) 1-26.

Eberhard, Wolfram. The supernatural in chinese folk-tales from chekiang. In **Humaniora, essays in literature, folklore, bibliography,** ny (1960) 335-341. Repr in **SCFRE** (1970) 67-72.

Eberhard, Wolfram. Volkspoesie an tempelwänden. **Sinica** 11.3/4 (mai-juli 1936) 127-130, rev engl tsl in author's **SCFRE** (1970) 97-112.

Eder, Matthias. Das jahr im chinesischen volkslied. **FS** 4 (1945) 1-160.

Edkins, Joseph. The books of the modern religious sects in north china. **ChRec** 19 (1888) 261-268, 302-310.

Eichhorn, Werner. Bemerkungen über einen taoistischen roman. In **SSM/FHF** (1979) 353-361.

Eichhorn, Werner. Wang chia's shih-i-chi. **ZDMG** 102, n.s. 27 (1952) 130-142. ''. . . dieser aus mythen, legenden und tatssachen kompilierten mirakel-historie.''

Eichler, E.R. The k'uen shih wan [ch'üan shih wen] or, the practical theology of the chinese. **ChRev** 11 (1882) 93-101, 146-161. Popular moral and religious tracts.

Eichler, E.R. Die religiöse tractliteratur der chinesen. **AMZ** 19 (1892) 499-511.

Eliasberg, Danielle. Quelques problèmes relatifs au roman de zhong kui. In **MS/CA** (1977) 129-134.

Eliasberg, Danielle. **Le roman du pourfendeur de démons.** Paris (1976) 425 p, 1 pl. Re Chung k'uei.

Erkes, Eduard. Der pfau in religion und folklore. **JSMVL** 10 (1926-51 sic) 67-73.

Erkes, Eduard (tsl) Das 'zurückrufen der seele' (chao hun) des sung-yüh. Text, übers und erläuterungen. Leipzig (1914)

Fang, Lienche Tu. Ming dreams. **TJ** n.s. 10.1 (july 1973) 55-72.

Ferguson, John C. Books on journeys to western regions. **CJ** 11.2 (aug 1929) 61-68. Re Hsüan chuang's ta t'ang hsi yü chi; li chih-ch'ang's ch'ang ch'un chen jen hsi yu chi; hsi yu chi; hou hsi yu chi; tsa chü hsi yu chi.

Fu, James S. The harmony of humors: relations of the pilgrims in his-yu chi. **APQCSA** 6.2 (autumn 1974) 28-42.

Fujino, Iwatomo. On chinese soul-inviting and firefly-catching songs: a study on chinese folklore. **ActaA** [tokyo] 19 (dec 1970) 40-57.

Galpin, F. Notes on the ethical and christian value of chinese religious tracts and books. **ChRec** 12.3 (may-june 1881) 202-217.

Garritt, J.C. Popular account of the canonization of the gods, illustrated. **ChRec** 30 (1899) 162-174. Feng shen yen-i.

Giles, Lionel. A t'ang manuscript of the sou shen chi. **NCR** 3 (1921) 378-385, 460-468.

Gordon-Cumming, C.F. Temple theatres. col 1, chap 15 in author's **WinC** (1886) 270-276.

Grube, Wilhelm (tsl) **Fêng-shên-yen-i. Die metamorphosen der goetter.** Leiden (1912) bd 1, xxiv + 304; bd 2, 305-657.

Grube, Wilhelm. Die huldigungsfeier der acht genien für den gott des langen lebens, ein chinesischer schattenspieltext. In **BMV** (1906) 1-4.

Grube, Wilhelm. Zur pekinger volkskunde. **Veröffentlichungen aus dem königlichen museum für völkerkunde** 7.1/4 (1901) 1-160.

Gützlaff, Dr (übers) mit mitgeheilt von prof Neumann. Sprüche und erzählungen aus dem chinesischen hausschatz. **ZDMG** 16 (1862) 628-650.

Haden, R.A. (tsl) The kan ying pien . . . The tractate on rewards and punishments by the great exalted. **EA** 3 (1904) 172-182.

Hales, Dell R. Dreams and the daemonic in traditional chinese short stories. In William H. Nienhauser, jr (ed) **Critical essays on chinese literature,** chin univ hk (1976) 71-88.

Hankey, Rosalie. Ghosts and shamanism in kwangtung. **CFQ** 2 (1943) 303-308.

Hankey Rosalie. California ghosts. **CFQ** 1 (1942) 155-177. Chin ghost stories coll in california.

Hawkes, David. The quest of the goddess. **AM** n.s. 13 (1967) 71-94. On the ch'u tz'u, Songs of the south. Repr with some rev in Cyril Birch (ed) **Studies in chinese literary genres,** univ california (1974) 42-68.

Hawkes, David. The supernatural in chinese poetry. In D. Grant and M. Maclure (ed) **The far east: china and japan,** univ toronto (1961) 311-324.

Heřmanová-Novotná, Zdenka. An attempt at linguistic analysis of the text of ta t'ang san-tsang ch'ü ching shih-hua. **ArchOr** 39 (1971) 167-189. Re text, preserved in japan and ed by lo chen-yü in 1916, narrating story of hsi yu chi.

Ho, Peng Yoke, Goh Thean Chye & Beda Lim. Lu yu, the poet-alchemist. Canberra, australian natl univ **occasional paper no 13, faculty of asian studies** (1972) 51 p Re ". . . poet's alchemical beliefs and activities . . . "

Ho, Peng Yoke, Goh Thean Chye & David Parker. Po chü-i's poems on immortality. **HJAS** 34 (1974) 163-186. Re the poet and alchemy.

Ho, Peng-yoke & Yu Wang-luen. Physical immortality in the early nineteenth-century novel ching-hua-yüan. **OE** 21.1 (june 1974) 33-51.

Hrdličková, Věnceslava. The motif of the god of the hearth and the division of the joint family in chinese chap-books. **Acta universitatis carolinae** (1968) 81-102.

Hsu, Jing & Wen-shing Tseng. Family relations in classic chinese opera. **IJSP** 20 (1974) 159-172.

Huang, Chun-ming. The forbidden puppets. **Echo** 2.9 (oct 1972) 24-34, col photos. Re the connection of marionettes with relig, among other things.

Huang, Joe C. Ideology and confucian ethics in the characterization of bad women in socialist literature. In **Deviance** (1977) 37-51.

Imbault-Huart, C. (tsl) Trois contes de fées traduits du chinois. **REO** 2 (1883) 281-286 (Extr du shen-nü chuan)

Iriya, Yoshitaka. Tsl by N.A. Waddell. Chinese poetry and zen. **EB** n.s. 6.1 (may 1973) 54-67.

Jameson, R.D. **Three lectures on chinese folkore.** Peking (1932) ix + 13 + 164 p.

Johnson, T.W. Far eastern fox lore. **AsFS** 33 (1974) 35-68.

Julien, Stanislas (tsl) **Livre des récompenses et des peines.** Paris (1835) (T'ai-shang kan-ying p'ien)

Kalvodová, Dana. Wang k'uei in hell: the metamorphosis of a chinese play. **Dodder** 2 (jan 1970) 46-48.

Keënyun yewheŏ sheteě or odes for children in rhyme, on various subjects, in thirty-four stanzas. **ChRep** 4 (oct 1835) 287-291. Tsl of text, which consists of moralistic verses.

Kopetsky, Elma E. (tsl) Two fu on sacrifices by yang hsiung: the fu on kanch'üan and the fu on ho-tung. **JOS** 10.2 (july 1972) 85-118. Re imperial sacrifices to the supreme one at kan-ch'üan palace; to sovereign earth at fen-yin in ho-tung; both took place in 13 b.c.

Koskikallio, T. The religious motive in the book of poetry (shih ching) **ChRec** 71.12 (dec 1940) 768-780.

Kroll, Paul W. Szu-ma ch'eng-chen in t'ang verse. **SSCRB** 6 (fall 1978) 16-30.

Kuo, Li-cheng. Tsl Linda Yee. The doll behind every mystic. **Echo** 4.7 (july-aug 1974) 15-18, 1 illus. Re camphor-willow god, chang-liu shen; incl author's retelling of a story fr liao-chai chih yi.

Kuo, Li-cheng. Tsl Scott Satterfield. Peopling the sorcerer's stable. **Echo** 5.6 (june 1975) 18-20, illus. Tale of the black magic called tsao-ch'u, "making animals."

Kuo, Mo-jo. And the jade-like firmament was cleared of dust. **CL** (may 1966) 118-122. Political observations on an incident in the white bone demon fr pilgrimage to the west.

Lamont, H.G. (tsl) An early ninth century debate on heaven: liu tsung-yüan's t'ien shuo and liu yü-hsi's t'ien lun. **AM** 18.2 (1973) 181-208; pt 2, **ibid** 19.1 (1974) 37-85.

Lévy, André. **Inventaire analytique et critique de conte chinois en langue vulgaire.** Paris, lre partie, lre vol (1978) 336 p; lre partie, 2e vol (1979) 464 p; 2e partie, ler vol (1981) 516 p.

Li, Lillian. Two california ghosts. **CFQ** 4 (1945) 278-280

Ling, Shun-sheng. Kuo shang and li hun of the nine songs and the ceremonies of head-hunting and head-feast. **ASBIE** 9 (1960) engl abrmt 451-461.

Liu, Ts'un-yan. **Buddhist and taoist influences on chinese novels. Volume 1: The authorship of the fêng shên yen i.** Wiesbaden (1962) viii + 326 p, index, pl.

Lo, Chin-t'ang. Popular stories of the wei and chin periods. **JOS** 17.1/2 (1979) 1-9.

Loewe, Michael. **Ways to paradise. The chinese quest for immortality.** London (1979) 270 p, illus, app, notes. Based on han dyn silk painting, tlv bronze mirrors, and representations of hsi wang mu.

Macgowan, John. **Chinese folk-lore tales.** N.Y. (1920) 197 p.

Mackerras, Colin. **The chinese theatre in modern times** London & univ mass (1975) See Index, Religion.

Mackerras, Colin. **The rise of the peking opera, 1770-1870.** Oxford univ (1972) See Index, Religion.

Mansfield, M.T. Chinese legends. **FLJ** 5 (1887) 124-127.

Martin, W.A.P. **The lore of cathay.** N.Y. (1901) repr taipe (1971) See Native tracts . . . 148-162.

Martin, W.A.P. The native tract-literature of china. **ChRec** 18 (1887) 329-334, 369-374.

Mathieu, Rémi (tsl) **Le mu tianzi zchuan.** Paris (1978) 320 p, incl étude critique.

McHugh, Tom (tsl) Chung kuei gives his sister in marriage. A Ch'ing dynasty kun chu play. **Echo** 6.7 (sept 1977) 45-52, illus.

Miller, Lucien. **Masks of fiction in dream of the red chamber. Myth, mimesis, and persona.** Univ arizona (1975) See Index for various pertinent subjects.

Mitsunori, Okuno. Chinese superstition in fiction and folklore. **Contemporary japan** 9 (1940) 1567-1577.

Moral tales of the treatise on response and retribution (t'ai shang kan ying p'ien) **OC** 19.9 (sept 1905) 547-562; 19.10 (oct 1905) 604-621. Tsl partly by Teitaro Suzuki and partly fr french version of Stanislas Julien; illus by chin artists.

Moule, G.E. (tsl) A guide to true vacuity. By yuen-yang-tsze. **JNCBRAS** 23 (1889) 9-22. A popular philosophical-religious tract on one sheet, from hangchow.

Mythological account of hiuen-tien shangti, the high ruler of the sombre heavens, with notices of the worship of shángtí among the chinese. **ChRep** 18.2 (feb 1849) 102-109. Fr sau shin ki (sou shen chi)

Mythological account of some chinese deities, chiefly those connected with the elements. Translated from the siú shin ke (sou shen chi) **ChRep** 19.6 (june 1850) 312-317.

Ng, Yong-sang. Pai ngo t'an. The legend of the macao passage. **CJ** 24 (1936) 202-204.

Ng, Yong-sang. The temple of no sorrows. A cantonese santa claus story. **CJ** 19 (1933) 280-284.

Oberle, A. Der hundertkopfdämon im volksglauben des westtales und des chinesischtibetanischen kontaktgebietes im osttale von kuei-te in der provinz ch'ing-hai. In **Ethnographische beiträge aus der ch'inghai provinz,** peking (1952) 222-233.

Odontius, L. Chinesische märchen. (Nemesis, gleichgesinnte seelen, seelenwanderung, o-ha) **OstL** 17 (1903) 798-799.

Paper, Jordan (comp) **An index to stories of the supernatural in the fa yüan chu lin.** Taipei (1973) ix + 29 p.

Pavie, Théodore. Yu-ki le magicien, Légende chinoise. **RDM** 6e sér, 9 (15 mars 1851) 1129-1144.

Pimpaneau, Jacques. Chinese medium cults and creativity in literature. In china soc of singapore, **China society 25th anniversary journal** (1975) 30-35.

Plaks, Andrew H. **Archetype and allegory in the dream of the red chamber.** Princeton univ (1976) See esp chap 1, Archetype and mythology in chinese literature, 11-26; chap 2, The marriage of nü-kua and fu-hsi, 27-42.

Plopper, Clifford H. **Chinese religion seen through the proverb.** Shanghai (1926) 381 p, illus. repr (1935) repr ny (1969)

Porkert, Manfred. Die Zweispältige rolle des chiang tzu-ya, der zentralfigur in feng-shen yen-i. **Sinologica** 11 (1970) 135-143.

Poseck, Helena von. Why the city god of yench'en has no skin on his face. **EA** 3 (1904) 169-171.

Review of the shin seën tung keën, a general account of the gods and genii; in 22 vols. **ChRep** 7 (1839) 505-525, 553-568.

Richard, Timothy (tsl) **One of the world's literary masterpieces, hsi yu chi, a mission to heaven. A great chinese epic and allegory by ch'iu ch'ang ch'un, a taoist gamaliel who became a prophet and advisor to the chinese court.** Shanghai (1913) xxxix + 362 + viii p, illus.

Richard, Timothy (tsl) One of the world's literary masterpieces. Introduction to a great chinese epic or religious allegory by ch'iu ch'ang ch'un born a.d. 1148 . . . **JNCBRAS** 44 (1913) 3-10. Re hsi yu chi.

Scarborough, William. The popular religious literature of the chinese. **ChRec** 13.4 (july-aug 1882) 301-307; 13.5 (sept-oct 1882) 337-355.

Schafer, Edward H. The auspices of t'ang. **JAOS** 83 (1963) 197-225. Re ". . . birds richly endowed with mana . . . the birds of auspices," with many illus passages fr t'ang lit.

Schafer, Edward H. The capeline cantos; verses on the divine loves of taoist priestesses. **AS** 32.1 (1978) 5-65.

Schafer, Edward H. Li po's star power. **SSCRB** 6 (fall 1978) 5-15.

Schafer, Edward. H. **Mao shan in t'ang times.** Boulder, colo (1980) 72 p, notes, diagram. SSCR monograph no 1.

Schafer, Edward H. **Pacing the void. T'ang approaches to the stars.** Univ california (1977) 352 p, illus, app, notes, bibliog, gloss, index.

Schafer, Edward H. The table of contents of the t'ai p'ing kuang chi. **ChLit** 2.2 (july 1980) 258-263.

Schafer, Edward H. Three divine women of south china. **ChLit** 1 (1979) 31-42.

Schafer, Edward H. A trip to the moon. **JAOS** 96.1 (jan-mar 1976) 27-37.

Schipper, K.M. The divine jester, some remarks on the gods of the chinese marionette theater. **ASBIE** 21 (1966) 81-94.

Schüler, W. Das chinesische volkstheater in religiöses bedeutung. **ZMK** 25 (1920) 27-38.

Schwarz, Ernst. Das drachenbootfest und die "neun lieder." **Wissenschaftliche zeitschrift der humbolt-universität zu berlin gesellschafts-und sprachwissenschaftliche reihe** 16 (1967) 443-452.

Sing shi páu yen. Precious words to awaken the age. By cháng lí chen. Published at canton 1848. **ChRep** 19.5 (1850) 233-241.

Sowerby, Arthur. The book of rewards and punishments. **ChRec** 48.1 (jan 1917) 7-20. Analysis of kan ying p'ien.

Sowerby, Arthur de Carle. Some chinese animal myths and legends. **JNCBRAS** 70 (1939) 1-20.

Steininger, Hans. **Hauch- und körperseele und der dämon bei kuan yin tze; untersuchungen zur chinesischen psychologie und ontologie.** Leipzig (1953) 93 p.

Stories about not being afraid of ghosts. **CL** 5 (may 1961) 72-83. Six stories fr bk of the same title.

Sung, Shi. Tsl Ma Kuo-hai. Interview with peiping opera actor sun yuan-pin. **Echo** 6.7 (sept 1977) 42-43.

Sung, Shi. Tsl Ho Ku-li. No-cha: the investiture of the gods. A short story. **Echo**, pt 1, 2.3 (mar 1972) 47-52; pt 2, 2.4 (apr 1972) 40-44.

Suzuki, Teitaro and Paul Carus (tsl) **T'ai-shang kan-ying p'ien.** Chicago (1906) repr la salle, ill (1950 and 1973) Popular tract.

Suzuki, Teitaro and Paul Carus (tsl) Yin wen chih. **OC** 19.8 (aug 1905) 477-493. **Yin wen chih.** Chicago (1906) repr la salle, ill (1950) Popular tract.

Tu, Wei-ming. Hsi-yu chi as an allegorical pilgrimage in self-cultivation. **HR** 19.2 (nov 1979) 177-184, Rev of Anthony Yü's tsl q.v. vol 1.

Turrettini, François (tsl) **Le livre des récompenses et des peines.** Génève (1889) T'ai-shang kan-ying p'ien.

Van der Loon, P. Les origines rituelles du théâtre chinois. **JA** 265.1/2 (1977) 141-168.

Van Over, Raymond (ed) **Chinese mystics.** NY etc (1973) xxx + 183 p. Sel fr taoist and budd texts.

Van Over, Raymond. **Taoist tales.** NY etc (1973) 250 p.

Ward, Barbara E. Not merely players: drama, art and ritual in traditional china. **Man** 14.1 (mar 1979) 18-39.

Watters, T. Chinese fox-myths. **JNCBRAS** 8 (1873) 45-65.

Webster, James. An analysis of the kan ying pien. **ChRec** 50.2 (feb 1919) 94-99.

Webster, James (tsl) **The kan ying pien . . . with full introduction, the text, translation, and notes.** Shanghai (1918)

Wen, Ch'ung-i. A study of the river god of the nine songs. **ASBIE** 9 (1960) engl summ 161-162.

Wen, Ch'ung-i. The supreme being and the natural gods in the nine songs. **ASBIE** 17 (1964) engl summ 70-71.

Wetterwald, Albert. Le diable sonneur de cloches. **RC** (1906) 24-41.

Whitaker, K.P.K. Tsaur jyr's 'luoshern fu.' (On the goddess of the luoh river) **AM** ser 3, 4 (1954) 36-56.

Wieger, Léon. Catéchisms taoïste (t'ai-shang kan-ying p'ien) In author's **Rudiments, 4. Morale et usages,** ho-kien-fou, 2nd ed (1905) 231-299.

Wilhelm, Hellmut. Wanderungen des geistes. **EJ** 33 (196) 177-200. Examples fr lit and the yi ching.

Williams, Mrs. E.T. Some popular religious literature of the chinese. **JNCBRAS** 33 (1900-01) 11-29.

Williams, F. Wells. Chinese folklore and some western analogies. **Annual report of the board of regents of the smithsonian institution** (1900) 575-600.

Willoughby-Meade, G. Ghost and vampire tales of china. **AR** 21 (1925) 690-700; 22 (1926) 113-148.

Wivell, Charles J. Myth and ritual patterns in king wu's campaign against king chou. **AsFS** 30.1 (1971) 31-37.

Wu Tsu-hsiang. On 'the pilgrimage to the west.' **CL** 1 (jan 1961) 115-125.

Yang, Hsien-i & Gladys Yang (tsl) The pilgrimage to the west (an excerpt from the novel) **CL** 1 (jan 1961) 126-172.

Yang, Hsien-i & Gladys Yang (tsl) Pilgrimage to the west (a chapter from the novel) **CL** 5 (may 1966) 100-117.

Yao, Tao-chung. Ch'üan chen taoism and yüan drama. **JCLTA** 10.1 (feb 1980) 44-56.

Yen, Yuan-shu (tsl) Yellow millet dream. A yuan dynasty play by ma chih-yuan. **Echo** 5.2/3 (feb-mar 1975) 13-23, 94. Re the 8 immortals.

Yetts, W.P. Taoist tales. **NCR** 2 (1920) 290-297.

Yip, Wai-lim. The taoist aesthetic: yu-yen tu-hua, the unspeaking, self-generating, self-conditioning, self-transforming, self-complete nature. In William Tay, Ying-hsiung Chou & Heh-hsiang Yuan (ed) **China and the west: comparative literature studies,** chin univ hk (1980) 17-32.

Yu, Anthony C. (tsl) The journey to the west. **Renditions** 13 (spring 1980) 21-39. Tsl of chap 64.

Yu, Anthony C. (tsl and ed) **The journey to the west.** Univ chicago, vol 1 (1977) xiii + 530 p, intro, notes; vol 2 (1978) 438 p, notes; vol 3 (1980) 453 p, notes; vol 4 (1983) 469 p, notes, index.

Yu, Anthony C. The monkey's tale. **University of chicago magazine** 70 (1977) 10-21. Tsl of hsi yu chi chap 27.

Yuan, Te-hsing. Dragons. Part 1: dragon tales. **Echo** 6.1 (july 1976) 45-56, illus.

37. SECTS, SECRET SOCIETIES & NEW RELIGIONS

Alabaster, Chaloner. The antiquity of freemasonry in china. **NCH** (5 feb 1860) 100-101.

Bach, A.H. Die triasgesellschaft. **FO** 2 (1903) 268-283.

Backhouse, Sally. Secret sons of the red eyebrows. **Orientations** 3.5 (may 1972) 36-44, illus.

Balfour, Frederic. Secret societies and their political signifi-cance. In author's **Waifs and strays,** london and shanghai (1876) 23-38.

Balfour, Frederic H. Secret societies in china. **JMGS** 7 (1891) 40-56. Same title in **Goldthwaite's geographical magazine** 4 (1892) 775-782.

Bauer, Wolfgang. **China und die hoffnung auf glück. Paradies, utopien, idealvorstellung.** München (1971) 703 s, zeittafel, anmerkungen, literaturverzeichnis, chin zeichenglossar. See rev art by Vitali Rubin in **TP** 59 (1973) 68-78. Engl tsl Michael Shaw, **China and the search for happiness,** ny (1976) 502 p.

Baynes, Herbert. Secret societies in china. **IAQR** 3rd ser, 6 (1898) 318-321.

Blake, Lady. The triad society and the restoration of the ming dynasty. **NC** 71 (1912) 667-687.

Blythe, Wilfred. **The impact of chinese secret societies in malaya.** London (1970) 14 + 566 p, bibliog.

Boyle, F. Chinese secret societies. **Harper's new monthly magazine** 83 (june-nov 1891) 595-602.

Brace, A.J. Some secret societies in szechwan. **JWCBorderResS** 8 (1936) 177-180.

G.M.C. The origin of the t'ien ti hwui. **NQ** 1 (1867) 55-58.

Candlin, George F. The associated fists. The society which caused the riots, and led to war in china. **OC** 14 (sept 1900) 551-561. About the boxers.

Castellane, le comte Boni de. Boxeurs et sociétés secrètes en chine. **RDM** 10e sér, 160 (1 août 1900) 689-700.

Chan, Hok-lam. The white lotus-maitreya doctrine and popular uprisings in ming and ch'ing china. **Sinologica** 10 (1969) 211-233.

Chao, Wei-pang. Secret religious societies in north china in the ming dynasty. **FS** 7 (1948) 95-115.

Chavannes, Édouard. La société des boxeurs en chine au commencement du XIXe siècle. **JA** 9e sér, 17 (1901) 164-168.

Ch'en, Chien-fu. Tsl Winfried Glüer. Christianity in china seen by a new confucian. **CF** 15.3 (autumn 1972) 144-161. "New confucian" refers to ch'en's new relig, founded in taipei.

Ch'en, Jerome. Secret societies. **Ch'ing-shih wen-t'i** 1.3 (feb 1966) 13-16.

Chesneaux, Jean. Chinese secret societies in the XIX-XX centuries. **Ch'ing-shih wen-t'i** 1.1 (may 1965) 5-8.

Chesneaux, Jean (ed) **Mouvements populaires et sociétés secrètes en chine aux xixe et xxe siècles.** Paris (1970) Engl version, **Popular movements & secret societies in china 1840-1950,** stanford univ (1972) 328 p, notes, bibliog, gloss, index. The two versions differ in contents: 9 papers of french version are not in engl edition; 1 paper in engl version was not in french ed; many papers substantially rev in engl versions. Engl ed abbrev **PMSS.**

Chesneaux, Jean. **Les sociétés secrètes en chine (XIXe et XXe siècles)** Paris (1965) 277 p, illus. Avec la collabora-tion de Marianne Rochline. Engl tsl Gillian Nettle: **Secret societies in china in the 19th and 20th centuries.** Hong kong and univ michigan (1971) 210 p, bibliog, chin char-acter index, index, illus.

A chinese secret society: the rise and growth of the 'ch'ing pang.' **China review** [london] 3 (1934) 35-37.

Comber, Leon. **An introduction to chinese secret societies in malaya.** Singapore (1957) 77 p, map, 12 pl.

Comber, Leon. **The traditional mysteries of chinese secret societies in malaya.** Singapore (1961) xii + 113 p, illus.

Concerning the tan tae hoey in singapore. **JIA** 6 (1852) 545-555. Personal account of visit to a meeting of the t'ien-ti hui near singapore.

Cordier, Henri. Les sociétés secrètes chinoises. **RE** 7.1/2 (1888) 52-72. Same title in **Revue bleue,** ann 39 (23 mars 1901) 365-369.

Culin, Stewart. The i hing or 'patriotic rising.' A secret society among the chinese in america. **Proc numismatic and antiquarian society of philadelphia** (1887-89)

Culin, Stewart. Chinese secret societies in the u.s. **JAFL** 3.8 (feb-mar 1890) 39-43.

Dardess, John W. The transformations of messianic revolt and the founding of the ming dynasty. **JAS** 29 (1970) 539-558.

DeKorne, John C. **The fellowship of goodness. T'ung shan she . . . A study in contemporary chinese religion.** Grand rapids, mich (1941) vi + 109p (publ by author in mimeo)

Dubarbier, Georges. Les sociétés secrètes en chine. **NR** 4e sér, 49 (1928) 31 et seq.

Dunstheimer, G.G.H. Deux études sur les religions chinoises. **ASR** 4 (juil-dec 1957) 133-142. Rev art on Vincent Y.C. Shih's Some chin rebel ideologies, **TP** 44.1/3, and Alan J.A. Elliott's **Chinese spirit medium cults in singapore** (1955) qqv.

Dunstheimer, Guillaume. Quelques aspects religieux des sociétés secrètes. **MPSSC** (1970) 69-73. Engl tsl, Some religious aspects of secret societies, in **PMSSC** (1972) 23-28.

Dunstheimer, G.G. Religion et magie dans le mouvement des boxeurs d'après les textes chinois. **TP** 47 (1959) 322-367.

Dunstheimer, G.G.H. Religion officielle, religion populaire et sociétés secrètes en chine depuis les han. In **EncyP:HR** vol 3, paris (1976) 371-448, bibliog.

Edkins, Joseph. The books of the modern religious sects in north china. **ChRec** 19.6 (1888) 261-268; 19.7 (1888) 302-310.

Edkins, J. Religious sects in north china. **ChRec** 16.7 (july 1886) 245-252.

Enjoy, Paul d'. Associations, congrégations et sociétés secrètes chinoises. **RIC** 7 (15 avr 1907) 440-452.

Enjoy, Paul d'. Congrégations et sociétés secrètes chinoises. **La revue** 52 (1 nov 1904) 75-89.

Fang, Fu-an. Almost everybody has his secret society in china. **CWR** (14 june 1930) 60.

Faure, David. Secret societies, heretic sects, and peasant rebellions in nineteenth century china. **Journal of the chinese university of hong kong** 5.1 (1979) 189-206.

Favre, Benoit. Les sociétés de frères jures en chine. **TP** 19 (1918-19) 1-40.

Favre, Benoit. **Les sociétés secrètes en china; origine—rôle historique—situation actuel.** Paris (1933) 222 p.

Fay, Donald. The international union of religions. **ChRec** 55.6 (june 1924) 361-366; 55.7 (july 1924) 155-159. Re a new relig of china.

Floris, George A. Chinese secret societies. **CR** 193 (june 1958) 319-322.

Gambo, Charles. Chinese associations in singapore. **JMBRAS** 39.2 (1966) 123-168.

Genähr, G. Gottsucher unter den chinesen (lung-hwa-sekte) **AMZ** 33 (1906) 38-44, 72-77, 117-129.

Genähr, J. Seekers after god amongst the chinese. **ChRec** 37.9 (sept 1906) 471-477; 37.10 (oct 1906) 548-555. Re relig sects.

Geoffrey, C.C. Red spears in china. **CSM** 22.4 (1927) 27-29.

Giles, Herbert A. **Freemasonry in china.** Amoy (1880) 34 p; 2nd ed shanghai (1890) 38 p with add.

Glick, Carl and Hong Sheng-hwa. **Swords of silence. Chinese secret societies, past and present.** N.Y. (1947) 292 p.

Glüer, Winfried. The new confucian—a modern religious movement. **CF** 15.3 (autumn 1972) 138-143. Re a new relig founded by ch'en chien-fu in taipei.

Grootaers, Willem A. Une séance de spiritisme dans une religion secrète à péking en 1948. **MCB** 9 (1948-51) 92-98.

Grootaers, Willem A. Une société secrète moderne, i-koan-tao. **FS** 5 (1946) 316-352.

Gutzlaff, Charles. On the secret triad society of china, chiefly from papers belonging to the society found at hong kong. **JRAS** 8 (1846) 361-367.

Hayes, James. More notes on tsuen wan. **JHKBRAS** 19 (1979) 204-213. On several temples, and a shrine for a "new relig" of the 19th century, the chun hung kan (chen k'ung chiao)

Heckethorn, Charles W. **The secret societies of all ages and countries.** London (1875) See vol 1, chap 6, 87 et seq; vol 2, 328.

Hodous, Lewis. The tao tê hsüeh shê, a modern syncretistic sect in china. **Actes 18e ICO, Leiden, 1931** (1932) 122-123.

Hoffman, Johann J. Oath taken by members of the triad society, and notices of its origin. **ChRep** 18.6 (june 1849) 281-295.

Hsiao, Kung-ch'üan. **Rural china: imperial control in the nineteenth century.** Univ washington (1960) See 229-235: Heretical sects.

Huberty, James F. The secret sects of shantung, with appendix. In **Records of the general conference of protestant missionaries in china,** shanghai (1890) 196-202.

Hugh, Albert Y. Significance of secret societies in chinese life. **CWR** 42 (10 sept 1927) 38-39.

Hutson, James (tsl) History of chinese secret societies. **CJ** 9 (1928) 164-170, 215-221, 276-282; 10 (1929) 12-16. Tsl fr chin tsl of jap work by Hirayama Amane.

Initiation ceremonies of the 'red spears.' **PT** n.s. 6 (1934) 147-151.

James, F.H. North-china sects. **ChRec** 30 (1899) 74-76.

James, F.H. Secret societies in shantung. In **Records of the 1890 missionary conference,** shanghai (1890)

Katschen, Leopold. Chinesische geheimgesellschaften. **Deutsche rundschau für geographie und statistik** 22 (1899-1900) 250-254.

Kesson, John **The cross and the dragon.** London (1854) See chap 17-18 on secret societies, 242-282.

Labadie-Lagrave, G. Les sociétés secrètes en chine. **TM** 6 (1900) 222-223, 230.

Leboucq, P. **Associations de la chine. Lettres du p. leboucq, missionaire au tché-ly-sud-est, publiées par un de ses amis.** Paris (ca 1875?) xiii + 312.

Leboucq, P. Les sociétés religieuses en chine. Tche-ly sud-est, village de iam-kia-sé, ler mars 1875. **ER** 19e ann, 5e sér, 8 (1875) 641-664.

Leboucq, P. Les sociétés secrètes en chine. District de X. . ., province de tche-ly, 27 février 1875. **ER** 19e ann, 5e sér, 8 (1875) 197-220.

Lewy, Guenter. **Religion and revolution.** Oxford univ (1974) See chap 3, heterodoxy and rebellion in traditional china, 57-69.

Li, Dun-jen. **The civilization of china from the formative period to the coming of the west.** NY (1975) See chap 4, Wei-shou. Buddhism during the north wei; chap 10 no 50, Origin of the lungmen society.

Liao, T'ai-ch'u. The ko lao hui in szechuan. **PA** 20 (1947) 161-173.

Llewellyn, Bernard. Secret societies of china. **CR** 181 (apr 1952) 217-220.

Lutschewitz, W. Die religiösen sekten in nordchina, mit besonderer berücksichtigung d. sekten in shantung. **OstL** 19 (1905) 203-207, 247-251, 291-293, 337-340.

Lyman, Stanford M. Chinese secret societies in the occident: notes and suggestions for research in the sociology of secrecy. **Canadian review of sociology and anthropology** 1 (may 1964) 79-102.

Lyman, Stanford, W.E. Willmott, and Ho Berching. Rules of a chinese secret society in british columbia. **BSOAS** 27.3 (1964) 530-539, illus.

Mabbett, Ian. Secret societies in imperial china. **Hemisphere** 16.11 (nov 1972) 7-11.

Mangrin, Ignace. Les boxeurs dans le tché-li sud-est. Tchang-kia-tchouang, 25 mars 1900. **Études** 84 (5 août) 1900) 366-399.

Masters, Frederic J. Among the highbinders. An account of chinese secret societies. **ChRec** 23 (1892) 268-273, 305-315.

Matgioï (A. de Pourvoirville) **l'Esprit des races jaune — le taoïsme et les sociétés secrètes chinoises.** Paris (1897) 32 p.

Miles, George. Vegetarian sects. **ChRec** 33 (1902) 1-10.

Millican, Frank R. (tsl) Religious elements in the esoteric societies of china. **ChRec** 58 (1927) 757-766. Tsl of art by Wang, Chao-hsiang: Chung-kuo pi-mi she-hui chung ti tsung-chiao, in **Wen-she yüeh-k'an** 2 (jan 1927) 41-54.

Milne, Dr. Communicated by Robert Morrison. Some account of a secret society in china entitled 'the triad society.' **Trans RAS** 1 (1827) 240-250. See also **ChRep** 14.2 (feb 1845) 59-69.

Morgan, W.P. **Triad societies in hong kong.** Hong kong (1960) 306 p, app, illus.

Morrison, Robert. A transcript in roman characters, with a translation, of a manifesto in the chinese language, issued by the triad society. **JRAS** 1 (1834) 93-95.

Muramatsu, Yuji. Some themes in chinese rebel ideologies. In A.F. Wright (ed) **The confucian persuasion,** stanford univ (1960) 241-267.

Mury, Francis. Les sociétés secrètes et le gouvernement chinois. **Revue des revues** 25 (15 juil 1900) 117-134, 17 gravures.

Naquin, Susan. **Millenarian rebellion in china. The eight trigrams uprising of 1813.** Yale univ (1976) 384 p, maps, 3 app, notes, sel bibliog, gloss-index. See rev by Timothy Jensen in **HR** 18.1 (aug 1978) 98-105.

Newbold, Lt. and Maj.-Gen. Wilson. The chinese secret triad-society tien-ti-huih. **JRAS** 6 (1840-41) 120-158.

North, Hart H. Chinese highbinder societies in california. **California historical society quarterly** 27 (mar 1948) 19-31.

Oath taken by members of the triad society, and notices of its origin. **ChRep** 18.6 (june 1849) 280-295.

Of the tea sect, translated from the peking gazette. **ICG** 1 (may 1817) 19-22. Re ch'ing-ch'a men chiao.

An Ordinance for the suppression of the triad and other secret societies in the island of hongkong and its dependencies. **ChRep** 14.2 (feb 1845) 57-59. Issued by John Francis Davis, governor, 8 jan 1845.

Origine des boxeurs [avec une lettre de mgr favier] **Revue française de l'étranger et des colonies** (août 1900) 464-471.

Ormond, McGill & Ron Ormand. **Religious mysteries of the orient.** Cranbury, n.j. (1976) See chap 8, The red swastika society of china, 111-116.

Overmyer, Daniel L. Boatmen and buddhas: the lo chiao in ming dynasty china. **HR** 17.3/4 (feb-may 1978) 284-302.

Overmyer, Daniel L. **Folk buddhist religion. Dissenting sects in late traditional china.** Harvard univ (1976) xi + 295 p, notes, bibliog, gloss, index.

Overmyer, Daniel L. A preliminary study of the tz'u-hui t'ang. **SSCRB** 4 (oct 1977) 19-40.

Palatre, P. La magie et le nénuphar blanc au kiangnan. **MC** 10 (1878) 434-441, 446-450, 458-465.

Pelliot, Paul. La secte du lotus blanc et la secte du nuage blanc. **BEFEO** 3.2 (1903) 304-317. See further: Notes additionelles sur . . . in **ibid** 4 (1904) 436-440.

Perry, Elizabeth J. Worshipers and warriors: white lotus influence on the nien rebellion. **Modern china** 2.1 (jan 1976) 4-22.

Pickering, W.A. Chinese secret societies and their origin. **JSBRAS** pt 1 no 1 (july 1878) 63-84; pt 2 no 3 (july 1879) 1-18.

Playfair, G.M.H. The lolao . . . secret society. **ChRev** 15 (1886-87) 129-130.

Porter, H.D. Secret sects in shantung. **ChRec** 17 (1886) 1-10, 64-73.

Pourvoirville, Albert de. La révolution et les sociétés secrètes en chine. **Revue de paris** (1 mars 1912) 119-132.

Prisco, Salvatore III. The vegetarian society and the huashan ku-t'ien massacre of 1895. **Asian forum** 3.1 (jan-mar 1971) 1-13.

Rankin, Mary L.B. The ku-t'ien incident (1895): christians versus the ts'ai-hui. **PC** 15 (dec 1961) 30-61.

Rape, C.B. Buddhistic brotherhood of the sacred army and the adventures of an american ship on the upper yangtsze. **CWR** 44 (17 mar 1928) 62-63.

Rawlinson, Frank. A study of the rebellions of china. **ChRec** 36 (1905) 107-117.

Richard, Timothy. The secret sects of china. **CMH** (1896) 41-45.

Richard, Timothy. Sects—chinese. In **HERE** vol 11, 309-315.

Rué, M. Sociétés secrètes en chine — la secte des trois-points au kouang-si. **MC** 38 (1906) 190-191.

Saglio, Charles. Les sociétés secrètes en chine. **Revue encyclopédique (larousse)** (1 sept 1900) 686-689.

Schipper, K.M. Le pays du milieu et la fin du monde. **Axes. Recherches pour un dialogue entre christian-isme et religions,** paris, 11.1 (1978) 32-42. Re a messianic sect of the middle ages based on cult of hsi wang mu.

Schlegel, Gustave. **Thian ti hwui. The hung league or heaven-earth-league. A secret society with the chinese in china and india.** Batavia (1866) x1 + 253, tables, illus. Repr N.Y. (1973)

Schram, Stuart R. Mao tse-tung and secret societies. **CQ** 27 (1966) 1-13.

Secret associations. **ICG** no 4 (1818) 87-88.

Secret societies among the chinese in singapore, with particulars of some of their late proceedings. Copied from the Singapore free press. **ChRep** 15.6 (june 1846) 330-306.

Les Sectes chinoises. **RIC** no 118 (21 janv 1901) 66-67.

Shek, Richard. The revolt of the zaili, jindan sects in rehe (jehol) **Modern china** 6.2 (apr 1980) 161-196. Re white lotus sects in north china.

Shih, Vincent. Some chinese rebel ideologies. **TP** 44.1/3 (1956) 150-226.

La Société des boxeurs en chine au commencement du XIXe siècle. **JA** 9e sér, 17 (1901) 164-168.

Les Sociétés secrètes en chine. **AEO** 6 (1883-84) 209-211.

Sparling, G.W. China's new religious sects. **West china missionary news** 26 (1924) 17-22.

Speed, John G. Chinese secret societies of new york city. **Harper's weekly** 44 (july 1900) 658.

Stanton, William. The triad society, or heaven and earth association. **ChRev** 21 (1892-93) 159-181, 217-230, 311-335, 378-399; 22 (1893-94) 429-447. See further same title publ as book, hong kong (1900) 124 p.

Stirling, W.G. The coffin breakers society. **JMBRAS** 4.1 (1926) 129-132.

Stirling, W.G. The red and white flag societies. **JMBRAS** 3.1 (1925) 57-61.

Tai, Hsuan-chih. Tsl by Ronald Suleski. Origin of the heaven and earth society. **Modern asian studies** 11.3 (july 1977) 405-425.

Tan, Hiang-ping. The singapore branch of the world red swastika society: a study in religion as a source for world unity. **CF** 14.4 (winter 1971) 131-141. Re Tao yüan society.

T'ang, Leang-li. The historical significance of the chinese secret societies. **PT** n.s. 3 (1932-33) 222-228.

Tien, Tsung. Chinese secret societies. **Orient** 3.2 (1952) 23-26; 3.3 (1952) 48-50; 3.4 (1952) 56-58; 3.5 (1952) 39-41; 3.6 (1953) 47-50.

Topley, Marjorie. The great way of former heaven; a group of chinese secret religious sects. **BSOAS** 26 (1963) 362-392, tables.

Topley, Marjorie. Notes on some vegetarian halls in hong kong belonging to the sect of hsien-t'ien tao (the way of former heaven) **JHKBRAS** 8 (1968) 135-148.

Twinem, P. de W. Modern syncretic religious societies in china. **JR** 5 (1925) 463-482, 595-606.

Wakeman, Frederic jr. The secret societies of kwangtung, 1800-1856. In **NCELYY** (1970) 127-160.

Ward, Barbara E. Chinese secret societies. In Norman MacKenzie (ed) **Secret societies,** london (1967) 174-203.

Ward, John S.M. and W.G. Stirling. **The hung society, or, the society of heaven and earth.** London (1925-26) 3 vol, diagr, illus. Repr ny (1973)

Welch, Holmes & Chün-fang Yü. The tradition of innovation: a chinese new religion. **Numen** 27.2 (dec 1980) 222-246. Re T'ien-te sheng-chiao, "the holy teaching of heaven's virtue."

Williams, S. Wells. Oath taken by members of the triad society, and notices of its origin. **ChRep** 18 (1849) 280-295.

Wylie, Alexander. Secret societies in china. **NCH** 165 (24 sept 1853) repr in **Shanghae almanac for 1854 and miscel.** Also repr in author's **Chinese researches** (1897) 110-146.

Yu, David C. A buddho-taoist sect in modern china. **HR** 11.1 (aug 1971) 157-160. Rev art on Lo Hsiang-lin's bk in chin, The spread of the chen-k'ung chiao in south china and malaya, hong kong (1962)

Yu, Shih-yu. **Religions secrètes contemporaines dans le nord de la chine.** Chengtu (1948) viii + 175 p, illus.

38. MODERN (PRE-1949) RELIGION

The anti-religion movement, symposium **CSPSR** 7.2. (1923) 103-113.

Bates, M. Searle. Religious liberty in china. **IRM** 35 (apr 1946) 165-173. Mostly on current situation under kuomintang govt.

Bellah, Robert N. The religious situation in the far east. **CRJ** 4 (june 1963) 95-117.

Braden, Charles S. **Modern tendencies in world religions.** N.Y. (1933) See chap 3, Modern tendencies in china, 87-135.

Braden, Charles S. Some present day religious tendencies in china. **OC** 42 (1928) 588-597.

Braden, Charles Samuel. **War, communism and world religions.** NY (1953) See chap 2, War, communism and the religions of china, 56-89.

Brou, Alexandre. Bulletin des missions chine: la défaite de confucius. **Études** 153 (20 nov 1917) 493-506.

Brou, Alexandre. La nouvelle chine et le culte de confucius. **RC** (janv-avril 1918) 3-15, illus.

Buck, John Lossing, Peasant movement. **CCY** (1928) 265-82.

Carus, Paul. Ceremony celebrated under the chinese republic in honor of confucius. **OC** 32.3 (mar 1918) 155-172, illus, extract fr Van Aalst's **Chinese music,** sec on sacrifices to confucius.

Chan, Wing-tsit. Modern trends in chinese philosophy and religion. In Joseph M. Kitagawa (ed) **Modern trends in world religions—paul carus memorial ymposium,** chicago (1959) 217-220.

Chan, Wing-tsit. **Religious trends in modern china.** Columbia univ (1953) xiii + 327 p, bibliog, gloss, chin character list, index.

Chang, Hao. **Liang ch'i-ch'ao and intellectual transition in china, 1890-1907.** Harvard univ (1971) See Index, buddhism; religion.

Chang, Neander S. The anti-religion movement. **ChRec** 54.8 (aug 1923) 459-467.

Chao, T.C. Christians and non-christians reply to the anti-religion movement. **ChRec** 53.12 (dec 1922) 743-748.

Chao, T.C. Present-day religious thought and life in china. In **CToday** 2nd ser (1926) 33-49.

Chao, T.C. Religious situation in china. **ChRec** 61.11 (nov 1930) 677-687.

Cheng, Ching-yi. Tsl J. Leighton Stuart. Translation of protest against the movement in favor of making confucianism a state religion. **ChRec** 44.11 (nov 1913) 687-692.

Chikusa, Tatsuo. Succession to ancestral sacrifices and adoption of heirs to the sacrifices: as seen from an inquiry into customary institutions in manchuria. In **CFL&SC** (1978) 151-175.

Ching, Julia. Confucius and his modern critics: 1916 to the present. **PFEH** 10 (1974) 117-146.

Couling, C.E. The oldest dress and the newest; or taoism in modern dress. **HJ** 22 (1924) 245-259.

Cressy, Earl H. A study in indigenous religions. In Orville A. Petty (ed) **Laymen's foreign missions inquiry,** supplementary series pt 2, **fact-finders' reports,** vol 5, **china,** n.y. and london (1933) 655-716.

Day, Clarence B. Contemporary chinese cults. **FEQ** 6 (1947) 294-299.

Day, Clarence B. Current values in peasant religion.
ChRec 63 (1932) 419-427.

Day, Clarence B. A unique buddhist-taoist union prayer
conference. **ChRec** 56.6 (june 1925) 366-369. Conference held at a monastery near hangchou for soldiers
who died in world war and for victims of tokyo-yokohama
earthquake.

DeKorne, John C. **The fellowship of goodness. T'ung
shan she . . . A study in contemporary chinese religion.**
Grand rapids, mich (1941) vi + 109 p (publ by author in
mimeo)

Doré, Henri. Le confucéisme sous la république. **La
chine** 28 (1922) 1533-1543; 29 (1922) 1559-1571.

Doré, Henri. Le confucéisme sous la république,
1911-1922. **NCR** 4 (1922) 298-319. See also same
author's Le culte de confucius sous la république
chinoise (1911-1922) **Études** 172 (20 août 1922)
433-448.

Drake, F.S. The tao yüan, a new religious and spiritualistic
movement. **ChRec** 54 (1923) 133-144. Same title in
TheE&theW 22 (1924) 66-75.

Eberhard, Wolfram. Neuere forschungen zur religion
chinas 1920-1932. **ARW** 33 (1933) 304-344. Engl tsl:
Studies of chinese religion 1920-1932, in author's **MSVC**
(1971) 335-399.

Edkins, Joseph. The books of the modern religious sects in
north china. **ChRec** 19 (1888) 261-268, 302-310.

Edwards, E.D. Religion in modern china. **PA** 28 (mar
1955) 79-81. Rev of W.T. Chan, **Religious trends in
modern china** q.v.

Elia, Pascal M. d' La religion et les religions d'après un des
plus grands lettrés contemporains [liang ch'i-ch'ao] **RC**
(janv-avril 1920) 278-287, illus.

Erkes, E. Ueber den heutigen taoismus und seine literatur.
Litterae orientales 53 (1933) 1-5. Offpr publ sep, leipzig
(1933) 10 p.

J.C.F. (John Ferguson) Restoration of confucius. **CJ** 22.3
(mar 1935) 102. Re nationalist govt decreeing ranks and
titles.

Franke, Otto. **Geistige strömungen im heutigen china.**
Berlin (1903-04) 29 p.

Franke, O. Das religiöse problem in china. **ARW** 17
(1914) Offpr publ sep, leipzig and berlin (1914) 32 p.

Hamilton, C.H. Religion and the new culture movement in
china. **JR** 1 (1921) 225-232.

Harlez, Charles Joseph. **La religion et les cérémonies
de la chine moderne.** Brussels (1894)

Hodous, Lewis. The chinese church of the five religions.
JR 4 (1924) 71-76.

Hodous, Lewis. A chinese premillenarian. **JR** 4 (1924)
592-599. Re t'ang huan-chang and the cult of the amal-
gamation of the 6 true religions; study of an 1822
manifesto by t'ang.

Hodous, Lewis. The ministry of chinese religions. **IRM** 25
(1936) 329-341.

Hodous, Lewis. Non-christian religious movements in
china. In M.T. Stauffer (ed) **The christian occupation of
china,** shanghai (1922) 27-31.

Hodous, Lewis. The tao tê hsüeh shê, a modern syncretistic sect in china. **Actes 18e ICO, Leiden 1931** 18
(1932) 122-123.

Hu, Shih. On observing the birthday of confucius. **ChRec**
66.3 (mar 1935) 153-158. Tsl fr tu-li p'ing-lun, 9 sept
1934; a diatribe against such observance.

Huntington, D.T. The religious writings of liang ch'i-ch'ao.
ChRec 38.9 (sept 1907) 467-475.

Johnston, Charles. A chinese statesman's view of religion.
HJ 7 (oct 1908) 19-26. Statesman is k'ang yu-wei.

Johnston, R.F. The religious future of china. **NC** 65 (nov
1913) 908-923.

Ku, Hung-ming. The religion of a gentleman in china.
CSM 17 (1922) 676-679.

Lancashire, Douglas. Confucianism in the twentieth
century. In Nicholas Tarling (ed) **China and its place in
the world,** univ auckland (1967) 26-42.

Lee, Hsi-dzen. Religious problems as viewed by chinese
themselves. **ChRec** 53.8 (aug 1922) 513-518. Expresses
author's own views.

Lim, Boon Keng. The religious revolution in china.
ChRec 57.2 (feb 1926) 95-102. On the current situation.

Löwenthal, Rudolf. **The religious periodical press in
china.** Peking (1940) 294 p.

Maclagan, P.J. Position and prospects of confucianism in
china. **IRM** 3 (apr 1914) 225-242.

Matgioï (E.A.P. de Pourvoirville) Le taoisme contemporain: sa hiérarchie, son enseignement, son rôle. **MCSJ**
19 (1889) 179-218.

Millican, F.R. Humanism in china. **ChRec** 65.11 (nov
1934) 677-683. Some thinkers of the present, represent-
ing both "relig" and "non-relig" humanism.

Millican, Frank R. Philosophical and religious thought in
china. **CCY** (1926) 423-469.

Moore, Frederick. President yuan shih-kai at the altar of
heaven. **Far eastern review** 11 (feb 1915) 349-354, 14
fig.

Peake, Cyrus H. China revives confucianism. **OC** 50 (1936) 24-31. Revival in context of current political situation.

Perrot, Albert. Le retour offensif de la vieille chine. Le confucianisme redevenu religion d'état. **Études** (20 mai 1914) 461-480 (juil 1914) 425-438, fig.

Porter, Henry D. A modern shantung prophet.**ChRec** 18.1 (1887) 12-21. Re Li hua-ch'eng.

Porter, Lucius C. **China's challenge to christianity.** NY (1924) See Spiritual quests, 140-178. Re contemp chin relig movements.

The Position and prospects of confucianism in china. **Chinese review** 1 (apr 1914) 50-51.

Rawlinson, Frank. China's answer to christianity. **ChRec** 58.1 (jan 1927) 40-51; 58.2 (feb 1927) 110-120, ref. On current relig conditions.

Rawlinson, Frank. Christians and other religionists in china. **ChRec** 64.12 (dec 1933) 794-807. Based on responses to questionnaire sent to 127 missionaries.

Rawlinson, Frank. Inter-religious cooperation in china. **ChRec** 65.11 (nov 1934) 695-707. Responses to a questionnaire, by 25 people.

Rawlinson, Frank J. Modern revolution and religion in china [1911-1927] **IRM** 18 (1929) 161-178.

Rawlinson, Frank J. **Revolution and religion in modern china. A brief study of the effects of modern revolutionary movements in china on its religious life.** Shanghai (1929) 97 p. 'modern' refers to period 1911-1927.

Reichelt, Karl Ludvig. Trends in china's non-christian religions. **ChRec** 65.11 (nov 1934) 707-714; 65.12 (dec 1934) 758-768.

Reid, Gilbert. Recent religious movements in china. **China mission year book** (1924) 59-66.

Reid, Gilbert. Trends in china's religious life. **CCY** (1926) 71-79.

Rousselle, Erwin. Der lebendige taoismus im heutigen china. **Sinica** 8 (1933) 122-131.

Rousselle, Erwin. Modern welt- und lebensanschauung in china. **Sinica** 6 (1931) 212-214.

Rousselle, Erwin, Seelische führung im lebenden taoismus. **EJ** 1 (1933) repr of author's orig publ in **CDA** 21 (1934) together with his Ne ging tu, "die tafel des inneren gewebes," ein taoistisches meditationsbild mit beschriftung, orig publ in **Sinica** 8 (1933) 207-216. Engl version of all three papers, entitled Spiritual guidance in contemporary taoism, in Joseph Campbell (ed) **Spiritual disciplines; papers from the eranos yearbooks,** ny (1960) 59-101, illus.

Roy, A.T. Attacks upon confucianism in the 1911-1927 period. **CCJ** 4.1 (nov 1964) 10-26.

Roy, A.T. Attacks upon confucianism in the 1911-1927 period (2) and (3) From a taoist lawyer: wu yü. **CCJ** 4 (may 1965) 149-163; 5 (nov 1965) 67-78.

Roy, A.T. The background of the confucian dilemma in the period 1927-47. **CCJ** 9.2 (may 1970) 182-201.

Roy, A.T. Confucian thought in the nineteen-thirties: ch'en li-fu—part I: his theory of the universe and of the significance of man. **CCJ** 7.1 (nov 1967) 72-89.

Roy, A.T. Confucian thought in the nineteen-thirties: ch'en li-fu—part II: application of his theory to social, cultural, and political questions. **CCJ** 8.1 (nov 1968) 63-92.

Roy, A.T. Liberal re-evaluation of confucianism in the 1911-1927 period. **CCJ** 6.1 (nov 1966) 79-100.

Shaw, Yu-ming. The reaction of chinese intellectuals toward religion and christianity in the early twentieth century. In **C&C** (1979) 154-182.

Slater, N.B. Religion in china today. **Religions** 44 (july 1943) 15-17.

La Suppression des processions en chine. **TM** 15 (1909) 14.

Ts'ai Yuan-pei. On religion and aesthetics. **PT** n.s. 4 (1933) 180.

Tsu, Y.Y. The confucian god-idea. In **CToday** 2nd ser (1926) 58-73.

Tsu, Y.Y. Prospect of religion in china. **ChRec** 67.7 (july 1936) 399-403. Brief look at current situation.

Tsu, Y.Y. Religion in china: toward a greater synthesis. **ChRec** 59.10 (oct 1928) 622-629. Brief survey of current relig situation.

Tsu, Y.Y. Trends of thought and religion in china today. **OC** 47 (1933) 433-452. Same title in **NO** (1933)

Tu, Wei-ming. Hsiung shih-li's quest for authentic existence. In Charlotte Furth (ed) **The limits of change: essays on conservative alternatives in republican china,** harvard univ (1976) 242-275, 396-400; repr in **H&SC** (1979) 219-256.

T'u, Hsiao-shih. What the chinese are thinking about religion. The attitude of a chinese literatus. **ChRec** 54.5 (may 1923) 273-276. The literatus is the author himself.

Twinem, P. de W. Modern syncretic religious societies in china. **JR** 5 (1925) 463-482, 595-606.

Vargas, P. de. The religious problem in the chinese renaissance. **IRM** 15 (1926) 3-20.

Wang, Ching-wei. Confucius and modern society. **ChRec** 65.11 (nov 1934) 683-689.

Wang, Hsing-kung. What the chinese are thinking about religion. **ChRec** 52.9 (sept 1921) 621-626.

Welch, Holmes. The chang t'ien shih and taoism in china. **JOS** 4 (1957-58) 188-212.

Welch, Holmes & Chün-fang Yü. The tradition of innovation: a chinese new religion. **Numen** 27.2 (dec 1980) 222-246. Re T'ien-te sheng-chiao, "the holy teaching of heaven's virtue"

Werner, E.T.C. Reform in chinese mourning rites. **NCR** 2 (1920) 223-247.

What "religion"means in china. A symposium. **ChRec** 58.11 (nov 1927) 703-705.

Wilhelm, Richard. Influence of the revolution on religion in china. **IRM** 2 (oct 1913) 625-642.

Williams, E.T. Confucianism and the new china. **HTR** 9.3 (july 1916) 258-285.

Yen, Hunter. Some modern chinese scholars and religion. **ChRec** 59.7 (july 1928) 414-421. Re Ts'ai yüan-p'ei, hu shih, liang su-ming, t'u hsiao-shih.

Youan chi kai, grand prêtre de ciel. **BAF** 15 (avr-juin 1915) 75-77.

Yu Shih-yu. **Religions secrètes contemporaines dans le nord de la chine.** Chengtu (1948) viii + 175 p, illus.

39. RELIGION IN PEOPLES REPUBLIC

Allen, Rodney F. & John A. Hutchinson. Has china changed teachers? Confucius and mao tse-tung. Study 4 in Robert A. Spivey, Edwin S. Gantad & Rodney F. Allen (ed) **Issues in religion,** menlo park, calif (1976) 89-121, illus photos.

Barry, Peter. A resurgence of feudal superstitious practices in china: a survey. **CF** 23.2 (1980) 71-80. **SCMP** for first 3 months 1980.

Bellah, Robert N. The religious situation in the far east. **CRJ** 4 (june 1963) 95-117.

Bergesen, Albert James. A durkheimian theory of "witch-hunts" with the chinese cultural revolution of 1966-1969 as an example. **JSSR** 17.1 (mar 1978) 19-29.

Bishop, Donald. Maoism as a religion. **RH** 10.1 (winter 1976) 26-30.

Bowker, John. **Problems of suffering in religions of the world.** Cambridge univ (1970) See 4, Marxism, sec Chinese marxism, 165-192.

Braden, Charles Samuel. **War, communism and world religions.** NY (1953) See chap 2, War, communism and the religions of china, 56-89.

Brandauer, Frederick P. Reflections on religion and the people's republic of china. **CF** 20.2 (1977) 72-83.

Bush, Richard C. The impact of communism on religions in china. In **Proc 11th ICHR, claremont, calif (1965)** vol 3 (1968) 57-72.

Bush, Richard C. jr. **Religion in communist china.** Nashville and n.y. (1970) 432 p, index.

Bush, Richard C. A religious dimension in chinese communist thought. In **C&C** (1979) 62-81.

Carroll, Ewing W. jr & Teresa Chu. Religion in china today. **EH** 19.6 (june 1980) 6-10.

Chan, W.T. Modern trends in chinese philosophy and religion. In Joseph Kitagawa (ed) **Modern trends in world religions,** la salle, ill (1959) 193-220.

Cheh, Chun. Confucius' doctrine of the mean is a philosophy opposed to social change. **PR** 17.15 (12 apr 1974) 16-20.

Chen, Chih-mai. Why peiping critizes confucius. **FCR** 25.3 (mar 1975) 19-23.

Chen, Chung-kuei. Respect for religious beliefs [in communist china] **CB** 449 (11 apr 1957) 6-10.

Chen, Kenneth K.S. Religious changes in communist china. **CC** 11.4 (1970) 56-62.

Chi, Lin. Anti-confucian struggles of peasant insurgents. **CL** 7 (july 1974) 86-92.

Chiang, Tien. The struggle between the confucians and legalists in the history of chinese literature and art. **CL** 7 (july 1975) 94-102.

China notes. (Periodical dealing mainly with religion and related topics on mainland china; many tsl) East asia dept, national council of churches, n.y. (sept-dec 1962 —) Abbrev **CN.**

China (people's republic) **RCDA** 13.5/6 (1974) 86-88. Re campaign against confucius and lin piao.

Chinese religious delegation. **RCDA** 18.10/12 (1979) 168. Delegation to 3rd world conference on relig and peace, princeton, n.j. aug 1979.

Ching, Julia. The new china: a dialectical response. **NC:CR** (1977) 3-24.

Ching, Yün-ko. Right opportunism and the thought of confucius. **SPRCM** 763-764 (2 nov—3 dec 1973) 47-54.

Christianity and the new china. South pasadena, calif (1976) 2 vol in 1. Vol 1, **Theological implications of the new china,** 200 p. Vol 2, **Christian faith and the chinese experience,** 204 p, app 28 p. Papers presented at conferences in sweden and belgium 1974.

Chu, Michael (ed) **The new china: a catholic response.** NY etc (1977) 165 p. Contributions sep listed in our bibliog. Abbrev **NC:CR.**

Chung, Tse & Hsin Sung. Is such an appraisal consistent with historical reality?—comment on the introduction to confucius in "an outline history of chinese philosophy" **SPRCM** 763-764 (26 nov—3 dec 1973)

Cole, A. Confucianism today. **Christianity today** 4.6 (21 dec 1959) 16-18, 25.

Confucius' reactionary ideas about music. **CL** 8 (aug 1974) 94-98.

Criticisms of lin piao and confucius. **CL** 6 (june 1974) 86-106. A sec of articles.

Croizier, Ralph C. (ed) **China's cultural legacy and communism.** N.Y. (1970) See chap 2 sec 3, Ting Chung: Repair of temples and preservation of cultural objects; chap 5, Religion, art by Holmes Welch, Ch'u Chung, and Joseph R. Levenson.

Crouch, Archie R. The religion of mao tse-tung. **CN** 14.3 (summer 1976) 25-26.

Dunn, Joe C.M. Celebrations in present-day china. **CF** 20.2 (1977) 84-88. Relig and other celebrations.

Dunn, Joe C.M. Why attack confucius now? **CF** 17.1 (1974) 41-47.

Eitner, Hans-Jürgen. "Sie ziehen es vor, sich an gott zu wenden": das kommunistische china im kampf mit der volksreligion. **Zeitwende; die neue furche** 32.5 (mai 1961) 320-326.

Erkes, Eduard. Die heutige stellung der religionen in china. **Numen** 3 (1956) 28-35.

Étiemble, René. Confucius et la chine contemporaine. **Évidences** (1954) 13-18.

Fan, Wen-lan. Confucius and the confucian theories he created. **CLG** 8.3 (winter 1975-76) 11-22.

Faricy, Robert. Mao's thought and christian belief. In **NC:CR** (1977) 44-80.

Faure, Edgar. **The serpent and the tortoise. Problems of the new china.** N.Y. (1958) Tsl fr french Lovett F. Edwards. See chap 15, The regime and the cults; chap 16, The regime and the cults (continued — the other cults) 129-156.

Feibleman, James K. **Understanding oriental philosophy. A popular account for the western world.** See pt 2, chap 28, chinese communism; chap 29, mao tse-tung, 155-171.

Feng, Yu-lan. On criticism of confucius and self-criticism of my past ideological inclination to honor confucius. **CEd** 7.1-2 (1974) 88-101; **SCMP** 5514 (12 dec 1973) 72-81.

Fitzgerald, C.P. Les communistes chinois et la religion jusqu'à la révolution culturelle. **Problèmes politiques et sociaux** 21 (22 mai 1970) 17-20.

Fitzgerald, C.P. Religion and china's cultural revolution. **PA** 40 (1967) 124-129.

Franke, Wolfgang. Der kampf der chinesischen revolution gegen den konfuzianismus. **NachrDGNVO** 74 (1953) 3-9.

Fu, Wen. Doctrine of confucius and mencius—the struggle that keeps women in bondage. **PR** 17.10 (8 mar 74) 16-18.

Fu, Yunlung. Tsl William A. Wycoff. Studies on confucius since 1949. **CSP** 12.2 (winter 1980-81) 25-51.

Glüer, Winfried. Contemporary confucianism. **CF** 13.1 (spring 1970) 17-33.

Glüer, Winfried. Religion in the people's republic of china. A survey of the official chinese press 1964-1967. **CF** 10.3 (1967) 34-57.

"Gods and ghosts are rubbish" **CN** 9.1 (winter 1970-71) 10.

Goldman, Merle. China's anti-confucian campaign, 1973-74. **CQ** 63 (sept 1975) 435-462.

Graf, O. Religion und 'religion' im china von heute. **NZM** 10 (1954) 96-108.

Grasso, Domenico. The new china and god's plan for salvation. In **NC:CR** (1977) 81-123.

Gregor, James A. & Maria Hsia Chang. Anticonfucianism: mao's last campaign. **AsSur** 19.11 (nov 1979) 1073-1092.

Harrison, James P. **The communists and chinese peasant rebellions. A study in the rewriting of history.** NY (1969) See pt 2, Communist analysis of the chinese peasant rebellions: chap 7, Religious attitudes, 165-189.

Herzer, Rudolf. Konfuzius in der volksrepublik china. **ZDMG** 119.2 (1970) 302-331.

Hinton, Harold C. Religion in china since 1949. In S. Chandrasekhar (ed) **A decade of mao's china,** bombay (1960)

Ho, Wellington. Religion versus atheism. **FCR** 14.12 (dec 1964) 45-49, illus.

Hsüan Mo. The chinese communists' evaluation of confucius and the political aims of their all-out campaign to "criticize confucius" (II) **CSP** 7.3 (spring 1976) 4-39.

Hsueh, Li-szu. Western han landlord class went from opposing to revering confucianism—criticism of tung chung-shu who trumpeted the doctrines of confucius and mencius. **PR** 19.8 (20 feb 1976) 11-15.

Huang, Joe C. Ideology and confucian ethics in the char-acterization of bad women in socialist literature. In **Deviance** (1977) 37-51.

Huang, Lucy Jen. The role of religion in communist chinese society. **AsSur** 11.7 (july 1971) 693-708. Abrmt repr in **CWayRel** (1973) 239-241.

Huang, Thomas Y. Current anti-confucius movement in communist china. **CC** 16.4 (dec 1975) 9-24.

Hunter, Neale. Is chinese communism godless? **CW** 212 no 1270 (jan 1971) 197-199.

Hunter, N. Religion and the chinese revolution. In **China. The peasant revolution.** NY (1972) 81-97.

"Iron girls" team of tachai brigade. We revolutionary women bitterly hate the doctrines of confucius and mencius. **SPRCM** 771-772 (25 mar—1 apr 1974) 36-38.

Jen, Chi-yü. Investigate religion and criticize theology. To commemorate the anniversary of the death of chairman mao. **CF** 20.3 (1977) 170-176. First public discussion of relig in china since cultural revol. See further, A conver-sation on Investigate religion . . . by Peter K.H. Lee, Joe C.M. Dunn, William Meacham, **ibid** 177-180.

Jen, Jiyu (Chi-yü) The struggle to develop a marxist science of religion. **CF** 22.2 (1979) 75-89. See further Ninian Smart, Towards a dialogue at the level of the science of religion . . . **ibid** 22.4 (1979) 219-222.

Jin, Jingfang. Tsl William A. Wycoff. On the question of methodology in the study of confucius. **CSP** 12.2 (winter 1980-81) 68-75.

Kandel, Barbara. A visit to the china taoist association. **SSCRB** 8 (fall 1980) 1-4. Visit made 24 july 1980.

Kao, Lu. To combat revisionism, it is necessary to criticize confucius. **SPRCM** 863-864 (22 mar—29 apr 1976) 33-39.

Kitagawa, Joseph M. One of the many faces of china: maoism as a quasi-religion. **JJRS** 1.2/3 (june-sept 1974) 125-141.

Kramers, R.P. Die lao-tsû-diskussionen in der chinesischen volksrepublik. **AS** 22 (1968) 31-67.

Kuo, Ch'i-yüan & Shih-yao Huang. Uncovering the reactionary essence of "do not do to others what you would not have them do to you" **SPRCM** 771-772 (25 mar—1 apr 1974) 26-28.

Kuan, Feng & Lin Lü-shih. Third discussion on confucius. **CSP** 2.4 (summer 1971) 246-263.

LaDany, L. China: signs of change in religious policy. **Worldmission** 24.2 (summer 1973) 35.40.

LaDany, L. Religious trends in china. **Social action** 19 (oct-dec 1969) 316-322.

LaDany, Ladislao. The tortuous history of the cult of mao. **CNA** 743 (7 feb 1969) 1-7.

Lee, Rensselaer W. III. General aspects of chinese communist religious policy, with soviet comparisons. **CQ** 19 (july-sept 1964) 161-173. Partially repr in **CWayRel** (1973) 232-235.

Lee, W.J. Religion's mainland ordeal. **FCR** 15 (july 1965) 15-20.

Levenson, Joseph R. The communist attitude toward religion. In Werner Klatt (ed) **The china model,** hong kong (1965)

Levenson, Joseph. The place of confucius in communist china. **CQ** 12 (oct-dec 1962) 1-18; repr in Albert Feuerwerker (ed) **History in communist china,** MIT (1968) 56-73.

Life and religion. **CNA** 717 (19 july 1968) 1-7.

Lin, Chih-hao. Lu hsun, a great fighter against con-fucianism. **CL** 4 (apr 1974) 81-88.

Lin, Tien-min. Is chinese communism incompatible with confucius? **RH** 9.2 (spring 1975) 62-63.

Liu, Kang-sheng. Why mao hates confucius. **FCR** 23.11 (nov 1973) 16-20.

Lohmann, T. Religion im alten und neueren china. **Theologische literaturzeitung** 85 (1960) 805-806.

Loi, Michelle. La vie et la mort en chine contemporaine. **Ethno-psychologie** 27.1 (mar 1972) 79-101.

London, Ivan D. and Mariam B. Attitudes of mainland youth toward traditional chinese customs and beliefs. **CC** 11.4 (dec 1970) 46-55.

Louie, Kam. **Critiques of confucius in contemporary china.** HK (1980) 186 p.

Lunar new year festival. **CN** 9.2 (spring 1971) 23.

MacInnis, Donald E. Maoism and religion in china today. In Donald R. Cutler (ed) **The religious situation: 1969,** boston (1969) 3-24.

MacInnis, Donald E. Maoism: the religious analogy. **Christian century** 85 (10 jan 1968) 39-42.

MacInnis, Donald E. Religion in china today. **CN** 16.2 (spring 1978) 21a-23a.

MacInnis, Donald. E. **Religious policy and practice in communist china. A documentary history.** NY & london (1972) 392 p, gloss, index.

MacInnis, Donald. Religious policy: statements of china's leaders. **CN** 10.1 (winter 1971-72)6-8.

Madsen, Richard. Religion and feudal superstition: implications of the prc's religious policy for the christian encounter with china. **CF** 22.4 (1979) 190-218.

Man controls "god of heaven" **CN** 9.2 (spring 1971) 23.

Maoism and religion in china today. N.Y. Missionary research library **Occasional bulletin** 19.9 (sept 1968) 1-12.

Martinson, Paul V. From reciprocity to contradiction: aspects of the confucian-maoist transformation. In **T&T** (1980) 185-218.

Mass criticism group of peking university and tsinghua university. Confucius the man. **SPRCM** 773-774 (22-29 apr 1974) 6-12.

Masson, Michel. Religious roots and implications of maoism. **Concilium** 126 (1979) 26-32.

Matthias, Leo L. Religionen im neuen china. **Merkur; deutsche zeitung für europäisches denken** 11.2 (feb 1957) 168-184.

Michael, Franz H. Ideology and the cult of mao. In Frank N. Trager and William Henderson (ed) **Communist china, 1949-1969: a twenty-year appraisal,** n.y. (1970) 27-44.

Moellering, Ralph L. Maoism and religion in china today. **Lutheran quarterly** 27 (may 1975) 155-159.

Moody, Peter R. jr. The new anti-confucian campaign in china: the first round. **AsSur** 14.4 (apr 1974) 307-324.

Myers, James T. Religious aspects of the cult of mao tse-tung. In **China after the cultural revolution,** vol 1, **Working papers,** centre d'étude du sud-est asiatique et de l'extrême-orient, bruxelles (1972) 231-247. See further Vol 2, **Discussions,** 69-77. Same title in **Current scene,** HK, 10.3 (10 mar 1972) 1-11.

Nanjing holds forum on atheism. **RCDA** 18.1/3 (1979) 23.

New changes in china's policy on religion by wen hua. **RCDA** 17.4/6 (1978) 76. Fr a HK newspaper.

Niu, Yu-hsien. Criticize thoroughly the "theory of genius" of confucius and mencius. **CEd** 7.1-2 (1974) 162-165; **Survey of china mainland press** 5529 (8 jan 74) 34-36.

Nivison, David S. Communist ethics and chinese tradition. **JAS** 16 (1956) 51-74.

O'Collins, Gerald. Christ and china. In **NC:CR** (1977) 124-145.

O'Connor, Patrick. 'Freedom of religion' in yenan. **China magazine** 17.4 (apr 1947) 25-28.

On the reactionary "jen doctrine" of confucius. **SPRCM** 902 (13 dec 76) 1-11.

Parish, William L. & Martin King Whyte. Life-cycle ceremonies and ritual life, chap 13 in joint authors' **VFCC** (1978) 248-272; The annual cycle of festivals, **ibid** 273-297.

La Question du confucianisme et le gouvernement de pékin. **BAF** 16 (oct-dec 1916) 175-176.

Ravenholt, Albert. **The gods must go!** AUFS: Far east (china) **AR-9-58** (1958) 7 p.

Religionen und religionspolitik im alten und neuen china. Frankfurt a.m. **China-analysen** 9 (1970) 46-96.

Religious research revived. RCDA 18.10/12 (1979) 171.

Robinson, David A. From confucian gentleman—to the new chinese 'political' man. In John Robert Nelson (ed) **No man is alien,** leiden (1971) chap 8, 149-161.

Roll,Christian. Die religionen im kommunistischen china. **Aussenpolitik** 15 (july 1964) 483-491.

Rubin, Vitali.The end of confucianism? **TP** 59 (1973) 68-78. Rev art on W. Bauer's **China und die hoffnung auf glück** q.v.

Rule, Paul. Is maoism open to the transcendent? In **NC:CR** (1977) 25-43.

Schilling, Werner. **Einst konfuzius heute mao tse-tung. Die mao-faszination und ihre hintergründe.** Weilheim/Oberbayem (1971) 329 s, anmerkungen, literaturverzeichnis, zur transkription chinesisches name, abkürzungen, personenverzeichnis.

Schram, Stuart R. Mao tse-tung and secret societies. **CQ** 27 (1966) 1-13.

Schwarz, Henry G. Some random thoughts on religion and religious policy in china. **Ajia kenkyūjo kiyō** 7 (1980) 1-39.

Selected articles criticizing lin piao and confucius. 2. Peking (1975) 229 p.

Sewell, William. Religion in china today. In **China and the west; mankind evolving,** ny (1970) 48-64. Personal experiences and reactions.

Shen, I-chen & Ting P'ei-jung. The doctrine of the golden mean is the philosophy of political swindlers. **SPRCM** 769-770 (25 feb-4 mar 1974) 53-55.

Shen, Ping-wen. **Chinese communist criminal acts in persecution of religions.** Taipei (1978) 133 p.

Shih, Yi-ko. In the forefront of the battle against con-fucianism. **CL** 7 (1975) 81-88.

Smart, Ninian. The bounds of religion and the transition from tao to mao. **Sri lanka journal of humanities** 1.1 (june 1975) 72-80.

Smart, Ninian. Towards a dialogue at the level of the science of religion: a reply to ren jiyu. **CF** 22.4 (1979) 219-222.

Sohier, A. La religion en chine populaire. In Centre d'étude des pays de l'est, institut de sociologie solvay, univ libre de bruxelles et centre national pour l'étude des pays à régime communiste (ed) **Le régime et les institutions de la république populaire chinoise,** brussels (1960) 138-151.

Some recent articles on religion in communist china. **CB** 510 (15 june 1958) 30 p.

Sovik, Arne. Religion, religious institutions and religious possibilities in china. **CN** 17.2 (spring 1979) 61-65.

Staiger, Brunhild. Die gesellschaftpolitische relevanz der diskussionen über konfuzius in der volksrepublik china. **IAF** 2.3 (juli 1971) 412-421.

Staiger, Brunhild. **Das konfuzius-bild im kommunis-tischen china; die neubewertung von konfuzius in der chinesisch-marxistischen gesichtsschreibung.** Wiesbaden (1969) 143 p.

Sullivan, Francis A. Theological implications of the "new china." In **NC:CR** (1977) 146-164.

Sumiya, Kazuhiko. The long march and the exodus: "The thought of mao tse-tung" and the contemporary sig-nificance of "emissary prophecy." Tsl fr jap Pharis Harvey, Hiroshi Shinmi and Tadashi Miyabe. In Bruce Douglass and Ross Terrill (ed) **China and ourselves; explorations and revisions by a new generation,** boston (1969) 189-223.

T'ang Lan. Tsl Elma E. Kopetsky. Discussing confucius should begin with a clear understanding of the nature of the society in which confucius lived. **CLG** 8.3 (winter 1975-76) 34-55.

Taussig, H.C. Religion and state in china. **EW** 11 (feb 1957) 12-14.

Third world conference on religion and peace (princeton, n.j.) **CF** 23.1 (1980) most of this issue concerns p.r.c. delegation which participated in conference aug-sept 1979.

Thomas, M.M. and M. Abel. Religion, state, and ideologies in china. In **Religion, state, and ideologies in east asia,** bangalore (1965) 15-30.

T'íen, K'ai. The laboring people's anti-confucius struggle in history. **SPRCM** 767-768 (21 jan-4 feb 1974) 34-42.

Trivière, Léon. La campagne contre le confucianisme en chine. **Études** (jan 1974) 805-829.

Tsai, Ching-yuan. Confucius versus communism. **FCR** 25.9 (sept 1975) 9-16.

Tu, Wei-ming. Confucianism: symbol and substance in recent times. **Asian thought and society** 1.1 (apr 1976) 42-66; repr in **H&SC** (1979) 257-296.

Two sources of morality: polarization of moral standards; factions, clans. **CNA** 864 (10 dec 1971) 1-7.

USJPRS reports:
Religion in communist china. NY-59/1 (19 apr 1958)
Selected translations on religions in china. DC-513-D (3 feb 1959) 4 p.
Selected translations of religious articles on communist china from **T'ien feng** nos 6 and 7. NY-1313-N (5 mar 1959) 51 p.
Selected articles [on religion in communist china] NY-1348 (11 mar 1959) 21 p.
Newspaper articles on activities of religious circles (communist china) NY-1454 (7 apr 1959) 25 p.
Articles [on religion in communist china] DC-828 (24 july 1959) 9 p.
Religious persecution in communist china. DC-952 (10 oct 1959) 9 p.
Translations of religious articles from chinese communist publications. NY-1184-N (1959) 43 p.
Translations of selected articles on religious theory and activity in communist china. NY-1210-N (1959) 23 p.
Translations of chinese communist articles on religion. DC-1150, 3192, 5108, 5474 (feb-sept 1960) 23, 8, 26, 12 p.

Urban, George R. (comp & ed) **The miracles of chairman mao; a compendium of devotional literature, 1966-1970.** Los angeles (1972) 182 p.

Varma, S.C. Religion under communism. **Indian journal of social research** 7.1 (apr 1966) 37-40.

Wang, Hsueh-wen. The development of the maosts' criticism of confucius movement. **I&S** 10.6 (mar 1974) 32-54.

Wang, Hsueh-wen. The maoists' criticism of mencius. **I&S** 10.10 (july 1974)

Wang, Hsueh-wen. The maoists' criticism of tung chung-shu. **I&S** 10.11 (aug 1974) 24-34.

Welch, Holmes. Changing attitudes toward religion in modern china. In **China in perspective,** wellesley, mass. (1967) 79-97.

Welch, Holmes. Facades of religion in china. **AsSur** 10.7 (1970) 614-626.

Welch, Holmes. The fate of religion. In Ross Terrill (ed) **The china difference,** ny etc (1979) 117-137.

Wen, Chun. Confucius' reactionary views on literature and art. **CL** 10 (oct 1974) 111-118.

Whitehead, Raymond L. Christ, salvation and maoism. **CN** 15.4 (fall 1977) 1-7. See further Creighton Lacy, A response to . . . **ibid** 7-10.

Whitehead, Raymond L. Christian terms in political use: salvation in the chinese revolution. **Worldmission** 24.2 (summer 1973) 22-32.

Whitehead, Raymond L. Enmity and ethics in the chinese revolution. **CF** 13.2 (summer 1970) 17-44.

Whitehead, Raymond L. Love and animosity in the ethic of mao. **CF** 17.2-3 (1974) 119-135.

Whitehead, Raymond L. Love and struggle in mao's ethic. **Christian century** 91.3 (23 jan 1974) 75-77.

Whitehead, Raymond L. Religion and social change in china today. In Steve S. K. Chin & Frank H. H. King (ed) **Selected seminar papers on contemporary china,** I, univ hk (1971) 179-198.

Wickeri, Philip L. Annotated listing of major articles on religion from the chinese press, january 1-june 30, 1980. **CF** 23.3-4 (1980) 174-179.

Wickeri, Philip L. Annotated listing of major articles on religion from the hong kong press, january 1-june 30, 1980. **CF** 23.3-4 (1980) 180-184.

Wickeri, Philip L. Morality and party reform: a problem in chinese ideology. **CF** 23.3-4 (1980) 141-149.

Woo, Franklin J. Another china visit: religion, the religious dimension, and religion surrogates. **CF** 16.3-4 (1973) 152-159.

Wu, An-chia. Disputes over interpretations of jen in the criticize-confucius movement. **I&S** 12.7 (july 1976) 81-100.

Wu, Ching-hsiung. The thought of confucius and chinese culture. **CSP** 8.1 (fall 1976) 77-88.

Wu, Tsung-jen. Religious persecutions by the maoist regime. **Asian outlook** 7.6 (june 1972) 25-29.

Wu, Yao-tsung. Problems of religious policy [in communist china] **CB** 449 (11 apr 1957) 1-5.

Wu, Yao-tsung. Religion is free in china. **CRecon** 1.6 (nov-dec 1952) 33-37.

Ya Han-chang. On the difference between the theist idea, religion, and feudal superstitions; incidentally, a reply to comrades yu hsiang and liu chün-wang. **SCMM** 413 (20 apr 1964) 1-7.

Ya, Han-zhang. Les options idéologiques de la liberté des croyances religieuses. **Problèmes politiques et sociaux** 21 (22 mai 1970) 4-9.

Yakovlev, M. A soviet view of the cult of mao tse-tung: the making of an idol. In George R. Urban (ed) **The miracles of chairman mao: a compendium of devotional literature 1966-1970,** los angeles (1972) 171-178.

Yang, C.K. **The chinese family in the communist revolution.** M.I.T. (1959) repr in author's **Chinese communist society: the family and the village,** m.i.t. (1965) See chap 10, Secularization of the family institution, 183-190.

Yang, Jung-kuo. Confucius – the thinker who stubbornly defends the system of slavery. **CEd** 7.1/2 (1974) 25-38; **SCMP** 5436 (14 aug 1973) 106-115.

Yu, Hsiang and Liu Chün-wang. The correct recognition and handling of the problem of religion. **SCMM** 410 (31 mar 1964) 41-49.

40. TAIWAN

Ahern, Emily M. The power and pollution of chinese women. In **WCS** (1975) 193-214.

Ahern, Emily M. Sacred and secular medicine in a taiwanese village: a study of cosmological disorders. In **MCC** (1975) 91-113. Same title in **CHAS** (1978) 17-39.

Aijmer, Göran. **The religion of taiwan chinese in an anthropological perspective.** Univ gothenburg (1976) 58 p.

Albrecht, Ardon and Go Sin-gi (tsl fr taiwanese) **A guidebook for christians on taiwanese customs and superstitions.** Taipei (1965) Tsl of a romanized bk written by taiwanese lutheran pastor.

Allen, Rodney F. & John A. Hutchinson. Has china changed teachers? Confucius and mao tse-tung. Study 4 in Robert A. Spivey. Edwin S. Gantad, & Rodney F. Allen (ed) **Issues in religion,** menlo park, calif etc (1976) 89-121, illus photos.

Ancient dance honoring the sage. **Vista** 4 (1975) 14-20.

Anderson, Mary M. Kuan yin: goddess of mercy. **Echo** 3.9 (oct 1973) 28-32, 55-56, col photos.

Baity, Philip C. The genesis of gods in taiwanese folk religion: a preliminary analysis. In **AR-HR** (1974) 33-47.

Baity, Philip C. The ranking of gods in chinese folk religion. **AsFS** 36.2 (1977) 75-84.

Baity, Philip Chesley. **Religion in a chinese town.** Taipei (1975) 307 p, gloss, ref cited, 2 maps.

Bans and banes. **Echo** 3.6 (june 1973) 26-31, illus. Re Fukienese taboos in taiwan.

Bauer, Wolfgang. Chinese glyphomancy (ch'ai-tzu) and its uses in present-day taiwan. In **LL&R** (1979) 71-96.

Best wishes for the new year of the horse. **FCR** 28.1 (jan 1978) col photo pic-story.

Cammann, Schuyler. On the decoration of modern temples in taiwan and hongkong. **JAOS** 88.4 (1968) 785-790. Criticism of W. Eberhard: Topics and moral values in chinese temple decorations q.v.

Cernada, E.C. & G. Cernada. Ethical judgments about induced abortion. **ASBIE** 41 (spring 1976) 47-59.

Cernada, George P. **Basic beliefs about a new human life and ethical judgment: family planning field workers in taiwan.** Univ mass intl area studies programs occ papers ser no 5 (1979) 46 p.

Chen, Chi-lu. Ancestral worship associations of the taiwan chinese. In **MS/CA** (1977) 53-58.

Chen, Chi-lu. An annual procession of tai-chion-ya-bio (a taoist temple) of hsin-chuang, taipei prefecture. **Studia taiwanica** 1 (1956) i-iv, illus.

Ch'en Chien-fu. Tsl Winfried Glüer. Christianity in china seen by a new confucian. **CF** 15.3 (autumn 1972) 144-161. "New confucian" refers to ch'en's new relig founded in taipei.

Chen, Chung-min. Ancestor worship and clan organiza-tion in a rural village of taiwan. **ASBIE** 23 (1967) engl summ 192-193.

Chen, Lucy H. (Ch'en Hsiu-mei) Spirit calling. In author's collection, **Spirit calling: tales about taiwan,** taipei (1962) 73-87. Fictional account of calling sick person's spirit by taoist priest.

Chen, Ying-chieh. She calms the winds and cures the sick. **FCR** 22.6 (june 1972) 19-22, photos. Re Matsu.

Chiu, Kun-liang. Tsl Robert Christensen. The city god's own theatrical troupe. **Echo** 6.1 (july 1976) 13-24, col photos.

Chow, L. Problem of funeral rites. **PrAnthro** 11 (sept-oct 1964) 226-228.

Chung, Chao-cheng. Tsl Ho Ku-li. Return to the sage pavilion. **Echo** 1.5 (may 1971) 15-19, illus. Re an old pavilion-like pagoda in taiwan.

Chung kuei. **Echo** 6.7 (sept 1977) special issue.

Cohen, Alvin P. Fiscal remarks on some folk religion temples in taiwan. **MS** 32 (1976) 85-158.

Collins, Valerie. Pilgrimage to peikang. **Echo** 1.5 (may 1971) 27-32, illus.

DeGlopper, Donald R. Religion and ritual in lukang. In **RRCS** (1974) 43-70.

Diamond, Norma. **K'un shen. A taiwan village.** N.Y. etc. (1969) See esp chap 6, The religious life in k'un shen, 84-107; but also passim.

Dodd, Jeremy. Temple of the dragons. **FCR** 21.6 (june 1971) 18-22. Lung shan ssu in taipei.

Eberhard, Wolfram. Religious activities and religious books in modern china. **ZMR** 49 (1965) Repr in author's **MSVC** (1971) 161-176.

Eberhard, Wolfram. **Studies in taiwanese folktales.** Taipei (1970) 193 p.

Eberhard, Wolfram. Topics and moral values in chinese temple decorations. **JAOS** 87.1 (1967) 22-32. Further see Eberhard's Rejoinder to schuyler cammann, **ibid** 88.4 (1968) 790-792.

Erdberg-Consten, Eleanor von. **Die architektur taiwans; ein beitrag zur geschichte der chinesen baukunst.** **R-WAW** vorträge G 189 (1973) 71 p, b-&-w and col photos.

Faurot, Albert. The oldest birthday party. **SJ** 2 (1975) 166-172. Birthday of confucius as celebrated in taiwan, korea and japan.

Festivals and pai pais. **Echo** 6.5 (feb 1977) 70.

Feuchtwang, Stephan. City temples in taipei under three regimes. In Mark Elvin & G. William Skinner (ed) **The chinese city between two worlds,** stanford univ (1974) 263-301.

Fisher, Tom. Feng shui: the occult science of geomancy. **Echo** 2.10 (nov 1972) 15-19, 54-55, photos.

Fisher, Tom. The peikang pai pai. **Echo** 3.3 (mar 1973) 21-25, col photos. Re Matsu festival.

Fisher, Tom. Trances, converts, and cures. **Echo** 2.6 (june 1972) 38-42, col photos. Cures at mother earth temple—ti mu miao—puli.

For man's humanity to man. **FCR** 28.7 (july 1978) Col photo pic-story on dragon-boats and races.

Freytag, Justus. **The church in villages of taiwan. The impact of modern society and folk-religion on rural churches.** Tainan (1969) 117 p, bibliog.

Gallin, Bernard. **Hsin hsing, taiwan: a chinese village in change.** Univ california (1966) See chap 8, Religion and magic in hsin hsing village, 231-269.

Gates, Alan Frederick. **Christianity and animism in taiwan.** San francisco (1979) x + 262 p, illus.

Glüer, Winfried. The new confucian—a modern religious movement. **CF** 15.3 (autumn 1972) 138-143. Re a new relig founded by ch'en chien-fu in taipei.

Gould-Martin, Katherine. Hot cold clean poison and dirt: chinese folk medical categories. **SSM** 12B.1 (jan 1978) 39-46.

Gould-Martin, Katherine. Medical systems in a taiwanese village: ong-ia-kong, the plague god as modern physician. In **MCC** (1975) 115-141. Same title (minus first phrase) in **CHAS** (1978) 41-67.

Hang, T. and J. Masson. Une enquête religieuse chez des étudiants de tainan (taiwan) **SM** 16 (1967) 99-115.

Harrell, C. Stevan. The ancestors at home: domestic worship in a land-poor taiwanese village. In **Ancestors** (1976) 373-385.

Harrell, C. Stevan. The concept of "soul" in chinese folk religion. **JAS** 38.3 (may 1979) 519-528.

Harrell, C. Stevan. When a ghost becomes a god. In **RRCS** (1974) 193-206.

Hegel, Robert. A day in the life of a taoist priest. **Echo** 1.10 (nov 1971) 34-38, 53-55, illus.

Hegel, Robert. For the glory of kuan ti. **Echo** 2.6 (june 1972) 28-35, illus. Re pai-pai at tahsi.

Hegel, Robert. Of men possessed and speaking gods. **Echo** 1.3 (mar 1971) 16-23, illus. Re tang-ki mediums.

Hegel, Robert. The seventh and eighth lords: china's divine bodyguards. **Echo** 1.7 (july-aug 1971) 14-19, illus.

Ho Ku-li. Fire walking in hsinchuang. **Echo** 2.1 (jan 1972) 18-24, illus.

Hou, Ching-lang. **Monnaies d'offrande et la notion de trésorerie dans la religion chinoise.** Paris (1975) 238 p, notes, bibliog, chin texts, pl, index, tipped-in samples of spirit money.

Hsiao, Ching-fen. The current situation of new religions in taiwan. Tainan, **Theology and the church** 10.2-3 (1971) 1-28.

Huang, Chun-ming. The forbidden puppets. **Echo** 2.9 (oct 1972) 24-34, col photos. Connection of marionettes with relig, among other things.

Huang, Chun-ming. Tsl Earl Wieman & Rick Johnston. The temple of a thousand steps. **Echo** 3.5 (may 1973) 34-42, illus. Re Chih nan kung in mucha, taipei.

Huang, Yung-sung. As told to Linda Wu. A man and the mountain. **Echo** 3.10 (nov 1973) 40-46, 59-60, col photos. Re a temple on wu-chih shan.

Hung, Joe. Religious activities on taiwan. **ACQ** 4.1 (spring 1976) 72-75.

Hwang, Teh-shih. An important characteristic of taiwan folk belief. **JCS** 6 (1969) 79-85.

Hwang, Teh-shih. One of the characteristics of taiwan folk religion. **JCS** 16-17 (1979) 63-68. The characteristic: "personalization" of nature spirits.

Jordan, David K. The chiaw of shigaang (taiwan): an essay in folk interpretation. **AsFS** 35.2 (1976) 81-107.

Jordan, David K. **Gods, ghosts and ancestors. Folk religion in a taiwanese town.** Univ calif (1972) xviii + 197 p, illus, gloss, bibliog, index.

Jordan, David K. Religion in bao-an: a case of godly possession. In Marc J. Swartz & David K. Jordan, **Culture, the anthropological perspective,** ny etc (1980) 298-308.

Jordan, David K. Two forms of spirit marriage in rural taiwan. **BTLVK** 127.1 (1971) 181-189.

Kaye, Lincoln. Scaling the ladder of swords. **Echo** 6.3 (nov 1976) 40-47, b-&-w and col photos. Exorcism by tang ki at a small temple in luchou.

Keupers, John. A description of the fa-ch'ang ritual as practiced by the lü shan taoists of northern taiwan. In **BTS-I** (1977) 79-94.

Kleinman, Arthur et al (ed) **Medicine in chinese cultures: comparative studies of health care in chinese and other societies.** Washington d.c. (1975) Art sep listed in our bibliog. Abbrev **MCC**.

Kleinman, Arthur. **Patients and healers in the context of culture. An exploration of the borderland between anthropology, medicine, and psychiatry.** Univ calif (1980) See passim. Based in large part on author's field experience in taiwan.

Kleinman, Arthur & Lilias H. Sung. Why do indigenous practitioners successfully heal. **SSM** 13B.1 (jan 1979) 7ff. Study of patients treated by shamans (tang-ki)

Kramer, Gerald P. and George Wu. **An introduction to taiwanese folk religions.** Taipei (1970) 71 p, tables, illus. Alleged to be an unauthorized tsl, without credit to author, of a work by Tung Fang-yuan, **Studies in the beliefs and practices of taiwanese folk religion** (Taiwan min-chien hsin-yang ssu-shen chih yen-chiu)

Kuo, Li-cheng. Chinese funerary arts. **Echo** 3.7 (july-aug 1973) 34-41, col photos. Re ming-ch'i.

Langlois, Jack. Festival of the lonely ghosts. **Echo** 3.7 (july-aug 1973) 16-21, illus.

Larre, Claude. Sécularization contre religiosité à l'est de l'inde. **RechScRelig** 63 (avr-juin 1975) 161-184. Taiwan is discussed 167-172.

Lévesque, Léonard. **Hakka beliefs and customs.** Tsl fr french Maynard Murphy. Taichung (1969) 113 p. Refers esp to hsinchu county.

Li Yih-yuan. Ghost marriage, shamanism and kinship behavior in rural taiwan. In **FRWVSP** (1968) 97-99.

Lighting the way for the spirits. **FCR** 20.3 (mar 1970) 37-44.

Lin, Heng-tao. Tsl Tom McHugh. Door gods. **Echo** 6.3 (nov 1976) 12-20, 32, b-&-w and col photos.

Liu, Chi-wan. The belief and practice of the wen-shen cult in south china and formosa. **PIAHA** (1963?) 715-722.

Liu, Chi-wan. Tsl Earl Wieman. Taiwan's plague gods. Part I: legends. **Echo** 6.6 (june 1977) 26-33, 50-51, illus.

Liu, Chi-wan. The temple of the god of epidemics in taiwan. **ASBIE** 22 (1966) engl summ 93-95.

Lungshan, a temple with four lives. **FCR** 30.2 (feb 1980) 29-32. Pic-story.

Mackay, George L. Ignorant and superstitious methods of curing disease in north formosa. **ChRec** 24.11 (nov 1892) 524-529.

McCreery, John L. The parting of the ways: a study of innovation in ritual. **ASBIE** 46 (autumn 1978) 121-137. Re individual differences in rituals as performed by taoists in taiwan.

Mollard, Sidney G. jr. Confucius and music. **EWCR** 3.3 (feb 1967) 31-39.

Neill, Peter. The dish saint, the skeptic, and the ghost. **Echo** 3.4 (apr 1973) 36-40, 56. Re a seance.

Novotney, John. Religious freedom in taiwan. **Church and State** 31.9 (oct 1978) 15-16.

O'Hara, Albert. Attitudes toward religion in the university-world of free china. **SM** 16 (1967) 75-98. Repr in author's collection: **RCCS** (1971) 111-134.

O'Hara, Albert R. A factual survey of taipei's temples and their functions. **JSS** 17 (1967) 323-337. Repr in author's collection: **RCCS** (1971) 91-109.

Overmyer, Daniel L. A preliminary study of the tz'u-hui t'ang. **SSCRB** 4 (oct 1977) 19-40.

Pas, Julian. Chinese religion rediscussed. **JHKBRAS** 19 (1979) 149-175. Rev art on Baity, **Religion in a chinese town** q.v. with further discussion on methodology.

Pas, Julian. Religious life in present-day taiwan: a preliminary report. **JHKBRAS** 19 (1979) 176-191.

Pasternak, Burton. Chinese tale-telling tombs. **Ethnology** 12.3 (july 1973) 259-273. ". . . deals with the relationship between grave composition and tomb sacrifices on the one hand, and lineage segmentation, lineage trusts, and the nature of relationships between living and dead members of the descent group on the other . . ."

Petrie, James. Tu ti kung. **Echo** 2.9 (oct 1972) 38-42, 56, photos.

Petterson, Richard. The native arts of taiwan. **Claremont quarterly** 11.3 (spring 1964) 49-58 + 12 p photos.

Quinn, Edward J. The taiwanese folk-values system. **Missiology** 1.3 (july 1973) 359-365.

Rebirth of kuanhsi's tai ho temple. **Echo** 2.10 (nov 1972) 23-31, photos.

Religion. In Stanford univ china project (comp) **Taiwan (formosa)** HRAF 1 (1956) 193-206.

Ross, D. A comparative study of religious symbolism among buddhists, adherents of folk or popular religion, protestants and catholics in taiwan. Ottowa, **Kerygma** 14 (1980) 101-116.

Saso, Michael. Chinese new year's customs in taiwan. **JCS** 4 (1964) 37-52.

Saso, Michael. A guide to the chuang-lin hsü tao-tsang. **JCS** 16-17 (1979) 9-28.

Saso, Michael. Lu shan, ling shan, and mao shan: taoist fraternities and rivalries in north taiwan. **ASBIE** 34 (autumn 1972) 119-147.

Saso, Michael. Red-head and black-head: the classification of the taoists of taiwan according to the documents of the 61st generation heavenly master. **ASBIE** 30 (1972) 69-82.

Saso, Michael. **Taiwan feasts and customs. A handbook of the principal feasts and customs of the lunar calendar on taiwan.** Hsinchu (1965) 3rd ed (1968) 95 p (mimeo)

Saso, Michael. The taoist tradition in taiwan. **CQ** 41 (jan-mar 1970) 83-102.

Schipper, Kristofer. Démonologie chinoise. In **Génie, anges et démons,** paris (1971) 403-429. 'Sources orientales' 8. Limited to treatment of fukien coast and taiwan.

Schipper, K.M. The divine jester; some remarks on the gods of the chinese marionette theater. **ASBIE** 21 (1966) 81-94, 2 p pl.

Schipper, K.M. **Le fen-teng. Rituel taoïste.** Paris (1975) Intro material 1-32, ref to sources in tao-tsang 33-38, notes 39-42, text in printed form, photos, text in calligraphy (facs) descr acc to author's notes taken at chiao in su-ts'o, taiwan, 26 mar 1967.

Schipper, Kristofer M. Neighborhood cult associations in traditional taiwan. In **CLIC** (1977) 651-676.

Seaman, Gary. Ethnographic film from the field to the classroom: film records of popular religion in china. **Chinoperl** 7 (1977) 106-135, bibliog.

Seaman, Gary. In the presence of authority: hierarchical roles in chinese spirit medium cults. In **NABCC** (1980) 61-74.

Seaman, Gary. **Temple organization in a chinese village.** Taipei (1978) 173 p, bibliog, char list, chronol, 2 maps.

Social values, patterns of living, and folk beliefs. In Stanford univ china project (comp) **Taiwan (formosa) HRAF** 1 (1956) 149-162.

Stevens, Keith. Ancestral images. **JHKBRAS** 18 (1978) 200-202. Suppl to author's art, Altar images from hunan and kiangsi, **ibid** 41-48.

Strickmann, Michel. History, anthropology, and chinese religion. **HJAS** 40.1 (1980) 201-248. Rev art on Michael Saso, **The teachings of taoist master chuang** q.v.

Sung, Lung-fei. Decorative art of the 'chiao tan' structure of sungshan. **ASBIE** 25 (1968) engl abrmt 219-224 + 18 p pl, illus.

Sung, Lung-fei. Two examples of the pilgrimage activities in taiwan. **ASBIE** 31 (1971) Engl summ 129-133, 20 p pl. Re pilgrimages to matsu temples.

Sung, Shi. Tsl Robert Hegel. The day they launched the floating lanterns. **Echo** 2.7 (july-aug 1972) 30-35, 53-54, illus. Re 7th month 15th day festival in chapei, near hsinchu.

Sung, Shi. Tsl Earl Wieman. On the road to peikang. **Echo** 3.3 (mar 1973) 26-33, 55-56, illus col photos. Re pilgrimage to matsu shrine.

Sung, Yu, Paintings of taoist and buddhist legends. **Echo** 2.5 (may 1972) 37-43, illus. Re some paintings in national palace museum.

Suzuki, Mitsuo. The shamanistic element in taiwanese folk religion. In **ExHum** (1976) 253-260.

Tang, Mei-chun. **Urban chinese families. An anthropological field study in taipei city, taiwan.** Natl taiwan univ (1978) See passim.

Temple carvings and sculptures in ancient style. **FCR** 22.11 (nov 1972) 33-44. Photo pic-story re carvings at a temple in sanhsi, outskirts of taipei.

Temples. **Echo** 5.4/5 (apr-may 1975) 18-27, 80-82, col photos. Re temples in manka, old sec of taipei.

Temples. **Echo** 5.8 (sept 1975) 40-52, b-&-w and col photos. Re old temples in tainan.

Thelin, Mark and Lin Wen-lang. Religion in two taiwanese villages. **JCS** 3 (1963) 44-57.

Thiele, Peter. Chinesische totenbräuche in nordtaiwan. **ZE** 100 (1975) 99-114.

Thompson, Laurence G. The cult of matsu. In author's **CWayRel** (1973) 196-201.

Thompson, Laurence G. Efficacy and afficacy in chinese religion. **SSCRB** 6 (fall 1978) 31-49.

Thompson, Laurence G. Funeral rites in taiwan. In author's **CWayRel** (1973) 160-169.

Thompson, Laurence G. Notes on religious trends in taiwan. **MS** 23 (1964) 319-350, map.

Thompson, Laurence G. P'eng-hu in mid-ch'ing times according to the p'eng-hu chi lüeh of hu chien-wei. **MS** 30 (1972-73) 166-219. See 193-212.

Thompson, Laurence G. Taiwanese temple arts and cultural integrity. **SSCRB** 8 (fall 1980) 70-78.

Thompson, Laurence G. Yu ying kung: the cult of bereaved spirits in taiwan. In **StAs** (1975) 267-277.

Tsai, Wen-hui. A study of divination in chinese temples in taiwan. **SyY:T&W** 6.2 (july 1968) 19-22.

Tseng, W.S. Psychiatric study of shamanism in taiwan. **AGP** 26 (1972) 561-565.

Tseng, Wen-shing. Traditional and modern psychiatric care in taiwan. In **MCC** (1975) 177-194.

Tuan wu. **Echo** 4.6 (june 1974) Special issue devoted almost entirely to this festival.

Unschuld, Paul Ulrich. **Die praxis des traditionellen chinesischen heilsysteme: unter einfluss des pharmazie dargestellt an den heutigen stand auf taiwan.** Wiesbaden (1973) viii + 182 p, illus.

Wang, Chin-hsing. Lantern festival. **Echo** 1.2 (feb 1971) 33-37, illus.

Wang, Lan. Tsl Margaret Mar. Chinese new year and its age-old customs. **Echo** 1.1 (jan 1971) 29-33, illus.

Wang, Shih-ch'ing. Religious organization in the history of a chinese town. In **RRCS** (1974) 71-92. The town is shulin near taipei.

Wang, Sung-hsing. Taiwanese architecture and the supernatural. In **RRCS** (1974) 183-192.

Wei, Henry Yi-min, & Suzanne Coutanceau. **Wine for the gods. An account of the religious traditions and beliefs of taiwan.** Taipei (1976) xi + 234 p, illus, table of festivals, gods and temples in engl, taiwanese, mandarin and char.

Welch, Holmes. The chang t'ien shih and taoism in china. **JOS** 4 (1957-58) 188-212, illus.

Welch, Holmes & Chün-fang Yü. The tradition of innovation: a chinese new religion. **Numen** 27.2 (dec 1980) 222-246. Re T'ien-te sheng chiao, ''the holy teachings of heaven's virtue''

Wheat, William T. Temple roof decorations. **Echo** 5.9 (oct 1975) 17-27, b-&-w and col photos, fig.

Wieman, Earl. The gods of nankunshen. **Echo** 3.6 (june 1973) 16-25, 54, illus.

Wolf, Arthur P. Aspects of ancestor worship in northern taiwan. In **Ancestors** (1976) 339-364.

Wolf, Arthur P. Gods, ghosts, and ancestors. In **RRCS** (1974) 131-182.

Wolf, Arthur P. (ed) **Religion and ritual in chinese society.** Stanford univ (1974) xii + 377p, ref, char list, index. Art sep listed in our bibliog. Abbrev **RRCS.**

Woodblock prints for the new year. **FCR** 25.2 (feb 1975) 29-32, col photos.

Wu, Agnes Chen-chung & Yu-hei Hu. Many ways to health: a study of 2,000 rural and urban taiwan families. **AJCM** 8.4 (1980) 313-330.

Wu, Linda. The biggest festival of them all. **Echo** 4.1 (jan 1974) 29-44, col photos. Re various chiao in different parts of taiwan.

Wu, Linda. Home, grand auntie, let's go home! **Echo** 4.4 (apr 1974) 19-38, 49-56, illus. Re pilgrimage to matsu shrine in peikang.

Wu, Linda. Race of the dragons. **Echo** 5.6 (june 1975) 7-17. A pic-story, some photos in col. Re tuan-wu rivalry betw 2 villages in i-lan.

Wu, Ping-chung. Matsu, goddess of the sea. **Echo** 1.1 (jan 1971) 12-17, illus.

Yao, Meng-chia & Lincoln Kaye. Grappling with the ghosts. **Echo** 6.2 (oct 1976) 13-18, 60, illus. Re lonely ghosts festival in taiwan past, and hengchun present.

Yao, Ruth. Temples of taiwan. **FCR** 14.4 (apr 1964) 13-20, illus.

41. OVERSEAS CHINESE (INCLUDING HONG KONG)

Anderson, E.N. jr. The changing tastes of the gods: chinese temple fairs in malaysia. **AsFS** 36.1 (1977) 19-30.

Anderson, Eugene N. jr. The happy heavenly bureaucracy. Supernaturals and the hong kong boat people. In **ESCBP** (1972) 11-19.

Anderson, Eugene N. jr. Sacred fish. **Man** n.s. 4 (1969) 443-449. Repr in author's collection: **Essays on south china's boat people,** taipei (1972)

Anderson, E.N. & Marja L. Feng shui: ideology and ecology. In **CE** (1973) 127-146.

Anderson, E.N. & Marja L. **Fishing in troubled waters. Research on the chinese fishing industry in west malaysia.** Taipei (1977) See chap 8, Oh lovely appearance of death: the deformation of folk religion, 165-189.

Anderson, E.N. & Marja L. Folk medicine in rural hong kong. In **CE** (1973) 121-126.

Baker, Hugh D. Burial, geomancy and ancestor worship. In **ASONT** (1965) 36-39.

Baker, Hugh D.R. **A chinese lineage village. Sheung Shui** [new territories, hong kong] Stanford univ (1968) 237 p, bibliog, gloss, index, photos. See passim.

Berkowitz, Morris J. & John H. Reed. Research into the chinese little tradition: a progress report. **JAAS** 6.3/4 (1971) 233-238. See also Berkowitz, Brandauer, & Reed, Study program on chinese religious practices in hong kong—a progress report, **CF** 11.3 (1968) 5-19.

Berkowitz, Morris J., Frederick P. Brandauer and John H. Reed. **Folk religion in an urban setting. A study of hakka villagers in transition.** Hong kong (1969) 167 p, maps, table, illus. Also publ in **CF** 12.3/4 (1969) 1-167.

Berkowitz, Morris J., Frederick P. Brandauer, and John H. Reed. Study program on chinese religious practices in hong kong — a progress report. **CF** 11.3 (1968) 5-19.

Blake, C. Fred. Death and abuse in marriage laments: the curse of chinese brides. **AsFS** 37.1 (1978) 13-33.

Blythe, Wilfred. **The impact of chinese secret societies in malaya.** London (1970) 14 + 566 p, bibliog.

Boxer, Baruch. Space, change and feng-shui in tsuen wan urbanization. **JAAS** 3 (1968) 226-240.

Brim, John A. Village alliance temples in hong kong. In **RRCS** (1974) 93-104.

Buck, Samuel (pseud) Chinese temples in hong kong. **Orient** 2.7 (1952) 27-29.

Burkhardt, Valentine R. **Chinese creeds and customs.** Hong kong, vol 1 (1953) 181 p; vol 2 (1955) 201 p; vol 3 (1958) 164 p; each vol with index, illus.

Cheng, Homer Hui-ming. **Chinese religious festivals in singapore.** Singapore (1949)

Choa, Gerald. Chinese traditional medicine and contemporary hong kong. In **TICHK** (1967) 31-35.

Cohen, Alvin P. A chinese temple keeper talks about chinese folk religion. **AsFS** 36.1 (1977) 1-17.

Comber, Leon. **Chinese ancestor worship in malaya.** Singapore (1956) 41 p, illus.

Comber, Leon. **Chinese magic and superstitions in malaya.** Singapore (1957) 50 p, illus.

Comber, Leon. **Chinese temples in singapore.** Singapore (1958) 110 p, illus.

Comber, Leon. **An introduction to chinese secret societies in malaya.** Singapore (1957) 77 p, map, illus.

Comber, Leon. **The traditional mysteries of chinese secret societies in malaya.** Singapore (1961) xii + 113 p, illus.

Concerning the tan tae hoey in singapore. **JIA** 6 (1852) 545-555. Account of visit to meeting of t'ien-ti hui near singapore.

Cooper, R.F. **Welcome to hong kong temples.** HK (1977) 95 p, illus col photos and drawings. Guide to 9 temples.

Culin, Stewart. Customs of the chinese in america. **JAFL** 3 (july-sept 1890) 191-200.

Culin, Stewart. **The religious ceremonies of the chinese in the eastern cities of the united states.** Philadephia (1887) 23 p, illus.

Delaney, Joan F. & Chan Ying-keung. A study of the role of religious organization in the kwun tong community. Chin univ hk (1973) 30 p.

Eberhard, Wolfram. Economic activities of a chinese temple in california. **JAOS** 82.3 (1962) 362-371.

Eberhard, Wolfram. A study of ghost stories from taiwan and san francisco. **AsFS** 33.2 (1971) 1-26.

Edmonds, Juliet. Religion, intermarriage and assimilation: the chinese in malaya. **Race** 10 (july 1968) 57-67.

Elegant, Robert (text) & Brian Blake (photos) Text: Men, gods and spirits; pic-essay: Buns for the spirits. In Elegant, Blake, & Editors of Time-Life books, **Hong kong,** amsterdam (1977) 95-127.

Elliott, Alan J.A. **Chinese spirit-medium cults in singapore.** Dept of anthropology, london school of economics and political science (1955) 179 p, illus.

Finn, D.J. Cult-objects from aberdeen (hong kong, china) in the lateran museum. **AL** 1 (1937) 35-68.

Franke, Wolfgang. Some remarks on the "three-in-one doctrine" and its manifestations in singapore and malaysia. **OE** 19 (1972) 121-130, tsl of 2 inscr, 10 photo pl.

Freedman, Maurice. Religion et adaptation social chez les chinois de singapore. **ASR** 7 (janv-juin 1959) 89-103.

Freedman, Maurice. A report on social research in the new territories of hongkong, 1963. **JHKBRAS** 17 (1976) See 218-236 on 'fung shui' Posthumous publ.

Gambo, Charles. Chinese associations in singapore. **JMBRAS** 39.2 (1966) 123-168.

Grout, G.C.W. Ceremonies of propitiation carried out in connection with road works in the new territories in 1960. **JHKBRAS** 11 (1971) 204-209.

Hankey, Rosalie. California ghosts. **CFQ** 1 (1942) 155-177. Chin ghost stories coll in california.

Hayes, James W. A ceremony to propitiate the gods at tong fuk, lantau, 1958. **JHKBRAS** 5 (1965) 122-124.

Hayes, James W. Chinese temples in the local setting, In **TICHK** (1967) 86-95.

Hayes, James W. Geomancy and the village. In **TICHK** (1967) 22-30.

Hayes, James W. A list of temples in the southern district of the new territories and new kowloon, 1899-1967. In **TICHK** (1967) 96-98.

Hayes, James. Local reactions to the disturbance of 'fung shui' on tsing yi island, hong kong, september 1977— march 1978. **JHKBRAS** 19 (1979) 213-216, 3 pl.

Hayes, James. Local reactions to the disturbance of 'fung shui' on tsingyi island, hong kong, march 1978— december 1980. **JHKBRAS** 20 (1980) 155-156.

Hayes, James. More notes on tsuen wan. **JHKBRAS** 19 (1979) 204-213. On several temples and a shrine for a new relig of 19th century, the chun hung kan (chen k'ung chiao)

Hayes, James W. Movement of villages on lantau island for fung shui reasons. **JHKBRAS** 3 (1963) 143-144.

Hayes, James W. Removal of villages for fung shui reasons. Another example from lantau island, hong kong. **JHKBRAS** 9 (1969) 156-158.

Hayes, James. Royal asiatic society—visit to tai mo shan, 3rd april 1976. Historical and general note. **JHKBRAS** 17 (168-179)

Hong, L.K. Association of religion and family structure; the case of the hong kong family. **Sociological analysis** 33 (spring 1972) 50-57, bibliog.

Hooyman and Vogelaar. Relation abrégée du tien-bing, vulgairement appelé la fête de morts, chez les chinois de batavia. **JA** 2 (1923) 236-243. Tirée des **Mémoires de la société de batavia** 6 (1792) et trad du hollandais.

Hoy, William. Native festivals of the california chinese. **Western folklore** 7 (1948) 240-250.

Jernigan, Homer L. Some reflections on chinese patterns of grief and mourning. **SEAJT** 15.1 (1973) 21-47. Re singapore chin.

Johnson, Graham E. From rural committee to spirit medium cult: voluntary association in the development of a chinese town. Canadian assoc for south asian studies, **Contributions to asian studies** 1 (1971) 123-143. See sec, Religious associations, 140-143. Re tsuen wan, new territories.

Kamm, John Thomas. Field notes on the social history of fung-shui of kam tin. **JHKBRAS** 17 (1977) See The fung-shui of kam tin, 215-216.

Kung, Chan-yuen. The development of the islet fu-t'ang men (fu tong mun) and the temples in various parts of the region. In Lo Hsiang-lin (ed) **Hong kong and its external communications before 1842,** hong kong (1963) 119-132.

Lan, Nio Joe. Chinese new year celebrations in java. **CJ** 24.3 (mar 1936) 149-153, illus photos.

Lan, Nio Joe. The dragon boat festival in west java. **CJ** 21.3 (sept 1934) 105-106, illus 3 photos.

Lan, Nio Joe. Fire-walking at a chinese temple in java. **CJ** 25.5 (nov 1936) 262-264, illus 3 photos.

Lee, Jon. Some chinese customs and beliefs in california. **CFQ** 2 (1943) 191-204.

Li, Lillian. Two california ghosts. **CFQ** 4 (1945) 278-280.

Lim, Thiam Hock. Kusu and unity. **CF** 14.4 (1971) 142-147. Re annual pilgrimages to kusu island and chin worship of "ethnically distinct" deities there. Kusu island is off singapore coast.

Littleton, L.A. Chinese mythology in san francisco. **OM** 2nd ser 1 (june 1883) 612-617.

Liu, David & James Hayes. Royal asiatic society—visit to the tang family graves on saturday, 11th december, 1976. **JHKBRAS** 17 (1977) 179-185, pl 45-53 at end of vol.

Lo, Dorothy and Comber, Leon. **Chinese festivals in malaya.** Singapore (1958) 66 p, bibliog, indexes, illus.

Lombard-Salmon, Claudine. A propos de quelques cultes chinois particuliers à java. **ArtsAs** 26 (1973) 243-264, illus 18 photos, 1 plan.

Lombard-Salmon, Claudine. La communauté chinoise de makasar, vie religieuse. **TP** 55 (1969) 241-297.

Loomis, A.W. Our heathen temples. **OM** 1 (nov 1868) 453-461. Re chin temples in san francisco.

Loomis, A.W. Holiday in the chinese quarter. **OM** 2 (feb 1869) 144-153.

Loomis, C. Grant. Chinese lore from nevada. **CFQ** 5 (1946) 185-196.

Lyman, Stanford M. Chinese secret societies in the occident: notes and suggestions for research in the sociology of secrecy. **Canadian review of sociology and anthropology** 1 (1964) 79-102.

Lyman, Stanford, Willmott, W.E. and Ho, Berching. Rules of a chinese secret society in british columbia. **BSOAS** 27.3 (1964) 530-539, illus.

Masters, Frederic J. Pagan temples in san francisco. **The californian** 2 (nov 1892) 727-741.

Mitchell, Robert E. Religion among urban chinese and non-chinese in southeast asian countries. **Social compass** 21.1 (1974) 25-44.

Moese, Wolfgang. Ancestor worship and ceremonies. In **CRWMS** (1979) 364-385, illus.

Moese, Wolfgang. Temples and religion. In **CRWMS** (1979) 303-363.

Mollard, Sidney G. jr. Confucius and music. **EWCR** 3.3 (feb 1967) 31-39.

Morgan, W.P. **Triad societies in hong kong.** Hong kong (1960) 306 p, illus.

Myers, John T. A hong kong spirit-medium temple. **JHKBRAS** 15 (1975) 16-27, 4 pl.

Myers, John T. Traditional chinese religious practices in an urban-industrial setting: the example of kwun-tong, hong kong. **IAF** 7.3/4 (1976) 355-377.

North, Hart H. Chinese highbinder societies in california. **California historical society quarterly** 27 (mar 1948) 19-31.

Notes on the chinese of pinang. **JIA** 7 (1854) 1-27.

Nyce, Ray. Chinese folk religion in malaysia and singapore. **SEAJT** 12 (spring 1971) 81-91.

An Ordinance for the suppression of the triad and other secret societies in the island of hongkong and its dependencies. **ChRep** 14.2 (feb 1845) 57-59. Issued by John Francis Davis, governor, 8 jan 1845.

Ormond, McGill & Ron Ormond. **Religious mysteries of the orient.** Cranbury, n.j. (1976) See chap 6, The spirit festival of the cheung chau junkers of hong kong, 81-98.

Pang, Duane. The p'u-tu ritual. In **BTS-I** (1977) 95-122.

Png (sic) P'oh-seng. The straits chinese in singapore: a case of local identity and socio-cultural accomodation. **JSEAHist** 10.1 (mar 1969) 95-114, photos.

Salmon, Claudine & Denys Lombard. **Les chinois de jakarta: temples et vie collective.** ?Ann arbor, mich: éditions de la maison des sciences de l'homme, publ by monograph (sic) (1980) lxxviii + 358 p, notes, app, bibliog, tables, pl.

Savidge, Joyce. **This is hong kong: temples.** HK (1977) 122 p, addresses of temples, index, illus col photos. Genl info re chin relig. Guide to 12 temples.

Schlegel, G. La fête de fouler le feu célébrée en chine et par les chinois à java, le treize du troisième mois, anniversaire du 'grande dieu protecteur de la vie' (pao ching [sheng] ta ti) **IAE** 9 (1896) 193-195, 1 pl.

Schlegel, Gustave. **Thian ti hwui. The hung-league or heaven-earth-league. A secret society with the chinese in china and india.** Batavia (1866) x1 + 253, 16 tables, illus.

Secret societies among the chinese in singapore, with particulars of some of their late proceedings. Copied from the singapore free press **ChRep** 15.6 (june 1846) 300-306.

Shen, D.C. "Fung shui" woodlands. **JHKBRAS** 14 (1974) 188-189. Repr fr **Wildlife conservation newsletter** 14 (oct 1971) publ by Agriculture, forestry and fisheries dept, hk govt.

Siu, Anthony K.K. Distribution of temples on lantau island as recorded in 1979. **JHKBRAS** 20 (1980) 136-139.

Smith, Carl T. Notes on chinese temples in hong kong. **JHKBRAS** 13 (1973) 133-139.

Smith, Carl T. Notes on tung wah hospital, hong kong. **JHKBRAS** 16 (1976) See Religious aspects of tung wah, 269-272.

Speed, John G. Chinese secret societies of new york city. **Harper's weekly** 44 (july 1900) 658.

Stevens, K.G. Chief marshall t'ien, patron of the stage, of musicians and wrestlers—east and south east china. **JHKBRAS** 15 (1975) 303-310.

Stevens, Keith G. Chinese monasteries, temples, shrines and altars in hong kong and macau. **JHKBRAS** 20 (1980) 1-33d, illus fig and photos.

Stevens, Keith G. The craft of god carving in singapore. **JHKBRAS** 14 (1974) 68-75.

Stevens, Keith. The immortal fan (cantonese: fan sin) **JHKBRAS** 18 (1978) 198-199.

Stevens, Keith. The saintly guo (sheng gong) **JHKBRAS** 18 (1978) 193-198.

Stevens, Keith G. Soul images and gods of the boat people. **AofA** 7.6 (1977) 52-61, b-&-w and col photos.

Stevens, Keith. Three chinese deities: variations on a theme. (With special reference to overseas chinese communities in south east asia) **JHKBRAS** 12 (1972) 169-195.

Stevens, Keith. Two examples of chinese religious involvement with islam. **JHKBRAS** 19 (1979) 199-202, 3 pl. In singapore and malaysia, and thailand.

Stevens, Keith G. Under altars (hsia-t'an) **JHKBRAS** 17 (1977) 85-100, pl 20-31 at end of vol.

Stirling, W.G. Chinese exorcists. **JMBRAS** 2 (1924) 41-47.

Stirling, W.G. The coffin breakers society. **JMBRAS** 4.1 (1926) 129-132.

Stirling, W.G. The red and white flag societies. **JMBRAS** 3.1 (1925) 57-61.

Strauch, Judith. A tun fu ceremony in tai po district, 1981: ritual as a demarcator of community. **JHKBRAS** 20 (1980) 147-153. The term tun fu is not in dictionaries.

Suryadinata, Leo. Confucianism in indonesia: past and present. **Southeast asia; an international quarterly** 3.3 (spring 1974) 881-903.

Tam, Janet L. Singapore trance men. **Orientations** 8.6 (june 1977) 4-5. Re spirit mediums.

Tan, Hiang-ping. The singapore branch of the world red swastika society: a study in religion as a source for world unity. **CF** 14.4 (winter 1971) 131-141. Re Tao yüan society.

The Sian Giap. Religion and overseas chinese assimilation in southeast asian countries. **Revue du sud-est asiatique** 2 (1965) 67-83.

The Temple of the supreme ruler, near sung wong toi, kowloon. **JHKBRAS** 19 (1979) 202-204.

Topley, Marjorie. Chinese occasional rites in hong kong. In **TICHK** (1967) 99-117.

Topley, Marjorie. Chinese religion and religious institutions in singapore. **JMBRAS** 29 (1956) 70-118.

Topley, Marjorie. Chinese rites for the repose of the soul. **JMBRAS** 25 (1952) 149-160.

Topley, Marjorie. Chinese traditional etiology and methods of cure in hong kong. In **AMS** (1976) 243-265.

Topley, Marjorie. Chinese women's vegetarian houses in singapore. **JMBRAS** 27.1 (1954) 51-67.

Topley, Marjorie. Cosmic antagonisms: a mother-child syndrome. In **RRCS** (1974) 233-250.

Topley, Marjorie. The emergence and social function of chinese religious associations in singapore. **CSSH** 3.3 (1961) 289-314. Same title in Lloyd A. Fallers (ed) **Immigrants and associations,** the hague (1967) 49-82.

Topley, Marjorie. Ghost marriages among the singapore chinese. **Man** 55 (1955) 29-30. See further same title + A further note, in **Ibid** 56 (1956) 71-72.

Topley, Marjorie. Is confucius dead? **FEER** 58 (21 dec 1967) 561-563.

Topley, Marjorie. Paper charms, and prayer sheets as adjuncts to chinese worship. **JMBRAS** 26 (1953) 63-80, illus.

Topley, Marjorie. Some basic conceptions and their traditional relationship to society. In **TICHK** (1967) 7-21.

Topley, Marjorie. Some occasional rites performed by the singapore cantonese. **JMBRAS** 24 (1951) 120-144.

Topley, Marjorie (ed) **Some traditional chinese ideas and conceptions in hong kong social life today.** Hong kong (1967) 145 p (Abbrev as **TICHK**)

Topley, Marjorie and James W. Hayes. Notes on shrines and temples of tai ping shan street area. In **TICHK** (1967) 123-141.

Topley, Marjorie and James W. Hayes. Notes on some vegetarian halls in hong kong belonging to the sect of hsien-t'ien tao (the way of former heaven) **JHKBRAS** 8 (1968) 135-148.

Tseung, F.I. Some aspects of fortune-telling in hong kong. In **TICHK** (1967) 60-72.

Vaughan, J.D. **The manners and customs of the chinese of the straits settlements.** Singapore (1879) repr taipei (1971) See index, passim.

Ward, John S.M. and W.G. Stirling. **The hung society, or, the society of heaven and earth.** London (1925-26) 3 vol, diagr, illus.

Welch, Holmes & Chün-fang Yü. The tradition of innovation: a chinese new religion. **Numen** 27.2 (dec 1980) 222-246. Re T'ien-te sheng-chiao, "the holy teaching of heaven's virtue"

Williams, George B, Daniel D. Wong & Brenda L. Wong. The chinese temples of northern california. In chin hist soc of america, san francisco, **The life, influence and the role of the chinese in the united states, 1776-1960** (1976) 293-296.

Wilson, B.D. Chinese burial customs in hong kong. **JHKBRAS** 1 (1960-61) 115-123.

Wolf, Arthur P. (ed) **Religion and ritual in chinese society.** Stanford univ (1974) See individual art sep listed in our bibliog. Abbrev **RRCS**.

Wong, C.S. **A cycle of chinese festivities.** Singapore (1967) xv + 204 p, notes, bibliog, index, illus. Chinese in malaysia.

Wynne, M.L. **Triad and tabur: a survey of the origin of chinese and mohammedan secret societies in the malay peninsula 1800-1935.** Singapore (1941)

Yeh, Sui Yen. Ma chu—the goddess of sailors. **ACSS** (1964-67) 35-38, 2 photos.

Yen, Ching-hwang. The confucian revival movement in singapore and malaya, 1899-1911. **JSEAS**, singapore, 7.1 (mar 1976) 33-57.

Young, W. The feast of lanterns at padang (sumatra) **ChRev** 9 (1880-81) 320-321.

42. COMPARISONS & INTERACTIONS

Addison, James Thayer. **Chinese ancestor worship. A study of its meaning and its relations with christianity.** n.p. (1925) 85 p.

Addison, James T. Chinese ancestor worship and protestant christianity. **JR** 5.2 (1925) 140-149.

Affinités des doctrines de lao-tse et du bouddha. Date incontestable de l'existence de lao-tse. Un savant prétend que lao-tse était un philosoph japonais. In **EM** 26 (d?) 343-344.

Ahern, Emily M. Sacred and secular medicine in a taiwanese village: a study of cosmological disorders. In **MCC** (1975) 91-113. Same title in **CHAS** (1978) 17-39.

Alexander, Edwin. The mountain and the valley, a comparative study of grace in the old testament and tao te ching. **CC** 20.3 (sept 1979) 71-84.

Alexandre, Noël. **Conformité des cérémonies chinoises avec l'idolatrie grecque et romaine.** Cologne (1700)

Amélineau, E. Les coutumes funéraires de l'égypte ancienne comparées avec celles de la chine. Dans **Études de critique et d'histoire, par les membres de la section des sciences religieuses de l'école des hautes études,** paris, 2e sér (1896) 1-34.

Arlington, L.C. Chinese versus western chiromancy. **CJ** 7 (1927) 67-76, 170-175, 228-235; 8 (1928) 67-76.

Barnes, W.H. Chinese influence on western alchemy. **Nature** 135 (1935) 824f.

Bellah, Robert N. Father and son in christianity and confucianism. **Psychoanalytic review** 52 (1965) 92-114. Repr in author's collection: **Beyond belief: essays on religion in a post-traditional world,** n.y. (1970) 76-99.

Bellah, Robert N. **Tokugawa religion. The values of pre-industrial japan.** Glencoe, ill (1957) 249 p, 3 app, bibliog, index. For many comparisons see Index, China.

Benton, Richard P. Tennyson and lao tzu. **PEW** 13.3 (1962) 233-240.

Benz, Ernst and Nambara Minoru (comp) **Das christentum und die nicht-christlichen hochreligionen. Begegnung und auseinandersetzung. Eine internationale bibliographie.** Leiden (1960) See 21-22, 46-51, 62, 79-82, 83-86.

Berling, Judith A. **The syncretic religion of lin chao-en.** Columbia univ (1980) 360 p, app, notes, gloss, sel bibliog.

Bernard Henri. l'Attitude du père matthieu ricci en face des coutumes et rites chinois. **RechScRelig** 28 (1938) 31-47. "Extrait du livre sur matthieu ricci et la société chinois de son temps"

Berndt, Manfred. Servanthood among para-christian and non-christian religions in hongkong. **CF** 14.4 (1971) 157-182.

Berthrong, John. "Suddenly deluded thoughts arise" **SSCRB** 8 (fall 1980) 32-55. Re mou tsung-san on neo-confucianism and t'ang budd philos.

Beyerhaus, Peter. The christian approach to ancestor worship. **Ministry** 6.4 (july 1966) 137-145.

Bocking, Brian. Neo-confucian spirituality and the samurai ethic. **Religion** 10 (spring 1980) 1-15.

Boüinais, Lt-Col. and A. Paulus. **Le culte des morts dans le céleste empire et l'annam comparé au culte des ancêtres dans l'antiquité occidentale.** Paris (1893) xxxiii + 267 p.

Braden, Charles S. **Jesus compared. Jesus and other great founders of religions.** Englewood cliffs, n.j. (1957) See Jesus and confucius, 108-131; Jesus and lao-tzu, 132-146.

Brewster, Paul G. Some parallels between the fêng-shên-yen-i and the shah-nameh and the possible influence of the former upon the persian epics. **AsFS** 31.1 (1972) 115-122.

Chan, Wing-tsit. Asian and western perspectives on religion. In brigham young univ, **Asian perspectives. Korea, japan, china, pakistan**, brigham young univ (1975) 21-29.

Chan, Wing-tsit. Chinese and western interpretations of jen (humanity) **JCP** 2 (1974-75) 107-129.

Chang, Aloysius. A christian interpretation of the god-concept in tao te ching. **CC** 15.1 (mar 1974) 16-28.

Chang, Aloysius. Does confucian jen mean christian love? **Worldmission** 24.4 (winter 1973-74) 50-56.

Chang, Aloysius. How christian are the chinese: are age-old indigenous values predisposing them to christian morality? **Worldmission** 24.3 (fall 1973) 46-50.

Chang, C. Essai d'une adaptation des exercices spirituels à l'âme chinoise. **SM** 7 (1950-51) 199-219.

Chang, Chi-yun. Ralph waldo emerson and confucius. **SAR** 1.3 (1975) 54-60.

Chao, Paul. Human nature and the concept of sin in confucianism and christianity. **CC** 16.2 (june 1975) 45-62.

Chao, T.C. Christianity and confucianism. **IRM** 17 (oct 1928) 588-600.

Chaudhuri, H. The concept of brahman in hindu philosophy [with a section on brahman, tao and t'ai-chi] **PEW** 4 (1954) 47-66.

Chen, Ivan. A comparative study of english and chinese customs and superstitions. **London and china express** 49 (14 nov 1907)

Chen, Joseph. Les doctrines chrétienne et confucéene de la piété filiale. **Laval théologique et philosophique** 19 (1963) 335-349.

Chiang, Liu. Some challenges of china's religions to christianity. **ChRec** 65.4 (apr 1934) 217-221.

Chikusa, Tatsuo. Succession to ancestral sacrifices and adoption of heirs to the sacrifices: as seen from an inquiry into customary institutions in manchuria. In **CFL&SC** (1978) 151-175.

Ching, Julia. Chinese ethics and kant. **PEW** 28.2 (apr 1978) 161-172.

Ching, Julia. **Confucianism and christianity: a comparative study.** Tokyo etc (1977) xxvi + 234 p, notes, bibliog, index.

Ching, Julia. Hyphenated christianity. **CN** 16.3 (summer 1978) 33-36. Re christianity and confucianism.

Ching, Julia. The new china: a dialectical response. In **NC:CR** (1977) 3-24.

Ching, Julia. Will confucianism survive? A critical re-assessment of the heritage. **CF** 18.4 (1975) 197-218.

Chochod, Louis. **Occultisme et magie en extrême-orient: inde, indochine, chine.** Paris (1949) 404 p, illus.

Christianity and the new china. South pasadena, calif (1976) 2 vol in 1. Vol 1, **Theological implications of the new china,** 200 p, Vol 2, **Christian faith and the chinese experience**, 204 p, app 28 p. Papers presented at conferences in sweden and belgium in 1974.

Chu, Michael (ed) **The new china: a catholic response.** NY etc (1977) 165 p. Papers sep listed in our bibliog. Abbrev **NC:CR.**

Clasper, Paul. Christian spirituality and the chinese context. **CF** 20.1 (1977) 2-17.

Clasper, Paul. Jungian psychology, taoism and christian faith. **CF** 21.1 (1978) 36-52. Re jung's ideas as expressed in the Wilhelm tsl, **The secret of the golden flower** q.v.

Clopin, Camille. Comparaison entre lao-tse, pythagore et confucius. Résultats définitif pour la chine des deux doctrines examinées par m. de milloué dans une conférence au musée guimet. **La géographie** 27.3 (1898) 285f.

Cohen, Maurice. Confucius and socrates. **JCP** 3.2 (mar 1976) 159-168.

Combaz, G. Masques et dragons en asie. **MCB** 7 (1939-45) 1-328.

Cordier, Henri. Le confucianisme et le shinto. **Revue de clergé français** 65 (1 fev 1911) 257-273.

Coulborn, Rushton. The state and religion: iran, india, and china. **CSSH** 1.1 (1958) 44-57.

Coyajee, Jehangir Cooverjee. **Cults and legends of ancient iran and china.** Bombay (1936) 308 p.

Crémazy, L. Le culte des ancêtres en chine et dans l'annam. **RIC** no 107 (1900) 1066-1068; no 108 (1900) 1088-1089.

Cressy, Earl Herbert. The christian message and the study of chinese religions. **ChRec** 53.4 (apr 1922) 238-241.

Danielli, M. The geomancer in china, with some reference to geomancy as observed in madagascar. **Folk-lore** 63 (1952) 204-226.

Dawson, Christopher. **Enquiries into religion and culture.** N.Y. (1934) See pt 2, chap The mystery of china.

DeKorne, John C. **Chinese altars to the unknown god. An account of the religions of china and the reactions to them of christian missions.** Grand rapids, mich. (1926) ix-xiii + 139 p, illus (publ by author in mimeo)

Dow, Tsung-i. Creativity as the self-realization of man's potential—the supreme value of man: marxian and confucian. Warsaw, **Dialectics and humanities. The polish philosophical quarterly** 5.4 (1978) 33-41.

Dumoulin, Heinrich. La mystique de l'orient et de l'occident. **BUA** 3e sér, 5 (1944) 152-202.

Duyvendak. J.J.L. A chinese 'divina commedia.' **TP** 41 (1952) 255-316. On lo mao-teng: san-pao ta-chien hsia hsi-yang chi [1597] a fictitious and fantastic account of the voyages of cheng ho.

Eberhard, Wolfram. A study of ghost stories from taiwan and san francisco. **AsFS** 33.2 (1971) 1-26.

Edgar, J.H. The sin bearer, a note on comparative religion. **JWCBorderResS** 3 (1926-29) 151.

Eliade, Mircea. The myth of alchemy. **Parabola** 3.3 (aug 1978) 6-23.

Erkes, Eduard. Chinesisch-amerikanische mythen-parallelen. **TP** 24 (1926) 32-53. See further E. von Sach: Einige bemerkungen zu Erkes's . . . **ibid** 382-383; Erkes: Zu E. von Sach's bemerkungen . . . **ibid** 25 (1928) 94-98.

Faricy, Robert. Mao's thought and christian belief. In **NC:CR** (1977) 44-80.

Fisher, Robert E. Tibetan art and the chinese tradition. **AofA** 5.6 (nov-dec 1975) 42-49, illus.

Folberth, Otto. **Meister eckhart und lao-tse. Ein vergleich zweier mystiker.** Mainz (1925) 119 p.

Ford, Eddy L. **A comparison of confucian and christian ideals.** Foochow (192?) 54 p.

Forke, A. Chinesische und indianische philosophie. **ZDMG** 98 (1944) 195-237 (Compares certain concepts: 1. Tao = brahman, das absolute; 2. Wu-wei = nivrtti, passivität; 3. Wei-hsin lun = māyā, idealismus; 4. Chinesische anklänge an sāmkhya und yoga)

Franke, Herbert. Indogermanische mythenparallelen zu einem chinesischen text der han zeit. In **MMDFL** (1963) 243-249.

Frey, H. **Les temples égyptiens primitifs identifiés avec les temples actuels chinois.** Paris (1909)

Fu, Charles Wei-hsun. Fingarette and munro on early confucianism: a methodological examination. **PEW** 28.2 (apr 1978) 181-198. See further Fingarette's Comments . . . **ibid** 223-226.

Fu, Charles Wei-hsun. Morality or beyond: the neo confucian confrontation with mahāyāna buddhism. **PEW** 23.3 (july 1973) 375-396.

Fukunaga, Mitsuji. 'No-mind' in chuang-tzu and in ch'an buddhism. **Zinbun** 12 (1969) 9-45.

Gallin, Bernard. Comments on contemporary sociocultural studies of medicine in chinese societies. In **MCC** (1975) 273-280.

Galpin, F. Notes on the ethical and christian value of chinese religious tracts and books. **ChRec** 12 (1881) 202-217.

Garvie, A.E. Mutual sharing. **IRM** 24 (1935) 181-192.

Gates, Alan Frederick. **Christianity and animism in taiwan.** San francisco (1979) x + 262 p, illus.

Gernet, Jacques. Christian and chinese world views in the fourteenth century. **Diogenes** 105 (spring 1979) 93-115.

Glasenapp, Helmuth von. **Die fünf grossen religionen.** Düsseldorf/köln (1951) See Schlussbetrachtung, indische und chinesische religiosität, 221-228.

Gould-Martin, Katherine. Medical systems in a taiwanese village: ong-ia-kong, the plague god as modern physician. In **MCC** (1975) 115-141. Same title (minus first phrase) in **CHAS** (1978) 41-67.

Graf, Olaf. **Tao und jen, sein und sollen im sung-chinesischen monismus.** Wiesbaden (1970) xii + 429 s, gloss, bibliog, index to names, general index. See rev by H.R. Schlette in **ZMR** 57.1 (1973) 60-64.

Grant, G.M. **Religions of the world in relation to christianity.** London (1894) Chap 3 and 4 deal with confucianism.

Grasso, Domenico. The new china and god's plan for salvation. In **NC:CR** (1977) 81-123.

Griffith, Gwilym O. **Interpreters of reality: a comment on heracleitus, lao tse and the christian faith.** London (1946) 106 p.

Guénon, René. Taoism and confucianism. **SCR** 6.4 (autumn 1972) 239-250.

Guignes, Joseph de. Observations sur quelques points concernant la religion et la philosophie des égyptiens et des chinois. **MAI** 40 (1780) 163-186.

Guimet, E. Lao-tzeu et la bráhmanisme. **Verhandlungen 2 CIHR, Basel, 1904,** bâle (1905) 168-183.

Gulik,R.H. van. Indian and chinese sexual mysticism. App I in author's **Sexual life in ancient china,** leiden (1961) 339-359.

Haar, Hans. **Bibliographie zur frage nach den wechsel-beziehungen zwischen buddhismus und christentum.** Berlin (1921) leipzig (1922) 47 p.

Hager, Joseph. **Panthéon chinois, ou, parallèle entre le culte religieux des grecs et celui des chinois. Avec des nouvelles preuves que la chine a été connue des grecs, et que les sérès des auteurs classiques ont été des chinois.** Paris (1806) 175 p, illus.

Hardon, John A. **Religions of the orient. A christian view.** Chicago (1970) See: Confucianism, 77-106.

Harlez, Ch. de. **La religion nationale des tartares orientaux, mandchous et mongols, comparée à la religion des anciens chinois, d'après les textes indigènes, avec le rituel tartare de l'empereur k'ien-long, traduit par la première fois. MCAM** 40 (1887) 216 p.

Heiler, F. Weltabkehr und weltrückkehr ausserchristlicher mystiker. 1. teil: Laotse und bhagavadgita. **Eine heilige kirche** 22 (1941) 181-213.

Hentze, Carl. **Objets rituels, croyances et dieux de la chine antique et de l'amérique.** Antwerp (1936)

Hentze, Carl. Die regenbogenschlange: alt-china und alt-amerika. **Anthropos** 61 (1966) 258-266, illus.

Hentze, Carl. Das ritual der wiederbelebung durch die "neue haut" (altchina—ocienien—amerika) **Sinologica** 6.2 (1961) 69-82, illus.

Hentze, C. Die tierverkleidung in erneuerungs- und initi-ationsmysterien (ältestes china, zircumpazifische kulturen und gross-asien) **Symbolon** 1 (1960) 39-86, illus.

Hentze, Carl. **Tod, auferstehung, weltordnung; das mythische bild in ältesten china, in den grossasiatisch-en und zirkumpazifischen kulturen.** Zürich (1955) 2 vol.

Hentze, Carl and Kim Chewon. **Ko- und chiwaffen in china und in amerika. Göttergestalten in der ältesten chinesischen schrift.** Antwerpen (1943) 59 p, pl.

Hessel, R.A.E. Calvin versus confucius: a sociological inquiry. **Japan christian quarterly** 26 (july 1960) 175-179.

Hodous, Lewis. Mo-ti and christianity. **IRM** 13 (apr 1924) 258-266.

Holbrook, Bruce. Chinese psycho-social medicine. Doctor and dang-ki: an inter-cultural analysis. **ASBIE** 37 (spring 1974) 85-110.

Holbrook, Bruce. Ethnoscience and chinese medicine, genuine and spurious. **ASBIE** 43 (spring 1977) 129-180.

Houtart, Francois H. Christian religions coming into confucian regions. **CF** 20.1 (1977) 18-32.

Howe, P.W.H. The bible and the chinese book of changes. **AP** 39 (aug 1968) 360-363.

Hsu, Francis L. K. **Americans and chinese. Reflections on two cultures and their people.** N.Y. (1953) 2nd ed (1970) See, in 2nd ed, chap 9 and 10.

Hsu, Francis L.K. **Clan, caste and club.** Princeton univ (1963) 335 p.

Hsu, Sung-peng. Lao tzu's conception of ultimate reality: a comparative study. **IPQ** 16.2 (june 1976) 197-217.

Huang, Wen-shan. On longevity. **ASBIE** 46 (autumn 1978) 139-150. Some comparisons of taoist and non-chin theories.

Hume, Robert E. **The world's living religions. With special reference to their sacred scriptures and in comparison with christianity.** N.Y. (1924) rev ed (1959) See chap 6 and 7.

Hwang, Bernard. Ancestor cult today. **Missiology** 5.3 (july 1977) 339-365.

Inglis, James W. Taoism from the christian standpoint. **ChRec** 46.10 (oct 1915) 595-599.

Iorio, Dominick A. (intro & tsl) **Nicholas malebranche: dialogue between a christian philosopher and a chinese philosopher on the existence and nature of god.** Washington d.c. (1980) 105 p, index. Malebranche (1638-1715) was a leading catholic cartesian philosopher.

Izutsu, Toshihiko. **A comparative study of the key philo-sophical concepts of sufism and taoism; ibn 'arabi and lao-tzu, chuang tzu.** Tokyo, keio gijuku daigaku, keio institute of cultural and linguistic studies, 2 vol (1967)

James, Edwin O. **The comparative study of religions of the east (excluding christianity and judaism)** Cambridge univ (1959) 32 p.

James T.W. Douglas. The christian approach to ancestor worship. **ChRec** 56.11 (nov 1925) 729-733.

Johnson, T.W. Far eastern fox lore. **AsFS** 33 (1974) 35-65.

Jones, E.E. The attitude of the chinese church toward non-christian festivals. **ChRec** 47.3 (mar 1916) 161-169.

King, Winston L. The way of tao and the path to nirvana. In **SA** (1963) 121-135.

Kleinman, Arthur et al (ed) **Medicine in chinese cultures: comparative studies of health care in chinese and other societies.** Washington d.c. (1975) Art sep listed in our bibliog. Abbrev **MCC**.

Kleinman, Arthur. Social, cultural and historical themes in the study of medicine in chinese societies: problems and prospects for the comparative study of medicine and psychiatry. In **MCC** (1975) 645-658.

Koo, Bon Myung. Thorough comparative studies on the morality of confucius and socrates. Seoul, **Journal of east and west studies** 4.2 (1975) 3-25.

Koppers, W. Der hund in der mythologie der zirkum-pazifischen volkes. **Wiener beiträge zur kultur-geschichte und linguistik** 1 (1930) 359-399. See rev art by Paul Pelliot in **TP** 28 (1931) 431-470.

Kramers, Robert. The sense of predicament in neo-confucian thought as a topic for christian reflection. **CF** 21.3 (1978) 107-114.

Krejci, Jaroslav. Religion and civilization: iran and china as two test cases of mutual interdependence and development. **CF** 19.3/4 (1976) 3-11.

Ku, Hung-ming. **The spirit of the chinese people.** Peking (1915) See essay of title name, 1-73, mostly on con-fucianism as chin substitute for relig. German tsl, **Der geist des chinesischen volkes,** jena (1924) See 41-106.

Kuong-hoa (Joseph Li) Die 'pietät' bei den völkern im orient und okzident. **Ecclesia apostolica** (1951) 40-56.

Lai, Whalen. The i-ching and the formation of the hua-yen philosophy. **JCP** 7.3 (sept 1980) 245-258.

Lanczkowski, Günter. Neutestamentaliche parallelen zu láo-tse's tao-te-king. In **Gott und die götter. Festgabe für erich fascher zum 60. geburstag,** berlin (1958) 7-15.

Laufer, Berthold. Columbus and cathay, and the meaning of america to the orientalist. **JAOS** 51 (1931) 87-103. Re mythol and relig resemblances.

Lee, Jung Young. Yin-yang way of thinking: a possible way for ecumenical theology. **IRM** 60 (july 1971) 363-370.

Lee, Peter K.H. An interpretive summary: "christianity and chinese humanism" **CF** 17.1 (1974) 48-53.

Legge, James. **Christianity and confucianism compared in the teaching of the whole duty of man.** London (1884) 36 p.

Legge, James. **Confucianism in relation to christianity.** Shanghai (1877) 12 p.

Legge, James. **The religions of china. Confucianism and taoism described and compared with christianity.** London (1880) 310 p.

Lew, Daniel Yu-tang. America and the new confucianism. **SAR** 5.1 (spring 1979) 8-21.

Liao, David Chia-en. Chinese religion and church growth. **CF** 15.3 (1972) 173-175.

Lie, Hwa-sun. **Der begriff skandalon im neuen testament und der wiederkehrgedanke bei laotse.** Bern & Frankfurt (1973) 252 s.

Liebenthal, Walter. Lord atman in the lao-tzu. **MS** 27 (1968) 374-380.

Lin, Timothy Tian-min. The concept of man in con-fucianism and christianity. **NEAJT** 14 (mar 1975) 20-24.

Lin, Timothy Tian-min. The confucian concept of jen and the christian concept of love. **CF** 15.3 (autumn 1972) 162-172.

Lin, Timothy Tian-min. Confucian filial piety and christian ethics. **NEAJT** 8 (mar 1972) 43-48.

Ling, Shun-sheng. Comparative study of the ancient chinese feng-shan and the ziggurat of mesopotamia. **ASBIE** 19 (1965) engl abrmt 39-51 + 10 p pl.

Ling, Shun-sheng. Dog sacrifice in ancient china and the pacific area. **ASBIE** 3 (1957) engl summ 37-40, illus.

Liu, C.H. On the dog-ancestor myth in asia. **SS** 1 (1941) 277-314.

Lo, Stanislaus Kuang. The meeting of christianity and confucianism. **ACQ** 5.1 (spring 1977) 36-40.

Lou, Dennis Wing-sou. Rain worship among the ancient chinese and the nahua and maya indians. **ASBIE** 4 (1957) 31-108, illus.

Lou, Tseng-tsiang (Dom Celestine) **Konfuzianer und christ.** Deutsche übertragung von Kaspar Hürlimann. Luzern (1947) 219 p, illus. Engl tsl by Michael Derrick, **The ways of confucius and christ,** london (1948) 140 p, illus.

MacLagan, Patrick J. **Chinese religious ideas: a christian valuation.** London (1926) 238 p.

Madsen, Richard. Religion and feudal superstition: implications of the prc's religious policy for the christian encounter with china. **CF** 22.4 (1979) 190-218.

Mahdihassan, S. A comparative study of greek and chinese alchemy. **AJCM** 7.2 (1979) 171-181.

Mahood, G.H. Socrates and confucius: moral agents or moral philosophers? **PEW** 21. (apr 1971) 177-188.

Malan, Saloman C. **A letter on the pantheistic and on the buddhistic tendency of the chinese and of the mongolian versions of the bible.** London (1856) 38 p.

Maspero, Henri. La société et la religion des chinois anciens et celles des tai modernes. In author's **HMRC** t 1, paris (1950) 139-194.

M'Clatchie M.T. The chinese on the plain of shinar, or a connection between the chinese and all other nations through their theology. **JRAS** 16 (1856) 368-435.

Mears, W.P. The philosophy, ethics, and religion of taoism. Chiefly as developed by chwang-tsze (a comparative sketch) **ChRev** 19 (1890-91) 225-242.

Medhurst, C. Spurgeon. **The tao teh king. A short study in comparative religion.** Chicago (1905) xix + 134.

Mégroz, R.L. Dream interpretation: chinese—greek—islamic. **AP** 6 (1935) 28-31.

Milloué, L. de. L'Astrologie et les différentes formes de la divination dans l'inde, en chine et au tibet. **CMG** (1899-1900 et 1900-01) 179-205.

Moran, J.A. Martin buber and taoism. **Judaism** 21 (winter 1972) 98-103.

Mori, Mikisaburō. Tsl Patrick James. Chuang tzu and buddhism. **EB** n.s. 5.2 (oct 1972) 44-69.

München-Helfen, Otto. Der schuss auf die sonnen. **WZKM** (1937) 75-95. Compares shooting of extra suns myth of china and other cultures in asia and america.

Mungello, David E. The reconciliation of neo-confucianism with christianity in the writings of joseph de prémare, s.j. **PEW** 26.4 (oct 1976) 389-410.

Murakami, Yoshimi. 'Nature' in lao-chuang thought and 'no-mind' in ch'an buddhism. **KGUAS** 14 (1965) 15-31.

Needham, Joseph. The elixir concept and chemical medicine in east and west. **JCUHK** 2.1 (june 1974) 242-265.

Needham, Joseph. Femininity in chinese thought and christian theology. **CF** 23.2 (1980) 57-70.

Neville, Robert. From nothing to being: the notion of creation in chinese and western thought. **PEW** 30.1 (jan 1980) 21-34.

Nevius, John L. **Demon possession and allied themes.** Chicago etc (1896) 494 p, indexes. Mostly chin cases, with some others for comparison.

Noël, Alexandre. **Conformité des cérémonies chinoises avec l'idolatrie grecque et romaine; pour servir de confirmation à apologie des dominicains missionaires de la chine** . . . Cologne (1700) 9 letters individually paginated.

Nyce, Ray C. The gospel and chinese religions today. **SEAJT** 14.2 (1973) 46-55.

O'Collins, Gerald. Christ and china. In **NC:CR** (1977) 124-145.

Ogilvie, Charles L. What can christianity give to china that other religions of china cannot give? **ChRec** 49.11 (nov 1918) 716-727.

M.C.P. Confucianism in its practical bearings upon the spread of christianity in china. **ChRec** 12.3 (may-june 1881) 218-224.

Pachow, W. Laotzû and gautama buddha; an enquiry into the authenticity of laotzû's mission to india. In **PFV** (1966) 293-303. Repr **ChBudd** (1980)

Pak, Hyobom. **China and the west. Myths and realities in history.** Leiden (1974) viii + 120 p. ". . . interacting forces of religion and politics"

Pakenham-Walsh, W.S. Memorials to the dead and their relation to christian practice. **ChRec** 41.4 (apr 1910) 264-268.

Park, O'Hyun. **Oriental ideas in recent religious thought.** Lakemont, ga (1974) See chap 5, Chinese religions and the religion of china, 155-185.

Pas, Julian F. Symbolism of the new light. Further researches into taoist liturgy: suggested by a comparison between the taoist fen-teng ritual and the christian consecration of the easter candle. **JHKBRAS** 20 (1980) 93-115.

Patai, R. Religion in middle eastern, far eastern, and western culture. **SWJA** 10 (1954) 233-254.

Pauthier, Georges. **Mémoire sur l'origine et propagation de la doctrine du tao, fondée par lao-tseu; traduit du chinois et accompagné d'un commentaire tiré des livres sancrits et du tao-te-king de lao-tseu, établissant la conformité de certaines opinions philosophiques de la chine et de l'inde; orné d'un dessein chinois; suivi de deux oupanishads des vedas, avec le texte sanscrit et persan.** Paris (1831) 79 p.

Pontynen, Arthur. Buddhism and taoism in chinese sculpture, a curious evolution in religious motifs. **FMB** 49.6 (june 1978) 16-21.

Poore, R. Ancestral worship in china and 'family worship' in england, as a practical basis of efficient state administration. **IAQR** (july 1894) 141-149. See also Eugène Simon, Une imitation . . . **La Réforme sociale** 2e sér, 8 (1893) 304-321.

Provine, Robert C. The sacrifice to confucius in korea and its music. **TKBRAS** 50 (1975) 43-69, illus.

Przyluski, J. Dragon chinois et naga indien. **MS** 3 (1938) 602-610.

Radhakrishnan, S. **India and china. Lectures delivered in china in may 1944.** Bombay (1944)

Rawlinson, Frank. China's answer to christianity. **ChRec** 58.1 (jan 1927) 40-51; 58.2 (feb 1927) 110-120, ref. Re current relig conditions.

Reichelt, G.M. Chinese religion and christianity. **Review & expositor** 58 (jan 1961) 25-34.

Reichelt, Karl Ludvig. Indigenous religious phrases that may be used to interpret the christian message. **ChRec** 58.2 (feb 1927) 123-126. Phrases fr budd and taoism.

Rhee, S.N. Fear god and honor your father and mother; two injunctions in the book of proverbs and the confucian classics. **Encounter** 26 (spring 1965) 207-214.

Roberts, John M. & Chien Chiao & Triloki N. Pandey. Meaningful god sets from a chinese personal pantheon and a hindu personal pantheon. **Ethnology** 14.2 (apr 1975) 121-148. A technical quantitative study.

Rosenkranz, G. Der geist europos und die religionen des ostens. **Zeitschrift für theologie und kirche** n.f. 47 (1950) 106-144.

Rosenzweig, Daphne Lange. Stalking the persian dragon: chinese prototypes for the miniature representations. **KdeO** 12.1/2 (1978-79) 150-176, illus.

Ross, D. A comparative study of religious symbolism among buddhists, adherents of folk or popular religion, protestants and catholics in taiwan. Ottowa, **Kerygma** 14 (1980) 101-116.

Rotours, Robert des. Confucianisme et christianisme. **Sinologica** 1 (1948) 231-245.

Rowley, Harold H. **Submission in suffering, and other essays in eastern thought.** Cardiff, univ wales (1951) 170 p, index.

Rule, Paul A. The confucian interpretation of the jesuits. **PFEH** 6 (sept 1972) 1-61.

Rule, Paul. Is maoism open to the transcendent? In **NC:CR** (1977) 25-43.

Rule, Paul A. Jesuit and confucian? Chinese religion in the journals of matteo ricci, s.j. 1538-1610. **JRH** 5 (1968) 105-124.

Sarkar, B.K. **Chinese religion through hindu eyes. A study in the tendencies of asiatic mentality.** Shanghai (1916) repr delhi (1975) xxxii + 331 p.

Sarkar, B.K. Confucianism, buddhism, and christianity. **OC** 33 (1919) 661-673.

Saussure, Léopold de. La cosmologie religieuse en chine, dans l'iran et chez les prophètes hébreux. **Actes CIHR, Paris, 1923,** paris (1925)

Scaligero, Massimo. Tao and grail: the search of earthly immortality. **E&W** 8 (apr 1957) 67-72.

Schmidt, P. Persian dualism in the far east. In **OSCEP** (1933) 405-406.

Schultz, J.P. Reciprocity in confucian and rabbinic ethics. **JRE** 2 (spring 1974) 143-150.

Schuster, C. A comparative study of motives in western chinese folk embroideries. **MS** 2 (1936-37) 21-80.

Senger, Nettie M. Christian attitudes in chinese religions. **ChRec** 57.7 (july 1926) 490-493.

Senger, N.M. Message of christianity to buddhism. **Brethren life & thought** 2 (1957) 22-29.

Shapiro, Sheldon. Morality and religious reformations. **CSSH** 18 (1976) 438-457. Incl chin comparisons.

Shastri, H.P. Hindu ideas and taoist texts. **AP** 10 (1939) 294-297.

Shaw, Yu-ming. The reaction of chinese intellectuals toward religion and christianity in the early twentieth century. In **C&C** (1979) 154-182.

Sheffield, D.Z. Christianity and the ethnic religions. **ChRec** 34.3 (mar 1903) 105-118.

Sheffield, D.Z. The ethics of christianity and of confucianism compared. **ChRec** 17 (1886) 365-379.

Sheffield, D.Z. The relation between christianity and heathen systems of religion. **ChRec** 14.2 (mar-apr 1883) 93-107.

Sherley-Price, Lionel D. **Confucius and christ: a christian estimate of confucius.** Westminster, engl (1951) 248 p, illus.

Shih, J. The tao: its essence, its dynamism, and its fitness as a vehicle of christian revelation. **SM** 15 (1966) 117-133.

Sih, Paul K.T. Mencius and st. thomas. Spiritually akin. **CC** 3.1 (1960) 87-100.

Simon, Eugène. Une imitation de la famille chinoise. Le major poore et les villages du wiltshire. **La réforme sociale** (16 août - 1 sept 1893) 304-321. See Poore, R. Ancestral worship in china and . . . .

Smart, Ninian. Maoism and religion.CF 18.4 (1975) 219-230. See also Philip Shen, Comments on professor ninian smart's paper, **ibid** 231-234; see further Smart's A reply to dr. shen's reply, **ibid** 19.1 (1976) 65-67.

Smith, Carl T. A heideggerian interpretation of the way of lao tzu. **CF** 10.2 (1967) 5-19.

Smith, Carl T. Radical theology and the confucian tradition. **CF** 10.4 (1967) 20-33.

Smith, D. Howard. Conflicting ideas of salvation in a.d. fifth century china. In Eric J. Sharpe & John R. Hinnells (ed) **Man and his salvation; studies in memory of s.f.g. brandon,** manchester univ (1973) 291-303.

Smith, D. Howard. Saviour gods in chinese religion. In **SG** (1963) 174-190.

Smith, Huston, Man and his fulfillment: china, india, and the west. **CF** 9.1 (1965) 19-23.

Smith, Robert J. Afterword. In **RRCS** (1974) 337-348. Reflections on comparison of totality of chin and jap relig.

Söderblom, N. **Die religionen der erde.** Halle a. saale (1905) 65 p.

Solomon, Bernard S. Meditation on two concepts of reality: biblical and taoist. **Tri-quarterly** 8 (winter 1967) 125-131.

Sowerby, Arthur de C. The chinese yuletide. **CJ** 7.6 (dec 1927) 271-273, illus. Compares aspects of Christmas and chin new year.

Sowerby, Arthur. Our attitude towards chinese religions. **ChRec** 48.5 (may 1917) 296-313.

Sparham, Charles G. **Christianity and the religions of china. A brief study in comparative religions.** London (1896) 24 p.

Speer, Robert E. **The light of the world. A brief comparative study of christianity and non-christian religions.** West bedford, mass (1911) See chap 3, Animism, confucianism and taoism, 121-176.

Stein, Rolf. Religious taoism and popular religion from the second to the seventh centuries. In **FT** (1979) 53-82.

Stevens, Keith. Two examples of chinese religious involvement with islam. **JHKBRAS** 19 (1979) 199-203, 3 pl. In singapore and malaysia and thailand.

Stewart, James Livingstone. **Chinese culture and christianity. A review of china's religions and related systems from the christian standpoint.** N.Y. etc (1926) 316 p, bibliog, index.

Sullivan, Francis A. Theological implications of the "new china" In **NC:CR** (1977) 146-164.

Sumiya, Kazuhiko. The long march and the exodus: "The thought of mao tse-tung" and the contemporary significance of "emissary prophecy." Tsl fr jap Pharis Harvey, Hiroshi Shinmi and Tadashi Miyabe. In Bruce Douglass and Ross Terrill (ed) **China and ourselves; explorations and revisions by a new generation,** boston (1969) 189-223.

Suppaner-Stanzel, Irene. Die ethischen ziele des taoismus und des existenzialismus. In festschrift, **Der mensch als persönlichkeit und als problem,** münchen (1963) 106-126.

T'an Yün-shan. **The universal mother in sino-indian culture and chinese universalism.** Santiniketan (1960) 19 p.

T'ang, Chün-i. Confucianism and chinese religions. In Moses Jung, Swami Nikhilanda, and Herbert W. Schneider (ed) **Relations among religions today. A handbook of policies and principles,** leiden (1963) 39-44.

Le Tao-teh-king. Identité des méthodes de lao-tse et du bouddha. Commentaire bouddhique du tao-teh-king. Lao-tse sous le nom de lauthu. **CISE** (1881) 765-771.

Thornberry, Mike. The encounter of christianity and confucianism: how modern confucianism views the encounter. **SEAJT** 10 (1968) 47-62.

Throop, Montgomery Hunt. Proverbs and the analects. A comparison of their teachings, moral and religious. **ChRec** 60.5 (may 1929) 323-330; 60.6 (june 1929) 371-378.

Tomkinson, L. Notes on the teachings of meh-tse and christianity. **ChRec** 58.8 (aug 1927) 489-497.

Tong, Lik Kuen. Confucian jen and platonic eros; a comparative study. **CC** 14.3 (sept 1973) 1-8.

Tong, P.K.K. Study of thematic differences between eastern and western religious thought. **Journal of ecumenical studies** 10 (spring 1973) 337-360.

Too-yu. The systems of foe and confucius compared, translated from the chinese. **ICG** no 5 (1818) 149-157.

Tseng, Wen-shing. Traditional and modern psychiatric care in taiwan. In **MCC** (1975) 177-194.

Tu, Wei-ming. An inquiry into wang yang-ming's four-sentence teaching. **EB** n.s. 7.2 (oct 1974) 32-48; repr in **H&SC** (1979) 162-178.

Übelhör, Monika. Geistesströmungen der späten ming-zeit, die als wirken der jesuiten in china begünstigten. **Saeculum** 23.2 (1972) 172-185.

Uno, T. The influence of chinese confucianism upon the spiritual life of japan. **YE** 3 (1927) 69-74; **PW** 3 (1927) 69-74.

Vlar, Alexandre. Lao-tse le nietzchéen. A propos du livre de la voie et la ligne droite. **Revue blanche** 27 (1902) 161-167.

Waidtlow, C. The identity of the ancient religions of china and scandinavia. **ChRec** 51.8 (aug 1920) 558-563; 51.9 (sept 1920) 623-628.

Welch, Holmes. Chinese omens for the christian clergy. **UUA Now** 150.12 (apr 1969) 22-25; repr **World buddhism,** colombo (aug 1969) repr **Cosmopolis,** madrid (sept 1969)

Whitehead, James D. & Yu-ming Shaw & N.J. Girardot (ed) **China and christianity. Historical and future encounters.** Univ notre dame (1979) xv + 293 p. See pertinent papers sep listed our bibliog. Abbrev **C&C.**

Whitehead, Raymond L. Christ, salvation and maoism. **CN** 15.4 (fall 1977) 1-7. See further, Creighton Lacy, A response to . . . **ibid** 7-10.

Whitehead, Raymond L. Christian terms in political use: salvation in the chinese revolution. **Worldmission** 24.2 (summer 1973) 22-32.

Wickersham, James. The religion of china and mexico compared. **American antiquarian and oriental journal** 19 (1897) 319-320.

Wienpahl, Paul. Spinoza and wang yang-ming. **RS** 5 (1969) 19-27.

Wilhelm, Richard. **Der mensch und das sein.** Jena (1931) 338 s. Re-issued as **Wandlung und dauer. Die weisheit des i ging,** düsseldorf-köln (1956) See passim.

Winter, H.J.J. Science, buddhism and taoism. **AP** 21 (may 1950) 206-208.

Wu, John C.H. **Chinese humanism and christian spirituality. Essays of john c.h. wu.** St. john's univ (1965) 227 p.

Wu, John C.H. The chinese soul and christian spirituality. **Worldmission** 2 (may 1951) 3-10.

Wu, Joseph S. Philosophy and revolution: confucianism and pragmatism. **PEW** 23.3 (july 1973) 323-332.

Wu, L.C. Tsl Z.S. Zia. Christianity in the light of confucian thought. **ChRec** 62.1 (jan 1931) 21-29.

Wyman, Mary. Chinese mysticism and wordsworth. **JHI** 10 (1949) 517-538.

Yang, Thaddeus. Tsl Fr McGlade. The chinese philosopher and st. thomas aquinas. **Worldmission** 3.1 (spring 1952) 40-51.

Yap, P.M. The possession syndrome; a comparison of hong kong and french findings. **BJP** 106 (1960) 114-137.

Yeh, Theodore T.Y. **Confucianism, christianity and china.** N.Y. (1969) 249 p, notes, bibliog.

Yen, Alsace. Shang-ssu festival and its myths in china and japan. **AsFS** 34.2 (1975) 45-86. Re purification rite.

Yen, Joseph C.Y. Christianity and confucianism: a brief survey of their central idea. Taipei, **Soochow journal of humanities** 2 (mar 1977) 158-164.

Yoon, Hong-key. The analysis of korean geomancy tales. **AsFS** 34.1 (1975) 21-34.

Young, John D. The cosmological gulf between china and the west. **CF** 23.2 (1980) 102-108.

Young, John D. An early confucian attack on christianity: yang kuang-hsien and his pu-te-i. **JCUHK** 3.1 (dec 1975) 156-186.

Young, John D. 'Original confucianism' versus neo confucianism: matteo ricci's chinese writings. In **MS/CA** (1977) 371-377.

Zia, N.Z. The common ground of the three chinese religions. **CF** 9.2 (1966) 17-34.

Zia, Rosina C. The conception of 'sage' in lao-tze and chuang-tze as distinguished from confucianism. **CCJ** 5 (may 1966) 150-157.

Zürcher, Erik. Buddhist influence on early taoism. **TP** 66.1/3 (1980) 84-147.

43. RELIGION & SOCIAL ORGANIZATION
(see also DEATH AND ANCESTRAL CULT; SECTS, SECRET SOCIETIES & NEW RELIGIONS; RELIGION IN PEOPLES REPUBLIC)

Ahern, Emily M. Affines and the rituals of worship. In **RRCS** (1974) 279-308.

Ahern, Emily M. The power and pollution of chinese women. In **WCS** (1975) 193-214.

Bergesen, Albert James. A durkheimian theory of "witch hunts" with the chinese cultural revolution of 1966-1969 as an example. **JSSR** 17.1 (mar 1978) 19-29.

Brim, John A. Village alliance temples in hong kong. In **RRCS** (1974) 93-104.

Cernada, George P. **Basic beliefs about a new human life and ethical judgment: family planning field workers in taiwan.** Univ mass intl area studies program occ papers ser no 5 (1979) 46 p.

Chang, Hao. **Liang ch'i-ch'ao and intellectual transition in china, 1890-1907.** Harvard univ (1971) See Index, Budd; Relig.

Chao, P. The mourning ritual within the chinese kinship system. **CC** 13.2 (june 1972) 49-71.

Chikusa, Tatsuo. Succession to ancestral sacrifices and adoption of heirs to the sacrifices: as seen from an inquiry into customary institutions in manchuria. In **CFL&SC** (1978) 151-175.

DeGlopper, Donald R. Religion and ritual in lukang. In **RRCS** (1974) 43-70.

Delaney, Joan F. & Chan Ying-keung. **A study of the role of religious organization in the kwun tong community.** Chin univ hk (1973) 30 p.

Durrant, Stephen W. The theme of family conflict in early taoist biography. Albuquerque, **Selected papers in asian studies,** western conference, assoc for asian studies vol 2 (1977) 2-8.

Erkes, Eduard. Der primat des weibes im alten china. **Sinica** 10 (1935) 166-176.

Feuchtwang, Stephan. School-temple and city-god. In **CLIC** (1977) 581-608.

Freedman, Maurice. On the sociological study of chinese religion. In **RRCS** (1974) 19-42.

Freedman, Maurice. Religion et adaptation sociale chez les chinois de singapore. **ASR** 7 (janv-juin 1959) 89-103.

Hong, L.K. Association of religion and family structure; the case of the hong kong family. **Sociological analysis** 33 (spring 1972) 50-57. bibliog.

Johnson, Graham E. From rural committee to spirit medium cult: voluntary association in the development of a chinese town. Canadian assoc for south asian studies, **Contributions to asian studies** 1 (1971) 123-143. See sec, Religious associations, 140-143. Re Tsuen wan, new territories.

Levy, Marion J. **The family revolution in modern china.** Harvard univ (1949) See chap 7, The modern kinship structure of integration and expression: integration, 247-257.

Mensching, Gustav. **Soziologie der grossen religionen.** Bonn (1966) See 2, Sociologie des chinesischen universismus, 42-53.

Miller, Alan L. The buddhist monastery as a total institution. **JRelSt** 72. (fall 1979) 15-29.

Molloy, S. Max weber and the religions of china: any way out of the maze? **British journal of sociology** 31.3 (1980) 377-400.

Pak, Hyobom. **China and the west. Myths and realities in history.** Leiden (1974) viii + 120 p. ". . . interacting forces of religion and politics . . ."

Pasternak, Burton. Chinese tale-telling tombs. **Ethnology** 12.3 (july 1973) 259-273. ". . . deals with the relationship between grave composition and tomb sacrifices on the one hand, and lineage segmentation, lineage trusts, and the nature of relationships between living and dead members of the descent group on the other . . ."

Quinn, Edward J. The taiwanese folk-values system. **Missiology** 1.3 (july 1973) 359-365.

Rawski, Evelyn S. Popular religion in east asia. **Peasant studies newsletter** 4.4 (oct 1975) 2-6. Rev art on E. Ahern, **Cult of the dead**; D. Jordan, **Gods, ghosts and ancestors** qqv; R.J. Smith, **Ancestor worship in contemporary japan**; A. Wolf (ed) **RRCS** q.v.

Rousselle, Erwin. Die frau in gesellschaft und mythos der chinesen. **NachrDGNVO** 49 (1939) 12-24; 50 (1939) 10-17. Same title in **Sinica** 16 (1941) 130-151, pl.

Schipper, Kristofer M. Neighborhood cult associations in traditional tainan. In **CLIC** (1977) 651-676.

Seaman, Gary. In the presence of authority: hierarchical roles in chinese spirit medium cults. In **NABCC** (1980) 61-74.

Seaman, Gary. **Temple organization in a chinese village.** Taipei (1978) 172 p, bibliog, char list, chronol, 2 maps.

Shapiro, Sheldon. Morality and religious reformation. **CSSH** 18 (1976) 438-457. Incl chin comparisons.

Shinohara, Koichi. 'Adjustment to the world' and 'rationalization' in max weber's study of chinese religious tradition. **Sciences religieux/Studies in religion** 18.1 (1979) 27-34.

Sjöhelm, Gunnar. Les limites entre la religion et la culture à l'occasion de l'interpretation de la religion antique. In Sven S. Hartman (ed) **Syncretism: based on papers read at the symposium on cultural contact, meeting of religions, syncretism held at abo on the 8th-10th of september, 1966,** stockholm (1969) 110-127.

Van der Sprenkel, O.B. Chinese religion. **British journal of sociology** 5 (1954) 272-275. Rev art on H.H. Gerth (tsl) Max Weber's **The religion of china** q.v.

Wang, Shih-ch'ing. Religious organization in the history of a chinese town. In **RRCS** (1974) 71-92. The town is shulin, a suburb of taipei.

Wang, Sung-hsing. Taiwanese architecture and the supernatural. In **RRCS** (1974) 183-192.

Watson, James L. Anthropological analysis of chinese religion. **CQ** 66 (june 1976) 355-364. Rev art on A. Wolf (ed) **RRCS** q.v.

Wolf, Arthur P. Gods, ghosts, and ancestors. In **RRCS** (1974) 131-182.

Wolf, Arthur P. (ed) **Religion and ritual in chinese society.** Stanford univ (1974) xii + 377 p, ref, char list, index. Art sep listed in our bibliog. Abbrev **RRCS.**

Wong, Yu-yui. 'The filial mourning head-dress society' in the villages of chang-i, shantung. Institute of pacific relations, research staff of secretariat (comp & tsl) **Agrarian china; selected source materials from chinese authors.** Univ chicago (n.d.--preface 1938) 204-207.

Woon, Yuen-fong. Social organization and ceremonial life of two multi-surname villages in hoi-p'ing county, south china, 1911-1949. **JHKBRAS** 17 (1977) 101-111.

Yang, C.K. **Religion in chinese society. A study of contemporary functions of religion and some of their historical factors.** Univ calif (1961) 473 p, notes, bibliog.

Zingerle, Arnold. **Max weber und china; herrschafts- und religionssoziologische grundlagen zum wandel der chinesischen gesellschaft.** Berlin (1972) 180 s.

44. CHINESE RELIGION AS A DISCIPLINE

Bergeson, Albert James. A durkheimian theory of "witch-hunts" with the chinese cultural revolution of 1966-1969 as an example. **JSSR** 17.1 (mar 1978) 19-29.

Eisenstadt, Samuel N. The implications of weber's sociology of religion for the understanding of the processes of change in contemporary non-european societies and civilization. **Diogenes** 85 (spring 1974) 83-111, bibliog.

Freedman, Maurice. On the sociological study of chinese religion. In **RRCS** (1974) 19-42.

Fu, Charles Wei-hsun. Fingarette and munro on early confucianism: a methodological examination. **PEW** 28.2 (apr 1978) 181-198. See further Fingarette's Comments. . . **ibid** 223-226.

Girardot, Norman J. Chinese religion and western scholarship. In **C&C** (1979) 83-111.

Girardot, Norman J. The problem of creation mythology in the study of chinese religion. **HR** 15.4 (may 1976) 289-318.

Holbrook, Bruce. Ethnoscience and chinese medicine, genuine and spurious. **ASBIE** 43 (spring 1977) 129-180.

Jen, Jiyu (Chi-yü) The struggle to develop a marxist science of religion. **CF** 22.2 (1979) 75-89. See further Ninian Smart, Towards a dialogue at the level of the science of religion . . . **ibid** 22.4 (1979) 219-222.

Kleinman, Arthur. Medical and psychiatric anthropology and the study of traditional forms of medicine in modern chinese culture. **ASBIE** 39 (spring 1975) 107-123.

Lai, Whalen. Toward a periodization of chinese religion. **SSCRB** 8 (fall 1980) 79-90.

Major, John S. Research priorities in the study of chinese religion. **HR** 17.3/4 (feb-may 1978) 226-243.

Meyer, Jeffrey F. Confucius as a zen master: on marrying content and method in teaching. In Ann Carr (comp) **The academic study of religion: 1975 proceedings,** annual meeting american academy of religion (1975) 7-15.

Pas, Julian. Chinese religion rediscussed. **JHKBRAS** 19 (1979) 149-175. Rev art on P. Baity, **Religion in a chinese town** q.v. with further discussion on methodology.

Rawski, Evelyn. Popular religion in east asia. **Peasant studies newsletter** 4.4 (1975) 2-6. Rev art on E. Ahern, **Chinese cult of the dead,** D. Jordan, **Gods, ghosts and ancestors** qqv; R.J. Smith, **Ancestor worship in contemporary japan;** A Wolf (ed) **RRCS** q.v.

Sakai, Tadao & Noguchi Tetsurō. Taoist studies in japan. In **FT** (1979) 269-287.

Seaman, Gary. Ethnographic film from the field to the classroom: film records of popular religion in china. **Chinoperl** 7 (1977) 106-135, bibliog.

Shinohara, Koichi. 'Adjustment to the world' and 'rationalization' in max weber's study of chinese religious tradition. **Sciences religieux/Studies in religion** 8.1 (1979) 27-34.

Sivin. Nathan. On the word "taoist" as a source of perpexity. With special reference to the relations of science and religion in traditional china. **HR** 17.3/4 (feb-may 1978) 303-330.

Sivin, N. Report on the third international conference on taoist studies. **SSCRB** 7 (fall 1979) 1-23.

Smart, Ninian. Towards a dialogue at the level of the science of religion: a reply to ren jiyu. **CF** 22.4 (1979) 219-222.

Smith, Richard J. An approach to the study of traditional chinese culture. **CC** 19.2 (june 1978) 47-78.

Watson, James L. Anthropological analyses of chinese religion. **CQ** 66 (june 1976) 355-364. Rev art on A. Wolf (ed) **RRCS** q.v.

Wills, John E. jr. State ceremony in late imperial china: notes for a framework for discussion. **SSCRB** 7 (1979) 46-57.

Zingerle, Arnold. **Max weber und china: herrschafts- und religionssoziologische grundlagen zum wandel der chinesischen gesellschaft.** Berlin (1972) 180 s.

45. MISCELLANEOUS

Ahern, Emily M. The power and pollution of chinese women. In **WCS** (1975) 193-214.

Ahern, Emily M. The problem of efficacy: strong and weak illocutionary acts. **Man** 14.1 (mar 1979) 1-17.

Anderson, E.N. & Marja L. Homage to the locality: religion in the agricultural landscape. In **CE** (1973) 147-166.

Bach, A.H. Glauben und aberglauben in china. **OstL** 2 (d?) 1087-1089, 1112-1113.

Berkowitz, Morris J. & John H. Reed. Research into the chinese little tradition: a progress report. **Journal of asian and african studies** 6.3/4 (1971) 233-238. See also Berkowitz, Brandauer & Reed, Study program on chinese religious practices in hong kong, a progress report, **CF** 11.3 (1968) 5-19.

Berndt, Manfred. Servanthood among para-christian and non-christian religions in hongkong. **CF** 14.4 (1971) 157-182.

Berthier, Brigitte. Le miroir brisé ou le taoïste et son ombre. **l'Homme** 19.3/4 (juil-dec 1979) 205-222. Re Taoism and femininity.

Bishop, Donald H. The international institute of shanghai, an eastern parliament of religions. **SCR** 6.3 (summer 1972) 152-176. Held in 1894.

Braden, Charles Samuel. **War, communism and world religions.** NY (1953) See chap 2, War, communism and the religions of china, 56-89.

Bulling, A Guttkind. A late shang place of sacrifice and its historical significance. **Expedition** 19.4 (1977) 1-11, illus.

C.C. Suttee in china. **All the year round** 6 (sept 1861) 538-541. Repr in **Chinese and japanese repository** (may 1862?) 457-461.

Canonization of a well. **ChRec** 3.6 (oct 1870) 155-156. By imperial edict.

Carmody, Denise Lardner. Taoist reflections on feminism. **Religion in life** 46.1 (summer 1977) 234-244.

Carmody, Denise Lardner. **Women and world religions.** Nashville, tenn (1979) See chap 3, East asian religions, 66-91.

Chan, Wing-tsit. The historic chinese contribution to religious pluralism and world community. In Edward J. Jurji (ed) **Religious pluralism and world community; interfaith and intercultural communication,** leiden (1969) 113-130.

Chan, Wing-tsit. The individual in chinese religions. In **SIEW** (1968) 181-198.

Chinese tables of merits and errors. **JIA** n.s. 2 (1858) 210-220. ". . . stated to be extracted from a chinese work called kung-kwo-kih, i.e. 'merits and errors scrutinized' . . ." Extracted fr **ICG** (1821)

Ching, Julia. The chinese religious sense. **CF** 21.4/22.1 (1978-79) 168-174. See further John D. Young, Regarding the chinese religious sense, **ibid** 22.3 (1979) 150-155.

Corwin, Charles. **East to eden? Religion and the dynamics of social change.** Grand rapids, mich (1972) See chap 2, China, 51-93. ". . . a phenomenological study of man as he appears in the . . . chinese . . . tradition"

Demiéville, Paul. **Choix d'études sinologiques 1921-1970.** Leiden (1973) xli + 633 p, bibliog of author 1920-1971 by Gisèle de Jong. Repr in 1 vol of many art relating to relig among other subj. Each repr is sep listed in our bibliog. Abbrev **CES.**

Demiéville, Paul. Momies d'extrême-orient. **Journal des savants** (janv-mars 1965) 144-170.

Doolittle, Justus. Missionary topics. Chap 17 in author's **SLC** vol 2 (1865) 394-417. Re certain beliefs and practices esp relevant to christian missionary efforts.

Doolittle, Justus. Priests of the three religions. Chap 9 in author's **SLC** vol 1 (1865) 236-254.

Douglas, R.K. Social and religious ideas of the chinese, illustrated in language. **Journal of the anthropological institute of great britain and ireland** 22 (1893-94) 159-173.

The Editor. The number of buddhists in the world. **ChRec** 14.6 (nov-dec 1883) 453-463. Concludes that "the great mass of the population of china is to be classified as confucianists"

Erkes, Eduard. Die profanisierung sakraler zeichen in der chinesischen schrift. **Wissenschaftliche zeitschrift der universität leipzig** 3 (1954) 413-416.

Evils of forming illegal associations; prohibition of magicians, leaders of sects, and teachers of false doctrines; renunciation of allegiance; the tea sect &c. **ChRep** 14.2 (feb 1845) 69-77.

Ferguson, John. **War and peace in the world's religions.** Oxford univ (1978) See chap 5, Religions of the far east, 62-77.

Foster, J.M. Some phases of religious development. **ChRec** 29.6 (1898) 266-269. Re Clan and village quarrel due to relig observances.

Franke, Herbert, Einige drucke und handschriften der frühen ming-zeit. **OE** 19 (1972) 55-64, 17 pl. Budd and taoist texts.

Franke, O. (tsl) **Kêng tschi t'u. Ackerbau und seidenge-winnung in china; ein kaiserliches lehr- und mahn-buch.** Hamburg (1913) mit 102 taf, 57 illus in text. See, Einleitung: ackerbau und seidengewinnung als ethische und religionsbildende elemente, 3-38.

Gen, Lewis. What legge thinks of confucius. **EH** 1.12 (june 1961) 44-46.

Heřmanová-Novotná, Zdenka. An attempt at linguistic analysis of the text of ta t'ang san-tsang ch'ü ching shih-hua. **ArchOr** 39 (1971) 167-189. Re text preserved in japan and ed by lo chen-yü in 1916, narrating story of hsi yu chi.

Ho, Lien-kwei. The cultural status of tortoise. **ASBIE** 16 (1963) engl summ 111-114.

Ho, Y.F. & L.Y. Lee. Authoritarianism and attitude toward filial piety in chinese teachers. **Journal of social psychology** 92 (1974) 305-306. Significant correlation was found.

Hodous, Lewis. The ministry of chinese religions. **IRM** 25 (july 1936) 329-341.

Hopkins, J. Castell. Chinese religions and national charac-teristics. **Canadian magazine of politics, science, art and literature** 5 (1895) 528-535.

Hsu, Dau-lin. Crime and cosmic order. **HJAS** 30 (1970) 111-125.

Hsu, Jing & Wen-hsing Tseng. Family relations in classic chinese opera. **IJSP** 20 (1974) 159-172.

Hutson, James. The domestic altar. **JNCBRAS** 49 (1918) 93-100.

Johnson, G.E. From rural committee to spirit medium cult: voluntary association in the development of a chinese town. Canadian assoc for south asian studies, **Contri-butions to asian studies** 1 (1971) 123-143. Re Tsuen wan, new territories.

Johnston, Reginald F. The religious future of china. **Nine-teenth century and after** 74 (nov 1913) 908-923.

Kaltenmark, Maxime. Religions de la chine. In **Problèmes et méthodes d'histoire des religions. Mélanges publiés par la section des sciences religieuses à l'occasion du centenaire de l'école pratique des hautes études,** paris (1968) 53-56.

Kuong-Hoa (Joseph Li) Die 'pietät' bei den völkern im orient und okzident. **Ecclesia apostolica** (1951) 40-56.

Larre, Claude. Sécularization contre religiosité à l'est de l'inde. **RechScRelig** 63 (avr-juin 1975) 161-184. Taiwan is discussed 167-172.

Lee, Hsing-tsun. A new look at taoism and buddhism **ACQ** 4.4 (winter 1976) 117-156. Author's orig interpre-tations.

Levy, Marion J. jr. **The family revolution in modern china.** Harvard univ (1949) See chap 7, The kinship structure of integration and expression: integration, 247-257.

Mark, Lindy Li. Orthography, riddles, divination and word magic: an exploration in folklore and culture. In **LL&R** (1979) 43-69.

Martin, W.A.P. The religious attitude of the chinese mind. **MRW** n.s. 4 (1891) 296-301.

Murphy, Gardner, and Lois B. Murphy (ed) **Asian psychology.** N.Y. and london (1968) See pt 2, The psychology of china, 127-177.

Needham, Joseph. Femininity in chinese thought and christian theology. **CF** 23.2 (1980) 57-70.

Niida, Noboru. The industrial and commercial guilds of peking and religion and fellow-countrymanship as elements of their coherence. **FS** 9 (1950) 179-206.

Park, O'Hyun. Chinese religions and the religion of china. **Perspectives in religious studies** 2 (fall 1975) 160-190. Re Martin buber's views.

Parrinder, Geoffrey. **Sex in the world's religions.** Oxford univ (1980) See chap 5, Chinese yin and yang, 77-102.

Pelliot, Paul. Les documents chinois trouvés par la mission kozlov à khara-khoto. **JA** sér 11, t 3 (1914) 503-518. Found in 1908; art briefly annotates the list, of which many are on chin relig.

Peyraube, Alain. Trois études sur les religions chinoises. **ASSR** 35 (janv-juin 1973) 151-157. Rev art on Doré, **Manuel des superstitions chinoises,** Gulik, **La vie sexuelle dans la chine ancienne,** Maspero, **Le taoïsme et les religions chinoises** qqv.

Raguin, Yves. Mediation dans le bouddhisme et le taoïsme. **SM** 21 (1972) 77-92.

Rawlinson, Frank. Some of china's life-sets. **ChRec** 57.5 (may 1926) 344-357. Art treats of "the spheres of human conflicts and cooperation, and religious expression"

Religion and poverty in china. **Methodist review** 77 (1895) 141-142.

Riboud, Krishna. Some remarks on the face-covers (fu-mien) discovered in the tombs of astana. **OA** n.s. 23.4 (winter 1977) 438-454. Tombs in turfan area, chin burials of six dyn period.

Roberts, John M. & Chien Chiao & Triloki N. Pandey. Meaningful god sets from a chinese personal pantheon and a hindu personal pantheon. **Ethnology** 14.2 (apr 1975) 121-148. A technical quantitative study.

Rowley, Harold H. **Submission in suffering, and other essays in eastern thought.** Cardiff, univ wales (1951) 170 p, index.

H.M.C.S. (tsl) Proclamation forbidding idol processions. **ChRec** 4.10 (1872) 267-269. Issued by acting gov-genl and lt-gov of fukien.

Seaman, Gary. Ethnographic film from the field to the classroom: film records of popular religion in china. **Chinoperl** 7 (1977) 106-135, bibliog.

Shih, J. Mediation in chinese religion. **SM** 21 (197) 77-92. Mostly concerned with li (ritual)

Sih, Paul K.T. Will confucianism thought (sic) survive in the modern age? **CC** 17.2 (june 1976) 27-30.

Sivin, N. Report on the third international conference on taoist studies. **SSCRB** 7 (fall 1979) 1-23.

Sjöholm, Gunnar. The boundaries between religion and culture with reference to the interpretation of ancient chinese religion. **CF** 13.4 (1970) 5-20.

Smith, Huston. Tao now: an ecological testament. In Ian G. Barbour (ed) **Earth might be fair. Reflections on ethics, religion, and ecology.** Englewood Cliffs, n.j. (1972) 62-81.

Stevens, Keith. Altar images from hunan and kiangsi. **JHKBRAS** 18 (1978) 41-48, illus b-&-w photos.

Sumiya, Kazuhiko. The long march and the exodus: "The thought of mao tse-tung" and the contemporary significance of "emissary prophecy." Tsl fr jap Pharis Harvey, Hiroshi Shinmi and Tadashi Miyabe. In Bruce Douglass and Ross Terrill (ed) **China and ourselves; explorations and revisions by a new generation,** boston (1969) 189-223.

T'ang, Chün-i. My option between philosophy and religion. **CSP** 5.4 (summer 1974) 4-38.

Tompkinson, Leonard. **Mysticism, ethics and service in chinese thought.** London (1956) 24 p.

Tsui, Bartholomew P. M. Ancient chinese prayers: a collection and study. **CF** 19.3/4 (1976) 48-97.

Tu, Wei-ming. Ultimate self-transformation as a communal act: comments on modes of self-cultivation in traditional china. **JCP** 6.2 (june 1979) 237-246.

Wasson, R. Gordon. **Soma. The divine mushroom of immortality.** Harcourt brace johanovich: printed in italy (1968) See chap 13, The marvelous herb [ling chih] 77-92, pl.

Wieger, Léon (tsl) Hymnes chinoises. **RechScRelig** 1 (1910) 359-372. Examples through the ages.

Williams, David Rhys. **World religions and the hope for peace.** Boston (1951) See chap 2, Mo ti and the will to peace.

Wolcott, Leonard and Carolyn. **Religions around the world.** Nashville and n.y. (1967) See chap 5, Chinese religions, 71-88. Juvenile level.

Wu, Pei-yi. Self-examination and confession of sins in traditional china. **HJAS** 39.1 (june 1978) 5-38.

Wurm, Paul. Religiöser eifer bei chines. buddhisten. **AMZ** 10 (1883) 501-503.

Yang, C.K. **The chinese family in the communist revolution.** M.I.T. (1959) repr in author's **Chinese communist society: the family and the village,** MIT (1965) See chap 10, Secularization of the family institution, 183-190.

Yang, Lien-sheng. (1) A note on the so-called tlv mirrors and the game liu-po. **HJAS** 9 (1947) 202-206; (2) An additional note on the ancient game liu-po. **Ibid** 15 (1952) 124-139. Both repr in author's collection, **Excursions in sinology,** harvard univ (1969) 138-165.

Yeh, E.K. The chinese mind and human freedom. **IJSP** 18 (1972) 132-136.

Young, John D. Regarding "the chinese religious sense" **CF** 22.3 (1979) 150-155. Response to art by Julia Ching in **ibid** 21.4/22.1 (1978-79) q.v.

PART THREE

Chinese Buddhism

1. REFERENCE WORKS
(See also **Studies of Texts & Terms;** also
Part One: **Bibliography**)

Akanuma, Chizen. **The comparative catalogue of
chinese āgamas and pali nikāyas (kan-pa shi-bu
shi-agon gosho-roku)** Nagoya (1929) 2nd ed tokyo
(1958) xvi + 424 p.

Anesaki, Masaharu. **The four buddhist āgamas in
chinese, a concordance of their parts and of the
corresponding counterparts in the pali nikāyas.** TASJ
35.3 (1908) 149 p.

Bagchi, P.C. **Le canon bouddhique en chine, les
traducteurs et les traductions.** Univ calcutta (publ in
paris) vol 1 (1927) vol 2 (1938) lii + 436 p.

Bagchi, P.C. **Deux lexiques sanskrit-chinois.** Univ
calcutta (publ in paris) vol 1: **Fan yu tsa ming, attributed
to li-yen; Fan yu ts'ien tsen wen, attributed to yi-tsing**
(1929) 336 p; vol 2: **Étude critique des deux lexiques**
(1937) 204 p.

Beal, Samuel. **The buddhist tripitaka as it is known in
china and japan. A catalogue and a compendious
report.** Printed for the india office. Devonport (1876)
117 p.

Beal, Samuel. Results of an examination of chinese
buddhist books in the library of the india office. **Trans 2nd
ICO london 1874,** london (1876) 132-162. See also
author's art, The buddhist works in chinese in the india
office library, **IA** 4 (1875) 90-101.

Brandon, S.G.F. (ed) **A dictionary of comparative
religions.** N.Y. (1970) See buddhist entries passim.

Chan, Wing-tsit. Chinese and buddhist religious
terminology. In Vergilius Ferm (ed) **Encyclopedia of
religion,** n.y. (1945) passim. Repr as pamphlet, n.y.
(1945) 36 p.

Demiéville, Paul (redacteur en chef) **Hôbôgirin.
Dictionnaire encyclopédique du bouddhisme d'après
les sources chinoises et japonaises.** Publié sous la
direction de S. Lévi et J. Takakusu. Fascicules i-iii (a-chi)
with fascicule annexe (tables de taishō issaikyō) In 4 pt (all
publ) tokyo (1929-37)

Demiéville, Paul. Manuscrits chinois de touen-houang à
leningrad. **TP** 51.4 (1964) 355-376.

Demiéville, Paul. **Récents travaux sur touen-houang.
Aperçu bibliographique et notes critiques.** Leiden
(1970) vi + 94 p.

Demiéville, Paul. Notes additionelles sur les éditions
imprimées du canon bouddhique. App to Paul Pelliot, **Les
débuts de l'imprimerie en chine,** rév et publ par Paul
Demiéville et R. des Rotours, paris (1953) 121-138. Repr
CEB (1973)

Demiéville, Paul. Sur les éditions imprimées du canon
chinois. **BEFEO** 24 (1924) 181-218.

Edkins, Joseph. Buddhist words and phrases. In **DV** vol 2,
pt 3, no 6, 221-229.

Edkins, Joseph. Handbook for the student of chinese
buddhism. **ChRec** 3.8 (jan 1871) 214-218. Rev of E.J.
Eitel's work q.v.

Eitel, E.J. **Handbook for the student of chinese
buddhism.** Hong kong (1870) viii + 224 p.

Eitel, Ernest J. **Hand-book of chinese buddhism, being a
sanskrit chinese dictionary with vocabularies of
buddhist terms in pali, singhalese, siamese, burmese,
tibetan, mongolian and japanese.** Hong kong, 2nd ed
rev and enl (1888) 231 p in 2 col. Repr san francisco
(1976)

Feer, Henri L. Introduction au catalogue spécial des
ouvrages bouddhiques du fonds chinois de la bibliothèqu
nationale. **TP** 9 (1898) 201-214.

Forke, A, **Katalog des pekinger tripitaka der
königlichen bibliothek au berlin.** Berlin (1916) 216 p.

Fou Si-hoa. Catalogue des pao-kiuan. **Mélanges
sinologiques** 2 (1951) 41-103.

Fujishima, Ryauon. Index des mots sanscrits-chinois
contenus dans les deux chapitres d'i-tsing. **JA** 8e sér, 13
(1889) 490-496.

Giles, Lionel. **Descriptive catalogue of the chinese
manuscripts from tun-huang in the british museum.**
London (1957) xxv + 334 p.

Giles, Lionel. **Six centuries at tun-huang. A short
account of the stein collection of chinese mss in the
british museum.** London (1944) 50 p, facs.

Grinstead E.D. **Title index to the descriptive catalogue
of chinese manuscripts from tunhuang in the british
museum** London (1963) 41 p.

Guignard, Marie-Roberte (ed) **Catalogue des manuscrits
chinois de touen-houang.** Paris vol 1 (1970) xxix + 407
p, 24 pl; items no 2001-2500.

Gutzlaff, Charles. List of the principal buddhistical works
from the pali, in chinese characters. **JRAS** 9 (1848)
207-213.

Hackmann, Heinrich. Alphabetisches verzeichnis zum kao
sêng ch'uan. **AO** 2 (1923) 81-112.

Hackmann, Heinrich. **Erklärendes worterbuch zum
chinesischen buddhismus. Chinesisch-sanskrit-
deutsch.** Von Heinrich Hackmann nach seinem
handschriftlichen nachlass überarbeitet von Johannes
Nobel. Leiden (1951-54) 1fg 1-6 (voranstlicher
gesarntungfang 12 lieferungen)

Haneda, T. and P. Pelliot. **Manuscrits de touen-houang, conservés à la bibliothèque nationale de paris et pub, par le toa-kokyukwai de changhai.** Kyoto (1926) 2 vol.

Inagaki, Hisao. **Index to the larger sukhāvatīvyūha sūtra. A tibetan glossary with sanskrit and chinese equivalents.** Kyoto (1978) xii + 269 p.

Julien, Stanislas. Concordance sinico-samskrite d'un nombre considérable de titres d'ouvrages bouddhiques, recueillie dans un catalogue chinois de l'an 1306, et publiée, après le déchiffrement et la restitution des mots indiens. JA 4e sér, 14 (1849) 353-446. Réimpr dans les **Mélanges de géographie asiatique et de philologie sinico-indienne,** paris (1864)

Julien, Stanislas. **Méthode pour déchiffrer et transcrire les noms sanscrits, qui se rencontrent dans les livres chinois.** Paris (1861)

Julien, Stanislas. Renseignements bibliographiques sur les relations des voyages dans l'inde et les descriptions du si-yu, qui ont été composées en chinois entre le Ve et le XVIIIe siècle de notre ère. JA sér 4, 10 (1847) 265-269.

Krueger, R. and E.D. Francis. **Index to lessing's lamaist iconography of the peking temple, yung-ho-kung.** Bloomington, ind (1966) 31 p.

Lalou, Marcelle. Onze années de travaux européens sur le bouddhisme (mai 1936-mai 1947) **Muséon** 61 (1948) 245-276.

Lancaster, Lewis. Buddhist literature: its canons, scribes, and editors. In Wendy Doniger O'Flaherty (ed) **The critical study of sacred texts,** berkeley, calif (1978) 215-230.

Lancaster, Lewis R. in collab with Sung-bae Park. **The korean buddhist canon: a descriptive catalogue.** Univ calif (1979)

La Vallée Poussin, L. de. **Catalogue of the tibetan manuscripts from tun-huang in the india office library. With an appendix on the chinese ms. by Kazuo Enoki.** Ed S.C. Sutton. London (1962) 318 p, 4 pl.

La Vallée Poussin, Louis de. Notes de bibliographie bouddhique. **MCB** 3 (1934-35) 355-407; 5 (1936-37) 243-304.

Ling, T.O. **A dictionary of buddhism.** NY (1972) Extracted fr S.G.F. Brandon (ed) **A dictionary of comparative religion,** ny (1970) See passim.

Maspero, Henri (ed) **Les documents chinois de la troisième expédition de sir aurel stein en asie centrale.** London (1953) xii + 268 p, 40 pl, index. Annot catalogue of materials in british museum. Documents fr tun-huang, lou-lan, turfan, tarim basin, khara-khoto.

Matsumoto, T. "Taishō shinshū daizōkyō" oder kurz "taishō issaikyō" **ZDMG** 88 (1934) 194-199. Contains "A. Die ausgabe der texte"; "B. Der bilder-atlas"

May, Jacques (redacteur en chef) **Hôbôgirin. Dictionnaire encyclopédique du bouddhisme d'après les sources chinoises et japonaises.** Publié sous la direction de Paul Demiéville. Fascicule 4 (chi-chotshusho) Paris et Tokyo (1967) iii + 72 + ix p, illus.

Mizuno, Kogen. An index to the pali texts translated into chinese. **Proceedings of the okurayama oriental research institute** 1 (1956) 14-26.

Nakamura, Hajime. A survey of mahayana buddhism with bibliographical notes. **JIC** 3 (1976) 60-145; 4 (1977) 77-135; 5 (1978) 89-138.

Nanjio, Bunyiu. **A catalogue of japanese and chinese books and manuscripts lately added to the bodleian library.** Oxford (1881) 28 col in 15 p.

Nanjio, Bunyiu [Nanjo, Bunyu] **A catalogue of the chinese translation of the buddhist tripitaka, the sacred canon of the buddhists in china and japan.** Oxford (1883) repr tokyo (1929) repr san francisco (1975) [ix] + xxxvi + 480 col.

Pelliot, Paul. Hôbôgirin (etc) Deuxième fascicule. (rev) **TP** 28 (1931) 95-104.

Rahder, Johannes. **Glossary of the sanskrit, tibetan, mongolian and chinese versions of the dasabhumika-sutra.** Paris (1928) 210 p.

Rosenberg, Otto. **Introduction to the study of buddhism according to the material preserved in japan and china. Part 1: Vocabulary. A survey of buddhist terms and names arranged according to radicals with japanese reading and sanscrit equivalents** . . . Tokyo (1916) x + 527 + 17 p.

Rosny, Léon de. Extraits d'un glossaire bouddhique sanscrit-chinois. **Lotus** 9 (juil 1890) 129-192.

Ross, E.D. **Alphabetical list of the titles of works in the chinese buddhist tripitaka. Being an index to bunyiu nanjio's catalogue and to the 1905 kioto reprint of the buddhist canon.** Calcutta (1910) xcvii + 97 p.

Ross, E. Denison (tsl) The preface to the fan-i-ming-i, a sanscrit-chinese glossary. **TP** 11 (1910) 405-409.

Schlegel, Gustave. **Catalogue of all buddhist books contained in the pitaka collection in japan and china.** With an alphabetical index by S. Fujii. Kyoto (1898)

Schmidt, G. von & T. Thilo & Taijun Inokuchi. **Katalog chinesisches buddhistischer textfragmente.** In collab with T. Inokuchi; app by A. Fujieda & T. Thilo. Vol 1 (1973) 209 p, 50 facsimiles, 34 tables. Berliner turfantexte 6.

Soothill, William E. and Lewis Hodous. **A dictionary of chinese buddhist terms.** London (1937) Same title, with add by Shih Sheng-kang, Liu Wu-long and Tseng Lai-ting, taipei (1962)

Suzuki, D.T. **An index to the lankavatara sutra (nanjio edition). Sanskrit-chinese-tibetan, chinese-sanskrit, and tibetan-sanskrit, with a tabulated list of parallel pages of the nanjio sanskrit text and the three chinese translations (sung, wei, and t'ang) in the taisho edition of the tripitaka.** Kyoto, 2nd ed (1934) 503 p.

Sykes, William H. On a catalogue of chinese buddhistical works. **JRAS** 9 (1848) 199-213.

Willemen, Ch. **Dharmapada. A concordance to udanavarga, dhammapada and the chinese dharmapada.** Bruxelles (1974) 56 p + xxxiii p chin text.

Willemen, Charles. **Udanavarga: chinese-sanskrit glossary.** ?Bruxelles (1975) ix + 101 p.

Wogihara [or Wogiwara or Ogiwara] Unrai. On the proposed supplement to the 'catalogue of the chinese translations of the tripitaka' by bunyiu nanjio. **Verh. 13th ICO** (1903) 62.

Yeh, Kung-cho,. Chinese editions of tripitaka. Natl central library, nanking, **Philobiblon** 1.2 (1946) 26-29.

2. GENERAL STUDIES

Abel-Rémusat, J.P. Observations sur la religion samanéene. In author's **Mélanges posthumes d'histoire et de littérature orientales** . . . paris (1843) 1-64.

Abel-Rémusat, J.P. Observations sur trois mémoires de m. deguignes insérés dans le tome xl de la collection de l'académie des inscriptions et belles-lettres, et relatifs à la religion samanéenne. **NouvJA** 7 (1831) 241 et seq.

Ampère, J.J. De la chine et les travaux de m.rémusat. **RDM** lère sér, 8 (1832) 373-405; 2e sér, 4 (1833) 249-275; **ibid** 561-595. Repr in author's work, **La science et les lettres en orient,** paris (?) (1865)

Bahm, Archie J. **The world's living religions.** Southern illinois univ (1964) See pt 2, religions of china and japan . . . buddhism 199-231.

Balfour, Frederic. A superficial view of buddhism. In author's **Waifs and strays** (1876) 134-142.

Ball, J. Dyer. **Is buddhism a preparation or a hindrance to christianity in china?** Hong kong (1907) 31 p.

Banerjee, Anukul Chandra. **Studies in chinese buddhism.** Calcutta (1977) 116 p, index.

Bazin, M. Recherches sur l'origine, l'histoire, et la constitution des ordres religieux dans l'empire chinois. **JA** 5e sér, 8 (1856) 105-174; also publ sep, paris (1861) 70 p.

Beal, Samuel. Buddhism in china. In **RSW** (1889 et seq) 166-179.

Beal, Samuel. **Non-christian religious systems.— buddhism in china.** London and n.y. (1884) viii + 263 p.

Benton, Warren G. Chinese buddhism. **PS** 38 (1890-91) 530-537.

Chambeau, Gabriel. Le bouddhisme chinois. **Études** 127 (5 juin 1911) 697-707. A propos du L. Wieger, **Bouddhisme chinois** q.v.

Ch'en, Kenneth K.S. **Buddhism: the light of asia.** N.Y. (1968) See chap 4, 7, 10-13.

Chou, Chung-i. The common points in the opinion of chinese buddhists and confucianists. **West and East** 14 (apr 1969) 8-10.

Clarke, James Freeman. Buddhism; or the protestantism of the east. **Atlantic monthly** 23 (1869) 713-728.

Dás, Baboo Sarat Chandra. Contributions on the religion, history, &c. of tibet. **JRASB** 50.1 (1881) See 8, Rise and progress of jin or buddhism in china, 87-99; 9, Ancient china, its sacred literature, philosophy and religion as known to the tibetans, 99-114.

Davrout, L. Le bouddhisme d'après un livre récent. **Revue apologétique** 1 (16 mai 1911) sep publ bruxelles (1911) 15 p. A propos de l'ouvrage du p. L. Wieger, **Bouddhisme chinois** q.v.

Demiéville, Paul. Le bouddhisme chinois. In **AC** 1 (1959) 162-166.

Demiéville, Paul. Le bouddhisme chinois. In **HCP:HR** (1970) 1249-1319.

Deshautesrayes. Recherches sur la religion de fo, professée par les bonzes ho-chang de la chine. **JA** 7 (1825) 150-173, 228-243, 311-317; 8 (1826) 40-49, 74-88, 179-188, 219-223.

Dubose, Hampden C. **The dragon, image and demon, or the religions of china: confucianism, buddhism, and taoism. Giving an account of the mythology, idolatry and demonolotry of the chinese.** London (1886) 463 p.

Dumoulin, Heinrich. Mahayana-buddhismus in ostasien und tibet. **Saeculum** 20 (1969) 253-258.

Dutt, Sukumar (ed) **Buddhism in east asia.** See under Lahiri, Miss Latika.

Edkins, Joseph. **Chinese buddhism. A volume of sketches, historical, descriptive, and critical.** London, 2nd ed (1879) 453 p, index. Repr san francisco (1976)

Edkins, Joseph. Notices of chinese buddhism (all in **NCH** (29 apr 1854 to 20 oct 1855) The various art collected and repr in **The shanghae miscellany** for 1855 and 1856.

Eitel, Ernest J. **Buddhism: its historical, theoretical, and popular aspects. In three lectures.** Hong kong, 2nd ed (1873) 130 p; 3rd ed (1884) 145 p.

Eitel, Ernest J. **Three lectures on buddhism.** Hong kong and london (1871) 38 p.

Everett, John R. **Religion in human experience.** London (1952) See chap 9, Chinese buddhism, 163-173.

Feibleman, James K. **Understanding oriental philosophy. A popular account for the western world.** NY (1976) See chap 24, Chinese buddhism, 131-136.

Finegan, Jack. **The archeology of world religions.** Vol 2: **Buddhism, confucianism, taoism.** Princeton univ (1952) 234-599, illus.

Foucaux, Philippe Édouard. Notices bouddhiques — 1. Le tripitaka des chinois et des japonais. 2. Le bouddhisme du nord et du sud. 3. Définition du nirvana par subhadra bhikshu. **Lotus** 9 (janv 1890) 50-61.

Friess, Horace L. and Herbert W. Schneider. **Religion in various cultures.** N.Y. (1932) See chap 5, Buddhism; sec 6, Chinese buddhism, 179-197.

Fu, Charles Wei-hsun. Mahāyāna buddhism (china) Chap 17 in Isma'īl Rāgī al Faruqui & David E. Sopher (ed) **Historical atlas of the religions of the world,** ny & london (1974) 185-194, bibliog, illus, map.

Fung, Yu-lan. **A history of chinese philosophy.** Tsl fr chin Derk Bodde. Princeton univ, vol 2 (1953) See chap 7-10.

J.G. et C.M. Bouddhisme chinoise. In **EUF** (1968) vol 3. See Bouddhisme, art 3, 482a-486a.

Grison, P. Le bouddhisme d'inde en chine. **FA** 16, no 158-159 (july-aug 1959) 1093-1103.

Groot, J.J.M. de. Der buddhismus [in china] In P.D. Chantepie de la Saussaye, **Lehrbuch der religions-geschichte** bd 1, tübingen (1905) 104-114.

Groot, J.J.M. de. Der buddhismus der chinesen. In **Kultur der gegenwart** tl 1, abtlg 3, 1, Die orientalische religionen, berlin and leipzig (1906) 184-192.

Groot, J.J.M. de. China. (Buddhism in) In **HERE** 3, 552-556.

Grootaers, W.A. Bouddhisme et christianisme en chine. **Bulletin des missions** (1951) 1-5.

Guenther, Herbert V. Buddhist sacred literature. **EncyB 3** (1974) **Macropaedia** vol 3, 431b-441a.

Guenther, Herbert V. Buddhist mysticism. **EncyB 3** (1974) **Macropaedia** vol 3, 414b-418b.

Guignes, Joseph de. **Recherches historiques sur la religion indienne et sur les livres fondamenteux de cette religion, qui ont été tr. de l'indien en chinois.** Paris (1773) 167 p.

Guignes, Joseph de. Recherches sur les philosophes appelés samanéens. **MAI** 26 (1759) 770-804.

Gutzlaff, C. Remarks on the present state of buddhism in china. **JRAS** 16 (1856) 73-92.

Hackmann, Heinrich F. **Buddhism as a religion: its historical development and its present conditions.** London (1910) 315 p. Tsl fr german, rev and enl.

Hackmann, Heinrich. **Der buddhismus.** Tübingen (1906) See chap 3, Der buddhismus in china, korea und japan.

Hackmann, Heinrich. Chinese buddhism and buddhist china. **ChRec** 41 (1910) 770-780.

Hackmann, Heinrich. Zum chinesischen buddhismus, hinterlassenes fragment. **AS** 5 (1951) 81-112.

Hamilton, C.H. Buddhism. In H.F. MacNair (ed) **China,** univ california (1946) 290-300.

Hardwick, Charles. Fo-ism or chinese buddhism. Pt 3 sec 3 in author's **Christ and other masters,** cambridge (1858) 321-346.

Harlez, Charles de. Le bouddhisme en chine. **La controverse et la contemporain** 4e sér, 2 (1884) 624-637; 5e sér, 4 (1885) 589-602.

Haydon, A. Eustace. The buddhist heritage of eastern asia. **OC** 46 (mar 1932) 158-184.

Henry, B.C. Buddhism in china. Chap 5 in author's **CD** (1885) 80-99.

Hodgson, B.H. **Illustrations of the literature and religion of the buddhists.** Serampore (1841) 220 p. Collection of 15 art orig publ in **JRASB.**

Horton, Walter M. Oriental religion: eastern asia, 3, buddhism in china. In Henry N. Wieman and Walter M. Horton, **The growth of religion,** chicago and n.y. (1938) 74-88.

Huang, Chia-cheng [François Houang] **Le bouddhisme de l'inde à la chine.** Paris (1963) 126 p.

Inglis, James W. The christian element in chinese buddhism. **IRM** 5 (oct 1916) 587-602.

Johnston, Reginald F. The buddhism of china. **OC** 28 (1914) 697-706.

Johnston, Reginald Fleming. **Buddhist china.** London (1913) 403 p, map, index, photos. Repr san francisco (1976)

Kawamura, Leslie S. & Keith Scott (ed) **Buddhist thought and asian civilization: essays in honour of herbert v. guenther on his sixtieth birthday.** Emeryville, calif (1977) Art on chin sep listed in our bibliog. Abbrev **BT&AC.**

Kim, Young Oon. **World religions.** Vol 3. **Faiths of the far east.** NY (1976) See Buddhism, 1-51, brief bibliog.

King, Winston L. The way of tao and the path to nirvana. In **SA** (1963) 121-135.

Kiyota, Minoru (ed) assisted by Elvin W. Jones. **Mahāyāna buddhist meditation: theory and practice.** Univ hawaii (1978) Art set listed in our bibliog. Abbrev **MBM.**

Klaproth, J. von. Ueber die fo-religion in china. **Asiatisches magazin** 1/2 (1802) 149-169.

Krause, Friedrich E.A. **Ju-tao-fo. Die religiösen und philosophischen systeme ostasiens.** München (1924) 588 p.

Krone, Rudolf. Der buddhismus in china. **Berichte der rheinischen missionsgesellschaft** 16 (1855) 241-255.

Lahiri, Miss Latika. China. Chap 9 in Sukumar Dutt, **Buddhism in east asia,** new delhi (1966) 127-158.

Lamairesse, E. **l'Empire chinois. — Le bouddhisme en chine et en thibet.** Paris (1894) 440 p.

Latourette, Kenneth Scott. Introducing buddhism. NY (1956) See 4, Buddhism in the east, 31-36; 5, Buddhism and rival faiths, 56-62.

Lewis, John. **The religions of the world made simple.** NY (1958) rev ed (1968) See chap 6, Buddhism in china and japan, 46-48; chap 7, Confucianism and taoism, 52-58.

Li, Dun J. (tsl) Buddhism. Chap 5 in tsl's anthology, **The essence of chinese civilization.** Princeton, n.j. etc (1967) 69-85. Tsl of sel pieces.

Liebenthal, Walter. The problem of chinese buddhism. **VBQ** ser 2, 18.3 (1953) 233-246.

Liebenthal, Walter. Was ist chinesischer buddhismus? **AS** 6 (1952) 116-129.

Martin, W.A.P. Is buddhism a preparation for christianity? **ChRec** 20.5 (1889) 193-203.

Martin, W.A.P. On reformed buddhism in china and japan. **IA** 11 (1882) 294-295.

Martinie, J.A. Chinese buddhism **Asia** 1 (mar 1951) 85-93.

McGovern, William M. **An introduction to mahayana buddhism, with especial reference to chinese and japanese phases.** London and n.y. (1922) 233 p, diagr.

McNulty, Henry A. The appeal of buddhism to the chinese mind. **ChRec** 49.4 (apr 1918) 235-242; 49.5 (may 1918) 301-309.

Mead, G.R.S. **Quests old and new.** London (1913) 338 p.

Migot, André. Le bouddhisme en chine. **FA:BPB** (1959) 697-716.

Milloué, L. de. **Le bouddhisme. Son histoire, ses dogmas, son extension et son influence sur les peuples chez lesquels il s'est répandu.** Lyon (1882) 23 p.

Milloué, Léon de. **Catalogue du musée guimet. Pt 1, Inde, chine et japon.** Précédé d'un aperçu sur les religions de l'extrême-orient et suivie d'un index alphabétique des noms des divinités et des principaux termes techniques. Paris and lyon (1883) lxviii + 323 p.

Minayeff, I.P. **Recherches sur la bouddhisme.** Tsl fr russian R.H. Assier de Pompignan. Paris (1894) 315 p.

Morgan, Kenneth W. (ed) **The path of the buddha. Buddhism interpreted by buddhists.** N.Y. (1956) 432 p, bibliog, gloss, index. See chap 4 and 5.

Morrison, Robert (tsl) Account of foe. Tr. from the san-kiao-yuen-liew, 'the rise and progress of the three sects.' In author's **Horae sinicae,** London, new ed (1817) 160-165. Orig ed london (1812)

Moule, Arthur E. Buddhism and taoism as they affect chinese life. Chap 6 in author's **NC&O** (1891) 163-192.

Müller, F. Max. The religions of china. 3. Buddhism and christianity. **NC** 48 (nov 1900) 730-742.

Murakami, S. Mahāyāna buddhism. **EB** 1 (1921) 95-108.

Nakamura, Hajime. **Parallel developments. A comparative history of ideas.** Tokyo (1975) xx + 567 p. On chin budd see passim.

Ōchō, Enichi. Studies in chinese buddhism. **JSR:HS** 11 (1960) 45-48.

Pachow, W. **Chinese buddhism: aspects of interaction and reinterpretation.** Lanham, md (1980) 260 p, notes, index. Collected essays on various topics. Abbrev ChBudd

Parker, E.H. **Buddhism in china.** London (1905)

Parker, E.H. Chinese buddhism. **IAQR** ser 3, 14 (july-oct 1902) 372-390. French tsl Louis de la Vallée Poussin: Le bouddhisme chinois, **Muséon** n.s. 4 (1903) 135-158.

Parrinder, E.G. **What world religions teach.** London etc (1963) See chap 7, Northern buddhism: salvation by faith, 64-71.

Parrinder, Geoffrey. **Worship in the world's religions.** London (1961) rev ed (1974) repr totowa, n.j. (1976) See pt 3, The far east, 1) Mahāyāna buddhism, 117-137.

Peeters,Hermes. **The religions of china. Confucianism, taoism, buddhism, popular belief.** Peking (1941) 64 p.

Piton, Charles. **Der buddhismus in china. Eine relig-ionsgeschichtliche studie.** Bâsle (1902) 32 s.

Pratt, James Bissett. **The pilgrimage of buddhism and a buddhist pilgrimage.** N.Y. (1928) 758 p. See chap 11-20.

Rao, K. Bhaskara. **Taoism and buddhism.** Vijayawata (n.d. —foreword 1971) vi + 86 p.

Reichelt, Karl L. **Meditation and piety in the far east.** London (1953) 170 p.

Reichelt, Karl L. **Religion in chinese garment.** London (1951) See chap 5, which is essentially a digest of author's **Truth and tradition** q.v.

Reichelt, Karl L. **The transformed abbott.** London (1954) 157 p.

Reichelt, Karl L. **Truth and tradition in chinese buddhism. A study of chinese mahayana buddhism.** Shanghai (1927) repr n.y. (1968) 330 p, index, illus.

Richard, Timothy. Chinese buddhism; its rise and progress; Edkins, Joseph. Chinese buddhism; its excellencies and defects. Two art under heading: Buddhism a preparation for christianity, in **CMH** (1896) 12-22.

Richard, Mrs Timothy. Re buddhism (untitled) Chap 3 in author's husband's **CbyM** (1907) 16-17.

Robinson, Richard H. Buddhism: in china and japan. In **ZCE** (1959) 321-347.

Robinson, Richard H. **The buddhist religion; a historical introduction.** Belmont, calif (1970)See chap 4, Developments outside of india, 77-99. 2nd ed, co-authored by Willard L. Johnson, encino & belmont, calif (1977) See chap 9, The buddhism of east asia, 145-183. 3rd ed by co-authors, belmont, calif (1982) See chap 10, East asian buddhism, 155-213.

Rosenkranz, Gerhard. **Der weg des buddha. Werden und wesen der buddhismus als weltreligion.** Stuttgart (1960)

Rosny, Léon de. Le bouddhisme dans l'extrême-orient. **Revue scientifique** 2e sér, 17 (20 dec 1879) 581-585.

Schott, Wilhelm. **Über den buddhismus in hochasien und in china. Akademie der wissenschaft zur berlin, philologische und historische abhandlungen 1844,** Berlin (1846) 161-288.

Stroup, Herbert. **Four religions of asia.** N.Y. (1968) See Buddhism, 115-168.

Tan Yun-shan. **Some aspects of chinese buddhism.** Santiniketan, india (1963) 22 p.

Too-yu. The systems of foe and confucius compared, translated from the chinese. **ICG** no 5 (1818) 149-157.

Tsukamoto, Zenryū. Buddhism in china and korea. In Kenneth Morgan (ed) **The path of the buddha** q.v. 182-236.

Tucci, Giuseppi. Buddhism. **EncyB 3** (1974) **Macropaedia** vol 3, 374a-403a.

Vail, Albert & Emily M. Vail. **Transforming light. The living heritage of world religions.** NY etc (1970) See chap 7, Lao tzu and confucius, 67-82; Buddhism in china, 83-91.

Vajra bodhi sea. A monthly journal of orthodox buddhism. Publ in City of ten thousand buddhas, talmage, calif by sino-american budd assoc. Text in chin and engl. All materials pertinent. Abbrev **VBS.**

Van Over, Raymond (ed) **Chinese mystics.** NY etc (1973) xxx + 183 p. Sel fr taoist and budd texts.

Völling, Arsenius. Der chinesische buddhismus und sein verfall. In Émile Charpentier (ed) **Semaine d'ethnologie religieux, compte-rendu, analytique de la IIme session tenus a louvain (27 août 4 septembre 1913)** Louvain (1914) 237-246.

Ward, C.H.S. **Buddhism.** Vol 2: **Mahāyāna.** London (1952)See Contents for several pertinent sec.

Wei, Francis C.-M. Buddhism as a chinese christian sees it. **IRM** 17 (1928) 455-463.

Wentworth, Erastus. Buddhism. In J.M. Reid (ed) **DR** (1884) 243-284.

Wieger, Léon. **Bouddhisme chinois.** 2 vol (1910-1913) repr (1940) (See entry under Texts in Translation)

Williams, E.T. Chinese buddhism. Chap 14 in author's **CYT** (1928) 289-315.

Winter, H.J.J. Science, buddhism and taoism. **AP** 21 (may 1950) 206-208.

Wu, John C.H. **Beyond east and west.** NY (1951) See chap 13, The lotus and the mud, 189-199.

Yang, Ming-che. Confucianism vs. tao and buddha. **FCR** 19 (jan 1969) 21-29.

Yule, Henry. Northern buddhism. **JRAS** n.s. 6 (1873) 275-277.

Zürcher, Erik. Buddhism in china. In Raymond Dawson (ed) **The legacy of china,** oxford (1964) 56-79.

3. TEXTS IN TRANSLATION

Bailey, D.R. Schackleton (tsl) **Mātṛceta. Śatapañcāśatka. Sanskrit text, tibetan translation and commentary, and chinese translation.** London (1951) xi + 237 p.

Bailey, H.W. (tsl) The pradakṣiṇā-sūtra of chang tsiang-kuin. In L. Cousins, A. Kunst & K.R. Norman (ed) **Buddhist studies in honour of i.b.horner,** dordrecht & boston (1974) 15-18.

Bapat, P.V. & A. Hirakawa (tsl) **Shan-chien p'i-p'o-sha: a chinese version by sanghabhadra of samatapā-sādikā, commentary on pali vinaya.** Poona (1970) lxiii + 588 p, intro, index chin words, genl index, app. corr and add.

Beal, Samuel. Brief prefatory remarks to the translation of the amitâbha sūtra from chinese. **JRAS** n.s. 2.1 (1866) 136-144.

Beal, Samuel (comp and tsl) **A catena of buddhist scriptures from the chinese.** London (1871) 436 p. Repr taipei (1970)

Beal, Samuel (tsl) Confessional of kwan-yin. An attempt to translate from the chinese a work known as the confessional service of the great compassionate kwan yin, possessing 1000 hands and 1000 eyes. **JRAS** n.s. 2.2 (1866) 403-425.

Beal, Samuel (tsl) **The fo-sho-hing-tsan-king. A life of buddha by asvaghosha bodhisattva translated from sanskrit into chinese by dharmaraksha, a.d. 420 and from chinese into english by samuel beal.** Oxford (1883) xxxvii + 380 p. Vol 19 of F. Max Müller (ed) 'Sacred books of the east.'

Beal, Samuel (tsl) The legend of dipankara buddha. Translated from the chinese (and intended to illustrate plates xxix and 1., 'tree and serpent worship.') **JRAS** n.s. 6 (1873) 377-395.

Beal, Samuel (tsl) A life of the buddha: translated from the p'u yao king . . . (suite) **BOR** 3.12 (nov 1889) 265-274; 4.1 (dec 1889) 12-15.

Beal, Samuel (tsl) The páramitá-hridaya sútra, or, the great páramitá heart sutra. **JRAS** n.s. 1.2 (1864) 25-28.

Beal, Samuel (tsl) **The romantic legend of sâkya buddha: from the chinese-sanskrit** . . . London (1875) xii + 395 p.

Beal, Samuel (tsl) **Suh-ki li-lih-kiu. The suhrillekha or 'friendly letter,' written by lung shu (nâgârjuna), and addressed to king sadvaha. Translated from the chinese edition of i-tsing.** London (1892) 51 p + 13 p chin text.

Beal, Samuel (tsl) The sutra of the forty-two sections, from the chinese. **JRAS** 19 (1862) 337-349.

Beal, Samuel (tsl) Text and commentary of the memorial of sakya buddha tathagata. By wong puh . . . with prefatory remarks by the rev. spence hardy. **JRAS** 20 (1863) 135-220.

Beal, Samuel (tsl) **Texts from the buddhist canon, commonly known as dhammapada, with accompanying narratives. Translated from the chinese** . . . London (1878) viii + 176 p. Repr san francisco (1977)

Beal, Samuel. Two chinese-buddhist inscriptions found at buddha-gayâ. **JRAS** n.s. 13 (oct 1881) 552-572.

Beal, Samuel (tsl) **Vajra-chhediká, the 'kin kong king' or 'diamond sutra.'** **JRAS** n.s. 1.1 (1864) 1-24.

Beal, Samuel and D.J. Gogerly. Comparative arrangements of two translations of the buddhist ritual for the priesthood, known as the prátimoksha, or pátimokshan. By the rev. s. beal from the chinese, and the rev. d.j. gogerly from the pali. **JRAS** 19 (1862) 407-480.

Behrsing, S. Das chung-tsi-king des chinesischen dirghâgama. Über. und mit anmerkungen versehen. **AM** 7 (1932) 1-149, 483; 8 (1933) 277. See also Weitere nachträge u. verbesserungen zu S. Behrsing, Das chung-tsi-king . . . **ibid** 8 (1933) 277.

Bhattacharya, Vidhushekhara. **Mahāyāna viṁsaka of nāgārjuna, reconstructed sanskrit text, the tibetan and chinese versions, with an english translation.** Calcutta (1931) ii + 44 p.

Birnbaum, Raoul. **The healing buddha.** Boulder, colo (1979) xviii + 253 p, illus 16 photo-pl, 4 app incl chin char list, bibliog, index.

Bischoff, F.A. (ed, tsl, comm) **Ārya mahābalanāma-mahāyānasūtra. Tibétain (mss de touen-houang) et chinois. Contribution à l'étude des divinités mineures du bouddhisme tantrique.** Paris (1956) 138 p, 4 facs.

BTTSoc (tsl) **The dharani sutra, with commentary.** San francisco (1976) 352 p.

BTTSoc (tsl) **The dharma flower (lotus) sutra, with commentary.** San francisco, 8 vol publ (1977-80) 2 further vol publ (1981-82) further vol forthcoming.

BTTSoc (tsl) **Entering the dharma realm.** San Francisco (1980) chap 39 of avatamsaka sutra, pt 1 and 2, further vol forthcoming.

BTTSoc (tsl) **Flower adornment (avatamsaka) sutra preface.** San francisco (1979) 131 p, 1 illus, index, chin text. Tsl of Ta-fang-kuang-fo hua-yen-ching ch'ien-shih. 4 vol of sutra publ (1981-83) further vol forthcoming.

BTTSoc (tsl) **A general explanation of the buddha speaks of amitābha sūtra by tripitaka master hsüan hua.** San francisco (1974) 159 p, index, illus.

BTTSoc (tsl) **A general explanation of the essentials of the śrāmaṇera vinaya and rules of deportment by tripitaka master hua.** San francisco (1975) 94 p, index.

BTTSoc (tsl) **A general explanation of the vajra prajñā pāramitā sūtra by dhyāna master hsüan hua.** San francisco (1974) 174 p, illus.

BTTSoc (tsl) **The heart sutra and verses without a stand. Commentary by hsüan hua.** San francisco (1978)

BTTSoc (tsl) **The shurangama sutra, with commentary.** San francisco, 5 vol publ (1977-80) 3 remaining vol publ (1981-83)

BTTSoc (tsl) **The sutra in forty-two sections.** San Francisco (1977) 114 p.

BTTSoc (tsl) **The sixth patriarch's sutra.** San Francisco (1977) 235 p.

BTTSoc (tsl) **Sūtra of the past vows of earth store bodhisattva. The collected lectures of tripitaka master hsüan hua.** NY (1974) 233 p, 1 col illus, gloss.

Chan, Wing-tsit (comp and tsl) **A source book in chinese philosophy.** Princeton univ (1963) See chap 20-26 for tsl buddhist texts, 336-449.

Chavannes, Édouard (tsl) **Cinq centes contes et apologues extraits du tripitaka chinois et traduit en français** . . . Paris, 3 vol (1910-11) Repr paris (1962) 4 vol in 3 (vol 4 is vol 1 of series: 'Bibliothèque de l'institut des hautes études chinoises') Orig ed, vol 1: xx + 428, vol 2: 449, vol 3: 395 p.

Chavannes, Édouard and S. Lévi (tsl) La notation de tréfonds (âlaya vijñāna) Extraits du fan yi min yi tsi, tok. 36, 11, 85a; chap. 16. In S. Lévi, **Un système de philosophie bouddhique: matériaux pour l'étude du système vijñāptimātra,** paris (1932) 125-173.

Chédel, A. (tsl) Le dhammapada, recueil de sentences bouddhiques. Extraits de versions chinoises. **MSGFOK** 5 (1934) 55-61.

Ch'en Kenneth K.S. A study of the svāgata store in the divāvadāna in its sanskrit, pali, tibetan and chinese versions. **HJAS** 9 (1945-47) 207-314.

Chou, Ta-fu. Three buddhist hymns. **SIS** 1 (1944) 85-98.

Chu, Ch'an (pseud for John Blofeld) (tsl) **The sutra of 42 sections and two other scriptures of the mahayana school.** London (1947) (The other two scriptures: The sutra of the doctrine bequeathed by the buddha; the sutra of the eight awakenings of the great ones)

Cook, Francis H. Fa-tsang's brief commentary on the prajñāpāramitā-hṛdaya-sūtra. In **MBM** (1978) 167-206.

Cools, J. (tsl) **Mahāyāna-sraddhotpāda-śāstra.** Bruxelles (1972) ix + 77 p, with chin text.

Csongor, B. Some chinese texts in tibetan script from tun-huang. **Acta orientalia academiae scientiarum hungaricae** 10 (1960) 97-140.

Davidson, J. LeRoy. **The lotus sutra in chinese art. A study in buddhist art to the year 1000.** Yale univ (1954) 105 p, bibliog, pl.

DeBary, William Theodore, with collab of Yoshito Hakeda and Philip Yampolsky (comp) **The buddhist tradition in india, china and japan.** N.Y. (1969) xxii + 417 p. Largely taken from the 3 vol: **Sources of indian, chinese, and japanese tradition,** columbia univ (1958, 1960, 1958) See chap 5-7 for tsl chin budd texts, 125-251.

DeBary, William T., W.T. Chan, and Burton Watson (comp and tsl) **Sources of chinese tradition.** Columbia univ (1960) See chap 15-17 for tsl buddhist texts, 306-408.

Demiéville, Paul. **Le concile de lhasa; une controverse sur le quiétisme entre bouddhistes de l'inde et de la chine au VIII. siècle de l'ère chrétienne.** Paris (1952) viii + 398 p, facs.

Demiéville, Paul (adapte et trad) **Mission paul pelliot. Documents conservés à bibliothèque nationale,** II: **Airs de touen-houang (touen-houang k'iu) Textes à chanter des VIIIe-Xe siècles.** Manuscrits reproduits en facsimilé, avec une introduction en chinois par jao tsong-yi. Adaptes en français avec la traduction de quelques textes d'air, par P. Demiéville. Paris (1971) 370, 58 pl.

Dumoulin, H. (tsl) Genninron [yüan-jen-lun] Tsung-mi's traktat vom ursprung der menschen. Aus die chinesischen übers, erlautet u. eingeleitet in zusammenarbeit mit S. Furuta u. T. Ibara. **MN** 1 (1938) 178-221.

Edkins, Joseph (tsl) A buddhist shastra, translated from the chinese; with an analysis and notes. **Journal of the shanghai literary and scientific society** 1 (june 1858)* 107-128. Text is i-lung-lu-ka lun. *The only vol publ under this title, which was changed to **JNCBRAS.**

Ensink, Jacob (tsl) **The question of rāṣṭrapāla. Translated and annotated.** Zwolle (1952) xxiii + 140 p, notes, 2 app. Two chin tsl utilized inter alia. See rev by Kenneth Ch'en in **HJAS** 47.1/2 (1954) 274-281.

Finot, Louis (tsl) **La marche à la lumière (bodhicaryāvatāra)** Paris (1920) 166 p.

Fischer, J. and Y. Takezo (tsl) **Vimalakīrtinirdeśa. Wei-ma-ch'ih so-shuo-ching. Das sutra vimalakīrti.** (Nach einem japanischen ms. von kawase kōzyun übers.) Tokyo (1969) 166 p. There apparently was an earlier edition (1944) 154 p.

Forte, Antonio. **Political propaganda and ideology in china at the end of the seventh century; inquiry into the nature, authors and function of the tunhuang documents. 6502 followed by an annotated translation.** Napoli, instituto universitario oriental (1976) 312 p. Text composed by a group of budd monks to legitimate ascension to throne of empress wu chao (r. 683-707) See rev by M. Strickmann in **EB** n.s. 10.1 (may 1977) 156-160.

Fung, Paul F. & George D. Fung (tsl) **The sutra of the sixth patriarch on the pristine orthodox dharma.** San francisco (1964) 187 p, notes, gloss.

Gauthiot, R. et P. Pelliot (tsl) **Le sutra des causes et des effets, texte sogdien de touen-houang, publié en facsimilé, avec transcription, traduction et commentaire par r. gauthiot, accompagné du facsimilé et de la traduction de la version chinoise par p. pelliot, et un glossaire sogdien-français-chinois par r. gauthiot et p. pelliot.** Paris (1914-1923) Mission pelliot en asie centrale; série linguistique, t 1.

Gemmell, W. (tsl) **The diamond sutra (chin-kang-ching) or prajña-pāramitā.** London (1912) xxxii + 117 p.

Goddard, Dwight (ed) **A buddhist bible.** N.Y. (1932) 2nd ed, rev and enl (1938) 677 p.

Graham, David C. (tsl) The book of causes and effects, buddhist. A translation. **ChRec** 60.9 (sept 1929) 584-593. Tsl of in-guoo-luh.

Graham, David C. (tsl) A simple talk on repeating the name of buddha. **ChRec** 59.8 (aug 1928) 490-498; 59.9 (sept 1928) 573-580. Tsl of budd tract, Nien-fo ch'ien-shuo.

Groot, J.J.M. de. **Le code du mahâyâna en chine, son influence sur la vie monacale et sur le monde laïque.** Amsterdam (1893) 271 p. Includes tsl of the 58 vows of the fan wang ching. Repr ny & london (1980)

Guignes, Joseph de (tsl) **Das buch des fo aus der chinesischen sprache. In's deutsche übersetzt (aus de guignes' histoire des huns)** Zürich (1791)

Hackmann, Heinrich (tsl) **Laien-buddhismus in china. Das lung shu ching t'u wên des wang jih hsiu. Aus dem chin. über., erläutert und beurteitr.** Gotha and stuttgart (1924) xvi + 347 s.

Hackmann, Heinrich (tsl) Die textgestalt des sutra der 42 abschnitt. **AO** 5 (1927) 197-237.

Hakeda, Yoshita S. (tsl) **The awakening of faith attributed to aśvaghosha.** Columbia univ (1967) 128 p, notes, selected bibliog, index.

Hamilton, Clarence H. (tsl) **Wei shih er shih lun . . . or, the treatise in twenty stanzas on representation-only, by vasubandhu. Translated from the chinese version of hsüan tsang, tripitaka master of the t'ang dynasty.** New haven, conn. (1938) 82 p.

Harlez, Charles de (ed and tsl) **Les quarante-deux leçons de bouddha, ou le king des xlii sections (sze-shi-erh-tchang-king). Texte chinois avec trad., introd. et notes.** Bruxelles (1899) 68 p. Being **MCAM** vol 59.

Harlez, Charles de. A sanskrit-chinese lexicon: mahāvyutpattih (pt 1) Tokyo (1901) **Rep. of the society for oriental research** 1-18.

Harlez, Ch. de (tsl) Vajracchedikâ (prajñāpāramitā). Traduite du texte sanscrit avec comparaison des versions chinoise et mandchoue. **JA** 8e sér, 18 (nov-déc 1891) 440-509.

Harlez, Ch. de. Vocabulaire bouddhique sanscrit-chinois . . . han-fan tsih-yao. Précis de doctrine bouddhique. **TP** 7 (1896) 356-396; 8 (1897) 129-154.

Hazai, Georg & Peter Zieme (hrsg) **Vajracchedikā. German, chinese and uigur. Selections. Fragmente der uigurischen version des jin'gangjing mit den gāthās des meister fu.** Nebst ein anhang von T. Inokuchi. Berlin (1971) 86 s, 61 facs, 40 taf.

Huber, Édouard (tsl) **Le prātimokṣasūtra des sarvāstivādins. Texte sanskrit par m. louis finot, avec la version de kumārajīva traduite en français par m. édouard huber.** Paris (1914) Repr fr **JA** sér 11, t 2 (nov-déc 1913) 465-558.

Humphreys, Christmas (ed) **The wisdom of buddhism.** N.Y. and evanston (1960) See chap, The new wisdom schools: china and japan, 156-210.

Hurvitz, Leon (tsl) Fa-sheng's observations on the four stations of mindfulness. In **MBM** (1978) 207-248.

Hurvitz, Leon (tsl) Hsüan-tsang and the heart scripture. In **PRS** (1977) 103-121.

Hurvitz, Leon (tsl) **Scripture of the lotus blossom of the fine dharma (the lotus sūtra) Translated from the chinese of kumārajīva.** Columbia univ (1976) xxviii + 421 p, preface, gloss, notes on the sanskrit text, index.

Hurvitz, Leon N. & Arthur E. Link (tsl) The prajñāpāramitā prefaces of tao-an. In **MSPD** t 2 (1974) 403-470.

Idumi, Hokei (tsl) Vimalakirti's discourse on emancipation. (Tsl fr chin vimalakīrti-nirdeśa) **EB** 2 (1923) 358-366; 3 (1924) 138-153, 224-242, 336-349; 4 (1926) 48-55, 177-190, 348-366.

Idzumi, Hōkei (tsl) **The suvarṇaprabhāsa sūtra.** Kyoto (1931)

Iwamoto, Yutaka (tsl) **Sumāgadhāvadāna** (incl chin version in transcription) Kyoto (1968) 262 p.

Jaworski, J. (tsl) l'Avalambanasūtra de la terre pure. **MS** 1 (1935-36) 82-107. With chin text.

Johnston, E.H. (tsl) The buddha's mission and last journey; **buddhacaratia,** xv to xxviii. (tsl of the tibetan and chin versions) **AO** 15 (1937) 26-62, 85-111, 231-292.

Katō, Bunnō (tsl) Rev by W.E. Soothill & Wilhelm Schiffer. **Myōhō-renge-kyō: The sutra of the lotus flower of the wonderful law. Translated from the chinese** . . . Tokyo (1971) xii + 440 p.

Katō, Bunnō, Yoshirō Tamura & Kōjirō Miyasaka (tsl) Rev by W.E. Soothill, Wilhelm Schiffer & Pier P. des Campana. **The threefold lotus sutra: Innumerable meanings; The lotus flower of the wonderful law; and Meditation on the bodhisattva universal virtue.** NY & Tokyo (1975) Preface by Nikkyō Niwano, intro by Yoshirō Tamura, editorial note. xix + 383 p, gloss.

Lamotte, Étienne. l'Alayavijñāna (le receptacle) dans le mahāyānasamgraha (chapitre ii) Asanga et ses commentateurs. **MCB** 3 (1934-35) 169-255.

Lamotte, Étienne (tsl) **La concentration de la marche héroïque (sūramgamasamādhisūtra)** Bruxelles (1965) xiii + 308 p. Being **MCB** vol 13.

Lamotte, Étienne (ed & tsl) **La somme du grand véhicule d'asaṅga (mahāyāna-saṃgraha)** T 1, **Versions tibétaine et chinoise (hiuan-tsang)** T 2, **Traduction et commentaire.** Louvain (1938-39)

Lamotte, É. (tsl) Le traité de l'acte de vasubandhu, karmasiddhi-prakana: traduction, versions tibétaine et chinoises; avec une introduction et un appendice, la traduction du chapitre XVII de la madhamakavrtti. **MCB** 4 (1935-36) 151-288.

Lamotte, Étienne (tsl) **La traité de la grande vertu de sagesse de nāgārjuna (mahāprajñāpāramitāśāstra)** two vol, Louvain (1944-49)

Lamotte, É. (tsl) **Vimalakīrtinirdeśa. l'Enseignement de vimalakīrti.** Louvain (1962) 503 p. Tsl fr tibetan of kandjur with the chin variants of hsüan chuang.

La Vallée Poussin, L. de (tsl) Documents d'abhidharma traduits et annotés. **BEFEO** 30 (1930) 1-28, 247-298. Same title in **MCB** 5 (1936-37) 1-187.

La Vallée Poussin, L. de (tsl) Documents madhyamaka. **MCB** 2 (1932-33) 1-146.

La Vallée Poussin, L. de (tsl) **Vijñaptimātratāsiddhi. La siddhi de hiuan-tsang.** Paris, 3 vol (1928-48) 873 p, index.

Lee, Pi-cheng (Lü Pi-ch'eng) i.e. Upasaka Chihmann (tsl) **The two buddhist books in mahāyāna.** London, 3rd ed (1939) 149 p. Tsl of hua-yen-ching p'u-hsien hsing-yüan-p'in (chap 39 of avatamsaka sūtra) and ching-t'u kang-yao (essentials of pure land)

Lévi, S. La légende de rama dans un avadâna chinois. In **MSL** (1937) 271-274.

Lévi, Sylvain (ed and tsl) **Mahākarmavibbaṅga (la grande classification des actes) et karmavibhaṅgago-padeśa). (discussion sur le mahākarmavibhanga). Textes sanscrits rapportés du nepal, édités et traduits avec les textes parallèles en sanscrit, en pali, en tibétain, en chinois et en koutcheen. Ouvrage illustré de 4 pl: le karmavibhaṅgagopadeśa sur les bas-reliefs de boroboudour, à java.** Paris (1932) 272 p, 4 pl.

Lévi, S. (tsl) Une poésie inconnue de roi harṣa çilâditya. In **MSL** (1937) 244-256.

Liebenthal, Walter (tsl) **The book of chao.** Peking (1948) 2nd rev ed hong kong (1968) 152 p. The **chao-lun** by seng-chao.

Liebenthal, Walter (tsl) **The sutra of the lord of healing (bhaishajyaguru vaiduryaprabha tathagata.** Peiping (1936) xii + 32 p. Same title, n.p. ?HK (n.d.) romanized min-nan (fukienese) text, engl tsl by Liebenthal. Also repr taipei (1962) tsl "erroneously attributed to prof. Chow Su-chia" rev by Shen Shou-liang; bilingual chin and engl text.

Lin, Li-kouang (tsl) **Avaiokitashimha. Dharma-samuccaya. Compendium de la loi. Recueil de stances. Extraites du saddharma-smrty-upasthāna-sūtra.** In 3 parts, paris (1946-73) 292, 424, 416 p. Revision de A. Bareau, J.W. de Jong et Paul Demiéville, avec des appendices par J.W. de Jong.

Link, Arthur E. The introduction to dhyāna-pāramitā by k'ang seng-hui in the liu-tu chi-ching. In **MSPD** t 2 (1974) 205-230.

Lu, K'uan Yü [Charles Luk] (tsl) **The śurangāma sūtra (leng yen ching) Chinese rendering by master paramiti of central north india at chih chih monastery. canton, china, a.d. 705, by ch'an master han shan (1546-1623)** London (1966) 262 p.

Lu, K'uan-yü (Charles Luk) tsl & ed. **The vimalakīrti nirdesa sūtra. (Wei mo chieh so shuo ching)** Berkeley & london (1972) xviii + 157 p, gloss.

MacDonald, Ariane (tsl) **Le maṇḍala du mañjuśrī-mūlakalpa.** Paris (1962) 191 p, with romanized tibetan text.

Masson-Oursel, Paul. Le yuan jen louen. **JA** 11e sér 5 (mars-avr 1915) 299-354.

Masuda, J. (tsl) Origin and doctrines of early indian buddhist schools. A translation of the hsüan-chwang version of vasumitra's treatise. **AM** 2 (1925) 1-78.

Masuda, Jiryo (ed) Saptaśatika-prajñāpāramitā. Text and hsüan-chwang's chinese version with notes. **Journal of taisho university,** vol 6-7 **(wogihara commemoration volume)** pt 2 (1930) 185-242, 1 pl.

Meynard. La marche à la lumière. **La chine** 35 (1923) 153-158. Rev with summ of Louis Finot (tsl) **Bodihičaryāvatāra** q.v.

Monumenta Serindica: Vol 1: **Chinese buddhist texts from tunhuang.** Kyoto (1958) Ed by the research society of central asian culture.

Mukherjee, Probhat Kumar (tsl) The dhammapada and the udānavarga. **IHQ** 11.4 (dec 1935) 741-760. App II, (engl) Translation of first chapter from last chinese translation of udānavarga, fa-chi-sung-ching, 753-760.

Müller, F. Max and Nanjio Bunyiu (ed and tsl) **Sukhâvativyûha. Description of sukhâvati the land of bliss.** (With two appendixes: 1, Text and translation of sanghavarman's chinese version of the poetical versions of the sukhâvati-vyûha; 2, Sanskrit text of the smaller sukhâvativyûha) Oxford (1883)

Naitō, Torajirō. Trois manuscrits de l'époque des t'ang récemment publiés au japon. **BEFEO** 2 (1902) 315-340.

Neumann, Charles F. (tsl) **The catechisms of the shamans; or, the laws and regulations of the priesthood of buddha, in china.** London (1831) 152 p. Tsl of treatise on the vinaya by chu-hung; it 'is very likely the earliest rendering into english of a chinese buddhist text,' acc. to Kenneth K.S. Ch'en: **Buddhism in china** q.v. p 544. German version, Der katechismus der schamanen . . . In **Zeitschrift f.d. historische theologie** 4 (1834) Publ sep, leipzig (1834) 70 p. Rev art in **ChRep** 1.6 (oct 1832) 285-289.

Nobel, J. (tsl) **Suvarnaprabhāsottamasūtra. I-tsing's chinesische version und ihre tibetische übersetzung.** Bd 1, I-tsing's chinesische version; bd 2, Die tibetische übersetzung. Leiden (1958)

Nogami, Shunjyo (tsl) Wu-liang-shou ching, translated from the chinese translation of·seng-k'ai, ts'ao-wei dynasty. **EB** n.s. 8.3 (nov 1957) 1-9; 8.4 (aug 1958) 10-17.

O'Brien, Paul W. (tsl) A chapter on reality from the madhyānta-vibhāgaçastra. **MN** 9 (1953) 277-303; 10 (1954) 227-269.

Ohara, Masatoshi. Questions of pe-suh, the brahman landlord. **HZ** 14.6 (1899) 38-44. Tsl fr chin text.

Ohara, Masatoshi. Vimalakîrti-nirdeśa-sûtra. **HZ** 13 (1898) 81-85, 121-132, 166-182, 219-229, 266-274, 307-312, 335-342, 373-380, 414-419, 453-469, 490-497.

Okakura, Kakuso (tsl) Chi ki (chik i) [sic] i.e. founder of japanese tendai chiso daishi: on the method of practicising concentration and contemplation. Pref note by William Sturgis Bigelow. **HTR** 16.2 (1923) 109-141.

Pachow, W. (tsl) A buddhist discourse on meditation from tun huang. **University of ceylon review** 21.1 (apr 1963) 47-62. Repr **ChBudd** (1980) Tsl of discourse of hung-jen.

Pachow, W. **A study of the twenty-two dialogues on mahayana buddhism.** Univ iowa (1979) 135 p, notes, index. Study and tsl of t'ang dyn work, ta-ch'eng erh-shih-erh wen. Same title in **CC** 20.1 (mar 1979) 15-64.

Paul, Diana Mary. **The buddhist feminine ideal. Queen srīmālā and the tathāgatagarbha.** Missoula, mont (1979) 246 p, notes, app on methodology. Study and tsl of chin text, srīmālādevī simhanāda sūtra.

Paul, Diana Y. **Women in buddhism. Images of the feminine in the mahāyāna tradition.** Berkeley, calif (1979) 333 p, gloss, bibliog, index. Tsl mostly fr chin texts.

Pelliot, Paul. Les versions chinoises du milindapañha. **BEFEO** 24 (1924) 1-258. Study and tsl.

Price, A.T. (tsl) **The diamond sutra or the jewel of transcendental wisdom.** London, 2nd ed (1955) 75 p.

Pruden, Leo (tsl) The ching-t'u shih-i-lun. **EB** n.s. 6.1 (may 1973) 126-157.

Pruden, Leo (tsl) A short essay on the pure land, composed by the dharma master t'an-luan. **EB** n.s. 8.1 (may 1975) 74-95.

Pye, Michael. The heart sutra in japanese context. In **PRS** (1977) 123-134.

Python, Pierre (tsl) **Vinaya-viniścaya-upāli-pariprcchā. Enquête d'upali pour une exégèse de la discipline. Trad. du sanscrit, du tibétaine et du chinois, avec introduction, édition critique des fragments sanscrits et de la version tibétaine, notes et glossaire. En appendice: texte et traduction de t. 1582, I, et du sugatapañcatrimśatstroda de mātṛceta.** Paris (1973) xxiii + 223 p, pl.

Radloff, W. (tsl) **Kuan-si-im pusar. Eine türkische übersetzung des xxv kapitels der chinesischen ausgabe des saddharmapundarīka.** St petersbourg (1911) viii + 119 p.

Rahder, J. **Daśabhūmika-sūtra seventh stage. (With comparisons with the tibetan and chinese versions.)** **AO** 4 (1926) 214-256.

Ramanan, K. Venkata (tsl) **Nāgārjuna's philosophy as presented in the mahā-prajñāpāramitā-śāstra.** Rutland, vt. etc (1966) 409 p, bibliog, notes, index.

Reuter, J.N. Some buddhist fragments from chinese turkestan in sanskrit and 'khotanese.' **Journal société finno-ougrienne** 30 (1913-18) 37 p, 9 pl.

Richard, Timothy (tsl) **The awakening of faith in the mahayana doctrine: the new buddhism, by patriarch ashvagosha.** Shanghai (1907) xxv + 45 p engl tsl; 46 p chin text. See further author's **New testament of higher buddhism.**

Richard, Timothy (tsl) **Guide to buddhahood. Being a standard manual of chinese buddhism.** Shanghai (1907) xxiii + 108 p. Manual is **hsüan fo p'u.**

Richard, Timothy (tsl) **The new testament of higher buddhism.** Edinburgh (1910) 275 p. Expanded version of author's **Awakening of faith in the mahayana doctrine** q.v.

Richard, Timothy. Synopsis of 'how to awaken faith in the mahayana school' by ma ming (died 100 a.d.) **JNCBRAS** 27 (1892-93) 263-278.

Robinson, Richard (tsl) **Chinese buddhist verse.** London (1954) 85 p, bibliog, notes, index of chin texts tsl.

Robinson, Richard H. (tsl) K.A.C. Soule (intro, annot & gloss) **The sutra of vimalakirti's preaching.** Berkeley, calif (1980) 200 p, gloss.

Schaeffer, Phil. (ed and tsl) **Nagarjuna, yuktisastika. Die 60 sätze des negativismus. Nach der chinesischen version übers. Mit photographischer reproduktion des chinesischen und tibetischen textes.** Heidelberg (1923)

Sekida, Katsuki (tsl) A.V. Grimstone (ed & intro) **Two zen classics: mumonkan and hekiganroku.** NY & tokyo (1977) 413 p, geneal table, index (all jap pronunciation)

Soothill, W.E. (tsl) **The lotus of the wonderful law or the lotus gospel: saddharma pundarika sutra, miao-fa lien hua ching.** Oxford (1930) repr san francisco (1977) xii + 275 p.

Suzuki, [Daisetz] Teitaro (tsl) **Açvaghosha's discourse on the awakening of faith in the mahāyāna. Translated for the first time from the chinese version.** Chicago (1900) xvi + 160 p. Repr san francisco (1976)

Suzuki, Daisetz T. (tsl) The hekigan roku—case two. **EB** n.s. 1.2 (sept 1966) 12-20.

Suzuki, Daisetz T. (tsl) On the hekigan roku ("blue cliff records") **EB** n.s. 1.1 (sept 1965) 5-21. Intro and tsl of "case one"

Suzuki, D.T. (tsl) Sutra in 42 sections. In Soyen Shoku (ed) **Sermons of a buddhist abbott,** chicago (1906) 3-21.

Tajima, R. **Étude sur le mahavairocana-sutra (dainichikyo), avec la traduction commentée du premier chapitre.** ?Paris (1936) viii + 186 p, pl, chin and tibetan texts, bibliog, index.

Takakusu, Junjirō (tsl) Pāli elements in chinese buddhism: a translation of buddhaghosa's samantapāsādikā, a commentary on the vinaya, found in the chinese tripiṭaka. **JRAS** (july 1896) 415-439.

Thomas, F.W., S. Miyamoto, and G.L. M. Clauson (tsl) A chinese mahāyāna catechism in tibetan and chinese characters. **JRAS** (1929) 37-76.

Thurman, Robert A.F. (tsl) **The holy scripture of vimalakīrti: a mahāyāna scripture.** Penn state univ (1976) 176 p, notes, gloss.

Tucci, Guiseppe (tsl) **The nyâyamukha of dignāga. The oldest buddhist text on logic. After chinese and tibetan materials.** Heidelberg (1930) 72 p. Repr san francisco (1976)

Tucci, Guiseppe (tsl) **Pre-dignāga buddhist text on logic from chinese sources.** Baroda (1929) Repr san francisco (1976)

Ui, H. (tsl) **The vaisesika philosophy according to the dasapadartha-sastra: chinese text, with introduction, translation, and notes.** Ed F.W. Thomas. London (1917) xii + 265 p. Repr san francisco (1977)

Utsuki, Nishū (tsl) **Buddhabhāṣita-amitāyuḥ-sūtra (the smaller sukhāvatī-vyūha). Translated from the chinese version of kumārajīva.** Kyoto (1924) 43 p.

Vajra bodhi sea. A monthly journal of orthodox buddhism. Publ in City of ten thousand buddhas, talmage, calif by sino-american budd assoc. Text in chin and engl. See passim. Abbrev **VBS.**

Vandier-Nicholas, Nicole (tsl) **Sariputra et les six maîtres d'erreur; facsimilé du manuscrit chinois 4524 de la bibliothèque nationale, présenté par nicole vandier-nicolas avec traduction et commentaire du texte.** Paris (1954) 3 p, 1, 32 p (Mission pelliot en asie centrale)

Waldschmidt, Ernst (tsl) **Die legende von leben des buddha. In auszügen aus den heiligen texten. Aus dem sanskrit, pali und chinesischen übers. u. eingeführt. Mit vielen zum teil farbigen illus. wiedergegeben nach tibetischen tempelbildern aus dem besitz des berliner museums für völkerkunde.** Berlin (1929) 248 p, 21 illus.

Waldschmidt, Ernst (tsl) **Das mahāvadānasūtra. Ein kanonischer text über die sieben letzten buddhas. Sanskrit, verglichen mit dem pali, nebst einer analyse der in chinesischer übers. über-lieferten parallel-versionen. T 2, Die textbearbeitung.** Berlin (1956)

Waley, Arthur (tsl) [Buddhist] texts originating in china and japan. In Edward Conze (ed) **Buddhist texts through the ages,** oxford (1954) 287-306.

Walleser, Max. **Prajñā pāramitā—die vollkommenheit der erkenntnis. Nach indischen, tibetischen und chinesischen quellen.** Göttingen (1914) 164 p.

Wang, Mu-sung (tsl) Dih Ping Tsze (preface) Sutra spoken by the sixth patriarch, wei lang, on the high seat of the gem of law (message from the east) **CC** 12.2 (june 1971) 1-90. Orig publ shanghai (1930)

Ware, J.R. (tsl) The preamble to the samgharakṣitavadana. **HJAS** 3 (1938) 47-67.

Watters, Thomas. Mr eitel's three lectures on buddhism. **ChRec** 4.3 (aug 1871) 64-68. Rev art.

Wayman, Alex & Hideko Wayman (tsl) **The lion's roar of queen śrīmālā: a buddhist scripture on the tathāgatagarbha theory.** Columbia univ (1974) xv + 142 p, intro, notes. Tsl fr "tibetan, chinese and japanese renditions and sanskrit fragments"

Wei, Tat (tsl) **Ch'eng wei-shih lun. The doctrine of mere-consciousness. By hsüan tsang, tripitaka-master of the t'ang dynasty. Translated from the chinese text by Wei Tat.** HK (1973) cxxxix + 818 p, forewords by Yin-shun and Lo Shi-hin, illus 7 pl; the 30 stanzas in sanskrit by master vasubandhu, ditto in Swami Chinmayananda's handwriting; chin and engl versions of the 30 stanzas; engl tsl and chin text facing throughout.

Weller, Friedrich (tsl) Das brahmajālasūtra des chinesischen dīrghāgama. **AS** 25 (1971) 202-264.

Weller, Friedrich (tsl) Buddhas letzte wanderung. **MS** 4 (1939-40) 40-84, 406-440; 5 (1940) 141-207.

Weller, Friedrich (tsl) Kāśyapaparivarta nach der djin-fassung verdeutscht. **MIOF** 12.4 (1966) 379-462.

Weller, Freidrich (tsl) Die sung-fassung des kāśyapapa-rivarta. Versuch einer verdeutschung. **MS** 25 (1966) 207-361.

Weller, Friedrich (tsl) Über den aufbau des pātikasuttanta. I: Der pali-text (d.n. xxiv). II: Übers. des chines. textes. **AMHAV** (1923) 620-639; **AM** 5 (1928) 104-140.

Wieger, Léon (tsl) **Bouddhisme chinois. Extraits du tripitaka, des commentaires, tracts, etc.** Mission de sienhsien, tientsin, 2 vol (1910-13) Repr peking (1940) 2 vol in 1. T 1: **Vinaya, monachisme et discipline. (Hinayana, véhicule inferieur)** 479 p; t 2: **Les vies chinoises du buddha,** 453 p. Chin texts with french tsl facing, illus.

Willemen, Charles (tsl) The chinese prajñāpāramitāhṛda-yasūtra. **Samadhi** 6.1 (jan-mar 1972) 14-22; 6.2 (apr-june 1972) 52-55; 6.3 (july-sept 1972) 102-115; 6.4 (oct-dec 1972) 152-166.

Willemen, Charles (tsl) **The chinese udānavarga. A collection of important odes of the law, fa chi yao sung ching.** Bruxelles, **MCB** 19 (1978) bibliog, intro, tsl, chin text.

Willemen, Charles (tsl) **Fa chu ching - dharmapada. Trad. annotée du 9e chapitre du taisho no. 210 correspondant au le chap. du dharmapada pali.** Kao-hsiung, taiwan (1973) 25 p.

Wong, Mow-lam (tsl) **Buddhabhashitamitayus sutra (the smaller sukhavativyuha). Chinese text and english translation.** Shanghai (1932)

Wong, Mow-lam (tsl) Vijñaptimâtratâ siddhi śāstra (nanjio no. 1197). Chapter I. Translated from the sanskrit into chinese by yuen chwang, and into english by wong mow-lam. **Chinese buddhist** 2 (1932) 1-57.

Wood, Liu Ming (tsl) A translation of the wu-chiao chih-kuan ("on the meditation of the five teachings") **JAC** 1 (1977) 84-125.

Yamaguchi, Susumu (tsl) Dignāga; examen de l'objet de la connaissance (ālambana-parīkṣā). Textes tibétain et chinois et trad. des stances et du commentaire, éclair-cissements et notes d'après le commentaire tibétain de vinītadeva en collaboration avec Henriette Meyer. **JA** 220 (janv-mars 1929) 1-65.

Ymaïzoumi, Y. et Yamata (tsl) O-mi-to-king ou soukhavati-vyouha-soutra d'après la version chinoise de koumarajiva. **AMG** 2 (1881) 39-64.

Yuyama, Akira (tsl) Svalpākṣarā prajñāpāramitā. In **BT&AC** (1977) 280-301. Reconstruction and tsl fr, inter alia, chin texts.

Zach, E. von. Notiz zu de harlez' vocabulaire bouddhique sanscrit-chinois [q.v.] (This rev followed by F. Weller: Bemerkungen zur vorstehenden notiz) **AM** 3 (1926) 569-573.

Zeuschner, Robert (tsl) The hsien tsung chi (an early ch'an (zen) buddhist text) **JCP** 3.3 (june 1976) 253-267. Intro & tsl.

4. STUDIES OF TEXTS AND TERMS

Abel-Rémusat, J.P. Note sur quelques epithètes descriptives de bouddha. **Journal des savants** 2e sér, 4 (oct 1819) 625-633.

Anesaki, Masaharu. The four buddhist āgamas and their pāli counterparts. **TASJ** 35 (1908) 1-149.

Anesaki, Masaharu. On the relation of the chinese āgamas to the pāli nikāyas. **JRAS** (1901) 895-900.

Anesaki, Masaharu. Der sagātha-vagga des samyutta-nikāya und seine chinesische versionen. **Verhandlung 13 ICO Hamburg (1902)** Leiden (1904) s 61. See also french version: Le sagāthavagga du samyutta-nikāya et ses versions chinoises, in **Muséon** n.s. 6 (1905) 23-37.

Anesaki, Masaharu. Sutta-nipāta in chinese. **JPTS** (1906-07) 51.

Bagchi, P.C. Buddhist studies in japan and the taisho edition of the chinese tripitaka. **New asia** 1.1 (1939) 16-20.

Bagchi, P.C. A fragment of the kāśyapa-samhitā in chinese. **Indian culture** 9 (1942) 53-64.

Bailey, Harold W. The pradakṣiṇā-sūtra of chang tsiang-kuin. In L. Cousins, Arnold Kunst & K.R. Norman (ed) **Buddhist studies in honour of i.b. horner,** dordrecht & boston (1974) 15-18.

Banerjee, A.C. Vinaya texts in chinese. **IHQ** 25 (1949) 87-94.

Bapat, P.V. Shan-chien-p'i-p'o-sha and the code of the early buddhist religieux. **Annals of the bhandarkar oriental research institute,** poona, 52 (1971) 1-30.

Bareau, André. A propos de deux traductions chinoises de brahma-jālasūtra du dīrghāgama. **MIHEC** 2 (1960) 1-4.

Bareau, A. Une confusion entre mahāsanghika et vātsīputrīya. **JA** 241 (1953) 399-406.

Bareau, André. l'Origine du dirgha-āgama traduit en chinois par buddhayaśas. In U. Ba Shin et al (ed) **Essays offered to g.h. luce in honour of his seventy-fifth birthday,** ascona (1966) vol 1, 49-58.

Bareau, André. The superhuman personality of buddha and its symbolism in the mahāparinirvāna-sūtra of the dharmaguptaka [from chinese text] In Joseph M. Kitagawa and Charles H. Long (ed) **Myths and symbols; studies in honor of mircea eliade,** univ chicago (1969) 9-21.

Bareau, A. Trois traités sur les sectes bouddhiques attribués à vasumitra, bhava et vinītadeva (ler partie) **JA** 242 (1954) 229-266; 2e partie **ibid** 244 (1956) 167-191 (no chin text used in 2e partie)

Baxter, Alexander. The awakening of faith. **ChRec** 54.10 (oct 1923) 584-595; 54.11 (nov 1923) 657-667.

Beal, Samuel. **Abstract of four lectures on buddhist literature in china, delivered at university college, london.** London (1882) xvi + 185 p, 5 pl.

Beal, Samuel. The age and writings of nagarjuna-bodhisattva. **IA** 15 (1886) 353-356.

Beal, Samuel. **The buddhist tripitaka as it is known in china and japan. A catalogue and compendious report.** Printed for the india office . . . devonport (1876) 117 p.

Beal, Samuel. On a chinese version of the sánkhya káriká, etc., found among the buddhist books comprising the tripitaka, and two other works. **JRAS** n.s. 10 (1878) 355-360.

Beal, Samuel. Results of an examination of chinese buddhist books in the library of the india office. **Trans 2nd ICO, London (1874)** London (1876) 132-162. See also author's art: The buddhist works in chinese in the india office library, in **IA** 4 (1875) 90-101.

Beal, Samuel. Some remarks on the suhrillekha or 'friendly communication' of nagarjuna-bodhisattva to king shatopohanna. **IA** 16 (1887) 169-172.

Bechert, Heinz. Über die "marburger fragmente" des saddharmapuṇḍarika. **AWGN** (1971: 1) 3-81.

Bendall, C.C. (ed) **Contributions to the study of the śikṣāsamuccaya derived from chinese sources.** St petersburg (1897-1902)

Bennett, A.G. Chinese translations of sanskrit buddhist literature during the 5th and 6th centuries. **MB** 66.1 (jan 1958) 2-10.

Bennett, A.G. Translations of sanskrit buddhist literature in china previous to the 5th century. **MB** 65 (1957) 77-82.

Bielefeldt, Carl & Lewis Lancaster. T'an ching (platform scripture) **PEW** 25.2 (apr 1975) 197-212. Rev art re hist of text and various tsl.

Boin, S(ara) A. An introduction to the teaching of vimalakīrti. **MW** 50.2 (aug 1975) 71-76.

Brough, John. Buddhist chinese etymological notes. **BSOAS** 38.3 (1975) 581-585.

Brough, John. The chinese pseudo-translation of ārya-sūra's jātakamālā. **AM** 11.1 (1964) 27-53.

Cerbu, A. Zigmund. A tun-huang version of the āśrayaparāvrtti. **Adyar library bulletin** 25 (1961) 40-48.

Chan, Wing-tsit. The lotus sutra. In W.T. DeBary (ed) **Approaches to the oriental classics,** columbia univ (1959) 143-165.

Chappell, David W. Introduction to the t'ien-t'ai su-chiao-i. **EB** n.s. 9.1 (may 1976) 72-86.

Châu, Thích-minh. **The chinese madhayama agama and the pali majhima nikaya; a comparative study.** Saigon (1964) 388 p.

Châu, Thích-minh. **Milindapanha and nagasena-bhikshusutra: a comparative study through pali and chinese sources.** Calcutta (1964) 127 p.

Ch'en, Kenneth K.S. A propos the feng-fa-yao of hsi ch'ao. **TP** 50 (1963) 79-92.

Ch'en, Kenneth K.S. A propos the mendhaka story. **HJAS** 16 (1953) 374-403.

Ch'en Kenneth K.S. Notes on the sung and yüan tripitaka. **HJAS** 14 (1951) 208-214.

Ch'en, Kenneth K.S. Some problems in the translation of the chinese buddhist canon. **TJ** n.s. 2.1 (1960) 178-188.

Chen, Tieh-fan. The sources of four tun-huang mss of the tso-chuan. **TP** 57.5 (1971) 302-204, photo of texts.

Cheng, Hsueh-li. Motion and rest in the middle treatise. **JCP** 7.3 (sept 1980) 229-244. Re Nāgārjuna's chung-lun.

Chi, Richard See Yee. **Buddhist formal logic. Part 1: a study of dignaga's 'hetucakra' and k'uei-chi's 'great commentary on the 'nyayapravesa.'** London (1969) 222 p, illus.

Chou, Ta-fu and P.C. Bagchi. New lights on the chinese inscriptions of bodhganā. **SIS** 1 (1944) 111-114.

Clark, Walter E. Some problems in the criticism of the sources for early buddhist history. **HTR** 23 (1930) 121-147.

Cook, Francis H. Fa-tsang's brief commentary on the prajñāpāramitā-hrdaya-sūtra. In **MBM** (1978) 167-206.

Corless, Roger G. The meaning of ching (sūtra?) in buddhist chinese. **JCP** 3.1 (dec 1975) 67-71.

Csongor, Barnabas. A chinese buddhist text in brāhmī script. **Unicorn** 10 (aug 1972) 36-77.

Demiéville, Paul. Apocryphes bouddhiques en chine. **ACF** 54 (1954) 246-249; 55 (1955) 237-241.

Demiéville, Paul. Le chapitre de la bodhisattvabhumi sur la perfection du dhyana. **Rocznik orientalistyczny** 21 (1957) 109-128. Repr in **CEB** (1973)

Demiéville, Paul. Deux documents de touen-houang sur le dhyâna chinois. In **EZT** (1961) 1-27. Repr in **CEB** (1973)

Demiéville, Paul. Manuscrits chinois de touen-houang à leningrad. **TP** 51.4/5 (1964) 355-376.

Demiéville, Paul. l'Origine des sectes bouddhiques d'après paramârtha. **MCB** 1 (1931-32) 15-64. Repr in **CEB** (1973)

Demiéville, Paul. Sur l'authenticité du ta tch'ing k'i sin louen. **BMFJ** 2.2 (1929) 1-78. Repr in **CEB** (1973)

Demiéville, P. Sur la mémoire des existences antérieures. **BEFEO** 27 (1927) 283-298. Fr various chin-budd texts.

Demiéville, Paul. Sur les éditions imprimées du canon chinois. **BEFEO** 24 (1924) 181-218. A pt of following art.

Demiéville, Paul. **Les versions chinoises du milindapanha.** Being **BEFEO** 24 (1924) 258 p, pl, tables.

Demiéville, Paul. La yogācārabhūmi de sangharaksa. **BEFEO** 44 (1947-50) 339-436.

Denlinger, Paul B. The buddhist arch at chü-yung-kuan: chinese transliterations of sanskrit. **JCS** 1 (1961) 66-74.

Dschi, Hiän-lin. On the oldest chinese transliterations of the name buddha. **SIS** 3 (1947) 1-9.

Dutt, Nalinasha (ed) with assistance of D.M. Bhattacharya . . . & Vidyavaridhi Shiv Nath Sharma. **Gilgit manuscripts** vol 1. Calcutta (1939) See Intro, 47-57: I. Bhaisajya-guru-sūtra: its chinese translations, its tibetan translations, popularity of bhaisajyaguru in china and japan, the contents of the sūtra. Also see ref to chin tsl in body of text.

Edgren, Sören. The printed dhāranī-sūtra of a.d. 956. **BMFEA** 44 (1972) 141-146, illus incl text photo.

Edkins, Joseph. Buddhist phraseology in relation to christian teaching. **ChRec** 9.4 (july-aug 1878) 283-295.

Edkins, Joseph. Notes of a correspondence with sir john bowring on buddhist literature in china. By prof. wilson. With notices of chinese buddhist works translated from the sanskrit. **JRAS** 16 (1856) 316-339.

Edmunds, Albert J. The chinese âgamas. With appeal to the japanese buddhists. **LD** 2 (1903) 21-23, 43-46.

Edmunds, Albert J. The chinese itivuttakam and its proof of the pali additions. **LD** 5 (1905) 85-86.

Eracle, Jean. Introduction au sūtra de la contemplation d'amitāyus. **Samadhi** 6.1 (jan-mar 1972) 2-13.

Feer, Léon. Introduction au catalogue spécial du fonds chinois de la bibliothèque nationale. **TP** 9.3 (1898) 201-214.

Finot, L. Manuscrits sanskrits de sāhana's retrouvé en chine. **JA** 225 (1934) 1-86.

Franke, Herbert. Einige druck und handschriften der frühen ming-zeit. **OE** 19 (1972) 55-64, 17 pl. Budd and taoist texts:

Franks, A.W. On some chinese rolls with buddhist legends and representations. Communicated to the society of antiquarians by a.w. franks. Westminster (1892) 6 p, 1 pl.Same title in **Archaeologie** 53, 2 sér, no 3, pt 1 (1892) 239-244, 1 taf.

Friese, Heinz. Das tao-yü-lu . . . des yao kuang-hsiao (1335-1418) **OE** 8 (1961) 42-58, 177-187.

Fuchs, Walter. Eine buddhistische tun-huang-rolle v.j. 673. In **Asiatica** (1954) 155-160, illus.

Fuchs, Walter. Die mandjurischen druckausgaben der hsin-ching (hrdayasūtra) mit reproduktion der vier- und fünfsprachigen ausgabe. **Abhandlungen für die kunde des morgenlandes herausgegeben von der deutschen morgenländischen gesellschaft** bd 39.3, wiesbaden (1970) 26 p, 47 pl.

Fuchs, Walter. Zur technischen organisation der übersetzungen buddhistischer schriften ins chinesiche. **AM** 6 (1930) 84-103.

Fujieda, Akira. The tunhuang manuscripts: a general description. **Zinbun** 9 (1966) 1-32; pt 2 **ibid** 10 (1969) 17-39, fig, tables.

Gard, Richard A. On the authenticity of the chung-lun. **JIBS** 3.1 (1954) 7-13.

Giles, Lionel. Dated chinese manuscripts in the stein collection. I. Fifth and sixth centuries a.d., **BSOAS** 7.4 (1935) 809-836; II. Seventh century a.d. **ibid** 8.1 (1936) 1-26; III. Eighth century a.d. **ibid** 9.1 (1937) 1-25; IV. Ninth century a.d. **ibid** 9.4 (1939) 1023-1046.

Giles, Lionel. **Descriptive catalogue of the chinese manuscripts from tun-huang in the british museum.** London (1957) xxv + 334 p.

Giles, Lionel. An illustrated buddhist sūtra. **BMQ** 11 (1936) 29.

Giles, Lionel. **Six centuries at tun-huang. A short account of the stein collection of chinese mss in the british museum.** London (1955) 50p, facs.

Gómez, Luis O. The bodhisattva as a wonder-worker. In **PRS** (1977) 221-261.

Goodrich, Luther Carrington. Earliest printed editions of the tripitaka. **VBQ** 19.3 (1953-54) 215-220.

Gulik, Robert Hans von. **Siddham: an essay on the history of sanskrit studies in china and japan.** Nagpur (1956) 2 vol, pl.

Haas, Hans. Tsungmi's yuen-zan-lun. Eine abhandlung über den ursprung des menschen aus dem kanon des chinesischen buddhismus. **ARW** 12 (1909) 491-532.

Hakayama, Noriaki. Mahāyānasaṃgrahopanibandhana (I) Its tibetan and chinese texts. Komazawa univ **Journal of the faculty of buddhism** 31 (mar 1973) 8-14.

Hakayama, Noriaki. On a verse quoted in the tibetan translation of the mahāyānasaṃgrahopanibandhana. **JIBS** 22.2 (mar 1974) 17-21. Comparison with chin version.

Hamilton, Clarence H. Buddhist idealism in wei shih er shih lwen. **EP** (1929) 99-115.

Hamilton, Clarence H. K'uei chi's commentary on wei-shih-er-shih-lun. **JAOS** 53 (1933) 144-151.

Harlez, Charles de. Man-han-si-fan-tsyeh-yao, a buddhist repertory in sanscrit, tibetan, mandchu, mongol, and chinese. **BOR** 2 (1887) 8-14, 49-55; 3 (1889) 69-72, 116-118, 143-144, 210-215, 232-239, 275-282; 4 (1890) 59-63, 112-116, 164-168, 188-192, 213-216, 238-240.

Hashimoto, Hokei. Concerning the philosophic influence of vimalakīrtinirdeśa sūtra upon chinese culture. **JIBS** 22.1 (dec 1973) 1-9.

Hashimoto, Hokei. The philosophic influence of the vimala-kīrti-nirdeśa-sūtra upon chinese culture. In **MS/CA** (1977) 143-154.

Havret, Henri. **T'ien-tchou, 'seigneur du ciel.' A propos d'une stèle bouddhique de tch'eng-tou.** Shanghai (1901) repr nendeln (1975) 30 p. (Variétés sinologiques no 19)

Hazai, Georg & Peter Zieme (hrsg) **Vajracchedikā. German, chinese and uigur. Selections. Fragmente der uigurischen version des jin'gangjing mit den gāthās des meister fu.** Nebst ein anhang von T. Inokuchi. Berlin (1971) 86 p, 61 facs, 40 taf.

Hoernle, A.F.R. **Manuscript remains of buddhist literature found in eastern turkestan. Facsimiles of mss. in sanskrit, khotanese, kuchean, tibetan and chinese with transcriptions, translations and notes, critical introductions and vocabularies.** Oxford (1916) vol 1 (all publ) 446 p, 22 pl.

Huber, Éd. Études de littérature bouddhique. **BEFEO** 4 (1904) 698-726; continued in **ibid** 6 (1906) 1-43, 335-340. Re certain chin tsl of indian texts; some tsl.

Hummel, A.W. An ancient chinese manuscript. (Mahāparinirvāṇa sūtra chüan 1-2) **QJCA** 3.4 (1946) 6.

Hurvitz, Leon. Additional observations on the 'defense of the faith.' In **EZT** (1961) 28-40.

Hurvitz, Leon. Fa-sheng's observations on the four stations of mindfulness. In **MBM** (1978) 207-248.

Hurvitz, Leon. The lotus sutra in east asia: a review of hokkeshisō. **MS** 29 (1970-71) 697-762.

Hurvitz, Leon N. & Arthur E. Link. Three prajñāpāramitā prefaces of tao-an. In **MSPD** t 2 (1974) 403-470.

Inaba, Shōjun. On chos-grub's translation of the chieh-shen-mi-ching-shu. In **BT&AC** (1977) 105-113.

Ivanovski, A.O. Sur une traduction chinoise du recueil bouddhique 'jātakamālā.' **RHR** 47 (1903) 298-335. Tsl fr russian M. Duchesne.

Iwai, Hirosato. The compilers of the ching-tu-pao-chu-chi. **TBMRD** 13 (1951) 47-86.

Iwamatsu, Asao. Prakritic aspects appearing in the chih ch'en's translation (1) **JIBS** 26.1 (dec 1977) 19-22. Re first tsl of mahāyāna texts in china.

Iwamatsu, Asao. Some names in pan chou san mei ching. **JIBS** 28.1 (dec 1979) 27-32.

Jan, Yün-hua. The fo-tsu-t'ung-chi, a biographical and bibliographical study. **OE** 10 (1963) 61-82.

Jong, J.W. de. A brief history of buddhist studies in europe and america. **EB** n.s. 7.1 (may 1974) 55-106; 7.2 (oct 1974) 49-82. See esp chap 4, Future perspectives, 70-82, re tsl of chin budd texts.

Jong, J.W. de. **Buddha's word in china.** Australian national univ (1968) 26 p (28th george ernest morrison lecture)

Jong, J.W. de. A propos du nidānasaṃyukta. In **MSPD** t 2 (1974) 137-150.

Kanaoka, Shōkō. On the word "pien" **TUAS** 1 (1961) 15-24. Re tun-huang mss.

Karlgren, Bernhard. Prononciation ancienne de caractères chinois figurant dans les transcriptions bouddhiques. **TP** 2e sér, 19 (1918-19) 104-121.

Kielhorn, F. Sanskrit manuscripts in china. **JRAS** (1894) 835-838. Repr in **Academy** 45 (16 june 1894) 498-499.

Kimm, Chung Se. Ein chinesisches fragment des prātimokṣa aus turfan. **AM** 2 (1925) 597-608.

Kimura, Mitsutaka. One aspect of the saddharmapundarīka sūtra sāstra. **Studies on buddhism in japan** 3 (1941) 71-80.

Kiyota, Minoru. Buddhist devotional meditation: a study of the sukhāvativyūhōpadesa. In **MBM** (1978) 249-296.

Kuroda, C. A note on the lankavatara sutra. **TJR** no 1 (1955) 91-94.

Kurumiya, Yenshu. A note of the seventeen distinctive names of saddharmapuṇḍārikasūtra. **JIBS** 25.2 (mar 1977) 24-28.

Lacouperie, Albert J. B. Terrien de. On hiuen-tsiang instead of yüan chwang, and the necessity of avoiding the pekinese sounds in the quotations of ancient proper names in chinese. **JRAS** (1892) 835-840.

Lai, Whalen. Limits and failure of ko-i (concepts-matching) buddhism. **HR** 18.3 (feb 1979) 238-257.

Lancaster, Lewis. Buddhist literature: its canons, scribes, and editors. In Wendy Doniger O'Flaherty (ed) **The critical study of sacred texts,** berkeley, calif (1978) 215-230.

Lancaster, Lewis R. The chinese translation of the aṣṭasāhasrikā-prajñāpāramitā-sūtra attributed to chih ch'ien. **MS** 28 (1969) 246-257.

Lancaster, Lewis R. An early mahāyāna sermon about the body of the buddha and the making of images. **AA** 36.4 (1974) 287-291.

Lancaster, Lewis R. The editing of buddhist texts. In **BT&AC** (1977) 145-151. Re chin tsl.

Lancaster, Lewis R. The oldest mahāyāna sutra: its significance for the study of buddhist development. **EB** n.s. 8.1 (may 1975) 30-41. Re the tao-hsing pan-jo ching, 2nd century a.d.

Lancaster, Lewis R. The story of bodhisattva hero (sadāprasudira) **TJ** n.s. 10.2 (july 1974) 83-90. Compares early chin version of aṣṭasāhasrikā prajñāpāramitā and extant sanskrit and later chin versions.

Laufer, Berthold. Origin of the word shaman. **American anthropologist** n.s. 19.3 (1917) 361-371.

La Vallée Poussin, Louis de. Brahma-jāla suttanta in chinese. **JRAS** (1903) 583.

La Vallée Poussin, Louis de. Les neuf kalpas qu'a franchi sākyamuni pour devancer maitreya. **TP** 26 (1929) 17-24.

La Vallée Poussin, L. de. Notes de bibliographie bouddhique. **MCB** 3 (1934-35) 355-407; 5 (1936-37) 243-304.

Lee, Shao-chang. The prajnaparamita hridaya sutra or 'essence of transcendental wisdom' (after hsuan chang, a.d. VIIth cent.) **JNCBRAS** 65 (1934) 150-151. Same title in **Orient et occident** (geneva) 1.11 (1935) 55.

Lethcoe, Nancy R. Some notes on the relationship between the abhisamālaṅkāra, the revised pañcaviṁśatisāhasrikā, and the chinese translations of the unrevised pañcaviṁśatisāhasrikā. **JAOS** 96.4 (oct-dec 1976) 499-511.

Lévi, S. Bilanga-dutiya. In **MSL** (1937) 405-412.

Lévi, Sylvain. Les éléments de formation du divyāvadāna. **TP** 8 (1907) 105-122.

Lévi, Sylvain. La légende de râma dans un avadâna chinois. In **MSL** (1937) 271-274.

Lévi, S. Un nouveau document sur le milindapraçna. In **MSL** (1937) 214-217.

Lévi, S. l'Original chinois du sutra tibétain sur la grande-ourse. **TP** 2e sér, 9 (1908) 453-454.

Lévi, Sylvain. Les saintes écritures du bouddhisme. Comment s'est constituée le canon sacré. **CMG** 31 (d?) 105-129.

Li, Jung-hsi. The stone scriptures of fang-shan. **EB** n.s. 12.1 (may 1979) 104-113. Re 15,143 slabs stored in cave in fang-shan county 75 kilometers southwest of peking, engraved betw 605/18 and 1621/27.

Liebenthal, Walter. New light on the mahāyāna-śraddhotpāda śāstra. **TP** 46 (1958) 155-216.

Liebenthal, Walter. Notes on the vajrasāmadhi. **TP** 44 (1954) 347-386.

Liebenthal, Walter. "One-mind-dharma." In **Tsukamoto hakase shōju kinen bukkyōshigaku ronshu [essays on buddhist history presented to professor z. tsukamoto]** kyoto univ (1961) 41-47.

Liebenthal, Walter. Sanskrit inscriptions from yunnan, I (and the dates of foundation of the main pagodas in that province) **MS** 12 (1947) 1-40, 8 pl.

Lin, Li-kouang. **l'Aide-mémoire de la vraie loi (saddharmasmrtyupashtanasutra). Recherches sur un sutra développé du petit véhicle.** Paris (1949) xv + 383 p. Introduction de P. Demiéville.

Link, Arthur E. The earliest chinese account of the compilation of the tripiṭaka. (I) **JAOS** 81.2 (1961) 87-103; (II) 81.3 (1961) 281-299.

Link, Arthur E. The introduction to dhyāna-pāramitā by k'ang seng-hui in the liu-tu chi-ching. In **MSPD** t 2 (1974) 205-230.

Link, Arthur E. Shyh daw-an's preface to saṅgharakṣa's yogācarabhūmisūtra and the problem of buddho-taoist terminology in early chinese buddhism. **JAOS** 77 (1957) 1-14.

Magnin, P. Une copie amidique du t'ien-t'ai tche-tchö ta che fa-yuan wen (une étude sur le manucrit p. 3183) In **Contributions aux études sur touen-houang,** paris (1979) 99-114.

Maître, Charles E. Notes de bibliographie chinoise. Une nouvelle édition du tripiṭaka chinois. **BEFEO** 2 (1902) 341-351.

Maître, Ch. E. Une nouvelle édition du tripiṭaka chinois. **BEFEO** 2 (1902) 341-351.

Maki, Itsu. On the chinese dhammapada with special reference to the preface attached thereto. **Hitotsubashi academy annals** 9 (1958) 109-121.

Makita, Tairyō. The ching-tu san-mei ching and the tun-huang manuscripts. **E&W** n.s. 21.3/4 (sep-dec 1971) 351-361. Tsl fr jap Antonio Forte, who also supplied footnotes.

Mártonfi, F. Yi-ching's buddhist sanskrit-chinese glossary; a source for t'ang phonology. **ActaOr** 23.3 (1974) 359-392.

Maspero, Henri. **Sur la date et l'authenticité du fou fa tsang yin yuan tchouan.** Angers (n.d.) 21 p.

Masson-Oursel. Paul. Le yuan jen louen. **JA** sér 11 (mars-avr 1915) 299-354. Re a 3-chap wk by tsung-mi (d. 841) on various budd doctrines.

Mather, Richard B. Wang chin's 'dhuta temple stele inscriptions' as an example of buddhist parallel prose. **JAOS** 83 (1963) 338-359.

Matsumoto, T. "Taishō shinshū daizōkyō" oder kurz "taishō issaikyō" **ZDMG** 88 (1934) 194-199. Contains "A. Die ausgabe der texte" and "B. Der bilder-altlas"

Matsumura, Hisashi. A propos de notes phonétiques dans le fo pen hing king. **JIBS** 25.1 (dec 1976) 32-34.

Meier, F.J. Neuerscheinungen zur buddhistischen geistesgeschichte. **Saeculum** 3 (1952) 319-340.

Meier, F.J. Probleme der chinesischen übersetzer des buddhistischen kanons. Glossen zu tao-an's leitsätzen für übersetzer. **OE** 19.1 (dec 1972) 41-46.

Millican, F.R. Chen ju. **ChRec** 55.2 (feb 1924) 115-119. See also Tai Hsü, The meaning of chen ju and ju lai, **ibid** 119-120.

Mironov, N.D. Buddhist miscellanea. **JRAS** (1927) 241-279. Re name kuan-yin.

Mironov, N.D. Nyāyāpraveśa. **TP** 28 (1931) 1-24.

Mizuno, Kōgen. On the pseudo-fa-kiu-king. **JIBS** 9.1 (1961) 9-16.

Mori, Sodō. On the fēn-bǐe-gōng-dé-lùn. **JIBS** 19.1 (dec 1970) 32-38.

Moule, G.E. "The awakening of faith" as included in the catalogue of christian literature society, shanghai. **ChRec** 42.6 (june 1911) 347-352. See also Timothy Richard, Some remarks on the foregoing paper, **ibid** 353-357.

Mukherjee, Probhat Kumar. The dhammapada and the udānavarga. **IHQ** 11.4 (dec 1935) 741-760. Udānavarga in chin is fa-chi-sung-ching.

Mukherji, Probhat Kumar [Mukhopādhyāya, Prabhāta-Kumārā] **Indian literature in china and the far east.** Calcutta (1932) 334 p.

Müller, F. Max. Chinese translations of sanskrit texts. **IA** 10 (1881) 121-122. Same title in author's **Chips from a german workshop,** 1,2nd ed (1868) 292-304.

Müller, F.W.K. Die 'persischen' kalendar-ausdrücke im chines. tripitaka. **SAWW** 155, pt 1 (1907) 458-465.

Murano, Senchu. The merits and demerits of the translation of chinese texts. **YE** n.s. 1.2 (spring 1975) 9-11. Re western tsl.

Murase, Miyeko. Kuan-yin as savior of men: illustration of the twenty-fifth chapter of the lotus sutra in chinese painting. **AA** 33.1/2 (1971) 39-74.

Mus, Paul. **La lumière sur les six voies. Tableau de la transmigration bouddhique d'après des sources sanskrites, pāli, tibétaines et chinoises en majeure partie inédites. T 1: Introduction et critique des textes.** Paris (1939) 360 p, 6 pl.

Musée Guimet. **Manuscrits et peintures de touen-houang; mission pelliot 1906-1909. Collections de la bibliothèque nationale et du musée guimet.** Paris (1947) 41 p, map.

Nagao, Gadjin M. An interpretation of the term samvriti (convention) in buddhism. In **SJV** (1951) 550-561.

Nakamura, Hajime. The influence of confucian ethics on the chinese translations of buddhist sutras. **SIS** 5.3/4 (1957) (Liebenthal festschrift) 156-170.

Nanjio, Buniyu [sic] Les versions chinoises du saddharma-puṇḍarīka. **PCIEEO** (1903) 110-112.

Nogami, Shunjyo. A study of the translatorship of the wu-liang-shou ching. **EB** 8.3 (nov 1957) 1-9.

Ōchō, Enichi. Tao-an on translation. **EB** 8.4 (aug 1958) 1-7.

Oetke, Claus. **Die aus dem chinesischen übersetzten tibetischen versionen des suvarṇaprabhāsasūtra: philologische und linguistische beiträge zur klassifizierenden charakterisierung übersetzter texte.** Wiesbaden (1977)

Osaki, Akiko. Abhūtvā-bhāva. **JIBS** 28.2 (mar 1980) 19-22. Re a chin phrase used to tsl a sautrāntika theory.

Pachow. Chuan tsi pai yuan king and the avadānaśataka. **VBA** no 1 (1945) 35-55.

Pachow. Comparative studies in the mahāparinibbāna-sutta and its chinese versions. **SIS** 1 (1944) 167-210; 2 (1945) 1-41.

Pachow. Development of tripitaka-translations in china. In **BCL** pt [vol] 1 (1945) 66-74. Repr in author's **ChBudd** (1980)

Pachow, W. A comparative study of the pratimoksa. **SIS** 4 (1953) 18-193; 5 (1955) 1-45.

Pachow, W. Development of tripitaka-translations in china. Repr in author's **ChBudd** (1980) 101-115; orig publ not stated.

Pachow, W. A study of the dotted record. Repr in author's **ChBudd** (1980) 69-86; orig publ not stated.

Pachow, W. **A study of the twenty-two dialogues on mahayana buddhism.** Univ iowa (1979) 135 p, notes, index. Study and tsl of t'ang dyn work, ta-ch'eng erh-shih-erh wen. Same title in **CC** 20.2 (june 1979) 35-110.

Pai, Hui. On the word 'cittavarana' in the prajñāpāra-mitā-hdrayasūtra. **SIS** 3 (1947) 131-139.

Parker, E.H. The diamond sutra (chin-kang-ching) **AQR** n.s. (ser 4) 2 (1913) 428-429.

Pas, Julian F. The kuan-wu-liang-shou fo-ching: its origin and literary criticism. In **BT&AC** (1977) 194-218.

Pas, Julian F. The meaning of nien fo in the three pure land sutras. **SR/SR** 7.4 (1978) 403-413.

Paul, Diana Mary. **The buddhist feminine ideal. Queen śrīmālā and the tathāgatagarbha.** Missoula, mont (1979) 246 p, notes, app on methodology. Study and tsl of chin text, śrīmālādevī simhanāda sūtra.

Pelliot, Paul. Encore un mot à propos du sutra des causes et des effets et de l'expression siang-kiao. **TP** 26 (1929) 51-52.

Pelliot, Paul. The kāçyapaparivarta. (Rev of 3 art publ by Stäel-Holstein and F. Weller) **TP** 32 (1936) 68-76.

Pelliot, Paul. Les noms propres dans les traductions chinoises du milindapañha. **JA** 11e sér, 4 (sept-oct 1914) 379-420.

Pelliot, Paul. Quelques transcriptions apparentées à cambhala dans les textes chinois. **TP** 20.2 (1920-21) 73-85.

Pelliot, Paul. Les stances d'introduction de l'abhidharma-hrdayaśāstra de dharmatrāta. **JA** 217 (1930) 267-273.

Pelliot, Paul. Le terme siang-kiao comme designation du bouddhisme. **TP** 25 (1928) 92-94.

Pelliot, Paul. Textes chinois sur pāṇḍuraṅga. **BEFEO** 3 (1903) 649-654.

Pelliot, Paul. Trois termes de mémoires de hiuan-tsang. In **EORL** (1932) t 2, p 423-431.

Pelliot, Paul. Les versions chinoises du milindapañha. **BEFEO** 24 (1924) 1-258. Study and tsl.

Petzold, Bruno. The completion of the new edition of the chinese tripitaka. **YE** 4 (1929) 193-196; **PW** 4 (1929) 521-524.

Petzold, Bruno. Die neuausgabe des chinesischen tripitaka. **NachrDGNVO** ?18 (1929) 13-18.

Pruden, Leo M. Some notes on the fan-wang-ching. **JIBS** 15.2 (1967) 915-925.

Przyluski, J. **The legend of emperor ašoka in indian and chinese texts.** Calcutta (1967) Tsl fr french with add notes and comments by D.K. Biswas.

Przyluski, J. and M. Lalou. Notes de mythologie bouddhique. 1. Yaksa et gandharva dans le mahāsamayasuttanta. 2. Les rgynd sum-pa manuscrits de touen-houang. 3. Les fils de brahmā. **HJAS** 3 (1938) 40-46, 128-136; 4 (1939) 69-76.

Przyluski, J. Le parinirvāna et les funérailles du buddha. Examen comparatif des textes. **JA** 11e sér, 11 (mai-juin 1918) 485-526; 11e sér, 12 (nov-déc 1918) 401-456. II: Vêtements de religieux et vêtements de rois, **ibid** 11e sér, 13 (mai-juin 1919) 365-430. [III] Les éléments rituels dans les funérailles du buddha, **ibid** 11e sér, 15 (janv-mars 1920) 5-54. Idem: Première partie, extrait du **JA** (1918-20) Paris (1920) 216 p.

Przyluski, J. Le partage des reliques du buddha. **MCB** 4 (1935-36) 341-367.

Reichelt, Karl Ludvig. Indigenous religious phrases that may be used to interpret the christian mesage. **ChRec** 58.2 (feb 1927) 123-126. Phrases fr budd and taoism.

Richard, Timothy. How to awaken faith in the mahayana school. **JNCBRAS** 27.2 (1892) 263-272. Synopsis.

Richard, Timothy. Some remarks on the foregoing paper. **ChRec** 42.6 (june 1911) 353-357. Re G.E. Moule, "The awakening of faith" as included in the catalogue of christian literature society, shanghai, **ibid** 347-352.

Richardson, Hugh E. "The dharma that came down from heaven": a tun-huang fragment. In **BT&AC** (1977) 219-230.

Saibaba, V.V.S. A brief look at the avatamsaka sūtra. **YE** 4.4 (autumn 1978) 28-33. Re hist and doctrine of the sūtra.

Saigusa, Mitsuyoshi. **Studien zum mahāprajñāpāramitā (upadeśa) śāstra. Inaugural-dissertation zur erlangung des doktorgrades der philosophischen fakultät der ludwig-maximilians-universität zu münchen vorgelegt von Mitsuyoshi Saigusa in münchen 1962.** Tokyo (1969) 239 p.

Sastri, S.S. Suryanarayana. The chinese suvarnasaptati and the matharavriti. **JOR** 5 (1932) 34-40.

Schlegel, G. Le terme bouddhique tu-p'i. **TP** 9 (1898) 269-271.

Schlegel, G. Les termes yü-lan-p'en et yü-lan-p'o. **TP** 2e sér, 2.2 (mai 1901) 146-148.

Schmidt-Glintzer, Helwig. **Das hung-ming chi und die aufnahme des buddhismus in china.** Wiesbaden (1976) viii + 212 p.

Schott, Wilhelm. Zur litteratur des chinesischen buddhismus. **Akademie der wissenschaft zu berlin, philologische und historische klasse, Abhandlungen 1873.** Berlin (1874) 37-65.

Sedgwick, Ellery. A chinese printed scroll of the lotus sutra. **QJCA** 6.2 (feb 1949) 6-9, pl, facs. With a note by Arthur W. Hummel.

Sen, Satiranjan. Two medical texts in chinese translation (In tripitaka) **VBA** 1 (1945) 70-95.

Smith, Helmer. En marge du vocabulaire sanskrit des bouddhistes. **Orientalia suecana** 2 (1953) 119-128; 3 (1954) 31-35; 4 (1955) 109-113.

Specht, Édouard. **Deux traductions chinoises du milindapañha.** Paris (1893) 25 p. Sub-title: Mélanges sinologiques ii. Introduction de Sylvain Lévi.

Stache-Rosen, Valentina. The upalipariprcchasutra, a vinaya text in chinese. In **B&J** (1976) 24-30.

Stäel-Holstein, A. von. On a peking, a st. petersburg, and a kyoto reconstruction of a sanskrit stanza transcribed with chinese characters under the northern sung dynasty. In **Studies presented to ts'ai yüan-p'ei on his 65th birthday,** peking, vol 1 (1933) 175-187.

Stäel-Holstein, A. von. On two recent reconstructions of a sanskrit hymn transliterated with chinese characters in the X century a.d. **Yenching journal of chinese studies** 17 (1935) 1-38, 2 pl.

Stein, Rolf A. Illumination subite ou saisie simultanée: note sur la terminologie chinoise et tibétaine. **RHR** 179 (jan-mar 1971) 3-30.

Su, Ying-hui. An analytical study of the tun-huang manuscripts with regard to their urbane or popular tastes. **CC** 20.1 (mar 1979) 95-99.

Sutherland, Joan. Li ho and the lankavatara sutra. **JAC** 2.1 (spring 1978) 69-102.

Suzuki, D.T. An introduction to the study of the lankavatara sutra. **EB** 5 (1929) 1-79.

Sykes, William H. On a catalogue of chinese buddhistical works. **JRAS** 9 (1848) 199-213.

Tai Hsü. The meaning of chen ju and ju lai. **ChRec** 55.2 (feb 1924) 119-120.

Tajima, R. **Étude sur le mahavairocana-sutra (dainichikyo), avec la traduction commentée du premier chapitre.** Paris (1936) viii + 186 p, pl, chin and tibetan texts, bibliog, indexes.

Takakusu, Junjirō. Buddhaghosa's samantapāsādikā in chinese. **JRAS** (1897) 113-114.

Takakusu, Junjirō. Chinese translations of the milinda pañho. **JRAS** (1896) 1-21.

Takakusu, Junjirō. The name of 'messiah' found in a buddhist book; the nestorian missionary adam, presbyter, papas of china, translating a buddhist sutra. **TP** 7.5 (1896) 589-591.

Takakusu, Junjirō. Notes on buddhist books. **JRAS** (1903) 181-183.

Takakusu, Junjirō. On the abhidharma literature of the sarvāstivādins. **JPTS** (1905) 67-146. See also author's art, The abhidharma literature, pali and chinese, **JRAS** (1905) 160-162.

Takakusu, Junjirō. **A pali chrestomathy; with notes and glossary giving sanskrit and chinese equivalents.** Tokyo (1900) 94 + 6 + 272 p.

Takakusu, Junjirō. Pali elements in chinese buddhism. A translation of buddhaghosa's samantapasadika, a commentary on the vinaya, found in the chinese tripitaka. **JRAS** 28 (1896) 415-439.

Takakusu, Junjirō. La sāṃkhyakārikā étudiée à la lumière de sa version chinoise. **BEFEO** 4 (1904) 1-65, 978-1064. See further next item.

Takakusu, Junjirō. La sāṃkhyakārikā étudiée à la lumière de sa version chinoise. **PCIEEO** (1902) 39-41. Same title in engl, in **Journal of the madras univ** 4.1 suppl (1932) 1-51; 5 (1933) 81-114. See preceding item.

Takakusu, Junjirō. A study of paramartha's life of vasu-bandhu; and the date of vasu-bandhu. **JRAS** (1905) 33-53.

Takakusu, Junjirō. The works of samgha-bhadra, an opponent of vasu-bandhu. **JRAS** (1905) 158-159.

Takasaki, Jikido. Structure of the anuttarāsrayasūtra (wu-shang-i-ching) **JIBS** 8.2 (mar 1960) 30-37.

Takasaki, Jikido. **A study on the ratnagotravibhāga (uttaratantra). Being a treatise on the tathāgatagarbha theory of mahāyāna buddhism.** Rome (1966) 452 p, app, indices. Incl tsl fr sanskrit text and comparison with tibetan and chin versions.

T'ang, Yung-t'ung. On ko-yi. the earliest method by which indian buddhism and chinese thought were synthesized. In W.R. Inge (ed) **Radhakrishnan: comparative studies in philosophy presented in honour of his 60th birthday,** london (1951) 276-286.

T'ang, Yung-t'ung. The editions of the ssu-shih-erh chang-ching. **HJAS** 1 (1936) 147-155.

Thomas, F.W. A buddhist chinese text in brāhmī script. **ZDMG** 91 (1937) 1-48.

Thomas F.W. Paramartha's life of vasubandhu and the date of kaniska. **JRAS** (1914) 748-751.

Thomas, F.W. and G.L.M. Clauson. A chinese buddhist text in tibetan writing. **JRAS** (1926) 508-526.

Thomas, F.W. and G.L.M. Clauson. A second chinese buddhist text in tibetan characters. **JRAS** (1927) 281-306. See further: Note supplementary to the article, 'A second chinese . . . ' in **ibid** 858-860.

Thomas, F.W., S. Miyamoto and G.L.M. Clauson. A chinese mahāyāna catechism in tibetan and chinese characters. **JRAS** (1929) 37-76.

Thomas, F.W. and H. Ui. 'The hand treatise,' a work of aryadeva. **JRAS** (1918) 267-310.

Tokiwa, Gishin. "The mind not in accord" of the mahayana faith awakening. **JIBS** 21.1 (dec 1972) 52-57.

Tokiwa, Gishin. The shin fugyū as expounded in the lankavatara. **JIBS** 24.1 (dec 1975) 6-11. Re a phrase, hsin pu chi, in the record of zen master lin-chi i-hsüan.

Tokunaga, Michio. A view of tariki (other power) in t'an-luan's ronchū (ching-t'u lun-chu) **JIBS** 22.2 (mar 1974) 22-27.

Tomomatsu, E. Sûtralamkâra et kalpanâmaṇditikâ. **JA** 219 (1931) 135-174, 245-337.

Tubyansky, M. On the authorship of nyāyapraveça. **Izvestiya akademiya nauk** ser 6, vol 20 (1926) 975-982.

Tucci, G. Is the nyayapravesa by dinnaga? **JRAS** (1928) 7-13.

Tucci, G. Un traité d'āryadeva sur le 'nirvana' des hérétiques. **TP** 24 (1926) 16-31.

Vajra bodhi sea. A monthly journal of orthodox buddhism. Publ in City of ten thousand buddhas, talmage, calif by sino-american buddhist assoc. Text in chin and engl. See passim. Abbrev **VBS.**

Vassiliev, Boris. 'Ju-shih lun' — a logical treatise ascribed to vasubandhu. **BSOAS** 8.4 (1937) 1013-1037.

Ventakasubbiah, A. On the grammatical work si-t'an-chang. **JOR** 10 (1936) 11-26.

Visser, M.W. de. **Ancient buddhism in japan. Sūtras and ceremonies in use in the seventh and eighth centuries a.d. and their history in later times.** Leiden, 2 vol (1935) See passim for chin tsl.

Visser, Marinus Willem de. The canon of chinese buddhism. **Museum** 11.1 (1903) col 1-5.

Waldschmidt, Ernst. Ein fragment der samyuktāgama aus den "turfan-funden" (m476) **AWGN** (1956) 45-54.

Waldschmidt, Ernst. Das upasensūtra, ein zauber gegen schlangenbiss aus dem samyuktāgama. **AWGN** (1957: 2) 27-44, 2 pl.

Waldschmidt, Ernst. Wunderkräfte des buddha. **AWGN** (1948: 1) 48-91.

Ware, J.R. Notes on the fan wang ching. **HJAS** 1 (1936) 156-161.

Ware, J.R. Studies in the divyāvadāna. **JAOS** 48 (1928) 159-165; 49 (1929) 40-51.

Ware, J.R. Transliteration of the names of chinese buddhist monks. **JAOS** 52 (1932) 159-162.

Watanabe, K. Aśvaghoṣa and the great epics. **JRAS** (1907) 664-665.

Watanabe, Kaikioku (or Kaikyoku) A chinese text corresponding to parts of bower manuscript. **JRAS** (1907) 261-266.

Watanabe, Kaikioku (or Kaikyoku) The nepalese nava dharmas and their chinese translations. **JRAS** (1907) 663-664.

Watanabe, Kaikioku (or Kaikyoku) The oldest record of the rāmāyana in a chinese buddhist writing (mahāvibhāsa) **JRAS** (1907) 99-103.

Watters, Thomas. The a-mi-t'o ching. **ChRev** 10 (1881-82) 225-240.

Watters, Thomas. Notes on the miao-fa-lien-hua-ching, a buddhist sutra in chinese. **JNCBRAS** n.s. 9 (1874) 89.

Watters, Thomas. The ta-yun-lun-ch'ing-yu-ching. **ChRev** 10 (1881-82) 384-395.

Weinstein, Stanley. On the authorship of the hsi-fang-yao-chüeh. **Trans ICfO Japan** 4 (1959) 12-25.

Weller, Freidrich. Das brahmajālasūtra des chinesischen dīrghāgama. **AsFS** 25 (1971) 202-264.

Weller, F. Über den aufbau des patikasuttanta. ii. Übersetzung des chinesischen textes. **AM** 5 (1930) 104-140.

Whitehead, James D. The "sinicization" of the vimalakīr-tinirdeśa sūtra. **SSCRB** 5 (spring 1978) 3-51.

Willemen, Charles. The prefaces to the chinese dharmapadas, fu-chü ching and ch'u-yao ching. **TP** 59 (1973) 203-219.

Wogihara (or Wogiwara or Ogiwara) Unrai. Contributions to the study of the śiksa-samuccaya derived from chinese sources. **Muséon** n.s. 5 (1904) 96-103, 209-215; 7 (1906) 255-261.

Wohlgemuth, Else. Über die chinesische version von aśvaghosas buddhacarita . . . fo-so-hing-tsan. **MSOS** 19 (1916) 1-75.

Wu, K.T. Chinese printing under four alien dynasties. **HJAS** 13 (1950) 441-457, 515-516. Re buddhist texts.

Yamada, Isshi. Anityatāsūtra. **JIBS** 20.2 (mar 1972) 30-35.

Yeh, Kung-cho. Chinese editions of the tripitaka. Natl central library, nanking, **Philobiblon**, 1.2 (1946) 26-29.

Zach, E. von. Einige bemerkungen zu pelliot's sūtra des causes et des effets. **TP** 25 (1928) 403-413.

5. THEORY AND DOCTRINE

Abel-Rémusat, J.P. Essai sur la cosmographie et la cosmogonie des bouddhistes, d'après les auteurs chinois. **Journal des savants** 2e sér, 16 (oct 1831) 597-610; 2e sér, 16 (nov 1831) 668-674; 2e sér, 16 (déc 1831) 716-731. See also author's **Mélanges posthumes d'histoire et de littérature orientales,** paris (1843) 65-131.

Abel-Rémusat, J.P. **Observations sur quelques points de la doctrine samanéenne, et en particulier sur les noms de la triade suprême chez les différents peuples bouddhistes.** Paris (1831) 67 p.

Aiyaswamisastri, N. Kwei-chi's note on alambana (object-cause) **SIS** 5.3/4, Liebenthal festschrift (1957) 1-8.

Andrews, Allan A. Nembutsu in the chinese pure land tradition. **EB** n.s. 3.2 (oct 1970) 20-45.

Bertholet, R. l'Astrobiologie et la pensée bouddhique. (l'Astrobiologie et la pensée d'asie: essai sur les origines des sciences et des théories morales) **RMM** 41 (1931) 509-529.

Birnbaum, Raoul. Introduction to the study of t'ang buddhist astrology: research notes on primary sources and basic principles. **SSCRB** 8 (fall 1980) 5-19.

Bloom, Alfred. The sense of sin and guilt and the last age [mappo] in chinese and japanese buddhism. **Numen** 14 (1967) 144-149.

Bodde, Derk. The chinese view of immortality; its expression by chu hsi and its relationship to buddhist thought. **RofR** 6 (1942) 369-383. Repr **ECC** (1981) 316-330.

Boin, S (ara) A. An introduction to the teaching of vimalakīrti. **MW** 50.2 (aug 1975) 71-76.

Chang, Carsun. Buddhism as a stimulus to neo-confucianism. **OE** 2.2 (1955) 157-166.

Chang, Garma C.C. **The buddhist teaching of totality. The philosophy of hwa yen buddhism.** Penn state univ (1971) xxv + 270 p, list of chin terms, gloss, index.

Chappell, David W. Chinese buddhist interpretations of the pure lands. In **BTS-I** (1977) 23-54.

Chung, Albert C. The mysticism of the buddhists. **CC** 5.1 (1963) 99-121.

Cook, Francis H. **Hua-yen buddhism. The jewel net of indra.** Penn state univ (1977) xiv + 146 p, notes, gloss, index.

Corless, Roger G. Monotheistic elements in early pure land buddhism. **Religion** 6.2 (1976) 176-189.

Day, Clarence B. **The philosophers of china.** N.Y. (1962) See chap 8, The inner development of chinese buddhism, 111-180.

Demiéville, Paul. Sur la mémoire des existances antérieures. **BEFEO** 27 (1927) 283-298.

Drake, F.S. A chat with buddhists. **ChRec** 67.5 (may 1936) 281-285.

Edkins, Joseph. The buddhist doctrine of future punishment. **Sunday at home** (july 1879)

Edkins, Joseph. The four elements. **ChRev** 16 (1888) 369-370.

Edkins, Joseph. The nirvana of the northern buddhists. **JRAS** n.s. 13 (jan 1881) 59-79. See also author's The nirvana according to northern buddhism, **Atti 4th ICO Florence, 1878,** vol 2, Florence (1881) 295-308.

Edkins, Joseph. Paradise of the western heaven. **ChRev** 17 (1888-89) 175-176.

Eitel, E.J. Amita and the paradise of the west. **NQ** 2 (1868) 35-38.

Eitel, E.J. A buddhist purgatory for women. **NQ** 2 (1868) 66-68, 82-85.

Eitel, E.J. The nirvana of chinese buddhists. **ChRec** 3 (1870-71) 1-6.

Fang, Li-t'ien. A tentative treatise on the buddhist philosophical thought of hui-yüan (334-416) **CSP** 4.3 (spring 1973) 36-76.

Fung, Yu-lan. **A history of chinese philosophy.** Tsl fr chin Derk Bodde. Princeton univ, vol 2, (1953) See chap 7-10.

Fung, Yu-lan **A short history of chinese philosophy.** Ed Derk Bodde. N.Y. (1948) See chap 21, The foundation of chinese buddhism, 241-254.

Gautier, Judith. **Les peuples étranges.** Paris (1879) See pt 2, sec l'Enfer, 221-231.

Glüer, Winfried. Salvation today—chinese interpretations. **CF** 16.1 (1973) 33-46. Genl considerations; confucianism; budd.

Gómez, Luis O. The bodhisattva as a wonder-worker. In **PRS** (1977) 221-261.

Gurij, P. Der buddhismus des mayâyâna . . . aus dem russischen übersetzt mit einer einleitung . . . von W.A. Unkrig. **Anthropos** 16-17 (1921-22) 343-359, 801-818; 18-19 (1923-34) 267-277.

Hackmann, Heinrich. **Chinesische philosophie. Mit einem bilde bodhidharmas.** München (1927) 406 s. See p 237-311.

Hakeda, Yoshito S. (tsl) **Kūkai; major works, translated with an account of his life and a study of his thought.** Columbia univ (1972) See chap 4, Enounter with master hui-kuo, 29-33; also pt 3, Major works of kūkai, passim.

Hamilton, Clarence H. Buddhist idealism in wei shih er shih lun. In **EP** (1929) 99-115.

Hamilton, Clarence H. Hsüan chuang and the wei shih philosophy. **JAOS** 51 (1931) 291-308.

Hamilton, Clarence H. The idea of compassion in mahāyāna buddhism. **JAOS** 70 (1950) 145-151.

Harlez, Charles J. de. Tathāgatha. **JRAS** (1899) 131.

Hsüan-hua. BTTSoc (tsl) **The ten dharma realms are not beyond a single thought.** San francisco (1976) 72 p. Budd cosmology with comm.

Hurvitz, Leon. Chih tun's notions of prajñā. **JAOS** 88 (1968) 243-261.

Hurvitz, Leon. The first systematizations of buddhist thought in china. **JCP** 2.4 (sept 1975) 361-388.

Hurvitz, Leon. The lotus sutra in east asia: a review of hokkeshisō. **MS** 29 (1970-71) 697-762. Rev art.

Hurvitz, Leon. Road to buddhist salvation as described by vasubhadra. **JAOS** 87 (1967) 434-486.

Jan, Yün-hua. Tsung-mi's theory of the "comparative understanding" (ho-hui) of buddhism. In **MS/CA** (1977) 181-186.

Kalupahana, David J. **Causality: the central philosophy of buddhism.** Univ hawaii (1975) xviii + 265 p, notes, bibliog, index of chin terms, genl index. A comparison of "the teachings on the problem of causation in the pali nikāyas and the chinese āgamas"

Katsumata, Shunkyō. Concerning various views of human nature. **TUAS** 1 (1961) 33-45. As found particularly in chin-budd texts.

Kung, Tien-min. Some buddhist and christian doctrines compared. **QNCCR** 5.2 (1961) 34-37.

Lai, Whalen. Chinese buddhist causation theories: an analysis of the sinitic mahāyāna understanding of pratītya-samutpāda. **PEW** 27.3 (july 1977) 241-264.

Lai, Whalen. Further development of the two truths theory in china. **PEW** 30.2 (apr 1980) 139-162.

Lai, Whalen. Illusionism (māyāvāda) in late t'ang buddhism: a hypothesis on the philosophical roots of the round enlightenment sūtra (yüan-chüeh-ching) **PEW** 28.1 (jan 1978) 39-52.

Lai, Whalen. The meaning of 'mind only' (wei-hsin): an analysis of a sinitic mahāyāna phenomenon. **PEW** 27.1 (jan 1977) 65-83.

Lai, Whalen. Sinitic understanding of the two truths theory in the liang dynasty. **PEW** 28.3 (july 1978) 339-352.

Lamotte, Étienne. Prophéties relatives à la disparition de la bonne loi. **FA:BPB** (1959) 657-668.

La Vallée Poussin, Louis de. Staupikam. **HJAS** 2 (1937) 276-289. Theory of stupa and its evolution.

La Vallée Poussin, Louis de. Studies in buddhist dogma: the three bodies of a buddha. **JRAS** (1906) 943 f.

Lee, Hsing-tsun. A new look at taoism and buddhism. **ACQ** 4.4 (winter 1976) 117-156. Author's personal views.

Lee, Pi-cheng [Lü Pi-ch'eng] (ed and tsl) **An outline of karma.** N.p. [publ by tsl] (1941?) 97 p.

Liang Ch'i-ch'ao. Kurzer überblick über die buddhistische psychologie . . . Tsl fr chin R. Wilhelm. **Sinica** 4 (1929) 18-27, 68-83.

Liebenthal, Walter. The immortality of the soul in chinese thought. **MN** 8 (1952) 327-397.

Link, Arthur E. Evidence for doctrinal continuity of han buddhism from the second through the fourth centuries: the prefaces to an shih-kao's grand sūtra on mindfulness of the respiration and k'ang seng-hui's introduction to "the perfection of dhyāna" In James B. Parsons (ed) **Papers in honor of professor woodbridge bingham: a festschrift for his seventy-fifth birthday,** san francisco (1976) 55-126.

Masaki, Haruhiko. On the principle of "negative-intermediation" seen in the interpretation of shan-tao's kuan-wu-liang-shou-fo-ching-shu—compared with that of the two famous phrases in an embroidered curtain depicting a land called tenju. **JIBS** 20.2 (mar 1972) 65-75.

Masson-Oursel, Paul. Les trois corps du bouddha. **JA** sér 11, t 1 (1913) 581-618.

Matsunaga, Alicia. **The buddhist philosophy of assimilation. The historical development of the honji-suijaku theory.** Tokyo (1969) See chap 3, Buddhist assimilation in china, 97-138.

Matsunaga, Daigan & Alicia Matsunaga. **The buddhist concept of hell.** NY (1972) 152 p, app, notes, bibliog, index. See esp sec 2, Description and analysis of the eight hells, drawn from chinese translations of saddharmasmṛti-upasthāna (chen-fa-hien-ch'u ching)

McGovern, William M. Buddhist metaphysics in china and japan. **Proc aristotelian society** n.s. 20 (1920) 157-166.

Meister, Peter Wilhelm. Buddhistische planetendar-stellungen. **OE** 1 (1954) 1-5, pl.

Mortier, F. Le bouddhisme et des variations doctrinales. **BSAB** 65 (1954) 197-202.

Mus, Paul. **La lumière sur les six voies. Tableau de la transmigration bouddhique d'après des sources sanskrites, pāli, tibétaines et chinoises en majeure partie inédites. T 1: Introduction et critique des textes.** Paris (1939) 360 p, 6 pl.

Nakamura, Hajime. Buddhist philosophy. In **EncyB 3** (1974) **Macropaedia** vol 3, 425a-431b.

Nakamura, Hajime. **Parallel developments. A comparative history of ideas.** Tokyo (1975) xx + 567 p. On chin budd see passim.

Nakamura, Hajime. A survey of mahāyāna buddhism with bibliographical notes. **JIC** 3 (1976) 60-145; 4 (1977) 77-135; 5 (1978) 89-138.

Nishi, Giyū. The concept and practice of the bodhisattva way. With special emphasis on the origin and meaning of the bodhisattva concept. **TUAS** 1 (1961) 59-71. Mostly as found in chin-budd texts.

Pachow, W. The controversy over the immortality of the soul in chinese buddhism. **JOS** 16.1/2 (1978) 21-38; repr in author's **ChBudd** (1980) 117-162.

Petzold, B. Mahāyāna. **OL** 41 (1938) col 600-607.

Pratt, J.B. Buddhism and scientific thinking. **JR** 14 (1934) 13-24.

Raguin, Yves. Médiation dans le bouddhisme et le taoïsme. **SM** 21 (1972) 77-92.

Reichelt, Karl Ludvig. The living seed in the ethical system of chinese buddhism. **ChRec** 60.5 (may 1929) 287-294.

Rotermund, W. **Die ethik lao-tse's mit besonderer bezugnahme auf die buddhistische moral.** Gotha (1874) 26 p.

Sakamoto, Yukio. The development of the theories on the buddhata in china. In **RSJ** (1959) 350-358.

Saso, Michael. Buddhist and taoist notions of transcendence: a study in philosophical contrast. In **BTS-I** (1977) 3-22.

Schott, Wilhelm. Die moral der buddh. chinesen. **MLA** 18 (1840) 445-451.

Schott, Wilhelm. Die verklärte welt des buddha amitabha. **MLA** 18 (1840) 321-322.

Ščuckij, J. Tsl fr russian W.A. Unkrig. Ein dauist im chinesischen buddhismus. **Sinica** 15.1/2 (1940) 114-129. Re Hui-yüan, 334-416 c.e.

Selby, T.G. Yan kwo, Yuk lik, or the purgatories of popular buddhism. **ChRev** 1 (1872-73) 301-311.

Servus. The paradise of fuh. **ICG** no 6 (1818) 194-200.

Shen, C.T. The five eyes: a study of buddhism. **CC** 10.3 (1969) 22-32.

Snellgrove, David L. Buddhist mythology. In **EncyB 3** (1974) **Macropaedia** vol 3, 418b-425a.

Stein, Rolf A. Nouveaux problèmes du tantrisme sino-japonaise. **ACF** 75e ann (1975) 481-488.

Stein, Rolf A. Quelques problèmes du tantrisme chinois. **ACF** 74e ann (1974) 499-508.

Suzuki, Beatrice Lane. What is mahāyāna buddhism? **EB** 1 (1921) 61-69.

Suzuki, D.T. Buddha in mahāyāna buddhism. **EB** 1 (1921) 109-122.

Suzuki, Daisetz T. Freedom of knowledge in chinese buddhism. **MW** 31 (1906) 12-18.

Suzuki, D.T. The natural law in the buddhist tradition. **NLIP** 5 (1953) 91-115.

'The systems of buddha and confucius compared' extracted from the **ICG** no 5, août 1818, 149-157. **ChRep** 2 (1833-34) 265 et seq.

Tai-hü. Über das nichtvorhandensein eines objectiven geistes. **Sinica** 4 (1929) 206-215.

Takakusu, Junjiro. **The essentials of buddhist philosophy.** Ed W.T. Chan and Charles A. Moore. n.p. [Honolulu] 1st ed (1947) 2nd ed (1949) 221 p, charts, index. Repr westport, conn (1973)

Takata, Ninkaku. The relations between esotericism and the tathāgatagarbha theory as seen in the shou-hu-kuo-chieh-chu-dhāraṇī-ching. **JIBS** 9.2 (mar 1961) 34-39.

Tamaki, Koshiro. The development of the thought of tathāgatagarbha from india to china. **JIBS** 9.1 (jan 1961) 25-33.

Thurman, Robert A.F. Buddhist hermeneutics. **JAAR** 46.1 (mar 1978) 19-40.

Tokiwa, Gishin. Criticism of shuko's (i.e. chu-hung) "universality-particularity-unobstructed" viewpoint by hakuin from his "dharma" standpoint. **JIBS** 20.2 (mar 1972) 85-92.

Tokunaga, Michio. A view of tariki ("other-help") in tan-luan's ronchū. **JIBS** 22.2 (mar 1974) 22-27.

Ui, H. **The vaiśeṣika philosophy.** London (1917)

Unno, Taitetsu. The buddhatā theory of fa-tsang. **Trans ICfO Japan** 8 (1963) 34-41.

Vajra bodhi sea. A monthly journal of orthodox buddhism. Publ in City of ten thousand buddhas, talmage, calif by sino-american buddhist assoc. Text in chin and engl. See passim. Abbrev **VBS**.

Verdú, Alfonso. **Dialectical aspects in buddhist thought; studies in sino-japanese mahāyāna buddhis** Univ kansas centre for east asian studies (1974) 273 p.

Waley, Arthur. References to alchemy in buddhist scriptures. **BSOAS** 6.4 (1932) 1102-1103.

Wei, Francis C.M. The doctrine of salvation by faith as taught by the buddhist pure land sect and its alleged relation to christianity. **ChRec** 51.6 (june 1920) 395-40**1** 51.7 (july 1920) 485-491.

Wilhelm, Richard. Einige probleme der buddhistischen psychologie. **Sinica** 4 (1929) 120-130.

Wogihara (or Wogiwara, or Ogiwara) Unrai. Bemerkungen über die nordbuddhistische terminologie im hinblick auf die bodhisattvabhūmi. **ZDMG** 58 (1904) 451-454.

6. HISTORY

Akira, Fujieda. The tun-huang manuscripts. In Donald D Leslie, Colin Mackerras & Wang Gungwu (ed) **Essays on the sources for chinese history,** australian natl univ (1973) univ so carolina (1975) 120-128.

Allen, Herbert J. The connexion between taoism, confucianism and buddhism in early days. **Trans 3rd ICHR,** Oxford (1908) vol 1, 115-119.

Allen, H.J. The first introduction of buddhism into china. **Academy** 40 (1891) 221.

Allen, Herbert J. Similarity between buddhism and early taoism. **ChRev** 15 (1886-87) 96-99.

Ampère, J.J. Histoire du bouddhisme: relation des royaumes bouddhiques, tr. du chinois par Abel Rémusat **RDM** 4e sér, 9 (15 janv 1837) 736-751. See also what is apparently german tsl: Zur geschichte des buddhismus. Aus der reise des chinesischen priester fa-hian. In **MLA** 12 (d?) 349-350, 354,355.

Anon. **History of the Chinese mahayana church.** Bangkok (1960) 30 p.

Aurousseau, L. Paul pelliot — 'meou-tseu ou les doutes levés' (etc.) **BEFEO** 22 (1922) 276-298.

Bagchi, P.C. The beginnings of buddhism in china. **SIS** (1944) 1-17.

Bagchi, Prabodh Chandra. **India and china: a thousand years of cultural relations.** Bombay, 2nd rev and enl ed (1950) n.y. (1951) 234 p, map, app, bibliog, index.

Bagchi, P.C. On foreign element in the tantra. **IHQ** 7 (1931) 1-16.

Bagchi, P.C. On the original buddhism, its canon and language. **SIS** 2 (1945) 107-135.

Bagchi, P.C. Some early buddhist missionaries of persia in china. **CalR** ser 3, vol 24 (1927) 60-64.

Balazs, Stefan. Der philosoph fan dschen und sein traktat gegen den buddhismus. **Sinica** 7 (1932) 220-234. Engl tsl H.M. Wright: The first chinese materialist, in Arthur F. Wright (ed) **Chinese civilization and bureaucracy. Variations on a theme** [collection of essays by Étienne Balazs, in engl tsl] yale univ (1964) 255-276.

Banerjee, Anukul Chandra. **Studies in chinese buddhism.** Calcutta (1977) 116 p, index.

Bareau, André. Indian and ancient chinese buddhism: institutions analogous to the jisa. **CSSH** 3 (1961) 443-451. ('Jisa' is tibetan for the principal land of the monastery)

Bauer, Wolfgang. **China und die hoffnung auf glück. Paradies, utopien, idealvorstellung.** München (1971) 703 s, zeittafel, anmerkungen, literaturverzeichnis, chin zeichenglossar. See rev art by Vitali Rubin in **TP** 59 (1973) 68-78. Engl tsl by Michael Shaw, **China and the search for happiness,** ny (1976) 502 p.

Bazin, Antoine P.L. Recherches sur l'origine, l'histoire et la constitution des ordres religieux dans l'empire chinois. **JA** 5e sér, t 8 (août 1856) 105-174.

Beal, Samuel. The buddhist inscription at keu-yung-kwan. **IA** 9 (1880) 195-196.

Beal, Samuel. Early buddhist missionaries in china. **Academy** 33 (28 jan 1888) 65.

Bechert, Heinz. Staatsreligion in den buddhistischen ländern. **IAF** 2.2 (apr 1971) See sec 3, China, 174-175.

Berval, René de. l'Expansion du bouddhisme en asie. **FA:BPB** (1959) 685-693.

Blofeld, John. Lamaism and its influence on chinese buddhism. **THM** 7 (1938) 151-160.

Bloom, Alfred. The sense of sin and guilt and the last age (mappo) in chinese and japanese buddhism. **Numen** 14 (1967) 144-149.

Bose, Phanindra Nath. **The indian teachers in china.** Triplicane, madras (1923) 148 p.

Brandauer, Frederick P. The encounter between christianity and chinese buddhism from the fourteenth century through the twentieth century. **CF** 11.3 (1968) 30-38.

Brandt, Philip. Buddhism in china. pt 1, The early stages, **Echo** 4.2 (feb 1974) 16-20, 52, map; pt 2, Gentry buddhism, **ibid** 4.3 (mar 1974) 19-23, 56-58, illus; pt 3, The north south split, **ibid** 4.5 (may 1974) 37-40, 52-55; pt 4, The tang dynasty, **ibid** 4.7 (july-aug 1974) 33-36.

Bras, Gabriel le. Quelques problèmes sociologiques de l'histoire du bouddhisme. **Archives de sociologie des religions** 11.21 (jan-juin 1966) 119-124.

Brough, John. Gândhârâ, shan-shan, and early chinese buddhist translations. **Tôhôgaku** 32 (1966) 164-172.

Carter, Thomas F. **The invention of printing in china and its spread westward.** Columbia univ (1925) rev ed (1931) 3rd rev ed (1955) See esp chap 4, The dynamic force that created the demand for printing, the advance of buddhism; chap 6, The beginnings of block printing in the buddhist monasteries of china; chap 8, The first printed book. The diamond sutra of 868.

Chan, David B. The role of the monk tao-yen in the usurpation of the prince of yen (1398-1402) **Sinologica** 6.2 (1959) 83-100.

Chan, Hok-lam. The white lotus-maitreya doctrine and popular uprisings in ming and ch'ing china. **Sinologica** 10.4 (1969) 211-233.

Chan, Wing-tsit. Transformation of buddhism in china. **PEW** 7.3/4 (oct 1957-jan 1958) 17-116. Repr in Charles K.H. Chen (ed) **Neo-confucianism, etc.: essays by Wing-tsit Chan,** hong kong (1969) 422-437.

Chan, Wing-tsit. Wang yang-ming's criticism of buddhism. In **WPDMD** (1968) 31-37.

Châu, Thích-minh. Some chinese contributions to buddhism. **MB** 69 (1961) 113-117.

Chavannes, Édouard. Communication sur l'inscription de kiu-yong koan. **Actes 10e ICO Geneva, 1894,** 5e sec, Leiden (1897) 89-93.

Chavannes, Édouard. Inscriptions et pièces de chancellerie chinoises de l'époque mongole. **TP** n.s. 5 (1904) 366-404. Documents dealing with controversy between buddhists and taoists.

Chavannes, Édouard. Les pays d'occident d'après le wei lio. **TP** n.s. 6 (1905) 519-571. Re intro of buddhism into china. See rev by P. Pelliot in **BEFEO** 6 (1906) 361-400; he also discusses various aspects of han buddhism.

Chavannes, Édouard. Le sûtra de la pario occidentale de l'inscription de kiu-yong-koan. In **Mélanges charles de harlez,** leiden (1869) 60-81.

Chavannes, Édouard et Sylvain Lévi. Note préliminaire sur l'inscription de kiu-yong koan. Première partie, Les inscriptions chinoises et mongoles, par E.C. Deuxième partie. Les inscriptions tibétaines, par S.L. **JA** 9e sér, 4 (sept-oct 1894) 354-373.

Ch'en, Kenneth K.S. Anti-buddhist propaganda during the nan-ch'ao. **HJAS** 15 (1952) 166-192.

Ch'en, Kenneth K.S. **Buddhism in china. A historical survey.** Princeton univ (1964) 560 p, bibliog, gloss, list of chin names, index.

Ch'en, Kenneth K.S. The buddhist contributions in neo-confucianism and taoism. In **TC** (1970) 155-160 (Excerpt from author's **Buddhism in china** q.v. 471-476).

Ch'en, Kenneth K.S. Buddhist-taoist mixtures in the pa-shih-i-hua t'u. **HJAS** 9 (1945) 1-12.

Ch'en, Kenneth K.S. Chinese communist attitudes towards buddhism in chinese history. **CQ** 22 (1965) 14-30; repr in Albert Feuerwerker (ed) **History in communist china,** MIT (1968) 158-174.

Ch'en, Kenneth K.S. **The chinese transformation of buddhism.** Princeton univ (1973) 345 p, bibliog, gloss, index. Mostly on budd and chin culture during t'ang dyn.

Ch'en, Kenneth K.S. Economic background of the hui-ch'ang persecution. **HJAS** 19 (1956) 67-105.

Ch'en, Kenneth K.S. Inscribed stelae during the wei, chin, and nan-ch'ao. In **StAs** (1975) 75-84.

Ch'en, Kenneth K.S. Neo-taoism and the prajñā school during the wei and chin dynasties. **CC** 1 (oct 1957) 33-46, bibliog.

Ch'en, Kenneth K.S. On some factors responsible for the anti-buddhist persecution under the pei-ch'ao. **HJAS** 17.1/2 (1954) 261-273.

Ch'en, Kenneth K.S. The role of buddhist monasteries in t'ang society. **HR** 15.3 (feb 1976) 209-230.

Ch'en, Kenneth K.S. The sale of monk certificates during the sung dynasty. **HTR** 49.4 (1956) 307-327.

Chia Chung-yao. The church-state conflict in the t'ang dynasty. In E-tu Zen Sun and John DeFrancis (ed) **Chinese social history; translations of selected studies,** washington d.c. (1956) 197-206. Art largely excerpted from diary of japanese monk ennin.

China institute. Ancient cultural contacts between china and india. **China institute bulletin** 6 (mar-apr 1942) 4-8, map.

Chou, Hsiang-kuang. **A history of chinese buddhism.** Allahabad (1955) 264 p.

Chuan, T.K. Some notes on kao seng chuan. **THM** 7 (1938) 452-468.

Clemen, K. Christliche einflüsse auf den chinesischen und japanischen buddhismus. **OZ** 9 (1920-22) 10-37, 185-200.

Conrady, August. Indisches einfluss in china im 4. jahrhundert v. chr. **ZDMG** 60 (1906) 335-351.

Conze, Edward. **A short history of buddhism.** London (1980) Orig publ as Buddhismo, in G. Tucci (ed) **Le civilta dell'oriente;** engl text publ bombay (1960) See chap 2 sec 7; chap 3 sec 6; chap 4 sec 5.

Cutts, Elmer H. Chinese-indian contacts prior to the latter half of the first century. **IHQ** 14 (1938) 486-502.

Daudin, Pierre. l'Idéalisme bouddhique chez wang wei. **BSEIS** 43.2 (1968) 1-152.

Davidson, J. LeRoy. Buddhist paradise cults in sixth century china. **JISOA** 17 (1949) 112-124.

Demiéville, Paul. A propos du concile de vaiśāti. **TP** 40 (1951) 239-296. Review Art.

Demiéville, Paul. Le bouddhisme sous les t'ang. **ACF** 52 (1952) 212-215; 53 (1953) 218-221. See also same title in **AC** t 1 (1959) 171-175.

Demiéville, Paul. **Le concile de lhasa. Une controverse sur le quiétisme entre bouddhistes de l'inde et de la chine au VIII-ème siècle de l'ère chrétien.** Paris (1952) viii + 398 p, facs.

Demiéville, Paul. l'Iconoclasme anti-bouddhique en chine. In **Mélanges d'histoire des religions offerts à henri-charles puech,** paris (1974) 17-25.

Demiéville, Paul. l'Origine des sectes bouddhiques d'après paramārtha. **MCB** 1 (1931-32) 15-64. Repr **CEB** (1973)

Dixon, Stanley H. Buddha or christ for china? **TheE&TheW** 23 (1925) 319-336. In part treats hist of chin budd.

Donner, Neal. The mahāyānization of the chinese dhyāna tradition. **EB** n.s. 10.2 (oct 1977) 49-64.

Drake, F.S. The shên-t'ung monastery and the beginning of buddhism in shantung. **MS** 4 (1939-40) 1-39.

Dubs, Homer H. The 'golden man' of former han times. **TP** 33 (1937) 1-14. See also idem, Post-script to dubs, The golden idol of former han times, in **ibid** 191-192.

Dubs, Homer H. Han yü and the buddha's relic: an episode in medieval chinese religion. **RofR** 9.1 (1946) 5-17.

Dutt, S. Migrations of buddhism over asia. In **Studies in asian history** (Proceedings of the asian history congress, new delhi, 1961) london (1969) 40-44.

Duyvendak, J.J.L. The dreams of the emperor hsüan-tsung. In **India antiqua** (1947) 102-108.

Eberhard, Wolfram. Die buddhistische kirche in der toba-zeit [Université d'ankara] **Revue de la faculté de langues, d'histoire et de géographie** 4 (1946) 308-311.

Edkins, Joseph. **The early spread of religious ideas especially in the far east.** Oxford (1893) 144 p.

Edkins, J. Religious persecution in china. **ChRec** 15.6 (nov-dec 1884) 433-444. Brief historical survey.

Eichhorn, W. (tsl) **Ch'ing-yüan t'iao-fa shih-lei. Beitrag zur rechtlichen stellung des buddhismus und taoismus in sung-staat. Übersetzung der secktion taoismus und buddhismus aus dem ch'ing yüan t'iao-fa shih-lei (ch. 50 und 51). Mit original text in faksimile.** Leiden (1968) 178 p.

Eliot, Charles. **Hinduism and buddhism. An historical sketch.** London (1921) repr (1954) 3 vol. See vol 2, bk 4: The mahayana; vol 3, chap 41-46.

Eliot, Charles. **Japanese buddhism.** London (1935) repr ny (1959) See chap 5, Buddhism in china, 142-176.

Farquhar, David M. Emperor as bodhisattva in the governance of the ch'ing empire. **HJAS** 38.1 (1978) 5-34.

Filliozat, Jean. Emigration of indian buddhists to indo-china c.a.d. 1200. In **Studies in asian history** (proceedings of the asian history congress, new delhi, 1961) london (1969) 45-48.

Filliozat, Jean. Le médecine indienne et l'expansion bouddhique en extrême-orient. **JA** 224 (1934) 301-307.

Finot, L. Kālidāsa in china. **IHQ** 9 (1933) 829-834.

Forte, Antonio. **Political propaganda and ideology in china at the end of the seventh century; inquiry into the nature, authors and function of the tunhuang document s. 6502 followed by an annotated translation.** Napoli, instituto universitario oriental (1976) 312 p. Re text composed by a group of budd monks to legitimate ascension to throne of empress wu chao (r. 683-707) See rev by M. Strickmann in **EB** n.s. 10.1 (may 1977) 156-160.

Franke, O. Die ausbreitung der buddhismus von indien nach turkestan und china. **ARW** 12 (1909) 207-220.

Franke, Otto. **Eine chinesische tempelinschrift au idikutšahri bei turfan (turkistan) üb. u. erklärt.** Berlin (1907) 92 s, 1 taf.

Franke, Otto. Das datum der chinesischen tempelinschrift von turfan. **TP** 2e sér, 10 (1909) 222-228.

Franke, Otto. Skt. mss. in china. **ChRev** 21 (1894) 204.

Franke, O. Taoismus und buddhismus zur zeit der trennung von nord und süd. **Sinica** 9 (1934) 89-113.

Franke, O. Zur frage der einführung des buddhismus in china. **MSOS** 13 (1910) 295-305. See rev by H. Maspero in **BEFEO** 10 (1910) 629-636.

Franke, Wolfgang. Some remarks on the "three-in-one doctrine" and its manifestations in singapore and malaysia. **OE** 19 (1972) 121-130, with tsl of 2 inscr and 10 photo pl.

Friese, Heinz. Der mönch yao kuang-hsiao . . . und seine zeit. **OE** 7.2 (1960) 158-184.

Fu, Charles Wei-hsun. Morality or beyond: the neo-confucian confrontation with mahāyāna buddhism. **PEW** 23.3 (july 1973) 375-396.

Fuchs, Walter. Zur technischen organization der übersetzungen buddhistischen schriften in chinesische. **AM** 6 (1930) 84-103.

Fujimoto ?Ryūgyō. Alleged contacts of christianity and buddhism in the t'ang dynasty. **Ryūkoku daigaku ronshū, journal of ryūkoku univ** 351 (mar 1956) 1-37.

Fukui, Fumimasa-Bunga. Buddhism and the structure of ch'ing-t'an. — A note on sino-indian intercourse. **CC** 10.2 (june 1969) 25-30.

Gard, Richard A. Why did the mādhyamika decline? **JIBS** 5.2 (1957) 10-14.

Gaspardone, E. Bonzes des ming réfugiés en annam. **Sinologica** 2 (1950) 12-30.

Gernet, Jacques. **Les aspects économiques du bouddhisme dans la société chinoise du Ve au Xe siècle.** Saigon (1956) See also rev by A.F. Wright, **JAS** 16.3 (1957) 408-414; D.C. Twitchett, **BSOAS** 19.3 (1957) 526-549; K. Ch'en, **HJAS** 20 (1957) 733-740.

Gimello, Robert M. Random reflections on the "sinicization" of buddhism. **SSCRB** 5 (spring 1978) 52-89.

Glüer, Winfried. The encounter between christianity and chinese buddhism during the nineteenth century and the first half of the twentieth century. **CF** 11.3 (1968) 39-57.

Goodrich, L. Carrington. Earliest printed editions of the tripitaka. **VBQ** ser 2 vol 19 (1953-54) 215-220.

Goodrich, L. Carrington. The revolving bookcase in china. **HJAS** 7 (1942-43) 130-161. Re invention and history of case for tripitaka.

Groot, J.J.M. de. **Sectarianism and religious persecution in china.** Amsterdam, vol 1 (1903) vol 2 (1904) repr taipei (1963) 2 vol in 1, 595 p.

Groot, J.J.M. de. Wu tsung's persecution of buddhism. **ARW** 7. (1904) 157-168.

Grünwedel, Albert. **Altbuddhistische kultstätten in chinesisch-turkistan. Bericht über archäologische arbeiten von 1906 bis 1907 bei kuća qarašahr und in der oase turfan.** Berlin (1912) 371 p.

Guelny, A. A propos d'une préface. Aperçu critique sur le bouddhisme en chine au 7e siècle. **Muséon** 13 (1894) 437-449; 14 (1895) 85.

Guignes, Joseph de. Recherches historiques sur la religion indienne, et sur les livres fondamentaux de cette religion; qui ont été traduits de l'indien en chinois. Première mémoire. Établissement de la religion indienne dans l'inde, la tartarie, le thibet & les isles. Second mémoire. Établissement de la religion indienne dans la chine, et son histoire jusqu'en 531 de jésus christ. Troisième mémoire. Suite de l'histoire de la religion indienne à la chine. **MAI** (1773-76) repr in **Histoire et mémoires AIBL** 40 (1780) 187-355.

Gundert, Wilhelm. Bodhidharma und wu-di von liang. **SJFAW** (1956) 48-66.

Haas, Hans. Ein wenig bekannter buddhistisches autor des alten china und sein werk. **Orientalische archiv** 1 (1910-11) 25-33.

Haenisch, Erich (ed and tsl) **Die viersprachige gründungsinschrift des tempels an-yüan-miao in jehol v. jahre 1765**. Wiesbaden (1951) 22 p, pl.

Haneda, A. Les conquérants tartares et le bouddhisme. **CHM** 1 (1954) 922-926.

Havret, Henri. **T'ien tchou 'seigneur de ciel.' A propos d-une stele bouddhique de tch'eng tou.**|Shanghai (1901) 30p. (Variétés sinologiques no 19) Same title in **Études** 89 (1901) 398-409, 546-553; repr nendeln (1975)

Hée, L. von. Le bouddha et les premiers missionaires en chine. **AM** 10 (1934) 365-372.

Hirano, Umeyo (tsl) Buddhism in the asuka-nara period. **EB** n.s. 7.1 (may 1974) 19-36.

Hodgson, B.H. (tsl) Introductions of buddhism in china. Translated from the 'tae-ping-kuang-ke.' **Asiatic journal and monthly register** no 5 (1831) 71.

Hodous, Lewis. The introduction of buddhism into china. In **The macdonald presentation volume,** princeton univ (1933) 223-235.

Holth, Sverre. The encounter between christianity and chinese buddhism during the nestorian period. **CF** 11.3 (1968) 20-29.

Houang, François. **Le bouddhisme de l'inde à la chine.** Paris (1963)

Hrdličková, V. The first translations of buddhist sutras in chinese literature and their place in the development of storytelling. **ArchOr** 26.1 (1958) 114-144.

Hsu, Sung-peng. **A buddhist leader in ming china: the life and thought of han-shan te-ch'ing, 1546-1623.** Penn state univ (1979) 409 p.

Hu, Shih. The indianization of china. In **Independence, convergence, and borrowing in institutions, thought and art,** harvard univ (1937) 239-246.

Huang Chia-cheng. **Le bouddhisme de l'inde à la chine.** Paris (1963) 126 p.

Hulsewé, A.F.P. Sidelights on popular buddhism in china in the fifth century. **Proc 7th ICHR Amsterdam, 1950,** amsterdam (1951) 139-141.

Hurvitz, Leon. The first systematizations of buddhist thought in china. **JCP** 2.4 (sept 1975) 361-388.

Hurvitz, Leon. 'Render unto caesar' in early chinese buddhism: hui-yüan's treatise on the exemption of the buddhist clergy from the requirements of civil etiquette. **SIS** 5.3/4 (1957) (Liebenthal festschrift) 80-114.

Hurvitz, Leon. Toward a comprehensive history of chinese buddhism. **JAOS** 89 (1969) 763-773.

Hurvitz, Leon (tsl) **Treatise on buddhism and taoism: an english translation of the original chinese text of wei-shu CXIV and the japanese annotation of tsukamoto zenryū.** Kyoto univ (1956) 25-103 p. See rev by L.S. Yang and K. Ch'en in **HJAS** 20 (1957) 362-382. See rev by Arthur E. Link, **JAOS** 78 (1958) 60-70.

I, Ying-ki. The secularization decree of emperor wu-tsung. **BCUP** 6 (1929) 119-124 (Refers to buddhists and nestorians)

Iida, Shotaro. A mukung-hwa in ch'ang-an—a study of the life and works of wonch'uk (613-696) with special interest in the korean contributions to the development of chinese and tibetan buddhism. In intl symposium commemorating the 30th anniversary of korean liberation **Proceedings,** seoul, natl acad of sciences (1975) 225-251.

Imaeda, Y. Documents tibétaine de touen-houang concernant le concile du tibet. **JA** 263.1/2 (1975) 125-146.

Imbault-Huart, Camille. Note sur l'inscription bouddhique et la passe de kiu-young-kouan près de la grande muraille. **REO** 2.4 (1884) 486-493.

Jan, Yün-hua. Buddhist historiography in sung china. **ZDMG** 114 (1964) 360-381.

Jan, Yün-hua. Buddhist relations between india and sung china. **HR** 6.1 (1966) 24-42; 6.2 (1966) 135-168.

Jan, Yün-hua. Buddhist self-immolation in medieval china. **HR** 4 (1965) 243-268.

Jan, Yün-hua. **A chronicle of buddhism in china, 581-960 a.d. Translation from monk chih-p'an's fo-tsu-t'ung-chi . . .** Santiniketan (1966) vi + 189 p + iii p.

Jan, Yün-hua. Kashmir's contribution to the expansion of buddhism in the far east. **IHQ** 37 (1961) 93-104.

Jan, Yün-hua. Some new light on kuśinagara from 'the memoir of hui-ch'ao.' **OE** 12.1 (1965) 55-63.

Kamstra, J.H. **Encounter or syncretism. The initial growth of japanese buddhism.** Leiden (1967) See chap 3.a, pt 1, China and buddhism, 142-185.

Kasugai, Shinya. The historical background of kumarajiva and his historical influence on chinese buddhism. **Philosophical quarterly** 31 (1958-59) 121-125.

Kennedy, J. The secret of kanishka. **JRAS** (1912) 665-688, 981-1019.

Kennedy, J. Sidelights on kanishka. The introduction of buddhism into china . . . **JRAS** (1913) 369-378.

Kimura, Ryūkan. **A historical study of hinayāna and mahāyāna and the origin of mahāyāna buddhism.** Calcutta univ (1927)

Kitagawa, Joseph M. Buddhism, history of. In **EncyB 3** (1974) **Macropaedia** vol 3, 402a-414b.

Kodera, Takashi James. **Dogen's formative years in china. An historical study and annotated translation of the hōkyō-ji.** London & henley (1980) xx + 257 p, chronol, tables, map, jap text.

Konow, S. Kālidāsa in china. **IHQ** 10 (1934) 566-570.

Kubo, Noritada. Prolegomena on the study of the controversies between buddhists and taoists in the yüan period. **TBMRD** 26 (1968) 39-61.

Lacouperie, Terrien de. How in 219 b.c. buddhism entered china. **BOR** 5.5 (1891) 97-105.

Lacouperie, Terrien de. The introduction of buddhism into china. **Academy** 40 (3 oct 1891) 389-390.

Lacouperie, Terrien de. The yueh-ti and the early buddhist missionaries in china. **Academy** (?) (31 dec 1897) 443-444.

Lahiri, Latika. Lung-man (sic) cave inscriptions and the popularity of maitreya bodhi sattva. In **B&J** (1976) 76-82.

Lamotte, É. Les premières missions bouddhiques en chine. **Académie royale belge bulletin, classe des lettres** 5e sér, 39 (1953) 220-231.

Lamotte, É. Sur la formation du mahāyāna. In **Asiatica** (1954) 377-396.

Lancashire, Douglas. Buddhist reaction to christianity in late ming china. **JOSA** 6.1/2 (1968-69) 82-103.

Lee, Peter H. Fa-tsang and uisang. **JAOS** 82.1 (1962) 56-59 + chin text 60-62.

Lévi, S. Les missions de wang hiuen ts'e dans l'inde. **JA** 9e sér, 15 (1900) 401-468. Re introduction of buddhism into china.

Lévi, Sylvain et Édouard Chavannes. Quelques titres énigmatiques dans la hiérarchie ecclésiastique du bouddhisme indien. **JA** 9e sér, 5 (1915) 193-223. Add et rectifications in **ibid** 6 (1915) 307-310.

Lévi, Sylvain et Édouard Chavannes. Les seize arhat protecteurs de la loi. **JA** 11e sér, 8 (juil-août 1916) 5-50; **ibid** (sept-oct 1916) 189-304.

Lewy, Guenter. Religion and revolution and the major traditions—(chinese) buddhism. In chap 2 of author's **R&Rev** (1974) 29-32.

Li, Dun J. (tsl) Wei shou, buddhism during the north wei. Chap 4 no 21 in tsl's anthol, **The civilization of china from the formative period to the coming of the west,** ny (1975) 134-143.

Li, Jung-hsi. The stone scriptures of fang-shan. **EB** n.s. 12.1 (may 1979) 104-113. Re 15,143 slabs stored in cave in fang-shan county, 75 kilometers southwest of peking; engraved betw 605/618-1621/1627.

Liang, Ch'i-ch'ao. **China's debt to buddhist india.** N.Y. (?1927) 15 p. With a biographical note by Herbert A. Giles.

Liebenthal, Walter. Chinese buddhism during the fourth and fifth centuries. **MN** 11.1 (1955) 44-83.

Liebenthal, Walter. **Sanskrit inscriptions from yünnan, and the dates of the foundation of the main pagodas in the province.** Peiping (1947) 40 p. See author's art, Sanskrit inscriptions from yünnan, **SIS** 5 (1955) 46-48.

Liebenthal, Walter, Shih hui-yüan's buddhism as set forth in his writings. **JAOS** 70 (1950) 243-259.

Link, Arthur E. Cheng-wu lun: the rectification of unjustified criticism. **OE** 8.2 (dec 1961) 136-165.

Link, Arthur E. Evidence for doctrinal continuity of han buddhism from the second through the fourth centuries: the prefaces to an shih-kao's grand sūtra on mindfulness of the respiration and k'ang seng-hui's introduction to "the perfection of dhyāna" In James B. Parsons (ed) **Papers in honor of professor woodbridge bingham: a festschrift for his seventy-fifth birthday,** san francisco (1976) 55-126.

Link, Arthur E. The earliest chinese account of the compilation of the tripiṭaka. **JAOS** 81 (1961) (I) 87-103; (II) 281-299.

Link, Arthur E. Professor tang yong-torng's 'various traditions concerning the entry of buddhism into china.' **PTA** 4 (1953) 31-93.

Link, Arthur E. Shih seng-yu and his writings. **JAOS** 80 (1960) 17-43.

Link, Arthur E. Shyh daw-an's preface to sangharakṣa's yogācarabhūmi-sūtra and the problem of buddho-taoist terminology in early chinese buddhism. **JAOS** 77 (1957) 1-14.

Link, Arthur E. and Tim Lee. Sun cho's yü-tao-lun: a clarification of the way. **MS** 25 (1966) 169-196.

Liu, Ts'un-yan. Lu hsi-hsing: a confucian scholar, taoist priest and buddhist devotee of the sixteenth century. **AS** 18/19 (1965) 115-142; repr in **LTY:SP** (1976)

Liu, Mau-tsai. **Kutscha und seine beziehungen zu china vom 2.jh v. bis zum 6.jh n.chr.** Wiesbaden (1969) See esp teil 1, b.2, Kutscha und der buddhismus in china, 77-99; t. 2, b, Nachrichten aus buddhisten quellen, 173-199.

Lo, Hsiang-lin. Sino-indian relations over the chiao-kwang route and new discoveries on buddhism and its art in the kwangtung-kwangsi areas in the tang dynasty. **CC** 1.3 (1958) 181-203.

MacGowan, D.J. An inscription from a tablet in a buddhist monastery at ningpo in china. **JRASB** 13 (1844) 113-114, pl.

Maejima, Shinji. The travels of a japanese buddhist priest in 13th century to yüan china. **JSR:HS** 10 (1959) 97-101.

Masaki, Haruhiko. The practice of buddhist austerities and its popularization in shan-tao and prince shotoku — in connection with śrīmālā and vaidehī. **JIBS** 16.2 (1968) 943-955.

Maspero, Henri. Comment le bouddhisme s'est introduit en chine. In author's **HMRC** Paris (1950) 195-211.

Maspero, Henri. Communautés et moines bouddhistes chinois au IIe et IIIe siècles. **BEFEO** 10 (janv-mars 1910) 222-286.

Maspero, Henri. Les origines de la communauté bouddhique de loyang. **JA** 225 (1934) 87-107.

Maspero, Henri. Le songe et l'ambassade de l'empereur ming. Étude critique des sources. **BEFEO** 10 (1910) 95-130.

Maspero, Henri. Report sommaire sur une mission archéologique au tchö-kiang. **BEFEO** 14 (1914) 1-75, 21 pl. Mostly re budd relics in chekiang.

Masunaga, Reiho. The place of dōgen in zen buddhism. In **RSJ** (1959) 339-349.

Mather, Richard. The conflict of buddhism with native chinese ideologies. **RofR** 20 (1955-56) 25-37; repr in **CWayRel** (1973) 77-86.

Mather, Richard B. Vimalakīrti and gentry buddhism. **HR** 8 (1968) 60-73.

Matsunaga, Yukei. A history of tantric buddhism in india with reference to chinese translations. In **BT&AC** (1977) 167-181.

Mayers, William Frederick. Chinese views respecting the date of introduction of buddhism. **NQ** 1 (1867) 52.

Meunié, Jacques. Le couvent des otages chinois de kanīska au kāpiśa. **JA** 234 (1943-45) 151-162.

Michihata, Ryoshu. A study of chinese buddhism in t'ang dynasty. **JSR:HS** 10 (1959) 54-56.

Modi, J.J. An iranian prince of the parthian dynasty as the first promulgator of buddhism in china. In **Jha commemoration volume,** poona (1937) 249-258.

Moule, A.C. Relics of the monk sakugen's visits to china 1539-1541 and 1547-1550. **AM** 3.1 (1952) 59-64.

Mukherjee, Probhat Kumar [Mukhopādhyāya, Prabhātā-Kumārā] **Indian literature abroad (china)** Calcutta (1928) 98 p.

Mukherjee, Probhat K. [Mukhopādhyāya, Prabhātā-Kumārā] **Indian literature in china and the far east.** Calcutta (pref 1931) iv + 2 + 334 + 18 + 4.

Mukhopādhyāya, Sujit. Sino-indian relations of old. **SIJ** 1 (july 1947) 77-94.

Murata, J. (ed) **Chü-yung-kuan. The buddhist arch of the 14th century a.d. at the pass of the great wall northwest of peking.** Kyoto (1958) 2 vol, 360 p, 110 pl, 34 illus, 4 charts. Text in 6 languages: sanskrit, tibetan, mongol, uighur, hsi-hsia, chin, and synopsis in engl.

Nakamura, Hajime. The transformation of buddhism in china. **East** 10.9 (nov 1974) 54-56, 59.

Needham, Joseph. Buddhism and chinese science. In Louis Schneider (ed) **Religion, culture and society,** n.y. etc (1964) 353-358. Excerpted from Needham's **Science and civilization in china,** cambridge univ, vol 2 (1956) 417-422, 430-431.

Niset, J. Bhiksu shih tao-an, la doctrine du bouddha et les droits de l'homme. **RDH** 10.1/2 (1979) 5-13.

Ohashi, Kaishun. Die spuren des buddhismus in china vor kaiser ming. **EB** 6 (1934) 247-278, 432-477; 7 (1937) 214-226.

Olschki, L. Manichaeism, buddhism and christianity in marco polo's china. **AS** 5 (1951) 1-21.

Orlando, Raffaello. Buddhism in the t'ang-hui-yao. **Annali della faculta di lingue & litterature straniere di ca'foscari,** venice 14.3 (1975) 265-276.

Overmyer, Daniel L. Folk-buddhist religion: creation and eschatology in medieval china. **HR** 12.1 (aug 1972) 42-70.

Overmyer, Daniel L. **Folk buddhist religion. Dissenting sects in late traditional china.**. Harvard univ (1976) xi + 295 p, notes, bibliog, gloss, index.

Pachow, W. Ancient cultural relations between ceylon and china. Repr in author's **ChBudd** (1980) 197-212; orig publ not stated.

Pachow, W. Buddhism and its relation to chinese religions. Repr in author's **ChBudd** (1980) 87-99; orig publ not stated.

Pachow, W. Development of tripitaka-translations in china. Repr in author's **ChBudd** (1980) 101-115; orig publ not stated.

Pachow, W. The voyage of buddhist missions to southeast asia and the far east. Repr in author's **ChBudd** (1980) 213-240; orig publ not stated.

Palatin, W. von. Kaiser t'ai-tsung's edikt gegen die bonzen und ihre klöster. **FO** 2 (1903) 181-183.

Pardue, Peter A. **Buddhism. A historical introduction to buddhist values and the social and political forms they have assumed in asia.** NY & london (1968) See chap 2, China, 53-80.

Parker, E.H. Early buddhism in china. **ChRec** 25 (1894) 224-234, 282-288, 343-347.

Parker, E.H. Notes on the history of buddhism in china. **JNCBRAS** 37 (1906) 198.

Paul, Diana. Empress wu and the historians: a tyrant and saint of classical china. In **VW** (1980) 191-206.

Pelliot, Paul. Deux titres bouddhiques portés par les religieux nestoriens. **TP** 2e sér, 12 (1911) 664-670.

Pelliot, Paul. Les kouo-che ou 'maîtres du royaume' dans le bouddhisme chinois. **TP** 2e sér, 12 (1911) 671-676.

Pelliot, Paul (tsl) Meou-tseu, ou les doutes levés. **TP** 19 (1918-19) 255-433. See rev by L. Aurousseau, **BEFEO** 22 (1922) 276-298.

Pelliot, Paul. Les mo-ni et le houa-hou-king. **BEFEO** 3 (1903) 318-378.

Pelliot, Paul. La secte du lotus blanc et la secte du nuage blanc. **BEFEO** 3.2 (1903) 304-317. See further, Notes additionelles sur . . . **ibid** 4 (1904) 436-440.

Pillai, A. Balakrishna. The 'kalpa' chronology in ancient china. **SIJ** 1 (july 1947) 117-146.

Piton, Charles. Der buddhismus in china und was wir von ihm für die christ. missionstätigkeit lernen können. **AMZ** 19 (1892) 118-126.

Pokora, Timoteus. An important crossroad of the chinese thought. **ArchOr** 29.1 (1961) 64-76. Re intro of buddhism.

Rachewiltz, Igor de. The hsi-yu lu by yeh-lü ch'u-ts'ai. **MS** 21 (1962) 1-128. Re controversy betw buddhists and taoists in yüan times.

Raguin, Yves E. Father ricci's presentation of some fundamental theories of buddhism. **CC** 10.1 (mar 1969) 37-43.

Reischauer, Edwin O. (tsl) **Ennin's diary. The record of a pilgrimage to china in search of the law.** N.Y. (1955) xvi + 454 p, character gloss, index, end-paper maps.

Reischauer, Edwin O. **Ennin's travels in t'ang china.** N.Y. (1955) xii + 341 p, notes, index, end-paper maps.

Rhie, Marylin M. **The fo-kuang ssu: literary evidences and buddhist images.** NY (1977) 274 p.

Runyan, Mary Edith. Beginning and spread of buddhism in china to the t'ang dynasty. **CCJ** 11.2 (oct 1972) 30-40.

Saha Kshanika. Some buddhist monks of central asian china. **MB** 77 (oct 1969) 341-342.

Sargent, G.E. The intellectual atmosphere in lingan at the time of the introduction of buddhism. In **HKS** (1967) 161-171.

Sargent, Galen E. **Tchou hi contre le bouddhisme.** Paris (1955) 158 p.

Sato, Chisui. The character of yün-kang buddhism. A look at the emergence of a state-supported religion in china under the northern wei. **TBMRD** 36 (1978) 39-83.

Saunders, Kenneth J. Buddhism in china — a historical sketch. **JR** 3 (1923) 157-169, 256-275.

Schlegel, G. Names of the 33 first buddhist patriarchs. **TP** 8.3 (1897) 341-342.

Schmidt-Glintzer, Helwig. Der buddhismus im frühen chinesischen mittelalter und der wandel der lebensführung bei der gentry im süden. **Saeculum** 23.3 (1972) 269-294.

Schmidt-Glintzer, Helwig. **Das hung-ming chi und die aufnahme des buddhismus in china.** Wiesbaden (1976) viii + 212 s.

Schubert J. Die viersprachige inschrift des buddhistischen klosters fa lun szü in mukden (im originaltext herausgegeben, übersetzt und erläutert) **AA** 5 (1935) 71-75, 251-255.

Seu, Kshtiti Mohan. India and china. Their union through buddhism. **VBQ** n.s. 1 (1935-36) 35-45.

Shih, Robert (tsl and annot) **Biographies des moines éminents (kao seng tchouan) de houei-kiao. Première partie: Biographies des premiers traducteurs.** Louvain (1968) xi + 177 p, followed by chin text.

Staël-Holstein, A.A. von. The emperor ch'ienlung and the larger śūraṅgama-sūtra. **HJAS** 1 (1936) 136-146.

Steininger, Hans. Der buddhismus in der chinesischen geschichte (zu den arbeiten von E. Zurcher, J. Gernet und A. F. Wright). **Saeculum** 13.2 (1962) 132-165.

Stevenson, J. Buddhist antiquities in china. **JBBRAS** 5 (1855) 408 et seq.

Suzuki, D.T. The recovery of a lost ms. on the history of zen in china. **EB** 6.1 (apr 1932) 107-110.

Tai-hü. Buddhistische studien. Der buddhismus in geschichte und gegenwort. **Sinica** 3 (1928) 189-196.

Takakusu, Junjirō. A study of chinese inscriptions. 1. Notes on the earliest chinese inscription found at buddhagayâ in india. **HZ** 12.5 (1897) 20-29.

Takakusu, Junjirō (tsl) Le voyage de kanshin en orient 742-754, par aomi-no mabito genkai, 779. **BEFEO** 28 (1928) 1-41, 441-472; 29 (1929) 47-62.

Tan, Chung. Ageless neighborliness between india and china: historical perspective and future prospects. **China report,** delhi, 15.1 (jan-feb 1979) 3-37.

Thiel, Joseph. Der streit der buddhisten und taoisten zur mongolenzeit. **MS** 20 (1961) 1-81.

Thomas, F.W. Three letters from buddhist kings to the chinese court in the fifth century. **JRAS** (1933) 897-905.

Todo, Kyoshun. The critical views, or the sense of uneasiness, in chinese buddhism and their relief — especially in the first half of the 6th century a.d. **JIBS** 10 (mar 1962) 1-6.

Tsukamoto, Zenryū. The buddha-image made by king udayana in china and japan. In **RSJ** (1959) 359-367.

Tsukamoto, Zenryū. The dates of kumārajīva and seng-chao re-examined. In **SJV** (1954) 568-584.

Tsukamoto, Zenryū. The early stages in the introduction of buddhism into china. **CHM** 5.3 (1960) 546-572.

Tucci, Giuseppe. A tibetan history of buddhism in china. In **Eduard erkes in memoriam 1891-1958,** leipzig (1962) 230.

Twitchett, D.C. The monasteries and china's economy in medieval times. **BSOAS** 19 (1957) 526-549.

Twitchett, D.C. Monastic estates in t'ang china. **AM** n.s. 5 (1956) 123-146.

Vandier-Nicolas, Nicole. Les échanges entre le bouddhisme et le taoïsme des han aux t'ang. In **AC** t 1 (1959) 166-170.

Wada, Sei. On the date of the spread of buddhism to the east. **TBMRD** 36 (1978) 27-38. Re intro of budd into china.

Wagner, Rudolf G. The original structure of the correspondence between shih hui-yüan and kumārajīva. **HJAS** 31 (1971) 28-48. Re taisho tripitaka no 1856.

Waley, Arthur. Did buddha die of eating pork? With a note on buddha's image. **MCB** 1 (1931-32) 343-354.

Waley, Arthur. New light on buddhism in medieval india. **MCB** 1 (1931-32) 355-376.

Walle, W. van de. Lay buddhism among the chinese aristocracy during the period of the southern dynasties. Hsiao tzu-liang (460-494) and his entourage. Leuven, belge, **Orientalia lovaniensia periodica** 10 (1979) 275-297.

Ware, James R. Once more the 'golden man.' **TP** 34 (1938) 174-178.

Ware, James R. (tsl) Wei shou on buddhism. **TP** 30 (1933) 100-181.

Watters, Thomas. Buddhism in china. **ChRec** 2 (1869) 1-6, 38-43, 64-68, 81-88, 117-122, 145-150.

Weinstein, Stanley. Imperial patronage in the formation of t'ang buddhism. In Arthur F. Wright & Denis Twitchett (ed) **Perspectives on the t'ang,** yale univ (1973) 265-306.

Weller, F. Die überlieferung des älteren buddhistischen schrifttums. **AM** 5 (1930) 149-182.

Whitehead, James D. The "sinicization" of the vimalakīrti-nirdeśa sūtra. **SSCRB** 5 (spring 1978) 3-51.

Witte, Johannes. **Das buch des marco polo als quelle für den buddhismus.** Berlin (1915) 71 p.

Wittfogel, Karl A. and Fêng Chia-shêng. **History of chinese society: liao.** Philadelphia (1949) See 291-309 on buddhism.

Wittfogel, Karl A. and Fêng Chia-shêng. Religion under the liao dynasty, 907-1125. **RofR** 12 (1948) 355-374.

Wright, Arthur F. **Buddhism in chinese history.** Stanford univ (1959) 144 p, selection of further readings, index, illus.

Wright, Arthur F. Domestication of buddhism in china. In Chang, Chun-shu (ed) **The making of modern china,** englewood cliffs, n.j. (1975) 159-170.

Wright, Arthur F. The economic role of buddhism in china. **JAS** 16 (1957) 408-414. A rev art on J. Gernet's **Les aspects économiques du bouddhisme . . .** q.v.

Wright, Arthur F. The formation of sui ideology In **CTI** (1957) 71-104.

Wright, Arthur F. Fu i and the rejection of buddhism. **JHI** 12 (1951) 33-47.

Wright, Arthur F. Hui-chiao as a chinese historian. **JIBS** 3.1 (1954) 1-6.

Wright, Arthur F. T'ang t'ai-tsung and buddhism. In Arthur F. Wright & Denis Twitchett (ed) **Perspectives on the t'ang,** yale univ (1973) 239-263.

Wu, K.T. Chinese printing under four alien dynasties. **HJAS** 13 (1950) 451-457, 515-516. Re buddhist texts.

Wylie, Alexander. On an ancient buddhist inscription at keu-yung-kwan, in north china. **JNCBRAS** 5 (1870) 14-44.

Wylie, Alexander. Remarks on some impressions from a lapidary inscription at keu-yung kwan on the great wall near peking. **JNCBRAS** n.s. 1 (1864) 133-136, 163-166.

Yamazake, Hiroshi. The study on buddhist policy of the sui dynasty. **JSR:LPH** 4 (1953) 231-233.

Yang, Lien-sheng. Buddhist monasteries and four money-raising institutions in chinese history. **HJAS** 13 (1950) 174-191. Repr in author's collection, **Studies in chinese institutional history,** cambridge, mass. (1963) 198-215.

Yang, Ming-che. China reinterprets buddhism. **FCR** 18 (dec 1968) 27-32.

Ying Ignatius. The secularization decree of wu tsung. **BCUP** 6 (1931) 119-124.

Yu, David C. Skill in means and the buddhism of tao-sheng: a study of a chinese reaction to mahāyāna of the fifth century. **PEW** 24.4 (oct 1974) 413-427.

Zach, E. von. Einige bemerkungen zur tempelinschrift von idikutśahri (im museum für völkerkunde, berlin) **AM** 2 (1925) 345-347. Re inscription in maitreya temple, turfan.

Zeuschner, Robert. The meaning of hīnayāna in northern ch'an. **EB** n.s. 8.2 (oct 1975) 37-49.

Zürcher, Erik. **The buddhist conquest of china. The spread and adaptation of buddhism in early medieval china.** Leiden (1959) vol 1: Text; vol 2: Notes, bibliog, indexes. Repr (1972) with add and corr.

Zürcher, Erik. Zum verhältnis von kirche und staat in china während der frühzeit des buddhismus. **Saeculum** 10 (1959) 73-81.

7. SCHOOLS (EXCEPT CH'AN)

Andrews, Allan A. Nembutsu in the chinese pure land tradition. **EB** n.s. 3.2 (oct 1970) 20-45.

Andrews, Allan A. **The teachings essential for rebirth. A study of genshin's ōjōyōshū.** Tokyo (1973) See chap 1, The beginning of nembutsu and its development in china, 1-29.

Armstrong, R.C. The doctrine of the tendai school. **EB** 3 (1924) 32-54.

Bandō, Shōjun. Shinran's indebtedness to t'an-luan. **SCR** 5.4 (autumn 1971) 221-234. Same title in **EB** n.s. 4.1 (may 1971) 72-87.

Blofeld, John. **Beyond the gods. Buddhist and taoist mysticism.** London and ny (1974) 164 p, short gloss.

Blofeld, John Calthorpe. Lamaism and its influence on chinese buddhism. **THM** 7.2 (1938) 151-160, photos.

Bloom, Alfred. **Shinran's gospel of pure grace.** Univ arizona (1965) On chin pure land patriarchs see 7-17.

The Book of tao. A brief outline of the esoteric schools of buddhist [sic] and tao in china. Theosophical publ house, adyar (1933) 24 p.

Chang, Garma C.C. **The buddhist teaching of totality. The philosophy of hwa yen buddhism.** Penn state univ (1971) xxv + 270 p, list of chin terms, gloss, index.

Chou, Yi-liang. Tantrism in china. **HJAS** 8 (1945) 241-332.

Cook, Francis. Causation in the chinese hua-yen tradition. **JCP** 6.4 (dec 1979) 367-385.

Cook, Francis H. **Hua-yen buddhism. The jewel net of indra.** Penn state univ (1977) xiv + 146 p, notes, gloss, index.

Cook, Francis H. The meaning of vairocana in huayen buddhism. **PEW** 22.4 (1972) 403-415.

Corless, Roger G. Monotheistic elements in early pure land buddhism. **Religion** 6.2 (1976) 176-189.

Demiéville, Paul. l'Origine des sectes bouddhiques d'après paramārtha. **MCB** 1 (1931-32) 15-64. Repr **CEB** (1973)

Dutt, S. The ten schools of chinese buddhism. In **HPEW** (1952) vol 1, 590-595.

Edkins, Joseph. Notice of the wu-wei-kiau . . . a reformed buddhist sect. **Trans China Branch RAS** 6 (1858) 63-69.

Eracle, J. **La doctrine bouddhique de la terre pure. Introduction à trois sūtras bouddhiques.** Paris (1973) 117 p.

Fujiwara, Ryosetsu. The conception of the nembutsu in shan-tao's pure land buddhism. **RDR** 394 (dec 1970) 69-94.

Fujiwara, Ryosetsu. The nembutsu. Its origin and development. **RDR** 383 (mar 1967) 28-54.

Fujiwara, Ryosetsu. Shan-tao's influence on later pure land buddhism. **RDR** 400/401 (mar 1973) 12-33.

Hackmann, Heinrich. Die schulen des chinesischen buddhismus. **MSOS** 14.1 (1912) 232-266.

Hakeda, Yoshito S. (tsl) **Kūkai; major works; translated, with an account of his life and a study of his thought.** Columbia univ (1972) See chap 4, Encounter with master hui-kuo, 29-33; also pt 3, Major works of kūkai, passim.

Hall, David A. The question of the 'left hand' path in china and japan. **YE** n.s. 4.1 (winter 1978) 19-29. Re tantrism.

Harlez, Charles de. The buddhist schools. **Dublin review** no 105, 3rd ser, vol. 22 (july 1889) 47-71. See also author's art, Les écoles bouddhistes, in **Science catholique** 5 (mai-juil 1890)

Hsüan-hua. BTTSoc (tsl) **Buddha root farm.** San francisco (1976) 72 p. Meditation by recitation of name of amitabha.

Hsüan-hua. BTTSoc (tsl) **Listen to yourself think it over.** San francisco (1978) Meditation instructions on name of kuan-yin and ch'an.

Hsüan-hua. BTTSoc (tsl) **Pure land and ch'an dharma talks.** San francisco (1972) 72 p.

Hurvitz, Leon. Chu-hung's one mind of pure land and ch'an buddhism. In **SSMT** (1970) 451-482.

Ingram, Paul O. **The dharma of faith: an introduction to classical pure land buddhism.** Univ press of america (1977) See chap 2, The chinese tradition, 22-44.

Ingram, Paul O. The symbolism of light and pure land buddhist soteriology. **Japan journal of religious studies** 1.4 (dec 1974) 331-344.

Julien, Stanislas. Listes diverses des noms des dix-huit écoles schismatiques qui sont sorties du bouddhisme. **JA** 5e sér, 14 (1859) 327-361.

King, Winston L. Hua-yen mutual interpenetrative identity and whitehead organic relation. **JCP** 6.4 (dec 1979) 387-410.

Lai, Whalen. The i-ching and the formation of the hua-yen philosophy. **JCP** 7.3 (sept 1980) 245-258.

Liebenthal, Walter. The world conception of chu tao-sheng. **MN** 12.1/2 (1956) 65-103; 12.3/4 (1957) 241-268.

Lo, Hsiang-lin. Transmission of the she-lun school of buddhism. **JOS** 1 (1954) 313-326.

Luk, Charles (Lu K'uan-yü) **The secrets of chinese meditation.** London (1964) 240 p. Self-cultivation according to several buddhist as well as taoist schools.

Miyuki, Mokusen. Chinese response to buddhism: the case of hua-yen buddhism. In **StAs** (1975) 221-260.

Nakamura, Hajime. The kegon sect of buddhism and its influence on asian cultures. **East** 11.1 (jan 1975) 15-18.

Oh, Kang-nam. Dharmadhātu—an introduction to hua-yen buddhism. **EB** n.s. 12.2 (oct 1979) 72-91.

Okakura, Kakuzo (tsl) Chi ki (chik i) [sic] i.e. founder of japanese tendai: chisho daishi: on the method of practising concentration and contemplation. Pref note by William Sturgis Bigelow. **HTR** 16.2 (1923) 109-141.

Ono, G. A note on tz'u-min's works and some points of his religious teaching. **PIAJ** 2.8 (1926) 361-363. Ching-t'u school.

Ono, Gemmyō. On the pure land doctrine of tz'u-min. **EB** 5 (1930) 200-213.

Pas, Julian. Shan-tao's interpretation of the meditative vision of buddha amitāyus. **HR** 14.2 (nov 1974) 96-116, gloss.

Petzold, Bruno. The chinese tendai teachings. **EB** 4 (1927-28) 299-347.

Petzold, Bruno. Tendai buddhism as modern world-view (chinese tendai) **YE** 4 (oct 1929) 281-304.

Robert, Jean-Noël. La secte bouddhique ten-dai (t'ien-t'ai) **Samadhi** 6.2 (apr-june 1972) 56-74.

Robinson, Richard H. **Early mādhyamika in india and china.** Univ wisconsin (1967) 347 p, documents, notes, bibliog, index.

Rousselle, Erwin. Die typen der meditation in china. **CDA** (1932) 20-46.

Sasaki G. What is the true sect of the pure land? **EB** 1 (1921) 167-179.

Sasaki, Genjun H. Hinayana schools in china and japan. **FA:BPB** (1959) 499-514.

Stein, Rolf A. Nouveaux problèmes du tantrisme sino-japonais. **ACF** 75e ann (1975) 481-488.

Stein, Rolf A. Quelques problèmes du tantrisme chinois. **ACF** 74e ann (1974) 499-508.

Suzuki, D.T. The development of the pure land doctrine. **EB** 3 (1924) 285-327.

Suzuki, Daisetz T. The madhyamika school in china. **Journal of the buddhist text society of india** 20.6 (1898) 23-30.

Tamaki, Kōshirō. The way of bodhisattvahood as viewed in t'ien-t'ai teaching. **TBMRD** 30 (1972) 35-53.

Tokunaga, Michio. A view of tariki in tan-luan's ronchū. **JIBS** 22.2 (mar 1974) 22-27.

Vajra bodhi sea. A monthly journal of orthodox buddhism. Publ in City of ten thousand buddhas, talmage, calif by sino-american budd assoc. Text in chin and engl. See passim. Abbrev **VBS.**

Wei, Francis C. M. The doctrine of salvation by faith as taught by the buddhist pure land sect and its alleged relation to christianity. **ChRec** 51.6 (june 1920) 395-401; 51.7 (july 1920) 485-491.

Wieger, Léon. **Amidisme chinois et japonais.** Hien-hien (1928) 51 p, illus.

8. INDIVIDUALS (EXCEPT CH'AN)

Broomhall, Marshall. **In quest of god. The life story of pastors chang and ch'u, buddhist priest and chinese scholar.** London etc (pref 1921) xiii + 190 p.

BTTSoc (tsl) **Records of the life of the venerable master hsüan hua.** San francisco, vol 1, on his life in china (1973) 96 p; vol 2, on his life in hk (1975) 229 p, further vol forthcoming.

Bush, Susan H. & Victor Mair. Some buddhist portraits and images of the lü and ch'an sects in twelfth- and thirteenth-century china. **AAA** 31 (1977-78) 32-51, illus.

Callahan, Paul E. T'ai hsü and the new buddhist movement. Harvard univ, **Papers on china** 6 (1952) 149-188.

Chan, Hok-lam. Liu pin-chung (1216-1274), a buddhist-taoist statesman at the court of khubilai khan. **TP** 53.1/3 (1967) 98-146.

Chavannes, Édouard. Seng-houei . . . +280 p.c. **TP** 10 (mai 1909) 199-212.

Chen, Gerald. Jian Zhen comes home. **EH** 19.6 (june 1980) 11-16, illus. "Visit" of lacquer statue of monk chien-chen fr tōshōdaiji, nara, to yangchou and peking.

Chen-hua. Tsl Denis Mair. Ed Chün-fang Yü. Random talks about my mendicant life: I. **CSA** 13.1 (fall 1980) 3-110 (entire issue) Sel tsl fr bk publ in kaohsiung (1965) by budd monk, about his life on mainland during mid-1940s. II. **ibid** 13.4 (summer 1981) 3-111 (entire issue)

Chen, Tsu-lung. **La vie et les oeuvres de wou-tchen (816-895): contribution à l'histoire culturelle de touen-houang.** Paris (1966) 165 p, app, bibliog, pl, cartes, index générale, index des termes chinois.

Chou, Hsiang-kuang. **T'ai hsu. His life and teachings.** Allahabad (1957) 74 p.

Chu, Pao-tang. Venerable tai-hsu and his buddhist refor-mation in modern china. **CC** 13.3 (sept 1972) 78-118.

Chuan, T.K. Some notes on kao seng chuan. **THM** 7 (1938) 452-468.

Dien, Albert E. Yen chih-t'ui (531-591+): a buddho-confucian. In **CP** (1962) 43-64.

Fang, Li-t'ien. A tentative treatise on the buddhist philo-sophical thought of hui-yüan (334-416) **CSP** 4.3 (spring 1973) 36-76.

Franke, Herbert. Zur biographie des pa-ta shan-jen. In **Asiatica** (1954) 119-130.

Friese, Heinz. Der mönch yao kuang-hsiao . . . und seine zeit. **OE** 7.2 (1960) 158-184.

Gundert, W. Die nonne liu bei we-schan. In **Asiatica** (1954) 184-197.

Haas, Hans. Ein wenig bekannter buddhistischer autor des alten china und sein werk. **Orientalisches archiv** 1 (1910-11) 25-33.

Hackmann, Heinrich. Ein heiliger des chinesischen buddhismus und seine spüren im heutigen china (tsi k'ae) **ZMK** 18 (1903) 65.

Hakeda, Yoshito S. (tsl) **Kūkai; major works, translated with an account of his life and a study of his thought.** Columbia univ (1972) See chap 4, Encounter with master hui-kuo, 29-33; also pt 3, Major works of kūkai, passim.

Hamilton, C.H. An hour with t'ai shu (sic), master of the law. **OC** 42 (mar 1928) 162-169.

Hamilton, Clarence H. Hsüan chuang and the wei shih philosophy. **JAOS** 51 (1931) 291-308.

Harlez, Charles d'. The buddhist schools. **Dublin review** no 105, 3rd ser, vol 22 (july 1889) 47-71. See also author's art: Les écoles bouddhistes, in **Science catholique** 5 (mai-juil 1890)

Held, Axel. **Der buddhistische mönch yen-ts'ung (557-610) und seine übersetsungstheories.** Univ köln (1972) 150 p.

Hsu, Sung-peng. **A buddhist leader in ming china: the life and thought of han-shan te-ching 1546-1623.** Penn state univ (1979) 409 p.

Hsu, Sung-peng. Han-shan te-ching: a buddhist interpre-tation of taoism. **JCP** 2.4 (sept 1975) 418-427.

Hurvitz, Leon. **Chih-i (538-597). An introduction to the life and ideas of a chinese buddhist monk.** Comprises **MCB** vol 12 (1962) 372 p.

Hurvitz, Leon. Chu-hung's one mind of pure land and ch'an buddhism. In **SSMT** (1970) 451-482.

Hurvitz, Leon. Hsüan-tsang and the heart scripture. In **PRS** (1977) 103-121.

Jan, Yün-hua. A buddhist critique of the classical chinese tradition. **JCP** 7.4 (dec 1980) 301-318. Re Tsung-mi (780-841)

Jan, Yün-hua. Conflict and harmony in ch'an and buddhism. **JCP** 4.3 (oct 1977) 287-302. Re Tsung-mi (780-841)

Jan, Yün-hua. Hui-ch'ao and his works: a reassessment. **IAC** 12 (1964)

Jan, Yün-hua. Nagarjuna, one or more? A new interpretation of buddhist hagiography. **HR** 10.2 (aug 1970) 139-155.

Jan, Yün-hua. Tsung-mi's questions regarding the confucian absolute. **PEW** 30.4 (oct 1980) 495-504.

Jan, Yün-hua. Tsung-mi's theory of the "comparative understanding" (ho-hui) of buddhism. In **MS/CA** (1977) 181-186.

Johnston, Reginald. A poet monk of modern china [su man-shu] **JNCBRAS** 63 (1932) 14-30.

Julien, Stanislas. Listes diverses des noms des dix-huit écoles schismatiques qui sont sorties du bouddhisme. **JA** 5e sér, 14 (1859) 327-364.

Laufer, Berthold. Zum bildnis des pilges hsüan tsang. **Globus** 88 (1905) 257-258.

Lee, Peter H. Fa-tsang and uisang. **JAOS** 82.1 (1962) 56-59 + chin text 60-62.

Liebenthal, Walter. A biography of chu tao-sheng. **MN** 11.3 (1955) 64-96.

Liebenthal, Walter. Shih hui-yüan's buddhism as set forth in his writings. **JAOS** 70 (1950) 243-259.

Liebenthal, Walter. The world conception of chu tao-sheng. **MN** 12.1/2 (1956) 65-104; 12.3/4 (1957) 241-268.

Lin, Li-kouang. Punyodaya (na-t'i), un propagateur du tantrisme en chine et au camboge à l'époque de hiuan tsang. **JA** 227 (1935) 83-100.

Link, Arthur (tsl) Biography of tao an. **TP** 46 (1958) 1-48.

Link, Arthur E. Hui-chiao's 'critical essay on the exegetes of the doctrine' in the kao seng chuan (lives of eminent monks) In **NCELYY** (1970) 51-80.

Link, Arthur E. Remarks on shih seng-yu's ch'u san tsang chi-chi as a source for hui-chiao's kao-seng chuan as evidenced in two versions of the biography of tao-an. **Oriens** 10.2 (1957) 292-295.

Liu, Ts'un-yan. Lu hsi-hsing: a confucian scholar, taoist priest and buddhist devotee of the sixteenth century. **AS** 18/19 (1965) 115-142; repr in **LTY:SP** (1976)

Liu, Wu-chi. **Su man-shu.** NY (1972) 173 p.

Luk, Charles (Lu K'uan-yü) (tsl) The 300th patriarch: great master seng-ts'an. **MB** 67 (1959) 22-23.

Magnin, P. **La vie et l'oeuvre de huisi (515-577) (Les origines de la secte bouddhique chinoise du tiantai)** Paris (1979) 289 p, 15 pl, bibliog.

Makita, Tairyō. Hui-yüan — his life and times. Tsl fr jap Philip Yampolsky. **Zinbun** 6 (1962) 1-28.

McAleavy, Henry. **Su man-shu, a sino-japanese genius.** London (1960) 51 p.

Millican, Frank. Buddhism in the light of modern thought as interpreted by the monk tai hsü. **ChRec** 57.2 (feb 1926) 91-94.

Millican, Frank R. T'ai-hsü and modern buddhism. **ChRec** 54.6 (1923) 326-334.

Monestier, Alphonse. The monk lu cheng-hsiang. **BCUP** 5 (1930) 11-21.

Niset, J. Bhiksu shih tao-an, la doctrine du bouddha et les droits de l'homme. **RDH** 10.1/2 (1977) 5-13.

Ono, Gemmyō. A note on tz'u-min's works and some points of his religious teachings. **PIAJ** 2.8 (1926) 361-363.

Ono, Gemmyō. On the pure land doctrine of tz'u-min. **EB** 5 (1930) 200-213.

Paul, Diana. Empress wu and the historians: a tyrant and a saint of classical china. In **VW** (1980) 191-206.

Rachewiltz, Igor de. Yeh-lü ch'u-ts'ai (1189-1243): buddhist idealist and confucian statesman. In **CP** (1962) 189-216.

Robinson, Richard H. Mysticism and logic in seng-chao's thought. **PEW** 8 (1958-59) 99-120.

Rousselle, Erwin. Das leben des patriarchen huineng. **Sinica** 5 (1930) 174-191.

Sargent, Galen E. (tsl) The śramana superintendent: t'an-yao and his times. **MS** 16 (1957) 363-396. A chap fr Tsukamoto Zenryū's book, **Shina bukkyōshi kenkyū hokugi-ken,** tokyo (1942)

Shih, Robert (tsl) **Hui-chiao. Biographies des moines éminents de houei-kiao. Kao seng tchouan, 1 partie. Biographies des premiers traducteurs.** Louvain (1968) xi + 177. Chin text and french tsl.

Soymié, Michel. Biographie de chan tao-k'ai. **MIHEC** 1 (1957) 415-422.

Su, Ying-hui. A study of the identify of monk wu (wu ho-shang) in the tunhuang manuscripts p.2913, p.4660 and s.1947v. **CC** 15.4 (dec 1974) 89-98.

Re Suzuki, Daisetz T. (1870-1966) **EB** 2.1 (aug 1967) Entire issue is in memoriam.

T'ai Hsü. Tsl by Frank Rawlinson. Buddhism and the modern mind. **ChRec** 65.7 (july 1934) 435-440.

T'ai Hsü. Tsl by Frank Rawlinson. The meaning of buddhism. **ChRec** 65.11 (nov 1934) 689-695.

Takakusu, Junjirō. K'uei-chi's version of a controversy between the buddhist and the sāmkhya philosophers. — An appendix to the translation of paramārtha's 'life of vasu-bandhu.' **TP** 2e sér, 5 (1904) 461-466.

Takakusu, Junjirō (tsl) The life of vasu-bandhu by paramārtha (a.d. 499-569) **TP** 2e sér, 5 (1904) 269-296.

Takaksu, Junjirō (tsl) Le voyage de kanshin en orient, 742-754, par aomi-no mabito kenkai, 779. **BEFEO** 28 (1928) 1-41, 441-472; 29 (1929) 47-62.

Tamaki, Kōshirō. The ultimate enlightenment of hui-yüan in lu-shan. **JIBS** 12.2 (1964) 1-12.

Tamura, Kwansei. Ganjin (chien-chen), transmitter of buddhist precepts to japan. **YE** n.s. 6.4 (autumn 1980) 4-6.

Tokunaga, Michio. A view of tariki in tan-luan's ronchū. **JIBS** 22.2 (mar 1974) 22-27.

Tschen, Yin-ko. Buddhistischer in den biographien von tsan tschung und hua to im san guo dschï. **TJ** 6 (1930) 17-20.

Tschen, Yuan. Johann Adam Schall von Bell und der bonze mu tschen-wen. **MS** 5 (1940) 316-328.

Tsukamoto, Zenryū. The dates of kumarajiva . . . and seng-chao . . . reexamined. Tsl fr jap Leon Hurvitz. In **SJV** (1954) 568-584.

Ui, Hakuju. Maitreya as an historical personage. In **Indian studies in honor of charles rockwell lanman,** cambridge, mass (1929) 95-101.

Unno, Taitetsu. The buddhatā theory of fa-tsang. **Trans 8th ICfO Japan** (1963) 34-41.

Vajra bodhi sea. A monthly journal of orthodox buddhism. Publ in City of ten thousand buddhas, talmage, calif by sino-american budd assoc. Text in chin and engl. See passim. Abbrev **VBS**.

Wagner, Rudolf G. The original structure of the correspondence between shih hui-yüan and kumārajīva. **HJAS** 31 (1971) 28-48. Re taisho tripitaka no 1856.

Walleser, Max. The life of nāgārjuna from tibetan and chinese sources. In **AMHAV** (1923) 421-455. Repr as book, delhi (1979) 43 p.

Weinstein, Stanley. A biographical study of tz'u-ên. **MN** 15.1/2 (1959) 119-149.

Wilhelm, Richard. Der grossabt schï tai hü. **Sinica** 4 (1929) 16.

Wright, A.F. Biography and hagiography. Hui-chiao's lives of eminent monks. In **SJV** (1954) 383-432.

Wright, Arthur F. Biography of the nun an-ling-shou. **HJAS** 15 (1952) 193-196.

Wright, Arthur F. Fo t'u teng . . . a biography. **HJAS** 11 (1948) 322-370.

Wright, Arthur F. Seng-jui alias hui-jui: a biographical bisection in the kao-seng chuan. **SIS** 5.3/4 (1957) (Liebenthal festschrift) 272-294.

Yu, David C. Skill in means and the buddhism of tao-sheng: a study of a chinese reaction to mahāyāna of the fifth century. **PEW** 24.4 (oct 1974) 413-427.

9. CH'AN

Abe, Masao. Zen and buddhism. **JCP** 3.3 (june 1976) 235-252.

Abe, Masao. Zen and compassion. **EB** n.s. 2.1 (aug 1967) 54-68. Re Lin-chi lu and chao-chou lu.

Addiss, Stephen. The art of chinese huang-po monks in japan. **OA** n.s. 24.4 (winter 1978) 420-432. Re calligraphy and painting.

Akiyama, Satoko. On the "kirigame" in sōtō-zen tradition. **JIBS** 21.2 (mar 1973) 45-49. Re "cut-paper" and its chin origins.

Arai, S. The origins of zen. **YE** 1.12 (may 1926) 395-397.

Bancroft, Anne. **Religions of the east.** NY (1974) See Zen buddhism, 143-180.

Bancroft, Anne. **Zen. Direct pointing to reality.** NY (1979) Text, 5-31; pl, 33-65, "themes" 65-95; profusely illus b-&-w and col. See passim.

Baumann, C. A few psychological aspects of ch'an buddhism. **AA** 8 (1940-45) 216-237.

Beautrix, P. **Bibliographie du bouddhisme zen.** Bruxelles (1969) 114 p.

Beautrix, Pierre. **Bibliographie du bouddhisme zen. Premier supplément.** Bruxelles (n.d.—sometime 1971-75) 119 p.

Belloni, Michel. Trois "cas" du pi yen lou. **Tch'an** (1970) 86-111.

Bendiek, J. Realität und illusion. Die frage nach der wirklichkeit der aussenwelt in frühen ch'an-buddhismus. **Franziskanische studien** 58.3/4 (1976) 330-352, bibliog, 3 pl.

Benl, Oscar. Der zen-meister dōgen in china. **NachrDGNVO** no 79-80 (1956) 67-77.

Bielefeldt, Carl & Lewis Lancaster. T'an ching (platform scripture) **PEW** 25.2 (apr 1975) 197-212. Rev art re hist of text and various tsl.

Blofeld, John. **Beyond the gods. Buddhist and taoist mysticism.** London & ny (1974) 164 p, short gloss.

Blofeld, John. Ch'an, zen or dhyana. **EH** 1.3 (nov 1960) 22-27.

Blofeld, John (tsl) **The path to sudden attainment. A treatise of the ch'an (zen) school of chinese buddhism by hui hai of the t'ang dynasty.** London (1948) 51 p.

Blofeld, John. Life in a zen monastery. In **Z&H** (1978) 38-47. Repr fr author's autobiog, **The wheel of life,** london (1959) 159-174.

Blofeld, John (tsl) **The zen teaching of huang po on the transmission of mind. Being the teaching of the zen master huang po as recorded by the scholar p'ei hsiu of the t'ang dynasty.** N.Y. (1959) 136 p, index. Rev and enl ed of tsl entitled **The huang po doctrine** . . . q.v. under Chu Ch'an below.

Blyth, R.H. **Zen and zen classics.** Vol 1, **From the upanishads to huineng.** Tokyo (1960) 126 p, ref books, frontispiece, chin and jap char. Tsl and discussions.

Blyth, R.H. **Zen and zen classics.** Vol 2, **History of Zen.** Tokyo (1964) x + 211 p, illus, chin and jap char, index.

Blyth, R.H. **Zen and zen classics.** Vol 3, **History of zen (nangaku—i.e. nan-hsüeh—branch)** Tokyo (1970) 185 p. Posthumous publ.

Blyth, R.H. **Zen and zen classics.** Vol 4, **Mumonkan (wu-men kuan)** Tokyo (1966) 340 p, illus, chin char, index. Posthumous publ.

Blyth, R.H. **Zen and zen classics.** Vol 5, **Twenty-five zen essays.** Tokyo (1962) 225 p, illus, index.

Blyth, R.H. The zenrinkushu. **YE** n.s. 12 (summer 1963) 8-11; 12 (autumn 1963) 2-6; (winter 1963) 6-9; 13 (spring 1964) 2-4; 13 (summer 1964) 2-4. Tsl fr a major coll of ch'an texts.

Briggs, William (ed) **Anthology of zen.** London & ny (1961) 300p. See various sel.

Brinker, Helmut. Ch'an portraits in a landscape. **AAA** 27 (1973-74) 8-29. Paintings of various dates.

Brinker, Helmut. **Die zen-buddhistische bildnismalerei in china und japan. Von den anfängen bis zum ende des 16. jahrhunderts. Eine untersuchung zur ikonographie, typen- und entwicklungsgeschichte.** Wiesbaden (1973) x + 279 s, 80 taf.

Bush, Susan H. & Victor Mair. Some buddhist portraits and images of the lü and ch'an sects in twelfth- and thirteenth-century china. **AAA** 31 (1977-78) 32-51, illus.

Chan, Wing-tsit (tsl) **The platform scripture.** N.Y. (1963) 193 p, notes, index.

Chang, Aloysius. The essence of zen. **CC** 18.4 (dec 1977) 49-55.

Chang, C.C. Ch'an and madamudra. **CC** 2.1 (1959) 10-16.

Chang, Chen-chi. Meditation of t'ieh-shan. In **Z&H** (1978) 94-97; repr from The nature of ch'an (zen) buddhism, **PEW** 6.4 (jan 1957) 333-355.

Chang, Chen-chi. The nature of ch'an (zen) buddhism. **PEW** 6 (1957) 333-355.

Chang, Chen-chi. **The practice of zen.** London (1960) 256 p, notes, bibliog. app, index.

Chang, Chung-yüan. Ch'an buddhism: logical and illogical. **PEW** 17 (1967) 37-59.

Chang, Chung-yüan. Ch'an master niu-t'ou fa-yung and his teachings on prajñāpāramitā. **CC** 7.1 (mar 1966) 32-50.

Chang, Chung-yüan. Ch'an teachings of fa-yen school. **CC** 6.3 (june 1965) 55-80.

Chang, Chung-yüan. Ch'an teachings of fa-yen school. **CC** 7.4 (dec 1966) 12-53.

Chang, Chung-yüan. Ch'an teachings of the yün-mên school. **CC** 5.4 (june 1964) 14-39.

Chang, Chung-yuan. Nirvana is nameless. **JCP** 1.3/4 (june-sept 1974) 247-274.

Chang, Chung-yüan. **Original teachings of ch'an buddhism, selected from the transmission of the lamp.** N.Y. (1969) 333 p, chart of eminent ch'an masters (594-990) bibliog, index.

Chang, Chung-yuan. Pre-rational harmony in heidegger's essential thinking and ch'an thought. **EB** n.s. 5.2 (oct 1972) 153-170.

Chang, Chung-yuan. A study of master lin-chi i-hsuan. **Psychologia** 6 (1963) 74-80.

Chang, Chung-yüan. Ts'ao-tung ch'an and its metaphysical background, with translations of the dialogues of the founders. **TJ** n.s. 5 (1965) 33-65.

Chang, Chung-yüan. Ways of experiencing ch'an. **Main currents in modern thought** 20 (jan-feb 1964) 57-61.

Chapin, Helen B. The ch'an master pu-tai. **JAOS** 53 (1933) 47-52.

Chapin, Helen B. Three early portraits of bodhidharma. **ACASA** 1 (1945-46) 66-68.

Chen, C.M. Comment on śamatha, samāpatti, and dhyāna in ch'an (zen) **PEW** 16.1/2 (1966) 84-87.

Ch'en, Jen-dau. **The three patriarchs of the southern school in chinese paintings.** Hong kong (1955) 8 p.

Chen, Shih-hsiang. Chinese poetics and zenism. **Oriens** 10 (1957) 131-139.

Cheng, Chung-ying. On zen (ch'an) language and zen paradoxes. **JCP** 1.1 (dec 1973) 77-102.

Cheng, Hsüeh-li. Zen and san-lun madhyamika thought: exploring the theoretical foundation of zen teachings and practices. **RS** 15.3 (sept 1979) 343-363.

Chi, R.S.Y. (tsl) Dialogue on zen by nan-ch'üan (nansen) **MW** 34 (1959) 117-123.

Chi, Richard S.Y. From the dialogues of shen-hui. **MW** 40.3 (nov 1965) 130-134.

Chou, H.K. **Buddhism and the chan school of china.** Allahabad? (1965) 24 p.

Chou, Hsiang-kuang. **Dhyana buddhism in china; its history and teaching.** Allahabad (1960) xii + 216 p, illus.

Chu, Ch'an [pseud for John Blofeld] **The huang po doctrine of universal mind, being the teaching of dhyana master hsi yün as recorded by p'ei hsiu, a noted scholar of the t'ang dynasty.** London (1947) 52 p. French tsl Y. Laurence: **Le mental cosmique selon la doctrine de huang po. Selon les annales de p'ei hsiu erudit bien connu sous la dynastie t'ang.** Adyar (1954) 144 p. See, for enlarged ed of engl work, under Blofeld, John, **The zen teaching of huang po . . .**

Chung, Albert Chi-lu. The chinese mind and zen buddhism. **CC** 3.4 (oct 1961) 64-73.

Claridge, Gordon. The ch'an school: an expression of orthodox buddhism. **Queensland historical review** 6.1 (1977) 1-5.

Cleary, Christopher (tsl) **Swampland flowers: the letters and lectures of zen master ta hui.** NY (1977) xxvii + 144 p.

Cleary, Thomas (tsl) **Sayings and doings of pai-chang.** Los angeles (1979) 144 p.

Cleary, Thomas (tsl) **Timeless spring. A soto zen anthology.** Tokyo & ny (1980) 176 p. Fr chin and jap texts.

Cook, Francis Dojun. **How to raise an ox. Zen practice as taught by zen master dogen's shobogenzo.** Los angeles (1978) 215 p. See passim.

Cools, A.J. Houei-neng. **Samadhi** 5.2 (jan-mar 1967) 15-19.

Dai, Bingham, Zen and psychotherapy. In **RS&P** (1973) 132-141, bibliog.

Demiéville, Paul. Deux documents de touen-houang sur le dhyāna chinois. In **EZT** (1961) 1-27. Repr in **CEB** (1973)

Demiéville, Paul. Les entretiens de lin-tsi. **Tch'an** (1970) 61-80.

Demiéville, Paul. Le miroir spirituel. **Sinologica** 1.2 (1948) 112-137.

Demiéville, Paul. Le recueil de la salle des patriarches, tsou-t'ang tsi. **TP** 56.4/5 (1970) 262-286. Text was composed 952.

Demiéville, Paul (tsl) **Shih i-hsüan. Entretiens de lin-tsi. Traduit du chinois et commentés par Paul Demiéville.** Paris (1972) 254 p.

Demiéville, Paul. Le tch'an et la poésie chinoise. **Tch'an** (1970) 123-136.

Donner, Neal. The mahāyānization of the chinese dhyāna tradition. **EB** n.s. 10.2 (oct 1977) 49-64.

Dumoulin, Heinrich. Bodhidharma und die anfänge des ch'an buddhismus. **MS** 10 (1945) 222-238. Same title in **MN** 7 (1951) 67-83.

Dumoulin, Heinrich. **The development of chinese zen after the sixth patriarch [hui-neng] in the light of mumonkan [wu men kuan]** N.Y. (1953) xxii + 146 p, tables. Tsl fr german art, Die entwicklung des chinesischen ch'an . . . q.v. with add notes and app by Ruth Fuller Sasaki.

Dumoulin, Heinrich. The encounter between zen buddhism and christianity. **JCS** 7 (1970) 53-63.

Dumoulin, Heinrich. Die entwicklung des chinesischen ch'an nach hui-neng im lichte des wu-men-kuan. **MS** 6 (1941) 40-72. For engl tsl see **The development of chinese zen . . .**

Dumoulin, Heinrich. **Der erleuchtungsweg des zen im buddhismus.** ?place (1976) Engl tsl John C. Maraldo, **Zen enlightenment. Origins and meanings,** ny & tokyo (1979) 175 p, 10 ox-herding pics, chin-jap equivalents, notes, bibliog, index.

Dumoulin, Heinrich. Das wu-men-kuan. 'Der pass ohne tor.' **MS** 8 (1943) 41-102.

Dumoulin, Heinrich. **Wu-men-kuan, der pass ohne tor.** Tokyo (1953) x + 64 p.

Dumoulin, Heinrich. **Zen. Geschichte und gestalt.** Bern (1959) 332 p, 16 pl. Engl tsl Paul Peachey: **A history of zen buddhism,** n.y. (1963) viii + 335 p, notes, bibliog, index.

Ecke, G. Concerning ch'an in painting. **ArtsAs** 3 (1956) 296-306, illus.

Evola, J. Zen and the west. **E&W** 6 (1955) 115-119.

Fontein, Jan and Money L. Hickman. **Zen painting and calligraphy.** Boston (1970) liv + 173 p, illus.

Fujimoto, ?Ryūgyō. On reading the development of chinese zen, by heinrich dumoulin & ruth fuller sasaki. **RDR** 347 (apr 1954) 39-43.

Fukunaga, Mitsuji. 'No-mind' in chuang-tzu and in ch'an buddhism. **Zinbun** 12 (1968) 9-45.

Fuller-Sasaki, Ruth. Tsl fr engl by Francis Ledoux. l'Usage du koan en chine. **Tch'an** (1970) 112-122.

Fung, Paul F. and George D. Fung (tsl) **The sutra of the sixth patriarch [hui neng] on the pristine orthodox dharma.** San francisco (1964) 187 p, notes, gloss.

Fung, Yu-lan. Ch'anism, the philosophy of silence. Being chap 6 in author's **A short history of chinese philosophy,** ed Derk Bodde, n.y. (1948)

Fung, Yu-lan. The inner-light school (ch'an tsung) of buddhism. Being chap 7 in author's **The spirit of chinese philosophy,** tsl fr chin E.R. Hughes, london (1947) 156-174.

C.G. Tch'an. In **EUF** (1968) vol 15, 769a-778c.

Garner, Dick. Skepticism, ordinary language and zen buddhism. **PEW** 27.2 (apr 1977) 165-182.

Gernet, J. Biographie de maître chen-houei du ho-tsö. **JA** 239 (1951) 29-68.

Gernet, Jacques. Complément aux 'entretiens du maître de dhyâna chen-houei (668-760)' **BEFEO** 44.2 (1947-50) 453-466.

Gernet, Jacques. Entretiens de chen-houei du ho-tsö. Extraits. **Tch'an** (1970) 21-34.

Gernet, Jacques. **Entretiens du maître de dhyâna chen-houei du ho-tsö (668-760)** Hanoi (1949) x + 126 p.

Gernet, Jacques. Les entretiens du maître ling-yeou du kouei-chau (771-853) **BEFEO** 45.1 (1951) 65-70.

Giles, Herbert A. Liao-yüan fo-yin. **NCR** 4 (1922) 36-37.

Gray, Terence. A metaphysical interpretation of takuan's letter to tajima no kami. **MW** 35 (1960) 103-106.

Gundert, W. (tsl) Bi-yän-lu. In **Meister yüan-wu's niederschrift von der smaragdenen felswand.** Munich (1960) chap 1-33.

Gundert, Wilhelm. Bodhidharma und wu-di von liang. In **SJFAW** (1956) 48-66.

Gundert, Wilhelm. Dasui's feuerige lohe. Das 29. beispiel des bi-yän-lu. **NachrDGNVO** 85/86 (1959) 9-17.

Gundert, Wilhelm (tsl) Das 35. kapitel des bi-yän-lu, übersetzt und erläutet. **MDGNVO** 44 teil 3 (1964) 1-25.

Gundert, Wilhelm (tsl) Fëng-hsüan's eiserner stier. Das 38. beispiel des bi-yän-lu. **OE** 12.2 (1965) 129-160.

Gundert, Wilhelm (tsl) Das neunte beispiel des bi-yän-lu. **NachrDGNVO** no 79-80 (1956) 8-14.

Gundert, Wilhelm (tsl) Die nonne liu bei we-schan; das 24. kapitel des bi-yän-lu, eingeleitet, übersetzt und erläutert. In **Asiatica** (1954) 184-197.

Gundert, Wilhelm (tsl) Pang's, des privatstudierten, schöne schneeflocken; das 42. beispiel des bi-yän-lu. **NachrDGNVO** 97 (1965) 13-28.

Gundert, Wilhelm (tsl) Das 47. kapitel des bi-yän-lu. **OE** 11 (1964) 127-141.

Gundert, Wilhelm (übers & erklärt) Das 51. kapitel der 'niederschrift aus smaragdenen felswand' (pi yen lu) In **Asien** (1971) 156-168.

Gundert, Wilhelm (tsl) Yang-schan's fünfaltenhörner; das 34. beispiel des bi-yän-lu. **OE** 9 (1962) 200-219.

Haimes, Norma. Zen buddhism and psychoanalysis—a bibliographic essay. **Psychologia** 15 (1972) 22-30.

Hasumi, Toshimitsu. **Élaboration philosophique de la pensée du zen.** Paris (1973) 243 p, bibliog.

Heifetz, Harold (ed) **Zen and hasidism. The similarities between two spiritual disciplines.** Wheaton, ill (1978) Three relevant items, sep listed in our bibliog. Abbrev **Z&H.**

Heng-k'ung. The hua-t'ou technique. **MB** 86 (1978) 235-236.

Hisamatsu, H.S. Eine erläuterung des lin-dji-zen. **NachrDGNVO** 85-86 (1959) 18-20.

Hisamatsu, Shin'ichi. On zen art. **EB** n.s. 1.2 (sept 1966) 21-33.

Hisamatsu, Shin'ichi. Tsl Gishin Tokiwa. **Zen and the fine arts.** Tokyo (1971) 400 p, 276 pl, notes to pl, biog notes, index.

Hisamatsu, Shin'ichi. Le zen et les beaux-arts. **ArtsAs** 6.4 (1959) 243-258, illus. Genl discussion of what is zen in art, incl chin.

Hisamatsu, Shin'ichi. Zen: its meaning for modern civilization. **EB** n.s. 1.1 (sept 1965) 22-47. Many chin masters quoted.

Hixon, Lex. **Coming home. The experience of enlightenment in sacred traditions.** Garden city, n.j. (1978) See chap 4, Ten seasons of enlightenment; zen ox-herding, 77-108, illus.

H(obson) R. L. Pu-tai ho-shang. **BMQ** 11 (1937) 112-113.

Holmes, Stewart W. & Chinyu Horiaka. **Zen art for meditation.** Rutland, vt & tokyo (1973) 115 p, 31 pl.

Hongo, Tameo. Mu-ch'i, zen monk painter. **APQCSA** 5.1 (summer 1973) 77-81, illus.

Hoover, Thomas. **The zen experience.** NY (1980) 286 p, historical chart, notes, bibliog, index, illus.

Houei-neng, le sutra de l'estrade; extraits du t'an king. **Tch'an** (1970) 15-20. Tsl fr engl version of Philip Yampolsky q.v.

Houlné, Lucien (tsl) **Houeï-neng, sixième patriarche du bouddhisme zen, discours et sermons d'après le sûtra de l'estrade sur les pierres précieuses de la loi fa-pao-t'an-king.** Paris (1963) 185 p.

Hsu, Sung-peng. **A buddhist leader in ming china: the life and thought of han-shan te-ching 1546-1623.** Penn state univ (1979) 409 p.

Hsu, Sung-peng. Han-shan te-ching: a buddhist interpretation of taoism. **JCP** 2.4 (sept 1975) 418-427.

Hsüan-hua. BTTSoc (tsl) **Listen to yourself think it over.** San francisco (1978) Meditation instructions on name of kuan-yin and ch'an.

Hsüan-hua · BTTSoc (tsl) **Pure land and ch'an dharma talks.** San francisco (1972) 72 p.

Hu, Shih. An appeal for a systematic search in japan for long-hidden t'ang dynasty source materials of the early history of zen buddhism. Kyoto, **Bukkyō to bunka,** (1960) 15-23.

Hu, Shih. Ch'an (zen) buddhism in china, its history and method. Is ch'an (zen) beyond our understanding? **PEW** 3.1 (1953) 3-24.

Hu, Shih. Development of zen buddhism in china. **CSPSR** 15 (1932) 475-505. Repr in **SIS** 3.3/4 (1949) 99-126; repr in W. Briggs (ed) **Anthology of zen** q.v.

Hui-Wan. Ch. Pönisch-Schoenwerth (übers) Prajñā ch'an. Buddhistische weisheit und meditation. **Yana** 32.1 (jan-feb 1979) 7-12.

Hurvitz, Leon. Chu-hung's one mind of pure land and ch'an buddhism. In **SSMT** (1970) 451-482.

Hyers, M. Conrad. The comic perspective in zen literature and art. **EB** n.s. 5.1 (may 1972) 26-46.

Iriya, Yoshitaka. Tsl N.A. Waddell. Chinese poetry and zen. **EB** n.s. 6.1 (may 1973) 54-67.

Izutsu, Toshihiko. The interior and exterior in zen buddhism. **EJ 1973** (1975) 581-618; repr in **TPZB.** Mostly fr chin sources.

Izutsu, Toshihiko. Meditation and intellection in japanese zen buddhism. In Yusuf Ibish & Peter L. Wilson (ed) **Traditional modes of contemplation and action,** tehran (1977) 275-304.

Izutzu, Toshihiko. The philosophical problem of articulation in zen buddhism. **Revue internationale de philosophie** 28 (1974) 165-183; repr in **TPZB.**

Izutsu, Toshihiko. The structure of selfhood in zen-buddhism. **EJ 1969** (1972) 95-150. Fr chin sources.

Izutsu, Toshihiko. **Toward a philosophy of zen buddhism.** Tehran (1977) 259 p. Coll of 7 essays, republ, all of which are listed sep in our bibliog. Abbrev **TPZB.**

Jan, Yün-hua. Conflict and harmony in ch'an and buddhism. **JCP** 4.3 (oct 1977) 287-302. Re Tsung-mi (780-841)

Jan, Yün-hua. Tsung-mi, his analysis of ch'an buddhism. **TP** 58.1/5 (1972) 1-54.

Kadowaki, J.K. **Zen and the bible. A priest's experience.** London (1980) 180 p. Tsl of jap bk orig publ tokyo (1977) Author is a jesuit.

Kalupahana, David J. **Buddhist philosophy. A historical analysis.** See app 2, Reflections on the relation between early buddhism and zen, 163-178.

Kasulis, T.P. Truth and zen. **PEW** 30.4 (oct 1980) 453-464.

Lai, Whalen. Ch'an metaphors: waves, mirror, lamp. **PEW** 29.3 (july 1979) 243-254.

Lai, Whalen W-L. Inner worldly mysticism: east and west. In **Z&H** (1978) 186-207.

Lanciotti, Lionello. New historic contribution to the person of bodhidharma. **AA** 12.1/2 (1949) 141-144.

Lee, Cyrus. Thomas merton and zen buddhism. **CC** 13.2 (june 1972) 35-48.

Lesh, T. Zen and psychotherapy: a partially annotated bibliography. **JHP** 10 (1970) 75-83.

Li, Chu-tsing. Bodhidharma crossing the yangtze river on a reed: a painting in the charles a. drenowatz collection in zürich. **AS** 25 (1971) 49-75, 15 pl, chin-jap gloss.

Liebenthal, Walter (tsl) Huang-po hsi yün, protokoll seiner einvernahme durch p'ei hsiu. **AS** 30 (1976) 1-44.

Liebenthal, Walter. The sermon of shen-hui. **AM** n.s. 3.2 (1952) 132-155.

Liebenthal, Walter (tsl) Yung-chia cheng-tao-ko or yung-chia's song of experiencing the tao. **MS** 6 (1941) 1-39.

Lin, Robert K. The concept of naturalness in taoism and ch'an (zen) **ACQ** 3.4 (winter 1975) 37-51.

Linssen, R. **l'Éveil suprême. Bases théoretique et pratique du bouddhisme ch'an, du zen du taoïsme et des enseignements de krishnamurti.** Bruxelles (1970) 160 p.

Liu, Guan-ying (tsl) **Der heilige als eulenspiegel (chi-kung-chuan, ausz.dt.) 12 abenteuer e. zenmeisters.** Basel and stuttgart (1958) 167 s, mit abb.

Lou, Kouan Yu & Francis Ledoux (tsl) Hsu yun. Essentiel de l'entraînement tch'an. **Tch'an** (1970) 137-149.

Lu, K'uan-yü (Charles Luk) **Ch'an and zen teaching.** London, ser 1 (1960) 225 p; ser 2 (1961) 254 p; ser 3 (1962) 306 p.

Lu, K'uan Yü (Charles Luk) **Practical buddhism.** London (1971) 167 p, gloss.

Luk, Charles (Lu K'uan-yü) **The secrets of chinese meditation.** London (1964) 240 p. Deals with both taoist and several schools of buddhist techniques incl ch'an. German tsl H.-U. Rieker, **Geheimnisse der chinesischen meditation,** zürich & stuttgart (1967) 296 s.

Luk, Charles (Lu K'uan Yü) **The transmission of the mind outside the teaching.** NY (1974) 191 p.

Masui, J. Approaches du tch'an (zen) **Revue philosophique de la france et de l'étranger** 164 (janv-mars 1974) 65-76.

Masunaga, Reiho. The gist of sōtō zen. **JIBS** 7.2 (1959) 19-35.

Masunaga, Reiho. Introduction to (dōgen's) butsudō and translation of text. Komazawa univ **Journal of the faculty of buddhism** 21 (oct 1962) 1-15. Traditions of chin ch'an masters.

Merton, Thomas. A christian looks at zen. Being the intro to John C.H.Wu: **The golden age of zen,** q.v. 1-28.

Merton, Thomas. Mystics and zen masters. **CC** 6.2 (mar 1965) 1-18. Same title incl in author's collection (which is itself also entitled **Mystics and zen masters**) n.y. (1961 et seq)

Mitchell, Donald W. Faith in zen buddhism. **IPQ** 20.2 (june 1980) 183-197.

Miura, Isshū & Ruth Fuller Sasaki. **Zen dust: the history of the koan and koan study in rinzai (lin-chi) zen.** NY (1966) xxii + 574 p, illus, maps, bibliog.

Miura, Isshū & Ruth Fuller Sasaki. **The zen koan. Its history and use in rinzai zen.** Kyoto (1965) 156 p, illus, index.

Mulder, Willem Zilvester. A note on pi yen chi (blue cliff collection) **China society annual,** singapore (1954) 27-29.

Murakami, Yoshimi. 'Nature' in lao-chuang thought and 'no-mind' in ch'an buddhism. **KGUAS** 14 (1965) 15-31.

Muralt, Raoul von (ed and tsl) **Wei lang. Das sutra des sechsten patriarchen.** Zürich (1958) 149 p.

Nagashima, Takayuki. Hypothesis: shen-hui was not acquainted with hui-neng. **JIBS** 25.1 (dec 1976) 42-46.

Nishitani, Keiji. Tsl N.A. Waddell. On the i-thou relation in zen buddhism. **EB** n.s. 2.2 (nov 1969) 71-87. In pt re blue cliff collection.

Nukariya, Kaiten. **The religion of the samurai. A study of zen philosophy and discipline in china and japan.** London (1913) See chap 1, History of zen in china, 1-27. Repr (1973)

Ogata, Sohaku. Bodhidharma, an indian master of dhyana who became the father of zen in china and japan. **YE** 9.4 (1943) 21-27.

Ogata, Sohaku. **Zenshu mu mon kan: a gateless barrier to zen buddhism.** Kyoto (1955) repr in author's **Zen for the west,** ny (1959) app, A new translation of the mu mon kan, 79-131.

Onda, A. Zen and creativity. **Psychologia** 5 (1962) 13-20.

Pachow, W. The spirit of zen buddhism. Repr in author's **ChBudd** (1980) 21-34; orig publ not stated.

Pachow, W. Zen buddhism and bodhidharma. **IHQ** 32.2/3 (1956) 329-337; repr in author's **ChBudd** (1980) 1-19.

Petzold, B. Was ist zen? **OL** 45 (1942) col 89-102.

Rousselle, E. (tsl) Buddhistische studien: das sūtra des sechsten patriarchen. **Sinica** 2 (1936) 131-137, 202-210.

Rousselle, E. Buddhistische wesenschau nach der lehre der meditationssekte. **CDA** (1931) 76-86.

Rousselle, E. (tsl) Das leben des patriarchen hui neng. **Sinica** 5 (1930) 174-191.

Rousselle, E. Die typen der meditation in china. **CDA** (1932) 20-46.

Rousselle, E. Vergeistigte religion. Nach der lehre der meditationssekte. (Buddhistische studien) **Sinica** 6 (1931) 26-34.

Sakamaki, Shunzo. Zen and intuited knowledge. **Etc.** 16 (1959) 203-207.

Sasaki, Ruth Fuller. A bibliography of translations of zen (ch'an) works. **PEW** 10.3/4 (1961) 149-168.

Sasaki, Ruth Fuller. Chia-shan receives the transmission from boatman-priest te-ch'eng. **Chicago review** 12.2 (summer 1958) 33-36.

Sasaki, Ruth Fuller (tsl) **The recorded sayings of ch'an master lin-chi hui-chao of chen prefecture.** Kyoto (1975) 123 p.

Sasaki, Ruth Fuller. **Zen: a method for religious awakening.** Kyoto (1959) 26 p.

Sasaki, Ruth Fuller, Yoshitaka Iriya & Dana R. Fraser (tsl) **The recorded sayings of layman p'ang. A ninth-century zen classic.** NY & tokyo (1971) 109 p, 6 illus, intro, suppl notes, sel bibliog, index.

Scharfstein, Ben-Ami. Salvation by paradox: on zen and zen-like thought. **JCP** 3 (1975-76) 209-234.

Schloegl, Irmgard (tsl) The record of rinzai. **MW** 49.1 (may 1974) 29-34; 49.3 (nov 1974) 38-42.

Schloegl, Irmgard (ed) **The wisdom of the zen masters.** NY (1975) 80 p. Fr chin and jap sources, some tsl by ed, some fr existing engl tsl.

Schloegl, Irmgard (tsl) **The zen teaching of rinzai.** Berkeley, calif (1976) 96 p. Tsl of lin-chi lu; japanizes all chin names.

Schmidt, J.D. Ch'an, illusion, and sudden enlightenment in the poetry of yang wan-li. **TP** 60.4/5 (1974) 230-281.

Schumacher, Stephan (übers & heraus) **Han shan. 150 gedichte vom kalten berg.** Düsseldorf/köln (1974) 192 s, 12 bildtag, kart.

Seckel, Dietrich. Mu-hsi: sechs kaki-fruchte; interpretation eines zen-bildes. **NachrDGNVO** 77 (1955) 44-55, pl.

Sekida, Katsuki (tsl) A.V. Grimstone (ed and intro) **Two zen classics: mumonkan and hekiganroku.** NY & tokyo (1977) 413 p, geneal table, index (all pronunciations in jap)

Seo, Kyung-bo. The history or legend of zen in india and china: according to the chodangjip. **Bulgyo hakpo; journal of the korean buddhist research institute** 8 (oct 1971) 372-401.

Shaw, R.D.M. (tsl) **The blue cliff records; hekigan roku, containing 100 stories of zen masters of ancient china.** London (1961) 299 p.

Shibata, Masumi. Le dialogue dans le zen chinois. **RMM** 64 (1959) 310-319.

Shibata, Masumi (tsl) **Wu-men-kouan. Passe sans porte. Texte essentiel zen.** Paris (1968) 2e éd rev and corr, 166 p.

Shibayama, Zenkei et al. Chinese zen: a dialogue. **EB** n.s. 8.2 (oct 1975) 66-93.

Shibayama, Zenkei. Tsl Sumiko Kudo. **Zen comments on the mumonkan.** NY (1974) 366 p, gloss, index.

Siren, Osvald. Ch'an (zen) buddhism and its relation to art. **Theosophical path** 44 (oct 1934) 159-176.

Snyder, Gary. A record of the life of the ch'an master po-chang huai-hai. In author's **Earth household,** ny (1969) 69-82.

Sowerby, A. de C.S. Legendary figures in chinese art. Tamo or bodhidharma. **CJ** 14.4 (apr 1931) 157-158, illus.

Speiser, Werner. Hu dschï-fu. **Sinica** 16 (1941) 152-161, pl. Re a ch'an painter.

Speiser, Werner. Liang K'ai. **OZ** 27.5/6 (1961) 159-168, 6 pl. Re a ch'an painter.

Speiser, Werner. Liang-tsüan (jap ryōzen) **Sinica** 13.5/6 (1938) 254-264, pl. Re ch'an painter.

Speiser, Werner. Yin-to-lo. **Sinica** 12 (1937) 155-160, illus. Re ch'an painter.

Speiser, Werner. Zum werk des mu-hsi. **OZ** 27.3/4 (1941) 95-115, 2 pl. Re ch'an painter.

Spiegelberg, Frederic. **Living religions of the world.** Englewood cliffs, n.j. (1956) See chap 12, Zen buddhism, 328-353.

Steger, E. Ecker. The no-philosophy of zen. **Personalist** 55.3 (summer 1974) 273-289. Quotes mostly fr chin texts.

Stryk, Lucien & Takashi Ikemoto (tsl) **Zen poems of china and japan; the crane's bill.** NY (1973) See China sec, 1-43.

Stunkard, Albert. Some interpersonal aspects of an oriental religion. **Psychiatry** 14.4 (nov 1951) 419-431. Re zen.

Re Suzuki, Daisetz T (1870-1966) **EB** 2.1 (aug 1967) Entire issue is in memoriam.

Suzuki, D.T. The awakening of a new consciousness in zen. **EJ** 23 (1954) 275-304.

Suzuki, D.T. The awakening of a new consciousness in zen. In **Man and transformation: papers from eranos yearbooks** 5 (1964) 179-202 + 10 pl.

Suzuki, Daisetz T. Comprehending zen buddhism. In G. Myers (ed) **Self, religion and metaphysics,** ny (1961) 122-126.

Suzuki, Daisetz Teitaro. **Essays in zen buddhism.** London, first ser (1927) 388 p, index, illus; second ser (1933) 367 p, index, illus; third ser (1934) 396 p, index, illus. First ser repr (1949) second ser repr (1953) third ser repr (1953). See all 3 vol passim.

Suzuki, Daisetz Teitaro. Christmas Humphreys (ed) **The field of zen. Contributions to the middle way, the journal of the buddhist society.** London (n.d. Foreword 1969) xvii + 105 p, photos of author. Incl obituary by ed; Early memories by author. On ch'an see passim.

Suzuki, Daisetz T. (tsl)The hekigan roku—case two. **EB** n.s. 1.2 (sept 1966) 12-20.

Suzuki, Daisetz Teitaro. **Introduction to zen buddhism.** Kyoto (1934) 152 p, illus. See passim.

Suzuki, D.T. The lankavatara sutra as a mahayana text in especial relation to the teaching of zen buddhism. **EB** 4 (1927-28) 199-298.

Suzuki, Daisetz Teitaro. **Living by zen.** Tokyo (1949) 235 p. rev ed tokyo (1971). See passim.

Suzuki, Daisetz Teitaro. **Manual of zen buddhism.** Kyoto (1935) 192 p, illus. See passim.

Suzuki, Daisetz T. (tsl) On the hekigan roku ("blue cliff records") **EB** n.s. 1.1 (sept 1965) 5-21. Intro and tsl of "case one"

Suzuki, D.T. The recovery of a lost ms. on the history of zen in china. **EB** 6.1 (apr 1932) 107-110.

Suzuki, Daisetz T. Rinzai on zen. **Chicago review** 12 (summer 1958) 12-16.

Suzuki, Daisetz T. The secret message of bodhidharma. **EB** 4.1 (july-sept 1926) 1-26.

Suzuki, Daisetz T. Eva van Hoboken (ed) **Sengai, the zen master.** Greenwich, conn (1971) 191 p, illus ink drawings and calligraphy, explanatory notes by Shokin Furuta. Pref notes by Sazo Idemitsu, Basil Gray & Herbert Read. Posthumous publ.

Suzuki, Daisetz T. Some aspects of zen buddhism illustrated by selections from the hekiganroku, the first book of the zen school of buddhism. **Studies on buddhism in japan** 1 (1939) 1-35.

Suzuki, Daisetz Teitaro. **The training of the zen buddhist monk.** Kyoto (1934) 161 p, illus. Repr ny (1959)

Suzuki, Daisetz T. Ummon (i.e. yün-men, 862-949) on time. **EB** n.s. 6.2 (oct 1973) 1-13. Posthumous publ.

Suzuki, D.T. Zen: a reply to hu shih. **PEW** 3 (1953) 25-46. Re Hu's art: Ch'an (zen) buddhism in china . . . **ibid** 3-24 q.v.

Suzuki, D.T. Zen and pragmatism — a reply. **PEW** 4 (1954) 167-174.

Suzuki, D.T. **Zen buddhism. Selected writings of D.T. Suzuki.** Ed William Barrett. N.Y. (1956) See passim.

Suzuki, D.T. Zen buddhism as chinese interpretation of the doctrine of enlightenment. **EB** 2 (1923) 293-347.

Suzuki, Daisetz T. Zen buddhism on immortality: an extract from the hekiganroku. **EB** 3 (1924-25) 213-223.

Suzuki, D.T. **The zen doctrine of no-mind. The significance of the sūtra of hui-neng.** Ed Christmas Humphreys. London (1969) 160 p.

Suzuki, Daisetz & Ueda Shizuteru. The sayings of rinzai (lin-chi) A conversation between Suzuki Daisetz and Ueda Shizuteru. **EB** n.s. 6.1 (may 1973) 92-110. Publ after suzuki's death.

Tch'an (zen) Textes chinois fondamentaux, témoignes japonais, expériences vécues contemporaines. Paris (1970) **Hermès** 7. Indiv art sep listed in our bibliog. Abbrev **Tch'an.**

Thich, Nhat Hanh. **Zen keys.** NY (1974) 185 p. Tsl of orig french ed, **Clefs pour le zen,** paris (1973)

Thich, Thien-an. **Zen philosophy, zen practice.** Emoryville, calif (1975) 179 p, 2 app, gloss.

Timmons, Beverly & Joe Kamiya. The psychology and physiology of meditation and related phenomena: a bibliography. **JTP** 2.1 (1970) 41-59.

Timmons, Beverly & Demetri P. Kanellakos. The psychology and physiology of meditation and related phenomena: bibliography II. **JTP** 6.1 (1974) 32-38.

Tokiwa, Gishin. Tathāgata garbha. **JIBS** 22.1 (dec 1973) 10-19. Re zen.

Tsujimura, Koichi and Hartmar Buchner (tsl) **Der ochs und sein hirte (kuo-an-shih-niu-tu, dt.) Eine altchines. zen-geschichte. Erl. von daizohkutsu rekidoh ohtsu.** Pfullingen (1958) 132 s, mit jap bildern aus d. 15. jahrhundert. Engl tsl M.H. Trevor: **The ox and his herdsman. A chinese zen text. With commentaries and pointers by master d.r. otsu and japanese illustrations of the fifteenth century,** tokyo (1969) 96 p, illus.

Tsukamoto, Zenryū, Shibayama Zenkei & Nishitani Keiji. Dialogue: chinese zen. **EB** 8.2 (oct 1975) 66-93.

Tu, Wei-ming. An inquiry into wang yang-ming's four-sentence teaching. **EB** n.s. 7.2 (oct 1974) 32-48; repr in **H&SC** (1979) 162-178.

Ueda, Shizuteru. Leere und fülle: shûnyatâ im mahâyâna buddhismus. **EJ 1976** (1980) 135-163. Explication of the "ten ox-herding pictures" with illus.

Vajra bodhi sea. A monthly journal of orthodox buddhism. Publ in City of ten thousand buddhas, talmage, calif by sino-american budd assoc. Text in chin and engl. See passim. Abbrev **VBS.**

Verdú, Alfonso. **Abstraktion und intuition als weg zur wahrheit in yoga und zen** . . . München (1965) 309 p.

Verdú, Alfonso. **Dialectical aspects in buddhist thought; studies in sino-japanese mahāyāna buddhism.** Univ kansas centre for east asian studies (1974) 273 p.

Verdú, Alfonso. The "five ranks" dialectic of the sōtō-zen school in the light of kuei-feng tsung-mi's "ariya-shiki" scheme. **MN** 21.1/2 (1966) 125-170.

Vessie, Patricia Armstrong. **Zen buddhism. A bibliography of books and articles in english 1892-1975.** Ann arbor, mich (univ microfilms intl) 1976.

Waddell, N.A. (tsl) A selection from the t'sao ken t'an ('vegetable-root discourses') **EB** 2.2 (nov 1919) 88-98.

Wai-dau and Dwight Goddard (tsl) **Buddhist practice of concentration; dhyana for beginners [by chih-i]** Santa barbara, calif (1934) 59 p. French tsl G. Constant Lounsberry: **Dhyana pour les débutants . . .,** paris (1944) 104 p.

Waley, Arthur. History and religion. **PEW** 5 (1955) 75-78. Re debate between Hu Shih and D.T. Suzuki.

Waley, Arthur. **Zen buddhism and its relation to art.** London (1922) 31 p.

Wang, L. (tsl) Houai-hai. l'Illumination subite. Extraits du po-chang kouang-lou. **Tch'an** (1970) 53-60.

Wang, L. (tsl) Houang-po. De la transmission de l'esprit. Extraits du wan ling lou. **Tch'an** (1970) 35-51.

Wang, L. & J.M. (tsl) Seng-ts'an. Sin-sin-ming (inscription sur l'esprit de foi) **Tch'an** (1970) 81-85.

Watts, Harold H. **The modern reader's guide to religions** N.Y. (1964) See Chinese and japanese religion: zen buddhism, 565-576.

Weller, Friedrich. Neues vom ch'an buddhismus und zwei worte dazu. **OL** 59 (july-aug 1964) 325-338.

Wienpahl, Paul. Ch'an buddhism, western thought, and the concept of substance. **Inquiry** 14.1/2 (1971) 84-101. Comparisons with spinoza.

Wong, Mou-lam (tsl) **Sutra spoken by the sixth patriarch, wei lang [hui neng] . . .** Shanghai (pref 1930) 76 p. New ed rev Christmas Humphreys: **The sutra of wei lang (or hui neng)** london (1944) further rev ed (1953) 128 p. Repr westport, conn (1973)

Wu, Chi-yü. A study of han-shan. **TP** 45 (1957) 392-450.

Wu, John C. H. Tsl Michel Bello. l'Enseignement de houei-neng. **Tch'an** (1970) 3-14.

Wu, John C.H. **The golden age of zen.** Taipei (1967) 332 p, notes, index; app: My reminescences [sic] of dr. Daisetz T. Suzuki. With intro by Thomas Merton: A christian looks at zen, 1-28.

Wu, John C.H. Hui-neng's fundamental insights. **CC** 6.4 (oct 1965) 42-55.

Wu, John C.H. Little sparks of zen. **CC** 8 (mar 1967) 1-31.

Wu, John C.H. Zen: its origin and its significance. **JCS** 6 (1969) 87-95.

Yamada, Kōun (tsl) **Gateless gate.** Los angeles (1979) xxiii + 283 + 10 p, 4 app incl gloss and lineage charts. Tsl and comm on wu-men-kuan.

Yamada, Reirin. The way of understanding zen: tung-shan and shen tsan. **YE** 6.24 (winter 1957) 5-7.

Yampolsky, Philip (tsl) **The platform sutra of the sixth patriarch (hui-neng). The text of the tunhuang manuscript with translation, introduction and notes.** Columbia univ (1967) 212 p. facs.

Yampolsky, Philip. Problems in the translations of the chinese zen materials. **ICfO** 5 (1960) 111-112.

Yanagida, Seizan. Tsl Ruth Fuller Sasaki. The life of lin-chi i-hsüan. **EB** n.s. 5.2 (oct 1972) 70-94.

Yasutani, Hakuun. Tsl C. Blacker. The five kinds of zen (based on tsung-mi's analysis) **MW** 35.4 (feb 1961) 147-150.

Yi, T'ao-t'ien (tsl) Records of the life of ch'an master pai-chang huai-hai. **EB** n.s. 8.1 (may 1975) 42-73.

Young-Merllié, Christine. La mystique des maîtres du tch'an. In **EMM** (1975) 243-260.

Yü, Chün-fang. Ta-hui tsung-kao (1089-1163) and kung-an ch'an. **JCP** 6.2 (june 1979) 211-235.

Yung, Hsi. **Buddhism and the chan school of china.** Tsl fr chin Chou, Hsiang-kuang. Allahabad (1965) 24 p.

Zaehner, R.C. **Concordant discord. The interdependence of faiths.** Oxford (1970) See chap 14, What is zen? 279-301.

Zeuschner, Robert (tsl) The hsien tsung chi (an early ch'an (zen) buddhist text) **JCP** 3.3 (june 1976) 253-267.

Zeuschner, Robert. The meaning of hīnayāna in northern ch'an. **EB** n.s. 8.2 (oct 1975) 37-49.

Zeuschner, Robert. A selected bibliography for ch'an buddhism in china. **JCP** 3.3 (june 1976) 299-311. Incl wk in western languages & jap.

Zeuschner, Robert B. (tsl) A sermon by the ch'an master ho-tse shen-hui. **MW** 49.3 (nov 1974) 45-47.

Zeuschner, Robert. The understanding of mind in the northern line of ch'an (zen) **PEW** 28.1 (jan 1978) 69-80.

10. SANGHA, MONACHISM & MONASTERIES

Aufhauser, Johannes B. Ein blick in buddhistische heiligtümer des fernen ostens. **Zeitschrift für buddhismus und vervandte gebiete** 6 (1924-25) 243-258.

Ball, J. Dyer. Tonsure (chinese) − 2. Buddhist. In **HERE** 12 (1921) 38-39.

Bapat, P.V. Shan-chien-p'i-p'o-sha and the code of conduct of the early buddhist religieux. **Annals of the bhandarkar oriental research institute** 52 (1971) 1-30.

Bazin, Antoine P.L. Recherches sur l'origine, l'histoire et la constitution des ordres religieux dans l'empire chinois. **JA** 5e sér, 8 (1856) 105-174; publ sep, paris (1861) 70 p.

Bleichsteiner, R. **Die gelbe kirche. Mysterien der buddhistischen klöster in indien, tibet, mongolei und china.** Wien (1937) 272 p, 83 pl.

Blofeld, John. Life in a chinese buddhist monastery. **THM** 8 (1939) 145-154.

Blofeld, John. Life in a zen monastery. In **Z&H** (1978) 38-47. Repr fr author's autobiography, **The wheel of life,** london (1959) 159-174.

Blofeld, John. **Mantras. Sacred words of power.** London & ny (1977) 106 p, illus. See esp chap 1-2.

la Bonzerie de kou-chan, près de fou-tcheou-fou (fokien). Par un dominicain, du couvent de lyon, ancien miss. en chine, 3 janvier 1870. **MC** 10 (1878) 81-83.

Buddhist monasteries of taiwan. I. Kuan-yin hill and ling-yün buddhist temple; II. Yuan tung shih, a nunnery. **New force** 2.4 (feb 1951) 20-25, illus photos.

Chambeau, Gabriel. Une visite aux monastères bouddhiques de kieou-hoa-chan. **Études** 130 (20 mars 1912) 785-798; 131 (5 avril 1912) 34-52.

Ch'en, Kenneth K.S. The role of buddhist monasteries in t'ang society. **HR** 15.3 (feb 1976) 209-230.

Chu, Ch'an (pseud for John Blofeld) Life in a ch'an monastery. **Buddhism in england** 16 (1941) 10-11.

Chü Tsan. A buddhist monk's life. **CRecon** 3.1 (1954) 42-44.

Curzon, George N. The cloister in cathay. **Fortnightly review** 49 (1888) 752-767.

Drake, F.S. The shên-t'ung monastery and the beginning of buddhism in shantung. **MS** 4 (1939-40) 1-39.

Dukes, Edwin J. A buddhist monastery. Chap 10 in author's **ELC** (1885) 214-229. Re monastery on kushan, fukien.

Dukes, Edwin J. Cremation of a buddhist priest. Chap 11 in author's **ELC** (1895) 230-236.

Dukes, J. and A. Fielde. Ein buddhist kloster in china. **EMM** n.s. 36 (1892) 57-71.

Durt, Hubert. The counting stick (śalākā) and the majority/minority rule in the buddhist community. **JIBS** 23.1 (dec 1974) 28-34.

The Editor. Initiation of buddhist priests. **ChRec** 9.3 (may-june 1878) 181-184. Eyewitness account of rites at kooshan, fukien.

Edkins, Joseph. The monasteries at pu-to. **NCH** 345 (7 mar 1856)

Edkins, J. Visit to the chan-t'an sï — monastery of the sandal-wood buddha. **ChRec** 7.6 (nov-dec 1876) 431-435. Temple in peking.

Eigner, J. Life in buddhist monasteries. **CJ** 28 (1938) 275-279.

Fei, Shih-tang. How to eat without eating meat. **Echo** 3.3 (mar 1973) 34-38. Re vegetarian meals at tsai ming budd temple in tahsi.

Fitch, D.F. In the 'monastery of the soul's retreat.' **Asia** 24 (1924) 524-527.

Goodrich, G. Nuns of north china. **Asia** 37 (1937) 90-93.

Gordon-Cumming, C.F. In a buddhist monastery. Vol 2, chap 23 in author's **WinC** (1886) 30-49.

Gordon-Cumming, C.F. Ningpo and the buddhist temples. **Century magazine** 24, n.s. 4 (may-oct 1882) 726-739, illus.

Graham, Dorothy. Pools for the preservation of life. **CW** 147 (1938) 536-542.

Gray, John Henry. **Walks in the city of canton.** HK (1875) repr san francisco (1974) See chap 3 for Hai-chwang-sze (honam budd temple) 33-75.

Groot, J.J.M. de. **Le code du mahayana en chine, son influence sur la vie monacale et sur le monde laïque.** Amsterdam (1893) 271 p.

Groot, J.J.M. de. Militant spirit of the buddhist clergy in china. **TP** sér 1, 2.2 (juin 1891) 127-139. Same title in **JNCBRAS** 26 (1894) 108-120.

Gundert, Wilhelm. Die nonne liu bei we-schan. In **Asiatica** (1954) 184-197.

Hackmann, Heinrich. Buddhist monastery life in china. **EA** 1.3 (sept 1902) 239-261. German version: Buddhistisches klosterleben in china, **FO** 1 (1902) 235-256.

Hackmann, Heinrich. Das buddhisten-kloster tien-dong in der chinesischen provinz che-kiang. **ZMK** 17 (1902) 173-178.

Hackmann, Heinrich. 'Pai chang ch'ing kuei.' The rules of buddhist monastic life in china. **TP** n.s. 9 (1908) 651-662. Same title in **Trans. 3rd ICHR Oxford, 1908,** vol 1, oxford (1908) p 137.

Hackmann, Heinrich. Die schulen des chinesischen buddhismus. **MSOS** 14 (1911) 232-266.

Hardy, Jacques and Ch. Lenormand. Le monastère du kou-chan [fukien] **Monde moderne** 29 (déc 1906) 206-214.

Harlez, Charles de. Une visite au monastère bouddhique de wu-tchin par pe-k'iu-yi. **Muséon** 12 (1893) 99-107, 197-212.

Hecken, Joseph van. Les lamaseries d'oto (ordos) **MS** 22 (1963) 121-168, illus, map.

Hsü, Vivian. Monks and nuns as comic figures in yüan drama. **Dodder** 2 (jan 1970) 10-12.

Hsüan-hua (comm) BTTSoc (tsl) **A general explanation of the essentials of the śrāmaṇera vinaya and rules of deportment.** San francisco (1975) 94 p, index. Tsl of ming dyn text by lien-ch'ih (i.e. chu-hung, 1532-1612)

Initiation of buddhist priests. **ChRec** 9.3 (may-june 1878) 181-184.

Irving, E.A. A visit to the buddhist and tao-ist monasteries on the lo fau shan. **BIM** 157 (mar 1895) 453-467.

Kiang, Alfred. A new life begins in the [buddhist] temples. **CWR** 116 (11 feb 1950) 173-174.

Lévy, Paul. **Buddhism: a mystery religion?** Univ london (1957) ny (1968) 111 p, index. Interpretations of ordination rituals.

Li, Rongxi. The guang-ji monastery. **YE** n.s. 6.4 (autumn 1980) 7-11. A temple in peking.

Little, Alicia Bewicke. Among chinese monasteries. **MacMillan's magazine** 81 (jan 1900) 201-208.

Little, Mrs Archibald. Buddhist monasteries; a chinese (buddhist nuns') ordination. Chap 17-18 in author's **IntC** (ca. 1900) 227-250.

Loi. Der mönch des klosters kilungsan. **OstL** 18 (1904) 163-165, 202-203, 243-247.

Maspero, Henri. Communautés et moines bouddhistes chinois au IIe et IIIe siècles. **BEFEO** 10 (1910) 222-232.

Maspero, Henri. Les origines de la communauté bouddhiste de loyang. **JA** 225 (1934) 87-107.

Matignon, J.J. l'Auto-crémation des prêtres bouddhistes. **Archives d'anthropologie criminelle** 13 (15 janv 1898); also in author's book, **Crime, superstition et misère,** lyon (1899) q.v. 143-156.

Miller, Alan L. The buddhist monastery as a total institution. **JRelSt** 7.2 (fall 1979) 15-29.

Peri, N. and H. Maspero. Le monastère de la kouan-yin qui ne vent pas s'en aller. **BEFEO** 9 (1909) 797-807 (P'u-t'o shan)

Prebish, Charles S. (tsl) **Buddhist monastic discipline: the sanskrit prātimoksa sūtras of the mahāsāmghikas and mūlasarvāstivādins.** Penn state univ (1975) 164 p, bibliog.

Prip-Møller, Johannes. **About buddhist temples.** Peiping (1931) 33 p, illus.

Prip-Møller, Johannes. **Chinese buddhist monasteries. Their plan and its function as a setting for buddhist monastic life.** Copenhagen and oxford univ (1937) repr univ hong kong (1967) 396 p, index, sketches, plans, elevations, photos.

Prip-Møller, Johannes. Streiflichter auf die entwicklung des bauplans chinesischer buddhistischer klöster in ihrem verhältnis zum buddhistischem kultus. **OZ** 24 (1938) 156-166.

Rhie, Marylin M. **The fo-kuang ssu: literary evidence and buddhist images.** NY (1977) 274 p, illus.

Sato, Mitso. The ceremony of the ordination and its understanding in chinese terms of the vinaya. **JIBS** 11 (1963) 1-8.

Saunders, Kenneth J. Buddhist monasticism and its fruits. **AP** 10 (1939) 229-234.

Thomson, J. A visit to yuan-foo monastery. **ChRec** 3.10 (mar 1871) 296-299.

Tiffany, Osmond jr. **The canton chinese.** Boston & cambridge (1849) See chap 10, The buddhist temple (honam) 180-191.

Tsu, Y.Y. (tsl) A diary of a buddhist nun. **JR** 7.5/6 (oct 1927) 612-618. From **Hai ch'ao yin** 3.11/12 (feb 1923) Repr in **CWayRel** (1973) 120-124.

Twitchett, D.C. The monasteries and china's economy in medieval times. **BSOAS** 19 (1957) 526-549.

Twitchett, D.C. Monastic estates in t'ang china. **AM** n.s. 5 (1956) 123-146.

Verdeille, Maurice (tsl) Le monastère de la montagne 'ou-tai' en révolution. **BSEIS** 70 (1919) 21-37, 2 pl. Extr par l'éditeur des 'siao-siao chouo' du livre intitulé 'liang shan po.'

Visit to two celebrated peking temples. **ChRec** 12.5 (sept-oct 1881) 363-372. In the western hills area: chih-t'ai-sz and pi-yun-sz.

Welch, Holmes. The buddhist career. **JHKBRAS** 2 (1962) 37-48.

Welch, Holmes. The chinese sangha, the good and the bad. **The buddhist annual** (Colombo) 1 (1964) 23-26.

Yang, Lien-sheng. Buddhist monasteries and four money-raising institutions in chinese history. **HJAS** 13 (1950) 174-191. Repr in author's collection: **Studies in chinese institutional history,** cambridge, mass (1963) 198-215.

Yorke, Gerald. **China changes.** London (1935) See chap 7 and 9 on buddhist monachism.

11. PILGRIMS

Abegg, Emil. Chinesische buddhapilger in indien. 2. Huan-tsang. **AS** 1-2 (1948) 56-79.

Abel-Rémusat, J.P. **Foë kouë ki ou relation des royaumes bouddhiques: voyage dans la tartarie, dans l'afghanistan et dans l'inde, exécuté, à la fin du IVe siècle, par chỷ fã hian. Traduit du chinois et commenté par m. Abel- Rémusat. Ouvrage posthume revu, complété, et augmenté d'éclaircissements nouveaux par mm. Klaproth et Landresse.** Paris (1836) lxviii + 424 p. See item by H.H. Wilson, Account of the foe kúe ki . . .

Abel-Rémusat, J.P. Mémoire sur un voyage dans l'asie centrale, dans le pays des afghans et des beloutches, et dans l'inde, exécuté à la fin du IVe siècle de notre ère, par plusieurs samanéens de la chine. **MAIBL** n.s. 13 (1831) 345 et seq. See also author's art: Voyage dans la tartarie, dans l'afghanistan et dans l'inde, exécuté à la fin du IVe siècle par plusieurs samanéens de la chine. **RDM** (1 janv 1832)

Allan, C.W. The priest hsuan tsang and the sian monuments. **ChRec** 39 (oct 1908) 576-577.

Bagchi, P.C. (tsl) **She-kia-fang-che.** Santiniketan (1959) 151 p.

Beal, Samuel. Indian travels of chinese buddhists. **IA** 10 (1881) 109-111, 192-199, 246-248.

Beal, Samuel (tsl) **The life of hiuen-tsiang. By the shaman hwui li. With an introduction containing an account of the works of i-tsing.** London (1911) xlvii + 218 p. Repr westport, conn (1973) san francisco (1974)

Beal, Samuel (tsl) **Si-yu-ki. Buddhist records of the western world. Translated from the chinese of hiuen tsiang (a.d. 629)** London (1884) vol 1, cviii + 242 p; vol 2, vii + 368 p. Beal's **Travels of fahhian and sung yun** q.v. is incorporated in this work. Repr as **Travels of hiouen-thsang,** calcutta (1957-58) 4 vol. Repr san francisco (1976)

Beal, Samuel. Some remarks on the narrative of fã-hien. **JRAS** n.s. 19 (1887) 191-206.

Beal, Samuel (tsl) **Travels of fah-hian and sungyun, buddhist pilgrims, from china to india (400 a.d.-518 a.d.)** London (1896) lxxiii + 208 p.

Beal, Samuel. Two chinese-buddhist inscriptions found at buddha gaya. **JRAS** n.s. 13 (1881) 552-572.

Bodh-Gayā inscriptions: See a ser of art and responses by Édouard Chavannes and Gustave Schlegel, the former publ in **RHR,** the latter in **TP:**

E.C.— Les inscriptions chinoises de B.-G. **RHR** 34.1 (1896)

G.S.— (same title) **TP** 7.5 (1896)

E.C.— La première inscr. chin. de B.-G. **RHR** 36.1 (1897)

G.S.— (same title) **TP** 8.5 (1897)

G.S.— Les inscriptions chin. de B.-G. ii. Première partie. **TP** 8.1 (1897)

G.S.— Les inscr. chin. de B.-G. ii. Deuxième partie. **TP** 8.2 (1897)

G.S.— Les inscr. chin. de B.-G. iii-iv. **TP** 8.3 (1897)

Boulting, Wiliam. **Four pilgrims: (1) hiuen tsiang . . .** London and n.y. (1920) viii + 256 p.

Chang, Kuei-sheng. The travels of hsüan chuang. **CC** 1.3 (1958) 86-123.

Char, S.U. Raghavendra. Ancient contacts between india and china with particular reference to buddhism. In **MS/CA** (1977) 45-52.

Châu, Thích-minh. **Hsuan tsang, the pilgrim and scholar.** Nha-trang (1963) 139 p.

Chavannes, Édouard. Gunavarman. **TP** n.s. 5 (1904) 193-206.

Chavannes, Édouard. l'Itinéraire de ki-ye. **BEFEO** 4 (1904) 75-81.

Chavannes, Édouard. I-tsing. In **La grande encyclopédie,** paris, vol 20 (1894) 1137.

Chavannes, Édouard. Voyage de song-yun dans l'udyāna et le gandhāra (518-522 apr j.-c.) **BEFEO** 3 (1903) 379-441. Note additionelle par Paul Pelliot, p 442.

Chavannes, Édouard (tsl) **Voyages des pèlerins bouddhistes. — Les religieux éminents qui allerent chercher la loi dans les pays d'occident, mémoire composé à l'époque de la grand dynastie t'ang par i-tsing.** Paris (1894) xxi + 218 p.

Ch'en, Kenneth K.S. Hsüan tsang. In **EncyB** vol 11 (1970)

Cunningham, Alexander. Verification of the itinerary of hwan thsang through ariana and india. With reference to major anderson's hypothesis of its modern compilation. **JRASB** 17 (1848) 476-488.

Cunningham, Alexander. Verification of the itinerary of the chinese pilgrim, hwan thsang, through afghanistan and india during the first half of the seventh century of the christian era. **JRASB** 17 (1848) 13-60.

Doré, H. Le grand pèlerinage bouddhique de lang-chan et les cinq montagnes de tong-tcheou. **NCR** 1.1 (mar 1919) 41-56; 1.2 (may 1919) 120-144; 1.3 (july 1919) 282-298; 1.5 (oct 1919) 457-479; 1.6 (dec 1919) 580-603; 2.1 (feb 1920) 44-46.

Douglas, Robert K. Fa-hien's description of the image of maitreya buddha (bodhisattva) **Athenaeum** (12 mar 1887) 359. Also see J. Legge's art on the image, **ibid** 390, 454.

Eckstein, Baron d'. Tsl Stanislas Julien. Mémoires sur les contrées occidentales . . . par hiouen thsang . . . tome premier. **JA** sér 5, t 10 (1857) 475-552. Rev art.

Edgar, J.H. Did hsüan tsang visit the west of china after his return from india? **JWCBorderResS** 3 (1926-29) 106.

Eigner, Julius. Strange ceremonies connected with buddhist pilgrimage to miao feng shan. **CJ** 30.3 (mar 1939) 168-172, illus photos, Temple in western hills near peking.

Enoki, Kazuo. Tsung-lê's mission to the western regions in 1378-1382. **OE** 19 (1972) 47-53.

Fa Hsien. Record of early buddhist countries. **CL** 3 (1956) 153-181, map.

Feer, Henri L. Les jatakas dans les mémoires de hiouen-thsang. **Actes du 11e ICO, Paris 1897,** t 1, sec 1, paris (1898) 151-169.

Ferguson, John C. Books on journeys to western regions. **CJ** 11.2 (aug 1929) 61-68. Re Hsüan chuang's ta t'ang hsi yü chi, li chih-ch'ang's ch'ang ch'un chen jen hsi yu chi, hsi yu chi, hou hsi yu chi, tsa chü hsi yu chi.

Finot, Louis. Hiuan-tsang and the far east. **JRAS** (jan 1920) 447-452.

Fujishima, Ryauon (tsl) Deux chapitres extraits des mémoires d'i-tsing sur son voyage dans l'inde. **JA** 8e sér, 12 (1888) 411-439.

Fujishima, Ryauon. Index des mots sanscrits chinois contenus dans les deux chapitres d'i-tsing. **JA** 8e sér, 13 (1889) 490-496.

Giles, Herbert A. (tsl) **Record of the buddhist kingdoms.** London (1877) Retsl as **The travels of fa-hsien (399-414 a.d.), or, record of the buddhist kingdoms.** Cambridge univ (1923) xvi + 96 p. Repr london (1956)

Gowen, Herbert H. The travels of a buddhist pilgrim, a.d. 399-414. **American antiquarian and oriental journal** 21 (1899) 3-13. Re fa hsien.

Grimes, A. The journey of fa-hsien from ceylon to canton. **JMBRAS** 19 (1941) 76-92, 4 charts.

Grousset, René. **Sur les traces du bouddha.** Paris (1929) 329 p, map, illus. Engl tsl Mariette Leon: **In the footsteps of the buddha,** london (1932) 352 p, map, indexes, illus (Hsüan chuang and yi-ching) Repr san francisco (1976)

Guignes, Joseph de. Recherches historiques sur la religion indienne. Second mémoire . . . **MAIBL** 40 (1780) 247-306.

Harlez, Charles de. Un pèlerin-missionaire bouddhiste au IVe siècle de notre ère. **La controverse et la contemporain** 11 (1887) 5-33.

Ho, Chang-chun. Fa-hsien's pilgrimage to buddhist countries. **CL** 3 (1956) 149-181.

Huber, É. l'Itinéraire de pèlerin ki-ye dans l'inde. **BEFEO** 2 (1902) 256-259.

Introduction to the buddhist library of huen chwang. By the emperor tai tsung a.d. 627-649. **JNCBRAS** 48 (1917) 115-117.

Jacquet, E. Examen de la traduction du fo koue ki, ouvrage posthume de m. Abel-Rémusat, compété par mm J. Klaproth et C. Landresse. **JA** sér 3, t 4 (août 1837) 141-179. The wk was apparently never finished.

Jan, Yün-hua. Hui ch'ao and his works: a reassessment. **IAC** 12 (jan 1964) 177-190.

Jinananda, B. Early routes between china and india. In **B&J** (1976) 265-271.

Julien, Stanislas (tsl) **Histoire de la vie d'hiouen thsang, et de ses voyages dans l'inde entre les années 629 et 645 de notre ère.** Paris (1851) 72 p. See further next item.

Julien, Stanislas (tsl) **Histoire de la vie de hiouen-thsang et de ses voyages dans l'inde depuis l'an 629 jusq'en 645, par hoëi-li et yen thsong; suivi de documents et d'éclaircissements géographiques tirés de la relation originale de hiouen-thsang.** Paris (1853) lxxxiv + 472 p.

Julien, Stanislas (tsl) **Mémoires sur les contrées occidentales, traduits du sanscrit en chinois, en l'an 648, par hiouen-thsang, et du chinois en français, par S.J.** Paris, vol 1 (1857) lxxviii + 493; vol 2 (1858) xix + 576.

Julien, Stanislas. Renseignements bibliographiques sur les relations des voyages dans l'inde et les descriptions du si-yu, qui ont été composées en chinois entre le Ve et le XVIIIe siècle de notre ère. **JA** 4e sér, 10 (1847) 265-269.

Julien, Stanislas (tsl) **Voyages des pèlerins bouddhistes.** Paris (1853-58) t 1: **Histoire de la vie de hiouen thsang et de ses voyages dans l'inde;** t 2 et 3: **Mémoires sur les contrées occidentales.** See foregoing items.

Klaproth, J. Reise des chinesischen buddhapriesters hiüan thsang durch mittel-asien und indien. **Sitzung der berliner geog. gesel.** (15 nov 1834) 8 p.

Lacouperie, Albert J.B. Terrien de. On hiuen-tsiang instead of yüan chwang, and the necessity of avoiding the pekinese sounds in the quotations of ancient proper names in chinese. **JRAS** (1892) 835-840.

Laidlay, J.W. **The pilgrimage of fa hian; from the french edition of the foe koue ki of mm. Rémusat, Klaproth, and Landresse with additonal notes and illustrations.** Calcutta (1848) viii + 373 p.

Lamiot, Louis (tsl) **Ta-t'ang-hsi-yu-chi. Esquisse du sy-yu, ou des pays á l'ouest de la chine.** Paris, 2 pt (1832)

Laufer, Berthold. Ein buddhistisches pilgerbild. **Globus** 86 (1904) 386-388.

Laufer, Berthold. Zum bildnis des pilgers hsüan tsang. **Globus** 88 (1905) 257-258.

Legge, James. The image of maitreya. **Athenaeum** (12 mar 1887) 390, 454. See art by R.K. Douglas above.

Legge, James (tsl) **A record of buddhistic kingdoms. Being an account by the chinese monk fa-hien of his travels in india and ceylon (a.d. 399-414) in search of the buddhist books of discipline.** Oxford univ (1886) repr (1964) index, illus, chin text in corean rescension. Repr san francisco (1975)

Legge, James. Sur un passage de la préface du . . . hsi yü ki. **Mémoires société études japonaises etc.** 5 (nov 1886) 263-266.

Lévi, Sylvain. Hiouen-tsang. In **La grande encyclopédie.**, paris, vol 20 (1894) 105-106.

Lévi, Sylvain. Les missions de wang hiuen-ts'e dans l'inde. **JA** (1900) 297-341, 401-468.

Lévi, Sylvain. Notes chinoises sur l'inde. **BEFEO** 2.3 (1902) 246-255; 3 (1903) 38-53; 4.3 (1904) 543-579; 5.3/4 (1905) 253-305.

Lévi, Sylvain. Wang hiuen-ts'ö et kaniska. **TP** 2e sér, 13 (1912) 307-309.

Lévi, Sylvain et Édouard Chavannes (tsl) Voyages des pèlerins bouddhistes. — l'Itinéraire d'ou-k'ong (751-790) **JA** 9e sér, 6 (1895) 341-384.

Lévy, Paul. Les pèlerins chinois en inde. In **FA:BPB** (1959) 375-436.

Li, Hsin-tsung. Hsuan chuang and chinese buddhism. **China today** 10.6 (june 1967) 13-17.

Li, Yung-hsi (tsl) **Monk hui-li: the life of hsuan tsang, the tripitaka-master of the great tzu-en monastery.** Peking (1959) 274 p.

Li, Yung-hsi (tsl) **A record of the buddhist countries by fa-hsien.** Peking (1957) 94 p, map.

Liétord. Le pèlerin bouddhiste chinois i-tsing et la médecine de l'inde au IIIe siècle. **Bulletin de la société française d'histoire de la médecine** 1 (1903) 472-487.

Mabbett, Ian W. Chinese buddhist pilgrims. **APQCSA** 11.2 (summer 1979) 4-12.

Meuwese, Catherine **l'Inde du bouddha. Vue par les pèlerins chinois sous la dynastie tang (VIIe siècle)** Paris (1968) 319 p, illus, map.

Moule, A.C. Relics of the monk sakugen's visits to china 1539-1541 and 1547-1550. **AM** 3.1 (1952) 59-64.

Neumann, Carl F. Pilgerfahrten buddhistischer priester von china nach indien. — aus dem chinesischen übersetzt, mit einer einleitung und mit anmerkungen versehen . . . **Zeitschrift für die historische theologie** 3 (1833) 66 p.

Nilakantasastri, K.A. The chinese pilgrims. In **FA:BPB** (1959) 437-448.

Pelliot, Paul. Deux itinéraires de chine en inde à la fin du VIIIe siècle. **BEFEO** 4 (1904) 131-413.

Pelliot, Paul. Note sur le récit de hiuan-tsang relatif à la légende de sou-ta-na. **BEFEO** 3 (1903) 334.

Pelliot, Paul. Trois termes de mémoires de hiuan-tsang. In **EORL** (1932) t 2, 423-431.

Petech, Luciano. La 'description des pays d'occident' de che tao-ngan. **MSPD** t 1 (1966) 167-190. See further, author's Note additionelle, **ibid** t 2 (1974) 399-402.

Raja, C.K. I-tsing and bhartthari's vakyapadiya. In **Dr s. krishnaswami aiyangar commemoration volume,** madras (1936) 285-298.

Rosthorn, A.V. Letter on hiouen-tsang's 'twelve chang.' **Wiener zeitschrift für die kunde des morgenländes** 10 (1896) 280-284.

Roussel, Romain. **Les pèlerinages à travers les siècles.** Paris (1954) 326 p. See . . . Bouddhistes . . . Taoïstes . . .

Sarkar, Himansu Bhusan. The travails of foreign journey between eastern india and china in the ancient and early medieval periods. **Journal of indian history** 52.1 (apr 1974) 101-125.

Sasaki, Kyōgo. A note on the study of the ta-t'ang hsi-yü-chi. **EB** 8.4 (aug 1958) 8-9.

Sastri, R.A. Nilakanta. The chinese pilgrims. **FA:BPB** (1959) 437-448.

Saunders, Kenneth J. Fa-hian in lanka. **IRM** 11 (july 1922) 401-405.

Schlegel, G. Itinerary to the western countries of wang-nieh in a.d. 964. **MCSJ** 21 (1893) 35-64.

Sen, A.C. Chinese pilgrims in ancient india. **IAC** 6.3 (jan 1958) 271-275.

Silabhadra, Bhikkhu. Fa-hien's indian travel. **MB** 49 (1941) 436-448.

Staël-Holstein, A. von. Hsüan-tsang and modern research. **JNCBRAS** 54 (1923) 16-24.

Stein, Mark Aurel. The desert crossing of hsüan-tsang, 630 a.d. **Geographical journal.** 54.5 (nov 1919) 265-277.

Stein, Mark Aurel. La traversée du désert par hiuan-tsang en 630 ap. j.-c. **TP** 20 (1921) 332-354.

Takakusu, Junjirō. Discovery of hiuen tsang's memorials. **YE** 2 (8 aug 1926) 75-77.

Takakusu, Junjirō. Fa-hian. In **HERE** 5 (1912) 678.

Takakusu, Junjirō. Hiuen tsang. A great traveller in india. **HZ** 12.11 (1897) 24-25.

Takakusu, Junjirō. **Kanshin's (chien-chên's) voyage to the east, a.d. 742-54, by aomi-no-mabito genkai (a.d. 779)** London (1925)

Takakusu, Junjirō (tsl) **A record of the buddhist religion as practised in india and the malay archipelago (a.d. 671-695) by i-tsing.** Oxford univ (1896) repr taipei (1970) lxiv + 240 p, map, notes, index.

Takakusu, Junjirō. Th. Watters: On yuan chwang's travels in india. **JRAS** (1905) 412-417. Review art.

Takakusu, Junjirō. Le voyage de kanshin au japon (742-754) **PCIEEO** (1902) 56-60.

Takakusu, Junjirō. Yuan-chwang, fa-hian and i-tsing. In **HERE** 12 (1921) 841-843.

Taylor, G. The marvelous genealogy of hsuen tseng. **ChRev** 17 (1889) 258-265.

Thomas, F.W. A chinese buddhist pilgrim's letters of introduction. **JRAS** (1927) 546-558.

Valentino, Henri. **Le voyage d'un pèlerin chinois dans l'inde des bouddhas . . .** Paris (1932) 243 p, map.

Waley, Arthur. **The real tripitaka and other pieces.** London (1952) See pt one, 9-130, on hsüan chuang; pt two, 131-168, on ennin and ensai.

Watters, Thomas. Fa-hsien and his english translators. **ChRev** 8 (1879-80) 107-116, 131-140, 217-230, 277-284, 323-341.

Watters, Thomas. **On yuan chwang's travels in india, 629-645 a.d.** Ed T.W. Rhys David and S.W. Bushell. London (1904) vol 1, 401 p; vol 2, 357 p; indexes, maps. Repr san francisco (1975).

Watters, Thomas. The shadow of a pilgrim, or, notes on the ta-t'ang hsi-yü-chi of yuan-chwang. **ChRev** 18 (1889-90) 327-347; 19 (1890-91) 107-126, 182-189, 201-224, 376-383; 20 (1891-92) 29-32.

Weller, Friedrich. Kleine beiträge zur erklärung fa-hsiens. In **AMHAV** (1923) 560-574.

Wethered, H. Newton. **The four paths of pilgrimage.** London (1947) See chap 4 sec 5-6 on hsuan-tsang, 182-191.

Wilson, H.H. Account of the foe kúe ki, or travels of fa hian in india, translated from the chinese by m. Rémusat. **JRAS** 5 (1839) 108-140. Repr in **ChRep** 9 (1840) 334-366.

Wilson, H.H. Summary review of the travels of hiouen thsang, from the translation of the si-yu-ki by m. Julien, and the mémoire analytique of m. Vivien de Saint-martin. **JRAS** 17 (1860) 106-137.

Wriggins, Sally. A monk's journey to the buddhist holy land. **Orientations** 10.10 (oct 1979) 54-57, illus chin woodcuts. Re Hsüan chuang.

Yule, Henry. Hwen t'sang [hsuan chuang] In **EncyB** 9th ed (1881) vol 12, 418-419.

12. RITES & PRAXIS, CULTS, IMPLEMENTS

Blofeld, John. **Mantras. Sacred words of power.** London & ny (1977) 106 p, illus. See esp chap 1-2.

Chinese rosary. **ICG** no 9 (1819) 138-139.

Davidson, J. LeRoy. Buddhist paradise cults in sixth century china. **JISOA** 17 (1949) 112-124.

Day, Clarence B. The cult of amitabha. **CJ** 33 (1940) 235-249. Repr **PRPCC** (1975)

Demiéville, Paul. Notes on buddhist hymnology in the far east. In **Buddhist studies in honour of walpola rahula,** london & sri lanka (1980) 44-61.

Devéria, G. Liturgie bouddhique. **REO** 1.2 (1882)

Dukes, Edwin J. Cremation of a buddhist priest. Chap 11 in author's **ELC** (1885) 230-236.

Duyvendak, J.J.L. The buddhistic festival of all-souls in china and japan. **AO** 5 (1927) 39-48.

Edkins, Joseph. Earnestness in chinese buddhism. **IA** 12 (1883) 104-110.

Edkins, Joseph. Mandal. **ChRev** 16 (1888) 369.

Edkins, Joseph. Religious devotion among buddhists. **Sunday at home** (may 1882)

Edkins, Joseph. Wooden fish as a buddhist implement. **ChRev** 16 (1888) 375.

Eigner, Julius. Strange ceremonies connected with buddhist pilgrimage to miao feng shan. **CJ** 30.3 (mar 1939) 168-172, photos. Temple in western hills near peking.

Eurius, O. Die gelübde der buddhisten und die ceremonie ihrer ablegung bei den chinesen. In Karl Abel (tsl) **Arbeiten der kaiserlich russischen gerandschaft zu peking** . . . [q.v. in Part One: General Studies] (1858) 315-419.

Filliozat, Jean. La mort voluntaire par le feu et la tradition bouddhique indienne. **JA** 251 (1963) 21-51.

Fritzen, Joachim. Das schlagzeug in der buddhistischen liturgischen musik chinas. **OE** 22.2 (dec 1975) 169-182, illus with musical ex.

Gernet, Jacques. Les suicides par le feu chez les bouddhistes chinois du Ve au Xe siècle. **MIHEC** 2 (1960) 527-558.

Graham, Dorothy. Dance of the whirling devils; huang ssu monastery, peking. **CW** 122 (feb 1926) 594-599.

Groot, J.J.M. de. Buddhist masses for the dead at amoy. **Actes, 6eICO Leide, 1883** leiden (1885) 1-120.

Groot, J.J.M. de. Miséricorde envers les animaux dans le bouddhism chinois. **TP** 3 (1892) 466-489.

Gulik, Robert Hans van. **Hayagrīva. The mantrayānic aspect of the horse-cult in china and japan.** Leiden (1935) 103 p, illus.

Hodous, Lewis. The universal rescue. **ChRec** 48.7 (july 1917) 434-439. Re p'u-tu of seventh month.

Hou, Ching-lang. **Monnaies d'offrande et la notion de trésorerie dans la religion chinoise.** Paris (1975) 238 p, notes, bibliog, chin texts, pl, index, tipped-in samples of spirit money.

Imbault-huart, Camille. Une cérémonie bouddhiste en chine: scène de la vie intime chinoise. **JA** 7e sér, 16 (oct-déc 1880) 526-533.

Iwai, Hirosato. The buddhist priest and the ceremony of attaining womanhood during the yüan dynasty. **TBMRD** 7 (1935) 105-161.

Jan, Yün-hua. Buddhist self-immolation in medieval china. **HR** 4.2 (1964-65) 243-268.

Jan, Yün-hua. Der buddhistische begräbnisritus. **Concilium** 4 (feb 1968) 144-146.

Johnston, R.F. Purification (chinese) In **HERE** 10, p. 470.

Johnston, R.F. Vows (chinese) In **HERE** 12, p 646.

Karutz, Richard. Von buddhas heiliger fuss-spur. **Globus** 89 (jan 1906) 21-25, 45-49.

Landon, Perceval. A remnant of buddha's body. **NC** 50 (aug 1901) 236-243.

La Vallée Poussin, Louis de. Staupikam. **HJAS** 2 (1937) 276-289. Theory of stupa and its origin.

Lessing, Ferdinand D. Skizze des ritus: die speisung der hungergeister. In Herbert Franke (ed) **Studia sino altaica: festschrift für erich haenisch zum 80. geburstag,** wiesbaden (1961) 114-119. Seventh month p'u-tu.

Lessing, Ferdinand D. Structure and meaning of the rite called the bath of the buddha according to tibetan and chinese sources. In **SSBKD** (1959) 159-171.

Lessing, Ferdinand D. The thirteen visions of a yogācārya. A preliminary study. **Ethnos** 15 (1950) 108-130.

Lessing, Ferdinand D. Wu-liang-shou . . . a comparative study of tibetan and chinese longevity rites. **ASBIHP** 28 (1957) 794-824.

Lévy, Paul. **Buddhism: a mystery religion?** Univ londor (1957) ny (1968) 111 p, index. Interpretations of budd ordination rituals.

Lisowski, F.P. The practice of cremation in china. **EH** 19.6 (june 1980) 21-24.

Liu, Chun-jo. Five major chant types of the buddhist service, gong-tian. **Chinoperl** 8 (1978) 130-160, app, transcriptions, musical scores.

Lombard-Salmon, Cl. Survivance d'un rite bouddhique à java: la cérémonie du pu-du (avalambana) **BEFEO** 62 (1975) 457-486, many photos.

Lucius. A bone of fuh. **ICG** no 12 (1820) 305-308.

MacGowan, D.J. Self-immolation by fire. **ChRec** 19 (1888) 445-451, 508-521. See further Errata and addenda, **ibid** 20 (1889) 31-32; also More self-immolation by fire at wenchow, **ibid,** 530.

MacLagan, P.J. Celibacy (chinese) In **HERE** 3, p 271.

Masaki, Haruhiko. The practice of buddhist austerities and its popularization in shan-tao and prince shotoku — in connection with śrimālā and vaidehī. **JIBS** 16.2 (mar 1968) 943-955.

Matignon, J.J. l'Auto-crémation des prêtres bouddhistes. **Archives d'anthropologie criminelle** 13 (15 janv 1898) also in author's **Crime, superstition et misère** q.v. 143-156.

Matignon, J.J. La transformation assise (tso-hua) **TP** 9.3 (1898) 230-232.

Mayers, W.F. The buddhist rosary and its place in chinese official costume. **NQ** (1869) 26-28.

Orcet, G. d'. Les moulins à prières dans l'inde, en chine et au japon. **Revue britannique** n.s. 1 (1882) 31-62.

Prip-Møller, J. Buddhist meditation ritual. **ChRec** 66.12 (dec 1935) 713-718.

Przyluski, J. Les rites d'avalambana. **MCB** 1 (1931-32) 221-225.

Reichelt, Karl L. (tsl) Extracts from the buddhist ritual. **ChRec** 59 (mar 1928) 160-170. Passages from ch'ang meng er sung.

Rousselle, E. Ein abhiṣeka-ritus im mantra-buddhismus. **Sinica-Sonderausgabe** (1934) 58-90; (1935) 1-23.

Rousselle, E. Der kult der buddhistischen madonna kuan-yin. **NachrDGNVO** 68 (1944) 17-23.

Saintyves, P. Le culte de la croix dans le boudhisme en chine, au nepal et au tibet. **RHR** 75 (janv-févr 1917) 1-52, fig.

Simpson, William. **The buddhist praying-wheel. A collection of material bearing upon the symbolism of the wheel and circular movements in custom and religious ritual.** London (1896) viii + 303 p.

Stein, Rolf A. Nouveaux problèmes du tantrisme sino-japonais. **ACF** 75e ann (1975) 481-488.

Stein, Rolf A. Quelques problèmes du tantrisme chinois. **ACF** 74e ann (1974) 499-508.

Stevens, Keith. Chinese preserved monks. **JHKBRAS** 16 (1976) 292-297, bibliog, 2 photos. Cases cited of buddhists, taoists, and non-monks also.

Suzuki, D.T. The kuan-yin cult in china. **EB** 6 (1935) 339-353.

Trautz, F.M. Eine erhebende musikaufführung am 'fünffachen stupa' (des wu-t'a-ssü bei peking) **AM** 2 (1925) 581-596.

Wiese, J. Selbstrerbrennung buddhistischer priester in china. **Asien** 7 (1909) 68-70.

Wood, Liu Ming. A translation of the wu-chiao chih-kuan ("on the meditation of the five teachings") **JAC** 1 (1977) 84-125.

Yetts, W. Perceval. Note on the disposal of buddhist dead in china. **JRAS** (july 1911) 699-725, pl.

Yü, Chung-(sic)fang (i.e. Yü, Chün-fang) Buddha-invocation (nien-fo) as koan. **JD** 2.2 (apr 1977) 189-203.

13. ART & ICONOGRAPHY

A. GENERAL

Art in the worship of the east. **FCR** 23.3 (mar 1973) 35-46. Pic-story.

Ball, Katherine M. **Decorative motives of oriental art.** London & ny (1927) 286 p, 673 illus. See passim.

Binyon, Laurence. Chinese art and buddhism. **Proc british academy** 22 (1936) 157-175. Also publ sep london (1936) 21 p, 9 illus.

Buddhistische kunst ostasiens. Ausstellung der museums für ostasiatische kunst der stadt köln, vom 11. april-13. oktober 1968. Museum für ostiatische kunst, köln (1968) 86 s, illus.

Burland, Cottie A. Buddhism in art at the berkeley galleries, nov. 1948-jan. 1949. **Asian horizon** 1.4 (winter 1948) 53-57.

Chavannes, Édouard. l'Exposition d'art bouddhique au musée cernuschi. **TP** (1913) 261-286, pl.

Chinese buddhist bronzes: a loan exhibition under the joint auspices of department of fine arts, freer fund, and museum of art, april 13-may 7, 1950. Univ michigan (1950) 15 p, 23 pl.

Chinesisch-buddhistische tempelkunst. Sonderausstellung in china-institut (frankfurt am main) **Sinica** 12 (1937) 261-264.

Coomaraswamy, Ananda K. What is common to indian and chinese art? **SCR** 7.2 (spring 1973) 75-91.

Corbet, R.G. Buddhism and art. **IAQR** (july-oct 1902) 114-120.

Focillon, Henri. **Art et religion — l'art bouddhique.** Paris (1921) xvi + 164 p, 24 pl.

Fontein, Jan. China. In **EncyWA** vol 3, 393a-466b. See passim, also relevant illus in sec at end of vol.

Fontein, Jan. Chinese art. In **EncyWA** vol 3, 466a-577a. Presented chronol by periods, and within each period by kind of art. See passim, also relevant illus in sec at end of vol.

Grousset, René. **Les civilisations de l'orient.** T 3, **La chine.** Paris (1930) Engl tsl Catherine A. Phillips, **The civilizations of the east.** Vol 3, **China,**, ny (1967) See chap 2, Buddhist influence in china, 147-278, illus.

Hackin, J., O. Sirén, L. Warner, and P. Pelliot. **Studies in chinese art and some indian influences.** London (1938) vii + 63 p, pl. Lectures at royal academy of arts in connection with the burlington exhibition of chinese art.

Hisamatsu, Shin'ichi. Tsl Gishin Tokiwa. **Zen and the fine arts.** Tokyo (1971) 400 p, 276 pl, notes to pl, biog notes, index.

Hisamatsu, Shin'ichi. Le zen et les beaux-arts. **ArtsAs** 6.4 (1959) 243-258, illus. Genl discussion of what is zen in art, incl chin.

Hui Wan (Ch. Pönisch-Schoenwerth, übers) Buddhistische kunst in china. **Yana** 32.6 (nov-dez 1979) 182-184.

Lommel, Andreas. **Kunst des buddhismus: aus der sammlung des staatlichen museums für völkerkunde in münchen.** Zurich (1974) 250 p.

Ludwig, Ernst. Lama temples in peking. 1. Yung-hô-kung. **EA** 1 (1902) 81-103. See also Pekinger lamaserails (yung-hô-kung) in **FO** 1 (1902) 105-125.

Milloué, Léon de. **Catalogue du musée guimet. Pt 1: Inde, chine et japon. Précédé d'un aperçu sur les religions de l'extrême-orient et suivie d'un index alphabétique des noms des divinités et des principaux termes techniques.** Paris (1883) lxviii + 323 p.

Moore, Albert C. **Iconography of religions: an introduction.** Philadelphia (1977) See chap 6, Religions of east asia . . . china, 170-180.

Petrucci, R. l'Art bouddhique, en extrême-orient d'après les découvertes récentes. **GBA** (sept 1911) 193-213.

Petrucci, Raphael. Buddhist art in the far east and the documents from chinese turkestan. **BM** 18 (1910-11) 138-144, 2 photos.

Petrucci, R. l'Exposition d'art bouddhique au musée cernuschi. **BAAFC** 5 (1913) 223-229.

Ridley, Michael. The art of buddhism. **AofA** 2.1 (jan-feb 1972) 13-18, illus. Incl china.

Scott, Alexander. Buddhistic art. **Museum journal** 5 (1914) 58-61.

Seckel, Dietrich. **Buddhistische kunst ostasiens.** Stuttgart (1957) 383 s, 204 abh, 2 ktn.

Seckel, Dietrich. **Kunst des buddhismus. Werden, wanderung und wandlung.** Baden-baden (1964) Engl tsl Ann E. Keep: **The art of buddhism,** n.y. (1964) 331 p, app, maps, bibliog, index, illus.

Segalen, Victor. Bouddhisme chinois. **RAA** 3 (1926) 119-122.

Sickman, Laurence. Notes on later chinese buddhist art. **Parnassus** 11.4 (1939) 12-17.

Sirén, Osvald. Ch'an (zen) buddhism and its relation to art. **Theosophical path** (oct 1934) 159-176.

Soper, Alexander C. Literary evidence for early buddhist art in china, 1. **OA** 2.1 (1949) 28-35. Same title, 2. in **AA** 16 (1953) 83-110.

Soper, Alexander C. **Literary evidence for early buddhist art in china.** Ascona (1959) 296 p, indexes. See rev by Paul Demiéville **OL** 60.1/2 (1965) 82-86, repr in **CEB** (1973).

Swann, Peter C. **Chinese monumental art.** N.Y. (1963) also french ed (1963) 276 p, 157 pl, maps and fig, bibliog, index. Photos Claude Arthaud and François Hébert-Stevens.

Tucci, Giuseppe. Buddhism. In **EncyWA** vol 2, 670b-703a. See passim, also relevant illus in sec at end of vol.

Warner, Langdon. A chinese exhibition at cleveland museum of art. **BM** 56 (apr 1930) 205-211, 2 pl.

B. ICONOGRAPHY—MOTIFS

Behrsing, S. Der heiligenschein in ostasien. **ZDMG** 103 (1953) 156-192.

Beltran, A. **Symbolism of oriental religious art.** Los angeles (1953) 122 p, illus. See passim.

Bouillard, G. **Notes divers sur les cultes en chine: les attitudes des buddhas.** Pékin (1924) 28 p, pl.

Bouillard, G. Notes diverses sur les cultes en chine. **La chine** 60 (1924) 239-247; 65 (1924) 227-232.

Bunker, Emma C. Early chinese representations of vimalakirti. **AA** 30.1 (1968) 28-52.

Cammann, Schuyler. The four great kings of heaven — part 2. **JWCBorderResS** 11 (1939) 78-84.

Carus, Paul. The fish in brahmanism and buddhism. **OC** 25.6 (june 1911) 343-357, illus. See further author's art, The fish as a mystic symbol in china and japan, **ibid** 25.7 (july 1911) 385-411, illus.

Chapin, Helen B. A study in buddhist iconography; six-armed form of cintamaniçakra avalokiteśvara. **OZ** 18 (1932) 29-43, 111-129; 21 (1935) 125-134, 195-210; corrigenda, 12 (1936) 69-70; illus, bibliog.

Chapin, Helen B. Yunnanese images of avalokiteśvara. **HJAS** 8 (1944) 131-186, 16 pl, bibliog.

Chinesisch-buddhistische tempelkunst. Sonder-ausstellung in china-institut (frankfurt am main) **Sinica** 12 (1937) 261-264.

Clapp, F.M. Arhats in art. **Art studies** 3 (1925) 95-130.

Cohn, W. **Buddha in der kunst ostasiens.** Leipzig (1925) 5 + lxiv + 253 p illus.

Davidson, J. LeRoy. The origin and early use of the ju-i. **AA** 13.4 (1950) 239-249.

Davidson, J. LeRoy. A problem in skulls. **Parnassus** 11.1 (1939) 33-35. Iconography.

Dumoutier, Gustave. Le swastika et la roue solaire dans les symboles et dans les caractères chinois. **RE** 4.4 (1885) 319-350.

Edmunds, W. **Pointers and clues to the subjects of chinese and japanese art.** London (1934) 706 p, illus. See passim.

Erkes, Eduard. Zum problem der weiblichen kuanyin. **AA** 9 (1946) 316-320, illus.

Fontein, J. **The pilgrimage of sudhana. Study of gandavyūha illustrations in china, japan and java.** The hague (1967) 237 p, 64 pl.

Franks, A.W. On some chinese rolls with buddhist legends and representations. **Archaelogia** 2nd ser, pt 3.1 (1892) 239-244.

Gaillard, Louis. **Croix et swastika en chine.**Shanghai (1893) 282 p (Variétés sinologiques no 3)

Getty, Alice. **The gods of northern buddhism.** Oxford univ 1st ed (1914) 2nd ed (1928) repr of 2nd ed (1962) liv + 220 p, bibliog, index, 67 pl. See rev by Kanaoka Shuyu, **CRJ** 5.3 (sept 1964) 207-220.

Goepper, Roger. Some thoughts on the icon in esoteric buddhism of east asia. In **SSM/FHF** (1979) 245-254.

Hée, Louis van. Le témoignage de l'occident. **AA** 1 (1925) 217-226.

Hitchman, F. Buddhistic symbols on chinese ceramics. **OA** n.s. 8 (1962) 15-20, illus.

Huntington, Harriet E. The sixteen buddhist arhats. **AofA** 7.2 (1977) 62-71, illus with b-&-w and col photos.

Lancaster, Lewis R. An early mahayana sermon about the body of the buddha and the making of images. **AA** 36.4 (1974) 287-291.

Lessing, Ferdinand D. **Yung-hô-kung. An iconography of the lamaist cathedral in peking with notes on lamaist mythology and cult.** Stockholm (1942) 179 p, fig, plan, app, notes, bibliog, pl.

Lim, K.W. Studies in later buddhist iconography. **BTLVK** 120.3 (1964) 327-341.

Lotus. **Echo** 4.8 (sept 1974) 45-49, 55-56.

Mallman, Marie Thérèse de. A propos d'une coiffure et d'un collier d'avalokiteśvara. **OA** 1 (spring 1949) 168-176, illus.

Mallman, Marie Thérèse de. **Étude iconographique sur mañjuśri.** Paris (1964) 284 p, 16 pl.

Mallman, Marie Thérèse de. Notes sur les bronzes du yunnan représentant avalokiteśvara. **HJAS** 14 (1951) 567-601, illus.

Manabe, Shunshō. The expression of elimination of devils in the iconographic texts of the t'ang period and its background. **JIBS** 15.2 (mar 1967) 907-914, pl.

Marchal, H. The flying (quivering) flame in the decorations of the far east. In **New IA,** extra ser 1 (1939): **A volume of eastern and indian studies, presented to f.w. thomas,** 148-151.

Marchand, Ernesta. The development of the aureole in china in the six dynasties period. **OA** n.s. 20.1 (spring 1974) 66-74, illus.

Meister, P.W. Buddhistische planetendarstellungen in china. **OE** 1 (1954) 1-5.

Milloué, L. de. Le svastika. **CMG** 31 (d?) 83-103.

Minamoto, H. l'Iconographie de la 'descente d'amida.' Tsl fr jap R. Linossier. In **EORL** (1932) 99-130.

Pander, E. **Iconographie du bouddhisme.** Pekin (1933) 45 p, illus.

Przyluski, J. Études indiennes et chinoises. **MCB** 2 (1932-33) 307-332; 4 (1935-36) 289-339.

Przyluski, J. (tsl) La roue de la vie à ajanta. **JA** 11e sér, 16 (1920) 313-331. Tsl of vinaya of mūla-sarvāstivādin by yi-tsing.

Rowland, Benjamin, jr. **The evolution of the buddha image.** N.Y. (1963) 140 p, 68 p.

Rowland, Benjamin, Jr. The iconography of the flame halo. **BFoggMA** 11 (june 1949) 10-16, illus.

Saunders, E. Dale. **Mudrā. A study of symbolic gestures in japanese buddhist sculpture.** N.Y. (1960) 296 p, notes, bibliog, index, fig, pl.

Saunders, E. Dale. Symbolic gestures in buddhism. **AA** 21 (1958) 47-63.

Scherman, L. Sanskrit letters as mystical symbols in later buddhism outside india. In **A&T** (1947) 55-62.

Schmidt, H. Die buddha des fernöstlichen mahāyāna. **AA** 1 (1925) 6-31, 98-120, 176-190, 245-258; 2 (1927) 11-29, 123-132, 165-179, 265-277.

Seckel, Dietrich. Die beiden dvârapâla-figuren im museum rietburg, zürich. **AA** 25 (1962) 23-44, pl.

Snellgrove, David L. (genl ed) **The image of the buddha.** UNESCO (1978) See IV, 5, China: growth and maturity, 204-226, illus.

Soper, Alexander C. Japanese evidence for the history of architecture and iconography of chinese buddhism. **MS** 4.2 (1940) 638-678.

Sowerby, Arthur de C.S. Legendary figures in chinese art. The five hundred lo-han **CJ** 15.4 (oct 1931) 172, illus.

Sowerby, Arthur de C.S. Legendary figures in chinese art. Mi-lo fo, the laughing buddha. **CJ** 14.6 (june 1931) 287.

Sowerby, Arthur de C.S. Legendary figures in chinese art. Tamo or bodhidharma. **CJ** 14.4 (apr 1931) 157-158, illus.

Soymié, Michel. Notes d'iconographie chinoise: 1. Les acolytes de ti-tsang. **ArtsAs** 14 (1966) 45-78, pl. Continued in **ibid** 16 (1967) 141-170.

Stiassny, M. Einiges zur 'buddhistischen madonna.' **JAK** 1 (1924) 112-119. Same title in **Cicerone** 15 (1923) 1011-1020. Illus. Re kuan-yin.

Tucci, G. Buddhist notes. **MCB** 9 (1948-51) 173-220. Re evolution of kuan-yin in art and texts.

Ward, W.E. The lotus symbol: its meaning in buddhist art and philosophy. **JEAC** 11 (1952-53) 135-146.

Watters, Thomas. The eighteen lohan of chinese buddhist temples. **JRAS** (apr 1898) 329-347; repr separately shanghai (1925) 45 p, portraits of the lohan.

Wegner, M. Ikonographie des chinesischen maitreya. **OZ** 15 (1929) 156-178, 216-229, 252-270, illus.

Wilson, Thomas. The swastika, the earliest known symbol, and its migrations . . . **U.S. national museum report for 1894** (smithsonian institution) 757-1011, pl 1-25, fig 1-374. Issued sep washington, d.c. (1896)

Wu, Feng-p'ei. The conch-shell trumpet of the esoteric buddhism. **NPMB** 3.5 (nov-dec 1968) 1-2, illus.

C. SPECIFIC TEMPLES

Abraham, A. Art treasures of a hangchow pagoda. **CJ** 26 (1937) 12-13.

Arlington, L.C. The pai ma ssŭ or "white horse monastery" **CJ** 4.3 (mar 1926) 123-124, photos.

Art treasures rediscovered (Ping-ling ssù, monastery in kansu) **CRecon** 2.4 (1953) 25-27.

Bouillard, Georges. **Le temple des lamas. Temple lamaïste de yung ho kung à pékin: description, plans, photos, cérémonies.** Peiping (1931) 127 p.

Bridgman, E.C. A picture of the precious porcelain pagoda in the recompensing favor monastery of kiangnan (commonly known as the porcelain tower) **ChRep** 13 (1844) 261-265.

Bulling, A. Buddhist temples in the t'ang period. **OA** n.s. 1 (1955) 79-86, 115-122, illus.

Burn, D.C. **A guide to lunghwa temple. With brief notes on chinese buddhism.** Shanghai (1926) 62 p, illus.

Cook, T. The great buddha of kiating. **JWCBorderResS** 7 (1935) 36-39.

Dahlmann, Joseph. In den pagoden pekings. **OstL** 18 (1904) 782-785.

Dodd, Jeremy. Temple of the dragons. **FCR** 21.6 (june 1971) 18-22, illus. Taipei's lung shan ssu.

Drake, F.S. The shên-t'ung monastery and the beginning of buddhism in shantung. **MS** 4 (1939-40) 1-39.

Dumoutier, Gustave. Les bouddhas des pagodes de quan-am et de chuan-dè. **RGI** 17 (1892) 219-220.

Ecke, G. Ergänzungen und erläuterungen zu professor Boerschmanns kritik von 'the twin pagodas of zayton' [q.v.] **MS** 2 (1936-37) 208-217.

Ecke, G. Once more, shen-t'ung ssu and ling-yen ssu. **MS** 7 (1942) 295-311.

Eskelund, K.J. Ten thousand ages gone in a night. **CJ** 27.1 (july 1937) 6-8, photos. Re Wan shou ssu, peking, burned down 29 apr 1937.

Gray, John Henry. **Walks in the city of canton.** HK (1875) repr san francisco (1974) See chap 3 for Hai-chwang-sze (honam temple) 33-75.

Hildebrand, Heinrich. **Der tempel ta-chüeh-sy (tempel des grossen erkenntnis) bei peking.** Berlin (1897) 36 s, 87 text-abb, 12 taf.

Hurst, R.W. The chao chung temple at pagoda anchorage **ChRev** 16 (1887-88) 177-179.

Lartigue, J. Le sanctuaire bouddhique de long-hong-sseu à kiating. **RAA** 5 (1928) 35-38.

Latham, A. Le temple de fa-hai-sse. **GBA** 6e sér, 18.2 (1937) 253-257.

Lee, J.G. Chih-hua-ssu, the temple of wisdom, peking. **PMB** 53 (1958) 29-32, illus, plan.

Liang, Ssu-ch'eng. China's oldest wooden structure: fo-kuang ssu, the temple of buddha's light. **Asia** 41 (july 1941) 384-387, illus. See same author's China's oldest wooden building, **El palacio** 48 (1941) 166-167.

Lovegren, L.A. Measurements of the kiating big buddha. **JWCBorderResS** 5 (1932) 102-103.

Ludwig, Ernst. Lama temples in peking. 1. Yung-hô-kung **EA** 1 (1902) 81-103. See also Pekinger lamaserails (yung-hô-kung) in **FO** 1 (1902) 105-125.

Lung shan temple. **Echo** 2.8 (sept 1972) 34-38, 59, col photos, plan. In taipei.

MacGowan, John. Mountain temples. Chap 11 in author's **L&S** (1909) 125-135.

Melchers, Bernd. **China. Der tempelbau. Die lochan von ling-yän-sï; ein hauptwerk buddhistischer plastik.** Hagen i.w. (1921) 47 p text, 73 p photos of temple, 45 p photos of sculpture, 37 p drawings, photos and arch plans of temple.

Pantoussoff, N. Le temple chinois 'bei-iun-djuan,' dans la passe d'ak-su, province d'ili (vièrny, turkestan russe) **Revue des études ethnographiques et sociologiques** 1 (août 1908) 398-403, 2 pl.

Sirén, Osvald. A chinese temple and its plastic decoration of the 12th century. In **EORL** (1932) t 2, 499-505, pl lvi-lxiv.

Soper, Alexander C. Hsiang-kuo-ssû, an imperial temple of northern sung. **JAOS** 68.1 (1948) 19-45.

Soper, Alexander C. A vacation glimpse of the t'ang temples of ch'ang-an; the ssu-t'a chi by tuan ch'eng-shih. **AA** 23.1 (1960) 15-40.

Sprague, Roger. The most remarkable monument in western china. **PS** 83 (1913) 557-566. Re temple and great buddha in kiating.

Tiffany, Osmond jr. **The canton chinese.** Boston & cambridge (1849) See chap 10, The buddhist temple (honam) 180-191.

Tschepe, A. Der tempel hsing-fu-sze. **FO** 3 (1904?) 257-259.

Wong, C.S. **Kek lok si, temple of paradise.** Singapore (1963) 131 p. On a famous temple, chi-lo ssu, in penang.

Yang, Yu. Art treasures of the ping-ling-ssu temple. **PC** 15 (1953) 28-30.

Zacher, J. Die tempelanlagen am südabhang des richthofenbirges, erläutert am beispiel von yen-hu-chai-tzu. **FS** 8 (1949) 270-276.

D. ARCHITECTURE (EXCEPT PAGODAS)

Beylié, L. de. **l'Architecture hindoue en extrême-orient.** Paris (1907) 416 p. Illus de Tournois et Doumenq.

Boerschmann, Ernst. **Die baukunst und religiöse kultur der chinesen.** Vol 1, **P'ut'o shan.** Berlin (1911) 203 p, 33 pl, fig.

Boerschmann, Ernst. Chinese architecture and its relation to chinese culture. **Annual reports of the smithsonian institution** (1911) Tsl fr **ZE** 42 (1910)

Boerschmann, Ernst. **Chinesische architektur.** Berlin (1925) 2 vol.

Bulling, A. Buddhist temples in the t'ang period. **OA** n.s. 1 (1955) 79-86, 115-122.

Chambers, William. **Designs of chinese buildings.** London (1757) facs repr farnborough, engl (1969) See, Of the temples of the chinese, 1-5; Of the towers [taa = t'a, or pagodas] 5-6, pl 1-5.

Hsing, Fu-ch'uan. The transition period of chinese early buddhist architectures and their backgrounds. **CC** 21.4 (dec 1980) 57-68.

Ito, C. Architecture (chinese) In **HERE** vol 1 (1908) 693-696.

Liang, Ssu-ch'eng. China's oldest wooden structure. **Asia** 41 (july 1941) 384-387, illus. T'ang temple on wu-t'ai shan, shensi. Same title in **El palacio** 48 (1941) 166-167.

Parmentier, H. Origine commune des architectures hindoues dans l'inde et en extrême-orient. **Études asiatiques** 2 (1925) 199-242.

Prip-Møller, Johannes. **Chinese buddhist monasteries. Their plan and its function as a setting for buddhist monastic life.** Copenhagen and oxford univ (1937)repr univ hong kong (1967) 396 p, index, sketches, plans, elevations, photos.

Prip-Møller, Johannes. The hall of ling ku ssu, nanking. **Artes** (copenhagen) 3 (1934) 171-211, illus, folding plans.

Prip-Møller, Johannes. Streiflichter auf die entwicklung des bauplans chinesischer buddhistischer klöster in ihrem verhältnis zum buddhistischen kultus. **OZ** 24 (1938) 156-166.

Soper, Alexander C. Architecture. Being pt 2 of Laurence Sickman and Alexander Soper, **The art and architecture of china,** harmondsworth, middlesex, engl (1956) 2nd ed with add (1960) 205-288; notes 307-310; gloss 313; bibliog, index, fig, pl.

Soper, Alexander C. Four columns from a chinese temple. **Honolulu academy of arts, special studies** 1 (apr 1947) illus.

Soper, Alexander C. Japanese evidence for the history of architecture and iconography of chinese buddhism. **MS** 4.2 (1939-40) 638-678.

Stein, Rolf. Architecture et pensée religieuse en extrême-orient. **ArtsAs** 4.3 (1957) 163-186, illus.

Thilo, Thomas. **Klassische chinesische baukunst: strukturprinzipien und funktion.** Vienna (1977) 252 s, taf, anhang, karte. See passim for budd and taoist architecture.

E. PAGODAS

Abraham, A. Art treasures of a hangchow pagoda. **CJ** 26 (1937) 12-13.

Alley, Rewi. Pagodas and towers in china. **EH** 2 (may 1962) 20-28, illus.

Bareau, André. La construction et le culte des stūpa d'après le vinayapiṭaka. **BEFEO** 50.2 (1962) 229-274.

Boerschmann, E. **Chinesische pagoden.** Berlin (1931) illus.

Boerschmann, Ernst. **Die baukunst und religiöse kultur der chinesen.** Vol 3: **Pagoden; pao-t'a.** Berlin and leipzig (1931) 288 p, illus.

Boerschmann, Ernst. Eisen-und bronzepagoden in china. **JAK** 1 (1924) 223-235.

Boerschmann, E. K'ueising türme und fengshuisäulen. **AM** 2 (1925) 503-530.

Boerschmann, Ernst. Pagoden der sui- und frühen t'angzeit. **OZ** n.f. 11 (1924) 195-221.

Boerschmann, Ernst. Pagoden im nördlichen china unter fremden dynastien. In Hans H. Schaeder (ed) **Der orient in deutscher forschung,** leipzig (1944) 182-204.

Boerschmann, Ernst. Die pai t'a von suiyüan: eine nebenform der t'ienningpagoden. **OZ** n.f. 14. 24 (1939) 185-208.

Bouchot, J. La grande pitié des pagodes en chine. **La chine** 2 (1922) 97-106; 12 (1922) 250-264.

Bowen, A.J. 'The porcelain tower' (Description in engl bk of 1698) **CJ** 5 (1926) 77-81.

Bridgman, E.C. A picture of the precious porcelain pagoda in the recompensing favor monastery of kiangnan (commonly known as the porcelain tower) **ChRep** 13 (1844) 261-265.

Brousse, Jean de la. Les t'a, tours chinoises après l'introduction du bouddhisme. **RC** (avr 1922) 110-123, illus; (juil 1922) 169-176; (oct 1922) 223-230, fig.

Buhot, J. l'Origine des pagodes sur plan hexagonal. **RAA** 13 (1939-42) 36-41.

Buhot, J. Stupa et pagode: une hypothèse. **RAA** 11 (1937) 235-239.

Chambers, William. **Designs of chinese buildings.** London (1757) facs repr farnborough, engl (1969) See Of the towers [taa = t'a, or pagodas] 5-6 pl 1-5.

Chen, Tsung-chou. Pagodas. **China pictorial** no 5 (may 1963) 28-31, illus.

Chinese pagodas. **JNCBRAS** 46 (1915) 45-57.

Combaz, G. l'Évolution du stūpa en asie. Contributions nouvelles et vue d'ensemble. **MCB** 3 (1934-35) 93-144.

Combaz, G. l'Évolution du stūpa en asie: étude d'architecture bouddhique. **MCB** 2 (1932-33) 163-305.

Combaz, G. l'Évolution du stūpa en asie: les symbolismes du stūpa. **MCB** 4 (1935-36) 1-125.

Cumine, E.B. The chinese pagoda. **CJ** 31 (1939) 160-163.

Ecke, G. Erganzungen und erläuterungen zu professor Boerschmanns kritik von 'the twin pagodas of zayton' [q.v.] **MS** 2 (1936-37) 208-217.

Ecke, Gustav. Structural features of the stone-built t'ing pagoda. A preliminary study. Chapter ii: Brick pagodas in the liao style. **MS** 1 (1935-36) 253-276; 13 (1948) 331-365.

Ecke, Gustav. Two ashlar pagodas at fu-ching in southern fu-chien. **BCUP** 8 (1933) 49-66.

Ecke, G. and P. Demiéville. **The twin pagodas of zayton. A study of later buddhist sculpture in china.** Harvard univ (1935) viii + 95 p, maps, pl. Photographs and intro G. Ecke; iconography and history P. Demiéville.

Finot, L. and V. Goloubew. Le fan-tseu t'a de yunnan fou. **BEFEO** 25 (1925) 435-448.

Franz, Heinrich Gerhard. Pagode, stūpa, turmtempel. Untersuchen zum ursprung der pagode. **KdeO** 3 (1959) 14-28, illus.

Gray, John Henry. William G. Gregor (ed) **China.** London (1878) illus with sketches. See vol 2, chap 21, Pagodas, 87-98.

Groot, J.J.M. de **Der thupa, das heiligste heiligtum des buddhismus in china.** Berlin (1919) viii + 96 s, 6 taf.

Hobson, H.E. (tsl) The porcelain pagoda of nanking. Translation of the historical portion of a pictorial sheet engraved and published by the buddhist high priest in charge of the pao-en temple. Tsl of the devotional portion by W.A.P. Martin. **JNCBRAS** 23 (1888) 31-38.

Hoech, G.T. Der ursprung der pagoden, topen und zwiebelkuppeln. **Zeitschrift für bauwesen** 44 (1914) hft 7-9, col 524-542.

Liang, Ssu-ch'eng. Five early chinese pagodas. **Asia** 41 (aug 1941) 450-453, 7 illus.

Liebenthal, Walter. Sanskrit inscriptions from yunnan I (and the dates of foundation of the main pagodas in that province) **MS** 12 (1947) 1-40, 8 pl.

March, Benjamin. The lintsing pagoda. **CJ** 5 (1926) 250-252.

Meurs, H. van. Alter und symbolische bedeutung der stupa. **OZ** 27 (1941) 32-45.

Milne, William C. **Life in china.** London (1858) See pt 4, chap 3, On pagodas, 429-471.

Milne, William C. Pagodas in china. A general descrption of the pagodas in china. (?) **Trans china branch RAS** 5 (1854) 17-63.

Moule, A.C. The lei feng ta. **JRAS** (1925) 285-288.

Oelmann, F. Der ursprung der pagode. **Sinica** 6 (1931) 196-199.

Prip-Møller, Johannes. On the building history of pao shu t'a, hangchow. **JNCBRAS** 67 (1936) 50-57.

Sawamura, Sentarō. Die stupa im bezirk des shao-lin-ssu. **OZ** 12 (1925) 265-272.

Soper, Alexander C. Two stelae and a pagoda on the central peak, mt. sung. **ACASA** 16 (1962) 41-48.

Williams, S. Wells. Pagodas in and near canton; their names and time of their erection. **ChRep** 19 (1850) 535-543.

F. SCULPTURE

Adams, P.R. A sui dynasty bodhisatva. **AQ** 15 (1952) 85-86.

Ashton, Leigh. **An introduction to the study of chinese sculpture.** London (1924) xvii + 108, 63 pl.

Bachhofer, Ludwig. Die anfänge der buddhistischen plastik in china. **OZ** n.s. 10 (1934) 1-15, 107-126, bibliog.

Bachhofer, Ludwig. Zur geschichte der chinesischen plastik vom bis 14.jhd. **OZ** n.s. 14 (1938) 65-82, 113-136.

Banks, Michael. Religion and art in the northern wei dynasty. **AofA** 10.4 (july-aug 1980) 68-74, illus. Re ming-ch'i and budd sculpture.

Bell, Hamilton. An early bronze buddha. **BM** 25 (1914) 144-153, 2 pl.

Boerschmann, Ernst. Steinlöwen in china. **Sinica** 13.5/6 (1938) 217-224, fig.

The Buddha of measureless light and the land of bliss. A chinese buddhist group in bronze. **BMFA** 24 (1926) 2-10.

Bunker, Emma C. Early chinese representations of vimalakīrti. **AA** 30 (1968) 28-52, illus.

Bunker Emma C. The spirit kings in sixth century chinese buddhist sculpture. **ACASA** 18 (1964) 26-37, illus.

Caswell, James O. The "Thousand-buddha" pattern in caves XIX and XVI at yün-kang. **ArsO** 10 (1975) 35-54, 8 pl.

Chavannes, Édouard. **Mission archéologique dans la chine septentrionale.** T 1: Première partie: La sculpture à l'époque des han, paris (1913) 290 p, pl. T 2: Deuxième partie: La sculpture bouddhique, paris (1915) 291-614, pl. There are 2 add vol pl: Première partie, pl i-cclxxxvi, paris (1909); Deuxième partie, pl cclxxxvii-cccclxxxviii, paris (1909) See also: Note sur les 488 planches de sa mission, **TP** 10 (1909) 538-547 (There is a small literature on this famous mission, which we do not list)

Chen, C.M. **Buddha's statues in the yunkang caves.** Berkeley, calif (1977) 24 p.

Chen, Gerald. Jian zhen comes home. **EH** 19.6 (june 1980) 11-16, illus. "Visit" of lacquer statue of monk chien chen fr tōshōdaiji, nara, to yangchou and peking.

Chow, Fong. Chinese buddhist sculpture. **BMMA** n.s. 23 (1964-65) 301-324, illus.

Cohn, W. A chinese buddha-image of the year 1396. **BM** 77 (?1940) 14-20.

Cook, T. The great buddha of kiating. **JWCBorderResS** 7 (1935) 36-39. See also **ibid** 5, 102-103, art by L.A. Lovegren, Measurements of the kiating big buddha.

Davidson, Martha. Great chinese sculpture in america. **ANA** (1939) 71-74, 174-176.

Demiéville, Paul. Notes d'archéologie chinoise. 1, l'inscriptions de yun-kang; 2, Le bouddha du k'o chan; 3, Les tombeaux des song meridioneaux. **BEFEO** 25.3/4 (1925) 449-468.

Dohrenwend, Doris. Royal ontario museum, far eastern department: arts of buddhist asia. **AofA** 9.2 (mar-apr 1979) 62-76, illus. In part concerned with chin sculpture.

Drake, F.S. The wei dynasty sculptures of yellow-stone cliff in shantung. **CJ** 25.4 (oct 1936) 194-203, illus with 3 fig and photos.

Ecke, G. Ananda and vakula in early chinese carvings. **SIS** 5.3/4 (1957) (Liebenthal festschrift) 40-46, illus.

Ecke, G. On some buddhist images at the honolulu academy of arts. **AS** 21 (1967) 24-30, pl.

Ecke, G. A throning sakyamuni of the early t'ang period. **OA** 5 (1959) 165-169.

Ecke, G. and P. Demiéville. **The twin pagodas of zayton. A study of later buddhist sculpture in china.** Harvard univ (1935) viii + 95 p, maps, pl. Photographs and intro G. Ecke; iconography and history P. Demiéville.

Erkes, E. Ahnenbilder und buddhistische skulpturen aus altchina. **JSMVL** 5 (1913) 26-32, illus.

Fernald, Helen E. A buddhist stone sculpture from t'ien-lung shan, shansi, 8th century a.d. **BROMA** 22 (sept 1954) 1-3, illus facing p 12.

Fernald, Helen E. A chinese buddhistic statue in dry lacquer (late yuan-early ming) **MJ** 18.3 (1927) 284-294. Offpr, univ pennsylvania, univ museum (1927) 10 p.

Fischer, O. Chinesische buddh- und bodhisatvaköpfe. **JAK** 1 (1924) 159-164.

Fischer, O. **Chinesische plastik.** München (1948) 200 p, 136 pl.

Fong, Mary H. Buddhist cave sculpture at lung-men. **AofA** 10.4 (july-aug 1980) 82-88, illus.

From maitreya to sakyamuni: the gilt-bronze buddha of the wei dynasty. **ACASA** 19 (1965) 63-65, illus.

Fu, Tien-chun. The rock sculptures of lungmen. **CL** 5 (may 1962) 65-71, illus.

Fu, Tien-chun. The sculptured maidens of the tsin temple. **CL** 4 (apr 1962) 92-98.

Gabbert, Gunhild. **Buddhistische plastik aus china und japan. Bestandskatalog des museums für ostasiatische kunst der stadt köln.** Wiesbaden (1972) xviii + 522 s, illus, app, index-gloss.

Gangoly, O.C. A fragment of chinese buddhist sculpture. **Rupam** 33-34 (jan-apr 1928) 1, 1 pl.

Gray, Basil & William Watson. A great sui dynasty amitabha (with the inscription) **BMQ** 16.3 (oct 1951) 81-84.

Griswold, A.B. Prolegomena to the study of the buddha's dress in chinese sculpture. With particular reference to the rietberg museum's collection. **AA** 26 (1963) 85-131, pl 1-28. See further pt ii, **ibid** 27 (1964-65) 335-348, pl 29a-40.

Grünwald, Michael. Geistige und stilistische konvergenzen zwischen frühbuddhistischen skulpturen und religiöser plastik des frühen mittelalters in europa. **AA** 9 (1946) 34-67, illus.

Ho, Wai-kam. Notes on chinese sculpture from northern ch'i to sui. Part 1: Two seated stone buddhas in the cleveland museum. **AAA** 22 (1968-69) 6-55.

Ho, Wai-kam. Three seated stone buddhas. **BCMA** 53.4 (apr 1966) 83-102, illus.

Hollis, Howard C. A head from the lung men caves. **BCMA** 35 (sept 1948) 159-161, illus.

Jayne, H.H.F. Amitabha altar group. **UPUMB** 7 (apr 1939) 2-9, illus.

Jayne, H.H.F. Early chinese stone sculpture. **Pennsylvania museum bulletin** 214 (jan 1929) 15-25.

Jayne, H.H.F. Maitreya and guardians. **UPUMB** 9 (jan 1941) 2-8, 4 illus.

Jayne, H.H.F. A tile relief of a bodhisattva. **Pennsylvania museum bulletin** 214 (jan 1929) 25-29.

Joyce, T.A. A chinese bodhisattva. **BM** 42 (1923) p 130, photo on p 110.

Joyce, T.A. Note on a gilt bronze figure of padmapani in the british museum. **Man** 22 (1922) 33.

Keeble, F.H.G. Buddhistic images of china. **International studio** 75 (sept 1922) 514-521. Re sculptures in various museums.

Kelley, Charles F. A buddhist triad of the t'ang dynasty. **BAIC** 24 (may 1930) 60-63.

Kemp, Craig Charles. Kuan yin. **Lizzadro museum quarterly** (spring-summer 1972) 24-31. Illus of several examples in nephrite and jade.

Kim, Won-yong. An early chinese gilt bronze buddha from seoul. **AA** 23.1 (1960) 67-71.

Kingman, S. More precious than rubies; bodhisattva head from the caves of t'ien lung shan, china. **Asia** 34 (aug 1934) 498-499.

Klee, Th. Die plastik in den höhlen von yün-kang, lung-mên und kung-hsien. **OZ** 7 (1918-19) 31-56.

Lao, Kan. Six tusked elephants on a han bas-relief. **HJAS** 17 (dec 1954) 366-369.

Lee, Sherman E. Five early gilt bronzes. **AA** 12.1/2 (1949) 5-22.

Lee, Sherman E. The golden image of the newborn buddha. **AA** 18.3/4 (1955) 225-237, illus.

Lee, Sherman E. Kleinkunst, two early chinese wood sculptures. **AAA** 20 (1966-67) 66-68, illus. Re a kuan yin and a taoist fig.

Lee, Sherman E. & Ho Wai-kam. A colossal eleven-faced kuan-yin of the t'ang dynasty. **AA** 22.1/2 (?1958) 121-137.

Leuridan, Thre. Sur une statuette chinoise du musée de roubaix, la déese pou-ssa. **Mémoires de la société d'émulation de roubaix,** t 5.

Liebenthal, Walter. An early buddhist statue from yünnan. **IHQ** 32 (1956) 352-353.

Lindsay, J.H. The makara in early buddhist sculpture. **JRAS** (1951) 134-138, pl. Re a monster fish.

Lippe, Aschwin. A gilt-bronze altarpiece of the wei dynasty. **ACASA** 15 (1961) 29-31.

Little, D.B. A chinese stone lion from lung-mên datable to a.d. 680-1. **BMFA** 38 (1940) 52-53.

Lobsiger-Dellenbach, W. Statuaire des song méridionaux (chine) **AS** 10 (1956) 105-113.

Lodge, John E. The buddha of measureless light and the land of bliss; a chinese buddhist group in bronze. **BMFA** 24 (1926) 2-10, illus. Dated 593.

Mahler, Jane Gaston. An assembly of lung-men sculpture. **AAA** 24 (1970-71) 70-75. Re items in sackler coll.

March, Benjamin. Detroit's bronze maitreya. **Art in america** 18 (1930) 144-150. See also: Maitreya (n. wei bronze) **BDetIA** 12 (nov 1930) 14-16.

March, Benjamin. New chinese sculptures. **BDetIA** 11 (nov 1929) 20-25.

Matics, Kathleen. Thoughts pertaining to the "maitreya" image in the metropolitan museum. **E&W** n.s. 29.1/4 (dec 1979) 113-126.

Melchers, Bernd. **China. Der tempelbau. Die lochan von ling-yan-si; ein hauptwerk buddhistischer plastik.** Hagen i.w. (1922) 47 p text, 73 p photos of temple, 45 p photos of sculpture, 37 p drawings, photos and plans of temple.

Migéon, Gaston. Une sculpture chinoise classique, collection rockefeller à new york. **Revue de l'art** 55 (1929) 57-62, 5 illus, 1 pl.

Mizuno, S. **Bronze and stone sculpture of china.** Tokyo (1960)

Mizuno, S. **Chinese stone sculpture.** Tokyo (1950) 33 p, pl, maps.

Munsterberg, Hugo. **The art of the chinese sculptor.** Tokyo and rutland, vt (1960) 32 p, 12 col pl.

Munsterberg, Hugo. Buddhist bronzes of the six dynasties period. **AA** 9.4 (1946) 275-315.

Munsterberg, Hugo. Chinese bronzes of the t'ang-period. **AA** 11.1/2 (1948) 27-45.

Munsterberg, Hugo. **Chinese buddhist bronzes.** Rutland, t (1967) 192 p, illus.

Munsterberg, Hugo. Chinese buddhist bronzes of the kamakura museum. **AA** 19 (1956) 101-110.

Murdoch, W.G.B. Buddhist sculpture of china. **American magazine of art** 18 (sept 1927) 461-470.

Nachhofer, L. Die anfänge der buddhistischen plastik in china. **OZ** 10 (1934)

Nagahiro, Toshio, Eun Hyun Yum & Takeshi Kuno. **Great sculpture of the far east.** NY (1979) On chin budd sculpture and caves, see 11-22 and pl. Mostly an album.

A Note on two chinese buddhist dedicatory groups. **BMFA** 26 (1928) 57-60.

Pelliot, Paul. Un bronze bouddhique de 518 au musée du louvre. **TP** 24 (1926) 381-382.

Pelliot, Paul. Une statue de maitreya de 705. **TP** 28 (1931) 381-382.

Perrault, J. Chinese bodhisattvas. **International studio** 80 (jan 1925) 291-300, illus. Re various sculptures in ny metropolitan museum of art.

Plumer, James M. China's ancient cave temples. Early buddhist sculpture in the northwest. **CJ** 22 (1935) 52-57, 104-109, illus.

Pontynen, Arthur. Buddhism and taoism in chinese sculpture, a curious evolution in religious motif. **FMB** 49.6 (june 1978) 16-21.

Poor, Robert. Chinese-buddhist sculpture: a figure of kuan-shih-yin. Minneapolis institute of arts, **Bulletin** 58 (1969) 19-28.

Priest, Alan. **Chinese sculpture in the metropolitan museum of art.** N.Y. (1944) 81 p, pl. Photos by Tet Borsig. Repr ny (1974)

Priest, Alan. A collection of buddhist votive tablets. **BMMA** 26 (1931) 209-213.

Priest, Alan. A note on kuan ti. **BMMA** 25 (1930) 271-272, illus.

Priest, Alan. A stone fragment from lung mên. **BMMA** 36 (1941) 114-116.

Priest, Alan. Two buddhist masterpieces of the wei dynasty. **BMMA** 34 (1939) 32-38.

Rao, M. Basava. A buddhist image from china. Maharaja sayajirao univ of baroda, **Journal** 16 (mar 1967) 249-250, illus.

Reitz, S.C.B. A bronze-gilt statue of the wei period. **BMMA** 21 (1926) 236-240.

Reitz, S.C.B. A chinese lacquered lohan statue. **BMMA** 22 (1927) 134-136.

Rhie, Marylin M. Aspects of sui k'ai-huang and t'ang t'ien-pao buddhist images. **E&W** n.s. 17.1/2 (mar-june 1967) 96-114, illus pl.

Rhie, Marylin M. Some aspects of the relation of 5th century chinese buddha images with sculpture from n. india, pakistan, afghanistan and central asia. **E&W** n.s. 26.3/4 (sept-dec 1976) 439-461, illus.

Rousselle, Erwin. Die typischen bildwerke des buddh-istischen tempels in china. **Sinica** 6 (1931) 70-125; 7 (1932) 62-71, 106-116; 8 (1933) 62-77; 9 (1934) 203-217; 10 (1935) 120-136, 153-165.

Rowland, Benjamin. Chinese sculpture of the pilgrimage road. **BFoggMA** 4.2 (mar 1935)

Rowland, Benjamin. Indian images in chinese sculpture. **AA** 10.1 (1947) 5-20, illus.

Rowland, Benjamin. Notes on the dated statues of the northern wei dynasty and the beginning of buddhist sculpture in china. **AB** 19.1 (1937) 92-107.

Salmony, Alfred. **Chinese sculpture: han to sung. The j. klijkamp and e. monroe collections.** N.Y. (1944) 57 p, 28 pl.

Salmony, Alfred. **Chinesische plastik.** Berlin (1925) xi + 172 p, 129 illus.

Salmony, Alfred. Delimiting questions in indian and chinese sculpture. **EArt** 1 (1929) 153-156, 225-233, illus.

Scherman, Lucian. **Frühbuddhistische steinskulpturen in china.** München (1921) 11 p mit abb.

Seckel, Dietrich. Die beiden dvârapâla-figuren im museum rietburg, zürich. **AA** 25 (1962) 23-44, pl.

Segalen, Victor. Bouddhisme chinois. **RAA** 3 (1926) 119-122. Re author's visit to lung-men, feb 1914.

Segalen, Victor. **The great statuary of china.** Univ chicago (1978) See chap 7, The Buddhist heresy, 119-128. Posthumous publ.

Sickman, Laurence. Monsters and elegance: nine centuries of chinese sculpture. **Apollo** (mar 1973) 240-247, illus.

Sickman, Laurence. Painting and sculpture. Being pt 1 of Laurence Sickman and Alexander Soper, **The art and architecture of china,** harmondsworth, middlesex, engl (1956) 2nd ed with add (1960) See chap 8-10, 12, 14; notes, gloss, bibliog, index, fig, pl.

Sirén, Osvald. **Chinese sculpture from the fifth to the fourteenth centuries.** London (1925) 4 vol. French ed paris (1925)

Sirén, Osvald. Chinese sculpture of the sung, liao, and chin dynasties. **BMFEA** 14 (1942) 45-64.

Sirén, Osvald. Chinese sculpture of the transition period. **BMFEA** 12 (1940).

Sirén, Osvald. **Chinese sculptures in the von der heydt collection.** (museum rietberg, zurich) Zurich (1959) 189 p, 66 pl. Descr catalog, text in german and engl.

Sirén, Osvald. A chinese temple and its plastic decoration of the 12th century. In **EORL** (1932) t 2, 499-505, pl lvi-lxiv.

Sirén, Osvald. **A history of early chinese art.** Vol 3: **Sculpture.** London (1930) French ed paris and bruxelles (1930)

Sirén, Osvald. Studien zur chinesischen plastik der post-t'ang-zeit. **OZ** n.f. 4 (1927-28) 1-2, 16 taf.

Sirén, O. Three stages in the evolution of chinese sculpture. **RAA** 12 (1938) 86-90, ilus.

Soper, Alexander. Chinese sculptures. **Apollo** 84 (aug 1966) 103-112, illus. From avery brundage collection.

Soper, Alexander C. Some late chinese bronze images (eighth to fourteenth centuries) in the avery brundage collection, m.h. deyoung museum, san francisco. **AA** 31 (1969) 32-54.

Sprague, R. Most remarkable monument in western china. **PS** 83 (dec 1913) 557-566. Great buddha at yung hsien, kiating,ssuchuan.

The Statue of a bodhisattva from yün-kang. **BMMA** 17 (1922) 252-255.

Stone carvings at ta-tsu. Peking (1958) 228 p, 205 pl.

Su, Ying-hui. Chinese stone sculpture since chin and han dynasties. **CC** 3.2 (1960) 45-54.

Sudzuki, Osamu. Chinese stone lions in tenri museum. **TJR** 7 (dec 1965) 8-24, illus.

Swann, Peter C. **Chinese monumental art.** N.Y. (1963) French ed (1963) 276 p, 157 pl, maps, fig, bibliog, index. Photos by Claude Arthaud and François Hébert-Stevens.

Tani, Nobukazu. On the stone images of buddha from the pao-ch'ing-ssu temple. **Kokka** 499 and 501 (jun and aug 1932) 161-164, 239-256, pl.

Tizac, H. d'Ardenne de. **La sculpture chinoise.** Paris (1931) 49 p, 64 pl.

Tokiwa, D. Buddhist monuments in china. **PIAJ** 2 (1926) 93-95.

Tomita, Kojirō. The chinese bronze buddhist group of a.d. 593 and its original arrangement. **BMFA** 43 (june 1945) 14-19, 5 illus.

Tomita, Kojirō. The tuan fang altarpiece and the accessories dated a.d. 523. **BM** 87 (1945) 160-164.

Tomita, Kojirō. Two chinese sculptures from lung-mên. **BMFA** 35 (1937) 2-4.

Trubner, H. A bodhisattva from yün-kang. **AQ** 11 (1948) 93-105.

Trubner, H. Three important buddhist images of the t'ang dynasty. **AA** 20.2/3 (1957) 102-110.

Tunhuang painted sculptures. Peiching (1978) chin and engl text, 85 col pl, folio size.

Vogel, J. Ph. Études de sculpture bouddhique. **BEFEO** 8 (1908) 487-500, illus.

Warner, Langdon. An introduction to the bronze statuettes of the far east. **Parnassus** 9.1 (1937) 18-20.

Watson, William. A dated buddhist image of the northern wei period. **BMQ** 22.3/4 (1960) 86-88.

Wegner, M. Eine chinesische maitreya-gruppe vom jahre 529. **OZ** 15 (1929) 1-4.

Welch, William. Notes on some bronze buddhas from pekin. **Transactions and proceedings of the new zealand institute** 37 (1905) 208-211.

Wenley, A.G. Radiocarbon dating of a yünnanese image of avalokitesvara. **ArsO** 2 (1957) 508.

Willetts, William. **Chinese art.** Harmondsworth, middlesex, engl (1958) See vol 1, chap 5, Sculpture, 293-391 and pl.

Willetts, William. **Foundations of chinese art from neolithic pottery to modern architecture.** London (1965) See chap 5, Sculpture: six dynasties and early t'ang, 173-228, incl pl 119-151.

Yetts, W.P. **The george eumorfopoulos collection: Catalogue . . .** vol 3: **Buddhist sculpture:** London (1929)

G. STELAE

Böttger, Walter. Weitere buddhistische votivstelen aus dem alten china im besitz der museum für völderkunde zu leipzig. **JSMVL** 25 (1968) 92-102.

Chavannes, Édouard. **Six monuments de la sculpture chinoise.** Being vol 2 of **ArsA** (1914) texte 40 p, 52 pl.

Ch'en, Kenneth K.S. Inscribed stelae during the wei, chin, and nan-ch'ao. In **StAs** (1975) 75-84.

Chicago art institute. **A chinese buddhist stele of the wei dynasty in the collection of the art institute of chicago.** Chicago (1927) 5 p, pl.

Fernald, Helen. An early chinese sculptured stela of 575 a.d. **EArt** 3 (1931) 73-111.

Gatling, E.I. A dated buddhist stele of 461 a.d. and its connections with yün kang and kansu province. **AA** 20 (1957) 241-250.

Havret, Henri. **T'ien-tchou 'seigneur du ciel.' A propos d'une stèle bouddhique de tch'eng-tou.** Shanghai (1901) 30 p, (Variétés sinologiques no 19) Same title in **Études** 89 (1901) 398-409, 546-553. Repr nendeln (1975)

Kuntze, Hertha. Eine votif-stele aus dem jahre 538. **Tribus** 11 (1962) 85-87, illus.

Mather, Richard B. Wang chin's 'dhuta temple stele inscriptions' as an example of buddhist parallel prose. **JAOS** 83 (1963) 338-359.

Pal, Pratapaditya. Notes on a so-called t'ang dynasty votive tablet. **AAA** 20 (1966-67) 71-75.

Peat, Wilbur D. A chinese buddhist stele. **Bulletin of the john herron institute,** 39 (oct 1952) 31-34.

Rhie, Marylin M. A t'ang period stele inscription and cave XXI at t'ien lung shan. **AAA** 28 (1974-75) 6-33, illus.

Roberts, Laurance P. A stele of the north wei dynasty. **Parnassus** 7.2 (1935) 13-15.

Sickman, Laurence. A sixth-century buddhist stele. **Apollo** (mar 1973) 220-225.

Sirén, Osvald. Two chinese buddhist stelae. **ACASA** 13 (1959) 8-12, illus.

Soper, Alexander C. A t'ang parinirvāna stele. **AA** 22.1/2 (?1958) 159-169.

Soper, Alexander C. Two stelae and a pagoda on the central peak, mt. sung. **ACASA** 16 (1962) 41-48.

H. PAINTING (INCLUDING WOODCUTS AND FRESCOES)

Addiss, Stephen. The art of chinese huang-po monks in japan. **OA** n.s. 24.4 (winter 1978-79) 420-432. Re calligraphy and painting.

Andrews, F.H. **Wall paintings from ancient shrines in central asia recovered by sir aurel stein.** Oxford univ (1948) xxiv + 128 p, illus, folding map, portfolio of 32 pl.

Awakawa, Yasuichi. **Zen painting.** Tsl fr jap John Bester. Tokyo (1970) 184 p, 139 illus. German tsl Dorothea Javorsky: **Die malerei des zen-buddhismus. Pinsel-striche des unendlichen,** münchen (1970) 184 p.

Bachhofer, L. Die lohan-bilder der städtlischen sammlungen zu freiburg im breisgau. **Pantheon** 5 (1930) 93-97, supply 19-20, illus, engl summ.

Bachhofer, Ludwig. 'Maitreya in ketumati' by chu hao-ku. In **India antiqua** (1947) 1-7, pl.

Boston museum of fine arts. Dept of asiatic art. **Catalogue of a special exhibition of ancient chinese buddhist paintings, etc.** Boston (1894) 37 p. Intro Ernest Fenollosa.

Brasch, K. **Zenga (zen-malerei)** Tokyo (1961) 192 s, 108 taf.

Brinker, Helmut. Ch'an portraits in a landscape. **AAA** 27 (1973-74) 8-29. Paintings of various dates.

Brinker, Helmut. **Die zen buddhistische bildsmalerei in china und japan von den anfängen bis zum ende der 16. jahrhundert.** Wiesbaden (1973) x + 279 p, 126 pl.

Burckhardt, Titus. **Sacred art in east and west.** Bedfont, middlesex, engl (1967) French version **Principes méthodes de l'art sacré,** lyon (1958) See chap 6, Landscape in far eastern art, 134-142. Mostly on zen painting.

Carus, Paul. Wu tao tze's nirvana picture. The buddha's nirvana, a sacred buddhist picture by wu tao tze. **OC** 16.3 (mar 1902) 163-166, illus.

Chandra, Lokesh. **Buddha in chinese woodcuts.** Delhi (1973) Chin text, Shih-chia ju-lai ying-hua shih chi, illus with 100 folio-size blockprints. Author and d unkn; Nakamura Hajime thinks it is fr ming dyn.

Chang, Cornelius P. Kuan-yin paintings from tun-huang: water-moon kuan-yin. **JOS** 15.2 (1977) 140-160, 5 pl.

Chang, Dai-chien. Tun huang frescoes and i. **APQCSA** 8.2 (autumn 1976) 43-45.

Chapin, Helen. A long roll of buddhist images. **JISOA** 6 (1938) 26-67. See further same title as revised by Alexander C. Soper, with his Foreword and excursus on the text of the nan chao t'u chuan, in **AA** 32 (1970) 5-41 and 33 (1971) 75-142, 157-199, 259-306; sep publ ascona (1971) 142 p text, 58 pl-pages.

Chapin, Helen B. Three early portraits of bodhidharma. **ACASA** 1 (1945-46) 66-98.

Ch'en, Jen-dao. **The three patriarchs of the southern school in chinese painting.** Hong kong (1955) 8 p.

Cohn, W. Amida-bilder in der ostasiatischen kunstsammlung. **Berliner museum** 54 (1933) 75-80.

Cohn, W. Ein chinesisches kuanyin-bild. **Berliner museum** 49 (1928) 70-74.

Coq, Albert von le. Peintures chinoises authentiques de l'époque t'ang provenant du turkestan chinois. **RAA** 5 (1928) 1-5, illus.

Dietz, E. Sino-mongolian temple painting and its influence on persian illumination. **Ars islamica** 1 (1934) 160-170.

Eastman, A.C. A chinese fresco of kuan yin. **BDetIA** 9 (apr 1928) 81-83.

Ecke, G. Concerning ch'an in painting. **ArtsAs** 3 (1956) 296-306, illus.

Fernald, Helen E. Another fresco from moon hill monastery (honan) **MJ** 19 (1928) 109-129.

Fernald, Helen E. Chinese frescoes of the t'ang dynasty in the [toronto] museum (from a honan monastery: moon hill) **MJ** 17 (1926) 229-244.

Fernald, Helen E. Two sections of a chinese fresco newly acquired, belonging to the great kuan yin wall. **MJ** 20 (june 1929) 119-129.

Fong, Wen. **The lohans and a bridge to heaven.** Freer gallery. **Occasional papers** 3.1 (1958) xii + 64 p, illus.

Franke, Herbert. Zur biographie des pa-ta shan-jen. In **Asiatica** (1954) 119-130.

Giles, Lionel. An illustrated buddhist sutra. **BMQ** 11 (1936) 29.

Grimm, Martin (ed) **Das leben buddhas: ein chinesisches holzschnitt fragment.** Frankfurt-am-main (1968) 58 p. Re a chin col woodcut collection of the life of buddha, d 1793.

Hadl, Richard. Langdon Warner's: Buddhist wall paintings. **AA** 9 (1946) 160-164.

Hongo, Tameo. Mu-ch'i, zen monk painter. **APQCSA** 5.1 (summer 1973) 77-81, illus.

Hummel, Siegbert. Guan-yin in der unterwelt. **Sinologica** 2 (1950) 291-293. Description of a scroll.

Hummel, Siegbert. Vom wesen der chinesischen tusch-malereien aus des sung-zeit. **JSMVL** 11 (1953) 12-22, 5 fig.

Hummel, S. Zur frage der aufstellung buddhistischer bildwerke zentral- und ostasiens. **JSMVL** 10 (1926-51 sic) 50-57.

Jenyns, Soame. **A background to chinese painting.** London (1935) See chap 2, The influence of religion, 35-88.

Karetzky, Patricia Eichenbaum. The recently discovered chin dynasty murals illustrating the life of the buddha at yen-shang-ssu, shansi. **AA** 42 (1980) 245-252, illus.

Kelley, Charles F. A chinese buddhist fresco. **BAIC** 25 (nov 1931) 110-111.

Lalou, M. Trois aspects de la peinture bouddhique. **AIPHO** 3 (1935) 245-261.

Laufer, Berthold. Zum bildnis des pilgers hsüan tsang. **Globus** 88 (1905) 257-258.

Lessing, Ferdinand. The eighteen worthies crossing the sea. Stockholm [**reports of the sino-swedish expedition, viii. ethnography** 6] (1954) 109-128, 6 pl.

Li,Chu-tsing. Bodhidharma crossing the yangtze river on a reed: a painting in the charles a. drenowatz collection in zürich. **AS** 25 (1971) 49-75, 15 pl, chin-jap gloss.

Lippe, Aschwin. Buddha and the holy multitude.**BMMA** n.s. 23 (1964-65) 325-336, illus, diagr, map, bibliog. Re monumental murals fr kuang-sheng-ssu in shansi, now in several u.s. museums.

Loehr, Max. **Chinese landscape woodcuts from an imperial commentary to the tenth-century printed edition of the buddhist canon.** Cambridge, mass. (1968) 114 p, notes, chin characters, bibliog, index, 41 pl.

March, Benjamin. A tun-huang buddhist painting. **BDetIA** 10 (may 1929) 109-111.

Matsumoto, Yeiichi. On some amulet pictures from tun-huang. **Kokka** 482 (1931) 3-6; 488 (1931) 249-254, illus.

Müller, H. Der divaraja des wei-ch'ih i-seng. **OZ** 8 (1919-20) 300-309.

Murase, Miyeko, Kuan-yin as savior of men: illustration of the twenty-fifth chapter of the lotus sutra in chinese painting. **AA** 33.1/2 (1971) 39-74.

Nagahiro, T. On wei-ch'ih i-sêng — a painter of the early t'ang dynasty. **OA** n.s. 1 (1955) 70-74.

Pelliot, Paul. Les déplacements de fresques sous les t'ang et le song. **RAA** 8 (1934) 201-228.

Pelliot, Paul. Les fresques de touen-houang et les fresques de m. eumorfopolous. **RAA** 5 (1928) 143-163, 193-214, illus.

Petrucci, Raphaël. Les peintures bouddhiques de touen-houang (mission stein) **AMG** (1916) 115-150, illus.

Pommeranz-Liedtke, Gerhard (hrsg) **Kuan-hsiu: Die sechzehn lohans; eine berühmte bildnisreihe der chinesisch-buddhistischen kunst.** Leipzig (1961) 51 p (chiefly illus)

Rousselle, E. Buddhistische studien. Die typischen bildwerke des buddhistischen tempels in china. **Sinica** 7 (1932) 62-71, 106-116; 8 (1933) 62-77; 9 (1934) 203-217; 10 (1935) 120-165. Publ sep as: **Von sinn der buddhistischen bildwerke in china,** darmstadt (1958)

Sasaguchi, Rei. A dated painting from tun-huang in the fogg museum. **AAA** 26 (1972-73) 26-49. Maitreya's paradise.

Schnitzer, Joseph. Chinesisch-buddhistische höllenbilder. **Wissen und leben** 2 (1909) 379-384.

Seckel, D. Grundzüge der buddhistischen malerei. **MDGNVO** 36, teil c (1945) 1-115.

Seckel, Dietrich. Mu-hsi: sechs kaki-fruchte; interpretation eines zen-bildes. **NachrDGNVO** no 77 (1955) 44-55, pl.

Sickman, Laurence. An early chinese wall-painting newly discovered. **AA** 15 (1952) 137-144, illus.

Sickman, Laurence. Painting and sculpture. Being pt 1 of Laurence Sickman and Alexander Soper, **The art and architecture of china,** harmondsworth, middlesex, engl (1956) 2nd ed with add (1960) See esp chap 13, 20-21; notes, gloss, bibliog, index, fig, pl.

Sickman, Laurence. Wall paintings of the yuan period in kuang-shêng-ssǔ, shansi. **RAA** 11 (1937) 53-67.

Sirén, Osvald. Three chinese buddhist paintings. **Parnassus** 9.3 (1937) 25-28.

Soper, Alexander C. Early buddhist attitudes toward the art of painting. **AB** 32.2 (1950) 147-155.

Speiser, Werner. Hu dschï-fu. **Sinica** 16 (1941) 152-161, pl. Ch'an painter.

Speiser, Werner. Liang k'ai. **OZ** 27.5/6 (1941) 159-168, 6 pl. Ch'an painter.

Speiser, Werner. Liang-tsüan (jap ryōzen) **Sinica** 13.5/6 (1938) 254-264, pl. Ch'an painter.

Speiser, Werner. Yin-to-lo. **Sinica** 12 (1937) 155-160, illus. Re ch'an paintings.

Stein, Marc Aurel. Specimens from a collection of ancient buddhist pictures and embroideries discovered at tun-huang. **Journal of indian art and industries** n.s. 15 (1912) 60-66, 4 pl.

Su, Ying-hui. The buddhist art of the tunhuang caves in china. **APQCSA** 2.3 (winter 1970) 28-33.

Su, Ying-hui. A comparative study on the contour techniques of wall-paintings found in tunhuang, ajanta, sigiriya and polonnaruwa. **APQCSA** 7.1 (summer 1975) 10-12.

Sung, Yu. Paintings of taoist and buddhist legends. **Echo** 2.5 (may 1972) 37-43, illus. Re some paintings in natl palace museum, taiwan.

Suzuki, Daisetz T. Eva van Hoboken (ed) **Sengai, the zen master.** Greenwich, conn (1971) 191 p, illus ink drawings and calligraphy, explanatory notes by Shokin Furuta. Pref notes by Sazo Idemitsu, Basil Gray & Herbert Read. Posthumous publ.

Tomita, Kojirō. Two chinese paintings depicting the infant buddha and mahāprajapati. **BMFA** 42 (feb 1944) 13-20, 7 illus.

Tomita, Kojirō. Two more dated buddhist paintings from tun-huang. **BMFA** 26 (1928) 11.

Vandier-Nicolas, N. avec le concours de Mmes. Gaulier, Leblond et Maillard et M. Jera-Bezard. **Bannières et peintures de touen-houang conservés au musée guimet.** Paris (1974) xxiii + 435 p, pl. A second vol with same title plus **Planches.** Paris (1976) 252 p, 134 pl. Mission Paul Pelliot vol 14 & 15.

Waley, Arthur. Chinese temple paintings. **BM** 41 (1922) 228-231. Paintings in ch'ang-an and lo-yang temples mentioned and described in chang yen-yuan's records of painting in successive ages (a.d. 847)

Watson, William (ed) **Mahayanist art after a.d. 900: proceedings of a colloquy held 28 june-1 july 1971 at the perceval david foundation of chinese art.** London (1971) 5 + 104 p, 19 pl.

White, William Charles. **Chinese temple frescoes. A study of three wall-paintings of the thirteenth century.** Univ toronto (1940) xvii + 230 p, pl, illus.

White, William Charles. Chinese temple frescoes. Number one. Constituting **BROMA** no 12 (july 1937) 32 p, illus. Included in author's book, above, chap 12.

Xia, Yuchen. Liang kai's "eight eminent monks" **CL** (may 1980) 95-97, col pl of painting.

Yetts, W.P. Some buddhist frescoes from china. **BM** 51 (1927) 121-128.

Zhang, Anzhi. "Vimalakirti expounds buddhist sutras" by li gonglin. **CL** 1 (jan 1980) 97-100, col pl of painting.

I. HISTORICAL EMPHASIS

Alexandrian, Sarane. Ex-voto pour bouddha. **Connaissance des arts** 253 (mar 1973) 60-67, col pl. Re tun-huang banners in paris museum.

Bulling, A. Buddhist temples in the t'ang period. **OA** n.s. 1 (1955) 79-86, 115-122, illus.

Bush, Susan H. & Victor H. Mair. Some buddhist portraits and images of the lü and ch'an sects in twelfth- and thirteenth-century china. **AAA** 31 (1977-78) 32-51, illus.

Coq, A. von le. **Die buddhistische spätantike in mittelasien.** Berlin (1922-33) 7 vol.

Davidson, J. LeRoy. Buddhist paradise cults in sixth century china. **JISOA** 17 (1949) 112-124.

Davidson, J. LeRoy. **The lotus sutra in chinese art. A study in buddhist art to the year 1000.** Yale univ (1954) 105 p, bibliog, 40pl.

Davidson, J. LeRoy. Traces of buddhist evangelism in early chinese art. **AA** 11.4 (1948) 251-265, illus.

Ghose, Hemendra Prasad. Indian art in the far east. **CalR** (oct 1903) 287-313.

Liang, Ssu-ch'eng. China's oldest wooden structure. **Asia** 41 (july 1941) 384-387, illus. Re t'ang temple on wu-t'ai shan.

Lo Hsiang-lin. Sino-indian relations over the chiao-kwang route and new discoveries on buddhism and its art in the kwangtung-kwangsi areas in the tang dynasty. **CC** 1.3 (1958) 181-203.

Rhie, Marylin M. **The fo-kuang ssu: literary evidences and buddhist images.** NY (1977) 274 p, illus.

Soper, Alexander C. South chinese influence on the buddhist art of the six dynasties period. **BMFEA** 32 (1960) 47-112, 18 pl.

Waley, Arthur. **Zen buddhism and its relation to art.** London (1922) 31 p.

With, Karl. Suiko. Über den beginn der buddhistischen kunst in ostasien. **Zeitschrift für buddhismus und verwandte gebiete** 4 (1922) 190-196.

J. MISCELLANEOUS

Allen, William Dangaix. A secular portrait art hidden in china's temples. **CJ** 16.6 (june 1932) 314-319, illus with photos. Esp re budd art.

A Chinese priest of the t'ang dynasty. **EB** 10 (1922) 23-24. Pottery grave figure.

Coomaraswamy, Ananda K. and F.S. Kershaw. A chinese buddhist water vessel and its indian prototype. **AA** 3 (1928) 122-141.

Denés, Françoise. **Catalogue raisonné des objets en bois provenant de dunhuang et conservés au musée guimet.** Paris (1976) 81 p.

Hickman, Money L. Notes on buddhist banners. **BMFA** 71 (1973) 4-20, illus.

Hisamatsu, Shin'ichi. On zen art. **EB** n.s. 1.2 (sept 1966) 21-33.

Hobson, R.L. Two pottery lokapalas, **BMQ** 7 (1933) 83. T'ang grave figures.

Jera-Bezard, Robert. Six triangles sur soie inédits de la collection paul pelliot. **La revue du louvre et de musées de france** 28.4 (1978) 230-235, illus.

Karmay, Heather. **Early sino-tibetan art.** Warminster, engl (1975) 128 p, 69 pl. See rev by M. Strickmann in **Annali dell'instituto orientale di napoli** 39 (1979) 506-513.

Kopf des mönchs ki-tsi besser bekannt unter dem namen pu-tai. **Sinologica** 8.1 (1964) 10, pl. Bronze.

A Large pottery lohan of the t'ang period. **BMMA** 16 (1921) 15-16, 120.

Lerner, Martin. A seventh-century chinese buddhist ivory. **BCMA** 55 (nov 1968) 294-302, illus.

Miao, D.F. The discovery of t'ang dynasty figures at lo chih. **CJ** 18.4 (apr 1933) 188-191, illus with photos. Lo chih is "a small town situated about ten miles southwest of quinsan (k'un-shan)" Clay fig found in temple called pao shen ssu.

Munsterberg, Hugo. A buddhist reliquary in the musée guimet. **OA** 12 (1966) 231-233, illus.

Polonyi, P. Chinese sutra covers in the collection of the ferenc hopp museum of eastern asiatic arts in budapest. **AO** (budapest) 23.1 (1970) 85-106.

Pope, John. A chinese buddhist pewter with a ming date. **ACASA** 16 (1962) 88-91, illus.

Sarre, F. Eine chinesische pilgerflasche der t'angzeit. **Pantheon** 14 (1934) 273-276.

Simmons, P. An eighteenth century priest robe. **BMMA** 29 (1934) 7-8.

Soper Alexander C. A buddhist travelling shrine in an international style. **E&W** 15 (1965) 211-225, pl.

Turner, Gerald. Á magic mirror of buddhist significance. **OA** 12 (1966) 94-98, illus.

Vandier-Nicolas, N. avec le concours de Mmes. Gaulier, LeBlond et Maillard et M. Jera-Bezard. **Bannières et peintures de touen-houang conservés au musée guimet.** Paris (1974) xxiii + 435 p, pl.A second vol with same title plus **Planches.** Paris (1976) 252 p, 134 pl. Mission Paul Pelliot vol 14 & 15.

Wolf, Marion. The lohans from i-chou. **OA** n.s. 15.1 (1969) 51.57, illus.

14. CAVES AND MOUNTAINS

A. GENERAL

Akiyama, Terukazu and Matsubara Saburo. **Arts of china. Buddhist cave temples; new researches.** Tsl fr jap Alexander C. Soper. Tokyo and palo alto, calif. (1969) 248 p, chron, bibliog, map, col and bl-&-wh pl.

Brankston, A.D. Buddhist cave temples from china to ellora. **AR** 34 (1938) 497-509.

Doré, Henri. Le grand pèlerinage bouddhique de lang-chan et les cinq montagnes de tung-tcheou. **NCR** 1 (1919) 41-56, 120-144, 282-298, 457-479, 588-603; 2 (1920) 44-68, pl.

Fontein, Jan. China. In **EncyWA** vol 3, 393a-466b. See passim, also relevant illus in sec at end of vol.

Klee, Th. Die plastik in den höhlen von yün-kang, lung-mên, und kung-hsien. **OZ** 7 (1918) 31-56.

Nagahiro, Toshio, Eun Hyun Yum & Takeshi Kuno. **Great sculpture of the far east.** NY (1979) On chin budd sculpture and caves, see 11-22 and pl. Mostly an album.

Perzynski, Friedrich.**Von chinas göttern. Reisen in china.** München (1920) 260 s 80 bildtaf.

Petrucci, Raphael. Buddhist art in the far east, and the documents from chinese turkestan. **BM** 18 (dec 1911) 138-144, 2 photos.

Soper, Alexander C. Imperial cave-chapels of the northern dynasties. **AA** 28 (1966) 241-270, illus, fig.

Swann, Peter C. **Chinese monumental art.** N.Y. (1963) french ed (1963) 276 p, 15 maps and fig, bibliog, index, 157 pl. Photos Claude Arthaud and François Hébert-Stevens.

Tokiwa, Daijo and Sekino Tadashi. **Buddhist monuments in china.** Tokyo (1926-28) 6 vol text; 6 vol pl.

Tucci, Giuseppe. Buddhism. In **EncyWA** vol 2, 670b-703a. See passim, also relevant illus in sec at end of vol.

B. YÜN-KANG

Adam, M. Les grottes de yün kang. **La chine** 66 (1924) 350-364.

Alley, Rewi & R. Lapwood. China's ancient cave temples: a visit to the yun kang caves and ta-t'ung fu. **CJ** 23.5 (nov 1935) 274-276, illus with map and photos.

Bishop, D.F. We visit the cave temples of yun-kang. **Japan** 19.4 (1930) 9-11, 48-49, illus.

Boode, P. A visit to the yün kang caves. **TOCS** (1937-38) 55-62.

Caswell, James O. The "Thousand-buddha" pattern in caves XIX and XVI at yün-kang. **ArsO** 10 (1975) 35-54, 8 pl.

Chang, Y.H. (photog) The yunkang caves. **EH** 5.4 (1966) 8 p photos betw 12-21.

Committee in charge of cultural relics & the institute for the preservation of the yunkang caves of shansi province (comp) **The yunkang caves.** Peking (1977) chin text, 107 pl, engl version 29 p.

Cox, Leonard B. **The buddhist cave temples of yün-kang and lung-mên.** Australian national univ (1957) 14 p, 5 pl (george e. morrison lecture in anthropology no 18)

Crane, L. Buddhist treasures in the shansi mountains. **Asia** 31 (1931) 434-438.

Demiéville, Paul. Notes d'archéologie chinoise. 1,
l'Inscriptions de yun-kang; 2, Le buddha du k'o chan; 3,
Les tombeaux des song méridionaux. **BEFEO** 25.3/4
(1925) 449-468.

Drake, F.S. Yün-kang: the buddhist caves of the fifth
century a.d. in north china . . . report of the archaeological survey . . . of the tōhō bunka kenkyūsho (rev art)
JOS 2 (1955) 324-337.

Eigner, J. The grandeur of the yun kang caves. **CJ** 25
(1936) 315-317.

Gabain, Annemarie v. Die fliegenden genien von yün-
kang, verkörperung geistiger freude. **NachrDGNVO** no
97 (june 1965) 7-12, pl.

Geelmuyden, N. The yun-kan [sic] caves, one of
buddhism's earliest manisfestations in china. **Journal of
the siam society** 46.1 (1958) 37-45.

Giles, W.R. Cave temples in china. Exquisite sculpture
revealed in mountain caves. **Asia** 18 (mar 1918) 234-236,
illus.

Les grottes de yün-kang. l'Art des wei. Pékin (192?)
6 p, pl.

Hansford, S. Howard. The stone buddhas of yün-kang.
GM 14 (jan 1942) 134-141, illus, map.

Institute for the preservation of yunkang antiquities, shansi
(comp) **The yunkang caves.** Peking (1973) 5 p of text, 25
b-&-w pl.

Kaul, T.N. The caves of yun kang. **United asia** 5 (1953)
313-314.

King, Gordon. **The buddhist cave temples at yünkang.**
Peiping (1935) 12 p, illus.

Klee, Th. Die plastik in den höhlen von yün-kang, lung-
mên und kung-hsien. **OZ** 7 (1918-19) 31-36.

Krueger, Hans-Ewald. The caves at tatung. **CJ** 31.2 (aug
1939) 91-94, photos.

Mizuno, Seiichi. Archaeological survey of the yün-kang
grottoes. **ACASA** 4 (1950) 39-60.

Mizuno, Seiichi and Nagahiro Toshio. **Yün-kang: the
buddhist cave-temples of the fifth century a.d. in north
china. Detailed report of the archaeological survey
carried out by the mission of the tōhōbunka
kenkyūsho, 1938-45.** Kyoto (1951-56) 16 vol text, 16 vol
pl, engl and jap text.

Mullikin, Mary A. The buddhist sculptures at the yun kang
caves. **Studio** 108 (1934) 65-70, illus.

Mullikan, Mary Augusta. **Buddhist sculptures at the yun
kang caves. Text and illustrations by Mary Augusta
Mullikan, with additional illustrations by Anna H.
Hotchkis.** Peiping (1935) 66 p, illus.

Mullikan, Mary Augusta. China's great wall of sculpture.
Man-hewn caves and countless images form a colossal art
wonder of early buddhism. **NGM** 73 (mar 1938) 313-348,
illus.

Musée Cernuschi. **Yun-kang et nara. Documents photo-
graphiques sur l'art bouddhique.** Paris (1952) 34 p, illus.

Poon, Walter, text & photos. Yun gang's giant buddhas.
Orientations 10.5 (may 1979) 19-23, col-photos.

Read, B.E. Yun kan [sic]; buddhist temple-caves. **Orient**
1.8 (mar 1951) 19-21.

Sato, Chisui. The character of yün-kang buddhism. A look
at the emergence of a state-supported religion in china
under the northern wei. **TBMRD** 36 (1978) 39-83.

Shinkai, Taketarō and Nakagawa Tadayori. **Rock-
carvings from the yun-kang caves, selected by shinkai
taketarō and nakagawa tadayori.** Photos Yamamoto
Akira and Kishi Masakatsu. Tokyo (1921) 16 p, 200 pl.
Intro in jap and engl.

Sowerby, Arthur de C.S. China's sacred mountains. **CJ**
22.2 (feb 1935) 64-65.

Yashiro, Yukio. The present state of the yünkang caves.
BEA no 15 (1941) 3-12.

Yin, Wen-tsu. Restoration of the yunkang caves. **CL** 5
(may 1978) 104-111, illus.

C. LUNG-MEN

Chavannes, Édouard. Le défilé de long-men dans la
province de ho-nan. **JA** 9e sér, 20 (1902) 133-158, 6 fig.

Cox, Leonard B. **The buddhist cave temples of yün-
kang and lung-mên.** Australian national univ (1957) 14 p,
5 pl (george e. morrison lecture in anthropology no 18)

Fong, Mary H. Buddhist cave sculpture at lung-men. **AofA**
10.4 (july-aug 1980) 82-88, illus.

Fu Tien-chun. The rock sculptures of lungmen. **CL** 5 (may
1962) 65-71, illus.

Giles, W.R. Cave temples in china. Exquisite sculpture
revealed in mountain caverns. **Asia** 18 (mar 1918)
234-236, illus.

Klee, Th. Die plastik in den höhlen von yün-kang, lung-
mên und kung-hsien. **OZ** 7 (1918-19) 31-36.

Kuck, F.W. The cave-temples of lung men. **CJ** 18.6 (june 1933) 343-344, illus with 16 photos taken during author's visit in 1931.

Lahiri, Latika. Lung-man (sic) cave inscriptions and the popularity of maitreya bodhi sattva. In **B&J** (1976) 75-82.

Mahler, Jane Gaston. An assembly of lung-men sculpture. **AAA** 24 (1970-71) 70-75. Re items in sackler coll.

Mizuno, S. and T. Nagahiro. **A study of the buddhist cave-temples at lung-mên, honan.** Tokyo (1941) 482 p, jap and engl. App 1: Z. Tsukamoto's Buddhism under the northern wei dynasty.

Pelerzi, E. **Les grottes de longmen.** Shanghai (1923) 99 p, illus.

Ségalen, Victor. Bouddhisme chinois. **RAA** 3 (1926) 119-122. Re author's visit to lung-men in 1914.

Spruyt, A. Reminiscences of the édouard chavannes expedition. Evidences of early buddhism in china. The sacred mountain of lung-men. **Indian art and letters** 5.2 (1931) 103-110, 4 pl.

Spruyt, A. Souvenir d'un voyage à la montagne sacrée de long men. **MCB** 1 (1932) 241-262, 18 photos, 1 carte.

D. T'IEN-LUNG SHAN

Boerschmann, E. Die kultstätte des t'ien lung shan. **AA** 1 (1925) 262-279.

Lartigue, J. Le sanctuaire bouddhique de t'ien-long-chan. **RAA** 1 (1924) 3-9.

Rhie, Marylin M. A t'ang period stele inscription and cave XXI at t'ien lung shan. **AAA** 28 (1974-75) 6-33.

Vanderstappen, Harry and Marylin Rhie. The sculpture of t'ien lung shan: reconstruction and dating. **AA** 27 (1964-65) 189-220, 81 pl.

E. O-MEI SHAN

Bonin, Charles-Eudes. Le mont omei. **Bulletin de géographie historique et descriptive** 1 (1899) 64-75.

Cammann, Schuyler. Temples in the clouds, mount omei. **Travel** 78 (1942) 4-10.

Dent, R.V. To mount omei by way of the yangtze gorges. **CJ** 21.4 (oct 1934) 164-169, illus photos.

Eigner, Julius. The sacred mountains of china: the pilgrimage to omei shan. **CJ** 22.1 (jan 1935) 20-23, illus photos.

Franck, Harry A. **Roving through southern china.** NY & london (1925) See chap 23, To the summit of sacred omeishan, illus photos.

Graham, David C. Recent changes among the temples of mt. omei. **JWCBorderResS** 8 (1936) 175-176.

Hart, Virgil C. **Western china. A journey to the great buddhist centre of mount omei.** Boston (1888) 306 p.

Hayes, L. Newton. A trip to sacred mount omei. **ChRec** 48.8 (aug 1917) 515-519.

Hooker, Charles. Moods of mount omei. **CJ** 11.4 (oct 1929) 183-184.

Hsu, Chih. Climbing mount omei. **CL** 11 (nov 1961) 93-96.

Johnston, R.F. **From peking to mandalay.** N.Y. (1908) See chap 6, Mount omei and chinese buddhism, 54-81; chap 7, Mount omei, 82-111.

Kemp, E.G. Mount omi. Chap 17 in author's **FC** (1909) 182-194.

Kendall, Elizabeth. **A wayfarer in china.** Boston & ny (1913) See chap 9, Omei shan, the sacred, 180-201.

Little, Archibald J. **Mount omi and beyond. A record of travel on the thibetan border.** London (1901) xiv + 272 p, map. Same title in **NCH** 26 may 1893) 76-78, 809, 881, 926, 964 (5 jan 1894) 19-20.

Little, Mrs. Archibald. The sacred mountain of omi. Chap 19 in author's **IntC** (ca 1900) 251-264.

Madrolle, Claudius. **Le mont omei, lieu de pèlerinage bouddhique.** Paris (1914) 16 p, cartes.

Migot, A. Les temples bouddhiques de mont o-mei (o-mei chan) **ArtsAs** 4 (1957) 20-34, 131-142.

Payne, Jessie E. Where buddhism still reigns. **ChRec** 62.11 (nov 1931) 713-715. Visit to omei shan.

Phelps, Dryden L. (tsl) **Omei illustrated guide book. A new edition of the omei illustrated guide book, by huang shou-fu and t'an chung-yo, a.d. 1887-1891.** Pictures redrawn from the original plates by yü tzu-tan. Chengtu (1936) 353 p, text in chin and engl, illus. Repr univ hk (1974) with new preface by tsl.

Phelps, Dryden L. A sung dynasty document of mount omei. **JWCBorderResS** 11 (1939) 66-77. Intro, with 2 photos, and tsl of travel account by fan ch'en of sung dynasty.

Shields, E.T. Omei shan: the sacred mountain of west china. **JNCBRAS** 44 (1913) 100-109.

F. WU-T'AI SHAN

Alley, Rewi & R. Lapwood. The sacred mountains of china: a trip to wu t'ai shan. **CJ** 22.3 (mar 1935) 114-121, maps, photos.

Blofeld, John. The festival of the sacred mountain. **CJ** 28.1 (jan 1938) 25-37, photos.

David-Neel, A. The manjushri of wu t'ai shan. **JWCBorderResS** ser A.14 (1942) 25-30.

Fischer, E.S. **The sacred wu tai shan.** Shanghai (1925) 37 p, illus, map.

Hummel, Siegbert. Die fussspur des gautama-buddha auf dem wu-t'ai-shan. **AS** 25 (1971) 389-406, 3 taf, 20 pl.

Irving, Christopher. Wu-t'ai-shan and the dalai lama. **NCR** 1 (may 1919) 151-163.

Lamotte, Étienne. Mañjuśrī. **TP** 48 (1960) 54-96. On mañjuśrī and wu-t'ai shan.

Limpricht, W. Eine durchwanderung der wutaischan-ketten. **MSOS** 16 (1913) 141-176, fig.

Marchand, Ernesta. The panorama of wu-t'ai shan as an example of tenth century cartography. **OA** n.s. 22.2 (summer 1976) 158-173, illus. Re a mural in cave 61 at tun-huang.

Payne, Henry. Lamaism on wu tai shan. **ChRec** 60.8 (aug 1929) 506-510.

Rockhill, William W. A pilgrimage to the great buddhist sanctuary of north china [wu-t'ai shan] **Atlantic monthly** 75 (june 1895) 758-769.

Savage-Landor, A. Henry. A journey to the sacred mountain of siao-outai-shan, in china. **Fortnightly review** (sept 1894) 393-409. Repr in **Eclectic magazine** 123 (july-dec 1894) also repr in **Littel's living age** 203 (oct-dec 1894)

Swallow, R.W. A journey to wu tai shan, one of the meccas of buddhism. **JMGS** (1903) 173-182.

Verdeille, Maurice (tsl) Le monastère de la montagne 'ou-tai' en révolution. Extrait par l'éditeur des 'siao-siao chuou' du livre intitulé 'liang-shan-po.' **BSEIS** 70 (1919) 21-37, 2 pl.

G. P'U-T'O SHAN

Arène, Jules. Excursion à l'île sacrée de pou tou. **l'Explorateur** no 20.1 (1875)

Ein Ausflug nach die heilige insel putu. **Das ausland** 31 (1876)

Bock, Carl. l'Île sacrée du pouto (archipel de tchou-san ou chusan, chine) **Comptes rendus société géographie** (1891) 483-485.

Boerschmann, Ernst. **Die baukunst und religiöse kultur der chinesen; vol 1: P'u t'o shan.** Berlin (1911) 203 p.

Butler, John. Pootoo ancient and modern. **ChRec** 10.2 (mar-apr 1879) 108-124.

Crane, L. Honoring the goddess of mercy; pootoo, the island sanctuary of kuan yin. **Travel** 56 (mar 1931) 22-26.

Edkins, Joseph. The monasteries at pu-to. **NCH** 345 (7 mar 1856)

Fernandez, R.I. The island kingdom of buddha. **CJ** 34.4 (apr 1941) 169-172, photos.

Fitch, Robert F. **Pootoo itineraries.** Shanghai (1929) 90 p.

Fitch, Robert F. Puto, the enchanted island. **NGM** 89 (mar 1946) 373-384, illus.

Franke, O. Die heilige insel pu-to. **Globus** 63 (1893) 117-122.

Fryer, J. Gleanings about poo-too. **NCH** (8 aug 1868)

Gundry, R.S. **Sketches of excursions to chusan, poo-too . . . Nanking and kioto.** Shanghai (1876) ix + 116 p.

Gützlaff, C. Extract from gutzlaff's journal: journal of a voyage along the coast of china, from the province of canton to leaoutung in mantchou tartary; 1832-33. **ChRep** 2.2 (june 1833) 53-57.

Gützlaff, C. ['Philosinensis'] Remarks on buddhism; together with brief notices of the island of poo-to, and of the numerous priests who inhabit it. **ChRep** 2 (1833-34) 214-255.

H. [a letter about p'u-t'o shan] **NCH** 734 (1864)

Inveen, Emma. Pootoo: china's sacred island (ii) **EA** 3 (1904) 357-362.

Krieger. Putu, chinas heilige insel. **Koloniale rundschau** 1 (1909) 762-770.

Kupfer, Carl F. Pootoo: china's sacred island (i) **EA** 3 (1904) 264-281.

Mizande, François. Dans l'archipel des chu-san: pu-tu, l'île des pagodes ou la terre de bouddha. **TM** 18 (1912) 265-268, 273-276, carte et illus.

Natz, Marie. Eine pilgerfahrt nach pu-to. **OstL** vol 28 no 23 (1914) 21-23.

Nevius, Helen S.C. **Our life in china.** NY (1868) See chap 3, Pootoo—glance at the religions of china, 44-66.

Peri, N. and H. Maspero. Le monastère de la kouan-yin qui ne veut pas s'en aller [in p'u-t'o shan] **BEFEO** 9 (1909) 797-807.

P'u t'u, kuan yin's island. **CJ** 21.2 (aug 1934) 64-66, illus 8 photos.

Rees, I. A visit to putushan. **GM** 6 (1937) 67-72, illus.

Rondot, Natalis. **Excursion à l'île de pou-tou (province de tché-kiang) 7 et 8 octobre, 1845.** Reims (1846) 40p, 2 lith.

Stanley, Arthur. Putoshan. A draught at the well-springs of chinese buddhist art. **JNCBRAS** 46 (1915) 1-18, illus.

H. TUN-HUANG

Alexandrian, Sarane. Ex-voto pour bouddha. **Connaissance des arts** 253 (mar 1973) 60-67, col pl. Re tunhuang banners in paris.

Bohlin, B. Newly visited western caves at tun-huang. **HJAS** 1 (1935) 163-166.

Bonin, Charles-Eudes. Les grottes de mille bouddhas. **CRAIBL** pt 1 (mar-avr 1901) 209-217.

Chang, Cornelius P. Kuan-yin paintings from tun-huang: water-moon kuan-yin. **JOS** 15.2 (1977) 140-160, 5 pl.

Chang, Dai-chien. Tun huang frescoes and i. **APQCSA** 8.2 (autumn 1976) 43-45.

Chang, Shu-hung. The art treasures of tunhuang. **China pictorial** no 1 (jan 1956) 19-21, illus.

Chavannes, Édouard. Présentation du touen-houang che che yi chou. **CRAIBL** (juin 1910) 245-246.

Chen, Tsu-lung. **Éloges de personnages éminents de touen-houang sous les t'ang et les cinq dynasties.** Paris (1970)

Chen, Tsu-lung. Notes on the wedding ceremonies and customs observed in tun-huang in the second half of the ninth century. **E&W** n.s. 22.3/4 (sep-dec 1972) 313-327.

Chen, Tsu-lung. Table de concordance des numérotages des grottes de touen-houang. **JA** 250.2 (1962) 257-276.

Chen, Tsu-lung. **La vie et les oeuvres de wou-tchen (816-895). Contribution à l'histoire culturelle de touen-houang.** Paris (1966) 165 p, bibliog, indexes, map.

Chêng, Tê-k'un. **Tun-huang studies in china.** Chengtu (1947) 14 p.

Chou, Shao-miao and Wu Mi-feng (copyists) **Designs from the tunhuang caves.** Intro Wang Hsun. Peking (1956) 20 leaves in portfolio.

Demiéville, Paul. **Mission paul pelliot. Documents conservés à la bibliothèque nationale, II: Airs de touen-houang (touen-houng k'iu). Textes à chanter des VIIIe — Xe siècles. Manuscrits reproduits en facsimilé, avec une introduction en chinois par jao tsung-yi. Adaptes en français avec la traduction de quelques textes d'air, par p. demiéville.** Paris (1971) 370 p, 58 p.

Demiéville, Paul. Récents travaux sur touen-houang. Aperçu bibliographique et notes critiques. **TP** 56.1/3 (1970) 1-95.

Denés, Françoise. **Catalogue raisonné des objets en bois provenant de dunhuang et conservés au musée guimet.** Paris (1976) 8 1 p.

Excavation and protection of relics in tunhuang cave-temples. **Economic reporter** 2 (apr-june 1972) 26-28.

Fontein, Jan and Money L. Hickman. **Zen painting and calligraphy.** Boston (1970) liv + 173 p, illus.

Foreign languages press (comp) **Murals from the tunhuang caves.** Peking (1956) 20 pl in portfolio.

Forte, Antonio. **Political propaganda and ideology in china at the end of the seventh century: inquiry into the nature, authors, and function of the tunhuang document s.6502, followed by an annotated translation.** Napoli, instituto universitario oriental (1976) 312 p. Re text composed by a group of budd monks to legitimate ascension to throne of empress wu chao (r.683-707) See rev by M. Strickmann in **EB** n.s. 10.1 (may 1977) 156-160.

Fourcade, François. **Le peinture murale de touen-houang.** Paris (1962) 134 p, illus, maps, plans, table.

Friend, Robert. The caves of the thousand buddhas—tunhuang and the old silk road. **EH** 17.8 (aug 1978) 22-24, illus.

Fujieda, Akira. The tun-huang manuscripts. In **ESCH** (1973) 120-128.

Fujieda, Akira. The tunhuang manuscripts: a general description. **Zinbun** 9 (1966) 1-32; 10 (1969) 17-39, fig, tables.

Gray, Basil. **Buddhist cave paintings at tun-huang.** Photos J.B. Vincent; preface Arthur Waley. Univ chicago (1959) 83 p, 70 pl, notes on pl, bibliog.

Guignard, Marie-Roberte (ed) **Catalogue des manuscrits chinois de touen-houang.** Paris, vol 1 (1970) xxix + 407, 24 pl; items no 2001-2500.

Hadl, R. Langdon Warner's buddhist wall paintings. **AA** 9 (1946) 160-164.

Hejzlar, Josef. Recollections of tunhuang. **NO** 5 (feb 1966) 15-16, 4 p illus.

Imaeda, Y. Documents tibétains de touen-houang concernant le concile du tibet. **JA** 263.1/2 (1975) 125-146.

Jera-Bezard, Robert. Six triangles sur soie inédits de la collection paul pelliot. **La revue du louvre et de musées de france** 28.4 (1978) 230-235, illus.

Kanaoka, Shōkō. On the word "pien" **TUAS** 1 (1961) 15-24. Re tun-huang mss.

King, Yung-hua. Some current tun huang projects in taiwan and hongkong. **CC** 21.1 (mar 1980) 91-92.

Lao, Kan. The art of tunhuang. Tsl fr chin Ho Chien. **CC** 1 (oct 1957) 47-74.

Mair, Victor. Lay students and the making of written vernacular narrative: an inventory of tun-huang manuscripts. **Chinoperl** 10 (1980) 5-96, app.

March, Benjamin. A tun-huang buddhist painting. **BDetIA** 10 (may 1929) 109-111.

Matsumoto, Yeiichi. On some amulet pictures from tunhuang. **Kokka** 482 (1931) 3-6; 488 (1931) 249-254, illus.

Mibu, Taishun & Hirai Yuhkei. Present state of the mokau-ku cave temples at tunhuang. **JIBS** 28.2 (mar 1980) 1-12.

Mizuno, S. **Wall paintings of tun-huang.** Tokyo (1958)

Musée Cernuschi. **Relevés de touen-houang et peintures anciennes de la collection tchang ta-ts'ien.** Paris (1956) 25 p, 29 pl.

Musée Guimet. **Manuscrits et peintures de touen-houang; mission pelliot 1906-1909. Collections de la bibliothèque nationale et du musée guimet.** Paris (1947) 41 p, map.

Pelliot, Paul. Arthur waley: A catalogue of paintings recovered from tun-huang (etc) (rev art) **TP** 28 (1931) 383-413.

Pelliot, Paul. Une bibliothèque médiévale retrouvé au kan-sou. **BEFEO** 8 (1908) 501-529.

Pelliot, Paul. Les fresques de touen-houang et les fresques de m. eumorfopoulos. **RAA** 5 (1928) 143-163, 193-214, illus.

Pelliot, Paul. Les grottes des mille bouddhas. **JRAS** (1914) 421-426.

Pelliot, Paul. **Mission pelliot en asie centrale: les grottes de touen houang.** Paris (1914-24) 6 vol pl (no text)

Petrucci, R. Les peintures bouddhiques de touen-houang (mission stein) **AMG** (1916) 115-140, illus.

Plumer, James M. Tun huang: vision of buddhist glory as seen in irene vincent's photographs. **AQ** 14 (spring 1951) 56-57, illus.

Riboud, Mme Krishna et Gabriel Vial, avec le concours de Mlle. M. Hallade. **Tissus de touen-houang. Conservés au musée guimet et à la bibliothèque nationale.** Paris (1970) 443 p, 103 pl, charts (Mission paul pelliot no 13)

Richardson, Hugh E. "The dharma that came down from heaven": a tun-huang fragment. In **BT&AC** (1977) 219-230.

Sasaguchi, Rei. A dated painting from tun-huang in the fogg museum. **AAA** 26 (1972-73) 26-49. Maitreya's paradise.

Shen, I-chang, Sun Yu & Ronald J. Dickson (tsl) Chang dai-ch'ien's copies of the tun-huang cave paintings. **NPMB** 12.3 (july-aug 1977) 1-21.

Shor, Franc and Jean. The caves of the thousand buddhas. **NGM** (mar 1951) 383-415, illus.

Silva-Vigrier, Anil de. **Chinese landscape painting in the caves of tun-huang.** London (1967) 240 p, maps, tables, illus.

Soper, Alexander C. Representations of famous images at tun-huang. **AA** 27 (1965) 349-364, pl.

Stein, Aurel. **Serindia: detailed report of explorations in central asia and westernmost china.** Oxford univ (1921) 5 vol, pl.

Stein, Marc Aurel. Specimens from a collection of ancient buddhist pictures and embroideries discovered at tun-huang. **Journal of indian art and industries** n.s. 15 (1912) 60-66, 4 pl.

Stein, Aurel. **The thousand buddhas: ancient buddhist paintings from the cave-temples of tun-huang on the western frontier of china.** London (1921) 3 vol, pl. Facsimile ed ny (1980?)

Strassberg, Richard E. Buddhist storytelling texts from tun-huang. **Chinoperl** 8 (1978) 39-99, transcriptions bibliog.

Su, Ying-hui. The buddhist art of the tunhuang caves in china. **APQCSA** 2.3 (winter 1970) 28-33.

Su, Ying-hui. The buddhist art of wei, tsin, and southern and northern dynasties at tunhuang in china. **CC** 11.2 (june 1970) 55-61.

Su, Ying-hui. A comparative study on the contour techniques of wall-paintings found in tunhuang, ajanta, sigiriya and polonnaruwa. **APQCSA** 7.1 (summer 1975) 10-12.

Su, Ying-hui. **A collection of articles on tunhuang.** Taipei (1969) 80 p. Most of art in chin; 3 art in engl and abstracts of the others.

Su, Ying-hui. The dancing guidebook of tunhuang. **APQCSA** 12.1 (spring 1980) 47-49. A text fr 2 mss.

Su, Ying-hui. On the tunhuang science. **West and East** 9.6 (june 1964) 7-10; 9.7 (july 1964) 5-7, illus.

Su, Ying-hui. On the tunhuang studies. **CC** 17.1 (mar 1976) 63-92. Rev art. Same title in **APQCSA** (spring 1974) 34-55.

Su, Ying-hui. A study of the identity of monk wu in the tun-huang manuscripts. In **MS/CA** (1977) 305-318.

Su, Ying-hui. A study of the identity of monk wu (wu ho-shang) in the tunhuang manuscripts p. 2913, p. 4660 and s.1947v. **CC** 15.4 (dec 1974) 89-98.

Su, Ying-hui. The tun huang stone cave and the thousand buddha caves. **CC** 5.2 (oct 1963) 32-46, illus.

Tomita, Kojirō. A dated buddhist painting from tun-huang. **BMFA** 25 (1927)

Tomita, Kojirō. Two more dated buddhist paintings from tun-huang. **BMFA** 26 (1928) 11.

Tunhuang, Kansu, National Art Institute. The sacred grottoes of tunhuang. **China magazine** 19 (jan 1949) 28-42, illus.

Tunhuang painted sculptures. Peiching (1978) chin and engl text, 85 col pl.

Vandier-Nicolas, N. avec le concours de Mmes. Gaulier, Leblond et Maillard et M. Jera-Bezard. **Bannières et peintures de touen-houang conservés au musée guimet.** Paris (1974) xiii + 435 p, pl. A second vol with same title plus **Planches.** Paris (1976) 252 p, 134 pl. Mission Paul Pelliot vol 14 & 15.

Vincent, Irene Vongehr. **The sacred oasis. Caves of the thousand buddhas, tun huang.** London (1953) 114 p, map, bibliog, index, photos.

Waite, Arthur E. The shrine of a thousand buddhas. **Occult review** 15 (1912) 195-203.

Waley, Arthur. **A catalogue of paintings recovered from tun-huang by sir aurel stein, k.c.i.e., preserved in the british museum and in the museum of central asian antiquities, delhi.** London (1931) lii + 328 p, diagr. Rev Paul Pelliot, q.v. above.

Waley, Arthur. A legend about the caves of the myriad buddhas. **SIS** 5.3/4 liebenthal festschrift (1957) 241-242.

Wang, Hsün (intro) **Designs from the tun-huang caves.** Peking (1956) 4 p, 20 pl. Designs copied by Chou Shao-miao & Wu Mi-feng.

Warner, Langdon. **Buddhist wall-paintings. A study of a ninth-century grotto at wan fo hsia.** Harvard univ (1938) xv + 33 p, map, pl.

Warner, Langdon. **The long old road in china. Descriptive of a journey into the far west of china to discover and bring back famous buddhist frescoes and statuary.** N.Y. (1926) 176 p, illus.

Wright, Harrison K. The thousand buddhas of the tunhuang caves. **NCR** 4 (oct 1922) 401-407.

I. OTHERS

Chambeau, Gabriel. Une visite aux monastères bouddhiques de kieou-hoa-chan. **Études** 130 (20 mars 1912) 785-798; 131 (5 avr 1912) 34-52.

Doré, H. Le grand pèlerinage bouddhique de lang-chan et les cinq montagnes de tong-tcheou. **NCR** 1.1 (mar 1919) 41-56; 1.2 (may 1919) 120-144; 1.3 (july 1919) 282-298; 1.5 (oct 1919) 457-479; 1.6 (dec 1919) 580-603; 2.1 (feb 1920) 44-46, pl.

Edwards, R. The cave reliefs of ma hao (szechuan) **AA** 17 (1954) 5-28, 103-129.

Eigner, Julius. Strange ceremonies connected with buddhist pilgrimage to miao feng shan. **CJ** 30.3 (mar 1939) 168-172, photos. In western hills near peking.

Gordon-Cumming, C.F. The kushan monastery. Vol 1, chap 14 in author's **WinC** (1886) 257-269.

Imbault-Huart, Camille. Le pèlerinage de la montagne du pic mystérieux près de péking. **JA** 8e sér, 5 (jan 1885) 62-71. Re miaô-foung-chan and temple de fées.

Jayne, H.H.F. The buddhist caves of the ching ho valley. **EArt** (1928-29) 157-173, 243-261, illus.

Jen, Tso-wu. Grottoes of maichishan. **E&W** 5.3 (oct 1954) 210-212.

Jisl, Lumir. Mai-chi-shan, the throne of the gods. **NO** 2.5 (oct 1961) 143-144, 4 p pl.

King, Gordon. Wondrous cave temples of wu chou shan. **Illustrated london news** (10 oct 1931) 553.

Klee, Th. Die plastik in den höhlen von yün-kang, lung-mên und kung-hsien. **OZ** 7 (1918-19) 31-36.

Lapwood, E.R. The sacred mountains of china: t'ien t'ai shan, a home of buddhist philosophy in china. **CJ** 23.1 (july 1935) 29-36, map, photos.

Li, Jung-hsi. The stone scriptures of fang-shan. **EB** n.s. 12.1 (may 1979) 104-113. Re 15,143 slabs stored in fang-shan county, 75 kilometers southwest of peking; engraved betw 605/618-1621/1627.

Mather, Richard. The mystical ascent of the t'ien-t'ai mountains: sun cho's yu-t'ien-t'ai-shan fu. **MS** 20 (1961) 226-245.

Meech, S.E. A recent visit to the yün-shui tung [on shang-fang shan, about 140 li southeast of peking] **ChRec** 5 (1874) 339-347.

Mizuno, S. and T. Nagahiro. **The buddhist cave-temples of hsiang t'ang-ssû.** Kyoto (1937) 48 illus, 66 pl.

Mullikan, Mary Augusta. China's ancient cave temples, sui dynasty cliff and cave sculptures in shantung. **CJ** 22 (1935) 304-306.

Plumer, James M. China's ancient cave temples. Early buddhist sculpture in the northwest. **CJ** 22 (1935) 52-57, 104-109, illus.

Soymié, Michel. Le lo-feou chan. Étude de géographie religieuse. **BEFEO** 48.1 (1956) 1-139, 2 app, bibliog, index, map, illus.

Stein, Aurel. **Ruins of desert cathay: personal narrative of explorations in central asia and western-most china.** London (1912) 2 vol.

Sullivan, Michael. **The cave temples of maichishan.** Photos Dominique Darbois. With an account of the 1958 expedition to maichishan by Anil de Silva. Univ california (1969) 77 p text, 104 p photos [southern kansu]

Tao-chün (pseud for Martin Steinkirk) **Buddha and china: tsi-hia-schan.** Potsdam (1940) 30 p.

Teng, Chien-wu. The cave-temples of chingyang [kansu] **EH** 4.6 (1965) 6-15, 4 p photos.

Wu, Tso-jen. Grottoes of maichishan [southern kansu] **E&W** 5 (1954) 210-212. See same title in **CRecon** 3.3 (1954) 25-27.

Wu, Tso-jen. **The rock grottoes of maichishan.** (1954) 161 pl.

15. SPECIFIC DEITIES

Abegg, E. Der buddha maitreya. **MSGFOK** 7 (1945) 7-37.

Aufhauser, Johannes B. Avalokitesvara — kuan yin (kwannon) — maria. **OR** 10.13 (1929) 366-367.

Birnbaum, Raoul. **The healing buddha.** Boulder, colo (1979) xviii + 253 p, 16 photo-pl, 4 app incl chin char list, bibliog, index.

Bischoff, F.A. (tsl) **Arya mahābala-nāma-mahāyānasūtra. Tibétain (mss. de touen-houang) et chinois. Contribution à l'étude des divinités mineurs de bouddhisme tantrique.** Paris (1956) 138 p, 4 facs.

Blofeld, John. **Compassion yoga; the mystical cult of kuan yin.** London (1977) Alternative title, **Bodhisattva of compassion; the mystical tradition of kuanyin.** Boulder, colo (1978) 158 p, app, gloss, illus.

Borel, Henri. **Kwan yin. die göttin der gnade.** Tsl fr dutch Alfred Reuss. (1912) 72 p.

Carus, Paul. **Amitabha. A story of buddhist theology.** Chicago (1906) 121 p.

Chang, Cornelius P. Kuan-yin paintings from tun-huang: water-moon kuan-yin. **JOS** 15.2 (1977) 140-160, 5 pl.

Chinese buddhist association (comp) **Statues and pictures of gautama buddha.** Peking (1956) 32 pl.

David-Neel, Alexandra. The manjushri of wu t'ai shan. **JWCBorderResS** ser A, 14 (1942) 25-30.

Day, Clarence B. The cult of amitabha. **CJ** 33 (1940) 235-249. Repr **PRPCC** (1975).

Eitel, E.J. Amita and the paradise of the west. **NQ** 2 (1868) 35-38.

Eitel, E.J. The trinity of the buddhists in china. **NQ** 2 (1868) 115-117.

Erkes, Eduard. Zum problem der weiblichen kuanyin. **AA** 9 (1946) 316-320, illus.

Fuchs, Walter. **Der wille der kwan-yin. Eine chinesische legende.** Zürich and stuttgart (1955) 46 p, pl.

Hummel, Siegbert. Der pfauenbuddha. **Sinologica** 2 (1950) 234-241, pl.

Inglis, J.W. The vows of amida. A comparative study. **JNCBRAS** 48 (1917) 1-11.

Karutz, Richard. **Maria im fernen osten; das problem der kuan yin.** Leipzig (1925) 99 p, illus.

Kemp, Craig C. Kuan yin. **Lizzadro museum quarterly** (spring-summer 1972) 24-31. Illus of several ex in nephrite and jade.

Koerber, Hans Nordewin von. Kuan yin, the buddhist madonna. **Theosophical forum** 19 (1941) 6-16.

Lahiri, Latika. Lung-man (sic) cave inscriptions and the popularity of maitreya bodhi sattva. In **B&J** (1976) 75-82.

Lamotte, Étienne. Mañjuśrī. **TP** 48 (1960) 54-96. On mañjuśrī and wu-t'ai shan.

Laufer, Berthold. Defender of the faith: statue of the god, wei-t'o. **Asia** 34 (may 1934) 290-291. See also Defender of the faith and his miracles, **OC** 46 (oct 1932) 665-667.

Lee, Pi-cheng [Lü Pi-ch'eng] **Kwan yin's saving power; some remarkable examples of response to appeals for aid, made known to kwan yin by his devotees.** Collected, translated and edited by lee pi-cheng. Oxford (1932) 39 p.

Lévi, S. Maitreya le consolateur. In **EORL** (1932) 355-402.

Mallman, Marie Thérèse de. **Étude iconographique sur mañjuśrī.** Paris (1964) 284 p, 16 pl.

Mallman, Marie Thérèse de. **Introduction à l'étude d'avalokiteśvara.** Paris (1948) 384 p, 32 pl.

Mironov, N.D. Buddhist miscellanea. **JRAS** (1927) 241-252. Re the name avalokiteśvara and kuan-yin.

Murase, Miyeko. Kuan-yin as savior of men: illustration of the twenty-fifth chapter of the lotus sutra in chinese painting. **AA** 33.1/2 (1971) 39-74.

Mus, Paul. Thousand-armed kwannon: a mystery or a problem? **JIBS** 12 (1964) 1-33.

Pelliot, Paul. Le bhaisajyaguru. **BEFEO** 3.1 (1903) 33-37.

Pelliot, Paul. Une statue de maitreya de 705. **TP** 28 (1931) 381-382.

Peri, Noël. Le dieu wei-t'o **BEFEO** 16.3 (1916) 41-56.

Pohlman, W.J. Translation of a buddhist print descriptive of the one thousand hands, one thousand eyes, the all-prevalent and most merciful to-lo-ni (goddess of mercy) **ChRep** 15 (1846) 351-354.

Poor, Robert, Chinese-buddhist sculpture: a figure of kuan-shih-yin. Minneapolis institute of art, **Bulletin** 58 (1969) 19-28.

Rousselle, E. Der kult der buddhistischen madonna kuan-yin. **NachrDGNVO** 68 (1944) 17-23.

Schlegél, G. Ma-tsu-po . . . or koan-yin with the horsehead . . . **TP** 9.5 (dec 1898) 402-406.

Sowerby, A. de C.S. Legendary figures in chinese art. The five hundred lo-han. **CJ** 15.4 (oct 1931) 172, illus.

Sowerby, A. de C.S. Legendary figures in chinese art. Kuan yin, the goddess of mercy. **CJ** 14.1 (jan 1931) 3-4, illus.

Sowerby, A. de C.S. Legendary fgures in chinese art. Mi-le fo, the laughing buddha. **CJ** 14.6 (june 1931) 287.

Staël-Holstein, A. von. Avalokita and apalokita. **HJAS** 1 (1936) 350-362.

Suzuki, Beatrice Lane. The bodhisattvas. **EB** 1 (1921) 131-139.

Suzuki, D.T. The kuan-yin cult in china. **EB** 6 (1935) 339-353.

Takakusu, Junjirō. Kwan-yin. In **HERE** 7, p 763-765.

Tay, C.N. Kuan-yin: the cult of half asia. **HR** 16.2 (nov 1976) 147-177.

Tucci, G. Buddhist notes. **MCB** 9 (1948-51) 173-220. Re evolution of kuan-yin in art and texts.

Visser, Marinus Willem de. The arhats in china and japan. **OZ** 7.1/2 (1918) 87-102; 9 (1920-22) 116-144. Same title publ sep, berlin (1923) 215 p, pl.

Visser, Marinus Willem de. **The bodhisattva akāśagarbha (kokūzō) in china and japan.** Amsterdam (1931) 47 p.

Visser, Marinus Willem de. The boddhisattva ti tsang (jizo) in china and japan. **OZ** 2 (1913) 179-192, 266-305; 3 (1914) 61-92, 326-327.

Visser, Marinus Willem de. Die pfauenkönig (k'ung-tsioh ming wang, kujaku myō-ō) in china and japan. **OZ** 8 (1919-20) 370-387.

Watters, Thomas. The eighteen lohan of chinese buddhist temples. **JRAS** (apr 1898) 329-347. Same title publ sep, shanghai (1925) 45 p, illus.

Wegner, M. Ikonographie des chinesischen maitreya. **OZ** n.s. 5 (1929) 156-178, 216-229, 252-270.

16. POPULAR BUDDHISM— BUDDHIST STORIES

Allan, C. Wilfrid. Chinese picture tracts. **EA** 5 (1906) 94-98.

Basset, René. Les contes indiens et orientaux dans la littérature chinoise. **Revue des traditions populaires** 27 (sept 1912) 441-448. A propos des **Cinq cents contes** . . . de É. Chavannes, q.v.

Bassett, Beulah E. Lecture on chinese mythology. **JWCBorderResS** 5 (1932) 92-101. On hsi-yu-chi.

Belpaire, B. Un conte chinois d'inspiration bouddhique du IXe siècle a.d. **Muséon** 67 (1954) 373-395.

Brown, William. From sutra to pien-wen: a study of sudatta erects a monastery and the hsiang-mo pien-wen. Appendix, Sudatta erects a monastery (tsl) **TR** 9.1 (apr 1978) 67-101.

Chavannes, Édouard (tsl) **Cinq cents contes et apologues extraits du tripitaka chinois et traduit en français.** Paris (1910-11) 3 t: 428, 449, 395 p. Repr paris (1962) 3 t.

Chavannes, Édouard (tsl) **Contes et légendes du bouddhisme chinois.** Paris (1921) 220 p, table, illus. Préface et vocabulaire de Sylvain Lévi.

Chavannes, Édouard (tsl) Fables et contes de l'inde extraits du tripitaka chinois. **Actes 14eICO Algiers, 1905,** paris (1905) 84-145. Same title publ sep, paris (1905) 63 p.

Chavannes, Édouard. Une version chinoise du conte bouddhique de kalyânamkara et pâpaṃkara. **TP** 15 (oct 1914) 469-500.

Chavannes, Mme Édouard. **Fables chinoises de IIIe au VIIIe siècle de notre ère (d'origine hindoue) traduit par édouard chavannes . . . versifiées par mme. édouard chavannes.** Paris (1921) 95 p. Tiré des **Cinq cents contes . . . qv.**

Chinese tables of merits and errors. **ICG** no 3 (1821) 154-165, 205-206; repr **JIA** n.s. 2 (1858) 210-220.

Dykstra, Yoshiko Kurata. A comparative study of indian, chinese and japanese buddhist tales. **JIC** 7 (1980) 39-45.

Eder, M. Buddhistische legenden aus yünnan und kueichou. **FS** 1 (1942) 91-99.

Edkins, Joseph. Paradise of the western heaven. **ChRev** 17 (1888-89) 175-176.

Eitel, E.J. Amita and the paradise of the west. **NQ** 2 (1868) 35-38.

Eitel, E.J. A buddhist purgatory for women. **NQ** 2 (1868) 66-68, 82-85.

Eoyang, Eugene. Oral narration in the pien and pien-wen. **ArchOr** 46 (1978) 232-252.

Ferguson, John C. Books on journeys to western regions. **CJ** 11.2 (aug 1929) 61-68. Hsüan chuang's ta t'ang hsi yü chi; li chih-ch'ang's ch'ang ch'un chen jen hsi yu chi; hsi yu chi; hou hsi yu chi; tsa chü hsi yu chi.

Ferguson, J.C. The miraculous pagoda of pa li chuang. **CJ** 9 (1928) 230.

Gjertson, Donald E. **Ghosts, gods, and retribution: nine buddhist miracle tales from six dynasties and early t'ang china.** Univ mass asian studies comm occasional papers series no 2 (1978) 51 p.

Gjertson, Donald E. Rebirth as an animal in medieval chinese buddhism. **SSCRB** 8 (fall 1980) 56-69.

Grube, Wilhelm. Die chinesische volksreligion und ihre beeinflussung durch den buddhismus. **Globus** 63 (1893) 297-303.

Hackmann, Heinrich (tsl) **Laien-buddhismus in china. Das lung shu ching t'u wen des wang jih hsiu, übers.** Gotha and stuttgart (1924)

Hayes, Helen M. **The buddhist pilgrim's progress. From the shi yeu ki, 'the record of the journey to the western paradise,' by wu ch'eng-en.** London (1930) 105 p.

Heřmanová-Novotná, Zdenka. An attempt at linguistic analysis of the text of ta t'ang san-tsang ch'ü ching shih-hua. **ArchOr** 39 (1971) 167-189. Re text preserved in japan and ed by lo chen-yü in 1916, narrating story of hsi yu chi.

Hrdličková, V. The first translations of buddhist sutras in chinese literature and their place in the development of story telling. **ArchOr** 26.1 (1958) 114-144.

Hulsewé, A.F.P. Sidelights on popular buddhism in china in the fifth century. **Proc 7th ICHR Amsterdam, 1950,** amsterdam (1951) 139-141.

Julien, Stanislas (tsl) Apologues indiens traduits sur une ancienne version chinoise. **Revue orientale et américaine** 4 (1860) 461-463; 5 (1861) 306-308.

Julien, Stanislas (tsl) **Les avadânas contes et apologues indiennes inconnus jusqu'à ce jour suivis de fables, de poésies et de nouvelles chinoises.** Paris (1859) 3 t: xx + 240, viii + 251, 272 p.

Julien, Stanislas. Fables indiennes, traduites pour la première fois sur une ancienne version chinoise. **Revue orientale et américaine** 1 (1859) 20.

Lee, Shao Chang (tsl) **Popular buddhism in china.** Shanghai (1939) engl text 52 p; chin text 22 p. Contains tsl 10 buddhist poems, 32 proverbs, hsüan chuang's Essence of wisdom sutra (hsin ching), Diamond sutra (chin kang pan-jo po-lo-mi ching)

Leong, Y.K. and L.K. Tao. **Village and town life in china.** London (1915) See The popular aspect of chinese buddhism, 115-155.

Lin, Shuen-fu & Larry Schulz (tsl) **The tower of myriad mirrors. A supplement to journey to the west, by tung yueh (1620-1686)** Berkeley, calif (1978) 200 p, index chin terms.

Lo, Chin-t'ang. Popular stories of the wei and chin periods. **JOS** 17.1/2 (1979) 1-9.

Mair, Victor. Lay students and the making of written vernacular narrative: an inventory of the tun-huang manuscripts. **Chinoperl** 10 (1980) 5-96, app.

Matsunaga, Daigan & Alicia. **The buddhist concept of hell.** NY (1972) 152 p, app, notes, bibliog, index. Incl sec 2, Description and analysis of the eight hells, drawn fr chin tsl of saddharma smṛti-upasthāna (chen-fa-nien-ch'u ching)

Mensikov, L.N. Les paraboles bouddhiques dans la littérature chinoise. **BEFEO** 67 (1980) 303-336.

Mok, P.R. Tragic mountain. **Asia** 32 (1932) 503-507, 521-523; 37 (1937) 227-230, 240. Story of a monk's life and thought.

Moule, G.E. (tsl) A buddhist sheet-tract, containing an apologue of human life. Translated with notes. **JNCBRAS** n.s. 19 (1884) 94-102.

Odontius, L. (tsl) Zwei buddhistische märchen. **OstL** (1901) 599-601.

Overmyer, Daniel L. Boatmen and buddhas: the lo chiao in ming dynasty china. **HR** 17.3/4 (feb-may 1978) 284-302.

Overmyer, Daniel L. Folk-buddhist religion: creation and eschatology in medieval china. **HR** 12.1 (aug 1972) 42-70.

Overmyer, Daniel L. **Folk buddhist religion. Dissenting sects in late traditional china.** Harvard univ (1976) xi + 295 p, notes, bibliog, gloss, index.

The Paradise of fuh. 'An exhortation to worship fuh, and seek to live in the land of joy, situated in the west.' **ICG** no 6 (1818) 194-200.

Pavie, Théodore. Étude sur le sy-yeóu-tchin-tsuen, roman bouddhique chinois. **JA** 5e sér, 9 (1857) 357-392; 10 (1857) 308-374.

Ragha, Vira. **Chinese poems and pictures on ahimsā.** Nagpur (1954) 101 p.

Richard, Timothy. **One of the world's literary master-pieces, hsi-yu-chi, a mission to heaven. A great chinese epic and allegory by ch'iu ch'ang ch'un a taoist gamaliel who became a prophet and advisor to the chinese court.** Shanghai (1913) xxxix + 363 + viii p, illus.

Schmidt-Glintzer, Helwig. **Das hung-ming chi und die aufnahme des buddhismus in china.** Wiesbaden (1976) viii + 212 s.

Schnitzer, Joseph. Chinesisch-buddhistische höllenbilder. **Wissen und leben** 2 (1909) 379-384.

Selby, T.G. Yan kwo; yuk lik, or the purgatories of popular buddhism. **ChRev** 1 (1872-73) 301-311.

Sokei-an (Sasaki, Shigetsu) **The story of the giant disciples of buddha, ānanda and mahākaśyapa. From the chinese version of the sūtras of buddhism.** N.Y. (1931) 32 p.

Strassberg, Richard E. Buddhist storytelling texts from tun-huang. **Chinoperl** 8 (1978) 39-99, transcriptions, bibliog.

Takakusu, Junjirō. Tales of the wise man and the fool, in tibetan and chinese. **JRAS** (1901) 447-460.

Translation of a budhist (sic) print, (descriptive of the) one thousand hands, one thousand eyes, the all prevalent and most merciful to-lo-ní (goddess of mercy) **ChRep** 15.7 (july 1846) 351-354, with chin text.

Verdeille, Maurice (tsl) Le monastère de la montagne 'ou-tai' en révolution. Extr par l'éditeur des 'siao-siao chuou' . . . du livre intitulé 'liang-shan-po,.' **BSEIS** 70 (1919) 21-37, 2 pl.

Waley, Arthur (tsl) **Ballads and stories from tun-huang: an anthology.** London (1960) See 10, The buddhist pieces, 202-215; 11, Mu-lien rescues his mother, 216-235.

Waley, Arthur D. Hymns to kuan-yin. **BSOAS** 1 (1920) 145-146.

Whitaker, K.P.K. Tsaur jyr and the introduction of fannbay into china. **BSOAS** 20 (1957) 585-597.

Wood, C.F. Some studies in the buddhism of szechwan. **JWCBorderResS** 9 (1937) 160-179.

Yu, Anthony C. (tsl & ed) **The journey to the west.**Univ chicago, vol 1 (1977) xiii + 530 p, intro, notes; vol 2 (1978) 438 p, notes; vol 3 (1980) 453 p, notes; vol 4 (1983) 469 p, notes, index.

Yu, Anthony C. The journey to the west. **Renditions** 13 (spring 1980) 21-39. Tsl of hsi yu chi chap 64.

Yu, Anthony C. The monkey's tale. **University of chicago magazine** 70 (1977) 10-21. Tsl of hsi yu chi chap 27.

17. BUDDHISM & CHINESE CULTURE

Bagchi, P.C. Indian influence on chinese thought. In **HPEW** (1952) vol 1, 573-589.

Bauer, Wolfgang. **China und die hoffnung auf glück. Paradies, utopien, ideal vorstellung.** München (1971) 703 s. zeittafel, anmerkungen, literaturverzeichnis, chin zeichenglossar. See rev art by Vitali Rubin in **TP** 59 (1973) 68-78. Engl tsl Michael Shaw, **China and the search for happiness,** ny (1976) 502 p.

Belpaire, B. Un conte chinois d'inspiration bouddhique du IXe siècle a.d. **Muséon** 67 (1954) 373-395.

Birnbaum, Raoul. Introduction to the study of t'ang buddhist astrology: research notes on primary sources and basic principles. **SSCRB** 8 (fall 1980) 5-19.

Chang, Carsun. Buddhism as a stimulus to neo-confucianism. **OE** 2 (1955) 157-166.

Ch'en, Kenneth K.S. Buddhist-taoist mixtures in the pa-shih-i-hua t'u. **HJAS** 9 (1945-47) 1-12.

Ch'en, Kenneth K.S. Filial piety in chinese buddhism. **HJAS** 28 (1968) 81-97.

Ch'en, Kenneth K.S. Mahayana buddhism and chinese culture. **Asia** 10 (winter 1968) 11-32.

Chen, Shih-hsiang. Chinese poetics and zenism. **Oriens** 10 (1957) 131-139.

Chi, Hsien-lin. Lieh-tzu and buddhist sutras. **SS** 9.1 (1950) 18-32.

Chou, Hsiang-kuang. Buddhist studies in china and its impact on chinese literature and thought. **CC** 4.4 (mar 1963) 43-59.

DeBary, William Theodore. Buddhism and the chinese tradition. **Diogenes** no 47 (fall 1964) 102-124.

DeBary, William Theodore. Buddhism and the chinese tradition. **Proc26th ICO**, new delhi, jan 1964, 4 (1970) 105-118.

Demiéville, Paul. La pénétration du bouddhisme dans la tradition philosophique chinoise. **CHM** 3.1 (1956) 19-38. Repr **CEB** (1973).

Frodsham, J.D. Hsieh ling-yün's contribution to medieval chinese buddhism. **PIAHA** (1963) 27-55.

Gard, Richard A. Some aspects of the buddhist cultural arts. In **StAs** (1975) 443-456. Same title in **MB** 85.4/5 (apr-may 1977) 119-128, a "rev and expansion" of above art.

Grube, W. Chin. volksreligion u.i. beeinflussung durch d. buddhismus. **Globus** 63 (1893) 297-303.

Hashimoto, Hokei. Concerning the philosophic influence of vimalakīrti-nirdeśa sūtra upon chinese culture. **JIBS** 22.1 (dec 1973) 1-9.

Hashimoto, Hokei. The philosophic influence of the vimalakīrti-nirdeśa-sūtra upon chinese culture. In **MS/CA** (1977) 143-154.

Haydon, A. Eustace. The buddhist heritage of eastern asia. **OC** 46 (mar 1932) 158-184.

Hrdličková, V. The first translations of buddhist sutras in chinese literature and their place in the development of story-telling. **ArchOr** 26 (1958) 114-144.

Hsü, Vivian. Monks and nuns as comic figures in yüan drama. **Dodder** 2 (jan 1970) 10-12.

Hu, Shih. Buddhistic influence on chinese religious life. **CSPSR** 9 (1925) 142-150.

Huard, Pierre. Le bouddhisme et la médecine chinoise. **HM** 8.1 (1958) 5-51, illus.

Huber, E. Termes persans dans l'astrologie bouddhique chinoise. **BEFEO** 6 (1906) 39-43.

Hui-wan. Buddhism in chinese culture. **CC** 19.3 (sept 1978) 43-48.

Johnston, Reginald F. Han-shan (kanzan) and shih-tê (jittoku) in chinese and japanese literature and art. **TPJS** 34 (1936-37) 133-137.

Lee, Siow Mong. Chinese culture and religion. **Voice of buddhism** 6 (mar 1969) 6-10.

Lessing, Ferdinand D. Bodhisattva confucius. **Oriens** 10.1 (1957) 110-113.

Liebenthal, Walter. The problem of chinese buddhism. **VQB** 18 (1952-53) 233-246.

Lisowski, F.P. The practice of cremation in china. **EH** 19.6 (june 1980) 21-24.

Liu, Ts'un-yan. **Buddhist and taoist influences on chinese novels.** Vol 1: **The authorship of the fêng shên yen i.** Wiesbaden (1962) viii + 326 p, index, illus.

Lo, Ch'ang-p'ei. Indian influence on the study of chinese phonology. **SIS** 1.3 (1944) 117-124.

Maspero, Henri. Le dialecte de tch'ang-ngan sous les t'ang. **BEFEO** 20 (1920) 1-124. Influence of buddhism on language.

Mather, Richard. The conflict of buddhism with native chinese ideologies. **RofR** 20 (1955-56) 25-37; repr in **CWayRel** (1973) 77-86.

Mather, Richard. The landscape buddhism of the fifth-century poet hsieh ling-yün. **JAS** 18 (nov 1958) 67-79. Same title in **Trans ICfO** 2 (1957) 34-36 (summ)

Müller, F.W.K. Die persischen kalendarsdrücke im chinesischen tripitaka. **SAWW** 155 (1907) 458-465.

Nakamura, Hajime. The transformation of buddhism in china. **The East** 10.9 (nov 1974) 54-56, 59.

Needham, Joseph. Buddhism and chinese science. In Louis Schneider (ed) **Religion, culture and society,** n.y. etc (1964) 353-358. Excerpted fr Needham's **Science and civilization in china,** cambridge univ, vol 2 (1956) 417-422, 430-431.

Pachow, W. Buddhism and its relation to chinese religions. Repr in author's **ChBudd** (1980) 87-99; orig publ not stated.

Pachow, W. A study of the philosophical and religious elements in the red chamber dream. Repr in author's **ChBudd** (1980) 163-196; orig publ not stated.

Průšek, Jaroslav. Narrators of buddhist scriptures and religious tales in the sung period. **ArchOr** 10 (1938) 375-389; repr in author's collection: **Chinese history and literature; collection of studies,** dordrecht (1970) 214-227.

Przyluski, J. Les rites d'avalambala. **MCB** 1 (1931-32) 221-235.

Rees, J. Lambert. The three religions and their bearing on chinese civilization. **ChRec** 27 (1896) 157-169, 222-231.

Richard, Timothy. The influence of buddhism in china. **ChRec** 21.2 (feb 1890) 49-64.

Schmidt, J.D. Ch'an, illusion, and sudden enlightenment in the poetry of yang wan-li. **TP** 60.4/5 (1974) 230-281.

Schmidt-Glintzer, Helwig. Der buddhismus im frühen chinesischen mittelalter und der wandel der lebens-führung bei der gentry im süden. **Saeculum** 23.3 (1972) 269-294.

Sutherland, Joan. Li ho and the lankavatara sutra. **JAC** 2.1 (spring 1978) 69-102.

Sutherland, Joan. A preliminary study of chinese meditative poetry. **JAC** 1 (1977) 126-144.

Tan, Yun-shan. Buddhism, its impact on chinese religion and philosophy. **MB** 80.5/6 (may-june 1972) 290-296; 80.7 (july 1972) 331-340.

Watters, Thomas. **Essays on the chinese language.** Shanghai (1889) See esp chap 8 and 9, The influence of buddhism on the chinese language.

Wright, Arthur F. Buddhism and chinese culture: phases of interaction. **JAS** 17 (nov 1957) 17-42.

Wu, Chi-yü. A study of han-shan. **TP** 45 (1957) 392-450.

18. MODERN (pre-1949) BUDDHISM

Aufhauser, Johannes B. Ein blick in buddhistische heiligtümer des fernen ostens. **Zeitschrift für buddhismus und verwandt gebiete** 6 (1924-25) 243-258.

Aufhauser, Johannes B. Christentum und buddhismus in ringen am fernasien. **Bücherei der kultur und geschichte** 25 (1922)

Benz, Ernst. **Buddhism or communism. Which holds the future of asia?** Tsl fr german Richard and Clara Winston. N.Y. (1965) 234 p. Orig german ed: **Buddhas wiederkehr, und die zukunft asiens,** münchen (1963) 274 p.

Blanchet, C. Le congrès bouddhiste de shanghai. **RHR** 67 (mai-juin 1913) 397-398.

Blanchet, C. Une nouvelle édition du tripitaka chinois. **TP** n.s. 11 (mai 1910) 315-318.

Blofeld, John. **The jewel in the lotus. An outline of present day buddhism in china.** London (1948) 193 p.

Blofeld, John. **The wheel of life. The autobiography of a western buddhist.** London (1959) 263 p, index, illus.

Callahan, Paul E. T'ai hsü and the new buddhist movement. Harvard univ, **papers on china** 6 (1952) 149-188.

Chan, Wing-tsit. **Religious trends in modern china.** Columbia univ (1953) See chap 2-3.

Chao, Pu-chu. Buddhism in china. **FA:BPB** (1959) 717-730, photos.

Chen-hua. Denis Mair (tsl) Chün-fang Yü (ed) Random talks about my mendicant life: I. **CSA** 13.1 (fall 1980) 3-110 (entire issue) Sel tsl fr bk publ in kaohsiung (1965) by budd monk, about his life on mainland in mid-1940s. Pt II is in **ibid** 13.4 (summer 1981) 3-113 (entire issue)

Chou, Hsiang-kuang. **T'ai hsu: his life and teachings.** Allahabad (1957) 74 p.

Chu, Pao-tang. Venerate tai-hsu and his buddhist reformation in modern china. **CC** 13.3 (sept 1972) 78-118.

Day, Clarence B. A unique buddhist-taoist union prayer conference. **ChRec** 56.6 (june 1925) 366-369. Held at a monastery near hangchou for soldiers who died in world war and for victims of tokyo-yokohama earthquake.

Demiéville, Paul. Le bouddhisme et la guerre. Postscriptum à l'histoire des moines guerriers de japan de G. Renondeau. **MIHEC** 1 (1957) 347-385. Repr **CEB** (1973).

Edkins, Joseph. The recent visit of a chinese buddhist monk to india. **JNCBRAS** 31 (1896-97) 203.

Franke, Otto. Ein buddhistischer reformversuch in china. **TP** n.s. 10 (1909) 567-602.

Franke, Otto. Eine neue buddhistische propaganda. **TP** 5 (1894) 299-310.

Franke, Otto. Die propaganda des japanischen buddhismus in china. In author's **Ostasiatische neubildungen,** hamburg (1911) 158-165.

Fürrer, Arnold. Der buddhismus in seiner bedeutung für die gegenwärtige religiöse krisis in china. **ZMK** 29 (1914) 264-281.

Galetzki, Th. von. Buddhistische missionen japans in china und nordamerika. **Dokumente des fortschritte** 1.2 (1908) 1155-1160.

Glüer, Winfried. The encounter between christianity and chinese buddhism during the nineteenth century and the first half of the twentieth century. **CF** 11.3 (1968) 39-57.

Gutzlaff, Charles. Remarks on the present state of buddhism in china. Communicated by lieut. col. W.H. Sykes. **JRAS** 16 (1856) 73-92.

Hackmann, Heinrich. Ein heiliger des chinesischen buddhismus und seine spüren im heutigen china (Tsi k'ae) **ZMK** 18 (1903) 65.

Hamilton, Clarence H. Buddhism resurgent. **JR** 17 (1937) 30-36.

Hamilton, C.H. An hour with t'ai-shu (sic) master of the law. **OC** 42 (mar 1928) 162-169.

Hodous, Lewis. **Buddhism and buddhists in china.** N.Y. (1924) 84 p.

Hodous, Lewis. The buddhist outlook in china. **CSM** 21.6 (1926) 9-11.

Hosie, Lady. **Portrait of a chinese lady and certain of her contemporaries.** London (1929) See chap 18, Buddha, 183-194.

Johnston, Reginald F. A poet monk of modern china [su man-shu] **JNCBRAS** 43 (1932) 14-30.

Kuan, Chiung. Buddhism. In **The chinese year book, 1935-36,** shanghai (1935) 1510-16; **ibid, 1936-37,** shanghai (1936) 1445-50; **ibid, 1937,** shanghai (1937) 70-75.

Kupfer, Carl F. Buddhism in hwang mei. **EA** 2 (1903) 185-194.

McDaniel, C. Yates. Buddhism makes its peace with the new order. **Asia** 35.9 (sept 1935) 536-541.

Millican, Frank. Buddhism in the light of modern thought as interpreted by the monk tai hsü. **ChRec** 57.2 (feb 1926) 91-94.

Millican, Frank R. Buddhist activities in shanghai. **ChRec** 65.4 (apr 1934) 221-227.

(Millican, Frank R.) The challenge of buddhism. **ChRec** 60.5 (may 1929) 271-275.

Millican, Frank R. The present situation: among the buddhists. **ChRec** 59.9 (sept 1928) 599-601.

Millican, Frank R. T'ai-hsü and modern buddhism. **ChRec** 54.6 (1923) 326-334.

Oehler, W. Der buddhismus als volksreligion im heutigen china. **EMM** n.s. 55 (1911) 308-317.

Pratt, James Bissett. **The pilgrimage of buddhism and a buddhist pilgrimage.** N.Y. (1928) 758 p. See chap 11-20 for mahāyāna and chin buddhism.

Pratt, James Bissett. A report on the present condition of buddhism. **CSPSR** 8.3 (1924) 1-32.

Reichelt, Karl L. Buddhism in china at the present time and the new challenge to the christian church. **IRM** 26 (1937) 153-166.

Reichelt, Karl L. A conference of chinese buddhist leaders. **ChRec** 54.11 (1923) 667-669.

Reichelt, Karl Ludvig. Present-day buddhism in china. **ChRec** 60.10 (oct 1929) 647-651.

Reichelt, Karl Ludvig. Some present aspects of buddhism in china. **ChRec** 59.3 (mar 1928) 174-175.

Reichelt, Karl L. Special work among chinese buddhists. **ChRec** 51.7 (1920) 491-497.

Reichelt, Karl Ludvig. Trends in china's non-christian religions. **ChRec** 65.11 (nov 1934) 707-714; 65.12 (dec 1934) 758-768.

Rosenberg, Otto. **Die weltanschauung des modernen buddhismus im fernen osten. (Ein vortr. geh. in d. ersten buddh. ausstell. zu st. petersburg 1919 von prof. dr. O. Rosenberg.) Aus d. russ. übers. v. Ph. Schaeffer . . .** Heidelberg (1924) 47 s.

Roussel, Alfred. **Religions orientales. Première série. — Le bouddhisme contemporain.** Paris (1916) ix + 520 p.

Saunders, Kenneth J. Sketches of buddhism as a living religion. **JR** 2 (1922) 418-431.

Suzuki, Daisetz Teitarō. Impressions of chinese buddhism. **EB** 6.4 (mar 1935) 327-378. Re author's visit to china, summer 1934.

T'ai-hsü. Frank Rawlinson (tsl) Buddhism and the modern mind. **ChRec** 65.7 (july 1934) 435-440.

T'ai Hsü. **Lectures in buddhism.** Paris (1928) 92 p, illus.

T'ai-hsü. Frank R. Millican (tsl) The meaning of buddhism. **ChRec** 65.11 (nov 1934) 689-695.

Tai-Hü. Buddhistische studien. Der buddhismus in geschichte und gegenwart. **Sinica** 3 (1928) 189-196.

Tai, Ping-heng. Modern chinese buddhism. **ChRec** 56.2 (feb 1925) 89-95.

Tsu, Y.Y. Buddhism and modern social-economic problems. **JR** 14 (1934) 35-43.

Tsu, Yu-yue. Present tendencies in chinese buddhism. **JR** 1.5 (1921) 497-512.

Tsu, Y.Y. Present tendencies in chinese buddhism. In **CToday** 2nd ser (1926) 74-93.

Tsukamoto, Zenryū. Japanese and chinese buddhism in the twentieth century. **CHM** 6.3 (1961) 572-602.

Wei-huan. Buddhism in modern china. **THM** 9.2 (sept 1939) 140-155.

Welch, Holmes. Buddhism in china today. In Heinrich Dumoulin & John C. Maraldo (ed) **Buddhism in the modern world,** ny & london (1976) 164-178. Orig publ in german in Dumoulin (ed) **Buddhismus der gegenwart,** freiburg (1970) 95-106; and before that in **Saeculum** 20 (1969) 259-270.

Welch, Holmes. **The buddhist revival in china.** Harvard univ (1968) 385 p, app, notes, bibliog, gloss-index. With a section of photos by Henri Cartier-Bresson.

Welch, Holmes. Case histories of motivation: two modern chinese monks. **ZMR** 54.2 (apr 1970) 112-123.

Welch, Holmes. The foreign relations of buddhism in modern china. **JHKBRAS** 6 (1966) 73-99.

Welch, Holmes. **The practice of chinese buddhism, 1900-1950.** Harvard univ (1967) notes, bibliog, gloss, index, app, illus.

Wilhelm, Richard. Der grossabt schï tai hü. **Sinica** 4 (1929) 16.

Wilhelm, Richard. The influence of the revolution on religion in china. **IRM** 2.8 (oct 1913) 624-642.

Witte, H. Die wirkung der umwälzung in china auf den chinesischen buddhismus. **ZMK** 29 (1914) 19-22.

Witte, Johannes. Neues leben im ostasiatischen buddhismus. **ZMK** 41 (1926) 33-41.

Witte, Johannes. Die rede des führers der chinesischen vertreter auf dem buddhistenkongress in tokyo im nov. 1925. **ZMK** 41 (1926) 257-263.

Witte, Johannes. Zur propaganda des japanischen buddhismus in china und zur propaganda der religionen überhaupt. **Christliche welt** 27 (1915)

Wright, Arthur F. Buddhism in modern and contemporary china. In Robert F. Spencer (ed) **Religion and change in contemporary asia,** univ minnesota (1971) 14-26.

19. BUDDHISM UNDER COMMUNISM

Amritananda, Bhikku. **Buddhist activities in socialist countries.** Peking (1961) 89 p, illus.

Bapat, P.V. A glimpse of buddhist china today. **MB** 64 (1956) 388-392.

Benz, Ernst. **Buddhism or communism. Which holds the future of asia?** Tsl fr german Richard and Clara Winston. N.Y. (1965)

Bräker, Hans. Kommunismus und buddhismus. Zur religions und asienpolitik der sowjetunion und chinas. **Moderne welt** 8 (1967) 50-64.

Brook, Tim. Traveling to the trigram mountains: buddhism after the gang of four. **Contemporary china** 2.4 (winter 1978) 70-75.

Buddhists in new china. Peking (1956) 189 p, illus.

Buddhists in peking. **FEER** (21 nov 1963) 381-382.

Chao, P'u-ch'u. **Buddhism in china.** Peking (1957) 55 p, illus; rev ed (1960) 51 p, illus. See same title as art in **FA:BPB** (1959) 717-732.

Chao, P'u-ch'u. New ties among buddhists. **CRecon** 5 (apr 1956) 2-17, illus.

Chao, P'u-ch'u. The story of the buddha's tooth-relic. **CRecon** 8 (sept 1959) 36-37, illus.

Chen, Gerald. Jian zhen comes home. **EH** 19.6 (june 1980) 11-16, illus. "Visit" of lacquer statue of monk chien-chen fr tōshōdaiji, nara, to yangchou and peking.

Ch'en, Kenneth. Chinese communist attitudes towards buddhism in chinese history. **CQ** 22 (apr-june 1965) 14-30; repr in Albert Feuerwerker (ed) **History in communist china,** MIT (1968) 158-174.

Ch'en, Kenneth, K.S. Religious changes in communist china. **CC** 11.4 (dec 1970) 56-62. Mostly on buddhism.

Chih, Sung. Chinese buddhism yesterday and today. **PC** 22 (16 nov 1956) 31-35.

Chinese Buddhist Association, Peking, publications:
  a) **Buddhism in china** (1955) 4 p text, 24 col pl in portfolio.
  b) **Statues and pictures of gautama buddha** (1956) 8 p, pl.
  c) **Buddhists in china** (1956) 177 p.
  d) **Buddhists in new china** (1957) 189 p, chiefly illus.
  e) **The friendship of buddhism** (1957) 160 p.
  f) **The buddha tooth relic in china** (1961) 10 p, pl.

Chü Tsan. A buddhist monk's life. **CRecon** 3 (jan-feb 1954) 42-44.

Gard, Richard A. Buddhist trends and perspectives in asia. In **FA:BPB** (1959) 561-568.

Hsu, William. **Buddhism in china.** Hong kong (1964) 72 p, illus.

Jaltso, Shirob. New appearance of buddhism in china. **CB** 627 (18 july 1960) 26-30.

Kiang, Alfred. A new life begins in the [buddhist] temples. **CWR** 116 (11 feb 1950) 172-174.

Langerhans, Heinz. Die buddhistische renaissance. 2. In ceylon, burma, kambodscha — und china. **Frankfurter** 20 (nov 1965) 763-774.

Li, Rongxi. The guang-i monastery. **YE** n.s. 6.4 (autumn 1980) 7-11. In peking.

Migot, André. Situation des religions en chine populaire: bouddhisme et marxisme. In Centre d'étude des pays de l'est, institut de sociologie solvay, univ libre de bruxelles and centre national pour l'étude des pays à régime communiste (ed) **Le régime et les institutions de la république populaire chinoise,** brussels (1960) 39-55.

Price, Frank W. Communist china (buddhism in china) **Religion in life** 25 (fall 1956) 512-515.

Raguin, Yves. Nouvelle attitude des jeunes bouddhistes. **CMBA** 2 (dec 1950)

Sourcebook on buddhism in mainland china. Anon (tsl) **CSA** 3.4 (summer 1971) 195-267 (entire issue) **ibid** 4.1 (fall 1971) 3-37 (entire issue) **ibid** 4.2 (winter 1971-72) 83-162 (entire issue) Sel tsl fr bk publ by union research institute, hk, in collab with hk chin budd assoc and hk sangha assoc (1968)

Strong, John. Buddhism in china. **Atlantic monthly** 231.1 (jan 1973) 16-19, 22. Re contemporary situation.

Strong, John & Sarah Strong. A post-cultural revolution look at buddhism. **CQ** 54 (apr-june 1973) 321-330.

USJPRS reports:
   Articles on buddhist activities. DC-613
      (24 mar 1959) 1, a-b, 63 p.
   Articles on chinese buddhist theory and activity.
      NY-1461 (9 apr 1959) 1, a, 55 p.
   Translations from hsien-tai-fo-hsüeh (modern
      buddhism)JPRS-2638 (25 may 1960) 1, a, 19 p.

Watson, William. Buddhism in china. **Asian affairs** 61.3 (oct 1974) 331-333. Rev art on Holmes Welch, **Buddhism under mao,** q.v.

Welch, Holmes. Asian buddhists and china. **FEER** 40 (4 apr 1963) 15-21.

Welch, Holmes. Buddhism after the seventh [world federation of buddhists conference] **FEER** 47.10 (12 mar 1965) 433-435.

Welch, Holmes. Buddhism since the cultural revolution. **CQ** 40 (oct-dec 1969) 127-136.

Welch, Holmes. Buddhism: making the best of things. **FEER** (15 aug 1980) 1-2 and col photo on cover.

Welch, Holmes. Buddhism under the communists. **CQ** 6 (apr-june 1961) 1-14.

Welch, Holmes. Buddhismus in china. **Saeculum** 20 (1969) 259-270.

Welch, Holmes. Buddhists in the cold war. **FEER** 35.10 (8 mar 1962) 555-563, photos. Author's report on 6th world federation of buddhists conference that he attended nov 1961 in phnom penh.

Welch, Holmes. The deification of mao. **Saturday review** (19 sept 1970) 25, 50.

Welch, Holmes. Facades of religion in china. **AsSur** 10.7 (july 1970) 614-626.

Welch, Holmes. The reinterpretation of chinese buddhism. **CQ** 22 (apr-june 1965) 143-153.

Yang, I-fan. **Buddhism in china.** Hong kong (1956) 98 p.

Yu, David C. Buddhism in communist china: demise or co-existence? **Journal of the american academy of religion** 39.1 (mar 1971) 48-61. Survey of contemporary lit, both chin and western.

Yu, David C. Maoism and buddhism in china. **JSSR** 14.3 (sept 1975) 298-301.

20. TAIWAN & OVERSEAS (INCLUDING HONG KONG)

Baity, Philip Chesley. **Religion in a chinese town.** Taipei (1975) 307 p, gloss, ref cited, 2 maps.

Blofeld, John. Chinese buddhism with special reference to siam. In **Visakhapuju,** bangkok, budd assoc of thailand (may 1971) 47-57. Speech delivered to the siam soc.

Blofeld, John. **Mahayana buddhism in southeast asia.** Singapore (1971) 51 p, illus. "The purpose of this book is to describe mahayana buddhism as practised by the great chinese communities spread throughout southeast asia"

Bodhedrum Publications: **Buddhism in taiwan.** Taichung (n.d., ca 1959) 44 p, chiefly photos.

Buddhist monasteries of taiwan. I. Kuan-yin hill and ling-yün buddhist temple; II. Yuan tung shih, a nunnery. **New force** 2.4 (feb 1951) 20-25, photos.

Buddhists build another gateway to immortality. **FCR** 27.2 (feb 1977) 29-32. Pic-story on fo-kuang mt in tashu hsiang, kaohsiung hsien, col photos.

Chien, S.C. Buddhism: the chinese version. **FCR** 13 (may 1963) 37-43, illus.

Chu, Pao-t'ang. Buddhist organizations in taiwan. **CC** 10.2 (june 1969) 98-132, tables.

Dodd, Jeremy. Temple of the dragons. **FCR** 21.6 (june 1971) 18-22, illus. Re taipei's lung-shan ssu.

Edmonds, Juliet. Religion, intermarriage and assimilation: the chinese in malaysia. **Race** 10.1 (1968) 57-68.

Fei, Shih-tang. How to eat without eating meat. **Echo** 3.3 (mar 1973) 34-38. Re vegetarian meals at tsai ming budd temple in tahsi.

Hsiao, C.F. Some issues raised by the polemic writings of buddhists and christians against each other in taiwan. **SEAJT** 11 (autumn 1969) 52-63.

Kitagawa, Joseph M. Buddhism in taiwan today. **FA** 18 (1962) 439-444.

Kuo, Huo-lieh. Buddhism in taiwan today: attitudes toward changing society. **QNCCR** 5.2 (1961) 24-33. Same title in **SEAJT** 3.2 (oct 1961) 43-58.

Lee, H.T. New horizons of universe and life in buddhism. **Tamkang journal.** 6 (nov 1967) 267-289.

Lombard-Salmon, Claudine. Survivance d'un rite bouddhique à java: la cérémonie du pu-du (avalambana) **BEFEO** 62 (1975) 457-486, many photos.

Lung shan temple. **Echo** 2.8 (sept 1972) 34-38, 59, col photos, plan.

Ormond, McGill & Ron Ormond. **Religious mysteries of the orient.** Cranbury, n.j. (1976) See chap 7, Some buddhist insights from taiwan, 101-110. The "insights" consist entirely of photos with captions.

Page, William. Shihtoushan: lamp of buddha on a lion's flank. **Echo** 1.6 (june 1971) 13-17, illus.

Raguin, Yves. Buddhism in taiwan. In Heinrich Dumoulin & John C. Maraldo (ed) **Buddhism in the modern world,** ny & london (1976) 179-185. Orig publ in german in Dumoulin (ed) **Buddhismus der gegenwart,** freiburg (1970) 113-116, and before that in **Saeculum** 20 (1969) 277-280.

Raguin, Yves. Lion head mountain and buddhism in taiwan. **JCS** 8 (1971) 21-30.

Ross, D. A comparative study of religious symbolism among buddhists, adherents of folk or popular religion, protestants and catholics in taiwan. Ottowa, **Kerygma** 14 (1980) 101-116.

Tamney, Joseph B. A sociological approach to buddhism in singapore. **CF** 14.4 (winter 1971) 153-156.

Thera, Ananda Mangala. Buddha dhamma and singapore. **CF** 16.3/4 (1973) 142-151. Not specifically on chin; deals with budd missionary effort in singapore.

Tiang, Henry Lau Hwee. Buddhism and youth in singapore. **CF** 16.2 (1973) 101-103. Orig publ in **The young buddhist,** singapore (1972)

Tobias, Stephen F. Buddhism, belonging, and detachment—some paradoxes of chinese ethnicity in thailand. **JAS** 36.2 (feb 1977) 303-326.

Topley, Marjorie. Chinese women's vegetarian houses in singapore. **JMBRAS** 27.1 (may 1954) 51-67.

Trippner, J. Formosa's buddhismus und die rückkehr zum festland china. **NZM** 14 (1958) 304-305.

Wei Wu Wei. The passing away of a buddhist sage in taiwan. **MW** 38 (1964) 156-158.

Welch, Holmes. Buddhism in china today. In Heinrich Dumoulin & John C. Maraldo (ed) **Buddhism in the modern world,** ny & london (1976) 164-178. Orig publ in german in Dumoulin (ed) **Buddhismus der gegenwart,** freiburg (1970) 95-106; and before that in **Saeculum** 20 (1969) 259-270.

Welch, Holmes. Buddhist organizations in hong kong. **JHKBRAS** 1 (1960-61) 98-114.

Wong, C.S. **Kek lok si — temple of paradise.** Singapore (1963). On a famous temple, chi-lo ssu, in penang. 131 p, illus, app, index.

Yang, Ming-che. China reinterprets buddhism. **FCR** 18 (dec 1968) 27-32.

21. COMPARISONS & INTERACTIONS

Abe, Masao. Zen and buddhism. **JCP** 3.3 (june 1976) 235-252.

Affinités des doctrines de lao-tse et du bouddha. Date incontestable de l'existence de lao-tse. Un savant prétend que lao-tse était un philosophe japonais. In **EM** 26 (d?) 343f.

Aufhauser, Johannes B. Christentum und buddhismus in ringen am fernasien. **Bücherei der kultur und geschichte** 25 (1922).

Bagchi, P.C. Indian influence on chinese thought. In **HPEW** (1952) vol 1, 573-589.

Ball, J. Dyer. **Is buddhism a preparation or a hindrance to christianity in china?** Hong kong (1907) 31 p.

Bareau, André. Indian and ancient chinese buddhism: institutions analogous to the jisa. **CSSH** 3 (1961) 443-451 ('Jisa' is tibetan for the principal land of the monastery)

Berling, Judith A. **The syncretic religion of lin chao-en.** Columbia univ (1980) 360 p, app, notes, gloss, sel bibliog.

Bernard-Maître, Henri. La découverte du bouddhisme. (La découverte spirituelle de l'extrême-asie par l'humanisme européen) **FA** 10.2 (1954) 1141-1153.

Berthrong, John. "Suddenly deluded thoughts arise." **SSCRB** 8 (fall 1980) 32-55. Re mou tsung-san on neo-confucianism and t'ang budd philos.

Brandauer, Frederick P. The encounter between christianity and chinese buddhism from the fourteenth century through the seventeenth century. **CF** 11.3 (1968) 30-38.

Chang, Carsun. Sino-indian spiritual affinity. **IAC** 6.4 (apr 1958) 367-376.

Chang, Chung-yüan. Concept of tao in chinese culture. **RofR** 17.3/4 (1953) 115-132.

Chang, Chung-yuan. Pre-rational harmony in heidegger's essential thinking and ch'an thought. **EB** n.s. 5.2 (oct 1972) 153-170.

Châu, Thích-minh. **The chinese madhayama agama and the pali majhima nikaya; a comparative study.** Saigon (1964) 388 p.

Châu, Thích-minh. **Milindapañha and nagasenabhik-shusutra: a comparative study through pali and chinese sources.** Calcutta (1964) 127 p.

Chen, Gerald. Jian zhen comes home. **EH** 19.6 (june 1980) 11-16, illus. "Visit" of lacquer statue of monk chien-chen fr tōshōdaiji, nara, to yangchou and peking.

Clemen, K. Christliche einflüsse auf den chinesischen und japanischen buddhismus. **OZ** 9 (1920-22) 10-37, 185-200.

Demiéville, Paul. l'État actuel des études bouddhiques. **Revue de théologie et de philosophie** 14 (1927) 43-65.

Dietz, E. Sino-mongolian temple painting and its influence on persian illumination. **Ars islamica** 1 (1934) 160-170.

Dschi, Hiän-lin. Lieh-tzu and buddhist sutras. A note on the author of lieh-tzu and the date of its composition. **SS** 9.1 (1950) 18-32.

Dumoulin, Heinrich. The enounter between zen buddhism and christianity. **JCS** 7 (1970) 53-63.

Dumoulin, Heinrich. **Östliche meditation und christliche mystik.** München (1966) 340 p.

Dykstra, Yoshiko Kurata. A comparative study of indian, chinese and japanese buddhist tales. **JIC** 7 (1980) 39-45.

Edkins, Joseph. Buddhist phraseology in relation to christian teaching. **ChRec** 9.4 (july-aug 1878) 283-295.

Edmunds, Albert J. **Buddhist and christian gospels. Being gospel parallels from pali texts. Now first compared from the originals by** Albert J. Edmunds. **Third and complete edition — Edited with parallels and notes from the chinese buddhist tripitaka by M. Anesaki.** Tokyo (1905) philadelphia (1902; 1908; 1935) vol 2 (all publ?) 341 p, xiii + 230 p.

Eitel, E.J. Buddhism versus romanism. **ChRec** 3 (1870-71) 142-143, 181-183.

Erkes, Eduard. Kumārajīvas laotse kommentar. **ZMR** 50 (1935) 49-53.

Evola, J. Zen and the west. **E&W** 6 (1955) 115-119.

Fisher, Robert E. Tibetan art and the chinese tradition. **AofA** 5.6 (nov-dec 1975) 42-49, illus.

Franz, Heinrich Gerhard. Pagode, stūpa, turmtemple. Untersuchen zum ursprung der pagode. **KdeO** 3 (1959) 14-28, illus.

Fu, Charles Wei-hsun. Morality or beyond: the neo-confucian confrontation with mahayana buddhism. **PEW** 23.3 (july 1973) 375-396.

Fukunaga, Mitsuji. 'No-mind' in chuang-tzu and in ch'an buddhism. **Zinbun** 12 (1969) 9-45.

Galetzki, Th. von. Buddhistische missionen japans in china und nordamerika. **Dokumente des fortschritte** 1.2 (1908) 1155-1160.

Glüer, Winfried. The enounter between christianity and chinese buddhism during the nineteenth century and the first half of the twentieth century. **CF** 11.3 (1968) 39-57.

Grootaers, W.A. Bouddhisme et christianisme en chine. **Bulletin des missions** (1951) 1-5.

Gulik, R.H. van. Indian and chinese sexual mysticism. App I in author's **Sexual life in ancient china,** leiden (1961) 339-359.

Hackmann, Heinrich. Aufgabe des christentums gegen über dem buddhismus. **Christliche welt** 19 (1905) 565.

Holth, Sverre. The encounter between christianity and chinese buddhism during the nestorian period. **CF** 11.3 (1968) 20-29.

Hsiao, C.F. Some issues raised by the polemic writings of buddhists and christians against each other in taiwan. **SEAJT** 11 (autumn 1969) 52-63.

Hsu, Sung-peng. Han-shan te-ch'ing: a buddhist interpretation of taoism. **JCP** 2 (1974-75) 417-427.

Inglis, James W. The christian element in chinese buddhism. **IRM** 5. (oct 1916) 587-602.

Inglis, James W. The vows of amida. A comparative study. **JNCBRAS** 48 (1917) 1-11.

Johnston, Reginald F. Buddhist and christian origins. An appreciation and a protest. **Quest** 4 (oct 1912) 137-163.

Kadowaki, J.K. **Zen and the bible. A priest's experience.** London (1980) 180 p. Tsl of a jap bk orig publ tokyo (1977) Author is a jesuit.

Karmay, Heather. **Early sino-tibetan art.** Warminster, engl (1975) 128 p, 69 pl. See rev by M. Strickmann in **Annali dell'istituto orientale di napoli** 39 (1979) 506-513.

King, Winston L. Hua-yen mutual interpenetrative identity and whitehead organic relation. **JCP** 6.4 (dec 1979) 387-410.

King, Winston L. The way of tao and the path to nirvana. In **SA** (1963) 121-135.

Kung, Tien-min. Some buddhist and christian doctrines compared. **QNCCR** 5.2 (1961) 34-37.

Lai, Whalen. The i-ching and the formation of the hua-yen philosophy. **JCP** 7.3 (sept 1980) 245-258.

Lancashire, Douglas. Buddhist reaction to christianity in late ming china. **JOSA** 6.1/2 (1968-69) 82-103.

Lee, Cyrus. Thomas Merton and zen buddhism. **CC** 13.2 (june 1972) 35-48.

Lee, Shiu-keung. **The cross and the lotus.** HK (1971) 6 + 125 p, bibliog.

Linssen, R. **l'Éveil suprême. Base théoretique et pratique du bouddhisme ch'an, du zen du taoïsme et des enseignements de krishnamurti.** Bruxelles (1970) 160 p.

Malan, Saloman C. **A letter on the pantheistic and on the buddhistic tendency of the chinese and of the mongol versions of the bible.** London (1856) 38 p.

Martin, W.A.P. Is buddhism a preparation for christianity? **ChRec** 20.5 (1889) 193-203.

Masaki, Haruhiko. On the principle of "negative inter-mediation" seen in the interpretation of shan-tao's kuan-wu-liang-shou-fo-ching-shu compared with that of the two famous phrases in an embroidered curtain depicting a land called tenju. **JIBS** 20.2 (mar 1972) 65-75.

Matsunaga, Yukei. A history of tantric buddhism in india with reference to chinese translationa. In **BT&AC** (1977) 167-181.

Merton, Thomas. A christian looks at zen. Being the intro to John C.H. Wu: **The golden age of zen,** taipei (1967) 1-28.

(Millican, Frank) The challenge of buddhism **ChRec** 60.5 (may 1929) 271-275.

(Millican, Frank) The present situation: present-day buddhism in china. **ChRec** 64.8 (aug 1933) 536-537.

Morgan, Evan. The christian elements in buddhism. **ChRec** 42.1 (jan 1911) 19-28; 42.2 (feb 1911) 98-105.

Mori, Mikisaburō. Tsl Patrick James. Chuang tzu and buddhism. **EB** n.s. 5.2 (oct 1972) 44-69.

Murakami, Yoshimi. 'Nature' in lao-chuang thought and 'no-mind' in ch'an buddhism. **KGUAS** 14 (1965) 15-31.

Olschki, L. Manichaeism, buddhism and christianity in marco polo's china. **AS** 5 (1951) 1-21.

Pachow, W. Buddhism and its relation to chinese religions. Repr in author's **ChBudd** (1980) 87-99; orig publ not stated.

Pachow. Comparative studies in the mahāparinibbāna-sutta and its chinese versions. **SIS** 1 (1944) 167-210; 2 (1945) 1-41.

Pachow, W. A comparative study of the pratimoksa. **SIS** 4 (1953) 18-193; 5 (1955) 1-45.

Pachow, W. The controversy over the immortality of the soul in chinese buddhism. **JOS** 16.1/2 (1978) 21-38; repr in author's **ChBudd** (1980) 117-162.

Parker, E.H. Buddhism and christianity in china. **ChRev** 16 (1887) 188.

Pauthier, Georges. **Mémoire sur l'origine et la propagation de la doctrine du tao, fondée par lao-tseu; traduit du chinois et accompagné d'un commentaire tiré des livres sanscrits et du tao-te-king de lao-tseu, établissant la comformité de certaines opinions philosophiques de la chine et de l'inde; orné d'un dessein chinois; suivi de deux oupanishads des vedas, avec le texte sanscrit et persan.** Paris (1831) 79 p. See critical rev by Anon [Stanislas Julien?] in **NouvJA** 7 (1831) 465-493; further Pauthier's rebuttal in **ibid** 8 (1831) 129-158.

Pontynen, Arthur. Buddhism and taoism in chinese sculpture, a curious evolution in religious motif. **FMB** 49.6 (june 1978) 16-21.

Przyluski, J. Études indiennes et chinoises. **MCB** 2 (1932-33) 307-332; 4 (1935-36) 289-339.

Pye, Michael. The heart sutra in japanese context. In **PRS** (1977) 123-134.

Re, Arundel del. Amidism and christianity. **Marco polo** 3 (apr 1941) 68-81.

Rhie, Marylin M. Some aspects of the relation of 5th century chinese buddha images with sculpture from n. india, pakistan, afghanistan and central asia. **E&W** n.s. 26.3/4 (sept-dec 1976) 439-461, illus.

Ross, D. A comparative study of religious symbolism among buddhists, adherents of folk or popular religion, protestants and catholics in taiwan. (Ottowa) **Kerygma** 14 (1980) 101-116.

Rowland, Benjamin jr. Indian images in chinese sculpture. **AA** 10 (1974) 5-20, illus.

Sarkar, B. K. Confucianism, buddhism, and christianity. **OC** 33 (1919) 661-673.

Stuhr, P.F. **Die chinesische reichsreligion und die systeme der indischen philosophie in ihrem verhältnis zu offenbarungslehren. Mit rücksicht auf die ansichten von Windischmann, Schmitt und Ritter.** Berlin (1835) vi + 109.

Su, Ying-hui. A comparative study on the contour techniques of wall-paintings found in tunhuang, ajanta, sigiriya and polonnarawa. **APQCSA** 7.1 (summer 1975) 10-12, illus.

Takakusu, Junjirō. Tales of the wise man and the fool, in tibetan and chinese. **JRAS** (1901) 447-460.

Tamaki, Kōshirō. The development of the thought of tathāgatagarbha from india to china. **JIBS** 9.1 (jan 1961) 25-33.

Tamura, Kwansei. Ganjin (chien-chen), transmitter of buddhist precepts to japan. **YE** n.s. 6.4 (autumn 1980) 4-6.

Thurn, E. Buddhism in the pacific. **Nature** 105 (1920) 407.

Too-yu. The systems of foe and confucius compared, translated from the chinese. **ICG** no 5 (1818) 149-157.

Tu, Wei-ming. An inquiry into wang yang-ming's four-sentence teaching. **EB** n.s. 7.2 (oct 1974) 323-48; repr in **H&SC** (1979) 162-178.

Visser, Marinus W. de. The arhats in china and japan. **OZ** 7 (1918) 87-102; 9 (1920-22) 116-144. Same title publ sep, berlin (1923) 215 p, pl.

Visser, Marinus Willem de. **The bodhisattva akāśagarbha (kokūzō) in china and japan.** Amsterdam (1931) 47 p.

Visser, Marinus Willem de. The bodhisattva ti tsang (jizo) in china and japan. **OZ** 2 (1913) 179-192, 266-305; 3 (1914) 61-92, 326-327.

Visser, Marinus Willem de. Die pfauenkönig (k'ung-tsioh ming wang, kujaku myō-ō) in china and japan. **OZ** 8 (1919-20) 370-387.

Wei, Francis C.M. Buddhism as a chinese christian sees it. **IRM** 17 (1928) 455-463.

Wei, Francis C.M. The doctrine of salvation by faith as taught by the buddhist pure land sect and its alleged relation to christianity. **ChRec** 51.6 (june 1920) 395-401; 51.7 (july 1920) 485-491.

Wienpahl, Paul. Ch'an buddhism, western thought, and the concept of substance. **Inquiry** 14.1/2 (1971) 84-101. Comparisons with spinoza.

Witte, Johannes. Zur propaganda des japanischen buddhismus in china und zur propaganda der religion überhaupt. **Christliche welt** 29 (1915) 535-541, 609-663, 679-683, 705-706, 725-727.

Zürcher, Erik. Buddhist influence on early taoism. **TP** 66.1/3 (1980) 84-147.

22. MISCELLANEOUS

Birnbaum, Raoul. Introduction to the study of t'ang buddhist astrology: research notes on primary sources and basic principles. **SSCRB** 8 (fall 1980) 5-19.

Blofeld, John. **Gateway to wisdom. Taoist and buddhist contemplative and healing yogas adapted for western students of the way.** Boulder, colo (1980) See pt 2, Mahayana buddhist theory and practice, 91-197; 3 app, 201-214.

Brown, Homer G. How buddhists use their bible. **ChRec** 64.4 (apr 1933) 239-242.

Demiéville, Paul. **Choix d'études bouddhiques (1929-1970)** Leiden (1973) xli + 497 p, bibliog of author, 1920-1971, comp by Gisèle de Jong. Repr in 1 vol of 13 art and 4 rev; each repr is sep listed in our bibliog.

Demiéville, Paul. **Choix d'études sinologiques (1921-1970)** Leiden (1973) xli + 633 p, bibliog of author 1920-1971, comp by Gisèle de Jong. Repr in 1 vol of many art relating to relig among other subj; each repr is sep listed in our bibliog.

Demiéville, Paul. Notes on buddhist hymnology in the far east. In **Buddhist studies in honour of walpola rahula,** london & sri lanka (1980) 44-61.

Eberhard, Wolfram. Chinesische volkskalendar und buddhistischer tripitaka. **OL** 40.6 (1937) 346-349.

Editor. The number of buddhists in the world. **ChRec** 14.6 (nov-dec 1883) 453-463. Concludes that "the great mass of the population of china is to be classified as confucianists"

Fritzen, Joachim. Das schlagzeug in der buddhistischen liturgischen musik china. **OE** 22.2 (dec 1975) 169-182, illus with musical ex.

Gimello, Robert M. Apophatic and kataphatic discourse in mahāyāna: a chinese view. **PEW** 26.2 (apr 1976) 117-136.

Gimello, Robert M. Random reflections on the "sinici-zation" of buddhism. **SSCRB** 5 (spring 1978) 52-89.

Gómez, Louis O. The bodhisattva as a wonder-worker. In **PRS** (1977) 221-261.

Hall, Manly P. **The adepts in the eastern esoteric tradition.** Los angeles (1979) 113 p, illus. Re taoist, confucian and budd adepts.

Heřmanová-Novotná, Zdenka. An attempt at linguistic analysis of the text of the ta t'ang san-tsang ch'ü ching shih-hua. **ArchOr** 39 (1971) 167-189. Re a text preserved in japan and ed by lo chen-yü in 1916, narrating story of hsi yu chi.

Hung, W. Remfry. Devotion to heathenism. **ChRec** 32.5 (may 1901) 231-232. Author admires a budd pilgrim.

Lee, Hsing-tsun. A new look at taoism and buddhism. **ACQ** 4.4 (winter 1976) 117-156. Author's own views.

Liu, Chun-jo. Five major chant types of the buddhist service, gong-tian. **Chinoperl** 8 (1978) 130-160, app, transcriptions, musical scores.

Matsunaga, Daigan & Alicia Matsunaga. **The buddhist concept of hell.** NY (1972) 152 p, app, notes, bibliog, index. Incl sec 2, Description and analysis of the eight hells, drawn fr chin tsl of saddharma smrti-upasthāna sūtra (chen-fa-nien-ch'u ching)

Niset, J. Bhiksu shih tao-an, la doctrine du bouddha et les droits de l'homme. **RDH** 10.1/2 (1979) 5-13.

Paul, Diana. Empress wu and the historians: a tyrant and saint of classical china. In **VW** (1980) 191-206.

Paul, Diana. **Women in buddhism. Images of the feminine in the mahāyāna tradition.** Berkeley, calif (1979) 333 p, gloss, bibliog, index. Tsl mostly fr chin texts.

Raguin, Yves. Mediation dans le bouddhisme et le taoisme. **SM** 21 (1972) 77-92.

Rape, C.B. Buddhistic brotherhood of the sacred army and the adventures of an american ship on the upper yangtsze. **CWR** 44 (17 mar 1928) 62-63.

Staël-Holstein, A. von. On certain divine metamorphoses. **CJ** 4.2 (feb 1926) 57-61; 4.3 (mar 1926) 111-115. On indra, varuna, mitra and yama, incl their chin versions.

Su, Ying-hui. The dancing guidebook of tunhuang. **APQCSA** 12.1 (spring 1980) 47-49. A text fr 2 mss.

Suzuki, Daisetz T. Freedom of knowledge in chinese buddhism. **MW** 31.1 (may 1956) 12-18.

Re Suzuki, Daisetz T. (1870-1966) **EB** 2.1 (aug 1967) Entire issue in memoriam.

Waldschmidft, Ernst. Wunderkräfte des buddha. **AWGN** (1948: 1) 48-91.

Ware, James R. Transliteration of the names of chinese buddhist monks. **JAOS** 52 (1932) 159-162.

ADDENDA & CORRIGENDA

I.2.

Ogilvie, C.L. Chinese religions. In **Some aspects of chinese life and thought. Being lectures delivered under the auspices of peking language school 1917-1918,** shanghai & peking (n.d.) 69-95.

II.2.

Kohl, Louis von. Die grundlagen des altchinesischen staates und die bedeutung der riten und der musik. **Baessler-archiv** 17.2 (1934) 55-98.

II.5.

Schipper, K.M. Millénairismes et messianismes dans la chine ancienne. In **Understanding modern china. Proceedings of the 26th conference of chinese studies, european association of chinese studies,** rome (1979) 31-49.

II.6.

Jiang, P.Y.M. **The search for mind: ch'en pai-sha, pilosopher-poet.** Singapore univ (1980) 232 p. Ch'en pai-sha (Hsien-chang) 1428-1500, was a prominent literatus of the ming dyn.

II.13.

Kohl, Louis von. Die grundlagen des altchinesischen staates und die bedeutung der riten und der musik. **Baessler-archiv** 17.2 (1934) 55-98.

II.17.

Schipper, K. Science, magie et mystique du corps—notes sur le taoïsme et la sexualité. In **Jeux des nuages et de la pluie,** fribourg, (1969)

II.18.

Chavannes, Édouard. Le jet des dragons. **Mémoires concernant l'asie orientales** 3 (1919) 53-220, illus pl and reproductions of rubbings and texts.

III.3.

Robinson, Richard H. (tsl) **Chinese buddhist verse.** London (1954) repr westport, conn (1980) 85 p, bibliog, notes, index of chin texts tsl.

III.6.

Schmidt-Glinzer, Helwig. **Die identität der buddhistischen schulen und die kompilation buddhistischer universalgeschichten in china.** München (1980) 200 s.

III.7.

Magnin, P. **La vie et l'oeuvre de huisi, 517-577. Chez origines de la secte bouddhique chinoise du tiantai.** Paris (1979)

Schmidt-Glinzer, Helwig. **Die identität der buddhistischen schulen und die kompilation buddhistischer universalgeschichten in china.** München (1980) 200 s.

III.8.

Magnin, P. **La vie et l'oeuvre de huisi, 517-577. Chez origines de la secte bouddhique chinoise du tiantai.** Paris (1979)

III.9.

Gernet, Jacques. **Entretiens du maître de dhyāna chen-houei du ho-tsö (668-760)** Hanoi (1949) repr paris (1977) x + 126 p.

III.14(H)

Stein, Aurel. **The thousand buddhas: ancient buddhist paintings from the cave-temples of tun-huang on the western frontier of china.** London (1921) facs ed NY (1978) 66 p text, 23 col pl, 25 monochrome collotype pl.

III.22.

Amore, R.C. (ed) **Developments in buddhist thought: canadian contributions to buddhist studies.** Wilfrid laurier univ (1979) 196 p.

Index of Authors, Editors, Compilers, Translators, Photographers, Illustrators